IMI
Library

Sandyford Road, Dublin 16
Telephone: 01 2078513
Email: knowledge@imi.ie
http://www.imi.ie

FINANCE: THEORY AND PRACTICE

Professor Ann Marie Ward (BA(hons), Macc, FCA, PGCUT, PhD, FHEA)
School of Accounting, University of Ulster at Jordanstown

Published in 2008 by
Institute of Chartered Accountants in Ireland
Burlington House, Burlington Road
Dublin 4

Designed by Hurix Systems (www.hurix.com)
Printed by ColourBooks, Dublin, Ireland
The paper used in the printing of this book was produced from managed, renewable, plantation forests.

ISBN   978 0 903854 429

The opinions expressed in this publication are those of the author and do not necessarily represent the views of the ICAI. The text is designed to provide accurate and authoritative information in regard to the subject matter covered. It is sold on the understanding that the ICAI is not engaged in rendering professional services. If professional advice or other expert assistance is required, the services of a competent professional should be sought.

For my family - Martin, Thomas, Anna, Mary and Seamus.
And one other - This book will always remind me of Kieran.

ABBREVIATED CONTENTS

DETAILED CONTENTS

ACKNOWLEDGEMENTS

At the top of the list, I must thank Martin for looking after Thomas, Anna, Mary and Seamus and for being very supportive.

Thank-you also to Patrick Bourke who kindly gave permission to use extracts from Viridian Group PLC's annual report.

Thanks to Barry Quinn, the anonymous reviewers, and the publishing team.

Finally, thanks to Kieran for being Kieran.

PREFACE

The success of a company is influenced by the quality of its management team. Managers need many skills and a wide knowledge of various subject areas to enable them to direct a company; to keep it ahead of the competition and to keep its products in demand. Some people are natural entrepreneurs, who can successfully make the correct decisions without having explicitly studied subjects that support management. This text book aims to provide the reader with relevant business finance knowledge which should support financial decision making, whether the decision maker is already running an established company, or is starting a company. Having an appropriate knowledge of business finance is vital for value creation both within a business context and on an individual personal level.

This text is split into six sections. The first two sections provide foundation knowledge for the rest of the text. Sections three to six provide specific information and techniques that can be used in support of business finance decision making in key business areas. Unlike other accounting subjects, business finance pays particular attention to the time value of money. A basic understanding of discounting, perpetuities, annuities and terminal values are required; therefore, an appendix has been included in the text which deals specifically with financial mathematics techniques that are commonly used to adjust cash flows for the time value of money.

The text is written from the perspective of a business finance manager making decisions in a company. However, the same principles and theories can be applied to any entity that makes economic decisions (including an individual, a sole trader, a partnership, a limited company and a public limited company) and by anyone who makes financial decisions (for example a director, a board of directors, a management accountant, a financial accountant, a consultant, an owner, a manager).

PEDAGOGY

Sectionalised approach: This text is structured into six main sections. The first two sections provide foundation knowledge for the rest of the text. The other sections have been structured according to the key decisions faced when dealing with the management of business finance: namely the financing; investment and dividend decisions.

Learning objectives: In each chapter the expected competencies to be gained by readers are outlined at the outset.

Chapter clarity: Each chapter begins with an introduction which explains the flow and connection between topics included in the chapter. The body of each chapter provides detail and a conclusion sums up, by highlighting key points.

Real world examples: Where relevant and practical, real world examples are included to provide a link between theory and the business world. As this text is primarily targeted at an Irish and British audience, examples used are biased in respect of companies from these regions.

Viridian Group PLC: Viridian Group PLC gave permission to use extracts from their Annual Report. Viridian Group PLC is a Northern Ireland based company with businesses spanning both sides of the border. Most of the targeted readership should be familiar with the company and hence should be more interested in their disclosures and be better able to relate theory to practice.

Research: In some instances the views, theories and findings of research studies (performed primarily on UK and/or ROI data) are integrated into the discussion of a topic.

Newspaper articles: Reference is made to newspapers articles (mostly the Irish Financial Times, Belfast Telegraph, Financial Times), again to stress the relevance of the topic being discussed to practical daily business issues.

Worked examples: The worked examples increase in complexity as a chapter progresses. Each chapter ends with an examination standard question.

Key terms: When key terms are first defined in a chapter they are highlighted in **bold and italicised**. At the end of each chapter the key terms are summarised in a table. The reader should be aware of the key terms and should revisit the chapter when unable to define/explain the key term.

Websites: When relevant, lists of websites that can be visited by readers are provided.

Review questions: These questions are designed to assist readers in identifying and revising the key issues within each chapter. It is a way for readers to provide themselves with feedback on their understanding of each topic: as solutions are provided in appendix seven. The questions range from short quick fire questions, to examination standard questions.

Challenging questions: These questions are all examination standard. Successful completion of these questions demonstrates a thorough understanding of the issues covered in the chapter and indeed may refer to issues covered in preceding chapters. The solutions to these questions are available in a separate book: this is so the text can be used for educational purposes.

Mathematics made simple: This book does not try to derive mathematical formula, or to prove existing accepted models. In each instance the accepted approach is explained in simple terms using narrative. A formula is provided and an example of how to calculate the outcome of the formula using input variables is given.

Financial mathematics for assessing the time value of money: A brief explanation of the formulae and approaches for adjusting cash flows to take account of the time value of money has been included in appendix one. Examples are used to help readers understand the application of the formulae.

Key formulae: The key formulae referred to in the text are provided in alphabetical order in appendix two, for quick reference when readers are preparing the solution to a problem.

Index tables: Index tables have been provided in the appendices to save readers time, when they are adjusting cash flows for the time value of money.

Abbreviations: A list of abbreviations used in the text has been provided, for quick reference for readers.

Bibliography: The readers of this text can deepen their understanding of areas of interest to them, by sourcing other authors work. The bibliography contains text books, newspapers articles and academic literature that are considered relevant by the writer.

SECTION ONE
THE BUSINESS FINANCE SETTING

INTRODUCTION

1

Debt   10,000,000
Equity   15,000,000
Market Value 25,000,000

LEARNING OBJECTIVES

This chapter provides a brief overview of this text.

(For most readers the linkages between the sections and chapters will only become clear as knowledge of business finance increases.)

Introduction

This book is divided into six sections.

The first section, 'The Business Finance Setting', which includes this chapter, provides foundation knowledge for the rest of the text. Chapter two examines the role of business finance in strategic management decision making. In brief, chapter two explains the importance of having an appropriate business finance function for financial success. Business finance forms part of the strategic decision making process within a company: as such, the breadth of knowledge required by a business finance manager is wide. Financial decisions cross several disciplines including: economics, taxation, law and statistics. In addition, business finance managers need to work with financial and management accountants, hence require knowledge of their areas also. Chapter two explains the type of knowledge required from other subject areas that will influence business finance decision making.

Every decision can impact on several stakeholders and the behavioural reaction of stakeholders needs to be anticipated. This information can be obtained by considering their reactions in the past to similar decisions (research), analysing industry norms, or simply by contacting them to discuss the possible impact of a decision. Therefore, a business finance manager needs to be a skilled communicator and have knowledge of a variety of academic theories, for example: agency theory, pecking order theory, Modigliani and Miller's theories on capital structure and dividend policy, and Lintner's theory on dividend payout. A business finance manager also needs to have knowledge of the financial environment within which a company operates, as the external environment is a source of finance and ultimately values companies.

The second section, 'Financial Statement Analysis', contains one chapter, which introduces the financial statements: the income statement, the balance sheet and the cash flow statement. This chapter highlights the purpose of each statement, introduces ratio analysis as a tool to interpret financial data and outlines the weaknesses of financial statements.

The third section, 'Sources of Finance and the Financial Environment', concentrates on the first of the three key business finance decisions – how to finance a company's resource requirements. This section has four chapters, which split the sources of finance according to the duration of the finance requirement (short term; medium term; long term). The categories are loosely defined and some sources could be considered to fall within different categories depending on the terms established at the outset of the finance agreement. For example, a term-loan might be for: six months (short term); three years (medium term); or for 30 years (long term).

The first chapter in this section, 'Asset-Mix Decision, Finance-Mix Decision and Short-Term Sources of Finance', explains the fundamental principles underlying the financing of investments: namely to match the duration and repayment schedule of each source of finance, to the expected duration and pattern of cash inflows from an investment made. This chapter also describes the various types of finance that are available to meet short-term (less than one year) needs. Chapter five, 'Medium-Term Sources of Finance', provides information on a variety of sources of finance, with durations of between one to seven years. Long-term finance sources are assumed to be available for periods in excess of seven years. There are two main sources of long-term finance: debt and equity. These sources are explained in two chapters: chapter six, 'Long-Term Sources of Finance: Debt', and seven, 'Long-Term Sources of Finance: Equity'.

Each chapter in section three provides detailed information on the financial environment relevant to the source of finance being considered.

Companies obtain funding from financial institutions and financial markets. The main financial institutions which provide finance are: commercial banks, international banks, merchant banks, discount houses, acceptance houses, building societies, insurance companies and pension companies. The financial markets that provide finance are the equity markets (for example, the London Stock Exchange and the Irish Stock Exchange) and debt markets (for example, the bond markets). Obtaining finance can be difficult for emerging companies that have no track record; or for small to medium-sized companies that are growing quickly, have liquidity problems and are of insufficient size to be able to economically avail of finance from market sources. This financing gap is filled to some extent by venture capitalist companies and business angels. These providers may supply traditional sources of finance or what is termed 'mezzanine finance'. In brief, mezzanine finance is considered more risky, relative to conventional types of finance and sometimes is quite complicated, depending on the terms of the finance agreement.

The investment decision is deemed to be the most important decision in business finance. Therefore two sections are committed to an examination of investment decision making. The fourth section, 'Investment Decision Making: Working Capital', has four chapters, which cover the main working capital elements: inventory, trade receivables/payables, and cash. Working capital is both an investment decision and a source of finance. Chapter eight, 'Working Capital: An Introduction', outlines the underlying principles of working capital management, highlighting the importance of good working capital management. Various strategies that company management can adopt in their general approach to working capital management are outlined (namely conservative, neutral and aggressive stances). Chapter eight also builds on the fundamental principles of financing as detailed in the previous section, by explaining the characteristics of finance that should be utilised when financing a company's working capital requirement.

Chapter nine, 'Inventory Management', considers the various issues surrounding investing in inventory, including the influence of the type of product, cost of product and costs facing a company in respect of controlling and managing products. It also identifies suitable evaluation techniques to use to monitor inventory. For example, when inventory is categorised as being 'high-value items' or 'high-risk items', then it is likely that the economic order quantity model will be used to determine an optimum order quantity. This model helps to identify the most efficient level of inventory to hold and order to minimise costs. Efficiency is deemed to be congruent with the primary objective of a company – value creation – as explained in chapter two. The role of information technology in inventory control is also outlined.

Chapter ten, 'Trade Receivables/Payables Management', explains the importance of managing trade receivables (debtors) and trade payables (creditors). The cost of having an inappropriate policy in respect of either trade receivables or trade payables is examined, and ways to increase efficiency and reduce costs are suggested. Costs include: interest forgone on debts not collected in line with the credit agreement, bad debts, loss of discounts, factor costs, invoice discounting costs and loss of reputation. Recommendations are made in respect of establishing a sound credit policy and the importance of acting ethically towards customers and suppliers is highlighted. The role of information technology in the management of trade receivables and trade payables is outlined.

The final chapter in this section, chapter 11, deals with cash management. In finance, cash is king. A profitable company can be forced into liquidation if it runs out of cash. Therefore, cash flow management is vital to a company's survival and a key part of a company's overall business strategy. The earlier parts of chapter 11 stress the importance of good cash management and evaluate the costs and benefits to be gained from managing lodgements. This involves weighing up the gains to be made (interest saved) from lodging more frequently with the cost of additional lodgements. The chapter also evaluates the costs and benefits of holding cash on deposit, or in short-term securities, to obtain a high-interest return – against the requirement for cash to meet operational demands and the costs that would be incurred were the short-dated securities not encashed (overdraft interest; penalty costs). A statistical model, the Baumol model, is used as a tool to calculate the optimum amount to withdraw from shortdated securities to minimise the costs faced by a company. Investment appraisal is considered in terms of cash flows and all long-term strategic plans usually revolve around a long-term rolling cash budget; therefore the concluding part of this chapter focuses on the preparation of cash budgets.

In business finance, value creation in companies is dependent not only on the ability of management to maintain efficient levels of working capital, but is also related to the success of management in recognising capital projects that yield strong future returns. Section five, 'Corporate Value and Risk', focuses on the evaluation of investment decisions. The main themes covered include – capital investment appraisal, company valuation, company reorganisation (mergers and takeovers) and managing risk. A fundamental principle underlying investment appraisal of any kind is that cash generated should at least cover the cost of a company's finance. Therefore all projects should be discounted at a rate that covers the cost of a company's capital. The first chapter in this section, chapter 12, 'Cost of Capital', concentrates on how to calculate the weighted average cost of capital for a company. The chapter concludes by highlighting the uses and limitations of the resultant discount rate, and how in certain circumstances the weighted average cost of capital may not be the most appropriate rate to use for investment appraisal.

Chapter 13, 'Capital Investment Decision Making', concentrates on explaining and evaluating techniques that are commonly used for capital investment appraisal (accounting rate of return; payback period; net present value; internal rate of return). The basic techniques are adapted to provide solutions to situations where the capital available is restricted (capital rationing). The chapter also considers situations wherein projects are divisible, or mutually exclusive. The most common internal investment decision facing companies is when to replace an asset: as such, the latter part of this chapter focuses on the asset-replacement decision. Chapter 14, 'Capital Investment Decision Making: Incorporating Risk', extends knowledge gained from the previous two chapters by considering a variety of techniques designed to adjust the investment appraisal process for specific risk factors. The techniques covered are those most commonly used in practice: sensitivity analysis, scenario analysis, certainty equivalents and probability theory. Finally, the advantages of information technology in the investment-appraisal process are detailed.

No business finance decision can be considered in isolation. Investment appraisal decision making should be congruent with a company's overall objective – in this case to maximise equity holder wealth (value creation). To do this, all projects with a positive net present value should be accepted. However, the situation is complicated by the fact that the form of financing used may change the capital structure of a company. This change will affect the financial risk faced by current financiers, who will alter their required return in response to the new risk level. This process is not straightforward and there are two main opposing views on the relevance of a company's capital structure to company value. Modigliani and Miller initially theorised that capital structure was irrelevant to company value, suggesting that there was no optimal capital structure. Their argument is that the return required by debt and equity holders will change (equity is always more expensive than debt) when more debt is introduced, but the change in the proportions held by each type of finance provider will always result in the company having a constant weighted average cost of capital, hence constant value, as the larger proportion of cheaper debt compensates for the increased cost of equity. Modigliani and Miller later adapted their theory to take account of taxation – concluding that a company's optimal capital structure was when the company had very high levels of gearing (up to the point of bankruptcy).

In opposition to Modigliani and Miller, traditionalists argue that there is an optimal capital structure and changes to the capital structure will impact on the value of a company. Therefore, a company should strive to find out its optimal capital structure and should maintain this. This is a key corporate strategic issue. Chapter 15, 'Capital Structure', discusses the link between the capital structure of a company, the weighted average cost of capital, capital investment and company value. The opposing theories on the relevance of capital structure are outlined and the catalysts causing changes in the required return of the financiers – namely gearing and financial risk – are explained. The chapter concludes by returning to investment appraisal, adapting Modigliani and Miller's capital structure theory with tax to investment appraisal, so that the appraisal process can take into consideration the impact of a change in capital structure caused by the specific financing of a current project.

The earlier chapters in this section are relevant for all entities that are investing in capital projects, however, they do not cater for all the investment decisions that face large companies. Many large companies have branches, subsidiaries or business units in different countries throughout the world. In many instances, their investment decision involves external growth, whereby they purchase another entire company, or part thereof. To cater for this, Chapters 16 'Valuing Companies' and 17 'Company Reconstructions' take the investment decision a step further by focusing on the investment decision, where the investment decision involves investing in another company. When a company is involved in a merger or takeover, the stakes are much higher than if the company is considering capital investment internally. There are so many additional hurdles to this form of investment. Two are mentioned here (more are considered in the chapter). The first major concern is social in nature – the target company may have operated with different employee contracts, pensions and holiday entitlements, in addition, there may be redundancies. This can cause problems with performance in the future. Determining the impact is difficult. The second is increased risk – the projections that are commonly used to value investments are even more risky now because of information asymmetry. The finance manager has to rely on information that is historic and publicly available (financial statements) and on information provided by the company. The target company is certainly not independent, this increases the risks associated with using the data supplied. Chapter 16 focuses on the techniques to be applied when valuing a company and chapter 17 deals with major investment decisions including mergers, takeovers, joint ventures, divestures, etc. The advantages, disadvantages and mechanics of each of these forms of restructuring are outlined.

The last chapter in this section deals with risk. Though risk is prevalent in small entities, it is usually controlled by the owner-manager who is fully aware of the impact on the entities cash flows of changes in variables. There is little need for risk to be formally investigated, recorded and managed. In larger companies, however, risk is a critical factor that, if not managed, can result in the demise of the company. Because of this, many large companies have a treasury department which focuses on finance and cash management, including the risks associated with this. Chapter 18 'Managing Risk', focuses on the identification, evaluation and management of the main risks that a large multi-national company faces – namely, commodity price risk, exchange rate risk and interest rate risk. The concept of hedging risk exposures is introduced and some of the tools that can be utilised to hedge risk exposures are explained (namely derivative financial instruments – futures, forwards, swaps, options).

Section six, 'Dividend Decision and Shareholder Wealth Maximisation', deals with the third main business finance decision, 'What dividend should a company pay to its equity holders?' This section has one chapter, 'Dividend Policy', which examines and explains the different theories on dividend policy and the methods used to evaluate a company's dividend policy. In brief, Modigliani and Miller theorise that dividend policy is irrelevant, that a company is valued on the strength of its past decision making in respect of investments. As is outlined in chapter 15, Modigliani and Miller consider the financing of investments to be irrelevant, and also theorise that the treatment of the surplus funds from operating activities is irrelevant. Whether the funds are distributed as interest or dividends, or are retained should have no impact on company value.

Opposition to Modigliani and Miller argue that dividend policy does impact on company value. One argument is that retained earnings can be used for investment and, so long as the return earned from this investment exceeds the current weighted average cost of capital and the required return of the equity holders, then equity holders will be happy with a high retentions policy. Other arguments include the fact that the market expects a company to pursue a certain constant pattern in respect of dividend policy. However, equity holders will build up expectations as to the dividend. These expectations are impacted on by issues such as: changes in taxation, company liquidation, imperfect information, signalling, competitors' dividend policies, company investment plans or changes in the economy. When a company reacts in a manner different to what the equity holders expect, this may adversely impact on share price.

To summarise, this chapter provides tools to determine a company's dividend policy and to interpret it. It also discusses theories on the influence of changes to a company's dividend policy on company value and integrates the dividend decision on how it can impact on the financing and investment strategic decision making.

THE ROLE OF BUSINESS FINANCE IN STRATEGIC MANAGEMENT AND INFLUENCES ON BUSINESS FINANCE DECISION MAKING

2

LEARNING OBJECTIVES

Upon completing this chapter, readers should be able to:

♣ Demonstrate an understanding of strategic management;
♣ Explain how business finance supports strategic planning;
♣ Discuss various company objectives and explain the conflict that may arise between financial and non-financial objectives;
♣ Describe the role of the business finance manager – including the three key decision areas;
♣ Outline the qualities required in a business finance manager;
♣ Discuss internal and external influences on business finance decision making; and
♣ Explain market efficiency theory.

Introduction

Business finance is concerned with the financial evaluation of the use, or intended use, of a company's financial resources. Business finance provides information that can be used to aid company decision making. The theoretical objective of business finance is to ensure that decisions made are consistent with the overall strategic objective of a company. In this text, this strategic objective is assumed to be equity holder wealth maximisation, otherwise known as *value creation*. Having a strong business finance function within a company is vital for the successful strategic management of a company and strategic management is pivotal to the success of a company.

In recognition of the importance of strategic management to a company's success, the first part of this chapter explains strategic management, high-lighting the variety of strategic objectives a company might choose to pursue. Many companies pursue a finance-orientated primary objective. The attainment of this primary strategic objective is not as straight-forward as it might seem. Companies do not just pursue a single course of action without having regard for corporate strategies in respect of other areas, including non-financial issues. In many instances pursuit of secondary non-financial objectives will restrict the extent to which a company can achieve its primary financial objective. For example, ensuring employee welfare is maintained at a high level is costly and will certainly reduce the short-term profits of a company and possibly future earnings also. In addition, conforming with regulations and ethical codes of conduct will ultimately result in a company taking decisions that reduce profitability. However, acting ethically is usually regarded favourably by equity holders, who may act irrationally by supporting a less-profitable company with strong ethical practices.

The second part of this chapter introduces business finance in the context of its role in the support of strategic decision making. Successful business finance decision making requires a wide variety of knowledge of various other topics, such as: financial accounting (for example, to analyse perfor-mance); management accounting (for example, for budgeting); maths and statistics (for example, for assessing risk and return); law (for example; for knowing about the legal limitations on company distributions) and economics (for example, for determining the expected impact of interest rate movements). The business finance manager also requires knowledge of the financial environment, including financial institutions and financial markets as these are the main sources of finance for a company.

Company success

Many large companies are complex (for example, they might be conglom-erates, have foreign subsidiaries, joint ventures and many product lines) and hence require a very well formulated management structure, which allows relevant and reliable information to be communicated quickly from several lower level departments, through divisions to the central management team – the board of directors – and vice versa. Managers at the lower levels of a company are referred to as operational managers. *Operations management* deals with the day-to-day running of a company. This level of management provides information to assist strategic decision making within a company; for example by providing information on the expected costs and revenues of undertaking a certain action. Operational management activities also include monitoring actual outcomes against planned outcomes, taking steps to alleviate potential differences and providing feedback on corrective action and the progress of each plan to strategic management levels (members of the board of directors).

The board of directors is headed by a single person who is responsible for the overall management of the company – the Managing Director. Decisions taken at board of director level are termed 'strategic'. Company success is arguably related to strong strategic management. There are many studies and text books which emphasise the importance of strong, focused strategies in the successful management of a company. Business finance is central to successful strategic management. To place business finance in context, strategic management is briefly explained.

Strategic management

Strategic management focuses on company policy decision making. Strategic management aims to ensure that a company remains successful in the long term and acts to either take advantage of, or make changes to, the company's operations to ensure continued success in light of economic changes that are beyond a company's control. It does not deal with detailed issues such as operational or employee problems within a department – these types of issues are dealt with at operational management level. Strategic management takes a holistic view in respect of the company. It normally has several facets that hinge on a central core objective: the overriding aim of the company. In this text the assumed objective being pursued by companies is 'value creation'. However, in practice not all companies pursue value creation as their core objective (discussed later). Strategic management is different in different companies: examples of some of the more general themes that strategic decision making is classified into include corporate strategy, competitive strategy and operational strategy.

Corporate strategy

Successful companies normally have a clearly defined primary objective, sometimes referred to as the *'company mission'*. Formulating this statement is the most important strategic decision facing a board of directors. All other strategic and operational decision making is angled at achieving the primary objective. Another corporate strategy issue is determining the types of business the company should operate in. When a company is formed, this type of information is included as part of the objects of the company (detailed in the company's memorandum and articles of association). The board of directors have to obtain agreement from a company's equity holders before they can change the objects (business activities) of a company. Changing business activity may be achieved by acquiring another company, starting a new venture or exiting a market and selling the relevant portion of the company.

Corporate strategy also includes determining the capital structure of the company. The board of directors will have to decide on the source of finance to pursue, when the company needs to obtain external funds. Related to this is another key strategic decision, the dividend policy of the company. When a company pays a dividend, it reduces the amount of funds available for investment and hence growth. The board of directors has to balance the demands for distributions from equity holders with the availability of funds for financing new profitable projects which, if undertaken, would lead to higher growth and an increase in equity share price.

Competitive strategy

The ability to remain competitive is vital for company success. This does not necessarily mean having the cheapest price. A company can improve its competitive position by providing better quality products, a better variant of the product or a new product to do the same task. **Competitive strategy** focuses on how the company's 'strategic business units' compete in particular markets, supplying the resources required to the various parts of the company that operate in different markets and deciding whether to enter new markets or exit old markets. To enable the strategic managers to undertake successful strategic decision making, they require a sound knowledge of the industry that they operate in. This will support the strategic management team in identifying comparative advantages the company has over its competitors and putting in place a plan to exploit these advantages.

Industries are all different and the potential for companies within a particular industry to make a profit is largely controlled by competitive forces, both from within the industry and from other industries. Porter (1985) formulated a five-point list to capture competitive forces that he considers influence industry success:

Competitive forces (Porter 1985)

Threat of potential market entrants: When there are barriers to entering a particular industry. For example the need to invest a significant capital outlay to get started, having sufficient product differentiation, or sufficient economies of scale to allow the product to be sold at a competitive price. Then the potential profitability of companies within that particular industry will be higher. When a market is easily entered, more companies are likely to join, resulting in more competition (price wars). Existing companies are more likely to keep competitive prices, and hence keep profitability low, in an attempt to create a barrier to entry.

Existing competition: The type of industry will also impact on industry (hence company) success. An industry with homogenous products and homogenous cost structures (a high proportion of fixed costs) will be less profitable, as individual companies will find it more difficult to create a comparative advantage over their rivals, as they are evenly balanced. The extent of market share will be linked to individual company success in these circumstances.

Pressure from substitutes: Within every industry, companies come under pressure from direct competition for market share from other companies within the same industry. However, this is not the only competition some industries face; many whole industries are exposed to competition from other industries. The best example is energy. The coal industry once dominated the energy world. Now coal has been substituted to a large extent by the oil and electricity industries. Another example is the transport industry: the low budget air industry has successfully competed with the rail industry and the package holiday industry, to gain a large portion of the travel market.

Continued

Bargaining power of buyers: Buyers are not as loyal as they once were. Many buyers now price around before purchasing a product. Universities frequently change their preferred suppliers after a competitive tendering process. By playing companies within the same industry off each other, buyers ensure that individual company profitability and overall industry profitability is reduced.

Bargaining power of suppliers: The quantity of suppliers to an industry will influence the profitability of that industry. If an industry has few suppliers, then their dominant position leaves them in a stronger position to raise purchase prices and to provide a poorer quality service, with little chance of losing business. When an industry has many potential suppliers, competition will keep the purchase price down and the quality of service high.

Operational strategy

Operational strategy focuses on ensuring that operational and functional level goals and objectives are consistent with overall corporate strategies. For example, by ensuring that the finance department supports investments that are consistent with the company's long-term future plans, even if this means not investing in projects that reap larger short-term rewards.

Company objectives

As mentioned in the prior section, the most important strategic decision to make is to determine a company's primary objective, its 'mission'. The expected outcome of this mission is sometimes referred to as the 'vision' for the company. Company objectives are either financial or non-financial. Most companies will view non-financial objectives as secondary to financial objectives. In some instances, the pursuit of non-financial objectives will actually restrict the potential to maximise financial objectives.

Financial objectives
Financial objectives include the following:

Equity holder wealth maximisation
The objective, **equity holder wealth maximisation,** involves making decisions that will ultimately benefit the equity holders (owners) of

a company. As mentioned previously, this objective is also referred to as 'value creation'. When companies pursue value creation, the focus is on undertaking sustainable long-term investments that increase the future earnings potential of the company. This may mean turning down projects that have higher short-term returns. Market participants value a company based on its expected future earnings potential and the risks associated with obtaining those earnings, therefore the focus is on undertaking projects with strong long-term earnings which are not over a certain risk threshold.

Profit maximisation

Profit maximisation is a commonly pursued objective. ***Profit maximisation*** usually involves pursuing projects that provide a quick return in the short term. It is argued that this may damage the long-term earnings of a company, as there is less focus on the future direction a company takes. Pursuing profit maximisation may also put management under pressure to expose a company to higher levels of risk in an attempt to maximise profits – higher returns are usually correlated with riskier projects. Conversely, it is argued that pursuing a profit-maximising objective will create value; hence the equity holders' objectives will be met also. The argument is that the pursuit of 'equity holder wealth maximisation' as the primary objective, though resulting in long-term value creation might, in the short term, cause the company to report poor financial performance and may even cause the company to fall into financial difficulties and/or go out of business.

Growth

Growth in market share is pursued as a primary objective by some companies. Growth may bring with it economies of scale and, hence, result in value creation for equity holders in the long term. Growth also reflects corporate power, and dominant management teams may pursue growth as a means of maximising their own positions, not that of the company. Many non-profit-making or associational organisations pursue growth as a primary objective; for example, building societies and credit unions. Growth in these financial institutions is assumed to encapsulate a social measure – it reflects the fact that the benefits of the organisation's services are being enjoyed by a wider membership, increasing social welfare.

Alternative financial objectives

In some instances, profit-making companies will not pursue earnings-related objectives explicitly as their primary objective, though they will pursue policies that have financial outcomes in mind – risk reduction and efficiency are examples of this type of objective.

Risk reduction

Some industries are exposed to more risk than others. All industries that rely on research and development for future earnings are subject to high levels of risk. For example, the pharmaceutical industry and the oil exploration industry. Companies in these industries are likely to pursue risk-minimising objectives and have profit maximisation as a secondary objective. The potential earnings to be obtained if the research and development turns out to be successful can be great, as will the losses if the research and development is scrapped. Risk-reducing strategies may include portfolio diversification (whereupon the company becomes a conglomerate investing in several different industries to reduce overall risk) or may spread the risk (by sharing the investment with, for example, another pharmaceutical company or a venture capital company).

Efficiency

Some entities do not have income, for example, many public bodies. They have a budget which has to cover costs and enable the body to achieve social and financial targets. Efficiency in the use of funds to achieve the greatest social output is usually the primary objective of these types of organisations. The ultimate goal is to provide quality services at the lowest possible cost. Viridian Group PLC (once publicly owned) pursues different objectives for different aspects of its business. It does not have a group-wide primary objective, however. Its website states that:

> 'Viridian has played a leading role in promoting an all-island electricity market in Ireland. Viridian's strategy is strongly focused on Irish energy markets, maximising the efficiency of its regulated electricity infrastructure in Northern Ireland and growing an integrated energy business in competitive markets across Ireland, backed by its investment in power generation.'

Non-financial objectives
Social objectives

Some non-profit-making organisations and public sector bodies might pursue ***non-financial objectives*** as their primary focus. Examples might include growth in membership numbers, reduction in patient deaths, reduction in waiting lists or improved train punctuality.

Employee welfare

Having *employee welfare* as a secondary objective usually increases company costs as it involves paying fair wages, providing a solid pension and good holidays, adopting a strong health and safety policy, enabling the employees to advance their skills through training and education and providing good redundancy packages and retraining initiatives, when necessary. However, there are financial benefits also as employees are likely to remain in the company for longer, saving recruitment and training costs, and gain greater company-specific skills, which add value.

Trade relationships

Another social objective might be to create and maintain quality relationships with suppliers and customers. Some large companies are in a position of power in respect of the custom they provide to small companies. They could cause damage to small companies by demanding unreasonably low prices for supplies purchased, or could take long credit periods, leaving the supply companies in financial difficulty. Adhering to an agreed credit agreement will maintain a good relationship. In terms of dealings with customers, the focus might be on providing quality products, which are adequately supported by the company in terms of warranty.

Environmental policies

Other companies pursue *environmental policies,* opting to, for example, reduce pollution by planting trees for flights taken by employees, or by using recycled packaging. These steps will reduce the profitability of a company, yet help the environment.

Damaging objectives
Personal objectives

Senior directors might support decisions which maximise their financial position by, for example, ensuring that short-term profit targets are met and bonuses obtained. When a board pursues personal aspirations, it is more likely to make decisions which increase the company's short-term profitability and to be less concerned about the company's long-term earnings potential (referred to as *'short-termism'*).

Satisficing objectives

In terms of company objectives, *satisficing* would occur where a company's strategic management team pursues objectives that are aimed at keeping everyone happy by providing a satisfactory return to equity holders, and not at maximising the value of a company.

Changes in company objectives

The primary objective of a company may change over time. A young start-up company, for instance, may strive to achieve market share and hence pursue growth as the primary objective, changing to profit maximisation when a certain size has been reached. When a company's financial risk increases beyond a point that is deemed acceptable by the board, the primary financial objective may be to reduce gearing in the company. When a company gets into real financial difficulties and is forced into liquidation, the strategic aim might be to operate the business so as to minimise the costs of liquidation and provide the maximum return to the company's stakeholders (namely the employees, creditors, tax authorities, loan creditors, preference shareholders and equity holders) and to ensure that there is equity in the treatment of each group until the company is closed and final distribution takes place.

Business finance – company objectives

In business finance theory it is assumed that the primary objective of a company is to maximise company value. By doing this, the value of equity holders' holding will be maximised. **Equity holder value** is a combination of dividends received in the past and the current market value of shares held. **Equity holder return** is the dividend received in a period plus the capital gain made on the value of equity shares held over the period. Assuming only one objective is a simplistic approach to a complicated area. As mentioned in the previous section, there are a variety of financial and non-financial objectives and companies do not just pursue one objective – often several are considered important, with their importance changing in light of changes in the economy, the global market, the environment and even when individual director's change. In defence of assuming the pursuit of only one objective, it is argued that market forces cause a company's directors to pursue value-creation strategies, and this happens in the real world. Decision making that conflicts with equity holders' interests will not be tolerated by the market. Equity holders can elect to change the directors, or may even sell their shares causing company value to drop, which may result in the company becoming a target for a takeover bid (after which the directors will be made redundant). There is also a market for top level executives, with premium salary packages being paid for executives who have a proven track record in increasing company value.

It can also be argued that pursuing value creation has social benefits. The proportion of shares held by the general public is increasing, aided by the spread of the World Wide Web and platforms that allow trading to take place from an individual's home. The theory is that, if all companies pursue policies to increase their wealth, then society's wealth would increase also. In addition, many insurance and pension companies hold large stakes in the stock market. If the market performs well, then retired people will get higher pensions and insurance premiums will not have to be as high, which will increase society's wealth.

Strategic planning and company value

The elements that a board of directors will have to consider when formulating the company's *strategic plan* will be driven primarily by the company's mission and will be influenced by secondary financial and non-financial strategic objectives. In addition to considering the overall aims of the company, policy makers should also have regard for the business environment within which they operate, both internally and externally. As recommended by Turnbull (discussed later in this chapter), the approach to setting a strategic plan should focus on identifying the risks faced by a company and formulating strategies to minimise these risks. The external factors that may cause risk exposure include the environment (for example changes to regulation), the economy and changes within foreign markets. Internally, cost structure, employee morale, agency costs and gearing may cause risk exposure. The interaction of these various forces on the formulation of a strategic plan is set out in the following diagram. The primary objective is the overriding driver in the formulation of the strategic business plan; however, secondary objectives and identified risk exposures will also influence the plan.

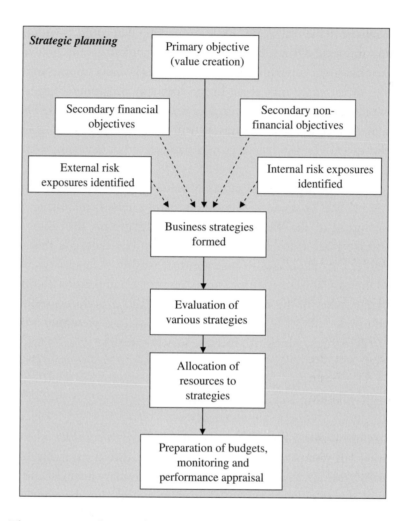

The strategic plan is denominated in financial terms and business finance is pivotal to all stages of the preparation and implementation of a strategic plan. Business finance is now explained.

Business finance explained

Sometimes referred to as *financial management, business finance* is concerned with financial decision making within a business. The decisions usually involve deciding on a course of action that will maximise the output received from a company's resources, ultimately resulting in an increase in the value of the company. Indeed, the objective of business finance decision making is assumed to be planning, raising and using resources in an effective and efficient manner, hence providing the maximum return to equity holders. As a company's primary objective is assumed to be value creation, the business finance objective is congruent with this aim. Most large companies have a finance function; within this department a business finance manager/director will have ultimate responsibility for business finance decision making. This role is now explained.

Role of the business finance manager

A business finance manager works with other managers to provide relevant information which is used by the board of directors for strategic decision making. Business finance normally involves making decisions in three key areas: investment, finance and dividend decisions.

Investment decision

The investment decision making process involves evaluating different projects. The business finance manager usually provides meaningful reports to the board of directors detailing expected outcomes and risks for each option. The appraisal methods adopted should allow the board of directors to make consistent comparisons across various options and easily identify those options that will result in the greatest value creation for the company.

Investment appraisal is deemed to be the most important decision facing a company, as it determines the future earnings potential of a company. The investment decision can be split into two types: internal and external. Internal decisions include asset replacements, new capital projects, working capital levels and surplus cash investment (short-term investments or portfolio theory) decisions. External investment decisions include merger and takeover decisions.

Finance decision

The business finance manager also has to concern himself with the source of finance to be used by a company for funding its investments. Each company can obtain finance by selling claims to its assets and future earnings in the marketplace. These claims are formalised into financial securities, which are categorised as either debt or equity. The holders of the financial securities are entitled to interest and capital repayments and dividends and capital growth. The return required by debt security holders is usually lower than equity security holders as they are exposed to less risk. Debt securities rank in front of equity securities when distributions are made and on the liquidation of a company. Interest has to be paid, whereas dividends can be waived. This means that debt, though cheaper, increases the financial risks faced by a company.

The overriding aim of the finance decision is to obtain the cheapest source of finance, without damaging overall company value. This is more complicated than it would first seem. For example, when too much debt is issued, equity holders are likely to react to the increased risk by either demanding a higher return or selling their shares. Therefore, when analysing the cost of a source of finance, the business finance manager not only has to take into account the cost of the new finance being obtained, but should also include the potential shift in the cost of the existing finance, in response to the new capital structure. Amount and timing are also important. The business finance manager has to provide the correct amount of finance: too much leaves a surplus that may not earn an appropriate return; too little exposes the investment to the risk of non-completion. If finance is received too early, it will not be utilised to earn a return, yet the financiers will have to be paid; if it is received too late, the investment will not be able to proceed as planned.

Dividend decision

Dividends are cash returns to equity holders. In practice, equity holders prefer a company to follow a stable dividend policy. When equity holders are happy with a company's dividend policy, they are more interested in holding shares in the company – this drives up share price, hence increasing company value. Deviations from a set dividend policy are also regarded favourably by equity holders in certain circumstances. For example, equity holders will react favourably when a company distributes surplus funds that are not being used to generate a return that is in excess of the cost of the company's capital. The distributed funds can be re-invested by the equity holders elsewhere to earn a higher return.

Relationship between the key decisions

Each of the key decisions cannot be taken in isolation and each decision will impact on the other two. Modigliani and Miller suggest that each company has two main sources of cash and two main uses of cash:

> ### Table to show sources and uses of cash in a company
>
> | Sources | Company Uses |
> | --- | --- |
> | Profits | Dividends |
> | Financing | Investments |

Dividends and investments are uses of finance and profits and financing are sources of finance. In all instances the sources should equal the uses. The basic relationship between the investment, financing and dividend decisions is given in a formula suggested by Modigliani and Miller:

$$P+F=D+I$$

Where: P = Profit

F = New financing

D = Dividends/distributions

I = Investment

It is argued that the interaction between the variables in the model affects company value and that the equation is constrained by various influences. For example, the availability of finance may depend on the current gearing of the company, its historic performance and its size. The variables are also related to each other; for example, the acceptability of an investment will depend on the cost of the chosen method of financing. An investment which can only be financed using an expensive source of finance, which will not cover the rate of return received from the investment, will most likely not be accepted, even though the return from the investment exceeds the current return earned by the company and the current cost of the company's capital.

As a source of finance, retained earnings have no issue costs and are quick and easy to obtain, and, as such, they are the preferred source of finance by decision makers. However, if a company uses retained earnings to finance an investment, this will reduce the amount available for dividends. Dividend policy usually influences a company's share price.

Equity holders like a company to adopt a steady dividend payout policy. Changes to the policy are likely to immediately affect share price, and, hence, company value. A volatile policy will also reduce the attractiveness of new equity share issues to market participants. Finally, the choice of profitable investments will affect the amount of future profits available for increased dividends.

Knowledge of the potential influence of each of the key decisions on each other and the consequences for company value is required for successful business finance decision making.

Qualities of a business finance manager

Business finance managers need to be strong communicators. They need to be able to transform data into information and to present this information in a meaningful manner to others. They have to attend board meetings when strategy is being discussed and to inform the board of the strengths, weaknesses, opportunities and threats in respect of each option. Collecting data about alternatives involves communicating across departments within a company, so the finance manager needs to establish communication channels with the purchasing, sales, credit control, inventory holding, production, marketing, financial accounting and management accounting departments.

In addition to strong communication skills and internal networks, a wide knowledge is required of subjects that extend beyond finance. These areas are explained now.

Financial accounting

Financial accounting centres on the preparation of financial statements that portray the historic results of a company for a period (in terms of profitability and cash-generation activities) and its financial position at a point in time. The finance manager needs to be able to interpret the financial statements of a company. The balance sheet reflects the sources of a company's finance and how that finance has been invested by the board of directors. The income statement shows the past performance of a company. This information can be used to analyse past decisions and to predict future profitability. The cash flow statement provides information on cash earnings and their sources, again useful information for predicting the future cash flow expectations for a company.

Management accounting

Management accounting focuses on accounting for decision making within a company. Management accounting pays particular attention to costs and their relationship to time and to output. Management accounting information on costs can help to inform finance decision making. The management accounting function will prepare budgets in respect of current operations and variance reports and will usually feed back reasons for variances to the board of directors. This information will be beneficial to business finance managers as it can highlight where prior finance projections were incorrect, or simply provide a better understanding of costs, leading to improved business finance decision making in the future.

Maths and statistics

The efficiency of a variety of options and the risk associated with these options can be formally assessed using quantitative techniques. For example, a cost minimisation model, the economic order quantity model, can be used to determine the optimal inventory order quantity, given a set level of demand, for a period. Expected values, standard deviations and variances can provide information on risk and return. Linear programming can help support decision making when there is capital rationing. However, it should be stressed that these techniques usually only add weight to a business finance manager's instinctive views as to the best option to pursue when deciding amongst a variety of options.

Law

When undertaking business finance decision making, knowledge of legislation and regulations affecting a company is mandatory. All companies have to comply with company law; public listed companies also need to comply with stock exchange rules. Legislation usually strives to protect stakeholders. For example, there are restrictions on the amount of dividends that a company can distribute. This law aims to protect loan creditors. Also a business finance manager has to be aware of the consequences of offering assets as security for debt. If the security is fixed, then those assets cannot be sold. When equity is being raised, there is a legal requirement to allow existing equity holders to retain their current equity holding proportion; they are given pre-emptive rights to purchase new share issues before the new issue is made available in the marketplace.

Taxation

There are different types of tax and a business finance manager needs to be aware of the different taxes as they will ultimately influence business finance decision making. Companies pay corporation tax on net earnings, therefore changes in corporation tax rates will alter expected future cash flows. Knowing what is tax deductible and what is not is also important – for example, depreciation is not tax-deductible, but capital allowances are. The differences in these two deductions can be material, particularly when the government gives first-year allowances for certain types of capital expenditure. In terms of financing, interest on debt securities is tax deductible (reducing its net cost to a company), whereas dividends are not. Given that equity holders value a company on the basis of expected future cash flows, changes to taxation will impact on company value.

As the objective of business finance is to maximise the wealth of ordinary equity holders, it is important that a business finance manager has knowledge of personal taxes. In respect of equity holdings, individuals face two taxes: capital gains tax and income tax. Finance managers should keep abreast of the changes in both taxes and consideration of the changes should be reflected in dividend policy. For example, when capital gains tax rates are low, the company may feel that it would be in its equity holders' interests to retain funds, reinvest them and cause their company share price to rise. Equity holders could than sell some shares and make a capital gain, which would be taxed at a lower rate than dividend income.

Economics

The business finance manager also has to have knowledge of economics. For example, an understanding of theories on the price elasticity of demand and the allocation of scarce resources should inform decisions in respect of new products; or changes to existing products. Understanding the relationship between inflation, interest rates and foreign exchange rates and the impact of changes to these variables on the markets will inform decision making, if sourcing finance. For example, when deciding on a loan product and the terms and type of interest rate to adopt, it is useful to have a reliable opinion on expected interest rate movements. When the finance manager expects that these rates will fall, a flexible interest option might be preferable; conversely when the finance manager expects interest rates to rise, a fixed-rate loan product might be more desirable.

Inflation also influences decision making, reducing the real return earned by a company.

Background influences on business finance decision making

Human behaviour
The finance manager has to be aware of conflicting objectives that can hinder decision making.

Conflict between internal departments
Conflict can arise between different departments within a company. This conflict might be caused, or accentuated, by an ineffective appraisal system. For example, if the purchasing department manager is rewarded for obtaining supplies at cheap rates, this will encourage bulk purchasing to obtain discounts. However, this causes a problem for the stores department manager who has to incur extra costs trying to maintain and insure the goods. If the stores manager is being appraised on the ability to minimise costs, conflict will arise. These sorts of issues arise in virtually every decision that impacts on more than one department. The business finance manager can introduce a more strategic viewpoint by, for example, weighing up the costs associated with having additional funds tied up in inventories and the increased costs of storing inventories, against the benefit gained from the discount received. The business finance manager can inform both departments of the most appropriate course of action, removing conflict.

Conflict between equity holders and creditors
Though the primary focus of business finance is to support decision making that creates value for equity holders, this should not be done at the expense of other legitimate stakeholders who also have claims on company assets. Creditors/debt financiers have invested in the company also and directors have a duty of care to ensure that their decision making does not put these financiers' claims at undue risk, even if the action would increase equity holder value. Debt financiers rank in front of equity holders when it comes to yearly distributions and on liquidation of a company; however, their return is capped, whereas the yearly and final distribution available to equity holders is not restricted. They can reap the balance of rewards available in each year and on liquidation. Conflict arises as pressure may

be exerted by equity holders to distribute excessive amounts, which may cause liquidity problems and an inability to pay the debt financiers in future years.

Many debt issuers protect themselves by building covenants into debt trust deeds. These covenants might legally restrict the level of dividend that can be distributed or restrict the gearing level of a company. The ethical stance of the board of directors in many instances also provides protection for debt holders (ethics is discussed later in the chapter).

Agency theory (the equity holder and director conflict)

It is one thing determining that the primary objective of a company should be value creation and getting board acceptance for this objective; it is another to encourage a board of directors to take decisions in support of this objective when the decision may cause them personal financial harm. For example, value creation will be enhanced by taking decisions that will maximise the long-run earnings of the company. However, these decisions may result in the rejection of other investments that provide higher short-term returns. Directors' bonus packages may be tied into short-term profitability. In addition, low returns and cash inflows in recent years might cause the liquidity of a company to deteriorate, increasing the financial risk associated with the company. Some directors may not wish to have their single source of income (their salaries) put at risk and so may oppose decisions that are not congruent with their own personal financial goals. This conflict is referred to in the relevant literature as 'agency theory'. *Agency theory* considers that directors are 'agents' who act on behalf of a 'principal': the equity holders. The directors should make decisions that fulfil equity holders' needs – namely value creation.

A commonly used method to encourage congruence between the aims of directors and equity holders is to align the financial rewards available to the board of directors with those of the equity holders. The financial rewards might include setting bonuses and rewards for meeting long-term performance targets. The performance targets might include achieving a certain growth in the earnings per share over a three-to-five year period, achieving a minimum return on equity over a three-to-five year period or achieving a minimum return on assets over a three to five year period. Another method is to award share options to directors as part of their salary package.

Share options allow the holder to purchase shares at a set price on a future date – usually in three-to-ten years' time. If management has performed well and taken decisions that maximise equity holder value, then share price on the exercise date will exceed the target price when the options were first issued. Management can then purchase the shares at the lower price and can either sell them immediately, realising a financial gain, or retain the shares and benefit from future capital value increases.

A problem with share option schemes is that they do not indicate whether an increased share price is due to genuine value creation caused by management decision making or whether it is due to positive changes in the economy. Equally so, they mask good performance when there has been a general downturn.

Every company incurs a considerable amount of expenditure in trying to reduce/monitor the agency problem. These costs are termed *'agency costs'* and include audit fees, costs associated with the remuneration committee and costs of aligning salaries with equity holder objectives. If the market were considered efficient (discussed later), this would hinder managers' motivation to make decisions that conflict with equity holders' objectives, as the actions of directors would be transparent. When directors act in conflict with equity holders' wishes, equity holders have two options. They can remove the directors or sell their shares. If sufficient numbers sell their shares, this will cause the value of the company to fall, making it a prime target for takeover. After a takeover occurs, the directors will be removed. In addition, directors operate in a competitive employment market. There is more demand for directors who have a proven track record of creating value. These directors can command high salaries.

Though equity holders are the owners of a company, they are not responsible for its governance. This responsibility falls firmly with company directors. Good corporate governance practices help to reduce agency conflicts.

Corporate governance

The rise in the importance of corporate governance
A number of high profile company scandals and collapses in Britain (Robert Maxwell, Mint and Boxed, Levitt, Polly Peck, BCCI, Barings bank), in Ireland (Powerscreen) and, more recently, in the United States

(WorldCom, Enron) have increased the attention afforded by regulators to the corporate governance of companies. The scandals reduced public confidence in financial reporting, the audit process and the worth of regulatory watchdogs (such as the London Stock Exchange and the government). To build confidence, the London Stock Exchange set up a committee, in 1991, to: investigate the responsibilities of executive and non-executive directors; determine whether an audit committee is required; clarify the principal responsibilities of auditors; and consider the responsibilities the board of directors has to other stakeholders. This committee issued a report in 1992: the first 'code of best practices' for the governance of a company. This report is known as the **Cadbury Report** after Sir Adrian Cadbury, the lead investigator. *Cadbury Report* defined corporate governance as:

'the system by which companies are directed and controlled'.

The *Cadbury Report* detailed the composition of a typical board of directors in a company with good corporate governance practices and outlined the board's recommended responsibilities. It suggested that the board of directors meet regularly, take steps to ensure that they have control of the company at all times and ensure that the board has sufficient segregation of duties so that no one director has ultimate control, as in the case of Robert Maxwell. The report recommended conditions to ensure the independence of non-executive directors (they should not be awarded share options as remuneration, have no dealings with the company and be able to obtain independent advice at the company's expense). The report recommended that executive directors (and non-executive directors) hold office for only three years, though they could be reappointed by equity holders. The report also recommended the establishment of two committees: a remuneration committee to deal with remuneration packages, and an audit committee to control the internal audit within a company. Companies listed on the London Stock Exchange have to disclose the extent of compliance with the *Corporate Report*. Non-PLCs are not required to disclose the extent of their compliance; however, it is recommended by professional accounting bodies that it be included.

The **Greenbury Report** (1995) strengthened some of the suggestions made in the *Cadbury Report* by recommending that all members of the remuneration committee be non-executive directors, and a remuneration report setting out all the remuneration details for each director (executive and non-executive) should be made available in the annual report of a company. A further report, the **Hampel Report** (1998), recommended that the role of the chairman and chief executive be segregated and that directors receive training on corporate governance. This report recommends that directors narrow their responsibilities to their primary duty – the enhancement of equity holders' value. These reports were integrated to form the **Combined Code** in 1999.

Corporate governance and risk
Risk is inherent in virtually every strategic decision taken by a company. Company value is affected by all prior strategic decisions. The market values a company based on its expected future income and the risk associated with achieving that income. When risk is high, market participants will value a company lower than it would, if risk were lower. Most boards direct specific attention to identifying the risks that a company faces and creating strategies to manage those risks. This may involve, for example, hedging transactions. The level of risk faced by a company is influenced by the nature of a business, its capital structure, foreign risk and exposures that might arise when there are changes in micro-economic conditions. For example, a manufacturing company that imports most of its supplies from one country, hires a labour force in another country (maybe a third world country) and exports its products to yet another country, will face far higher risks when compared to a similar company that purchases and sells its products in one country (that has a stable economy). Were the future expected income from both companies the same, the latter company would be valued at a premium by the market, due to its lower exposure to the various risks.

Corporate governance, risk and strategic management
Risk identification, evaluation and management have become more important over the past two decades. After the establishment of the *Combined Code* of practice for corporate governance, a working party was established to provide best practice guidance on how to comply with the *Combined Code*. This group was led by Nigel Turnbull and their recommendations were published in a report called *Internal Control – Guidance for Directors on the Combined Code* in 1999 (referred to as the **Turnbull Report**). The report suggests that a risk-based approach should be taken when establishing internal controls and when reviewing their effectiveness. The ethos of the report is not that a company should undertake a box-ticking exercise

to ensure compliance, but should embrace the principles of risk-based management as a means of increasing company value. This approach is captured by Sir Brian Jenkins, Chairman of the Corporate Governance Group of the ICEAW, in the preface to the guidance report: *Implementing Turnbull: A Board Room Briefing, 1999* when he stated:

> 'for directors the task ahead is to implement control over the wider aspects of business risk in such a way as to add value rather than merely go through a compliance exercise. There is also a need to get the buy-in of people at all levels of the organisation and to focus on risk management and internal controls in such a way as to improve the business.'

The *Combined Code* (1999) was updated in 2003 to include the *Turnbull Report* (1999) and the **Smith Report** (2003) and recently updated again (in 2005) by a working party lead by Douglas Flint. The findings of this recent review were that there is widespread support for the recommendations of Turnbull, with most companies adopting a risk-based approach to their strategic management. Indeed, the United States (US) Securities and Exchange Commission (SEC) has identified the Turnbull guidance as a suitable framework for reporting on a company's internal controls for financial reporting. The US legal requirements for disclosures in relation to internal controls are set out in section 404(a) of the Sarbanes-Oxley Act (2002) and the SEC's rules. In contrast to the US's 'rule based' approach, in the UK, the approach has remained 'principle based', with Flint recommending that this approach remain.

Evidence of the adoption of Turnbull can be found in the narrative part of most listed company's annual reports. For example Viridian Group PLC refer directly to the *Turnbull Report* in the introduction to their comments on their internal controls:

Viridian Group PLC Annual Report and Accounts 2005–2006

Corporate Governance Report
Internal Control
The Board has fully implemented the FRC's Internal Control: Revised Guidance for Directors on the Combined Code published in October 2005 (Revised Turnbull Guidance).

Viridian Group PLC explain their risk exposures under several headings. In the *Financial Review Report* explanations of 'liquidity and interest rate risk', 'foreign currency risk', 'commodity risk' and 'credit risk' are provided. As recommended by Turnbull, the *Corporate Governance Report* refers to the company's general risk-management procedures, the structure of which is provided in the following excerpt from *Viridian Group PLC's Annual Report (2005–06)*:

Viridian Group PLC Annual Report and Accounts 2005–2006

Corporate Governance Report
Risk management
The Group's strategy is to follow an appropriate risk policy, which effectively manages exposures related to the achievement of business objectives. The Risk Management Committee, chaired by the Group Finance Director, comprises a number of senior managers from across the Group and meets monthly to assist the Board in fulfilling its risk management and control responsibilities. It reports to the Audit Committee, the Executive Committee and the Board on a regular basis. The Committee regularly reviews individual business risk registers as well as registers covering a number of functional areas including group finance, treasury, regulatory affairs and procurement and also receives regular updates on IT governance arrangements. The Committee also reviews business continuity and IT disaster recovery arrangement and has responsibility for monitoring the Group's CSR strategy and programmes.

Risk issues are also addressed at management meetings through the review of risk registers. These meetings consider early warning signs or risks materialising and significant control failings or weaknesses.

The Executive Committee and the Board specifically consider the corporate risk register which sets out those risks which are managed at a corporate level and/or the management of which is determined by policy set at a corporate level.

Ethics, company objectives and business finance

In many instances, having regard to ethical practices might restrict the extent to which a company can achieve its primary objective. For example, in a global economy, there is much to be gained by companies who have products that can be made in countries that have no employment laws. For example, profits and company value will increase if a company is able to access cheap labour, or even child labour, for next to nothing (so long as the company does not advertise its policy in this area as this may cause an adverse reaction in the stock market, as equity holders are likely to react irrationally). In these circumstances, companies justify their actions by arguing that some income to a family is better than none, or by highlighting the fact that, though the salaries paid are low, they are higher than those paid by indigenous companies. Many companies also use some of their profits for social purposes in the communities that they are located in, by, for example, building schools, building churches, building hospitals or getting running water. These are all deemed to be signs of these companies acting ethically.

The use of bribery or corruption may be seen as part and parcel of normal trade within certain countries. In a global economy, when there is so much pressure to perform, directors may consider using unethical approaches to achieve a company's primary objectives. However, unethical behaviour cannot be defended on the grounds of it being normal practice in a country, nor can it be defended by the argument 'if I did not do it, someone else would' or 'we would lose the business to a competitor, who does it'.

Acting ethically in relation to company stakeholders is also in a company's long-term interest. By treating customers and suppliers correctly, future sales and supplies are being secured. Paying loan creditors the interest and capital repayments they are due on time will ensure that this source of finance can be used again in the future. Avoiding the practice of gearing the company unnecessarily just to make returns to equity holders, builds confidence in the management of the company, from creditors' perspectives. Showing concern for employee welfare (and acting on it) will ensure loyalty and increased effort from employees. By taking steps to reduce pollution, the health of employees will not deteriorate, which will reduce staff down time. In addition, the company's image will be improved and future sales may result. Equity holders should also be treated fairly; they should be kept well informed about a company's performance, future developments and strategies. Equity holders should not be surprised by the dividend that they are paid. If equity holders feel that they are being treated fairly, then the market will value the company higher and the equity holder body is more likely to support director decisions in the future.

Financial environment

Business finance managers and strategic decision makers also have to be aware of the financial environment and how external factors can impact on financial decision making. The *financial environment* encapsulates the *economic environment* within which a company operates and the *financial markets* in which a company's long-term funds are sourced and traded.

Economic influences

Inflation has been earmarked by governments as a major influence on a country's economic growth. When demand for a good outstrips supply, inflation results. In these circumstances, the supplier can increase the price of the good, without losing sales. The consequence is that the good becomes more expensive to purchasers who see the real value of their wages and capital fall. Purchasers will subsequently put pressure on their employers to increase their wages so that they can maintain their current spending power (capital maintenance). Due to the fall in the purchasing value of individuals' incomes, demand for products will fall. Individuals may become conservative and reduce overall spending, which will result in an economic down turn in the economy. When the purchaser is a company, pressure grows to increase the price of the end product, due to the increased production/supply costs. This may result in a loss of sales for the company and financial difficulties. When there are financial difficulties, companies will try to cut costs, which can mean job losses.

Interest rate changes are used as a means of controlling demand for goods. The assumption is that interest rate increases will reduce the overall spending power of consumers (who usually have a reasonable amount of debt), bringing demand for goods down to a level that discourages companies with excess demand from increasing prices. Therefore the price of goods does not increase, just the price of debt.

Foreign exchange rates are also of great influence to a company that imports supplies, exports goods, borrows or invests in other countries. When the value of a currency in one country rises, the subsequent cost of goods exported from that country increases, resulting in a loss of demand for the country's goods (assuming that demand is related to price) and vice versa.

Economic influences and business finance

Inflation and foreign exchange rate changes affect asset values, costs and revenues, making it difficult to accurately predict future cash flows (and so the outcomes from any financial decision making) with certainty. Where inflation causes the value of assets to rise, an additional financing requirement will result, as replacement assets (such as inventories, trade receivables or machinery) will be more expensive to purchase. Business finance managers should be aware of the financing implications of inflation and should ensure that sufficient financing is in place to meet future increased cash demands. Where inflation causes the costs of production to rise, an analysis of the impact on profitability should be undertaken. A strong knowledge of the competitive market for the good being sold by the company is vital, as the business finance manager would need to be able to estimate the reaction of customers and competitors to price changes. If this reaction is wrongly anticipated, the company could lose market share and profitability.

When interest rates increase, the required return by company financiers will also increase. This is because the risk-free rate of interest (the guaranteed return on a risk-free investment such as a bank deposit account) has increased, therefore the premium required by financiers (equity holders and debt holders) will increase the overall return expected. When the expected return by a company's financiers increases, the number of potential investments that can be undertaken by a company falls, as only those investments that cover the new higher required return by financiers will be accepted. All existing investment and assets will need to be reviewed and any that are not meeting the new higher required rate of return should be liquidated and utilised to reduce current debt levels. The cash outflow on debt finance cannot be waived, hence debt finance increases financial risk.

Company managers should also have hedging policies in place to reduce the exposure to loss in company value caused by changes in exchange rates.

One simple, yet commonly used, technique is to have a bank account located in the foreign country. Exchange rates can be fixed using derivative financial instruments such as forward rate contracts, futures contracts or swap contracts.

The markets and business finance

The financial environment also encapsulates the markets in which a company's long-term funds are sourced and traded. Having specific knowledge of economics and investment finance on their own is not sufficient; a finance manager also needs to have knowledge of the financial environment. A business finance manager needs to be able to predict the reaction of the market to, for example, the company dividend policy and any changes proposed to it (discussed in depth in chapter 19). Changes in capital structure will also be judged by the market (discussed in depth in chapter 15). A business finance manager needs to know how to raise equity and debt in the financial markets. To do this efficiently, a good knowledge of the equity markets and bond markets is required (discussed in depth in chapters 6 and 7). Knowledge of the sources of private equity and debt finance also supports business finance decision making (venture capital finance is discussed in chapter 5).

The demand for a company's shares determines the market value of that company, hence management should make efforts to promote trading in a company's shares as a means of increasing equity holder value. Therefore, business finance managers must not only strive to increase the long-term cash inflows of the company, but should also aim to create an efficient market for the company's shares. In an **efficient market**, share price encapsulates all the information that is currently available about a company and the economy. An efficient market is one that will promote confidence in the market and trade in shares, as equity holders will consider that the value of the quoted shares is fair and managers will believe that the amount received for a new issue is fair.

The efficient market hypothesis (EMH)

There are theories to suggest that speculative trading will not reap gains above average market gains. The theories are based on the 'information content of shares' and the interpretation of information that is available in respect of a company. The EMH theory suggests that competition between market participants wipes out excess profits that can be made from owning shares. Where market shares are mispriced, market participants will react quickly and buy or sell shares driving share price up or down depending on whether the shares are under or over priced. Therefore shares are priced at the value they are worth and no speculative gains or losses can be made by equity holders above and beyond the gains on the market overall, which responds to economic influences. It is assumed that share price includes all price-sensitive information there is about the company and reflects the impact of changes in the economy on the value of equity. In a nutshell, there is no information asymmetry. *Information asymmetry* is a term used to describe an information gap, or misinterpretation of information provided. In the context of the market price of shares, it usually refers to the misinterpretation of price-sensitive information, or the failure to provide this information by a company to the market.

In 1970, an economist, Fama, suggested that market efficiency be analysed using three levels of efficiency: weak-form efficiency, semi-strong-form efficiency and strong-form efficiency.

Weak-form efficiency

When markets are considered to be **weak-form efficient**, it means that the share price reflects all historic information in respect of a company. This form of market efficiency suggests that chartists (who chart the past pattern of performance of a company in an attempt to predict the future pattern of price movement to make gains) will not be successful, as market participants will be fully aware of all historic information and will know that selling shares when the price falls would be irresponsible, given that they know the share price will rise after a short period of time to a level beyond its initial position – hence there will not be a market for the shares and no excess gains can be made from speculative trading. According to this theory, investors who can anticipate future performance and investors with inside information can make excess returns.

Semi-strong-form efficiency

This goes further than weak-form efficiency. **Semi-strong-form efficiency** assumes that equity share price reflects all historic information in respect of a company and all publicly available information. If one equity holder reads a price-sensitive publication by the company, then all equity holders will read the information and interpret it in the same way, instantaneously. Therefore, there will not be a surge in trade for shares if, for example, a company issues a profit statement above what was initially publicised as expected, as the equity holders will require a premium to sell the shares, effectively cancelling the potential gain that could be made were the equity shares to be purchased at the price quoted before the announcement went public. According to this theory, only investors with insider knowledge will consistently make excess returns.

Strong-form efficiency

When a market is assumed to be **strong-form efficient**, equity share price is deemed to reflect all historic, publicly available and private information in respect of a company. Therefore, no market participant can make excessive gains above average market gains. This form of market has no information asymmetry and market participants with insider information cannot make returns in excess of the market.

Empirical research has indicated that markets are generally weak-form or semi-strong-form efficient and are typically not strong-form efficient. In practice, it is difficult to determine the extent of efficiency in markets or to pigeonhole markets into one of the aforementioned efficiency levels. Investors do make gains (and losses) suggesting that markets are not fully efficient. If markets were fully efficient there would be no need for investors at all, as anyone (without expert knowledge) would be able to purchase a portfolio of well balanced shares and perform as well as the markets. In reality, investors analyse financial statements and make adjustments for creative accounting, economic influences and the expected outcome of new investments, and then use the resultant figures to assist them in their decision on whether to buy, sell or hold a block of shares.

Government intervention

The welfare of companies within a country impacts on country wealth, therefore governments usually act to promote the growth and development of industries. Economic policy (discussed above – inflation, foreign exchange policies, employment, interest rates, importing and exporting), taxation (capital gains tax rates, corporation tax rates and income tax rates and capital allowances), grants and legislative changes are the main tools used by governments to influence company business finance decision making. Tax changes influence dividend, investment and finance policies. Grants influence investment decision making and changes to legislation enforce ethical and environmental responsibilities. For example, responsible reporting is encouraged by the Companies Acts for the benefit of stakeholders; employee welfare is protected by legislation on employment and health and safety; consumers are protected by consumer protection and consumer rights legislation and the environment is protected by environmental legislation and grants for environmentally friendly approaches.

Governments generally try to promote free markets and competition, and try to reduce regulation. However, in some instances they will intervene if it is in the interest of the overall industry or the economy. For example, where dominant players abuse their position, regulators (the Competition Commission, for instance) will intervene to ensure that customers and smaller companies within an industry are not being unfairly treated.

Globalisation

Business finance decision making needs to consider resources and markets that exist outside the country of residence. The current business world is global in its nature. Any business that fails to consider the advantages and disadvantages associated with the global economy and markets will not be serving their equity holders' interests to the full. For example, large multinational manufacturing companies can shift their labour-intensive production facilities to parts of the world that have lower salaries and running costs (for instance, the Fruit of the Loom textile manufacturing company moved some of its manufacturing from Ireland to Morocco). In the past, this sort of relocation would not have been attractive as the savings to be made would have been nullified by high risks and expensive transportation costs. Now companies spend increasing amounts of time and money building up relationships with governments and businesses in other countries. This practice helps to reduce foreign risks, as does the wide acceptance of the euro. Transportation costs have also fallen.

Advances in technology have been another driving force; the Internet and World Wide Web have enabled quick and effective communication across the globe, cheaply. In addition, the time differences between countries mean that 24-hour working days are possible if a company has branches located across the globe. The result is that outsourcing to foreign countries is regarded as a cost-saving business technique. For example, to reduce employee costs, many computer software companies use branches in India to write programming code and several telesales companies have moved operations overseas.

Conclusion

This chapter focuses on explaining the importance of business finance knowledge to the success of a company. This conclusion summarises briefly the key messages to be taken from the chapter.

Having appropriately qualified and experienced people leading a company influences its success. That is why directors in large public limited companies are awarded high salaries. These individuals determine company strategy, which is vital to company success. As directors are employed by equity holders, it is assumed that the main strategy adopted, in theory, is value creation – the maximisation of financial benefits to equity holders.

Business finance has a core role to play in value creation. The three main business finance decisions influence value creation. The investment decision determines the future operating cash inflows of the company, the finance decision deals with how to finance the investments and the dividend decision focuses on how equity holders' wealth will be influenced by the level of distributions made. These core decisions are interrelated and also impact on virtually all departments within a company (such as purchasing, sales, production, credit control, marketing and finance). Therefore, directors not only require knowledge of business finance, they also need to have a broad understanding of all the departments within a company.

As well as internal company-specific knowledge, decision makers will also require direct knowledge of specific subject areas that may influence a decision. These include law, taxation and economics. They also require knowledge of other subject areas, such as financial accounting, management accounting, maths and statistics, to assist in the evaluation process and analysis of the impact of decisions made. The decision makers also have to be aware of other influences such as business ethics (including agency theory and conflicts between equity holders and creditors) and environmental responsibilities. External factors also influence business finance decision making and the decision makers require knowledge of the economy and the financial environment, at both national and international levels.

Examination standard question

Worked example

Achieving the long-term financial objectives of a company will involve the business finance manager in making decisions regarding investment, financing and dividend policies.

REQUIRED

a)   Explain the nature of these three types of decision and the extent to which they are interrelated.

8 Marks

b)   In making each type of decision, discuss the information which you consider relevant to effective financial management.

8 Marks

c)   Indicate which of the three categories of financial decision you consider to be the most important, giving your reasons.

6 Marks

22 Marks

(ICAI, MABF II, Summer 1995, Question 5)

Solution

a) Investment Decisions

This category covers both internal and external investment. Internal investment in working capital may appear to be short term, but

Continued

---

working capital is a permanent requirement in any company, even though it is turned over and reconstituted in each trading cycle. Other investment decisions include the purchase of capital equipment, which are necessary to provide infrastructure – property, plant, equipment and a functioning organisation. Such acquisitions are also internal, but have a long-term effect. External investment includes the takeover or merger with companies external to the company, either in the same country or internationally.

The company's objective is most commonly assumed to be equity holder wealth maximisation and such investment decisions will be taken with reference to rates of return for the project (adjusted for risk). Other considerations would be the effect of the investment on cash flows and the feasibility of withdrawal from unsuccessful investments.

Financing Decisions

To avail of attractive investment opportunities, there must be suitable sources of finance available. These may include new share issues, loans, retained earnings or sales of assets. The costs of the different types of finance, as compared to the return promised by the investment, means that it is important to match the source of finance with the type of investment; the rule being long-term investment requires a long-term source of finance.

There are two main sources of finance: debt and equity. The interest on debt finance is tax deductible, so the effective cost of debt is the after-tax cost, which is usually less than the cost of equity. However, debt adds risk to the capital structure, as the interest must be paid irrespective of the results for the year. Dividends on equity share finance are optional and so in a bad year, no dividend need be distributed at all. Thus, apart from the cost of the type of finance and the suitability of it to the type of investment decision, there are other factors such as the impact of the type of finance on capital structure (gearing ratio) and on cash flow.

Continued

Dividend Decisions

The dividend decision is concerned with how much to distribute to equity holders. If profits are not distributed as dividends, they are retained and ploughed back into the company; this will result in capital growth and an increase in the share price of a company. When deciding how much to distribute, the main concerns will be the future cash requirements of a company, as well as the preference of equity holders for current income or future capital gains.

Sources and uses of cash	
Sources	*Company uses*
Profits	Dividends
Financing	Investments

From the above table, it can be seen that dividends and investments are uses of finance and profits and financing are sources of finance, i.e. sources = uses.

The basic relationship between investment, financing and dividend decisions is given by Modigliani and Miller in the following formula:

$$D+I=P+F$$

  D = Dividends
  I = Investment
  P = Profit
  F = New financing

There are subtle interactions between the decisions. The acceptability of an investment will depend on the cost of the chosen method of financing. A project which can only be financed using very expensive sources, which cannot be covered by the rate of return from the project, may have to be abandoned. If a company uses retained earnings for finance, this will affect the amount available for dividends. The dividend policy may affect the company's share price and consequently the possibility of financing investments by issuing shares. Finally, the choice of profitable investments will affect the amount of future profits available for increased dividends.

Continued

b) Investment Decisions

The information required for investment decision making might include the following:

Capital equipment and infrastructure
- estimated timing and amount of cash flows
- uncertainty surrounding cash flow estimates
- appropriate cost of capital/hurdle rate
- details concerning alternative projects
- impact on profitability

Investments in other companies via merger or takeover
- amount of liquid resources available for investment
- market rates of return
- desire to expand/diversify, e.g. declining sales
- levels of risk involved
- foreign issues

The investment in another company must promise a similar return to that obtained from the market in shares of a similar risk class.

Financing Decisions

The information required for financing decisions might include details on any of the following:

- available sources of finance
- current share price/state of the stock market
- current and forecast interest rates
- company's level of gearing
- cash flow implications, i.e. loan repayments, interest charges, dividends
- restrictions imposed by the articles of association
- security available
- restrictions imposed by other loan agreements

The state of the market would affect the decision as to whether to issue new shares. The current market price of shares could be low and

Continued

so a company would have to issue a lot of shares to raise the finance required, rather than waiting for a better share price or using another source of finance. Analysts can assist a company in this regard, in advising them as to whether the market is likely to be bullish or bearish in the future.

If interest rates are rising, a company is more likely to lock into fixed-interest loans or use equity finance or retained earnings, rather than debt. If interest rates are falling, a company is more likely to lock into variable rate debt.

Dividend Decisions

Typical information required when considering the dividend decision might include:

- profits available for distribution (according to the law on distributable profits)
- opportunities for the use of retained profits
- past dividend expectations
- impact of dividend policy on share price
- environment (boom or recession)
- dividend policy of other companies in the same industry sector
- cash liquidity
- possibility of maintaining the payout in the future
- loan agreement restrictions
- whether the directors need to send a signal to the market place

c) It is generally agreed that the investment decision is the most significant of the three types of decisions. The investment decision plays a major role in determining the long-term profitability of the business, as decisions made now produce returns in future years.

For this reason, inappropriate investment decisions will have a detrimental effect on future profits and may even influence the survival prospects of a company.

Additionally, large amounts of long-term finance will be tied up in a major investment and the company cannot afford to waste such

Continued

resources or endanger further share issues or borrowing facilities by investing in projects generating inadequate returns.

It is generally not possible to reverse investment projects without a significant loss of the initial investment. The degree of irreversibility will depend to a large extent on how specific the investment is to the company or industry concerned, e.g. an oil exploration field is not readily re-saleable, unless the price is substantially reduced.

For these reasons, it is reasonable to state that whilst financing and dividend decisions are also important, it is the investment decision that assumes primary importance in effective financial management.

KEY TERMS

Agency costs
Agency theory
Business ethics
Business finance
Cadbury Report
Combined Code
Competitive forces
Competitive strategy
Corporate strategy
Dividend decision
Economic environment
Efficient market
Efficient market hypothesis
Employee welfare
Environmental policies
Equity holder return
Equity holder value
Equity holder wealth
   maximisation
Finance decision
Financial environment
Financial management

Globalisation
Greenbury Report
Hampel Report
Investment decision
Information asymmetry
Mission statement
Non-financial objectives
Operations management
Operational strategy
Profit maximisation
Satisficing
Semi-strong-form efficiency
Short-termism
Smith Report
Strategic management
Strategic plan
Strong-form efficiency
Trade relationships
Turnbull Report
Value creation
Weak-form efficiency

WEBSITES THAT MAY BE OF USE

Information on corporate governance:
http://www.corpgov.net

Information on corporate governance (European Corporate Governance Institute):
http://www.ecgi.org/

Information on corporate governance (Institute of Directors):
http://www.iod.com

Information on corporate governance:
http://www.londonstockexchange.com

Information on agency theory:
http://moneyterms.co.uk/agency/

Information on how computer simulation can aid strategic management:
http://www.smginc.com/

REVIEW QUESTIONS

1. Define strategic management.
2. Provide three examples of non-financial objectives that a company might pursue.
3. Explain the relationship between financial and non-financial objectives.
4. Explain the three forms of market efficiency as suggested by Fama in 1970.
5. How might a government influence company business finance decision making?
6. Briefly explain the need for a business finance manager to have knowledge of taxation, law, mathematics and economics.
7. Enero Plc announces a breakthrough in computer memory storage devices that are so small they can be fitted to mobile phones. Knowledge of this information was secret up to the point of the announcement. The price of the share before the announcement was €/£5.00. Consider the following outcomes:

(a) Following the announcement, the price of each equity share jumps to €/£6.50 and then over the subsequent week falls to €/£5.75.

(b) Following the announcement, the price of each equity share jumps to €/£5.75 and stays there.

(c) Following the announcement the price of each equity share slowly climbs to €/£5.75.

REQUIRED

Which outcome indicates market efficiency? Which do not, and why?

8.   Write an essay to the board of directors of Alexander Ltd (they are concerned about the impact that changes in the economy may have on their business). The essay should cover three issues. The first two should explain:

(i) how changes in the economic environment might impact on the demand for the company's products and on the performance of the company; and

(ii) how changes in the economic environment would impact on business finance decision making.

The third issue is to respond to a suggestion made by one of the directors to you (the finance director) over tea:

Ian Smart informed you that a way to alleviate the impact of the expected downturn in the economy would be to open a factory in Tioeti (a fictional third world country). He suggests that with a couple of small bribes - to the right people, a suitable factory can be obtained and that the local indigenous population (from the age of five upwards) would be delighted to work for a mere fraction of the wages being paid in this country. This would reduce costs and increase profit margins, which would more than outweigh the expected reduction in sales units.

(iii) advise the board as to the appropriateness of this proposal.

Total <u>15</u> Marks
(ICAI, CAP 1, Mock 2007, Q7)

CHALLENGING QUESTIONS

1.   CORPORATE GOVERNANCE

a)   Explain what is meant by corporate governance, and why it is an important factor in determining the value of a company.

5 Marks

b)   List five characteristics of good corporate governance, outlining how each can enhance the value of a company.

10 Marks
Total 15 Marks
(ICAI, CAP 1, Pilot Paper: Finance, 2007, Q1)

2.   STOCK MARKET EFFICIENCY

a)   Why are new equity issues more common when the stock market index is high, relative to when it is low?

10 Marks

b)   Are the reasons provided in a) inconsistent with the efficient market hypothesis?

10 Marks
Total 20 Marks

3.   EFFICIENT MARKETS

a)   Describe the efficient market hypothesis and explain its three forms.

15 Marks

b)   Discuss the relevance of the hypothesis outlined in a) for the internal business finance management of public quoted companies.

10 Marks
Total 25 Marks

4.   NON-EXECUTIVE DIRECTORS

c)   Advise on the responsibilities of a non-executive director to a company and on the potential benefits of such an appointment to the company.

10 Marks
(ICAI, FAE, Extract from Autumn 1996)

SECTION TWO

FINANCIAL STATEMENT ANALYSIS

Chapter 3   **Financial Statement
Analysis**

FINANCIAL STATEMENT ANALYSIS

3

Debt	10,000,000
Equity	15,000,000
Market Value	25,000,000

LEARNING OBJECTIVES

Upon completing this chapter, readers should be able to:

- ♣ Calculate ratios to assess the financial performance, financial position and investment potential of a company;
- ♣ Make suggestions for differences in reported ratios: between similar companies; for the same company over time; and relative to industry averages;
- ♣ List the limitations of ratio analysis;
- ♣ Calculate the Z score of a company using Altman's failure prediction model; and
- ♣ Evaluate the usefulness of ratio analysis for predicting business failure.

Introduction

The most common technique for assessing company financial performance is ratio analysis. *Ratio analysis* summarises the relationships between key data entries from financial statements. Trends in ratios over time are usually calculated and interpreted as being indicative of how a company will perform in the future. Ratio analysis is widely used both in-house to evaluate performance and by external parties, including investors. Ratios can provide very useful information such as the ability of a company to survive and grow and can be used to indicate the efficiency of management. However, care needs to be taken when interpreting ratio results as the conditions in one company may change from year to year, and no two companies are the same. Therefore, ratio analysis should be used to spark investigation, to instigate the correct questions to be asked, or to limit the investigation of changes in performance and efficiency to key areas. Ratios should not be relied on solely to explain changes in the financial performance of a company.

This chapter begins by setting out the purpose of financial statements and examines how these documents can be utilised to help determine the financial position and performance of a company, over time. The chapter splits ratios that are commonly computed when analysing the financial performance of a company into three key areas that are of interest to an investor: company performance, financial position and investment potential. A proforma set of financial statements is provided at the end of the chapter and is used throughout the chapter to provide practical examples of how ratios can be used to interpret company performance, financial position and investment potential. Empirical literature on the use of ratio analysis in predicting corporate failure is briefly visited and the limitations of ratio analysis highlighted.

Financial statements

The annual report of a company is the core document used when evaluating company performance. The annual report can range from, four to five pages long for a sole trader, to over one hundred pages for plc's. A published annual report is primarily in two parts. The first part is mostly narrative and is used by directors and management of a company (agents/stewards) to communicate information directly to equity holders in respect of how they have discharged their stewardship of the company. It also provides information on the future direction, development and plans for a company. The narrative portion of annual reports, for plc's in particular, has expanded over the decades and now usually includes: a chairman's report; an operating and financial review; a remuneration report; a directors' report; a corporate governance report; and a chairman's review. Directors use these reports to reduce information asymmetry between the directors and the company's stakeholders. The reports provide information (financial and non-financial) on for example: the directors; directors' remuneration; corporate governance; the company's strategic objectives/principle aims including steps taken to meet them; major events occurring in the period; risks and uncertainties that might impact on the company; future developments; and material transactions. The narrative part of an annual report does not form part of a company's financial statements.

The second part of the published annual report, the financial statements, includes the historical results of a company. A company's past results are portrayed primarily in three statements: the income statement; the balance sheet; and the cash flow statement. An example of the typical layout of these statements is provided at the back of this chapter. The statements are accompanied by detailed notes (including accounting policies and the statement of changes in equity. In some instances, the latter might be included as a primary statement).

According to the IASB (1989) *'Framework for the Preparation and Presentation of Financial Statements'*:

> 'The objective of financial statements is to provide information about the financial position, performance and changes in financial position of an entity that is useful to a wide range of users in making economic decisions.'

The framework recognises some of the limitations inherent in financial statements for decision making:

> 'they do not provide all the information that users may need to make economic decisions since they largely portray the financial effects of past events and do not necessarily provide non-financial information'.

However, financial statements do provide useful information that an individual, with a reasonable understanding of business, should be able to decipher. The stewardship role of management can be assessed by reviewing the movement in the investments, assets and liabilities of a company. Management's accountability can be assessed by reference to the income statements, supplementary notes and the narrative reports included in the annual report such as the chairman's review or the directors' report.

Ratios are normally sub-divided into a minimum of three categories: performance, financial position and investment potential. Performance ratios focus on assessing the profitability of a company and the efficiency with which a company utilises its resources. Performance ratios are sometimes referred to as **operating ratios.** The financial position category examines the resources held by a company: its liquidity; solvency; and underlying financial structure. The final category, investment potential, focuses on assessing the earnings generated by a company. It investigates the extent of earnings distributed and conversely the amounts retained for capital growth.

Performance

The performance of a company can be analysed according to its profitability and its efficiency.

Profitability

To adequately assess company performance, it is vital to be able to interpret changes in company profitability, and indeed to compare a company's profitability to the profitability of other companies (in the same industry or in other industries). Information on profitability can help: to determine the impact of changes in the economic resources of a company on future profitability; to assess the ability of a company to generate cash flows from its current economic resources; and to predict the success/ failure of future investment decisions made by a company. Information on company profitability can be obtained from the income statement (see example at the back of the page). The *income statement* shows the income and related expenditure for a period. The income statement is split into sections. The first part contains information on the direct costs associated with products/services being produced – revenue less the cost of revenue. The resultant profit, or loss, is termed *gross profit*, or *gross loss*. The second part of the income statement deals with all overhead expenses that are not directly linked with the products being sold, these include administration and distribution expenses. These are totalled and deducted from gross profit to give *net profit*, or *profit before interest and tax* (PBIT). Then interest is removed to give *profit before tax* and finally tax is removed leaving *distributable profit*.

Each of the sub-total profit entries in the income statement provides valuable information to anyone who is trying to analyse the performance of a company (an investor). An investor can see, from looking at the income statement, the absolute size of profits made. A quick scan of the comparatives, allows an investor to determine whether profits have increased, or decreased in absolute terms. The following equation can be used to determine the percentage change in profits:

$$\frac{\text{Current year figure}}{\text{Prior year figure}} - 1 = \text{Growth\%}$$

Worked example 3.1   (Profit analysis: growth in profitability)

REQUIRED

Using the financial statements of ABC plc; calculate the percentage growth in profits.

Solution

The percentage increase in gross profits between 20X6 and 20X7 is:

$$\frac{\text{€/£7,000}}{\text{€/£6,200}} - 1 = 12.9\%$$

Profit has increased by 12.9% over the period: 1 January 20X7 to 31 December 20X7. [Note: Figures are in €/£'000s]

Where the percentage change in profits is positive, this is a good sign; however, it should be interpreted with caution as this formula does not take inflation into consideration. There is only real improvement if the growth rate exceeds the rate of inflation.

Gross profit margin
A commonly used ratio to provide information on gross profit is the gross profit margin; this is calculated as follows:

$$\frac{\text{Gross profit}}{\text{Revenue}} \times 100 = \text{Gross profit margin}$$

The *gross profit margin* is the percentage return made from each sale after direct product costs are deducted. It is sometimes referred to as the *contribution margin* – the contribution from revenue to cover a company's fixed costs and to pay financiers.

Worked example 3.2   (Profit analysis: gross profit margin)

REQUIRED

Using the financial statements of ABC plc; calculate the gross profit percentage for both years.

Solution

The gross profit percentage is:

$$20X7 \quad \frac{\text{€/£}20,000}{\text{€/£}50,000} \times 100 = 40.0\%$$

$$20X6 \quad \frac{\text{€/£}17,000}{\text{€/£}45,000} \times 100 = 37.8\%$$

The gross profit percentage has increased from 37.8% of sales value to 40.0% of sales value. [Note: Figures are in €/£'000s]

The gross profit margin varies between companies, though should be reasonably similar within specific industries. For example, the margin on petrol sales is very small – circa 5%; whereas the margin on grocery sales can range from 10–50% (average at 30%). When products turn over fast (for example, bread), the gross profit margin is usually low, whereas products that do no turn over fast have a higher gross profit margin (for example, jewellery). In general, a company's gross profit performance is best analysed with reference to the industry average, or with other companies selling similar products. Changes in the gross profit margin from year to year within one company should not be common and is likely to be as a result of inflation. Where a change in the margin does result, it may be due to: a change in the selling price of the product (for example, a fall in the margin may be as a result of the company reducing the selling price of its products to achieve more sales and more overall gross profit, but less gross profit per euro/pound of sale); a change in the purchase price of supplies – possibly from loss of discounts; wastage, theft, obsolescence of inventories; or a change in sales product mix.

Profit before interest and taxation (PBIT)

The next important profit figure is the PBIT. The PBIT highlights the return made by a company from its activities before taxation and the cost of financing the company are deducted. This figure is usually analysed in two ways: the first is to provide an indication of the overall PBIT made from each euro/pound of sale made (the *profit margin*); the second is to highlight the return the company has made for the financiers and owners of the company, the *return on capital employed (ROCE)*.

Net profit margin (profit margin)

The profit margin is calculated as follows:

$$\frac{\text{PBIT}}{\text{Revenue}} \times 100 = \text{profit margin}$$

Worked example 3.3   (Profit analysis: profit margin)

REQUIRED

Using the financial statements of ABC plc; calculate the profit margin for both years using profit before interest, tax and distributions.

Solution

The profit margin is:

$$20X7 \quad \frac{\text{€/£8,500} + \text{€/£1,000}}{\text{€/£50,000}} \times 100 = 19\%$$

$$20X6 \quad \frac{\text{€/£9,000} + \text{€/£1,000}}{\text{€/£45,000}} \times 100 = 22.2\%$$

The profit margin has fallen from 22.2% of sales value to 19.0% of sales value, over the year. This result would have been influenced by the increase in the gross profit margin (worked example 3.2); however, this benefit has been outweighed by increases in the fixed costs of the company, namely the: distribution; administration; and other costs, and the reduction in other income received. These costs require further scrutiny. [Note: Figures are in €/£'000s]

The profit margin is open to more variation than the gross profit margin as it encapsulates all the costs of a company, including fixed costs. Movements in the absolute amount of gross profit will impact on the profit margin. The gross profit margin could be considered to be more variable in nature, changing with the volume of transactions: whereas the costs deducted from gross profit (administration and distribution costs) when calculating the PBIT, are more fixed in nature. In addition, exceptional one-off costs are more likely to influence this ratio. Asset sales/write-offs are posted here, as are redundancy costs, bonuses and other such one-off expenses. When all the exceptional items are removed, this ratio can provide information on economies of scale, or inefficiencies. With an appropriate expenses analyses (i.e. individual expenses as a proportion of revenue) inefficient areas can be highlighted and measures put in place to reduce inefficiencies.

When analysing company performance a holistic approach has to be taken. For example, when a company changes its product price, to generate more revenue the resultant changes in the profitability ratios might be as follows: A lower sales price is likely to stimulate more revenue; however, will result in a lower reported gross profit margin, though higher overall profitability (net profit). Conversely, a high sales price is likely to reduce overall revenue and result in a high reported gross profit margin. However, the lower gross profit amount will result in lower overall profitability (net profit) as fixed costs will not have changed.

Return on capital employed (ROCE)

The ROCE ratio is sometimes referred to as the *primary ratio* and is regarded as the most important performance ratio – as it provides information on the return earned by a company on capital invested by investors (owners and financiers). Capital invested is commonly referred to as *capital employed*. Capital employed includes equity (equity share capital, reserves, share premium and other equity reserves) and long-term debt (debentures, loan stock, long-term debt, preference shares and any other long-term debt sources, including provisions for expenses extending beyond one year). Capital employed can be calculated by finding the sum of the book value of equity and debt, or can be calculated using 'total assets less liabilities due within one year'. The ROCE ratio is calculated as follows:

$$\frac{\text{PBIT}}{\text{Capital employed}} \times 100 = \text{ROCE\%}$$

> **Worked example 3.4** (Profit analysis: ROCE)
>
> **REQUIRED**
>
> Using the financial statements of ABC plc; calculate the ROCE for both years.
>
> **Solution**
>
> The ROCE is:
>
> $$20X7 \quad \frac{€/£8,500 + €/£1,000}{€/£40,500 + €/£25,000} \times 100 = 14.5\%$$
>
> $$20X6 \quad \frac{€/£9,000 + €/£1,000}{€/£29,500 + €/£21,500} \times 100 = 19.6\%$$
>
> The ROCE has declined from 19.6% of capital employed in 20X6, to 14.5% of capital employed, in 20X7. On the surface this means that the additional investment in resources has not yielded profit levels in line with those obtained prior to the investment.
>
> *Caution: information on the timing of the increase in resources would aid interpretation of this ratio, when increases occur near to the year end, the ratio should be adjusted to remove the new capital. Indeed, assets may have been sold just prior to the end of 20X6, causing the prior year ratio to be overstated and not reflective of the return received on the capital that was invested for the whole year. [Note: Figures are in €/£'000s]*

When analysing the ROCE, comparison should be made to prior year figures. The ratio should be adjusted where it is affected by exceptional items, so that like is compared with like. Obviously any increase in the reported percentage is a strong sign of performance, as the capital is producing more profit from each euro/pound invested. In addition, the ROCE should be compared to that reported by other companies in the same industry, as they will be affected similarly by changes in the economy. For example, suppose interest rates rise, causing demand for a company's products to fall. This will result in a fall in its

ROCE – which the markets would react negatively to. However, so long as a company's ROCE does not fall to the same extent as in other companies from the same industry – the company's performance will be treated in a positive light. Investors will interpret the comparative results across the companies and may conclude that the lower than average fall in the ROCE is a signal of strong management, who are adapting to the new economic conditions better than their competitors.

The ROCE should also be compared to the current risk-free rate of interest (bank borrowing rates, or government bond coupon rates). Investing in a company is always riskier than investing in debt; therefore, investors will assess whether the premium for investing in a company – a proxy of which might be the excess of the ROCE over the risk-free rate, is sufficient to warrant holding shares in a company. In addition, financiers will be keen to ensure that the ROCE is greater then the cost of debt. Excess returns are required, not only to pay interest on debt, but also to build up reserves, to repay loan capital.

Efficiency

The ROCE provides an indication of the profitability of a company and also its efficiency in the use the company makes of funds invested in it. The ROCE is broken down into a number of other ratios which help to pinpoint the source of changes in performance; or to highlight, weaknesses/strengths in performance. The ratios and their interrelationship with the ROCE are highlighted in the following diagram:

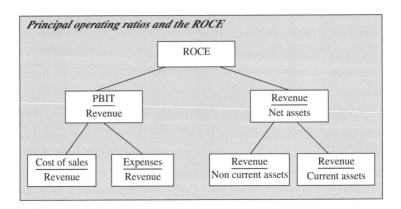

The left hand side ratios are considered to focus more on profitability, with those on the right hand side regarded as indicators of management efficiency in the use of assets to generate revenue.

Non-current asset turnover

The first of the efficiency ratios, the **non-current asset turnover ratio** (revenue to non-current assets), gives an indication of the amount of revenue being generated from each euro/pound invested in non-current assets. Care needs to be taken when interpreting this ratio as the value of non-current assets in different companies may differ, depending on accounting policies adopted. For example, some companies choose to revalue their assets, others do not. In these instances is it not meaningful to compare two companies that use different measurement bases. The non-current asset turnover ratio will always be lower in a company that revalues its assets, relative to one that does not, as will the ROCE. Differing depreciation policies may also lead to differences that relate to accounting adjustments, not indicators of efficiency. In addition, the timing of additions and disposals during the year will also complicate comparison of the ratio between different years for an individual company. Aside from these pitfalls this ratio provides a good indicator of the utilisation of non-current assets by management. Where turnover is low, assets can be scrutinised to determine if they are being utilised effectively to generate revenue, this process might highlight assets that are surplus to requirements. These can be sold, with little impact on operating activities, but resulting in a cash injection to a company, that can be utilised to produce more revenue.

Current asset turnover

The **current asset turnover ratio** highlights the revenue generated by each euro/pound invested in current assets. It provides an indication of the efficiency of the utilisation of current assets in the generation of revenue. Like the non-current asset turnover ratio, its comparability is influenced by accounting policies, for example, one company might use the first-in first-out method of inventory valuation, whereas another might use the last-in first-out method. When inventory is rising or falling in price – the two methods will result in different inventory values. The determination of the provision for doubtful debts is also subjective as is any provision for a fall in inventory value. Aside from these potential discrepancies, this ratio can provide a good indicator of management efficiency. Further information can be obtained by examining the individual components making up this ratio (inventories, trade receivables, trade payables). These are now considered in turn.

Inventory turnover

The ***inventory turnover ratio*** is a measure of the number of times inventory is turned over in a year, on average. It is expressed in months, weeks or days. Inventory is valued at the lower of cost or net realisable value and its turnover is relative to the total amount of purchased/manufactured goods that have been sold/used in the period (the cost of sales, or cost of goods produced). The ratio is calculated as:

$$\frac{\text{Cost of sales}}{\text{Inventory}} = \text{Number of times}$$

To find out the number of days that inventory is held for – divide 365 by the inventory turnover ratio (For months – divide 12 by the ratio; for weeks – divide 52 by the ratio).

Worked example 3.5   (Efficiency analysis: inventory turnover)

REQUIRED

Using the financial statements of ABC plc; calculate the inventory turnover rate for both years. Then calculate the number of days the inventory is held for in stores.

Solution

Inventory turnover is:

$$20X7 \qquad \frac{€/£30,000}{€/£6,000} = 5 \text{ times per year}$$

$$20X6 \qquad \frac{€/£28,000}{€/£5,000} = 5.6 \text{ times per year}$$

ABC plc's inventory turned over 5.6 times in 20X6 slowing to 5 times in 20X7. This means that inventory is held for 73 days (365/5) in year 20X7, compared to 65 days (365/5.6) in 20X6. Management were less efficient in their management of inventory in 20X7, hence store costs would have increased. [Note: Figures are in €/£'000s]

The type of inventory, its cost, and demand for the inventory will influence the amount held and the number of times inventory is turned over. The lower the amount of inventory held – the higher the number of times inventory turns over. A high turnover is generally considered efficient, as low inventory levels results in lower costs. A minimum level of inventory is required, as inventory levels that are too low, might lead to stock-outs and loss of contribution. Determining the optimum level of inventory to hold is discussed in depth in chapter nine.

Trade receivables period (debtors' ratio)
The *trade receivables period (debtors' ratio)* measures the average number of day's credit taken by customers. It might differ from the number of day's credit given, as some customers may not pay within the agreed timescale, whereas others may avail of discounts and pay early. The ratio is calculated as follows:

$$\frac{\text{Trade receivables}}{\text{Credit sales}} \times 365 = \text{Number of days credit taken by customers}$$

Worked example 3.6   (Efficiency analysis: trade receivables)

REQUIRED

Using the financial statements of ABC plc; calculate the trade receivables period for both years. Assume all sales are made on credit terms.

Solution

The trade receivables period is:

$$20X7 \qquad \frac{€/£8,000}{€/£50,000} \times 365 = 58.4 \text{ days}$$

$$20X6 \qquad \frac{€/£6,000}{€/£45,000} \times 365 = 48.67 \text{ days}$$

Continued

The number of day's credit taken by customers has increased from 48.67 days to 58.4 days. This may suggest that ABC plc is allowing longer credit terms to achieve greater sales volume. Longer credit is linked to increasing bad debts, which might result in increased administration costs for the company, or the increasing credit period may simply be an indication of a weakening of the credit control procedures. This needs further investigation, to highlight the main cause of the shift. [Note: Figures are in €/£'000s]

The trade receivables period is influenced by the type of industry a company operates in. Some companies trade mostly in cash (Sainsbury's, Tesco's), others allow credit – stipulating a credit period. However, in these scenarios credit can be extended by the customer (for example: builders merchant; motor factors) beyond an agreed period. Other companies have strict credit and payment terms (some breweries require their customers to enter into a direct debit arrangement. Therefore, the agreed credit period is rarely breached). When comparing the trade receivables ratio within an industry it is important to consider the days reported by similar companies only – not all companies in the same industry – as major differences between different types of company can occur, as highlighted earlier in this paragraph. Like most other ratios, this ratio should not be interpreted in isolation. A reduction in the trade receivable period might seem to be efficient; however, may have actually increased costs. For example, the reduction may have been achieved by allowing: a discount; or a shorter credit period at the outset. The result in both cases might be a fall in profitability. Techniques that can be used to determine an optimum credit policy are examined in depth in chapter ten.

Trade payables period (creditors' ratio)

The *trade payables period (creditors' ratio)* indicates the average number of day's credit taken by a company, from its suppliers. This may differ from the number of day's credit given by suppliers; as the company may elect to pay for supplies earlier, to avail of discounts; or may choose to pay after a longer period, due to having insufficient cash to cover the payments. The trade payables period is calculated as follows:

$$\frac{\text{Trade payables}}{\text{Credit purchases}} \times 365 = \text{Number of days credit taken by company}$$

Worked example 3.7   (Efficiency analysis: trade payables ratio)

REQUIRED

Using the financial statements of ABC plc; calculate number of day's credit taken in both years. You are informed that the opening inventory at the start of 20X6 was €/£5 million and that all purchases are on credit terms.

Solution

The trade payables period is:

20X7 $\dfrac{€/£5,500}{€/£30,000 + €/£6,000 - €/£5,000^*} \times 365 = 64.76 \text{ days}$

20X6 $\dfrac{€/£10,000}{€/£28,000 + €/£5,000 - €/£5,000} \times 365 = 130.35 \text{ days}$

*The required figure is credit purchases, where opening and closing inventory are known, purchases can be calculated from the cost of sales figure, as in this case.

The number of day's credit taken has fallen from 130.35 days to 64.76 days. This means that ABC plc is paying its suppliers 65 days earlier in 20X7, relative to 20X6. To analyse this correctly it would be beneficial to know the agreed credit terms between the parties. It may be that in the prior year ABC plc breached the credit terms and was loosing discounts and being penalised with interest charges, or higher prices. By paying on time, ABC plc may be availing of discounts, or a cheaper supplier. This explanation is consistent with the increased gross profit margin reported earlier in the chapter. [Note: Figures are in €/£'000s]

Influences on the trade payables period and advice as to the optimum credit period to take is provided in detail in chapter ten.

Financial position

The *balance sheet* contains the primary source of information on the financial position of a company. According to the IASB (1989) *'Framework for the Preparation and Presentation of Financial Statements'*:

> 'the financial position of an entity is affected by the economic resources it controls, its financial structure, its liquidity and solvency, and its capacity to adapt to changes in the environment in which it operates'.

Economic recourses of a company

Information on the economic resources a company controls and information on a company's ability to adapt, change and utilise these resources is vital to help an investor predict the ability of a company to generate future additional cash inflows, were they needed in the future. The *economic resources of a company* are its net assets (total assets less current liabilities). This information can be obtained from a company's balance sheet (an example is provided at the end of this chapter). The balance sheet is presented in a manner to aid interpretation of the data contained within. It has two sections. The top section details the assets of the company. Non-current assets are grouped together and are the first of the resources to be presented. The nature of these assets is highlighted as the balance sheet splits the total into tangible, intangible and investments. Next, current assets are listed. The second part of the balance sheet lists the equity and liabilities of a company. Equity is detailed first, followed by long-term liabilities, then current liabilities.

An analysis of the ability of a company to generate future additional cash flows from resources held can be obtained from the cash flow statement. In a set of financial statements, the *cash flow statement* is presented as a primary statement – located after the income statement and the balance sheet. It reports the cash flows generated by a company over a period, classified into operating, investing and financing activities. These classifications allow an investor to assess the impact of the three activities on the financial position, performance and adaptability of a company.

A proforma cash flow statement is reproduced at the end of this chapter. The three different activities are highlighted in bold. The *operating activities* section of a cash flow statement allows an investor to determine cash flows that have been generated from the every day running activities of a company, in particular it provides information on whether this has been sufficient to not only cover operating expenditure, but also to pay dividends, interest, capital commitments and to make new investments; without having to obtain additional external funding. The *investing activities* section allows the investor to see cash flows that have arisen in the period from investing activities. This provides an indication of the net investment in new resources made in the period, which should provide future economic benefits. This section includes details of the cash flows arising from the purchase or sale of non-current assets (including investment assets) and any trading in derivatives for speculative/trading purposes only. The final section, *financing activities*, records cash flows that occurred in the period in respect of changes in the financing of a company. This includes increases/decreases in equity and debt. This information is vital for predicting the future claims to be made by financiers on the cash flows of a company.

Two ratios are sometimes used to compare the disclosures from the income statement and the balance sheet with those from the cash flow statement. These are now explained:

Cash return on capital employed

The *cash return on capital employed* ratio is expressed as a percentage and is calculated as follows:

$$\frac{\text{Net cash flow from operating activities before interest and taxation}}{\text{Capital employed}} \times 100$$

This ratio provides information on the cash return on capital employed and can be compared to the profit return on capital employed to give an indication of the quality of profits earned.

> **Worked example 3.8**   (Cash flow analysis: cash return on capital employed)
>
> **REQUIRED**
>
> Using the financial statements of ABC plc; calculate the cash return on capital employed for both years.
>
> **Solution**
>
> The cash return on capital employed is:
>
> $$20\text{X}7 \quad \frac{€/£500}{€/£40{,}500 + €/£25{,}000} \times 100 = 0.76\%$$
>
> *Continued*

$$20X6 \quad \frac{€/£3,500^*}{€/£29,500 + €/£21,500} \times 100 = 6.86\%$$

*Estimate used.

In line with the reduction in the return on capital employed, the cash return from operating activities on capital employed has fallen from 6.86% in 20X6 to 0.76% in 20X7. The deterioration in cash from operating activities is a direct result of the company reducing its short-term liabilities by €/£7 million.

The problems highlighted earlier in respect of the timing of changes to capital employed are equally relevant for this ratio. Therefore, care need to be taken when interpreting the results. [Note: Figures are in €/£'000s]

Operating cash flow to total debt

The *operating cash flow to total debt* ratio is expressed as a percentage and is calculated as follows:

$$\frac{\text{Operating cash flow}}{\text{Total debt}} \times 100$$

This ratio provides information on the ability of a company to service its total debt from yearly cash flows. A high ratio provides a better sign of the solvency of a company.

Worked example 3.9   (Cash flow analysis: solvency)

REQUIRED

Using the financial statements of ABC plc; calculate the operating cash flow to total debt ratio for 20X7.

Solution

The operating cash flow to total debt ratio is:

Continued

$$20X7 \quad \frac{(€/£3,500)}{€/£25,000 + €/£10,000} \times 100 = -10\%$$

This result is a poor indicator of company solvency. Cash flows from other sources have been used to support the operating activities. If a company is not producing positive cash flows from its operating activities, it is unlikely to be able to meet the capital claims of debt financiers in the future. [Note: Figures are in €/£'000s]

Liquidity and solvency

Liquidity is a measure of the availability of cash to a company in the near future, after taking into account the commitments and liabilities of the company in the same time frame. This usually refers to the relationship between items that will be received as cash within one year (or are already cash); and items that will cause an outflow of cash within one year. *Solvency* is a term used to denote the availability of cash in a longer time frame to meet longer-term expected cash outflows and commitments. An analysis of the liquidity and solvency of a company will help an investor to determine the cash strength of a company in the short and long term.

Most companies use rolling cash budgets to manage their short and long-term cash requirements. These are the best source of information on expected liquidity and solvency. Cash budgets show the expected cash inflows and outflows, usually on a monthly basis (these are covered in depth in chapter 11). They can be used to highlight financing deficiencies and surpluses throughout a period. In terms of solvency they can be used to schedule the size that long-term loan repayments should be, or to determine whether a company can purchase an asset using its own internal cash flows, or whether it should obtain external funding.

External investors do not have access to cash budgets. They have to try to gauge the liquidity and solvency of a company from analysing its cash flow statement and from performing ratio analysis on its balance sheet. The crucial indicator of liquidity from the cash flow statement is the extent of net cash inflows received from operating activities. In addition, two key ratios can be calculated from the balance sheet, to provide an indication of the liquidity of a company. These ratios are called the, current ratio, and the quick or acid test ratio.

Current ratio

The *current ratio* provides a measure of the extent by which a company's current assets cover its current liabilities.

Current ratio = current assets : current liabilities

Worked example 3.10 (Liquidity analysis: current ratio)

REQUIRED

Using the financial statements of ABC plc; calculate the current ratio for both years.

Solution

The current ratio is:

20X7 €/£19,000 : €/£10,000 = 1.9 : 1

20X6 €/£22,000 : €/£17,000 = 1.29 : 1

The current ratio has increased from 1.29 : 1 to 1.9 : 1. This suggests that ABC plc is in a stronger liquid position, in 20X7. It now has €/£1.90 of current assets available to cover each €/£1 of current liability. This ratio would need to be compared to the industry average to determine whether the result is good, or not. Where the industry average is 1.5 : 1 then a ratio of 1.9 : 1 might indicate an overinvestment in current assets – hence inefficiencies. [Note: Figures are in €/£'000s]

In textbooks a benchmark ratio is 2 : 1 (i.e. twice as many current assets should be held relative to current liabilities); however, in practice the ratio is industry specific. It should always be greater than 1 to 1 but the margin over one, might differ. For example, manufacturing industries usually have to hold sufficient inventory to ensure that their production processes do not have to stop due to raw material shortages. They also have at any point in time, work in progress and finished goods – to meet orders as they fall due. Most manufacturers have to trade on credit terms with their customers, so will also have a substantial amount of trade receivables. Therefore, a large current ratio is expected for manufacturing entities.

A retail company, on the other hand, will only have finished good inventory. They usually trade on cash terms only – hence will have no trade receivables. Therefore, a much a lower current ratio is expected for a retail company, relative to a manufacturing company. A more meaningful evaluation of a company's liquidity position is to compare their current ratio with the average ratio for that type of company, within its industry. When a company's current ratio is less than the company specific industry average ratio, this may suggest that the company is having liquidity problems; whereas when it is greater than the company specific industry average it might highlight inefficiencies in the management of working capital – which will reduce company profits.

Quick/acid test ratio

The current ratio provides information to enable the user to determine the liquidity of the company over a period of several months to one year. Cash can be tied up, first in raw materials, then work in progress, then in finished goods – before being sold on credit, after which cash will be received. Depending on the length of time spent at each stage, the initial cash used to purchase raw materials may not result in a cash inflow for a long period of time. The *quick/acid test ratio* is used to provide an indication of the liquidity of the company in a very short time scale, as it removes the investment in inventory from the current ratio. Inventory is the least liquid current asset. Therefore, the quick/acid test ratio is a good measure of a company's ability to respond quickly when there are cash commitments to be serviced. The quick/acid test ratio is calculated as follows:

Quick/acid test ratio = (current assets − inventories) : current liabilities

---

Worked example 3.11   (Liquidity analysis: quick/acid test ratio)

REQUIRED

Using the financial statements of ABC plc; calculate the quick ratio for both years.

Continued

> **Solution**
>
> The quick/acid test ratio is:
>
> 20X7   (€/£19,000 − €/£6,000) : €/£10,000 = 1.3 : 1
>
> 20X6   (€/£22,000 − €/£5,000) : €/£17,000 = 1 : 1
>
> The current ratio has increased from 1:1 to 1.3:1. Consistent with the results of the current ratio, the quick ratio results suggest that ABC plc is in a stronger liquid position, in respect of its near cash assets also. It now has €/£1.30 of current assets available to cover each €/£1 of current liability. This ratio would need to be compared to the industry average to determine whether the result is good, or not. [Note: Figures are in €/£'000s]

A benchmark quick ratio outcome is commonly cited as 1 to 1 – all the current liabilities being covered by the most liquid current assets. An outcome of less than 1 to 1 would be indicative of liquidity problems, as the company is unable to service its current liabilities from its current assets. A return of greater than 1 to 1 might suggest that there are inefficiencies in the management of the company's working capital, which will affect the profitability of a company.

Financial structure

The equity invested and retained within a company and the long-term debt provided to a company make up its *financial structure*. In this text, a company's financial structure is referred to as its *capital structure*. Knowledge about the capital structure of a company is valuable when assessing a company's financial position, as it can be used to predict future sources of finance that the company might acquire and to make judgements on how profits and cash flows will be distributed among financiers in the future. Information on the financial structure of a company is available from its balance sheet. Information from the income statement can provide guidance on risk associated with a company's capital structure.

Gearing ratio

Gearing is the extent to which a company is financed by investors, who are not owners. Information on the sources of finance obtained by a company, from investors who are not owners, can be found in its balance sheet under the heading long-term liabilities. These sources typically include: preference shares; debentures; loan stock; long-term debt and other liabilities that extend beyond one year. The gearing ratio is calculated as follows:

$$\frac{\text{Long-term debt}}{\text{Long-term debt} + \text{equity}} \times 100 = \% \text{ of the company financed by debt}$$

Worked example 3.12   (Financial structure: gearing ratio)

REQUIRED

Using the financial statements of ABC plc; calculate the level of gearing in both years.

Solution

The level of gearing is:

20X7 $\qquad \dfrac{€/£25,000}{€/£40,500 + €/£25,000} \times 100 = 38.16\%$

20X6 $\qquad \dfrac{€/£21,500}{€/£29,500 + €/£21,500} \times 100 = 42.15\%$

In 20X6, 42.15% of the company was financed using debt sources; this has fallen to 38.16% by 20X7. A lower gearing ratio indicates lower financial risk. During the year the level of debt increased by €/£3.5 million, mostly as a result of an increase in long-term borrowings; however, the level of equity investment increased by a greater amount (€/£11 million). The equity increase came from two sources: a share issue provided a capital injection of €/£5 million;

Continued

> and €/£6 million of the €/£7 million profit made in the year was retained for future investment. Therefore, the financial structure of the company is in a stronger position at 31 December 20X7. [Note: Figures are in €/£'000s]

Like most ratios, a company's gearing should be compared to the average industry gearing level. A common rule of thumb is that a company should be able to cover its long-term debt from its equity. Management will view this ratio in a different light to external investors. When managers act to maximise equity holder value they will seek to manipulate the capital structure of a company so as to maximise its value (see chapter 15 for a detailed discussion of a theories on capital structure and value creation). External investors will use this ratio to highlight the financial risks associated with investing in a company. This will help them to decide if the return expected is fair, given the risk involved. Debt is considered to be riskier than equity as interest has to be paid, regardless of whether a company makes profits, or not. Dividends on the other hand do not, therefore debt is considered riskier.

The gearing ratio also informs an investor as to the potential of a company to raise future finance. If the gearing ratio is low, then a company will be able to obtain more debt. If the gearing ratio is high, the company will have difficulty raising more debt, and indeed more equity, as the equity market will require a premium for the additional risks involved with having higher gearing – making raising capital expensive.

Income gearing

If the level of debt is known then the expected future interest and preference dividend cash outflows can be determined. The extent by which a company can service the future cost of its debt can be estimated using the *income gearing ratio*. This is calculated as follows:

$$\frac{\text{Debt interest + preference dividends}}{\text{Profit before interest and tax}} \times 100 = \% \text{ of profit required to service debt}$$

Worked example 3.13 (Financial risk analysis: income gearing ratio)

REQUIRED

Using the financial statements of ABC plc; calculate the income gearing ratio for both years.

Solution

The income gearing ratio is:

$$20X7 \quad \frac{€/£1,000}{€/£8,500 + €/£1,000} \times 100 = 10.5\%$$

$$20X6 \quad \frac{€/£1,000}{€/£9,000 + €/£1,000} \times 100 = 10.0\%$$

The percentage of profits being used to cover debt interest has increased from 10.0% to 10.5%. The increase can be interpreted as an increase in the financial risk of the company; however, the ratio is low to start with. Debt financiers are providing about 40% of the finance for the company and only get 10% of profits. This is a strong sign for equity holders. [Note: Figures are in €/£'000s]

The income gearing ratio provides a measure of a company's ability to service its current debt. A high ratio indicates that a large proportion of the profits are required to cover the debt interest and preference share dividend, this can be interpreted as a sign of high financial risk. In addition, it would indicate that a company is limited in its ability to raise more debt as it currently has to use a high proportion of its distributable profits to cover current debt. The ratio is limited. It does not take into consideration loan repayments – a company may be able to repay interest and preference share dividends but not capital! In addition, the ratio is only reflective of one year's situation – unless the company's profits are steady from year to year. Where a company's profits fluctuate, the ratio should be evaluated over a longer time period.

Operating leverage

Operating leverage provides an indication of the risk associated with the extent of fixed costs in a company's operations. It is usually expressed as the *'degree of operating leverage'* – and indicates the effect of a change in revenue on a company's profit before interest and tax. The higher the degree of operating leverage the greater the increase in profits from an increase in revenue, conversely a reduction in revenue will have a larger impact in terms of falling profits, relative to a company that has a low degree of operating leverage. Therefore, the higher the degree of operating leverage, the riskier a company's cost structure. Operating leverage is calculated as follows:

$$\frac{\text{Contribution}}{\text{Net profits}} \times 100 = \text{degree of operating leverage}$$

Worked example 3.14   (Business risk analysis: operating leverage)

REQUIRED

Using the financial statements of ABC plc; calculate the degree of operating leverage for both years.

Solution

The degree of operating leverage is:

20X7 $\qquad \dfrac{€/£20,000}{€/£7,000} \times 100 = 285\%$

20X6 $\qquad \dfrac{€/£17,000}{€/£6,200} \times 100 = 274\%$

In line with the reduction in the net profit percentage (worked example 3.3), this ratio has picked up the increased risk associated with the higher proportionate level of fixed costs. The company is now in a riskier position that it was in 20X6, as the degree of operating leverage is higher, and any changes in the volume of revenue will have a larger impact now, than would have occurred had the fixed cost remained consistent with last year. [Note: Figures are in €/£'000s]

Investment potential

Potential investors need to be able to look at a company's financial statements and extract information that will allow them to make informed decisions as to the investment potential the company offers. Investors are interested in seeing their worth increase. This can be achieved by receiving dividends and/or increases in share price. Depending on their cash and tax position, some equity holders prefer dividends (low income band earners); others prefer to receive capital gains in the price of the share (high income band earners). The latter will have exhausted their income tax free personal allowance; however, may not have utilised their capital gains tax yearly tax free allowance. Being able to release the income from capital gains in a planned manner allows equity holders to minimise their personal tax expense. Earnings drive both dividends payable and capital growth, hence information on earnings and growth in earnings helps to inform investors about the overall return to be made from the purchase of shares. A couple of ratios are commonly calculated to provide information to an investor on a company's financial performance.

Earnings per share

The first indicator of performance that a potential equity holder will be interested in is a company's **earnings per share**. This ratio is simply the earnings that are available for distribution to equity holders after loan financiers and tax authorities claims have been settled – reported on an individual share basis. It is calculated as follows:

$$\frac{\text{Earnings after tax and preference dividends}}{\text{Number of ordinary shares in issue}} = \text{Earnings per share}$$

Worked example 3.15   (Investment potential: earnings analysis)

REQUIRED

Using the financial statements of ABC plc; calculate the earnings per share for both years. Assume that the nominal value of ABC plc's shares is €/£1 per share.

Continued

Solution

The earnings per share is:

20X7
$$\frac{€/£7,000}{€/£30,000} = 23.33c/p$$

20X6
$$\frac{€/£6,200}{€/£25,000} = 24.8c/p$$

In line with the reduction in the return on capital employed the earnings per share has fallen from 23.33c/p per share to 24.8c/p per share. Like the return on capital employed, the timing of the share issue is important, if it was not until the end of the year, the earnings per share may actually have increased to 28c/p per share (€/£7,000/€/£25,000); this information would need to be known before a proper evaluation could take place. [Note: Figures are in €/£'000s]

The earnings per share ratio is deemed to be so important to investors, that it is required to be disclosed either, on the face of the financial statements of a plc, or in the notes to the financial statements. In general, an increase in a company's earnings per share is seen as a positive sign about a company's future, hence will lead to an increase in a company's share price. However, this is not always the case, as is highlighted by the next example.

Worked example 3.16   (Investment potential: earnings per share)

Fernando plc raised €/£20 million of cheap debt at the beginning of 20X8. The company did increase its earnings per share in the year, primarily as a result of the additional return received from investing the €/£20 million raised, over and above the interest and tax that had to be paid on the additional earnings. The return, though higher than in previous years, was lower than equity holders' expectations.

The following data is available for Fernando plc just after the year end.

Continued

	20X7	20X8
Earnings per share	20c/p	22c/p
Price earnings ratio	9	7.5
Share price	180c/p	165c/p

REQUIRED

Earnings per share have risen between 20X7 and 20X8, yet share price has fallen. Why do you think this has occurred?

Solution

The fall in share price has arisen because the equity holders are disappointed in the performance of the company. Though the earnings per share have risen by 10% from 20c/p to 22c/p, this rise was not to the extent expected. Indeed, the question tells us that the increase is solely due to additional earnings being available for distribution from the investment of the new €/£20 million capital injection after all the associated costs (including interest and taxation) have been settled.

The reason for the expectation of additional earnings over and above the 22c/p is due to the increased financial risks now facing equity investors. The company has increased its debt levels by €/£20 million. Interest will have to be paid on this yearly, and the capital will have to be repaid at some point in the future. This has increased the fixed costs of the company and has moved the equity holders down the list of claimants in the event of the company being wound up – debt is always settled before equity. As a result of the higher risk, equity holders will require a higher return on their total equity investment. The return received is not higher, as expected – hence share price will fall as equity holders, unhappy with the risk return trade off, will sell their shares – driving down share price.
[Note: Figures are in €/£'000s]

Price earnings ratio

The *price earnings ratio* gives an indication of the number of years it would take to recover the current share price out of current earnings of the company. The ratio is calculated as follows:

$$\frac{\text{Market price per share}}{\text{Earnings per share}} = \text{Price earnings ratio}$$

Worked example 3.17   (Investment appraisal: price earnings ratio)

REQUIRED

Using the financial statements of ABC plc; calculate the price earnings ratio for both years. You are informed that the market price of the company's shares on 31 December 20X7 was 201c/p and on 31 December 20X6 was 173.6c/p.

Solution

The price earnings ratio is:

$$20X7 \quad \frac{201\text{c/p}}{23.33\text{c/p}} = 8.6$$

$$20X6 \quad \frac{173.6\text{c/p}}{24.8\text{c/p}} = 7$$

The price earnings ratio has increased from 7 to 8.6. This means that the market has more confidence in the future earnings of the company in 20X7 than it did in 20X6. The market must value the earnings potential of the new investment quite highly; this has increased demand for the shares and driven up share price from 173.6c/p to 201c/p. The current earnings per share are lower than those reported in the earlier year, though may not reflect the full earnings expected from the new investment. [Note: Figures are in €/£'000s]

The current market price of a share reflects the markets expectations about the future earnings of a company. Therefore, the price earnings ratio is a measure of market confidence in a company. A low price earnings ratio suggests that the market sentiment is that a company is unlikely to maintain earnings, or have growth in earnings; whereas a high price earnings ratio suggests that the market sentiment is that a company will be able to maintain its performance and indeed improve on it. As with all ratios, care needs to be taken if using the price earnings ratio to analyse two different companies. The price earnings ratio also reflects the market's consideration of the risk associated with investing in a company, – a risky company with high earnings is likely to have a lower price earnings ratio, compared to a less risky company with the same earnings. The market price will be less for the riskier company. Therefore, this ratio should not be used in isolation, when deciding on whether or not to invest in a company. The following table outlines some factors that influence a company's reported price earnings ratio:

Influences on a company's price earnings ratio

Earnings growth: Where a company has strong growth prospects this will lead to an increase in the price earnings ratio.

Quality of the company's net assets and earnings: Where the stock market feels that a company's net assets are undervalued, a higher price earnings ratio will be reported. In addition, a stable earnings pattern will also result in a higher price earnings ratio.

Financial risk: The price earnings ratio is inversely related to the gearing of a company. As gearing increases, equity holders required return increases, hence lowering the price earnings ratio.

Stock market: The current state of the stock market will influence the price earnings ratio. Where the market is bullish, this will push up the price earnings ratio, whereas the price earnings ratio will fall in a bear market.

Continued

State of the economy: General economic and financial conditions will impact on a company's price earnings ratio.

Industry: The type of industry is also influential, as is the company's standing within the industry.

Size: Related to the prior point, size is important. Larger companies will be expected to have steadier earnings.

Marketability: Unquoted shares have restricted marketability; hence a higher return is required for investing in them. This is reflected by them having a lower price earnings ratio.

Dividend ratios

Dividend per ordinary share

The **dividend per ordinary share** ratio calculates the annual individual monetary dividend amount that is distributed per ordinary share in issue. It is calculated as follows:

$$\frac{\text{Total ordinary dividend paid}}{\text{Number of ordinary shares in issue}} = \text{dividend per share}$$

Worked example 3.18   (Investment analysis: dividend per share)

REQUIRED

Using the financial statements of ABC plc; calculate the dividend per share for both years. Assume the dividend in the prior year was €/£800,000.

Solution

The dividend per share is:

$$20X7 \qquad \frac{\text{€/£1,000}}{\text{€/£30,000}} = 3.33\text{c/p per share}$$

Continued

$$20X6 \qquad \frac{€/£800}{€/£25,000} = 3.2c/p \text{ per share}$$

The dividend per share has increased from 3.2c/p per share to 3.33c/p per share, an increase of four percent in the year. [Note: Figures are in €/£'000s]

Dividend policy is covered in depth in chapter 19. At this early stage it is pointed out that the market usually expects a company to pay out a steady, but increasing, dividend per share. Hence, an investor would be interested in knowing the trend in the movement of this ratio over time.

Dividend yield

The *dividend yield* focuses on the value of the dividend to the equity holder. It calculates the return currently earned in the form of dividends only, from an investment in the company's shares. It is calculated as follows:

$$\frac{\text{Dividend per ordinary share}}{\text{Market price per ordinary share}} \times 100 = \text{dividend yield}$$

Worked example 3.19   (Investment analysis: dividend yield)

REQUIRED

Using the financial statements of ABC plc; calculate the dividend yield for both years. Assume the dividend in the prior year was €/£800,000 and the market price per share was 201c/p on 31 December 20X7 and 173.6c/p on 31 December 20X6.

Solution

The dividend yield is:

$$20X7 \qquad \frac{3.33c/p}{201c/p} \times 100 = 1.66\%$$

Continued

$$20X6 \qquad \frac{3.2c/p}{173.6c/p} \times 100 = 1.84\%$$

The dividend yield has fallen from 1.84% to 1.66%. Relative to the risk-free rate of interest this dividend yield is low; however, share price is rising indicating that the bulk of the return being made by equity holders, is capital gains. [Note: Figures are in €/£'000s]

The value of the dividend yield ratio is related to the amount of profits that are distributed, relative to the amount that are retained for growth. Normally this ratio produces a low result, which might be seen as poor given the increased risks associated with investing in equity, relative to risk-free investments. However, unless a company has a 100% payout ratio, this ratio will be low, as the additional return to equity holders will be in the form of capital growth, from the reinvestment of the profits. Therefore, it is not meaningful to analyse this ratio on its own as a determinant of company investment performance. To get a holistic view, capital growth also has to be considered.

Dividend cover

The *dividend cover* ratio indicates the extent by which profits after interest, tax and preference dividends can fall before the ordinary dividend is affected. The ratio is calculated as follows:

$$\frac{\text{Profit after taxation and preference dividends}}{\text{Ordinary dividends}} = \text{dividend cover}$$

Worked example 3.20   (Investment analysis: dividend cover)

REQUIRED

Using the financial statements of ABC plc; calculate the dividend cover for both years. Assume the dividend in the prior year was €/£800,000.

Continued

Solution

Dividend cover is:

$$20X7 \qquad \frac{€/£7,000}{€/£1,000} = 7 \text{ times}$$

$$20X6 \qquad \frac{€/£6,200}{€/£800} = 7.75 \text{ times}$$

Dividend cover is strong. In 20X6 profits covered dividends 7.75 times, falling to 7 times in 20X7. Even at the lower 20X7 level, profits would have to fall by 85% before the current dividend distribution would be affected. [Note: Figures are in €/£'000s]

The dividend cover ratio reflects the risk associated with a company being able to maintain its current policy in the future. If the ratio is low, then reductions in profit may compromise the ability of a company to pay out a steady, increasing, dividend. Therefore, an equity holder who is interested in receiving a constant stream of increasing dividends will not be interested in a company that has a low dividend cover ratio.

Payout ratio

The *payout ratio* is related to the dividend cover ratio; it provides an indication of the proportion of funds that are being distributed each year and therefore highlights the proportion that is being retained for growth. It is calculated as follows:

$$\frac{\text{Total ordinary dividend}}{\text{Earnings after taxation and preference dividends}} \times 100 = \text{payout ratio}$$

Worked example 3.21   (Investment analysis: payout ratio)

REQUIRED

Using the financial statements of ABC plc; calculate the payout ratio for both years. Assume the total dividend in the prior year was €/£800,000.

Solution

The payout ratio is:

$$20X7 \qquad \frac{€/£1,000}{€/£7,000} \times 100 = 14.28\%$$

$$20X6 \qquad \frac{€/£800}{€/£6,200} \times 100 = 12.9\%$$

The payout ratio has increased from 12.9% to 14.28%. This means that a greater proportion of the profits that are available for distribution, have been distributed in 20X7. Even so, distribution levels are quite low, indeed very low, for a plc. A low payout ratio means a high retentions ratio. In this case ABC plc retained 87.1% (1 − 12.9%) of their distributable profits in 20X6 and 85.72% (1 − 14.28%) in 20X7. The stock market and equity holders will be happy with this policy where the company is retaining funds for investment, or to reduce high gearing levels. [Note: Figures are in €/£'000s]

The retentions percentage is one minus the payout ratio. Alternatively it can be calculated using one divided by the dividend cover ratio.

Where the total dividend and distributable profits figure is not available the payout ratio can also be calculated from information in respect of an individual share, as follows:

$$\frac{\text{Dividend per share}}{\text{Earnings per share}} \times 100 = \text{payout ratio}$$

Though not always strictly the case, quoted companies usually have higher payout ratios relative to unquoted companies.

Business failures

Failure prediction models
Several empirical studies have suggested that a combination of financial ratios can be used to predict business failures. Beaver (1966) suggested that failure could be predicted at least five years in advance, using financial ratios. He reported that a mixture of ratios, including profitability ratios, were more effective in predicting failure than focusing solely on liquidity and solvency ratios. Altman (1968) produced a model based on factored ratio outcomes which he claimed could be used to predict business failure (***Altman's failure prediction model***). The outcome of this model is a measure of the financial health of a business and he called the measure the *'Z score'*. This model is calculated as follows:

$$Z = 1.2A + 1.4B + 3.3C + 0.6D + 1.0E$$

Where:
A = Working capital/total assets
B = Retained earnings/total assets
C = Profit before interest and tax/total assets
D = Market capitalisation/book value of debts
E = Revenue/total assets

Altman claimed that a company with a Z score of over 3 should remain solvent, whereas companies with a Z score of less than 1.8 were potential failures. Altman found that the model's prediction ability became more significant, closer to the event of failure.

Worked example 3.22   (Ratio analysis: failure prediction models)

REQUIRED

Using the financial statements of ABC plc; calculate the company's Z score using Altman's formula, for 20X7 only.

Solution

A: Working capital to total assets

$$\frac{€/£19,000 - €/£10,000}{€/£75,500} \times 100 = 11.92\%$$

B: Retained earnings to total assets.

$$\frac{€/£9,000}{€/£75,500} \times 100 = 11.92\%$$

C: Profit before interest and tax to total assets

$$\frac{€/£9,500}{€/£75,500} \times 100 = 12.58\%$$

D: Market capitalisation to book value of debts

$$\frac{€/£30,000 \times €/£2.01}{€/£35,000} \times 100 = 172\%$$

E: Revenue to total assets

$$\frac{€/£50,000}{€/£75,500} \times 100 = 66.22\%$$

The Z score is then $1.2(0.1192) + 1.4(0.1192) + 3.3(0.1258) + 0.6(1.72) + 1(0.6622) = 2.419$. Therefore using Altman's Z score methodology ABC plc is not regarded as being in danger of business failure. [Note: Figures are in €/£'000s]

Taffler and Tisshaw (1977) and Taffler (1983) manipulated the model suggested by Altman to achieve a predictor model, specific to UK companies, in the late 1970s. Like Altman they gave the greatest weighting (53 percent) to a profitability measure (profit before tax/current liabilities); considered financial leverage to be important (current liabilities/total assets), weighting it at 18 percent. They also included a liquidity measure (immediate assets minus current liabilities/operating costs minus depreciation) weighting it at 16 percent; and finally included a measure of the level of working capital investment in the company (current assets/total liabilities), weighting it at 13 percent.

Morris (1998) questions the usefulness of failure prediction models that are based on ratio analysis, suggesting that potential investors are already aware of the state of the company's affairs, and the model results add little to their decision making processes.

Analysis of accounting information over time

An analysis of accounting information over time might also provide valuable information when assessing the likelihood of business failure. The first indicator an investor will look for is the trend in reported profitability of a company. If a company reports losses for a number of years in a row, then the future is not positive, as a company's built up reserves will start to come under strain and liquidity problems are likely to occur. The second important characteristic to view in a company is its cost structure. A company with a high level of fixed costs (high degree of operating leverage), will be at greater risk when there is a decline in the company's revenue. Finally, a company may be growing and profitable; however, may be experiencing serious liquidity problems. The latter is a sign of overtrading, this happens when a company grows too fast without the appropriate financing. Overtrading can cause business failure.

Business overview

Where an investor has a more local knowledge of a company, or has been following the stories about a company in the press, then this can provide an indication of the company's financial health. Factors that might suggest a weak financial company might include: management infighting; imbalances in management boards (for example, too many sales directors, no finance directors);

poor accounting systems (in particular the lack of a planning, costing and budgetary system – a system may provide a lot of data, but little relevant information); static view (the company is not updating its products, or changing in line with advances made in other companies); high director and key member of staff turnover; over dependence on a limited number of products; increasing credit periods being taken; and general lack of information. A strong company is likely to advertise their strengths as a marketing tool; a weak company may not want to attract any attention.

Conclusion (including the limitations of ratio analysis)

Along with reading financial statements, ratio analysis is the most commonly used technique to evaluate the financial performance, position, adaptability and investment potential of a company. Ratios examine the relationship between the elements within a set of financial statements to allow the reader to make more informed decisions as to the profitability, efficiency, liquidity, solvency, financial risk and investment potential of a company, than would be possible from just viewing the statements. Ratios can be used to examine: the performance of one company over time; the performance of a company relative to its budgeted/expected performance; and how a company has performed relative to other companies in the same industry. It can also be used to compare the results of different sized entities, though care needs to be taken when interpreting this. For example, it is easier for a small entity to achieve a higher growth figure relative to a large company, yet its actual increase in sales might be one thousand times less than the growth achieved by the large company.

Indeed, interpreting ratios always needs to be undertaken with care. For example, increased profitability might be regarded as a strong sign of performance, but closer analysis might reveal that a large part of the reported profitability came from the sale of an asset – a one-off event. Another example is where the profit margin might have increased; however, the return of capital employed reduced as the new investment is generating less profit than existing assets – the result is that investors are getting less return on each euro/pound invested in the company, even though the company is regarded as more profitable.

In addition to the risk of mis-interpreting the results of ratio analysis, there are other limitations associated with the source of the data – the financial statements. The balance sheet is a 'snap shot' of the business assets and liabilities at a point in time, the balance sheet may not be reflective of a company's normal structure. This problem is accentuated when the company's trade is seasonal as the balance sheet will differ greatly, depending on the stage of the seasonal cycle at which the financial statements are prepared. Ratio analysis is more meaningful in companies that have constant operations throughout a year. Even so, when a company has a constant pattern of trade, ratio analysis is limited on a stand alone basis. Ratio analysis is most beneficial when interpreting the performance of a business over time, or when comparing the results of one company with another similar company.

Ratio analysis is used to assess past performance and also to help with decision making in respect of the future. In this respect ratio analysis is limited as the primary financial statements are based on historic data, which might not be the best reflection of the likely outcomes in the future. The narrative part of an annual return, which contains the financial statements, provides some information on the future developments and research undertaken by the company; however, this information is general, usually has little detail, and is not subject to audit. Details of key individuals are provided; however, other important information such as staff turnover, staff morale levels and the efficiency of staff are not provided. Though the limitations of ratio analysis for investment appraisal are many, they are known; hence an investor will still find them useful. The key is to use a holistic approach to the appraisal of a company, wherein a combination of analysing the financial statements using analytical review, reading the narrative parts of the annual return, calculating ratios, reading the press in respect of the company and if privileged enough, interviewing management, will provide a good foundation to inform decision making.

Examination standard question

Worked example 3.23

Aragon (a bank) has recently received a request for a term loan from one of its customers, Valencia plc, a company listed on the Alternative Investment Market of the London Stock Exchange. Valencia plc's directors have requested a further €/£6 million (five year floating rate) term loan at an initial interest rate of 12% per annum, in order to purchase new equipment. The equipment will not materially change the company's current average percentage return on investment. Valencia plc's turnover increased by 9% during the last financial year. Prior to receiving the request the regional commercial manager of Aragon had conducted a review of Valencia plc's financial position, and had decided to ask Valencia plc's management to reduce the company overdraft by 25% within the next six months.

Summarised financial statements for Valencia plc are as follows:

	20X7 €/£'000	20X6 €/£'000
Assets		
Non-current assets		
Property, plant and equipment (property revalued)	16,060	14,380
Current assets		
Inventories	31,640	21,860
Trade receivables	24,220	17,340
Investment	8,760	10,060
Cash and cash equivalents	1,700	960
	66,320	50,220
Total assets	82,380	64,600

Continued

Equity and Liabilities
Equity attributable to the equity
   holders of the parent

Share capital	3,800	3,800
Retained earnings	16,900	13,500
Total equity	20,700	17,300

Non-current liabilities

Long-term borrowings	6,000	–
Debentures	16,000	16,000
Total non-current liabilities	22,000	16,000

Current liabilities

Overdraft	16,340	13,220
Trade and other payables	20,920	15,280
Current taxation	2,420	2,800
Total current liabilities	39,680	31,300
Total liabilities	61,680	47,300
Total equity and liabilities	82,380	64,600

Extract information from the income statement of Valencia plc

	20X7 *€/£'000*
Revenue	99,360
Profit before interest and taxation	10,760
Finance costs	3,840
Profit before tax	6,920
Income tax expense	2,420
Profit for the period	4,500
Dividend paid in the year	1,100

The company's debentures are currently trading at €/£96.50 and ordinary 10c/p shares at €/£1.50.

Continued

Comparative ratio information for Valencia plc's industry (averages)

	20X7
Share price	€/£51.20
Dividend yield	2.5%
Dividend payout ratio	50%
Gross asset turnover	1.4 times
Earnings per share	17.8 pence
Gearing	52.4%
Acid test	1:1
Interest cover	4 times
Return on revenue (PBIT)	9%
Return on investment	16.5%

REQUIRED

a) You are a consultant for Aragon. You are required to produce a reasoned case explaining why the bank should request a 25% reduction in the company's overdraft.

9 Marks

b) You are a consultant for Valencia plc:

(i) Prepare a reasoned case to present to Aragon in support of the new term-loan; and

7 Marks

(ii) Make recommendations to the board of Valencia plc in respect of how you think the company's financial position might be improved.

9 Marks
Total 25 Marks

(Clearly state any assumptions made. All assumptions must relate to all parts of the question).

(ICAI, MABF II, Manual, 1998)

Continued

Solution

Profitability	20X7 €/£'000	20X6 €/£'000	Industry
Return on investment	$\dfrac{10,760}{42,700+16,340}=18.22\%$	–	16.5%
Return on revenue	$\dfrac{10,760}{99,360}=10.83\%$	–	9%
Asset turnover	$\dfrac{99,360}{82,380}=1.2$	$\dfrac{91,156^*}{64,600}=1.41$	1.4
Liquidity			
Current ratio	$\dfrac{66,320}{39,680}=1.67{:}1$	$\dfrac{50,220}{31,300}=1.6{:}1$	–
Acid test ratio	$\dfrac{66,320-31,640}{39,680}=0.87{:}1$	$\dfrac{50,220-21,860}{31,300}=0.91{:}1$	1:1
Trade receivables period	$\dfrac{24,220\times365}{99,360}=88.97\text{ days}$	$\dfrac{17,340\times365}{91,156}=69.4\text{ days}$	–
Inventory holding period (using sales)	$\dfrac{31,640\times365}{99,360}=116.23\text{ days}$	$\dfrac{21,860\times365}{91,156}=87.5\text{ days}$	–
Trade payables period (using sales)	$\dfrac{20,920\times365}{99,360}=76.85\text{ days}$	$\dfrac{15,280\times365}{91,156}=61.2\text{ days}$	–
Solvency			
Gearing	$\dfrac{22,000}{22,000+20,700}=51.5\%$	$\dfrac{16,000}{16,000+17,300}=48\%$	52.4%
Interest cover	$\dfrac{10,760}{3,840}=2.8\text{ times}$	–	4 times
Investment ratios			
Earnings per share	$\dfrac{4,500}{38,000}=11.84\text{ c/p}$	–	–
Dividend per share	$\dfrac{1,100}{38,000}=2.89\text{ c/p}$	–	–
Price earnings ratio	$\dfrac{150}{11.84}=12.67\text{ times}$	–	20 times

*€/£99,360,000/1.09 = €/£91,256,000

Continued

Bank's perspective

a) Reasons for requiring a reduction in the bank's overdraft include:

(i) The bank has a large risk exposure in respect of the overdraft and term-loan. The overdraft has increased substantially in the past year from €/£13.22 million to €/£16.34 million. If the overdraft is unsecured then the risks are even higher.

(ii) Valencia plc is highly geared, with long-term debt representing 51.5% of the company's total long-term financing. This has increased from the prior year due to long-term borrowing, though is below the industry average of 52.4%. However, it might be more appropriate to assume that the overdraft is a long-term source of finance as it is unlikely that the Valencia plc can repay it in the short term, or on demand. If the overdraft is included this ratio increases to 89.79%. This means that Valencia plc is seriously over-geared.

(iii) Valencia plc's liquidity ratios are also not strong. The current ratio has increased from 1.6 to 1 to 1.67 to 1, however, the more liquid measure, the acid test ratio, has fallen from 0.91 to 1 to 0.87 to 1. This ratio is lower than the industry average of 1 to 1.

(iv) The working capital ratios have all deteriorated, suggesting that inefficiencies are occurring. The trade receivables period has increased from 69.4 days to 88.97 days – nearly three weeks extra credit being allowed. This means that more cash is tied up in trade receivables, in addition a longer credit period may lead to a larger proportion of bad debts. The inventory holding period has also increased from 87.5 days to 116.23 days. More cash is tied up in inventories this year relative to last year. Given the company's debt position this is unacceptable. Inventories are being held for about three months. Holding inventory for longer means that higher levels of inventory are held, this leads to increased storage costs, as well as there being a higher risk of damage, or obsolescence. Suppliers are being paid within 76.85 days, an increase of 15 days on last year's

Continued

average of 61.2 days. This increase in the credit period taken will be a source of cash to the company. However, taking extended credit periods without agreement will negatively affect any goodwill that exists between Valencia plc and its suppliers. This may cause Valencia plc to loose discounts and to fall down the suppliers list of customers that they provide a quality service to.

(v) The investment in trade receivables has increased by €/£6.88 million, the investment in inventory by €/£9.78 million and the level of trade payables has increased by €/£5.64 million. This means that an additional €/£11.02 million is tied up in working capital. Were the levels of working capital in line with the increase in revenue, then the additional investment should only have been a further €/£2.152 million ((€/£17.34 million + €/£21.86 million − €/£15.28 million) × €/£99.360 million/€/£91.156 million). Therefore the increase in the overdraft (€/£3.12 million) and the long-term loan (€/£6 million) would not have been necessary.

(vi) The asset turnover ratio has also fallen from 1.41 to 1.2 over the past year. The industry average was also 1.4. This decline suggests that the assets this year are not being utilised as effectively as they were last year as each euro/pound invested in assets is yielding less revenue.

(vii) The market is also pessimistic about Valencia plc's future as indicated by the low price earnings ratio of 12.67, relative to the industry average price earnings ratio of 20.

To summarise, Valencia plc should reduce its overdraft as it seems to have arisen due to inefficiencies in the management of working capital and assets. The bank is currently over exposed with a very high debt to equity mix (when the overdraft is taken into consideration).

b) Reasons for granting a further €/£6 million five-year floating rate term loan at an initial interest rate of 12% per annum to purchase new equipment include:

(i) Valencia plc is more profitable than the average company within the industry. It provides a return on investment of

Continued

18.22% compared to the industry average of 16.5% and a return on sales of 10.83% compared to the industry average of 9%. Comparative figures were not available, though should be sought as the pattern of profitability would help to inform the decision making process.

(ii) The new loan will cost the company 12%, this is less than the return currently being earned by the company on the investment to date (18.22%); therefore, if the new assets are to generate a return similar to that currently being generated, company value should increase as should the price earnings ratio.

(iii) The machinery that the company proposes to purchase may be offered as security for the additional loan, this will reduce Aragon's credit exposure.

(iv) The gearing ratio has been calculated using book values; it could be argued that a more appropriate means of valuing the components of the gearing ratio, is market values. If these were to be utilised gearing would now be 27.33%[1]. When the overdraft is taken into consideration this increases to 39.86%[2]. This revised gearing ratio shows the bank's exposure to be much lower than reported when book values are used (the ratios were 51.5% for gearing without the overdraft and 89.79% with the overdraft).

1. Calculation of gearing without the overdraft.

$$\text{Market value of debentures} = €/£16 \text{ million} \times €/£96.5/€/£100$$
$$= €/£15.44 \text{ million}$$

$$\text{Total market value of debt} = €/£6 \text{ million} + €/£15.44 \text{ million}$$
$$= €/£21.44 \text{ million}$$

$$\text{Market value of equity} = 38 \text{ million} \times €/£1.50 = €/£57 \text{ million}$$

$$\text{Gearing} = €/£21.44 \text{ million}/(€/£21.44 \text{ million} + €/£57 \text{ million}) = 27.33\%$$

2. Gearing with the overdraft

$$\text{Total debt} = €/£21.44 \text{ million} + €/£16.34 \text{ million}$$
$$= €/£37.78 \text{ million}$$

Continued

Gearing = €/£37.78 million/(€/£37.78 million
+ €/£57 million) = 39.86%

c) The following points are suggested to help Valencia plc improve its financial position:

(i) The management of working capital needs to be totally reviewed. There appears to be plenty of opportunity to reduce trade receivables, inventory and cash levels. The period of credit taken from suppliers should not be increased any further, indeed a review of the impact of the increase in the credit period taken over the past year should be undertaken to determine if the discounts lost exceed the opportunity cost of retaining the funds for the 15 days longer before payment.

(ii) The funds generated from the reduction in working capital levels could be used to reduce the overdraft, or to finance the purchase of the new machine. When deciding on this, it is important to compare the cost of the overdraft at present with the cost of the new loan (12%). The flexibility of the overdraft should be taken into consideration. Valencia plc is making good profits and should be able to generate cash quickly; therefore, having the ability to repay debt quickly might be a reason to opt for keeping the overdraft and using the cash from the reduction in working capital to finance the purchase of the new machinery. However, before this decision can be made cash flow projections should be prepared and the pattern of cash requirements and surpluses for the coming five years ascertained.

(iii) Valencia plc could consider a further input of equity. However, this is an option for the future. At the present time, Valencia plc's shares might be undervalued (given the low price earnings ratio). Were the efficiencies in working capital to come to fruition, the market might regard the company's expected performance with more confidence, causing the price earnings ratio to rise, and share price to rise. Shares could be issued when the share price has reached an acceptable level. [Note: Figures are in €/£'000s]

KEY TERMS

Altman's failure prediction model
Acid test ratio
Balance sheet
Capital employed
Capital structure
Cash flow statement
Cash return on capital employed
Creditors' ratio
Current asset turnover ratio
Current ratio
Debtors' ratio
Degree of operating leverage
Dividend cover
Dividend per ordinary share
Dividend yield
Earnings per share
Economic resources of a company
Financing activities
Financial structure
Gearing
Gross profit margin
Income gearing ratio
Income statement

Inventory turnover ratio
Investing activities
Liquidity
Net profit margin
Non-current asset turnover
Operating activities
Operating cash flow to total debt
Operating leverage
Payout ratio
Price earnings ratio
Primary ratio
Profit before interest and tax
Quick ratio
Ratio analysis
Return on capital employed
Solvency
Trade payables ratio
Trade receivables ratio
Z score

PROFORMA INCOME STATEMENT

Income statement for ABC plc for the year ended 31 December 20X7

(This example classes expenses by function)

	20X7 €/£'000	20X6 €/£'000
Revenue	50,000	45,000
Cost of sales	(30,000)	(28,000)
Gross profit	20,000	17,000
Other income	1,000	2,000
Distribution costs	(5,000)	(4,000)
Administration costs	(6,000)	(5,000)
Other expenses	(2,000)	(1,000)
Finance costs	(1,000)	(1,000)
Share of profit of associates	1,500	1,000
Profit before tax	8,500	9,000
Income tax expense	(1,500)	(2,800)
Profit for the period	7,000	6,200

PROFORMA BALANCE SHEET

Balance sheet for ABC plc as at 31 December 20X7

	20X7 €/£'000	20X6 €/£'000
Assets		
Non-current assets		
Property, plant and equipment	50,000	40,000
Goodwill	1,000	1,000
Other intangible assets	3,000	3,000
Investments in associates	2,000	2,000
Available-for-sale investments	500	–
	56,500	46,000
Current assets		
Inventories	6,000	5,000
Trade receivables	8,000	6,000
Other current assets	2,000	3,000
Cash and cash equivalents	3,000	8,000
	19,000	22,000
Total assets	75,500	68,000
Equity and Liabilities		
Equity attributable to the equity holders of the parent		
Share capital	30,000	25,000
Other reserves	1,000	1,000
Retained earnings	9,000	3,000
Minority interest	500	500
Total equity	40,500	29,500
Non-current liabilities		
Long-term borrowings	20,000	15,000
Deferred tax	2,000	3,000
Long-term provisions	3,000	3,500
Total non-current liabilities	25,000	21,500
Current liabilities		
Trade and other payables	5,500	10,000
Short-term borrowings	1,000	2,000
Current portion of long-term borrowings	2,000	2,000
Current tax payable	500	1,000
Short-term provisions	1,000	2,000
Total current liabilities	10,000	17,000
Total liabilities	35,000	38,500
Total equity and liabilities	75,500	68,000

PROFORMA CASH FLOW STATEMENT

(Direct method)

Cash flow statement for ABC plc for the year ended 31 December 20X7

	20X7	
	€/£'000	€/£'000
Cash flows from operating activities		
Cash receipts from customers	48,000	
Cash paid to suppliers and employees	(47,500)	
Cash generated from operations	500	
Interest paid	(1,000)	
Income tax paid	(3,000)	
Net cash from operating activities		(3,500)
Cash flows from investing activities		
Purchase of property, plant and equipment	(12,500)	
Proceeds from sale of equipment	2,000	
Interest received	200	
Dividends received	800	
Net cash used in investing activities		(9,500)
Cash flows from financing activities		
Proceeds from issue of share capital	5,000	
Proceeds from long-term borrowings	5,000	
Payment of finance lease liabilities	(1,000)	
Dividends paid	(1,000)	
Net cash used in financing activities		8,000
Net increase in cash and cash equivalents		(5,000)
Cash and cash equivalents at the start of the year		8,000
Cash and cash equivalents at the end of the year		3,000

Note: comparatives are also provided in financial statements allowing the reader to determine changes in the generation of cash flow and its use over a two year period.

REVIEW QUESTIONS

1.   How does inflation affect ratio analysis?
2.   What is the difference between solvency and liquidity?
3.   The following are the summarised financial statements of Alpha and Omega, two companies which operate in the same industry:

	Alpha €/£m	Omega €/£m
Summarised balance sheet		
Non-current assets	790	1,000
Current assets		
Inventories	1,200	1,800
Trade receivables	720	1,200
Bank	190	–
	2,110	3,000
Total assets	2,900	4,000
Equity and liabilities		
Equity and reserves		
Capital	1,160	1,756
Profits	340	404
	1,500	2,160
Non-current liabilities		
Loan	500	–
Current liabilities		
Trade payables	900	1,040
Bank overdraft	–	800
Total current liabilities	900	1,840
Total liabilities	1,400	1,840
Total equity and liabilities	2,900	4,000

Continued

	Alpha		Omega	
	€/£m	€/£m	€/£m	€/£m
Summarised Income statement				
Revenue		6,000		7,200
Less: cost of goods sold				
Opening stock	1,000		1,500	
Add: purchases	4,760		5,916	
	5,760		7,416	
Less: closing stock	1,200	4,560	1,800	5,616
Gross profit		1,440		1,584
Less: Expenses				
Overhead Expenditure		1,100		1,180
Net Profit		340		404

REQUIRED

a) Using ratio analysis, comment on the profitability, efficiency, liquidity and gearing of BOTH companies; and

17 Marks

b) List three limitations of ratio analysis for the purposes of inter-preting financial statements.

3 Marks

Total **20 Marks**

SECTION THREE

SOURCES OF FINANCE AND THE FINANCIAL ENVIRONMENT

ASSET-MIX DECISION, FINANCE MIX DECISION AND SHORT-TERM SOURCES OF FINANCE

LEARNING OBJECTIVES

This chapter is mostly descriptive. Upon completing the chapter, readers should be able to:

- Explain the importance of achieving an optimal asset mix;
- Explain the difference between permanent and temporary current assets;
- Discuss various approaches to asset mix (neutral, conservative, aggressive);
- Explain the finance mix choices available and discuss various approaches (matching, flexible, restrictive);
- Discuss general influences on the cost of finance;
- List institutions that provide short-term finance;
- List and explain internal short-term sources of finance;
- List and discuss short-term sources of finance from banks, other financial intermediaries and the money markets; and
- Outline short-term sources of finance for the sale of goods on credit to foreign customers.

Introduction

Every company's balance sheet splits the company's assets into two categories: non-current (fixed assets) and current assets. *Non-current assets* are assets that are deemed to have a life of more than one year, whereas *current assets* are expected to be realised as cash within one year.

All assets have to be financed. Finance is categorised into three classifications according to the term of the finance instrument. A finance instrument's *term* is the length of time the finance is arranged for. The three finance classifications are: short term, medium term and long term. ***Short-term finance*** is considered to include all types of finance that offer a term of up to one year. ***Medium-term finance*** is considered to have a term of between one and seven years and ***long-term finance*** is any source of finance with a term of over seven years. The last two classifications are considered in the three chapters that follow this one. Sources of finance cannot be neatly pigeonholed according to their term; in reality, there is overlap. For example, leases are commonly regarded as being medium-term sources of finance, yet a computer can be leased for a week and a building may be leased for 20 years.

This chapter starts by discussing generic costs and benefits associated with obtaining and maintaining finance and, in particular, highlights the differences in costs and benefits between short-term and long-term sources of finance. The latter part of the chapter describes the most common forms of short-term finance; in particular bank-sourced, short-term finance.

Non-current assets versus current assets

Characteristics of non-current assets

As mentioned in the introduction, non-current assets are assets with a life of more than one year. They are usually a result of a conscious strategic management decision to invest funds in capital items for operating activities (such as buildings, machinery, motor vehicles, fixtures and fittings) or for investment purposes (for example, obtaining a portfolio of shares, investment properties or business ventures). In all instances, the expected return should exceed the average cost of the company's funds and the return that could be obtained from other opportunities, if higher (see chapter 12 for a deeper discussion of this decision). Due to their nature, non-current assets are generally not very liquid relative to current assets. For example, it may take considerable time to prepare a building for sale, particularly where it has been purpose built for the company's needs. Indeed, its 'value in use' to the company may be greater than the building's 'net saleable value' in the market. The sale process can also be costly. Take property, for example – the costs of sale may include preparation of the property for sale (which may be substantial where the property is custom built), advertising and estate agents' fees (usually a percentage of the sale price). Even the more liquid form of non-current assets, long-term marketable securities, will incur early settlement fees and broker costs if realised before maturity.

Lack of liquidity also increases the risk associated with investing in non-current assets, as the return from most non-current asset investments is susceptible to changes in the financial environment. For example, if a company manufactures luxury goods and a recession begins, production will slow down and the resale value of the machines will fall. Each machine might have been costly to purchase, hence the relative impact of the recession on the company is high. A change in technology will have the same impact, as will changes in trends or fashions. Obtaining a portfolio of non-current assets across various complementary and negatively correlated business projects might spread and reduce the risk to a company's future, were one long-term project to fail.

Characteristics of current assets
Current assets encapsulate a company's investment in inventories, trade receivables, short-term financial securities and cash. Current assets have a lower return when compared with non-current assets. For example, monies held in a bank account will provide a marginal return as will monies in short-term monetary securities. However, investment in working capital can range from being a cost – for example, when there are inventory shortages (stock outs) – to being a return – when additional sales result from the policy being pursued, i.e. providing longer credit terms relative to competitors. An appropriate investment in current assets is required to service the operating activities of a company. Current assets are quite liquid: for example, marketable securities can be agreed for periods ranging from overnight to one year. There is a penalty if these securities are encashed before their agreed maturity date. (The management of marketable securities is discussed in chapter 11). Trade receivables (debtors) are also a liquid source of funds and are usually converted into cash within an agreed credit period (the management of trade receivables is discussed in chapter 10). Finally, inventory is the least liquid current asset; it usually has the longest cash conversion cycle (the management of inventory is discussed in chapter 9). In a manufacturing company, raw materials have to be held to service the production process. Once they enter the production process, raw materials become work in progress; when that work has been completed, they form part of finished goods that are available for sale. These goods are most likely sold on credit and thereafter become trade receivables.

Current assets, if managed appropriately (see chapter 8 for more detail), are not as risky as non-current assets, because they are not as prone to losses resulting from changes in the environment or to a downturn in a particular company or product. Where there is notice of a downturn or reduction in demand, inventories can be reduced, minimising the overall loss if, for example, a product line were to be dropped.

Optimal asset mix

A business finance manager should aim to hold the correct mix of assets by balancing the carrying costs associated with holding current assets with the shortage costs that may occur when investment in current assets falls. The *carrying cost* associated with investing in current assets is an *opportunity cost*, in that it reflects the revenue lost, had the funds been invested in non-current assets. *Shortage costs* include all those costs that result from current asset levels being kept too low. These include: lost sales when there are stock outs; disruption in production caused by stock outs; lost sales caused by the credit period on offer being too tight; default payments being required when money securities have to be encashed before their maturity; overdraft interest when the cash account runs out; defaulting on loan repayments; and, the most severe cost of all, the company being put into liquidation by its creditors because of lack of liquidity.

The following inventory economic order quantity cost graph portrays the relationship between the two types of costs and highlights the optimum level of current assets to hold:

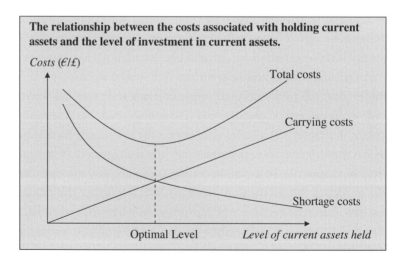

The relationship between the costs associated with holding current assets and the level of investment in current assets.

Costs (€/£)

Total costs

Carrying costs

Shortage costs

Optimal Level   *Level of current assets held*

In this example, the optimal level of current assets to hold is the amount at which the total cost of holding current assets is minimised.

The differences in these costs and how they change relative to the change in the investment in current assets will influence the asset mix investment policy.

Current assets: investment policies

There are typically three polarised policies that are prevalent in finance text books in relation to the investment of a company in its current assets. They are referred to as the aggressive, neutral and conservative policies. These terms are also used in relation to a company's working capital policy, which underlies the investment in current assets (see chapter 8 for more detail), and are also used in relation to the finance policy adopted by a company (see later in this chapter). The *neutral policy* is sometimes referred to as the *traditional policy*. The typical pattern of costs of a company pursuing this policy would be similar to those reflected in the above graph.

When the carrying costs of current assets are low relative to shortage costs, a *conservative policy* should be adopted. The conservative policy is sometimes referred to as a *flexible policy*. This involves holding higher levels of current assets (inventories, trade receivables, marketable securities and cash). The patterns of costs, which may stimulate a business finance manager to pursue a conservative policy, are portrayed in the following graph:

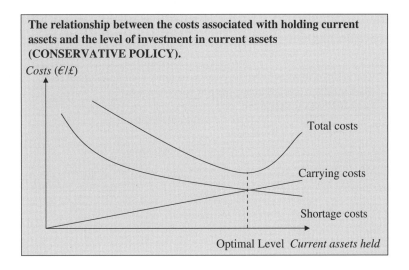

The relationship between the costs associated with holding current assets and the level of investment in current assets (CONSERVATIVE POLICY).

Costs (€/£)

Total costs

Carrying costs

Shortage costs

Optimal Level   *Current assets held*

To reiterate, this policy is appropriate where the carrying cost of current assets is not high. This may be the case when there are not many profitable investment opportunities and the return to be earned from long-term equity or money market investments is not high. This is most likely the case when the economy is in recession. Shortage costs will also be lower, as the risk of stock outs is lower due to higher inventory levels. In addition, a company is more likely to obtain high sales levels, because of higher inventory levels and attractive long credit periods. Companies pursing this policy may be able to charge a higher sales price or to disallow a discount. On the downside, there may be increased bad debts. The conservative policy is characterised by a high ratio of current assets to total assets. Another indicator is where there is a high ratio of current assets to sales.

The third policy that may be adopted is the *aggressive* or *restrictive policy*. This is where a company holds low levels of current assets, if any at all. It is characterised by a company having a low ratio of current assets to total assets, and a low ratio of current assets to sales. This policy should be pursued when the carrying cost of current assets is high relative to the shortage costs. This is likely to happen when an economy is in boom and the carrying costs – or opportunity cost – of investing in current assets is high as there are many alternative high-return investment opportunities available. In addition, shortage costs are not as high as they would be under the neutral or conservative situations. Again, this would be the case when the economy is in boom as a lost sale from having a stock-out is easily substituted by another sale. In these circumstances, demand is high, outstripping supply. The patterns of costs that would support a finance manager pursuing this type of policy are portrayed in the following graph:

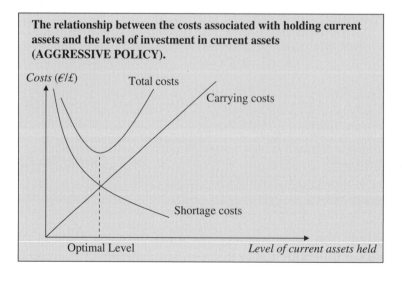

The relationship between the costs associated with holding current assets and the level of investment in current assets (AGGRESSIVE POLICY).

Costs (€/£)   Total costs   Carrying costs

Shortage costs

Optimal Level   *Level of current assets held*

Other influences on asset mix

The nature of the business

Some industries have to carry higher proportions of non-current assets to service their core operational activities. For example, manufacturers are likely to operate from bespoke premises, which normally have to be built by the company, as the cost of getting a landlord to provide a bespoke building is high. The production process usually requires a substantial investment in plant and equipment. These non-current assets are likely to be a permanent feature of a manufacturing company's balance sheet. The investment in inventories will also form a significant proportion of the current asset investment, as the costs associated with having a stock-out are high.

On the other hand a software development company can operate with relatively low levels of operational non-current assets and can invest surplus funds into new projects, achieving faster growth, or can spread their risk by purchasing shares in other types of entities or by investing in long-term marketable securities. Due to the nature of their business, software companies can rent premises (standard office space is required) and lease their hardware requirements. The main non-current asset likely to be found in the balance sheets of a software development company is development expenditure (intangible asset), a riskier type of non-current asset when compared with tangible assets. The life of capitalised development expenditure may be volatile as it is linked to the potential economic benefits that are expected from the project. Where earnings expectations fall or viability is called into question, an immediate write down will result.

Seasonal nature of revenue

Where a company has a constant pattern of revenue throughout the year, its investment in current assets can remain constant. However, where the company has seasonal fluctuations in its trade, levels of current assets will vary.

Managerial attitude to risk

Holding low levels of current assets is regarded as a risky strategy, as a company is more likely to have liquidity issues. This may not be an attractive policy to management, even in a boom economy where this policy works best, as there may be long-term repercussions. Such repercussions include loss of supplier goodwill resulting from taking too long a credit period, loss of goodwill with the bank as a result of breaching the overdraft too often and loss of customer goodwill because of inconsistent supply of the product due to stock outs. Therefore, though the most profitable strategy in the short term may be to pursue an aggressive policy, management may opt for a long-run view and hold higher levels of current assets.

The finance mix

A company's *finance mix* refers to the proportion of a company's assets that are financed by short-term, medium-term and long-term finance.

The structure of assets from a finance perspective

Investment in non-current assets is a long-term financial commitment. Investment in current assets is a commitment for a short period of time, usually less then one year. However, a portion of the investment in current assets is permanent (though constantly turning over) as a company always requires inventories to sell, must provide credit and must have sufficient liquidity to pay operational costs such as wages. Therefore, a long-term investment in **permanent current assets** is required. Few companies have constant demand and constant costs, there is usually some seasonal variation or surge in costs. For example, in winter utility costs might be higher due to poor weather conditions, or revenue may increase because of Christmas. This results in a company having a requirement to build up **temporary current assets** to service increased demand, or increased costs. For example, before Christmas there may be a build up of inventory, which will be run down over the Christmas and January sales period.

The following graph depicts the possible pattern of investment in a company's assets, where the company is not experiencing any growth.

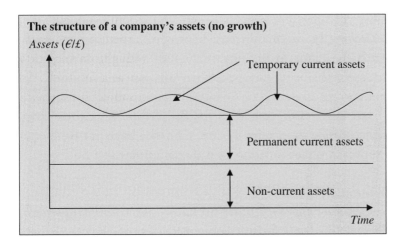

Where a company experiences growth, the structure of its assets will change in line with the pattern portrayed in the following graph. Additional finance will be required for the increased investment in total assets.

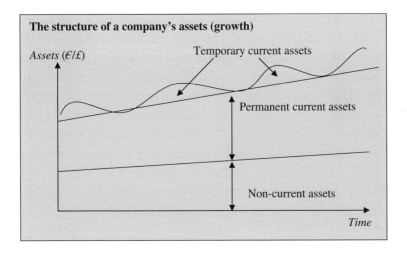

Finance mix: three policies

There are three approaches to the financing of a company's assets: matching approach; conservative approach; and aggressive approach. These are discussed in turn.

Matching approach

The ***matching approach***, otherwise known as the ***hedging approach***, aims to match the terms of the finance sourced with the maturities of the investment/assets being financed. Therefore, non-current assets and permanent current assets will be financed using mostly long-term and, possibly some short-term, sources of finance. Temporary current assets will be financed using short-term sources of finance, such as a bank overdraft. This approach is best suited to a steady economy.

Conservative approach

The ***conservative approach***, otherwise known as the ***flexible approach***, aims to fully match the peak finance requirement of a company using long-term sources of finance. This means that non-current assets and permanent and temporary current assets are all financed by long-term and medium-term sources of finance. When the temporary current asset requirement reduces, there is an excess of funds available. These are invested in temporary marketable securities. Under this policy, the company never has liquidity issues, though it will have higher interest and finance costs and higher debt capital repayments. This policy is most suitable when there is a recession, as it will be more difficult to obtain short-term funds quickly and, given the increased risk, these funds are likely to be more costly than they would be if the economy were in boom. In a recession, customers may take longer to pay and more might default, hence the company cannot be fully reliant on trade receivables as a reliable source of finance. Finally, suppliers will give premium discounts for quick payment, so having surplus funds available will increase profitability. In addition, the company will have a comparative advantage over others who do not have readily available funds, when speculative opportunities arise.

Aggressive approach

The ***aggressive approach***, otherwise known as the ***restrictive approach***, aims to maximise the level of short-term finance and to minimise the level of long-term finance that a company uses. Short-term sources are used to finance all temporary current asset requirements, a portion of the permanent current asset requirements and, in extreme cases, some of the non-current asset requirements. This approach will result in a company having little or no cash. It usually conducts its business using a large overdraft and takes a long time to pay its suppliers. Liquidity is likely to be a problem and the company will be prone to failure if the bank withdraws its support, regardless of its profitability. This approach will only be successful when the economy is in boom because customers are more likely to pay on time, bad debts are lower, interest rates are lower, the bank manager is more likely to have an optimistic view and creditors will not be too annoyed at late payments.

Is there an optimal finance mix?

When managing the finance mix, the objective should be to determine the optimal investment level in short-term, medium-term and long-term sources of finance. This will require an investigation into the costs and benefits to be obtained from the various alternative approaches. This process will involve investigating the trade-off between an aggressive and a conservative approach and coming up with the best option that minimises costs, hence maximising equity holder wealth. However, there are various factors that may restrict or influence the approach that is pursued. These are now discussed.

Attributes of finance with different terms

The strategies outlined in the previous paragraphs are polarised examples of extreme finance approaches. In reality, companies will select policies that are closer to the matching approach, though veer towards the polarised approaches slightly. Several factors influence the decision on whether to raise short-term or long-term finance. Each different type of finance, regardless of its term, has differing costs and benefits and these are outlined under the specific finance type in the chapters in this section. Some of the generic factors that influence the decision to opt for long-term or short-term finance are now outlined. This should aid understanding of the motivation for business finance managers to pursue either the aggressive, matching or conservative approaches.

Set-up costs
Set-up costs are the initial costs that are incurred in obtaining finance. These include costs such as bank commission, broker fees and administration fees. Short-term finance has lower set-up costs relative to long-term

finance, due to having lower credit risk – as the term of finance is shorter, the risk of default is lower.

Interest costs
Short-term sources of finance normally have lower interest costs relative to long-term sources. The relationship may be similar to that represented in the following graph:

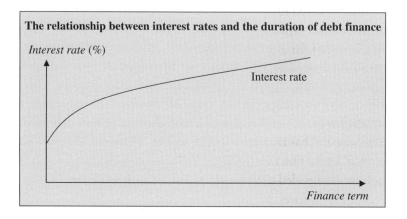

The relationship between interest rates and the duration of debt finance

Interest rate (%)

Interest rate

Finance term

As there is more risk associated with providing finance for longer periods of time, the premium or interest rate charged is higher. The interest differential between short-term and long-term sources of finance is said to be a result of the *'liquidity preference theory'*. This theory suggests that borrowers prefer to obtain long-term finance as this is less risky for them. However, lenders prefer to provide short-term finance as this is less risky for them. Therefore, to encourage lenders to provide long-term finance, a premium has to be given in the form of increased interest rates. Another theory suggests that long-term finance attracts a higher interest rate due to the influence of inflation. Long-term rates are adjusted upwards to take account of expected inflation – the higher rate equates to a real rate, which is similar to that charged on short-term finance. This is known as the *'pure expectations theory'*.

Type of finance
This is discussed in more detail under each specific type. Some sources of finance are more costly to set up than others. Tradable market sources, such

as equity and tradable debt, are more costly to arrange than non-marketable sources, such as bank debt. For example, issuing equity may involve holding meetings with current equity holders, preparing and publicising a prospectus, paying broker fees and commission and substantial managerial time.

Size of company

Small companies may find it more difficult to raise long-term finance. They may not be quoted on the stock exchange. Even if they are, it may not be economical to issue shares or tradable debt securities. Large companies are also restricted to an extent, as they have to be careful not to deviate from their optimal capital structure (see chapter 15). Small companies are more likely to opt for a mixture of medium-term and short-term finance to service their investment needs and are more likely to source their needs from suppliers, banks and finance houses.

Security available

Where a company has tangible assets, these can be provided as **security** to a finance provider for finance received. The assets act as a form of guarantee, in that the finance provided has a charge, or first claim to the proceeds, when an asset is sold. This reduces the risks associated with providing finance and usually brings down the cost of finance. Therefore, the cost of finance is influenced by the type of assets held by a company. Assets such as land or property are regarded as attractive for providing security (land and property normally increase in value), whereas intangible assets (which are subject to variation in value and are susceptible to economic changes) are not as attractive.

Gearing

Gearing is a measure of the proportion of the company that is financed by debt sources relative to equity sources (see chapters 3 and 15 for further information on gearing). A high level of gearing is indicative of high **financial risk**. Debt sources of finance are regarded as more risky than equity sources of finance, as debt capital is repayable and has an interest cost. Therefore, debt levels will impact on the liquidity and profitability of a company. The current level of financial risk influences the costs (set-up and interest) of new sources of finance.

Business risk

Different companies have different cost structures. Some have higher proportions of fixed costs, hence have higher business risk, whereas other companies have predominately variable costs and hence have lower business risk. The sensitivity of a company's cost structure can be measured using the operating leverage ratio (see chapter 3). Business risk also encapsulates the sensitivity of a company's activities to changes in the financial environment (for example, inflationary increases or changes in exchange rates). The elasticity of demand for a company's products will also influence business risk. The higher the level of business risk associated with a company, the higher the cost of finance.

Customer credit rating

A customer's credit rating is also important (see chapter 10 for a fuller discussion of this). A company that is well established, with a strong history in terms of performance and financial management, can negotiate lower set-up costs and interest costs relative to a company that is just starting out and has no credit history, or a company that has a poor credit history. Companies without a track record will incur hidden costs, in addition to the set-up and interest fees. These costs may include providing quarterly accounts, regular review meetings and having their decision making curbed by restrictive covenants (see chapter 6 for a discussion of restrictive covenants).

Providers of short-term finance

There are two main approaches to obtaining finance. The first is ***intermediation***, whereby finance is arranged through financial institutions, such as commercial banks or merchant banks. The type of finance obtained can range from an uncomplicated overdraft, which is provided internally by the financial intermediary, to a piece of paper (a bill), which can be traded for cash in the money markets. The second approach, ***disintermediation***, is where the financial intermediary's role is bypassed, with companies going direct to the money markets or stock exchanges to obtain finance. The latter is restricted to large, reputable companies seeking large amounts of finance.

As explained earlier, small and medium-sized companies are usually restricted to short-term and medium-term sources of finance as they are unlikely to have the critical mass to substantiate having a large treasury department and hence do not have the expertise or time to administer the raising of finance directly. Therefore they are likely to meet their finance needs through intermediation (i.e. from the national clearing banks, foreign-owned clearing banks or consortium banks). These financial intermediaries will arrange finance internally, using acceptance houses, discount houses and the money markets.

Acceptance houses

Acceptance houses are mostly merchant banks that take in short-term deposits and issue longer-term loans. They may not even have to pay out funds, but may provide a guarantee to pay a set amount on a set date. This guarantee can then be sold by a customer, who pays the acceptance house a commission for providing the guarantee. They mostly deal with financial intermediaries on behalf of themselves and their customers, though they have a growing relationship with large corporate companies. In terms of short-term sources of finance, acceptance houses trade in term loans, bills of exchange, acceptance credits, commercial paper and certificates of deposits (in all currencies). These types of short-term finance are discussed below. The role of acceptance houses is vital in ensuring that a liquid market for short-term paper finance exists.

Discount houses

Like acceptance houses, discount houses also create liquid markets for short-term financial products. **Discount houses** buy and sell short-term financial instruments such as Government securities (treasury bills, local authority bills), commercial paper, certificates of deposit, bills of exchange and acceptance credits. They operate in a similar manner to a stock exchange or bond market and quote prices at which they are willing to trade. The dealers are usually other discount houses, merchant banks and major banks (most major banks have a discount house department). The dealers purchase and sell these bills on behalf of their own organisation, large companies, pension companies and insurance companies.

Short-term sources of finance

The rest of this chapter explains the main sources of short-term finance that are available internally, through intermediation, and independently (disintermediation).

Internally generated sources of short-term finance

Internally generated finance is the easiest and most commonly used source of short-term finance. There are two potential sources of funds: expense accruals and working capital. These are now discussed in turn.

Expense accruals

All accruals are a source of finance, as the service, or good, is consumed in advance of payment being required. For example, electricity is used to create products and sales, yet the meter is only read quarterly, resulting in the company receiving free finance for the first day's electricity for 90 days. Then it takes time for the invoice to be generated, after which a period of credit is allowed. Therefore, the utility company may be allowing a real credit period of more than 120 days for the first day's electricity supply. Another example is Pay as You Earn (PAYE) – tax deducted from employees' wages on behalf of the government. This tax is deducted from wages weekly, but is only paid to the government every two weeks (ROI), monthly (NI) or quarterly (when a company does not have many employees). VAT is similar; it is collected from customers on sales made, but is not paid to the government until a set period has elapsed (in the ROI this is every two weeks or monthly; in NI, VAT has to be paid quarterly). Depending on the timing of the receipt of cash on the credit sale, VAT may even be a drain on the company's funds (if the debt is not received before the company has to pay the VAT). When this happens, the company has to finance the VAT payment. In these circumstances, an arrangement might be possible with the tax authorities to delay payment. Corporation tax is another free source of finance. Though profits are made, the tax on profits does not have to be paid until nine months after the year end. Indeed, it is possible to arrange with the tax authorities to pay the tax owed by instalments after this date, although interest is charged on the outstanding balance.

In addition to these internal sources, companies can arrange credit deals with financial intermediaries to fund the payment of major accruals, such as tax, VAT, accounting and audit fees or insurance fees. A financial intermediary might agree to pay the debt, after which the company pays the financial intermediary the amount outstanding (plus interest) over a short-term period, ranging from one month to twelve months. This is usually a costly source of finance, with the financial intermediary charging a high rate of interest relative to the base rate.

Working capital

The company can manage its working capital to release funds in the short term. When a company makes a sale on credit, it is effectively providing a loan to the customer for an agreed period. If the credit terms have not been strictly administered in the past and the customers have become slack in paying on time, then emphasis could be put on making the credit-collection system more efficient (see chapter 10). This will get funds in quicker. Another option is to put incentives in place to encourage customers to pay their accounts quicker than the agreed credit terms. Such an incentive could involve offering a discount. Discounts are a costly form of finance, as the effective yearly interest rate of even a low discount is quite high, usually more than an overdraft rate, and the decision should only be taken if it is beneficial for the company. Providing credit is a complicated decision that takes many factors into account (see chapter 10). The crux of the decision is to weigh up the loss of sales that would result from reducing the credit period with the finance, administration and bad debt costs that would be saved. In addition, liquidity and the ease of sourcing finance are major influences.

Trade receivables can also be used as security for finance raised through a financial intermediary (discussed later in this chapter).

Trade payables

Trade payables, or creditors, are a vital source of finance for a company. This is the other side of the coin to trade receivables. It is where a company obtains supplies on credit without having to pay for them for an agreed period of time. The period and amount of credit allowed depends on the industry, regional norms, the bargaining strength of the two companies and the type of product. A company with products that turn over quickly typically has a short credit period, whereas a company with products that have a low turnover usually has a longer credit period (see chapter 10 for a full discussion on trade credit and the influences on it). Trade credit can be used as a further source of credit where a company takes longer than the agreed period to pay the amount owing. This is best done with agreement from the supplier, as goodwill might be reduced otherwise. This is a simple, convenient and cheap source of finance, so long as discounts are not lost. It is flexible and is available to all companies regardless of size.

Worked example 4.1   (Discounts)

Gate plc has an overdraft facility of up to €/£1 million. The bank charges 10% on the outstanding balance. Gate plc is not near its limit. Verano plc (a supplier) offers Gate plc a 2% discount if it pays its account within ten days. Gate plc currently takes 50 days' credit.

REQUIRED

a)   Calculate whether it would be more beneficial for Gate plc to pay Verano plc in sufficient time to avail of the discount, or to take the full 50 days.

b)   Assume the information relates to an invoice for €/£100,000. Show the benefit to the company of both options.

Solution

a)   This question involves working out the effective yearly cost of each option to Gate plc.

Discount
The cost of the discount is: $2\%/(100\% - 2\%) = 0.0204\%$ for a 40 (50 − 10) day period.
Number of 40-day periods in a year is: $365/40 = 9.125$ times.
Therefore the effective annual interest rate is: $(1.0204)^{9.125} - 1 = 20.23\%$

Overdraft
The effective annual interest rate on the overdraft is 10%. Therefore the company will be better off extending its overdraft and paying Verano plc within 10 days to avail of the discount.

Continued

b)   *Discount*

Taking the discount option will result in a reduction in the amount to be paid by the company of €/£100,000×2%= €/£2,000.

Overdraft

If the company does not take the discount, but elects not to have to pay the funds until day 50, then the company will save interest on the additional 40 days that the €/£100,000 can remain in the bank. The daily rate of interest (i) is:

$$(1+i)^{365} = 1.1$$

$$i = \sqrt[365]{1.1} - 1$$

$$i = 0.00026$$

Therefore the total interest saving for 40 days is 0.00026×40= 0.0104 (1.04%).

The total saving in interest to the company will be €/£100,000× 1.04%=€/£1,040.

Therefore, the company will be €/£960 better off by taking the discount and incurring the additional interest cost.

Short-term finance sourced from financial intermediaries

Traditional bank sources

The most common types of finance provided by banking institutions are bank overdrafts and loans. Bank overdrafts are granted for short periods of time, though are commonly rolled over on review dates and are used by some companies as permanent sources of finance. Term loans can range from short-term loans to long-term mortgages. Banks also provide finance secured on a company's trade receivables and inventory, though this is less common. In all instances, banks assess the credit risk associated with providing finance and vary the terms according to this risk assessment. This section starts by considering the lending decision from a bank manager's perspective, then information required to inform this decision is outlined. Finally, various forms of finance provided by banks are explained.

Lending decision

Banks normally consider two aspects of each lending decision. The first involves determining whether the borrowing company can afford to make repayments. This is a *going concern issue*. Most banks try to ensure that they are not the cause of their client going out of business: this would be counterproductive for both parties. The second involves the recoverability of capital in the event of the company going into liquidation (*liquidation issue*). Banks have been criticised in the past for focusing on ensuring there has been sufficient security for their loans. This meant that many small companies with low levels of tangible assets found it difficult to attain debt at reasonable rates. Banks have been urged to give precedence to affordability and to support their clients, rather than ensuring that loans are secured on property. In most instances, banks write into the finance agreement a right to appoint a receiver, if the payments go into arrears. In reality, banks will try to reschedule the finance to both suit the company and still ensure that the debt does not end up bad.

The following information may be requested from a company by a bank to assist them in making their lending decision. The quantity of information required depends on the size of the loan requested. The information is normally presented as part of a *business plan*.

Business plan contents

Requirements

The introduction to a business plan should set out the *finance requirement* being requested. This will identify the *amount*, *interest structure* (overdrafts are normally variable rate; term loans can be variable or fixed rate), *term*, *purpose* of the funds and *source of repayment*. The main body of the business plan should refer to projections in the appendices which provide details of the repayment structure. This allows the bank to assess the company's ability to meet the repayment commitment.

Purpose of the finance

The company should highlight the investment it plans to undertake. Examples include: purchasing machines, a factory, land or a business; increasing working capital for growth; or undertaking a long-term contract such as a construction job. Banks generally prefer *self-liquidating* loans. These loans are stand alone in that they are not dependent on cash flows from current operating activities and assets for repayment, but can be repaid from the proceeds of the investment. For example, a loan to construct a ship for a customer can be repaid using revenue from stage and final payments. This information would be highlighted in projections (see below).

Background information on the company

The plan should document the *ownership structure* of a company, detailing whether it is a single company or part of a group. If the latter, it should specify whether the company is a parent company, a subsidiary, a joint venture or an associate. Share ownership details should be provided. In addition, the internal management structure could be provided.

Credit worthiness

To assess the credit worthiness of a company, a bank manager will need to get a 'feel' for the company. Therefore the business plan might include a *brief history* of the company, including what it trades in, the main products, when it started, location(s), growth/restructuring, profitability (this section would refer to financial statements that would be included in an appendix to the business plan, as would key accounting ratios), markets and employment statistics. The latter list is not exhaustive. People are also important and *managerial talent* is an intangible asset that has value; however, this value is not quantified and does not form part of a set of financial statements. Therefore, banks should be made aware of the strengths of the management team. The business plan could include the curriculum vitae of key personnel. In addition, this section could mention the names of key suppliers that the company has been trading with over a long period of time. These could be suggested as good sources of *trade references*.

Business stake

The plan should outline the commitment being made by the company to the investment being suggested. The larger the portion of the investment being committed by the company, the less risk attached to the lending decision. This is regarded as a positive signal by a bank.

Security

The business plan should highlight whether the company has assets that can be used for security. Loans can either be *secured* (otherwise known as a *committed line of credit*) or *unsecured* (otherwise known as an *uncommitted line of credit*). Unsecured loans are more risky to the bank, hence more costly, than secured loans. Security is usually of three types: fixed security, floating security and third-party guarantees. *Fixed security* is where debt is secured on a specific asset. In this instance, the bank would have a legal charge over the proceeds of the asset to the tune of the finance that has been advanced. *Floating security* is a general charge over the assets of a company. The bank has a legal charge over the proceeds of all the assets of a company and will receive funds to clear the finance that is outstanding, from any proceeds that are left after fixed security lenders have been repaid. *Third-party guarantees* are usually sought where a company has insufficient assets to provide adequate security. In these instances, related companies such as parent companies, associates, subsidiaries and joint ventures can guarantee the finance. Other commonly used third-party guarantees (used mostly by smaller companies) are personal guarantees from directors, whereby directors' private assets are used as security. Banks are not allowed to form a charge over a person's private home, but can place a legal charge over other assets.

The *type of asset* being used for security also impacts on the lending decision. Assets that do not have a volatile market value, and that generally appreciate in value, are viewed in a more positive light by banks, particularly property. Where a company has assets that could be used for security, then a schedule of these can be included in the appendix to the business plan, with up-to-date valuations, where appropriate.

Projections

Most business plans include cash flow projections in the appendix. *Cash flow projections* help banks assess the *affordability* of the bank overdraft or loan. They should show that the company will be generating sufficient liquid funds from operating activities to cover operating expenses, other expected outflows and capital and interest repayments. They are normally quite detailed and show monthly (or quarterly) cash inflows, outflows and the resultant expected cash balance. They should be for either the period of the debt being requested (if short term) or for a period of up to five years, whichever is the shorter. The projections could include *scenario analysis*, showing the worst-case, most-likely and best-case scenarios, and *sensitivity analysis* – an analysis of the impact of changes to variables used in the cash flow, such as sales price. Any assumptions made when preparing the projections should be included and explained.

Financial statements

Budgeted financial statements should also be prepared, showing the expected net income for each quarter/year and the expected balance sheet on the dates chosen. These statements should tie in with the cash flow projections. In addition (to help the bank manager assess the reasonableness of the budgeted income statements, balance sheets and cash flows), copies of the last three years' audited financial statements could be included in the appendix.

Some texts refer to the seven Cs of lending as a good acronym for remembering key information being sought by lenders.

The seven Cs of lending

1. Character
2. Capacity
3. Capital
4. Conditions
5. Customer relations
6. Competition
7. Collateral

(Source: White, L.R., (1990))

The various types of finance available from banking institutions are now explained.

Overdrafts

Normally banks provide customers with a bank account, which is a secure way of pooling and managing money. Bank customers deposit funds and withdraw them at a later date. Normally, the amounts that can be withdrawn are limited to the sum of the prior deposits made. An *overdraft* is where the bank allows its customer to withdraw more than was deposited, up to an agreed limit. The bank will start to charge interest on the account when the balance becomes negative, and will do so for every day that the account is in arrears. Overdrafts are normally unsecured and are legally *repayable on demand*. This means that a company has to be able to clear the overdraft immediately if requested to do so by the bank. In practice, this is rarely the case. Banks normally provide assurances that the facility will be in place for periods of up to a year, when the situation is reviewed and another agreement is reached. It is not in any bank's interest to demand repayment without notice, as they will put their customer under financial pressure, which may put them out of business – this will have a negative impact on the bank's reputation. Some banks have gone further than giving assurances, by making their overdrafts not repayable on demand, for example the Nationwide. They have agreed to give their customers notice when they propose to remove an overdraft facility.

As overdrafts are arranged for short periods, it is recommended that they are self-liquidating, in that they are only used to finance short-term requirements that will repay the finance obtained. An overdraft is a flexible form of finance, with an overall low interest rate cost. This is due to the fact that interest is only charged on the amount outstanding, not the full amount of the facility, and is calculated on a daily basis. The rate is variable and normally ranges between 1.5% and 5% above the bank's base rate, depending on the bank's credit assessment. Debt interest is tax deductible. There are other costs associated with an overdraft, such as an arrangement fee. This is usually about 1% of the facility being requested. In addition, the facility is reviewed periodically and the review usually incurs a fee.

If the agreed overdraft limit is breached, the consequences are punitive. The bank can refuse to honour cheques or payments made by a company. This may sour the relationship between a company and a supplier, who received a cheque in good faith – the supplier will be charged by its bank for dealing with the unpaid cheque. In addition, the supplier may lose interest or even breach its overdraft limit, incurring penalties. Breaching an overdraft limit also sends a negative message to the bank manager, as it is a sign of a deteriorating financial position or poor cash management. This will impact on a bank's willingness to provide future credit. It may also impact on a company's credit rating, causing it problems when negotiating credit from suppliers in the future. When an overdraft limit is breached, the bank immediately charges a referral fee for each and every payment made whilst the limit is breached. In addition, the rate of interest on the whole overdraft increases to rates of up to 15% or more, above the bank's base rate. In the worst-case scenario, the bank may withdraw the facility.

Short-term loans

Over the past two decades, companies in the UK and Ireland have changed their short-term lending habits, from predominant use of overdrafts to a greater use of short-term loans. Short-term loans are usually provided for periods of up to one year and are earmarked for a specific purpose. They are usually secured and provide a lender with confidence that repayment will not be demanded by the bank, unless the payments go into default. The interest rate charged is usually lower than the rate changed an overdraft, typically ranging from 1.5% to 3% above the bank's base rate. However, it is charged on the full amount of the loan, even if not in use, unless a predetermined draw-down timetable has been agreed. There is usually an arrangement fee, which can be up to 3% of the amount borrowed. The fees depend on the bargaining power of each of the parties. Getting the terms right at the outset is very important, as deviations from the agreement can be costly. Early repayment will incur a penalty.

If properly predicted, short-term loans can be reasonably flexible. There may be a facility to repay in such a manner as to match predicted cash flows. There are various off-the-shelf, short-term loan products with pre-defined repayment terms that may suit certain types of companies. For example, *balloon payment* terms involve agreements to repay the interest and only a small portion of the capital during the term of a loan – the majority of capital is repaid at the end. *Bullet payment* terms are where interest is paid throughout the term of the loan and capital is paid at the end. A *pure discount only* payment pattern involves only one repayment, at the end of the agreed term. This repayment will encapsulate all the accumulated interest and capital that is outstanding. This is usually used for large projects that do not have recurring revenue, but periodic lump sum payments. The loan advance is determined by the bank based on the lump sum to be received by them in the future and the discount rate required. The advance is the present value of the future lump sum discounted at the required rate of return (interest rate) by the bank.

Normal repayment loans that pay the interest and capital back on an annuity basis can also be tailored, with the possibility of arranging interest-only payments for the first few months, payment breaks or repayments timetabled to match the cash flows of the company.

Interest can either be fixed or variable. *Fixed interest rate* loans are usually more expensive than variable rate loans, though have the advantage of reducing uncertainty in respect of cash outflows, as the interest charge does not change when base rates change. When interest rates rise, they benefit the borrower; when interest rates fall, they benefit the bank. The initial fixed rate offered by the bank will take future expectations about interest rates into account. In *variable interest rate* loans, the interest rate is usually pegged to the bank's base rate, which usually moves in line with the Euribor (Euro Inter-Bank Offered Rate) (ROI), or LIBOR (London

Inter-Bank Offer Rate) (UK). The repayments on variable interest rate loans will increase when base rates increase and fall when base rates fall.

The bank will usually require more information from a company when deciding on whether to grant a term loan, relative to an overdraft, as the risk is higher. To reduce the risk, some banks write restrictive covenants into loan agreements. These may limit the company's ability to raise more debt or to pay dividends beyond a certain level, if at all. Overdrafts are legally repayable on demand, whereas loans are not – unless repayments fall into arrears. This means that they are more costly to set up due to increased administration charges.

Factoring

In the last two decades, banks have achieved strong growth in factoring. *Factoring* is where an outside company, usually a financial institution, provides finance to a company on the strength of its trade receivables. The factor obtains legal right to the proceeds of the trade receivables. In effect, a company is selling its future trade receivables, in exchange for up-front finance. Up to 80% of the book value of trade receivables can be obtained under a factor agreement. The factor rate is usually higher than an over-draft rate, ranging from 2% to 5% plus, above the bank's base rate. The margin charged by a factor company is influenced by their credit assess-ment of the lender. There are three main forms of factoring: non-recourse factoring; factoring with recourse; and confidential factoring.

Non-recourse factoring
Non-recourse factoring is the 'all-singing, all-dancing service', whereby a fac-tor provides up-front finance on every credit sale made, takes over the whole administration of the sales ledger and provides credit protection. This type of factoring is the most expensive, with the factor charging a service fee of typically 0.5% to 3% of total credit sales value. They may also charge a standard administration fee. The fee will be influenced by the expected number of transactions, level of late payers and bad debts. The service pro-vided by a factor includes assessing the credit worthiness of potential credit customers, reviewing the credit worthiness of current customers, preparing invoices, preparing statements and chasing late payments. Factor companies specialise in this type of activity, and hence are likely to be more efficient and successful at chasing late payments, compared with many company's

in-house credit departments. This may reduce the costs of the lender and also free up management time, which can be devoted to other issues.

The most identifiable feature of non-recourse factoring is the fact that the risk of bad debts are taken over by the factor company. This removes uncertainty for the company. However, the factor company decides whether a credit sale should be made or not. Given this, a factor company is more likely to turn away potentially profitable sales, to restrict their own exposure to bad debts. This may cause conflict between a company and a factor company. The usual procedure when a credit sale is made under a factor agreement is as follows:

Non-recourse factoring (steps)

1. The factor agrees which customers can receive credit and specifies the credit limit and period. The company may have some input into this decision process.
2. The company makes a sale, delivers the goods and informs the factor company, which issues an invoice.
3. The factor company transfers cash of up to 80% of the invoice amount to the company's bank account.
4. When the customer cheque is received by the company, it is immediately forwarded to the factor who cancels the debt owing on the invoice, deducts interest due for the period on the outstanding 80%, deducts a service charge and any other agreed fees and refunds the balance to the company.
5. The factor sends out statements and chases up customers who have not paid within the specified credit period. The factor writes up the sales day books and sales ledger and sends regular statements and reports to the company.

With-recourse factoring
With-recourse factoring is similar to non-recourse factoring – the only difference is that the company retains the right to chase up overdue debts that have breached their credit limit and retains responsibility for bad debts. This overcomes the conflict that may arise between a factor company and the lending company under a strict non-recourse factoring arrangement,

as the factor is likely to restrict credit to poor payers, whereas the company may recognise that the customers are slow payers, but are still profitable sales. In addition, it overcomes problems that may arise when a factor is used to chase up overdue trade receivable accounts. The use of an outside third party may upset customers and damage the relationship between the customer and the company.

With-recourse factoring (steps)

1. The company agrees which customers can receive credit and specifies the credit limit and period. The factor may have some input into this decision process.
2. The company makes a sale, delivers the goods and informs the factor company, which issues an invoice.
3. The factor company transfers cash of up to 80% of the invoice amount to the company's bank account.
4. When the customer cheque is received by the company, it is immediately forwarded to the factor who cancels the debt owing on the invoice, deducts interest due for the period on the outstanding 80%, deducts a service charge and any other agreed fees and refunds the balance to the company.
5. Where a customer does not pay their account within the agreed credit limit, the factor informs the company and requests that they pursue the debt.
6. If the debt is still not received after a predetermined time period (agreed between a factor and the company), then the company is called upon to make good the debt and costs to the factor company.
7. If the debt turns out to be bad, the company may claim the loss from their credit protection insurance (the latter can be provided by factor companies).

Confidential factoring

Using factor companies as a source of finance is expensive and, hence, is usually only used when a company has exhausted its overdraft facility and still requires additional short-term funds. As this is the case, the use of a factor company can be interpreted as a sign of liquidity problems. This makes the company riskier to grant credit to, and so may affect the company's ability to obtain credit. To counteract this problem, a company can enter into a confidential factoring agreement. Under a *confidential factoring agreement*, the factor's involvement is not visible; the company remains responsible for the administration of the trade receivables ledger and issues invoices, statements and letters, using its own stationery. The company still sells the trade receivables to the factor; however, it acts as an agent for the factor company in the collection of the debts. This agreement will have lower service and administration fees relative to the prior two types of factoring.

Confidential factoring (steps)

1. The company agrees which customers can receive credit and specifies the credit limit and period. The factor may have some input into this decision process.
2. The company makes a sale, delivers the goods, issues the invoice and informs the factor company.
3. The factor company transfers cash of up to 80% of the invoice amount to the company's bank account (so long as they agree to accept the invoice).
4. When the customer cheque is received by the company, it is immediately banked and a settlement cheque/transfer is sent to the factor company to cover the debt, interest and charges that are outstanding on the invoice.
5. Where a customer does not pay their account within the agreed credit limit, the company informs the factor and pursues the debt.
6. If the debt is still not received after a predetermined period of time (agreed between the factor and the company), then the company is called upon to make good the debt and costs to the factor company.
7. If the debt turns out to be bad, the company may claim the loss from their credit protection insurance (the latter can be provided by most factor companies).

Factoring: summary of advantages and disadvantages

The key advantage of factoring is that it is a quick source of short-term funds, which fluctuates in line with credit sales. In addition set-up costs are low relative to other forms of finance, the only sources of security required are trade receivables, the finance can be obtained without the factor company placing restrictive covenants on the company's other decisions, the finance is not repayable on demand and where the factor takes over the administration of trade receivables, savings can be made within the company and managerial time can be devoted elsewhere.

On the downside, factoring is costly. The interest rates charged are usually in excess of overdraft rates and the service fees can be high. Profitable sales can be lost due to strict credit control, or the factor will not provide finance against certain credit invoices as the factor will only be interested in taking over clean accounts. In addition, trade receivables cannot be encumbered by any other debt. Factor companies are usually only interested in large value invoices and the use of a factor may cause suppliers to reassess the credit period they allow to the company, due to perceived increased liquidity risk.

Worked example 4.2   (Factoring)

Enero plc has been set up for the purpose of importing commodities which will be sold to a small number of reliable customers. Sales invoicing is forecast at €/£300,000 per month. The average credit period for this type of business is 2.5 months.

The company is considering factoring its accounts receivable under a full factoring agreement within recourse. Under this agreement, the factor will charge a fee of 2.5% on total invoicing. He will give an advance of 85% of invoiced amounts, at an interest rate of 13% per annum.

The agreement should enable Enero plc to avoid spending €/£95,000 per annum on administration costs.

REQUIRED

As the company finance director, you are responsible for strategic financial management. For the next board meeting you need to:

   a) calculate the annual net cost of factoring; and

Continued

b) discuss the financial benefits of such an agreement, having regard to a current interest rate on bank overdrafts of 12.5%.

(10 Marks)
(ICAI, Questions and Answers book, 2000/2001)

Solution

a) *Note: An incremental approach has been adopted in this solution.*
Annual sales   €/£300,000 × 12 = €/£3,600,000

		€/£
Fee	€/£3,600,000 × 2.5% =	(90,000)
Interest:		
Amount advanced		
€/£3,600,000 × 85% = €/£3,060,000		
Charges		
€/£3,060,000 × 13% × 2.5/12 =		(82,875)
Administrative costs saved		95,000
Net cost per annum		(77,875)

b) An alternative source of finance is a bank overdraft. Assuming 85% of the invoiced amount is the amount of finance required (so that like is being compared with like).

	€/£
Cost of finance (bank)	
€/£3,060,000 × 12.5% × 2.5/12 =	(79,688)
Annual net cost of factoring	(77,875)
Annual benefit of factoring	1,813

Factoring: other financial benefits.

(i) Factoring offers flexibility as sales volumes fluctuate. If sales increase, additional finance is automatically received.

(ii) Bad debts are not lost money to Enero plc, as the factoring agreement in this instance is without recourse.

(iii) A semi-fixed cost of administration is removed from Enero plc's costs and fluctuations in sales volumes can easily be accommodated.

Worked example 4.3 (Factoring)

REQUIRED

Summarise the services that may be obtained from a factor.

(5 Marks)
(ICAI, Questions and Solutions manual, 2000/01)

Solution

Factors collect trade debts on behalf of client companies.

The various services provided by a factor include:

- relieving a trading company of an administrative function for invoicing and debtor collection;
- providing finance on the face value of invoices;
- covering bad debts (if the arrangement is 'without recourse'); and being confidential, so the customer is not aware of the arrangement.

Invoice discounting

Similar to factoring, *invoice discounting* is the sale of selected credit sales invoices to a financial intermediary, usually a bank. The bank normally provides finance secured on the invoice of about 75% to 80% of the invoice value. The credit period allowed can range for periods of up to 90 days. The borrowing company collects the amounts owing on the invoice and forwards the full amount to the invoice discounter who takes out the capital sum advanced to the company, the interest due and any set up fee or administration fee, and returns the balance to the company. This form of finance is more expensive than a conventional overdraft. The interest rates typically range from 3% to 6% above the bank base rate and the administration fee is typically 0.5% of the finance allowed. The company retains more control over this method of finance relative to a factoring agreement, as the company selects the invoices to discount, decides on the frequency of undertaking each transaction, administers the debt collection and is responsible for any bad debt that might occur on the invoice. Customers are usually unaware that an invoice discounter is involved, whereas under a standard factoring arrangement (not confidential factoring), customers know a factor is administering the debt.

Inventory financing

Inventory financing is where banks and/or other financial institutions provide finance using a company's inventory as security. Five types of arrangement exist: blanket lien, trust receipt, warehouse receipt, terminal warehousing and field warehousing. These are explained in brief:

Blanket lien
In some instances a lender will hold a charge against a company's total inventory balance – this is known as having a *blanket lien* over the inventory. The company is free to sell the inventory, reducing the benefit of this lien as a form of security.

Trust receipt
A *trust receipt* arrangement affords more protection to the lender. In this instance a company signs a trust receipt promising to hold inventory in trust for the benefit of a lender. The lender may physically inspect the inventory from time to time. When the inventory is sold, the revenue goes to the lender to settle the debt. The difference between the sums received for the inventory and the amount advanced on the strength of the value of the inventory is the cost of finance.

Warehouse receipt
Under a *warehouse receipt* arrangement, a lender takes physical and legal possession of the inventory and receives revenue from the sale of the specific inventory to settle the debt. As is the case under a trust receipt, the finance cost to a company (and the return to a lender) is the difference between the sale value of the inventory and the amount advanced to the company.

Terminal warehousing
Terminal warehousing is a similar arrangement to a warehouse receipt arrangement – the inventory is physically moved to a lender's warehouse.

However, it is more expensive, as the borrowing company agrees to pay a third party to manage and monitor the inventory. The inventory is released when the lending company receives payment for the goods.

Field warehousing

Field warehousing is a mixture of a trust receipt and terminal warehousing. Under a *field warehousing* arrangement, the inventory remains in the possession of the borrowing company. However, it is monitored by a third party at the borrowing company's expense. The inventory is only released from stores when the lender authorises the third party to do so.

Banks: Other forms of finance

Banks are also players in the money markets and can offer most of the products discussed below. In addition, banks, though not providing specific products, have a role to play in reducing the risk of products, by acting as guarantor for companies. These arrangements are discussed below.

Raising finance using the money markets

There are three main methods of raising finance from the money markets. They all involve issuing a bill of some description. *Bill finance* refers to paper documents that are similar to IOUs. The bill usually sets out the terms of the IOU; for example, usually a bill states that the issuer will pay the holder of the bill a set amount of money on a set date in the future. This bill is then traded in the money markets (between the commercial banks, discount houses and acceptance houses, depending on the particular bill). There are three main types of bill finance: bills of exchange, acceptance credits and commercial paper. These are now discussed in turn.

Bills of exchange

A *bill of exchange* is defined in the Bills of Exchange Act 1882 as:

> 'an unconditional order in writing, addressed by one person to another, signed by the person giving it, requiring the person to

whom it is addressed to pay on demand, or at a fixed or determinable future time, a sum certain in money to or to the order of a specified person, or to bearer'.

Historically, bills of exchange were used when goods were sold overseas and were in transit for long periods of time. The seller prepares a bill, which is signed by a purchaser as being agreed. This is a legal contract in which the purchaser has to pay the seller or holder a sum agreed for the goods (stipulated on the bill of exchange) at a future date (usually when the goods are expected to be received by the purchaser). This means that no funds exchange hands while the goods are in transit. The seller can then sell the bill to obtain finance and usually receives a discounted amount for the bill. Discount houses and commercial banks are the most frequent traders of bills. The discount given is the interest cost of the finance.

Bills of exchange can be arranged for domestic supplies and can cover periods of up to 180 days. The most frequent duration is 90 days and bills are usually for amounts of over €100,000/£75,000. The discount usually reflects a margin over the Euribor or LIBOR of between 1.5% and 4%. When credit difficulties arise, the holder of the bill usually has recourse to both the seller of the goods and the purchaser. It is not uncommon for the seller of the bill to take out credit insurance on the debt; where this is the case, the discount is usually less, reflecting the reduced risk.

Bills of exchange (steps)

1. The company sells goods to the customer (purchaser).
2. The company draws up a bill of exchange stating the amount owed by the customer, the customer's details, the settlement date and who the debt should be made payable to (usually the holder). This is sent to the customer.
3. The customer signs the bill of exchange and writes 'accept' on the bill. The customer returns the bill to the company.
4. The company can hold the bill until funds are received or can sell the bill in the money markets, at a discount.
5. The holder of the bill contacts the customer and agrees payment details for the due date.

Worked example 4.4 (Bills of exchange)

A €/£100,000 bill, dated three months from now, is sold by Egg plc to a commercial bank at 2% discount.

REQUIRED

Calculate the effective yearly cost of the bill to Egg plc.

Solution

The cost of the finance to Egg plc is a loss of 2% out of 100% for a three-month period. This represents a cost of 2%/98%=2.04% for three months.

Yearly, then, this equates to an effective annual interest cost of:

$$(1.0204)^4 - 1 = 8.4\%$$

This represents the cost to Egg plc and the return received by the commercial bank.

Acceptance credits

An acceptance credit is similar to a bill of exchange, except it is not attached to an underlying sale, is prepared by the company wishing to raise finance and is guaranteed by their bank. An *acceptance credit* bill is a legal document prepared by a company, which states that its bank will pay a set amount on a specified date in the future to the holder of the document. After it is prepared, the bank signs or stamps the agreement. At this juncture, the company pays the bank a commission for using its name as guarantor. This commission is typically between 0.5% and 1% of the face value of the bill. The fee for the guarantee is quite low. The guarantee is an off-balance-sheet commitment by the bank. It is a contingent liability and, as such, is not accrued for in the liabilities of the bank. The bill is then sold in the money markets by the company, usually to another bank, acceptance house or discount house, for cash at a discounted price.

The bank pays the holder of the bill on the specified day and collects the debt due to it from the company by the agreed terms (the company may pay the bank the full amount on a specified date or the balance may be paid to them in instalments). This is a separate arrangement and will include interest and commission for the additional source of finance. Alternatively, the balance can be rolled over into a new acceptance credit bill. Acceptance credits usually attract a lower discount rate than bills of exchange because of the lower risk resulting from having a bank guarantee. Indeed, they can be cheaper than an overdraft. Acceptance credit arrangements are not repayable on demand. Once sold, the borrowing company (seller) is hedged against interest rate movements and the discount cannot change. Acceptance credits are usually prepared for a minimum amount of €400,000/£250,000 and can range in duration from 30 to 180 days.

Government-backed notes that are issued by local authorities are examples of acceptance credits. In these instances, the government acts as guarantor.

Acceptance credits (steps)

1. The company prepares an acceptance credit declaring that its bank will pay a specified sum on a set date in the future. This is sent to the bank.
2. The bank signs the acceptance credit confirming that it will guarantee payment of the sum on the specified date. The bank returns the bill to the company.
3. The company pays the bank a commission for the guarantee.
4. The company sells the acceptance credit bill in the money markets, at a discount.
5. On the due date, the bank pays the holder of the acceptance credit the full amount on the bill.
6. The company pays the bank on the same day or prepares another acceptance credit (the proceeds of which are used to repay the bank), or makes an arrangement to repay the bank in instalments (this part can be quite flexible).

Worked example 4.5   (Acceptance credits)

A plc wishes to raise some finance using the money markets. It approaches its bank who agrees to guarantee an amount, limited to €/£500,000. A commission of 0.5% is payable for this service on the amounts of facility used. A plc prepares an acceptance credit agreement, the terms of which are that the bank agrees to pay €/£400,000 in three months' time to the holder of the bill. A plc has agreed to repay €/£425,000 to the bank in one year's time in respect of the bill. A plc sells the bill on the money markets at 8% discount.

REQUIRED

Calculate:
a)   the effective yearly cost of the discount rate given by the money markets to A plc;
b)   the return earned by the bank by agreeing to accept repayment from A plc in one year's time (this will represent the cost to A plc also); and
c)   the overall cost of the arrangement to the company.

Solution

a)   The company will receive €/£368,000 now in respect of the acceptance credit.
The return on the discount is: $8\%/(100\% - 8\%) = 8.7\%$ for three months.
The number of three-month periods in a year is: $12/3 = 4$ times.
Therefore, the effective annual interest rate is: $(1.087)^4 - 1 = 39.6\%$.
b)   The return received by the bank (cost to the company) of providing nine months' credit is as follows:
€/£25,000/€/£400,000 $= 6.25\%$ for a period of nine months.
The number of nine-month periods in the year is: $12/9 = 1.33$.
Therefore, the effective annual interest rate is: $(1.0625)^{1.33} - 1 = 8.4\%$.

Continued

c) The overall cost of the finance to the company is:
€/£425,000 − €/£368,000 = €/£57,000 + €/£2,500
€/£59,500/€/£368,000 = 16.168% for a 12-month period.

Commercial paper

A *commercial paper* bill is legal commitment by a company to pay a set amount on a specified date. The paper is traded directly in the money markets by the company and is a perfect example of disintermediation, as the company can cut out the role of the bank or financial intermediary. The company issuing the commercial paper should have sufficient in-house expertise to set up the documentation and does not necessarily require the debt to be guaranteed, making this a cheap form of short-term finance. The cost of commercial paper is typically the Euribor or LIBOR rate, plus 0.15% to 1% (depending on the company's reputation). Most commercial paper transactions are in multiples of over €750,000/£500,000 and their terms can range from 7 to 364 days. Only large, reputable companies that are quoted on the stock exchange can raise finance in this manner. They usually have net assets of over €75/£50 million.

A company with a strong reputation has a reduced need for a bank guarantee; however, in many instances the commercial paper being issued is guaranteed by a bank. Banks will normally agree a *'revolving underwriting facility'*; wherein the bank guarantees the issuing of commercial paper at a specified rate in the commercial paper market, for an agreed period of time. The company can then issue several short dated bills up to the limit of the agreed facility. The bank usually is more involved in this arrangement and sells the bills on behalf of the company at the specified rate in the money market. The bank purchases any bills not taken up by the money market. The company pays the bank a fee for the guarantee and commission on the sale of the bills.

A downside to bill finance is that it is not flexible. If an issuer runs into liquidity problems, repayment terms will not be changed – the market will require repayment of the bill – whereas finance obtained directly from a bank can be renegotiated.

International trade

Low-risk transactions: background

Most large companies export goods and import supplies from other countries. Exporting is riskier than domestic trading due to greater uncertainty when dealing with overseas companies, as it is more difficult to assess their credit standing. In addition, there are country-specific risks (such as the risk of war or recession) and currency risks. Where an importer's reputation is strong and the country in which they are located is regarded as being low risk, then transactions can be open account. An ***open account*** arrangement is not too different from the type of agreement found in domestic credit sales. A written credit agreement between two parties to a trade, about the settlement amount and date, is prepared. This is usually the only documentation that is required and cuts costs, as shipping documentation or bills conferring conditions as to transfer of legal title to the goods, are not required. This is termed *'clean bill collection'*. If the importer defaults on the agreement, the exporter can pursue the debt through the legal system. Most internal European trade is undertaken by open account arrangement. The invoices that are issued can be used to obtain finance in the same manner as in domestic transactions, though this may be more costly, as there are additional risks. In particular, export invoice discounting and export factoring are common sources of finance. The latter is now discussed.

Export factoring

Export factoring is virtually the same as domestic factoring. It can be set up with-recourse or as non-recourse; the only exception is that the factor takes over foreign currency exchange risk. The factor purchases the credit invoices, which might be denominated in a foreign currency, and pays the exporter a set portion of this up front, in the domestic currency. This hedges a portion of the credit transaction against future exchange rate movements. This additional feature increases the cost of factoring, making the service fees more expensive than domestic factor service fees. Another influence on fees is the additional time that is required to assess the credit worthiness of importers. Many factors have branches in other countries and this helps with this assessment. Those that do not, and who still provide export factoring, are usually members of an international factoring organisation such as '*factors chain international*'. This organisation will provide information to help a domestic factor company assess the credit risk of an importer.

High-risk transactions: role of bills in international finance

Where there is doubt as to the reputation of an importer, or there are concerns regarding currency risk or country risk, then a credit sale is normally processed by an intermediary (usually a bank) using carefully predetermined document flows or bills that are agreed by both parties to the transaction. As goods can be in transit for a long period of time, shipping documentation which includes information affecting the timing of transfer of legal title to the goods is also written into each sale arrangement. A *bill of lading* is usually prepared; this is a shipping document that transfers title of the goods. There will be periods when neither the exporter nor importer has physical possession of the goods – therefore having adequate transit insurance is important. Three main types of bills or arrangements are commonly used in exporting arrangements: letters of credit, bills of exchange or forfaiting.

Documentary letter of credit

A *documentary letter of credit* is a bank guarantee (importer's bank) to pay the amount on the letter of credit at a set time to the exporter, providing certain conditions are met in respect of the delivery of the goods (their type, quantity, quality, price and timing of shipment and delivery). The letter of credit is prepared by the importer, accepted by their bank and delivered to the exporter, who can then sell it to their bank at a discounted rate to raise finance. Payment on documentary letters of credit can be immediate (*sight drafts*) or follow an agreed credit term (*term drafts*).

There are two types of documentary letters of credit: an irrevocable documentary letter of credit and a revocable letter of credit. An *irrevocable documentary letter of credit* provides an exporter with the most protection. It is prepared by the importer, guaranteed by their bank and sent to the exporter's bank, who signs as having accepted it. An accepted irrevocable documentary letter of credit is known as a *confirmed documentary letter of credit*. This is a legally binding arrangement detailing the payment to be made, the documents to be delivered and the range of dates that the documents should be received by. This contract cannot be altered or cancelled without the consent of all parties. An irrevocable documentary letter of credit is usually requested by an exporter where the uncertainties are greatest. It is expensive for the importer to set it up and importers normally bargain for a lower product price to compensate for the additional costs. The document flows are very important to banks – more important than the goods. If the relevant documents are not received within the time frames specified in the letter of credit, then the exporter's bank may not accept payment. The legal title of the goods, as conferred by the bill of lading, normally goes to the importer's bank. They usually do not release title until they are paid by the importing company.

A less expensive, but more risky option, for an exporter is to require a *revocable documentary letter of credit*. This letter of credit is not legally binding, cannot be confirmed by the exporter's bank and can be altered or cancelled at any time by the importer, without having to give any notice to the exporter. A deterrent to this type of letter of credit turning bad is the involvement of the importer's bank, which (if reputable) will not wish to be associated with transactions that are cancelled.

Letter of credit (steps)

1. A sale is agreed between an exporter and an importer.
2. The importer prepares a letter of credit stating the amount and date to pay the exporter. This is guaranteed by their bank (the importing bank). The legal title to the goods will pass to the importing bank (they will hold the bill of lading).
3. If irrevocable, the importer's bank forwards the letter of credit to the exporter's bank for acceptance. If revocable, the bank forwards the letter of credit to the exporter.
4. The exporter delivers the products and presents the sight draft/term draft of the letter of credit (or their bank does so on their behalf) at the importer's bank, which pays the specified amount.
5. The importer's bank then passes title of the goods to the importer.
6. The importer pays the bank the capital outlay plus any commission and interest (if there is a timing difference).

Export bill of exchange

An *export bill of exchange* is the same as a bill of exchange used for domestic transactions (discussed earlier in the chapter). The exporter prepares the bill, which is addressed to the importer, specifying the amount and date the bill should be settled. This bill is then sent to the importer (usually through banking channels) who accepts the bill by signing it and writing that it is accepted. Only when the bill is accepted, will the exporter start to transport the goods. The exporter retains legal title (bill of lading). When the goods arrive in the importer's country, the bill of exchange is presented to the importer before legal title to the goods passes (the bill of lading is held until the conditions of the bill of exchange are fulfilled). If it is a sight draft, the importer has to pay immediately; if it is a term draft, the importer has the specified term to pay the bill. The exporter can sell the bill of exchange to its bank at a discount when it needs to raise short-term finance. A sight draft is used when the reputation of the importer is uncertain. Export bills of exchange are not as costly as documentary letters of credit.

Forfaiting

Forfaiting is a medium-term source of export finance. This is used where an importer has a long-running trading arrangement with an exporter. The importer prepares a series of bills detailing amounts owed for goods ordered from the exporter. Individual bills are for periods of up to six months; however, the arrangement is usually established for periods of up to five years. The exporter takes the bills to a forfaiter (a bank) who buys the bills at a discount. The bills are usually guaranteed by the importer's bank and are without recourse. Therefore, the exporter is fully hedged against credit risk. The discount taken by the bank varies depending on the credit rating of the importer, the reputation of their bank, currency exposure, if any, and country risk. Forfaiting can be expensive, though the exporter is usually aware of the cost up front and can increase the product price to take account of the increased cost.

Conclusion

The first part of this chapter deals with the current and non-current asset mix. The costs associated with holding different types of asset are outlined and other potential influences on the levels to hold, such as industry norms, nature of the products, seasonality of sales, the state of the economy and managerial attitude, are considered. The second part of the chapter deals with the finance mix a company should use to finance its investments (asset mix). This considers the portion of short-term, medium-term and long-term finance a company should source. Theoretically, a matching approach is deemed to be most appropriate, wherein the term of the finance should match the term of the investment; other policies are also explained.

The third part of the chapter describes the various forms of short-term finance that are available to a company. The variety is wide, and the products on offer from financial intermediaries range from simple to quite complicated.

Examination standard question

Worked example 4.6

POPPET Ltd. ('POPPET') is a manufacturing company. It sells goods for a total value of €/£500,000 per annum to regular customers. In order to secure this business, the company is flexible on debt collection and, on average, customers take 60 days to pay.

The company needs to improve its cash flow situation and does not want to wait a full 60 days to collect its debts. Invoice discounting has been put forward as an option to secure early payment. An invoice discounter has agreed to purchase the debts. The invoice discounting agreement involves the immediate cash payment of 70% of the face value of each invoice. The balance will be paid after 60 days less:

- an administration charge of 0.6% of turnover accepted by the discounter; and
- interest of 12% per annum on outstanding debts.

REQUIRED

a)   Explain THREE principal differences between factoring and invoice discounting.

4 Marks
Continued

b)   Calculate the annual percentage cost of POPPET's proposed invoice discounting.

8 Marks

c)   If POPPET could secure alternative short-term finance at an annual rate of 15%, should it proceed with invoice discounting or accept the alternative?

2 Marks

d)   Outline briefly TWO other ways in which POPPET might use its trade receivables to improve cash flow.

4 Marks
Total 18 Marks
(ICAI, MABF II, Autumn 2000, Q6)

Solution

a)   Factoring and invoice discounting are ways in which a company can obtain cash from its trade receivables, without waiting for the period of credit to expire. The principal differences between the two are as follows:

- *Invoice discounting involves purchasing only selected invoices:* Invoice discounting involves the discounter purchasing only selected invoices, perhaps just one. With factoring, the entire debtors ledger is sold to the factoring company.

- *Invoice discounting is only concerned with providing finance on customer accounts. It is not involved in sales administration:* Invoice discounting involves the purchase of invoices by the discounter. The discounter will immediately advance cash, up to 80% of the face value of the invoices. Unlike factoring, which involves the purchase of the debtors ledger, it assumes no responsibility for the administration of the accounts receivable or the collection of debts.

- *The selling company retains responsibility for bad debts with invoice discounting:* As mentioned above, invoice

Continued

discounting is simply the advance of finance on certain invoices. The discounting company does not take responsibility for the collection or non-collection of debts. With factoring, the selling company may retain responsibility for non-collection of bad debts, but the possibility of the discount company taking that responsibility exists if a non-recourse arrangement is put in place.

b)   Cost to POPPET Ltd. of invoice discounting:

- Administration charge of 0.6% of turnover accepted by the discounter
  If the discounter has agreed to accept all invoices of POPPET Ltd. in the year, then the accepted turnover is €/£500,000
  Therefore the administration charge will be €/£500,000 × 0.6% = €/£3,000

- Interest of 12 % per annum on outstanding debts
  Total interest will be the amount advanced by the interest rate.
  The amount advanced is: €/£500,000 × 70% × 60/365 = €/£57,534
  Therefore, the interest charge will be €/£57,534 × 12% = €/£6,904

  The total cost is €/£9,904 (€/£3,000 + €/£6,904)

  Total cost as a percentage of sales (€/£9,904/€/£500,000) = 1.98%
  Total cost as a percentage of funds advanced (€/£9,904/€/£57,534) = 17.21%

c)   The cost of invoice discounting at 17.21% per annum is higher than the cost of the alternative short-term finance (15%). POPPET Ltd. should, from a financial perspective, choose the short-term finance option. Non-financial factors should also be considered, such as the reputation and trading history of the finance provider.

Continued

d) Ways (other than invoice discounting) that the company may use its trade receivables to improve cash flow (TWO suggestions are required):

Factoring: Factoring effectively involves the selling of a company's trade receivables. Typically, a factoring company will advance the selling company a percentage of the value of trade receivables on making the arrangement and will then advance more cash to the seller as the debts are recovered. The advantage to the seller of this form of finance is that they can acquire cash immediately; however, it is an expensive form of finance as the fees etc. of the factoring company can be high. In addition, often factoring arrangements are with-recourse in that, if the debts cannot be recovered, the factoring company has recourse to the selling company, that is, the selling company bears the cost of bad debts.

Bill of exchange: A bill of exchange is a form of IOU. It is a document drawn up by the seller of goods detailing the date and the amount of payment. The bill of exchange is sent to the purchaser of the goods who signs it and returns it to the seller. The seller can then either hold the bill until maturity and claim payment from the purchaser or sell the bill at a discount in the market and get cash immediately.

Short-term bank finance: The company could use its trade receivables as security for acquiring a short-term loan or the extension of an overdraft facility with a bank.

Offer settlement discounts to customers: The company may offer early settlement discounts to customers to encourage early payment of debts. This would enhance the cash flow of the company.

With regard to each option for cash flow improvement listed above, the cost of the approach versus the benefits should be evaluated.

KEY TERMS

Acceptance credit
Acceptance house
Aggressive approach/policy
Balloon payment
Bill finance
Bill of exchange
Blanket lien
Bullet payments
Business plan
Clean bill collection
Commercial paper
Committed line of credit
Confidential factoring
Confirmed documentary letter of credit
Conservative approach/policy
Current assets
Discount houses
Disintermediation
Documentary letter of credit
Export bill of exchange
Export factoring
Factoring
Field warehousing
Finance mix
Financial risk
Fixed interest
Fixed security
Flexible approach/policy
Floating security
Forfaiting
Gearing
Going concern issue
Hedging approach
Intermediation
Inventory financing
Invoice discounting
Irrevocable documented letter of credit

Letter of credit
Liquidation issue
Liquidity preference theory
Long-term finance
Maturity approach
Medium-term finance
Neutral policy
Non-current assets
Non-recourse factoring
Open account
Overdraft
Ownership structure
Permanent current assets
Pure discount only loan
Pure expectations theory
Repayable on demand
Revolving underwriting facility
Scenario analysis
Security
Self-liquidating loans
Sensitivity analysis
Short-term finance
Shortage costs
Revocable letter of credit
Restrictive approach/policy
Temporary current assets
Term
Terminal warehousing
Traditional policy
Trust receipt
Third-part guarantees
Uncommitted line of credit
Unsecured
Variable interest
Warehouse receipt
With-recourse factoring

REVIEW QUESTIONS

1. Explain the difference between current assets and non-current assets.
2. Explain the difference between permanent current assets and temporary current assets.
3. What are the costs that have to be balanced when deciding on the most appropriate asset mix?
4. Outline the main characteristics of the neutral, flexible and restrictive policies in relation to asset mix choice.
5. Outline the main characteristics of the matching, flexible and restrictive policies in relation to finance mix choice.
6. Explain the term 'disintermediation'.
7. List two types of institutions that provide short-term finance.
8. List four forms of short-term finance that can be provided by banks.
9. What is the difference between factoring and confidential factoring?
10. NEWMAN plc has been experiencing continuing difficulties with the collection of debts from its customers. The managing director has requested a report detailing the main debt-collection techniques available in the domestic market.

    ### REQUIRED

    Critically evaluate the costs and benefits associated with each of the following:

    a) Factoring
    b) Invoice discounting

    8 Marks
    (ICAI, MABF II, Summer 1997, Q7)

11. What type of credit arrangement would you recommend to an exporter who is concerned about the reputation of a potential foreign customer?

CHALLENGING QUESTIONS

1.   TIGA SALES Ltd.

TIGA SALES Ltd. ('TIGA') sells to the general public by way of cata-logue, telephone and internet sales. The Credit Controller of TIGA has been reviewing the sales ledger and credit balances as well as the proce-dures in the credit control section.

The results of the Credit Controller's review are summarised in the table below. TIGA divides its sales into three separate geographic regions (Area 1, Area 2 and Overseas Area) and the sales for each region in €/£ millions is given in the table below.

The average outstanding balances over the year for customers in the various areas are also shown in the table below, e.g. in Area 1 the average balance is €/£500 and there are 10,000 customers in that area. The cost of collecting, or attempting to collect, outstanding amounts varies from area to area, with overseas customers costing the greatest amount. In spite of the efforts of the credit department, 22% of the total sales to the overseas area turn out as bad debts during the course of the year (as can be seen from the table below).

All products sold by TIGA produce a contribution of 25% of selling price from which collection costs, bad debts and selling costs have to be deducted. These vary by area also – from the table below it can be seen that the overseas area requires 8% of revenue to be spent on selling costs in order to achieve a sale.

Area	Sales €/£m	Average balance outstanding per customer €/£	Number of customers	Collection costs (% of average balance) %	Bad debts (% of area sales) %	Selling costs (% of area sales) %
Area 1	80	500	10,000	0	0	2
Area 2	70	300	30,000	8	18	6
Overseas Area	60	600	17,000	10	22	8

The Credit Controller has had discussions with DOMBA Ltd. ("DOMBA"), a factoring company that believes it can improve the overall profitability of TIGA by introducing better credit control procedures and incorporating new and strict guidelines for sales personnel to follow, which will speed up debt collection and reduce the bad debt problem. It will charge an annual sum of €/£3,500,000 for its administration, thereby cutting out all the existing collection costs.

DOMBA has offered to take over the administration of the sales ledger, debt collection and general management of trade receivables. It will not take over any losses arising from bad debts. It will lend funds to TIGA at 8% p.a. for the amount and period of the outstanding debtor balances, e.g. for every Area 1 customer it will lend €/£500 at 8% per annum. It predicts that its operating efficiency and credit guidelines for sales personnel will cut the bad debts percentages in respect of Area 2 and Overseas Area customers to 8% and 10%, respectively. It will also mean that total overseas sales will decline by €/£20 million, with a proportionate effect on balances outstanding.

The existing interest rate on TIGA's overdraft is 7% per annum.

REQUIRED

a)   Prepare a table of results which show the various revenues and costs for each Area under both the existing approach and the suggested DOMBA plan for TIGA.

13 Marks

b)   Write a brief report, including your recommendation, on your findings in a) above for the Credit Controller of TIGA.

5 Marks

c)   Outline the advantages and disadvantages of using short-term debt, as opposed to long-term debt, in the financing of working capital.

_4 Marks
Total _22 Marks
(ICAI, MABF II, Summer 2006, Q5)

2.   ABC Ltd.

a)   ABC Ltd. offers its goods to customers on 30 days' credit – subject to satisfactory trade references. It also offers a 2% discount, if payment is made within ten days of the date of invoice.

REQUIRED

(i)   Calculate the cost to the company of offering the discount, assuming a 365 day year.

(ii) Compare offering discounts to customers to encourage early settlement of bills, with using debt factors.

(iii) Describe two methods, other than debt factoring, that a company might use to obtain finance using trade receivables as security.

15 Marks

b)   Two aspects of working capital policy which require managerial decisions are the level of current assets and manner in which they are financed.

REQUIRED

Discuss aggressive, moderate and conservative policies in these areas.

10 Marks

25 Marks

(ICAI, Questions and solutions manual, 2000/01)

3.   RAPHAEL Ltd.

RAPHAEL Ltd. is a small engineering company which has annual credit sales of €/£2.4m. In recent years, the company has experienced credit control problems. The average collection period for sales has risen to 50 days, even though the stated policy of the company is for payment to be made within 30 days. In addition, 1.5% of sales are written off as bad debts each year.

The company has recently been in talks with a factor company. The factor is prepared to make an advance to the company equivalent to 80% of debtors, based on the assumption that all customers will, in future, adhere to a 30-day payment period. The interest rate for the advance will be 11% per annum. The trade debtors are currently financed using a bank overdraft, which has an interest rate of 12% per annum. The factor will take over the credit control procedures of the company and this will result in a saving to the company of €/£18,000 per annum. However, the factor will make a charge of 2% of sales for this service. The use of the factoring service is expected to eliminate the bad debts incurred by the company.

Raphael Ltd. is also considering a change in policy towards payment of its suppliers. The company is given credit terms which allow a 2.5% discount providing the amount due is paid within 15 days. However, Raphael Ltd. has not taken advantage of the discount opportunity to date and has, instead, taken a 50-day payment period, even though suppliers require payment within 40 days. The company is now considering the payment of suppliers on the fifteenth day of the credit period in order to take advantage of the discount opportunity.

REQUIRED

a) Calculate the net cost of the factor agreement to the company and state whether, or not, the company should take advantage of the opportunity to factor its trade debts.

10 Marks

b) Explain ways in which factoring differs from invoice discounting.

6 Marks

c) Calculate the approximate annual percentage cost of forgoing trade discounts to suppliers and state what additional financial information the company would need in order to decide whether, or not, it should change its policy in favour of taking the discounts offered.

5 Marks

d) Discuss any other factors which may be important when deciding whether, or not, to change the existing policy towards payment of trade creditors.

4 Marks
Total 25 Marks
(ICAI, Questions and solutions manual, 2000/01)

MEDIUM-TERM SOURCES OF FINANCE

5

Debt 10,000,00
Equity 15,000,00
Market Value 25,000,00

LEARNING OBJECTIVES

This chapter is mostly descriptive. Upon completing the chapter, readers should be able to:

- ♣ Describe and evaluate various forms of medium-term finance;
- ♣ List the advantages and disadvantages of hire purchase finance;
- ♣ Outline the difference between hire purchase finance and lease finance;
- ♣ Define finance leases and operating leases;
- ♣ Explain the difference between finance leases and operating leases;
- ♣ List the advantages and disadvantages of lease finance; and
- ♣ Explain the purpose of the 'government backed finance scheme'.

Introduction

Finance that is repayable within one year is regarded as short term. Finance repayable between one and seven years is considered to be medium-term financing. Finance repayable for periods extending beyond seven years is considered to be long term. The lines between what is classified as short, medium and long term are blurred. Some of the sources of finance discussed in the last chapter can extend for periods beyond one year; whereas some of the sources discussed in this chapter may be organised for periods of beyond seven years. Conversely, some sources that are typically categorised as long term are structured for periods of less than seven years. For example, some large organisations (companies, governments or financial institutions) issue medium-term bond debt for periods of between two and ten years. The Deutsche Bank defines medium-term bonds as:

> 'fixed interest securities with a maximum term of four years, issued by central/local government and credit institutions' (http://www.deutsche-bank.de/lexikon/2447.html).

As bond issues are normally considered long-term sources of finance, they are covered in chapter six: 'Long-Term Sources of Finance: Debt'.

Medium-term sources of finance can be utilised by all sizes and types of company. However, medium-term sources are regarded as a more important source of finance for small and medium-sized companies, as they have restricted access to long-term sources. This is due to barriers of entry that exist in relation to some long-term sources. For example, the costs associated with raising equity on a stock exchange are prohibitive for small and medium-sized companies that wish to raise a limited amount of capital. Indeed, large companies prefer to utilise medium-term sources relative to long-term sources, as these sources are cheaper and easier to obtain.

This chapter considers the main sources of medium-term finance: term loans (these were explained in detail in the previous chapter so are revisited in brief), hire purchase and leasing agreements.

Term loans/revolving credit facilities

As mentioned in the previous chapter, term loans can be arranged for periods of over one year. The interest charged can be either fixed or variable and there usually is an arrangement fee. The interest rate and arrangement fee is influenced by the creditworthiness of a company, the base rate and whether there is security for the loan, or not (the quality of the assets being used as security will also influence the rate). Loan repayments can be tailored to match the cash inflows received from the asset or investment for which the funds were used. It is not uncommon for term loans to have a *grace period* (initial period with no repayments), repayment breaks or increasing repayment amounts. The most common types of repayment schedule are balloon repayment loans or bullet repayment loans (explained in the last chapter). When a company organises a standard term loan, a repayment profile is arranged and capital, once repaid, cannot be accessed again.

Banks can also provide revolving credit facilities. A *revolving credit facility* is like a hybrid between a term loan and an overdraft facility. It is normally secured on the working capital of a company, though this is not a requirement – many large companies have a revolving facility that is unsecured. Repayments are made to reduce the capital element of the debt; however, the capital that has been repaid can be accessed again over the agreed life of the facility up to the original agreed sum. A company needs to give the bank notice of its intention to draw down an additional sum up to the limit of the committed total. As banks have to keep sufficient funds in reserve to service this type of finance, it is more costly than a straightforward term loan. The additional cost comes in the form of a commitment fee. This is usually a percentage of the undrawn balance. In all other respects, the costs are the same as those for a term loan.

Hire purchase

A *hire purchase agreement* is a form of finance, whereby the ownership of an asset being purchased on credit, passes from a supplier (the company selling the asset) to a finance house. The finance house then rents the asset to the purchaser. Ownership passes from the finance house to the purchaser when the final instalment is paid. The finance company that legally owns the asset and provides the finance is called the *hirer*. The company possessing and using the asset for the period of the agreement (the purchaser) is called the *hiree*. The arrangement is shown in the following diagram.

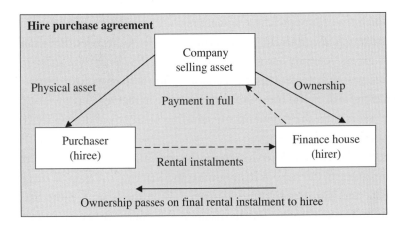

Hirer companies usually specialise in hire purchase and leasing transactions. In the UK they are normally affiliated to the Finance and Leasing Association (FLA), a body that lobbies government, accounting standards setters and others, on their behalf. Most commercial banks have a subsidiary that deals solely with this type of financing transaction, although many large companies also have their own financial subsidiary to cater for their hire purchase and leasing business.

Hire purchase agreements are usually for periods of between one and five years, though this depends on the useful economic life of the asset being financed. Assets financed in this manner typically have a useful economic life of less than ten years. Examples include motor vehicles, equipment (factory plant and machinery and agriculture equipment), fixtures and household goods. A hire purchase agreement usually involves the hiree having to pay a down payment and sign a legal contract committing the hiree to the payment of a predetermined number of periodic set payments to the hirer. This agreement is legally binding and usually provides for the transfer of legal title to the asset (from the hirer to the hiree) on the last payment.

The rental instalments are sufficient to pay off the whole capital that the hirer has spent on the asset, plus provide a profitable return. The hirer has the right to gain repossession of the asset if the hiree defaults on payment. If default occurs, the hiree loses all rights to the asset and has no claim on the payments made to date. The right of repossession may not protect the hirer in certain circumstances. For example, where the hire agreement is for a long period of time, but the asset becomes obsolete, then the hirer runs the risk of the hiree defaulting on the agreement on purpose, as the asset is no longer of use. To reduce exposure to this type of risk, the term of hire purchase agreements are usually arranged for periods that are much less than the useful economic life of the asset. For example, motor car agreements are usually for three to four years, yet most motor vehicles will still have a useful economic life left after four years. This reduces the risk of the hiree defaulting on the agreement, as the asset is of higher value than the payments outstanding at any time during the agreement period.

Another potential risk to the hirer is the condition of the asset on hire; the hiree assumes all the risks of maintaining and insuring the asset. If this is not adequate and the asset becomes damaged, then the hiree is more likely to default on the agreement. In this instance, the asset that can be repossessed may not be in a fit state for resale or rehire. Therefore, hire purchase is an expensive form of finance, as some of the risks associated with ownership stay with the hirer (deterioration in the asset value and condition) and a premium for these additional risks is factored into the rental payments. In addition, it is costly to terminate the agreement as penalty payments may be built into the hire purchase agreement.

The companies selling the assets (who recommend the hire purchase companies) usually do not fully explain the true cost of this form of finance to potential customers. The marketing approach adopted focuses on affordability (for example, this fridge will only cost you £7/€10 per week) and usually advertisements disclose the flat rate of interest being charged, not the annual percentage rate (APR). The APR can be over twice the flat rate of interest, as the flat rate does not take into consideration any of the capital repayments that have been made when working out the interest, whereas the APR calculates interest based on the reducing balance of capital after each repayment. This is highlighted in the following example.

Worked example 5.1   (Hire purchase)

Amarillo plc is in negotiations to purchase a machine for €/£500,000 on 1 January 2008 from Exit plc. The sales representative at Exit plc informs Amarillo plc that he can get finance for the sale from Exit Hire Finance Ltd. at the rate of 8%, to be repaid over the next three years in three equal yearly instalments.

REQUIRED

a)   Calculate the yearly payments to be made by Amarillo plc (assuming a flat rate of 8%) to the hire purchase company.

b)   Using these repayment amounts, calculate the effective APR being charged by Exit Hire Finance Ltd.

c)   Assume that Amarillo plc can get a term loan with an APR of 10%. This term loan will also have three repayments at the end of each year. What will the yearly cash outflow be, if the term loan is selected instead of the hire purchase finance? What will the cash flow implication of this option be to Amarillo plc?

Continued

Solution

a)   Interest repayment each year
     will be: (€/£500,000 × 8%)   €/£40,000
     Capital repayment each year
     will be: (€/£500,000/3)   €/£166,667
     Total yearly repayment: €/£206,667

b)   Find the yearly interest rate, given the repayments that result
     in a present value of the capital being advanced.

$$\text{Present value} = \text{annuity} \times \text{annuity factor}$$

     Where the present value is €/£500,000 and the annuity is
     €/£206,667 over three years.

$$€/£500,000 \quad = €/£206,667 \times \text{Annuity factor}$$
$$\text{Annuity factor} = €/£500,000/€/£206,667$$
$$\text{Annuity factor} = 2.419$$

     Use the annuity tables – look along the three-year annuity
     column. 2.419 lies between 11% (2.4437) and 12% (2.4018).
     Therefore the effective interest rate being used is: 11% +
     (2.4437 − 2.419)/(2.4437 − 2.4018) = 11.64%.

c)   In this instance, the yearly interest rate is given (therefore using
     the tables you can get the annuity factor: three years at 10%).
     The present value of the capital being advanced is also given.
     The requirement asks you to calculate the annuity payment.

$$\text{Present value} = \text{annuity} \times \text{annuity factor}$$
$$€/£500,000 \quad = \text{Annuity} \times 2.487$$
$$\text{Annuity} \quad\quad = €/£500,000/2.487$$
$$\text{Yearly repayment is: } €/£201,045$$

     The cash benefit of using the term loan over the hire purchase
     option is €/£5,622 per year (€/£206,667 − €/£201,045).

Although hire purchase is usually an expensive option, it is commonly used by companies.

Advantages to a hiree company of using hire purchase

Easy to arrange: The vendor has a prearranged agreement with a finance house and is trained in the documentation.

Quick source of finance: Hire purchase is usually arranged at the point of sale and is in place by the time the asset is delivered.

Availability: Hire purchase finance is usually available when other sources are not. As ownership does not pass until the end of the agreement, the asset itself forms the security for the finance arrangement.

Cash flow certainty/budgeting is easier: Unlike variable rate finance, hire purchase finance is fixed rate, hence repayment amounts will not fluctuate when interest rates change. As the cash outflows are known with certainty, this leads to easier, more reliable budgeting.

Not repayable on demand: Unlike an overdraft, hire purchase finance is not repayable on demand. Therefore it does not increase the liquidity risk of the hiree. The only time the agreement becomes repayable on demand is when the hiree defaults on payments.

Cash flow advantages: The hiree gets use of the asset immediately, without having to make a major cash outlay to acquire it.

Tax relief: The hiree qualifies for tax relief on the interest element of the rental and for capital allowances on the capital value of the asset being financed.

Ownership: The hiree automatically gains legal ownership of the asset at the end of the hire purchase agreement. The asset can then be utilised further in the company to generate income or can be sold.

The disadvantages of using hire purchase to a hiree are as follows:

Disadvantages to a hiree company of using hire purchase finance

Cost: Hire purchase agreements are usually quite expensive relative to other forms of finance, such as term loans.

Lack of flexibility: Hire purchase agreements are not flexible and the hirer has the right to repossess an asset, if a payment is missed.

Cancellation is costly: The hire purchase agreement usually includes costly fixed penalties, were the agreement to terminate, and may include surcharges in the eventuality of contractual payments being missed.

Maintenance/insurance: The hiree assumes responsibility for the maintenance, upkeep and insurance costs associated with the asset.

Risks of ownership: The risks associated with the ownership of the asset transfer to the hiree. If the asset were to be destroyed, the rental agreement payments would still have to be met. If the agreement were to be terminated, default charges would result.

Underutilisation: Rental payments have to be met even when the asset is not in use.

Accounting and tax treatment of assets purchased using hire purchase
The substance of a hire purchase transaction is that it is a form of financing. Most of the risks and rewards associated with asset ownership pass to the hiree at the outset of the agreement, as the hiree has full control over the asset. If the asset generates more revenue than anticipated, it falls to the hiree; likewise where the asset is not being used, the hiree bears the opportunity loss. The hiree will also treat the asset like any other fully owned asset, having to maintain it, insure it and service it. Therefore, from the outset, it is considered, both for accounting and tax purposes, that the hiree owns the asset and it is accounted for in exactly the same way as any other asset that is purchased outright.

Accounting treatment of hire purchase transactions: hiree
The asset is capitalised into non-current assets and is depreciated over its useful economic life in a manner that reflects the reduction in its useful economic life.

The amount to be capitalised will be the purchase price of the asset and an equivalent sum will be capitalised as finance debt. When each hire payment is made, it will be split between the repayment of the debt balance and the interest payable for the period. Therefore, the income statement will have a depreciation charge and a finance interest charge in respect of the transaction. The accounting treatment is provided in the next example.

Worked example 5.2   (Accounting for hire purchase transactions: hiree)

Corter plc has taken delivery of a machine worth €/£50,000. This is being financed using hire purchase from Hire Ltd. The repayments are four equal instalments of €/£17,500 over the next four years (starting at the end of this year).

REQUIRED

a)   Calculate the interest rate implicit in this agreement.
b)   Outline the accounting treatment on the purchase of the asset in the books of Corter plc, assuming that the asset has a useful economic life of ten years and generates income evenly over the ten-year period. Ignore deferred taxation.
c)   Outline the accounting treatment for the first rental payment that is made at the end of the year in Corter plc's books.

Solution

a)   Find the yearly interest rate, given the repayments that result in a present value of the capital being advanced.

$$\text{Present value} = \text{annuity} \times \text{annuity factor}$$

Where the present value is €/£50,000 and the annuity is €/£17,500 over four years

€/£50,000   = €/£17,500 × Annuity factor
Annuity factor = €/£50,000/€/£17,500
Annuity factor = 2.8571

Continued

Use the annuity tables, look along the four-year annuity column. 2.857 lies between 14% (2.914) and 15% (2.855). Therefore, the effective interest rate is: $14\% + (2.914 - 2.857)/(2.914 - 2.855) = 14.97\%$ (round to 15%).

b) The accounting treatment when the asset is first obtained and the agreement signed will be to increase non-current assets by €/£50,000 and to bring a hire purchase finance creditor of €/£50,000 into the balance sheet. This balance will be split between payments due within one year and payments due after this time scale.

The asset will be depreciated using the straight-line method over its useful economic life of ten years. Therefore, the depreciation charge released to the income statement will be €/£5,000 and the net book value of the asset at the year end will be €/£45,000.

c) The first payment of €/£17,500 will come out of Corter plc's bank account, hence this will be reduced. This payment will cover the interest for the year and will also pay off some of the capital balance. The interest will be a full year at $15\% = €/£50,000 \times 15\% = €/£7,500$, with the remaining €/£10,000 coming of the capital balance. Therefore, at the year end the balance on the finance hire purchase creditor will be €/£40,000 (in the next year the €/£40,000 figure will be used to calculate the yearly interest).

In the first year, the income statement will have a depreciation charge of €/£5,000 and a finance charge of €/£7,500 in relation to this asset. The balance sheet will have €/£45,000 in non-current assets and €/£40,000 in liabilities. Capital repayable within the next year (€/£11,500) will come under current liabilities (€/£17,500 − €/£6,000 (€/£40,000 × 15%)), with the balance of €/£28,500 (€/£40,000 − €/£11,500) forming part of non-current liabilities.

Taxation treatment: hiree

The tax authorities in the ROI and in NI treat assets obtained using hire purchase finance as though they are legally owned by the hiree at the start of the contract. In this respect, the hiree is not able to claim a tax-deductible expense for the full amount of the rental payment; however, the hiree can claim an allowance on the capital value of the asset and also gets a tax deduction for the interest paid. The tax allowance on assets is called a capital allowance. This is the tax authority's equivalent of depreciation. Depreciation is not an allowable expense for taxation purposes; however, a capital allowance is. In most instances, capital allowances are calculated using a standard method and rate – 25% reducing balance – though variations do occur. For example, in some years the government may make a special ruling to have a first-year allowance, which is in excess of the 25%; it may be set at 50%, with the 25% reducing balance method applying after the first year. The tax deduction allowed by the tax authorities will result in a saving for the hiree. The extent of this saving is dependent on the tax rate applying at the time. The higher the tax rate, the higher the saving from the tax deduction. It should also be noted that a tax deduction in a particular year is only possible if the company is profitable. The next example considers the tax saving that is available to a company from undertaking a hire purchase agreement.

Worked example 5.3 (Tax implications of hire purchase assets: hiree)

Corter plc has taken delivery of a machine worth €/£50,000. This is being financed using hire purchase. The repayments are four equal instalments of €/£17,500 over the next four years (starting at the end of this year). This equates to an APR of 15%. Assume that the corporation tax rate for this type of company is 30% per annum and that capital allowances are 25%. Ignore deferred taxation.

REQUIRED

a)   Calculate the tax deduction (for the first year) that the company would receive if it was to purchase the asset using cash reserves.
b)   Calculate the tax deduction (for the first year) that the company would receive if it was to purchase the asset using hire purchase.
c)   Calculate the after-tax interest rate implicit in this agreement.

Continued

Solution

a) The tax-deductible capital allowance on this asset will be €/£50,000 × 25% = €/£12,500. Assuming that Corter plc is profitable, this will result in a tax saving in the first year of €/£3,750 (€/£12,500 × 30%).

b) The capital allowance will remain the same (€/£12,500). However, the finance interest paid is also tax deductible. The interest is €/£7,500 (see example 5.2). Therefore, the new tax deduction is €/£6,000 ((€/£12,500 + €/£7,500) × 30%). This increased tax deduction means that the finance element of the hire purchase contract is not as expensive as it might first seem.

c) The fact that interest is tax deductible reduces its overall cost to $i(1-t)$, where i is the interest rate and t is the corporation tax rate. Therefore, the net cost of the hire purchase interest in this instance is $15\%(1-30\%) = 10.5\%$.

Accounting treatment for hire purchase transactions: hirer

The hiree will obtain the asset from the supplier, who sells it immediately to the hirer for the sales price. At this stage, the hirer pays the selling company (the supplier) in full. The overall impact of the hire purchase transaction to the hirer is to reduce the bank and to create a debtor for the capital amount that is receivable over the term of the hire purchase contract from the hiree. Each rental receipt will contain a portion that reduces the debtor balance; the remaining portion is finance interest income (revenue in the hirer's income statement). The next example expands on example 5.2 by looking at the accounting treatment from a hirer's point of view.

Worked example 5.4   (Accounting for hire purchase assets: hirer)

Corter plc has taken delivery of a machine worth €/£50,000. This is being financed using hire purchase from a company called Hire Ltd. The repayments to Hire Ltd. are four equal instalments of €/£17,500 over the next four years (starting at the end of this year). The APR is 15%.

Continued

REQUIRED

a) Outline the accounting treatment on establishment of the hire purchase agreement in the books of Hire Ltd.

b) Outline the accounting treatment for the first rental instalment received at the end of the year in the books of Hire Ltd.

Solution

a) The accounting treatment when the asset is first obtained and the agreement signed is to reduce the bank by €/£50,000 and to create a debtor (hire purchase receivable), of €/£50,000. This will be split between payments receivable within one year and payments receivable after this time.

b) The first payment of €/£17,500 will be lodged to the bank account, increasing its balance. This receipt covers the interest for the year and some of the capital balance. The interest will be a full year at 15% (€/£50,000 × 15%), €/£7,500, with the remaining €/£10,000 reducing the total debtor amount receivable. Therefore, at the year end, the balance on the total finance hire purchase debtor account will be €/£40,000.

In the first year, the income statement of Hire Ltd. will have finance interest income on hire purchase contracts of €/£7,500 in relation to this asset. The balance sheet will have a €/£40,000 debtor in assets. This will be split between current assets and non-current assets. The capital receivable within the next year, €/£11,500, will come under current assets (€/£17,500 − €/£6,000 (€/£40,000 × 15%)), with the balance €/£28,500 (€/£40,000 − €/£11,500) forming part of non-current assets.

Taxation treatment: hirer

The hirer will be taxed on the hire purchase interest income receivable in each year.

Leasing

The International Accounting Standard 17 *'Leases'* (IAS 17) defines a *lease* as:

> 'an agreement whereby the lessor conveys to the lessee, in return for a payment or series of payments, the right to use an asset for an agreed period of time'.

Leasing is similar in some respects to hire purchase, though is more commonly used. The FLA recorded £87.3 billion in new finance lease agreements in 2005. According to the FLA website, leasing accounts for 25.5% of all unsecured lending in the UK (www.fla.org.uk). The Irish Bankers Federation (IBF) reports that 37% of all assets purchased in the UK by small and medium-sized enterprises are acquired using leasing and hire purchase agreements; in the ROI this figure is 59% (*IBF Bank Brief* – Spring 2006).

A *leasing agreement* is similar to a hire purchase agreement; a company wishing to acquire an asset approaches the selling company, which sells the asset immediately to a third party (a finance house). The finance house then leases the asset to the purchasing company. The finance house is usually a member of the FLA and may be a subsidiary of a commercial or merchant bank, or a subsidiary of the corporation selling the asset. The company taking possession of the asset is called the *lessee* and the finance house that takes ownership of the asset (but not possession) is called the *lessor*. The selling company is no longer involved in the transaction (unless there is a warranty agreement or a fault with the asset) after the initial sale is made, as the lessor pays them for the asset at the outset. The selling company records the profit made on the sale in the same manner as for any other sale. The process is portrayed in the following diagram.

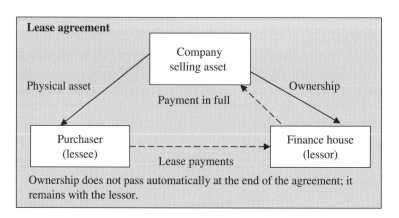

There are two different types of leases: finance leases and operating leases. These are accounted for differently and have different tax treatments.

Finance lease

According to IAS 17, a finance lease is a lease that:

'transfers substantially all the risks and rewards incidental to ownership of an asset. Title may or may not eventually be transferred'.

In some texts, a finance lease is sometimes referred to as a *capital lease* or a *full payout lease*. These names reflect key differences between a finance lease and an operating lease. When a finance lease is obtained, the asset is capitalised in the books of the lessee and the lessee pays the full price for the asset, more or less, over the term of the lease period. Both types of leases are similar in that they fall within the definition of a lease detailed in the previous section and involve a form of rental agreement, whereby the lessee gains possession of the asset and pays lease rentals to the lessor. The main difference between a finance lease and an operating lease is that operating leases usually specify only a *primary lease period*, whereas finance leases usually also include a *secondary lease period*. The purchase price of the asset plus finance cost is usually recovered from the payments made during the primary lease period, with the secondary lease being for a 'peppercorn' rent. This allows a lessee to use the asset for the duration of its useful economic life, which is usually for a longer period of time than the primary lease period.

To help classify which type of lease an agreement is, it is important to look at the substance of the transaction, not the legal position. IAS 17 provides examples of situations that help to determine whether a lease is a finance lease or not. These are highlighted in the next figure.

Finance lease indicators (IAS 17)

Ownership characteristics: Where the risks and rewards associated with ownership, such as down time, obsolescence, maintenance and insurance, transfer to the lessee.

Continued

Transfer of ownership: Where ownership transfers at the end of the lease term to the lessee.

Option to purchase asset at bargain price: Where the lessee has the option to buy the asset at the end of the lease term for a price that is less than the asset's expected fair value at this date, and the price is such that it is clear from the outset that it would make economic sense for the lessee to do so.

Lease term: Where the lease term is for substantially all of the asset's useful economic life.

Present value of the minimum lease payments: Where the present value of the minimum lease payments equates to all, or substantially all, of the asset's fair value at the inception of the lease.

Bespoke assets: Where the asset being leased is of such a specialised nature that it is highly improbable that it will be leased a second time.

Secondary lease rentals: Where the lease agreement has secondary lease rentals that are substantially lower, so as to make it economical (at inception), and probable, that the lessee will continue the lease agreement into the secondary term.

Cancellation: Where the lease agreement confers very high financial penalties (the lessor's loss on the agreement) on the lessee for breach or cancellation of the agreement.

Asset price fluctuations: Where these accrue to the lessee.

Worked example 5.5   (Classifying lease agreements)

Ruby Ltd. wants to lease a machine which is manufactured by Wax Ltd. The fair value of the machine is €/£500,000. Finance House Ltd. agrees to purchase the machine from Wax Ltd., and lease it to Ruby Ltd. on the following terms:

12 payments of €/£50,000, payable quarterly in advance, after which, six further annual payments of €/£5 per year in arrears are required.

Continued

REQUIRED

a)   Describe the pattern of these lease payments.
b)   Calculate the interest rate that is implicit in this agreement.
c)   What type of lease is this?

Solution

a)   The period during which the 12 lease payments of €/£50,000 are paid is called the primary lease period. In subsequent years, only a nominal rental is charged for the use of the asset; this is called the secondary lease period.

b)   Present value=annuity amount×annuity factor*
      *The secondary lease rentals are ignored in this instance as they are immaterial.

      €/£500,000=€/£50,000×annuity factor (assume 12 years, then multiply the rate by four to get a more reflective yearly rate) Annuity factor for 12 years is ten. The annuity factor tables disclose that the annuity rate for 12 years with an annuity factor of ten is 3% (rounded). This is for a three-month period. This equates to a yearly rate of 12% ($3\% \times 4$). A more precise rate is 12.55% ($(1.03)^4 - 1$).

c)   The lease is a finance lease. The agreement has both a primary and a secondary lease period, with only a nominal rental agreed for the secondary period. This makes it highly probable that Ruby Ltd. will continue with the lease after the primary period. In addition, the return earned by Finance house Ltd. is consistent with returns on this type of debt finance.

Accounting for finance leases: lessee

When an asset is treated as obtained under a finance lease, the asset is regarded as being under the control of the lessee and not the lessor (the legal owner), hence the substance of the transaction is that an asset purchase is assumed in the books of the lessee – financed by the lease company. Therefore, the lease is treated just like any other form of finance.

In the books of the lessee, the transactions will show the purchase of the asset from the lessor company. The asset will be capitalised at the minimum of its fair value or the present value of the minimum lease payments into non-current assets and depreciated over the asset's useful economic life (if it is not reasonably certain that the asset will remain in the possession of the lessee at the end of the primary lease term, then the asset should be depreciated over this shorter period). Each payment that is made will comprise two parts: the finance lease interest charge for the year, based on the implicit interest rate, and a capital repayment. The accounting entries are the same as those expected in the books of a hiree company in a hire purchase agreement. See worked example 5.2. The accounting treatment is captured by the following extract from RYANAIR's *Annual Report and Financial Statements (2005)*.

RYANAIR Annual Report and Financial Statements 2005

Statement of Accounting Policies (extract)
Leases
Assets held under finance leases are capitalised in the balance sheet and are depreciated over their estimated useful lives. The present values of the future lease payments are recorded as obligations under finance leases and the interest element of the lease obligation is charged to the profit and loss account over the period of the lease in proportion to the balances outstanding.

Taxation treatment for finance leases: lessee
The taxation treatment is the exact same as that outlined for the hiree company who purchases an asset using a hire purchase agreement. See example 5.3.

Accounting treatment for finance leases: lessor
The accounting treatment for finance leases in the books of lessor companies is the same as that outlined earlier in the chapter for hirer companies in respect of hire purchase transactions. To summarise, in the books of the lessor the transactions will show the purchase of the asset from the selling company and subsequent sale to the lessee usually on the same day on credit.

The debtor account for the monies due from the lessee is a balance sheet account, called 'finance receivable'. This represents the present value of the minimum lease receipts receivable over the period of the lease. Each year when lease income is received, it will go towards reducing the finance receivables account and providing yearly finance interest income (calculated as the average finance lease receivable balance for the year multiplied by the interest rate that is implicit in the finance lease agreement). The finance interest income is posted to the income statement (see example 5.4).

Taxation treatment for finance leases: lessor
The taxation treatment is exactly the same as that outlined for a hirer company (see the hire purchase section above). The lessor company is taxable on lease interest income receivable in the year.

Operating leases

IAS 17 defines an *operating lease* as:

'a lease other than a finance lease'.

These types of lease arrangements are usually entered into when the lessee does not wish to use an asset for its entire useful economic life – for example, where they only require the asset for the length of a particular job (e.g. construction industry) or where the asset is specialised and requires specialist knowledge for its maintenance (e.g. a hospital scanner in the health service) or where the asset is subject to technological change and the lessee does not have staff with the expertise, or time, to keep the company's equipment maintained and up to date (e.g. computer equipment or photocopiers).

The main characteristics of an operating lease are that an operating lease agreement can be cancelled more easily than a finance lease agreement with lower penalties. Operating lease agreements are usually for short periods of time and the lessor has the ability to lease the asset to another company at the end of the lease agreement, or enter into another lease agreement with the same company. Finally, the lessor maintains and insures the asset. As the risks incident with ownership remain with the lessor, the substance of this type of lease arrangement is that it is regarded as a hire contract. The duration of an operating lease agreement ranges from a few weeks or days, to about three or four years.

Relative to finance leases, operating leases are regarded as more advantageous to a lessee. This has resulted in a long-term headache for the International Accounting Standards Board (IASB). They would like both finance leases and operating leases to be accounted for using the same approach – the approach used for accounting for finance leases. The use of operating leases as off-balance-sheet finance is commonly used in many industries, in particular the airline and retail industries. The accounting implication of capitalising operating leases would be material for many companies. This has led to fierce lobbying from industry representatives against the proposed treatment.

The disadvantages to the lessee of using operating leases as a form of finance are now outlined.

Disadvantages of operating lease rentals to the lessee

Expensive: The lessor retains the risks (and rewards) associated with the ownership of the asset being leased. As the risks to the lessor are greater, operating leases are usually expensive – more expensive than finance leases. This is the main disadvantage.

Loss of asset: Where the lessee runs into difficulty in paying the lease payments, they may lose the asset.

The main advantages of using operating leases as a form of finance are as follows:

Advantages of an operating lease to a lessee

Cancellation: They are easier and less costly to cancel relative to a finance lease.

Quick and easy to obtain: They are usually arranged at the point of sale of the asset or when ordering the asset.

Possession of asset: The lessee can obtain immediate possession of the asset, without any major initial cash outlay.

Continued

No security required: The asset acts as security; therefore, the lessor can take possession of the asset if the payments are in default.

Finance of last resort: Operating leases can be obtained when the company cannot get finance elsewhere. This is more important for small emerging companies that do not have a strong track record or have insufficient security or cash. It is effectively a method of gaining access to an asset using 100% finance.

Reduced running costs: Maintenance and insurance costs usually remain with the lessor.

No obsolescence risk: The risk of obsolescence remains with the lessor. If the asset becomes obsolete, then the agreement can be cancelled or not renewed.

Tax relief: The full rental payment is tax deductible.

Cash flow planning and budgeting: Some operating lease agreements are arranged on a set rental basis, making the budgeting process easier.

Cash management: Some rentals are arranged and have a fixed and variable element: a fixed standing rental and a charge per unit used. This means that the rental will move in line with income, assuming more activity from the leased asset results in more revenue.

No restrictive covenants: There are not usually any restrictive covenants written into lease agreements.

Off-balance-sheet finance: An operating lease agreement ties the company into paying a future stream of payments; however, the present value of this liability is not accrued in the financial statements (it is disclosed).

Cheaper: Where the lessee is loss making, an operating lease arrangement may be cheaper for them, relative to a finance lease arrangement, as the lessor can pass on the tax benefits that are available for purchasing capital items. This results in lower rentals.

Accounting treatment for operating leases: lessee

An operating lease is regarded as a hire contract and IAS 17 states that the cost should be:

> 'released to the income statement on a straight-line basis over the term of the lease, unless another systematic basis is more representative of the time pattern of the user's benefit'.

The asset is not capitalised. The accounting treatment as recommended by IAS 17 has been applied in Viridian Group plc's accounts. See the following extract from their 2005/06 annual report and accounts.

Viridian Group plc Annual Report and Accounts 2005–2006

Accounting Policies
Operating Lease Contracts
Leases are classified as operating lease contracts whenever the terms of the lease do not transfer substantially all the risks and benefits of ownership to the lessee.

Rentals payable under operating leases are charged to the income statement on a straight-line basis over the lease term.

The Group has adopted International Financial Reporting Interpretations Committee (IFRIC) 4 'Determining Whether an Arrangement Contains a Lease' in these accounts.

Taxation treatment for operating leases: lessee

The full amount of the lease charge for the period is allowable for tax purposes. Therefore, the implicit interest rate underlying the lease agreement is reduced by the tax rate.

Accounting treatment for operating leases: lessor

The lessor will purchase the asset from the selling company and will capitalise it into the relevant category of non-current asset. The asset will be depreciated over its expected useful life in a manner to reflect the reduction in its useful economic life. The lease income receivable will be released to the income statement on a straight-line basis, which may be a different basis to the cash receipts received.

Taxation treatment for operating leases: lessor
The lessor will be taxed on the lease income relating to the period; though will be able to obtain a tax deduction (capital allowances) on the capital value of the asset.

Sale and leaseback agreements

Another common source of medium-term finance is where a company sells an asset and then leases that asset back again. The sale may be made to a newly established subsidiary company that has been formed to raise equity capital. The parent company sells the asset to the subsidiary and enters a lease agreement, committing to pay lease rentals in return for the use of the asset. This sort of arrangement is regarded as a finance lease and is accounted for as such. As a means of obtaining finance, it is a way to source cash without upsetting the equity equilibrium in the parent company, whilst retaining control over the asset.

In other instances, an asset might be sold to an external company and leased back. The agreement can either be a finance lease or an operating lease. The risk with this agreement is that the lease payments in the period beyond the lease term may get very costly. RYANAIR use this type of finance to obtain aircraft. Indeed, some finance houses specialise in providing lease finance for aircraft. A subsidiary of GE Capital, GE Commercial Aviation, has 225 airline customers all around the world (http://www.gecas.com) and has a branch at Shannon, Ireland. On their website, they advertise the benefit of obtaining aircraft using operating leases:

GE Capital: The advantages of obtaining aircraft using operating leases

1. Lowers cash outlays, which preserves working capital.
2. Fleet flexibility to introduce new routes or aircraft types.
3. Flexibility to increase or reduce capacity quickly.
4. No residual value risk.
5. Newer aircraft models with no need for pre-delivery payment or significant down payments with the manufacturers.
6. Off-balance-sheet finance.

(http:www.gecas.com)

Factors influencing the decision to use leasing as a source of finance

Leasing should be used as a source of finance when it is cheaper than other sources. The cost of a lease will depend on the tax situation of the lessee and the lessor. Where the lessee is loss making and cannot avail of tax benefits, it might be worthwhile negotiating an operating lease so that the lessor can avail of the capital allowances and can pass the benefit on to the lessee, in the form of lower payments. Another influence on the cost of a lease will be competition amongst finance houses and interest rates. When interest rates are low, lessors are likely to reduce the required rate of return on a lease agreement.

In all instances, a company should look at the project or asset requiring finance: it should be viable and have passed investment appraisal thresholds laid down by the company. This will normally involve discounting the project using the after-tax implicit rate in the lease agreement (where this is above the company's cost of capital and there is capital rationing). The tax shield is only relevant where a company makes profits. The method of financing should not change the cost of capital.

Government-backed finance schemes

An initiative established by the government in the UK to provide medium-term debt finance to small and medium-sized companies is the **government-backed finance scheme**. This scheme is a joint venture between the Department of Trade and Industry and a number of participating lenders. In these instances, the government guarantees up to 75% of loans, to small or medium-sized companies that are less than five years old. Loans are capped at £250,000 and cannot extend beyond ten years. The company sourcing the loan pays a 2% premium on the outstanding loan balance. This is collected by the participating bank and paid over to the Department of Trade and Industry.

Conclusion

The most commonly used medium-term finance by companies is debt finance. Term loans, hire purchase agreements and leasing agreements are commonly used by all sizes of companies, though larger companies can also source medium-term debt by selling bonds with maturities of less than seven years. The cost associated with each type of finance varies, depending on the individual agreement, and will usually be reflective of the risks that are inherent within the agreement, the credit standing of the company seeking credit and their ability to obtain finance from a range of sources.

Examination standard question

Worked example 5.6

REQUIRED

a)   Describe briefly the meaning and usage of

(ii) 'Finance leases' and 'hire purchase contracts'.

6 Marks
(ICAI, MABF II, Autumn 2005, Extract from Q6)

Solution

a)   (ii) **Finance leases and hire purchase contracts**

Finance lease
Leases can be either finance leases or operating leases. Finance leases are lease agreements between the user of a leased asset (the lessee) and a provider of finance (the lessor) for most, or all, of the asset's expected useful life.

Example
Suppose a company decides to obtain a company car and to finance the acquisition by means of a finance lease. A car dealer will supply the car. A finance house will agree to act as lessor in a finance leasing arrangement, and so will purchase
Continued

the car from the dealer and lease it to the company. The company will take possession of the car from the car dealer and make regular payments (monthly, quarterly, six-monthly or annually) to the finance house under the terms of the lease.

These are the important characteristics of a finance lease:

- The lessee is responsible for the upkeep, servicing and maintenance of the asset. The lessor is not involved in this at all.
- The lease has a primary period, which covers all or most of the useful economic life of the asset. At the end of this primary period, the lessor would not be able to lease the asset to someone else, because the asset would be worn out. The lessor must therefore ensure that the lease payments during the primary period pay for the full cost of the asset, as well as providing the lessor with a suitable return on his investment.
- It is usual at the end of the primary period to allow the lessee to continue to lease the asset for an indefinite secondary period, in return for a nominal rent, sometimes called a 'peppercorn' rent.

Returning to the example of the car lease, the primary period of the lease might be three years, with an agreement by the lessee to make three annual payments of €/£6,000 each. The lessee will be responsible for repairs and servicing, road tax, insurance and garaging.

Attractions of leasing
The attractions of leases to the supplier of the equipment, the lessee and the lessor are as follows:

- The supplier of the equipment is paid in full at the beginning. The equipment is sold to the lessor and, apart from obligations under guarantees or warranties, the supplier has no further financial concern about the asset.
- The lessor invests finance by purchasing assets from the supplier and makes a return out of the lease payments from the lessee. Provided that a lessor can find lessees willing to pay the amounts he wants to make his return, the lessor can make good profits.

Continued

- Leasing might be attractive to the lessee:

  (i) Where the lessee does not have enough cash to pay for the asset, and would have difficulty obtaining a bank loan to buy it, or

  (ii) Where the finance lease is cheaper than a bank loan.

Hire purchase

Hire purchase is another form of instalment credit finance. There are two basic forms of instalment credit, whereby an individual or company purchases goods on credit and pays for them by instalments.

- 'Lender credit' occurs when the buyer borrows money and uses the money to purchase goods outright.
- 'Vendor credit' occurs when the buyer obtains goods on credit and agrees to pay the vendor by instalments. Hire purchase is an example of vendor credit.

Hire purchase is similar to leasing, with the exception that ownership of the goods passes to the hire purchase customer on payment of the final credit instalment.

Hire purchase agreements nowadays usually involve a finance house.

- The supplier sells the goods to the finance house.
- The supplier delivers the goods to the customer who will eventually purchase them.
- The hire purchase arrangement exists between the finance house and the customer.

The finance house will nearly always insist that the hirer should pay a deposit towards the purchase price, perhaps as low as 10% or as high as 33%. The size of the deposit will depend on the finance company's policy and its assessment of the hiree. This is in contrast to a finance lease, where the lessee might not be required to make any large initial payment.

Continued

An industrial or commercial company can use hire purchase as a source of finance. With industrial hire purchase, a business customer obtains hire purchase finance from a finance house in order to purchase a non-current asset. Goods bought by companies on hire purchase include company vehicles, plant and machinery, office equipment and farming machinery. Hire purchase arrangements for fleets of motor cars are quite common and most car manufacturers have a link with a leading finance house, so as to offer hire purchase credit whenever a car is bought.

When a company acquires a capital asset under a hire purchase agreement, it will eventually obtain full legal title to the asset. The hire purchase payments consist partly of 'capital' payments towards the purchase of the asset and partly of interest charges.

KEY TERMS

Capital lease

Finance lease

Full payout lease

Government-backed financial scheme

Grace period

Hire purchase agreement

Hiree

Hirer

Lease

Leasing agreement

Lease term

Lessee

Lessor

Operating lease

Primary lease period

Revolving credit facility

Sale and leaseback agreements

Secondary lease period

WEBSITES THAT MAY BE OF USE

Statistics on financing can be obtained on the Bank of England's website:
http://www.bankofengland.co.uk/

The British Bankers Association (BBA) website:
http://www.bba.org.uk/

A UK government help website provides information on sources of medium-term finance:
http://www.businesslink.gov.uk/

The Finance and Leasing Association (FLA) in the UK:
http://www.fla.org.uk/

The Institute of Bankers in Ireland website:
http://www.institue-of-bankers.com

The Irish Bankers Federation (IBF) website:
http://www.ibf.ie

REVIEW QUESTIONS

1. Explain the term 'revolving credit facility'.
2. List briefly the advantages and disadvantages of hire purchase agreements from a hiree's perspective.
3. List the main motives for using lease finance.
4. Bargain Ltd. wishes to obtain a delivery lorry using hire purchase. The lorry has a useful economic life of four years. They approach a manufacturer, who arranges a hire purchase contract with a finance house. The finance house purchases the lorry for €/£60,000. The hire purchase agreement requires that Bargain Ltd. pay a down payment of €/£10,000. The agreement states that interest at the rate of 10% per annum on the remaining €/£50,000 will be charged and the capital should be repaid in three equal annual instalments.
    Given that the 10% is the flat interest rate, what will Bargain Ltd.'s yearly repayments be?

5.   What are the key differences between a finance lease and an operating lease?

6.   You work as a self-employed financial consultant. One of your clients has approached you for advice regarding short-term and medium-term sources of finance.

REQUIRED

Prepare a report for your client covering the following:

a)   Discuss ANY THREE factors which should be considered when selecting an appropriate source of finance.

6 Marks

b)   Outline the main features of each of the following sources of finance:

(i)   Bank overdraft.

3 Marks

(ii)   Medium-term bank loan.

3 Marks

(iii)   Hire purchase.

4 Marks

(iv)   Leasing.

3 Marks

Presentation Mark   **1 Mark**

Total 20 Marks

(ICAI, MABF I, Summer 2002, Q6)

CHALLENGING QUESTIONS

1.   ALRIGHT & BILSON PLC

ALRIGHT & BILSON PLC is a chemical company which has recently had legal difficulties over its pollution record. The company is assessing a proposal to acquire new equipment to improve waste disposal. The equipment would cost €/£500,000, have an economic life of four years and, at the end of year four, is expected to have a disposal value of €/£50,000. The equipment will dispose of waste more efficiently and is expected to generate cost savings of €/£200,000 in each of the four years.

The company is currently entirely equity financed and its equity holders require a return of 10% after allowing for all taxes. The company is subject to a corporation tax rate of 30% and, if the equipment is purchased, a 25% straight-line writing down allowance is available. Assume that corporation tax is payable one year after the financial year end.

REQUIRED

a)   Evaluate the financial returns from the acquisition of the equipment and state whether the acquisition should be made.

8 Marks

For the purpose of answering part b), assume that the equipment should be acquired. The equipment can be acquired in two ways:

> (i) The equipment can be purchased using a four-year bank loan at a pre-tax interest cost of 7% per annum.

> (ii) The equipment can be leased with a rental payment of €/£70,000 at the end of each of the four years.

REQUIRED

b)   Calculate which of the two methods presented is the most cost effective for the company.

8 Marks

c)   Set out and critically assess the arguments put forward in favour of using operating leases for obtaining equipment.

6 Marks
Total 22 Marks
(ICAI, MABF II, Summer 1999, Q5)

2. AHOGHILL Ltd.

a) Briefly explain the main features of a sale and leaseback transaction.

5 Marks

AHOGHILL Ltd. is a finance house. It is approached by RANDALSTOWN Ltd., an equity financed company, operating in the private education industry, with a request to arrange a lease for the purchase of a new internet system of computer based learning (including the equipment). The outlay will be €/£10 million. The equipment and software is expected to become obsolete in four years time and will have no scrap value. The investment has a positive net present value when operating cash flows are discounted at the company's current cost of capital (which is the equity holders' required rate of return).

AHOGHILL Ltd. would finance the purchase by borrowing the €/£10 million at an interest rate of 10% (gross rate before tax). The transaction would take effect on the last day of the accounting year. The first lease payment will also be received on that day.

Under the terms of the lease agreement, AHOGHILL Ltd. would also provide maintenance services, valued by RANDALSTOWN Ltd. at €/£600,000 per year. These services have no cost to AHOGHILL Ltd. as they currently have several technicians who are not working at full capacity, and are not expected to do so for the four-year period.

REQUIRED

b) Calculate the minimum rental AHOGHILL Ltd. should charge RANDALSTOWN Ltd., to break even. *(RANDALSTOWN Ltd. and AHOGHILL Ltd. pay tax at 30%. The tax authorities allow a writing down allowance on this type of system of 25%.)*

6 Marks

Assume the rental proceeds, and AHOGHILL Ltd. charges an annual rental of €/£3.5 million.

REQUIRED

c) Calculate whether, using purely financial criteria, RANDALSTOWN Ltd. should lease the asset or borrow in order to purchase it outright *(assume that RANDALSTOWN Ltd. can obtain bank finance at 12.85% gross)*:

(i) Ignoring the benefit of the maintenance savings.

6 Marks

(ii) Allowing for the maintenance savings.

3 Marks
Total **20** Marks

3.   JENNA Ltd.

c)   Outline TWO medium-term sources of finance that would be suitable to finance the purchase of a new machine.

6 Marks
(ICAI, MABF II, Summer 2001, Q6)

LONG-TERM SOURCES OF FINANCE: DEBT

6

Debt   10,000,000
Equity   15,000,000
Market Value 25,000,000

LEARNING OBJECTIVES

This chapter is mostly descriptive. Upon completing the chapter, readers should be able to:

* Explain the benefits of term loans;
* Outline the key characteristics of bond debt;
* List the advantages and disadvantages of bond debt;
* List factors that will influence the level of debt to source;
* Discuss factors that influence the market value of bonds;
* Describe methods that can be used by a company to finance the redemption of debt;
* Explain the difference between debentures and loan stock;
* Calculate the value of redeemable and irredeemable bonds;
* Calculate the cost of redeemable and irredeemable bonds; and
* Explain the terms securitisation; mezzanine finance and eurobonds.

Introduction

There are two main sources of finance: equity and debt. Equity is considered in the next chapter, whereas this chapter focuses on long-term debt sources. Debt finance is cheaper to obtain than equity finance and, therefore, is more popular. In particular, the costs associated with obtaining bank finance are low. The costs of issuing tradable bonds are higher; however, they are not as high as the costs associated with an equity issue. Debt is less risky for an investor, but is more risky from a company's perspective. This financial risk is attributable to the fact that interest on debt is a fixed cost, which affects a company's earnings per share and its liquidity. In addition, debt has to be repaid, whereas equity does not.

This chapter starts by explaining the common characteristics of long-term debt finance, before discussing the various options that are available to a company. The most popular option, the term loan, is discussed first. As bank finance is discussed in depth in the previous two chapters, its treatment in this chapter is brief. The bulk of this chapter deals with bond finance. Bonds are introduced, common characteristics are identified and different types are outlined. The methods companies put in place to ensure that they can afford to redeem bonds are described, as are the roles of trust deeds, covenants and credit-rating companies. The differences between debentures and loan stock are highlighted and the calculation of the value and cost/return of redeemable and irredeemable bonds is outlined. This enables the reader to work out whether, or not, it is worthwhile investing in a bond. The latter part of this chapter explains securitisation (how companies can package assets into tradable securities and sell them to obtain cash), mezzanine finance (hybrid finance) and project finance (finance raised for a specific project) and outlines international sources of long-term debt.

Debt

The two main sources of long-term debt are bank loans and bonds. There are other less common sources of finance that are *hybrid* in nature. Hybrid sources usually start off as debt instruments and then convert into equity instruments when certain conditions are fulfilled. The principles of financing outlined in chapter four, 'Asset-Mix Decisions, Finance-Mix Decisions and Short-Term Sources of Finance', also apply to long-term debt. For example, the term of the debt and repayment schedule should be planned to match the cash flows that are generated from the investment that was purchased by the debt. The cost of debt will be influenced by the perceived risk of default and any factors that may cushion this risk, such as the availability of tangible assets as security or credit insurance.

To protect investors and companies seeking to purchase assets that may have a legal encumbrance, company law requires that a central record is kept of all charges held on company assets. When debt is secured, this is registered with the Registrar of Companies, who maintains a *Register of Charges Against the Assets of Companies*. This register is open to public inspection and solicitors normally request searches for charges on particular assets, when they are being purchased by their clients, to ensure they are free of any encumbrance.

Term loans

Term loans are advances made by a lender to a borrower for a predetermined period. They can be provided by one lender (usually a bank, insurance company or pension company) or syndicated. *Syndicated loans* are usually large in size and are provided by several lenders (through one main lead bank who administers the loan) to a company. The reason for getting several parties involved in one transaction is to spread the credit risk across several lenders. Long-term 'term loans' are normally secured on assets and are referred to as *mortgage loans*. Companies usually prefer this type of debt to bond debt as it is quick to obtain, flexible in its terms (both at the outset and for the duration of the loan agreement), less costly, is not repayable on demand and is available to all sizes of company. Another attraction is that any asset used as security for a term loan remains under the legal ownership of the borrower; therefore, the rewards associated with owning it, such as capital appreciation, accrue to them. On the downside, the asset cannot be sold and permission is usually required from the lender to change the use of the asset – for example, if the company wishes to rent a building it owns.

The costs of a long-term loan are similar to those discussed for shorter term loans. The costs include an arrangement fee and a yearly interest charge, which can be either fixed rate or variable rate. Interest is tax deductible so reduces the tax bill each year, providing the company is in profit. The interest rate is influenced by the risks associated with the debt. Risk is affected by the reputation of the borrower, the availability of security and guarantees, the quality of management and the risk of the project. A more detailed business plan is required, relative to a business plan used to obtain shorter-term debt, as there is more information asymmetry in long-term loan decisions. The bank has less information about the future of the company and the business plan can be used to provide this information to the bank. Lenders can write restrictive covenants into the loan agreement (discussed later) to protect the liquidity of the company until the loan is repaid. As mentioned in the last chapter, a variety of repayment schedules can be arranged including repayment breaks, bullet payments and balloon payments, depending on the needs of the borrower.

Term loans are the main source of debt finance used by companies in Northern Ireland and the ROI. A newspaper article by Alan Bridle (2005) highlights the results of a Federation of Small Businesses report that stated that companies located in NI have higher dependency on bank and government support for finance than their counterparts in the rest of the UK, and are less reliant on their own resources and savings (equity).

Bonds

Bonds are simply tradable loans arranged by a borrower and bought by investors. They can be redeemable or irredeemable. Redeemable bonds normally have a maturity of between seven and 30 years, although the period can be either shorter or longer. Irredeemable debts do not have a maturity date, though they commonly are redeemed at the borrower's request. Bonds can be sold by way of a public issue, in which the company has to undertake similar steps to those followed when issuing equity (the company will have to prepare a prospectus, apply to the stock exchange and provide financial statements to the lenders, at least annually). These bonds are traded in the secondary market of the London Stock Exchange (UK) and in the official list of the Irish Stock Exchange (ROI). The other option is a private issue through a financial intermediary to a limited number of lenders. These bonds are not tradable on the secondary markets of the stock exchange, but can be traded in private deals between bond brokers.

In October 2003, an Irish food company, Greencore plc, borrowed $302 million in a private debt placement to nine US insurance companies. The placement was oversubscribed by up to three times the requirement

(O' Halloran, 2003). As the deal was a private placing, Greencore plc did not need to pay for a credit rating. In addition, at this time, the loan rates were more competitive in the US and demand was higher relative to a local issue (they would have had to pay a higher coupon).

Unlike the equity stock exchange, trading in the bond market is more about liquidity. The margin to be made on each deal is not great; however, the size of the deal usually results in a huge gain, or loss, to the trader. Bond brokers can make large sums of money, or can lose a fortune, as in the case of Nick Leeson when he worked for Barings bank in 1996.

> 'He had £100 million of Baring bank's money to invest in standard merchant banking activities; however, he made huge losses trading in the derivatives market'.

Glaxo plc closed its treasury department in 1994 because of losses incurred in the bond markets and in 2006 Nick Maounis, founder of the hedge fund *Amaranth* apologised to its investors for losing $6 billion in just a few days:

> 'We feel bad about losing our own money. We feel much worse about losing your money' (Hotten, 2006).

The issue price a corporation asks for a bond flotation is influenced by the price of government bonds, the price of similar risk bonds, the volatility of interest rates, the type of bond being issued (secured, unsecured, coupon, redeemable or convertible) and the extent of covenants within the trust deed. Bonds on the London Stock Exchange are issued in sterling and sometimes UK companies provide bonds in foreign markets, which are termed *bulldog bonds*. They are also traded in sterling.

Another underlying feature of bonds is how they are administered by a company. Bonds can either be 'registered' or 'bearer'. The details of the owners of *registered bonds* are included in a register within the issuing company. The register is a formal record of who has claims against the company and is also used to distribute coupon payments. Details of the owners of *bearer bonds*, on the other hand, are not kept by the company. These bonds are issued with coupons attached and the bearer (holder) has to present these coupons to the company, or their bank, to receive payment. The anonymity of these bonds makes them more attractive to investors, who are willing to accept a lower coupon. On the downside, were the bearer to lose a bond, or have it stolen, it is difficult to prove ownership, whereas a registered bond can be reissued. Though there are a variety of different kinds of bonds, most have common characteristics.

Common bond characteristics

Nominal value: Bonds all have a predetermined ***nominal value***. This is also known as the ***par value*** and is the set amount which will be paid by a company on the redemption of the bond. In the UK and Ireland, the nominal value is normally £100/€100. Having a consistent nominal bond value in each jurisdiction assists investors when comparing various bond options.

Coupon rate: Each bond will have a coupon rate attached to it. This is the interest that is payable on the bond. It is usually semi-annual, though variations exist. The amount paid by the borrower is the coupon rate multiplied by the nominal value. The coupon rate does not change when the market value of the bond changes.

Redemption value: Redeemable bonds have a predetermined redemption value. This is usually set at the nominal amount (£100/€100). However, it can include a premium.

Redemption date: Redeemable bonds have a predetermined redemption date, or range of dates, within which redemption can take place.

Variations of the most common characteristics are possible. The coupon can be a fixed percentage or can be pegged to the base rate or inflation. In some instances, the coupon rate may be pegged to the price of a commodity such as oil or gold. Therefore, the company's fortunes help determine the coupon it has to pay. For example, if a major expense of the company is oil, then the bond coupon may be set to vary with oil price such that when the commodity price goes down, the coupon rate goes up and vice versa. This means that when oil goes down, the company's costs fall, leaving more cash to pay the higher coupon.

Bond repayment

A company can take several approaches to ensure that it has sufficient liquidity to redeem bonds when they fall due.

Sinking fund

Many companies set up a ***sinking fund***. This is where a company puts a certain amount of cash into a separate investment fund each year, which earns a return. The theory is that the capital being input each year (an annuity), plus the return earned on the fund being built up over the period of the bond, will be sufficient to repay the bond issue on its redemption date. The calculation of the annuity is provided in the next example.

Worked example 6.1   (Sinking fund)

A company has decided to set up a sinking fund to provide sufficient funds to redeem a bond issue. The trust deed states that a total of €/£1,000,000 should be paid to the bond holders, on redemption of the bonds in ten years time. The trustees of the sinking fund have informed the company that they can guarantee a return of 12% on the sums invested over the next ten years.

REQUIRED

Calculate the amount that should be input by the company to the sinking fund, every six months, to ensure that the €/£1,000,000 is repaid in full from the proceeds of the sinking fund.

Solution

There will be 20 repayments, earning a payment rate of 6% (12%/2) every six months.
The terminal value of an annuity for 20 payments at 6% is 36.786 (see tables)

Continued

Therefore, the amount required to be input every six months (X) is:

$$X \times 36.786 = €/£1,000,000$$
$$X = €/£27,184$$

As long as the sinking fund earns the target return (12%), then a transfer of €/£27,184 every six months for 20 years will result in the sinking fund having a terminal value of €/£1,000,000.

Stagger repayments

A company may set a redemption period, not a specific date. For example, instead of redeeming bonds in 2010, a bond may have redemption dates ranging from 2010 to 2015. Within this period, the company can decide which bonds to redeem and the dates to redeem – the bond holder has to agree.

Purchase the bonds

Another approach that can be used by companies is to repurchase the bonds in the markets when they have the funds available to do so. This reduces the coupon payable and the capital sum required on the redemption date. Where a company wishes to purchase more bonds than are for sale in the markets, they can make an offer to the existing bond holders. The amount offered is usually the market price of the bond – though it may be at the nominal value (if higher) or may include a premium.

Issue irredeemable bonds

A company may set a policy of issuing only irredeemable bonds and redeeming the bonds when it has the funds to do so. If a company has a history of redeeming irredeemable bonds, the market will value the bonds as though they were redeemable – though the value is reduced due to the uncertainty of not having a set redemption date.

Issue of capital

Strong companies can redeem one issue of bonds using the finance raised by a new issue of bonds, on current terms. Alternatively, they may redeem the bonds using the proceeds of a stock issue. In these instances, the bond holders may be offered the right to exchange the bonds for equity stock. An exchange is not permitted where bonds were issued at a discount, unless the shares issued are reduced in number to take account of the discount (in this instance, there will be no premium to the new equity holders). This is to ensure that the new equity holders are not given benefit to the detriment of existing equity holders.

> **Reasons companies choose to redeem bonds before redemption date**
>
> When market interest rates fall, the bond becomes an expensive source of finance.
>
> When the company's net cash inflows are better than were anticipated when they were planning the redemption schedule for the bond issue.
>
> Changes in tax laws may increase the cost of the bond finance, making it attractive to redeem the bonds.
>
> The company directors may make a strategic decision to change the capital structure of the company to one that is less geared.
>
> The company may be in default of the restrictive covenants written into the trust deeds (see below) and may be forced to redeem the bonds early.
>
> The directors may see the covenants attached to a bond as hindering the future development of the company and so redeem the bond to allow them to widen the investment portfolio of the company.

Investors may not be happy to go along with the redemption plans of a company as they may have their cash requirements timed around the steady coupon receipts and there may not be suitable alternative investments available. Regardless, when a company decides to redeem its bonds, bond holders have to cooperate.

Trust deeds

When a company issues bonds, a *trust deed* is established, which sets out the terms of the contract between the company and the bond holder and establishes the identity of the trustee and their powers. The trustees of a bond are normally the issuing broker house or financial institution.

They usually monitor the company's behaviour throughout the term of the bond and ensure that it complies with the terms of the trust deed. In the event of default, the trustee will try to solve the issue. They may try to broker an agreement between the bond holders and the company, which usually involves rescheduling the coupon and redemption payments to suit the company. Where this is not possible, the trust deed normally gives the trustee the power to appoint a receiver.

The trust deed is also used as a means of reducing the risk of a bond, in that it can contain conditions or benchmarks that the company must achieve, or otherwise be considered to be in default. These conditions are known as *restrictive covenants* and can either be *negative covenants* or *positive covenants*. The main aim of restrictive covenants is to curb the financial activities of a company to ensure that sufficient liquidity and reserves are maintained to protect bond holders, who do not have a vote in company meetings. The most common forms of restrictive covenants are now listed:

Examples of negative restrictive covenants written in trust deeds

Security: The trust deed may restrict the sale or use of an asset where the asset is being used as security for the bonds.

Financial ratios (interest cover): It is common for a trust deed to limit a company's ability to take on more debt, by stipulating that the interest cover ratio should be maintained at a minimum of three or four times.

Financial ratios (gearing): It is common for a trust deed to place a restriction on the ratio of debt to total assets or debt to net assets or debt to shareholders funds.

Financial ratios (liquidity): Other benchmark financial ratios to protect liquidity include working capital ratios, current ratios and some are pegged to cash-denominated benchmarks, such as annual cash flow to annual interest and redemption payments.

Sinking funds: Some trust deeds require that the company creates a sinking fund, to ensure that sufficient funds are put aside by the company to redeem the bonds on the redemption date.

Continued

Place restrictions or limits on future bond issues: Normally, subordinate (lower rated) bond issues are allowed, but not superior debt or bonds.

Dividend restrictions: The trust deeds may place restrictions on the level of dividend that can be distributed. This is to ensure that there is sufficient liquidity to pay interest and capital repayments.

Share redemption: Some trust deeds place restrictions on a company's ability to redeem shares, or issue options, during the term of the bond debt.

There is a wealth of literature that suggests that management alter their behaviour, or their accounting practices, in response to restrictive covenants. Restrictive covenants usually restrict a company's ability to raise more finance by not allowing them to become more geared. This usually restricts management ability to invest, as they do not have sufficient cash generated from current activities. This restriction might be detrimental to the value of the company. Research on companies subject to restrictive covenants has shown that management will use a variety of means to relax restrictive covenants, including changing accounting policies. Companies with restrictive covenants are more likely to revalue their tangible assets and capitalise development expenditure (Whittred and Zimmer, 1986). However, most bond holders are aware of the loosening impact of these accounting adjustments and place restrictions on them within the trust deeds (Whittred and Zimmer, 1986). For example, revaluations are usually only allowed on land and buildings and the valuation must be performed by an independent valuer before the financial statements are finalised. Some trust deeds state that only tangible assets can be included in the assets part of the gearing ratio/ratio used as a restrictive covenant. See also: Whittred and Chan (1992); Brown, Izan and Loh (1992); and Henderson and Goodwin (1992).

Examples of positive restrictive covenants written in trust deeds

Accounting information: Providing financial statements and other information as predetermined in the trust deeds on a regular basis to bond holders.

Continued

Coupon: Paying a specified coupon amount (fixed or variable) within a specified range of dates.

Redemption value: Repaying the nominal amount that has been borrowed on a specified date or within a range of agreed dates.

The more restrictive covenants a trust deed contains, the less risk to the bond holder – therefore these bonds will be valued higher by the market. Other risk-reducing features may include a requirement to obtain credit insurance, security, a guarantee from a parent company or personal guarantees from directors. In these instances, the bonds are usually referred to as **guaranteed loan stock**. In addition to market restrictions, the level of debt that a company can raise is usually limited by its articles of association.

Bond ranking/credit rating

When a company undertakes a large public bond issue, it may consider it worthwhile to pay to have the issue rated by one of the specialist credit-rating companies such as Moody's, Standard and Poor's, and Fitch IBCA. These companies rate bonds from a triple A score (strongest) to a D which stands for default (some only rate as far as Bbb). There are varying ratings between these scores including AA, A, BBB, BB, B, C … and so on. Anything graded BBB or above is considered to have hit the investment grade and any bond rated below BBB is regarded as being a junk bond (discussed below). When an investment grade bond is re-rated as a junk bond, it is referred to as a *'fallen angel'*. In 2002, the Irish Company Elan plc saw its bonds downgraded by Moody's from B2 to Caa2, one of the lowest speculative grades, amid worries that the company would be unable to repay $2.4 billion of debt. The downgrading came about after it emerged that Elan plc had excluded $1 billion of off-balance-sheet debt from its US accounts (Bream and Firn, 2002). Elan plc was, at one time, Ireland's largest company (in terms of market capitalisation); however, in 2002 its shares lost 96% of their value.

Having a strong rating helps the marketability of a bond issue and reduces the costs associated with an issue. The rating depends on the interest and redemption default risks associated with the bond issue.

Therefore, factors such as the type of industry, whether the bond is secured or unsecured, gearing levels within the company, the current cash flow position of the company and the sensitivity of cash flows to changes in economic variables, such as interest or inflation, will influence the credit score awarded.

Debentures/loan stock

In GB and Ireland, bond issues are usually termed debentures or loan stock. The names highlight the difference between the two types of bond issue, in terms of the lien that they have over the assets of an issuing company.

Debentures

Debentures are bonds that are secured on the assets of the issuing company. The security can either be fixed to a specific asset, or assets, or floating over all assets in general (in the US, debentures are usually unsecured bonds, with only those bonds referred to as **mortgage debentures** or **mortgage bonds** being secured). Where the security is floating in nature, the bond is usually referred to as a **loan note**. With such security, management have more freedom over company assets. When the company breaches or defaults on any of the covenants within the trust deed, the floating charge crystallises into a fixed charge and the assets cannot be sold, or have their use changed, without the permission of the trustee or the receiver appointed by the trustee. Moreover, the receiver may sell the assets to redeem the bonds.

Loan stock

In GB and Ireland, **loan stock** usually refers to unsecured long-term bonds with coupons payable at intervals over the life of the bond. In the US, these are called **loan notes**. Because they are not secured, they are regarded as higher risk when compared to debentures and hence are more expensive for a company to service – they usually have a higher coupon rate.

Bond ranking: liquidation

When a company goes into liquidation, bonds do not have equal claim to its assets. The different types are ranked, with the highest ranking bonds having their claims met first. The general rule is that debentures, which are secured, qualify first and debentures with a fixed lien over a specific asset rank in front of debentures that have a floating lien over the general assets of a company. In addition, where there are several debenture issues, the earliest ranks first, unless the trust deeds of subsequent issues rank those issues in front of the earlier issues (covenants written into the trust deeds of the earliest debenture issues usually ensure that no subsequent bond issues are allowed, unless they are subordinate). Loan stock ranks below debentures and is also ranked in order of age; the earliest issues are considered superior to later issues. The ranking is not only important when a company is in liquidation, but also applies to coupon payments. The oldest debentures have their coupon paid first, the youngest loan stock coupons are paid last. When debentures or loan stock are ranked below other bonds, they are referred to as either *junior bonds* or *subordinated bonds*.

Plain vanilla bond

The most straightforward bond is the **plain vanilla bond**. This can also be called the '*straight bond*' or the '*bullet bond*'. These bonds are either redeemable or irredeemable. **Redeemable bonds** usually have an annual or semi-annual fixed coupon rate and a predetermined redemption value and date. In these instances, the company sells the bonds to an investor, receives money immediately and, in return, pays a stream of coupon payments and a final lump sum on the redemption date (usually the nominal value). **Irredeemable bonds** do not have a redemption date and the company only commits itself to paying the coupon rate either annually or semi-annually, depending on the initial terms of the bond. In practice, most companies redeem these bonds when it suits them. An example of the different types of long-term debt finance used by a large company, Viridian Group plc, is included at the end of this chapter.

Bond valuation

Valuing redeemable bonds

Redeemable bonds are valued at the present value of future stream of steady income (the coupon) for a set period (this is an annuity), plus a final redemption payment discounted at the bond holder's required rate of return. This return will be the same as the return on bonds in comparable companies. The following formula can be used to determine the market value of the bond (or what it should be):

$$P_0 = \frac{I_1}{(1+r)} + \frac{I_2}{(1+r)^2} + \cdots\cdots + \frac{R_n}{(1+r)^n}$$

Where P_0 is the market value of the bond in year 0, r is the discount rate or return on the bond, I is the annual coupon paid by a company (coupon rate multiplied by the nominal value), R is the redemption value of the bond and n is the number of years to maturity.

Worked example 6.2   (Valuing redeemable bonds)

ABC plc has €/£2,000,000 of 8% bonds that are due for redemption in three years' time. The expected return by bond holders is 5%.

REQUIRED

Calculate the equilibrium market value for a single bond.

Solution

The bond holder will pay a market price that equates to a return of 5% on an annuity of €/£8 (€/£100 × 8%) for three years, plus a final payment of €/£100 in three years.

$$P_0 = (€/£8 \times 2.723^*) + \frac{100}{(1.05)^3}$$

*This is the annuity factor for three years at 5%.

$$P_0 = €/£108.17 \text{ per bond}$$

The market value of a bond will vary over the life of the bond and is impacted on by many factors including the following:

Influences on the market value of bonds

1. Whether the bond is secured on assets of the company.
2. Whether the coupon is fixed rate or variable rate.
3. The extent of restrictive covenants.
4. The nature and return being allowed by bonds issued from similar companies with similar risks.
5. Coupon rates on offer in government-issued bonds (the risk-free rate).
6. Market interest rates.
7. The redemption value (nominal or with a premium).
8. On issue, demand for a bond will be influenced by the issue price, which may be at a premium or discount.

Return on redeemable bonds/cost of redeemable bonds

When investors are considering whether to purchase particular bonds or not, they will calculate the return the bond is currently providing, given the term to redemption, the market price the bond is currently trading at and the coupon receivable. In the case of redeemable bonds, the return has two elements, the yearly return and the capital gain (or loss) that will be made on the price of the bond. A quick way to work out the return is to use the following formula:

$$r = \frac{I_1}{P_0} + \frac{(R - P_0)/n}{P_0}$$

Where r is the return on the bond, I is the coupon received, P_0 is the current market price, n is the number of years to maturity and R is the redemption price of the bond.

Worked example 6.3   (Approximate cost of redeemable bonds)

ABC plc has €/£2,000,000 of 8% bonds that are due for redemption in five years' time. The bonds are currently trading at €/£80.

REQUIRED

Calculate the approximate yield received by bond holders, given an income tax rate of 40%.

Solution

The bond holder will receive €/£8 per year after investing €/£80. A quick guide to this yearly return is:

$$r = \frac{8(1-0.40)}{80} = 6\%$$

The bond will be held for five years, at which point the company will redeem the bond at its nominal value of €/£100. The capital return per year is estimated at:

$$\text{Capital return (estimate)} = \frac{€/£100 - €/£80}{5} = €/£4 \text{ per year}$$

This represents a capital gain of approximately $\dfrac{€/£4}{€/£80} = 5\%$ each year

Therefore, the overall approximate return is about 11% (6% + 5%), assuming the investor can avail of an exemption from capital gains tax.

The method used in the last example is quick and simple. It does not take into account the time value of money. To determine accurately the return of a redeemable debt instrument, the technique 'the internal rate of return' (covered in depth in chapter 13, 'Capital Investment Decision Making') should be used.

Worked example 6.4   (Cost of redeemable bonds)

ABC plc has €/£2,000,000 of 8% bonds that are due for redemption in five years time. The bonds are currently trading at €/£80.

REQUIRED

Calculate the approximate yield being received by bond holders, given an income tax rate of 40%.

Solution

The bond holder will receive €/£8 per year after investing €/£80 and will also receive €/£100 from the company in five years time. The aim is to work out the discount rate that equates the present value of this stream of payments to zero. The first rate selected is 10%.

(As this results in a negative net present value, a higher discount factor is chosen for the second rate to try. As the first guess has resulted in a net present value that is close to zero, the second guess is marginally higher, at 11%.)

Year	Cash flow	Discount factor	Present value	Discount factor	Present value
	€/£	Try 10%	€/£	Try 11%	€/£
0	80	1.000	80	1.000	80.00
1–5	(8 (1 − 0.40))	3.791	(18.20)	3.696	(17.74)
5	(100)	0.621	(62.10)	0.593	(59.30)
			(0.30)		2.96

Using interpolation, the precise rate is obtained:

$$10\% + \frac{-0.30(11-10)}{-0.30-(-2.96)} = 10.09\%$$

Valuing irredeemable bonds

Irredeemable bonds are valued by treating the coupon as being receivable in perpetuity. The value is obtained using the following formula:

$$P_0 = \frac{I}{r}$$

Where P_0 is the market value of the irredeemable bond at time 0, I is the annual coupon and r is the discount rate, or yearly return/yield required by bond holders. The market value of irredeemable bonds will be affected by the same factors that influence the market value of redeemable bonds (listed previously).

Worked example 6.5   (Valuing irredeemable bonds)

ABC plc has €/£2,000,000 of 8% irredeemable bonds. The expected return by bond holders is 5%.

REQUIRED

Calculate the equilibrium market value for a single bond.

Solution

The bond holder will pay a market price that equates to a return of 5% on a payment of €/£8 (€/£100 × 8%) in perpetuity:

$$P_0 = \frac{8}{0.05}$$

$$P_0 = €/£160 \text{ per bond}$$

A value greater than the nominal value is expected, as the yearly return of 8% greatly exceeds the bond holders' required return of 5%, hence they will pay more for the bond.

When a company decides to issue bonds, it needs to get the issue price correct, otherwise the bond will not sell. The company has to work out what the bond holders' return is for the type of bond being issued. To do this, it is common to look at the return bond holders are willing to pay for a similar bond, in a similar risk company. This next example highlights how to do this.

Worked example 6.6   (Calculating the issue price)

ABC plc wants to issue €/£2,000,000 of 8% irredeemable bonds. It is unsure of the issue price to market the bonds at. A similar company, XYZ plc, has already in issue 6% irredeemable bonds. These are currently trading at €/£80.

REQUIRED

Calculate the issue price ABC plc should include in its prospectus in respect of its bonds to achieve a full sell-out of the bonds in a public issue (ignore tax).

Solution

The return being earned by the bond holders of XYZ plc is:

$$r = \frac{€/£6}{€/£80} = 7.5\%$$

Therefore, ABC plc should set its issue price at an amount that, at a minimum, provides a return of 7.5%. The price is:

$$P_0 = \frac{€/£8}{0.075} = €/£106.67$$

The existing market will pay €/£106.67 for this future stream of interest payments. It is up to ABC plc to determine whether to issue the bonds at a value lower than this to make the bonds attractive to bond holders, ensuring a complete sell-out quickly.

Return on irredeemable bonds/cost of irredeemable bonds

The cost of servicing coupons on bonds is reduced by the tax saving as the coupon is tax deductible (so long as a company is profit making and has sufficient profits to obtain a full tax benefit). In these instances, the cost of a bond to a company is reflected by the following formula:

$$r = \frac{I(1-t)}{P_0}$$

Where r is the cost of the bond (after tax) to the company, I is the annual interest payment, t is the tax rate and P_0 is the market value of the bond. This formula can also be used to find the actual return being sought by bond holders, who have different marginal rates of tax.

Worked example 6.7   (Irredeemable debt: after-tax cost to the company)

ABC plc has €/£2,000,000 of 8% irredeemable bonds in issue. These are currently trading at €/£80. ABC plc pays tax at 30%.

REQUIRED

Calculate the cost of this debt to ABC plc.

Solution

The cost of the bond to ABC plc is:

$$r = \frac{€/£8(1-0.30)}{€/£80} = 7\%$$

Bond holders who purchase irredeemable bonds will be subject to income tax on the coupon earned. As the bond is not redeemed, they will only have to pay capital gains tax if they sell the bond at a premium above the rate they paid for the bond, on the difference between the selling price and the buying price. This will also only be payable if the bond holder does not have, or has exhausted, the yearly capital gains tax allowance.

Zero coupon bonds

Some bonds pay their coupon every three months; others pay no coupon at all. The latter are termed **zero coupon bonds** or **deep discount bonds**. Zero coupon bonds are sold at a large discount to their par value and do not pay any coupon to the holder. This means that the income to the investor is only in the form of a capital gain, either on the sale or redemption of the bond. Therefore, the demand and marketability of this type of bond will be affected by the tax differential between capital gains tax and income tax. It will be more attractive to investors who are higher rate tax payers, as they are better able to manipulate capital gains and have a tax-free capital gains allowance, which can be used each year.

The next example shows how to calculate the return being offered by a zero coupon bond.

Worked example 6.8   (Zero coupon bonds)

Marta plc issues 100,000 bonds at a price of €/£60 to be repaid at their nominal value of €/£100 in six years time.

REQUIRED

Calculate the annualised rate of return from the capital gain if the bond is held to maturity for the full six years.

Solution

The approach is to find the discount (compound interest rate) 'r' which would be achieved if €/£60 were to be invested now to achieve a terminal value payment of €/£100 in six years time.

This is represented by the following equation:

$$€/£60(1+r)^6 = €/£100$$

This can be rearranged to:

$$r = \sqrt[6]{100/60} - 1$$
$$r = 0.089 (8.9\%)$$

Continued

Alternatively, it can be rearranged as:

$$\frac{\text{€}/\text{£}60}{\text{€}/\text{£}100} = \frac{1}{(1+r)^6}$$

$$0.6 = ?$$

By reading the discount tables, it can be seen that the present value discount factor of 0.6, given the term is six years, lies between 8% and 9%. Interpolation can then be used to determine the exact rate.

The discount factor for six years at 8% is 0.630.

The discount factor for six years at 9% is 0.596.

Therefore, the rate of return before tax is:

$$= \frac{0.630 - 0.6}{0.630 - 0.596}$$

$$= 0.88\% \text{ more return over and above the}$$
$$8\% \text{ resulting in an overall return of}$$
$$8.88\% \text{ (before taxation)}$$

The following formula can be used to calculate the annualised return from an investment in zero coupon bonds.

$$r = \sqrt[n]{\frac{R}{IP}} - 1$$

Where r is the annualised return, R is the redemption value, IP is the issue price and n is the number of years to maturity.

Securitisation

Securitisation is a term used to describe the packaging of a company's claim to future income into tradable securities and the selling of that claim to third parties, in the markets, for a price. The packaging usually takes the form of a bond and the price is the coupon being paid and/or the capital appreciation on the price of the bond (if issued below par) between the date of issue and the date of redemption. Securitisation is widely used by banks to gain finance, which is secured on their claim to interest and repayment cash flows from mortgage holders. The right to income from mortgages is sold as securities in the markets for up-front cash. This process ensures that a bank's liquidity remains intact. The following diagram encapsulates the steps involved in the securitisation of a bank's assets (i.e. their claim to future income). These securities are sometimes referred to as *asset-backed securities*.

Securitisation of claims (steps)

1. The bank provides the mortgage holders with the capital to buy their house (€/£10 million). The debt is secured on the mortgage holders' properties.
2. The mortgage holders pay the bank set up fees, interest and capital (interest, say 6%).
3. The bank sells the future stream of income (interest and capital) in the markets as bonds with a coupon of 5% (issue price is typically below par, whereas redemption is at par) for, say, €/£9 million. The bank now has sufficient capital to keep awarding mortgages.
4. The bank pays the bond holders 5% each year and the nominal value of the issue (€/£10 million) on redemption.

The bank has the potential to make profits where the mortgage set-up fees exceed the issue costs, where the coupon paid to the bond holders is less than the interest being paid by the mortgage holders (in this example, this is 1%) and where the capital repayments made throughout the life of the mortgage are invested and the sum of the capital and its return exceed the redemption value of the initial issue on maturity (€/£10 million).

The legal right to the stream of mortgage payments passes to the bond holders, though the bank administers the whole process. The bank may also guarantee the payments, so that the process is not affected by bad debts. These are called *without-recourse asset-backed securities*. In some instances, the bank provides partial guarantees and this issue is termed *limited-recourse asset-backed securities*. The assets (i.e. the claim to future payments from mortgage holders) are usually removed from the bank's balance sheet and placed in a new fund, or an entity is set up specifically to administer the whole process (the entity is called a *special purpose entity)*. Securitisation emerged in relation to mortgage claims in the U.S. Mortgages claims are still the dominant type of securitisation. It is also used to package and sell commercial paper claims, car loan claims, credit card claims and export credit claims.

Mezzanine finance

Mezzanine finance is the term used to encapsulate long-term, high-risk, high-return financing. This type of finance is usually sought after all other debt sources have been exhausted and a company does not wish to issue equity (an equity issue is usually more expensive and may upset the control equilibrium within a company). The finance can be hybrid in nature – usually starting as debt, but having the option to convert to equity at some point in the future if the project or company succeeds. The finance is unsecured. As the finance is riskier, the premium or coupon rate is high. In the initial years, this type of finance is regarded as debt, hence it ranks in front of equity when it comes to yearly distributions of surpluses (interest is paid before dividends) and if the company goes into liquidation, the debt holders are paid after other creditors, but before the equity holders. This means that, though the finance is risky, it is not as risky from an investor's viewpoint as equity. When a company does well, the investors can convert their holding into equity and thereafter enjoy high dividends and/or capital gains in share price. The main types of mezzanine finance are junk bonds, convertible bonds and preference shares. Mezzanine finance is most commonly sought when there is a management buy out, a takeover, a merger, recapitalisation within a company to finance growth, when plcs go private or when a project requiring finance is capital intensive. Generally, about 20%–30% of the financing provided for these types of projects is mezzanine finance. The bulk of the finance requirement is usually provided by banks (50%–60%) or by another source of debt, with only 10%–20% being invested as equity.

Junk bonds

Junk bonds are low-grade, risky bonds, that carry a high coupon (about 5% higher than AAA rated bonds) and the potential to make a strong capital gain on issue price. These bonds normally have a rating of below BBB. Investors find them attractive as there is the potential to make large returns. Indeed, a proportion of investors' investment pots are usually targeted at speculative investment opportunities, such as junk bonds. Junk bonds may be plain vanilla, convertible or have warrants attached (see below) to them.

Convertible bonds

A **convertible bond** is a type of hybrid finance. It starts off as a plain vanilla bond and, rather than being redeemed, can be converted into equity (usually at a premium: for example, the premium might be that the shares are converted at a predetermined share price or at a rate of 10%–30% above the prevailing share price). There is much terminology surrounding convertible bonds and this is now outlined, in brief.

Convertible bonds: terminology

Conversion date: The date bonds can be converted to equity.

Conversion price: Calculated as the par value of the bond divided by the number of shares the bond can be converted into.

Conversion ratio: The number of shares that will be obtained from one bond on conversion, for example, 13 for 1.

Conversion value: Market value of shares that the bond can be converted into. Calculated as the conversion ratio × market value per share.

Conversion premium: This represents the premium over and above the market price of the shares that bond holders have to accept, to obtain the shares. It is calculated as:

$$\frac{\text{Conversion price per share} - \text{market price per share}}{\text{Market price per share}}$$

When share prices rise, the value of a convertible bond increases and it is more likely that the bond holder will convert on maturity. In these circumstances, the conversion premium is likely to be small.

Worked example 6.9   (Convertible debt)

Oslo plc's equity shares are currently trading at €/£2.50. It issues 15-year convertible 7% bonds, with a fixed conversion price of €/£4.00.

REQUIRED

a)   Calculate the conversion ratio.
b)   Calculate the conversion premium at the time of issue.
c)   In ten years time the share price has increased to €/£3.50. Calculate the new conversion premium.
d)   Under what circumstances are the bond holders likely to convert their bonds into equity share capital?
e)   If the shares were to rise in value to €/£5.00, what would the conversion value be?

Solution

a)   The conversion ratio is €/£100/€/£4.00=25 shares for each bond.

b)   The conversion premium at the time of issue is:

$$\frac{€/£4.00 - €/£2.50}{€/£2.50} = 60\%$$

c)   The new conversion premium will fall to:

$$\frac{€/£4.00 - €/£3.50}{€/£3.50} = 14.28\%$$

Continued

d)   The bond holders are likely to convert their bonds to equity share capital if the share price keeps rising and the conversion premium falls. A good scenario for the bond holder would be where the conversion premium is zero, in that the conversion price is the same as the market price, at the date of conversion. It is even better for the bond holder if the share price increases to a value above the fixed conversion price. The current equity holders would not be happy with this result.

e)   The conversion value of one bond in this instance will be: €/£5.00×25=€/£125. In this scenario, the bond holder will have made a capital gain on his investment in the convertible bonds.

Current equity holders do not normally like it when their company issues convertible debt, due to the fact that at some stage in the future their earnings per share will be diluted, as will their holding. In addition, as highlighted in the above example, the market value of shares may rise above the anticipated conversion price. To overcome this problem, some companies issue the convertible debt as a rights issue first, allowing existing equity holders the first chance to purchase the bonds.

Convertible bonds are attractive to companies, as they are generally more marketable than plain vanilla bonds, the coupon is usually lower than a normal bond (the conversion right is considered to have value) and the interest is tax deductible. Convertible bonds also have cash flow benefits, as conversion does not result in a cash outflow. In addition, when the bonds are converted, gearing is reduced. Companies use this option when they wish to raise equity finance, but consider that the current share price is undervaluing the company; the hope is that the share price will be more reflective of management's view of company value by the time conversion is due. However, if the company does not perform as management expect, it is left with a source of finance that has fixed yearly outflows (the coupon) and a large cash outflow on the conversion date if the bond holders elect to redeem the bonds, rather than convert them.

Investors generally like convertible shares; they are able to invest in a risky venture and be ranked higher than the equity holders when it comes to yearly distributions and liquidation payments. They have the option to redeem the bonds if the company does not perform as expected, yet can convert them to equity share capital if the company does perform. In addition, they can sell the bonds in the markets at any time.

Warrants

Warrants give the holder the right to subscribe for a specified number of equity shares in the company at some specified time in the future, or when the company meets set performance targets. They have their own value and can be bought and sold separately from the security to which they are attached. Their value is quite low and investors usually find it worthwhile keeping them, as the reward is high if the company performs well. For example, an investor who purchases junk bonds may have five warrants attached to each, giving him the right to purchase five shares in three years time at a cost of €/£3.00. The market value of each share is currently €/£2.00. Each warrant could be sold today for 10c/p. If, in three years time, share price rises to €/£4.00, the investor will make a large gain. The investor can purchase the shares for €/£3.00 and sell them immediately for €/£4.00. This is a way of rewarding those investors who invest in the company when it is risky to do so.

Project finance

When a large company (or a consortium of companies) undertakes a new major project, it is common for it to set up a separate legal entity to deal solely with that particular project. The separate legal entity, usually backed by the parent company, seeks project finance. *Project finance* is finance obtained to fund a specific project. The project is usually large – for example, the building of a bridge, a motorway, an oil rig or a dam – with easily separable cash inflows and outflows. The parent company usually issues equity to help fund the project and the remainder of the finance is sourced from a bank (usually by a syndicated loan) or the bond markets. The bonds are issued by the new separate legal entity, but may be guaranteed by the parent company (*with-recourse financing*). If the parent company does not provide a guarantee, this is called *non-recourse financing*. The terms of the bonds or bank debt are usually designed to be self-liquidating or self-servicing (wherein the cash inflows from the project repay the interest or coupon and capital repayments or redemption payments). The project is the determining influence on the ability to obtain finance, with the guarantee from the parent company usually only regarded as security (this helps the project obtain cheaper funding). The reputation of the parent will also impact on the credit risk assessment.

Project finance is usually more expensive than conventional loans from a lender. Conventional loans are usually made to a company that has a diversified portfolio of projects (the business the company has built up over years which reduces risk). However, the advantages to companies of raising project finance usually outweigh the costs. The advantages include: the risk associated with taking on a major project is transferred to a new legal entity; high levels of debt can be obtained to finance the project, yet not be included in the parent company's balance sheet; when the project is located in a foreign country, local banks and markets can be used to source finance, which may promote greater acceptance in the country; and having a separate legal entity, with its own agreement with the financiers, does not complicate the company's own finances. This is particularly relevant when more than one company has an interest in a project.

International sources of finance

Many large companies make strategic decisions to issue bonds on foreign markets. They do this where there is high demand for bonds in these markets and the coupon rate is competitive. However, a low coupon rate is usually a false economy, as there is a greater risk of a capital loss when it comes to the repayment of the bond, because of exchange rate movements. The bonds are usually issued in the currency of the country of the market that they are being issued in and are termed *Eurobonds*. The name has nothing to do with Europe – it denotes any bond issued in a different currency to the country of the issuer. Being issued in another currency means that the company is open to foreign exchange risk (in most instances, companies will have a business interest in the country the bond is issued in. Selling bonds in the currency of this country will reduce exposure to currency risk, to some extent). The interest on Eurobonds is usually fixed, is paid annually and is paid gross. Where the interest rate is variable, bonds are referred to as *Floating Rate Notes* (FRN). Eurobonds and FRNs are tradable and usually have fewer restrictive covenants and less disclosure demands, relative to UK or ROI debt issues.

Most companies source the cheapest type of debt and then use interest rate and currency swaps to tailor the structure of the debt to suit their needs (see the extract from Viridian Group plc 2005/06 annual report and accounts at the end of this chapter).

Conclusion

One of the key decisions a finance manager has to face is how to finance investments. Research has shown that there is a preference for using internal sources (discussed in the next chapter) and that debt is the next preferred option, with bank loans being more attractive to issuing bonds (pecking order theory). The driving influence in the decision is cost. However, there are hidden costs with debt. Companies with high levels of debt have greater financial risk and operating risk or leverage risk. This may influence operational activities and cause equity holders to demand a higher return. High levels of debt may even tie the hands of managers when they wish to invest in further projects (restrictive covenants). The decisions regarding the amount and source of debt to obtain are more complicated than they might seem initially. Finance managers have to weigh up the pros and cons of each potential source in light of current gearing levels, ownership structure and stability of future cash flows from operating activities.

Examination standard question

Worked example 6.10

'In recent years it has been rare for medium or long-term debt to be issued at a fixed interest rate; a floating (or variable) rate of interest, usually a few percentage points different from some variable base interest rate, has become much more common.'

REQUIRED

Outline briefly, from the viewpoint of corporate financial management, the main advantages and disadvantages of floating rate debt.

6 Marks

An engineering company with €/£60 million of assets believes that it is at the beginning of a three-year growth cycle. It has

Continued

a total debt to assets ratio of 16%, and expects revenues and net earnings to grow at a rate of 10% per annum and its share price to rise at 30% per annum over the three-year period. The company will require additional financing amounting to €/£6 million at the start of the period and another €/£3 million by the middle of the third year. The economy is at the beginning of a general upturn and, by the middle of the third year, money and capital costs will show their characteristic pattern near the peak of an upturn in the economy.

REQUIRED

Advise the company how the two amounts of additional financing should be raised.

6 Marks

A chemical company has been growing steadily. Currently, it requires €/£2 million of new capital equipment to increase sales from €/£40 million to €/£50 million over the next two years. When additional working capital requirements are taken into account, the total additional financing required during the first of these two years will be €/£5 million. Profits will remain unchanged in Year 1 but will rise by 50% in Year 2. The shares are currently selling on a price earnings ratio of 20. The company can either borrow straight debt at 7.5% per annum or convertible debt at 6.75%. The present debt to total assets ratio is 25%.

REQUIRED

Advise the company as to which form of finance it should employ.

6 Marks
Total 18 Marks
(ICAI, MABF II, Autumn 1996, Q6)

Continued

Solution

The advantages of using floating rate debt are:
- Interest rates will reduce if economic conditions improve.
- The rate of interest will reflect the actual economic climate.

The disadvantages of using floating rate debt are:
- Interest rates may increase.
- Uncertainty surrounds the amounts of the repayments.
- The cash budget will be difficult to complete, due to the uncertainty surrounding the interest rate outflows.

The engineering company is in good shape financially and seems to have low gearing (16%), when expressed as the debt to total assets ratio. As the economy begins a three-year growth cycle, interest rates may be currently low, but will rise as the first year elapses. Therefore, the company should raise the €/£6 million using fixed rate debentures. To avoid any increase in gearing, the company might consider issuing them as convertible debentures (so long as the agreement reached with the convertible debenture holders does not damage current equity holder value). From the company's viewpoint, the use of debt is cheaper than equity, because of the tax deductibility of interest.

The company's share price is beginning to rise and is expected to peak at the end of the three-year period. Therefore, the company should wait until it is at its peak and then issue new ordinary shares to raise the €/£3 million required by the middle of the third year. The higher the share price, the fewer new shares will have to be issued and the less the dilution in control. Very often after a period of growth, a company may be slightly under capitalised, so the addition to the permanent capital base of the company provided by the new equity should be welcomed as good financial management.

The current gearing of the company, measured as the debt to total assets ratio, is low so the company can take on more debt

Continued

without increasing the risk to either debt or equity holders. The convertible debenture is the cheapest option, at 6.75%, a full 0.75% cheaper than straight debt. The expected growth in profits over the two-year period should ensure that sufficient funds will be available to repay the debt. The option to convert will eliminate the interest payments and the gearing ratio will also fall after conversion has taken place. The industry is very volatile and forecasting profits can be hazardous. Therefore, the share price might fall, should profits take a downturn. The price earnings ratio of 20 is very high and indicates market confidence. However, it can also indicate susceptibility to an attractive takeover offer. The issue of shares now would also be a possible option, if the share price was expected to fall. However, if the share price is only beginning to rise, it would be expensive for the company to issue the shares now, as more shares than necessary would have to be issued. On balance, convertible debt should be used, as it also offers the flexibility of being easy to adjust, should the company have made errors in computing the amount of finance required for the equipment.

KEY TERMS

Asset-backed securities
Bearer bonds
Bonds
Bond credit rating
Bulldog bonds
Bullet bond
Conversion date
Conversion premium
Conversion price
Conversion ratio
Conversion value
Convertible bond
Debentures
Debt
Deep discount bonds
Eurobonds
Fallen angel
Floating rate notes
Guaranteed loan stock
Irredeemable bonds
Junior bonds
Junk bonds
Limited-recourse securities
Loan notes
Loan stock
Mezzanine finance

Mortgage bond
Mortgage debentures
Mortgage loans
Negative covenants
Nominal value
Non-recourse financing
Par value
Plain vanilla bonds
Positive covenants
Project finance
Recourse financing
Redeemable bonds
Registered bonds
Restrictive covenants
Securitisation
Sinking fund
Special purpose entity
Straight bond
Subordinate bonds
Syndicated loans
Term loans
Trust deed
Warrants
Without-recourse securities
Zero coupon bonds

EXTRACT FROM THE ANNUAL REPORT AND ACCOUNTS OF VIRIDIAN PLC 2005/06

20. Other Financial Liabilities

	Note	Group		Company	
		2006 £m	2005 £m	2006 £m	2005 £m
Current					
Interest payable on Eurobond		6.4	6.4	–	–
Interest payable on EIB loan		0.3	0.3	–	–
Interest payable on revolving credit facility		0.1	0.1	–	–
Huntstown bank loan facility		6.0	5.9	–	–
Loan notes		–	0.1	–	–
Intra-group loans	29	–	–	148.6	164.2
Redeemable B shares		0.8	–	0.8	–
		13.6	12.8	149.4	164.2
Non-current					
Eurobond		173.0	172.9	–	–
EIB loan		100.0	100.0	–	–
Huntstown bank loan facility		113.9	125.0	–	–
Revolving credit facility		57.1	39.1	57.1	39.1
		444.0	437.0	57.1	39.1

Loans and other borrowings outstanding are repayable as follows:

	Group		Company	
	2006	2005	2006	2005
	£m	£m	£m	£m
In one year or less or on demand	13.6	12.8	149.4	164.2
In more than one year but not more than two years	6.5	6.1	–	–
In more than two years but not more than five years	180.0	161.0	57.1	39.1
In more than five years	257.5	269.9	–	–
	457.6	449.8	206.5	203.3

The principal features of the Group's borrowings are as follows:

– the Eurobond is repayable in 2018 and carries a fixed interest rate of 6.875%;

– the £100m EIB loan is repayable in 2009 and carries a floating interest rate based on LIBOR. The weighted average interest rate during the year was 4.59% (2005 - 4.60%);

– the €171.7m (£119.9m) Huntstown bank loan facility (2005 - €190.3m (£130.9m)) is repayable in semi annual instalments to 2017. This bank loan is secured over the assets of Huntstown and carries interest fixed at 6.43% through interest rate swaps.

In addition the Group has revolving credit facilities of £225m which mature in 2010 and can be drawn in Sterling or Euro. The facilities carry a floating interest rate based on LIBOR/EURIBOR as appropriate. At 31 March 2006, €81.8m (£57.1m) (2005 - €56.8m (£39.1m)) had been drawn on these facilities, and the interest on €18.7m had been fixed through interest rate swaps. The weighted average interest rate was 3.25% (2005 - 2.99%).

At 31 March 2006, the Group had undrawn committed borrowing facilities of £167.9m (2005 - £185.9m) in respect of which all conditions precedent had been met.

The directors consider that the carrying amount of loans and other borrowings equates to fair value with the exception of the Eurobond which had a fair value at 31 March 2006 of £199.3m (2005 - £196.7m) based on current market rates.

REVIEW QUESTIONS

1. What is the purpose of restrictive covenants?
2. What is a trust deed?
3. List five methods a company can use to repay €/£1 billion of bonds on their redemption.
4. What do you call a bond that was once rated as an AAA, but subsequently rated as a Caa, by a bond credit-rating agency?
5. Calculate the annual amount that should be input by a company to a sinking fund that earns 15% per annum, to ensure that it can repay bonds with a nominal value of €/£2,500,000 in 15 years time. The bonds are to be redeemed at a premium of 5%.
6. An investor is currently viewing the irredeemable bonds of Jock plc to determine whether or not to invest in the bonds. The bond holders' required rate of return (gross) is 8%. Jock plc's 9% redeemable bonds are currently trading at €/£90. The coupon is paid annually and is due in one year's time.

REQUIRED

Determine whether the investor should invest in Jock plc.

7. Jock plc currently has a 10% bond outstanding which will be redeemed in two years at €/£100. The current market value of this bond is €/£95 and interest is paid semi-annually.

REQUIRED

Calculate the return on this bond.

8. Hola plc issues 1,000,000 bonds at a price of €/£50 to be repaid at their nominal value of €/£100 in ten years time.

REQUIRED

Calculate the annualised rate of return from the capital gain if the bond is held to maturity for the full ten years.

CHALLENGING QUESTIONS

1.   GREENWOOD Ltd.

GREENWOOD Ltd. is hoping to expand its business. The company runs a very successful job recruitment agency. Extracts from the company's financial statements for the last two years are as follows:

INCOME STATEMENT EXTRACT

	20X1	20X0
	€/£'000	€/£'000
Revenue	2,250	1,350
Profit after tax	763	485
Dividends	538	440

BALANCE SHEET EXTRACT

	Note	20X1	20X0
		€/£'000	€/£'000
Non-current assets	(1)	350	250
Net current assets		390	315
		740	565
Issued share capital (€/£1 ordinary shares)		250	250
Reserves		340	165
Long-term bank loan		150	150
		740	565

Note: (1) Non-current assets comprise motor vehicles, furniture and fittings and computers. The company does not own its premises.

The directors are hoping to raise €/£2 million in long-term finance to implement the proposed expansion of the company. They are looking at a number of financing options including the following:

(1)   Bank term loan
(2)   Retained earnings
(3)   Venture capital
(4)   Redeemable debentures

REQUIRED

a) Outline the characteristics of ANY THREE of the sources of finance listed above.

10 Marks

b) Prepare a report for the directors of GREENWOOD Ltd. outlining the more appropriate method, or methods, of financing from the list above, having regard to the particular circumstances of the company. Your report should contain reasoned arguments for the method or methods selected.

8 Marks
Total 18 Marks
(ICAI, MABF II, Autumn 2002, Q7)

2. BINTULU plc

a) Explain what you understand by the terms 'operational gearing' and 'financial gearing'.

4 Marks

b) Why do different levels of gearing exist in different industries? Briefly explain your answer and your understanding of why these differences arise.

6 Marks

BINTULU plc is a middle sized quoted company which manufactures plastics.

The last two years have been very successful for the company following on from a period of static profits. The company now has surplus cash of €/£100 million. Its factories are not operating at 100% capacity. It has no immediate plans for major investment projects.

The following table shows a comparison between various ratios for the company and for the plastics industry as a whole.

	BINTULU	Industry
Debt ratio	28%	32%
Debt interest coverage	3.6×	2.9×
Dividend yield	4.4%	4.6%
Dividend cover	3.4×	3.2×
Market capitalisation	€/£1,000 million	

REQUIRED

c)   Write a report to the Finance Director of BINTULU plc advising
     him on alternative courses of action in respect of the surplus cash;
     set out clearly your recommendation as to the best course of action
     to follow. Describe the factors you have taken into account in your
     analysis.

                                                        7 Marks
Presentation mark   **1 Mark**
                                              Total 18 Marks
                           (ICAI, MABF II, Summer 2003, Q6)

LONG-TERM SOURCES OF FINANCE: EQUITY CAPITAL

7

Debt   40,000,000
Equity   15,000,000
Market Value 25,000,000

LEARNING OBJECTIVES

This chapter is mostly descriptive. Upon completing the chapter, readers should be able to:

♣ Explain the risk of equity to an investor, relative to other sources of finance;

♣ Outline the risk of equity from a company's perspective;

♣ Understand the difference between the book value, nominal value and market value of equity;

♣ List and describe various types of equity;

♣ Describe the main equity markets in the UK and the ROI;

♣ List the advantages and disadvantages of flotation;

♣ Describe the main approaches used to raise equity in the markets (on initial joining and subsequent to this);

♣ Explain the characteristics, advantages and disadvantages of preference shares from a company's and an equity holder's perspective.

♣ Discuss the role of venture capitalists and business angels in closing the finance gap; and

♣ Describe government initiatives that have been used to promote investment in high-risk ventures, in the UK and the ROI.

Introduction

Equity finance is one of the most important long-term sources of finance to companies. It is the least risky source of finance, from a company's perspective, yet the most risky investment to make, from an investor's viewpoint. This chapter is written from the viewpoint of a company and considers equity in terms of a source of finance, not as an investment. Sourcing equity is not straightforward for a company; there are different types of equity finance and different methods of obtaining equity. Some avenues (such as public issues) are closed to some companies. The decision on whether to grow and raise equity is strategic and needs to take the following into account: the risks involved (including market risk, business risk and finance risk); the ownership structure of the company (control); the period of time the finance is required for; whether the funding from equity finance matches the finance requirements; and the current gearing of the company.

This chapter tries to shed some light on the equity finance options available to different types of companies. It starts by explaining equity in general terms and then splits the discussion into public equity (quoted) and private equity (not quoted). Public equity is mainly sourced from the equity markets; therefore, the UK and ROI markets are explained and the process involved in obtaining a public listing is outlined. The advantages and disadvantages to a company that result from becoming listed are also discussed. The various approaches available on an initial public offering are detailed, with diagrams being used to show the role of issuing houses in the process. A myriad of stakeholders and advisers, apart from the issuing house, are involved in the process of raising equity and these roles are detailed in brief. Then the options available to an already listed company, to raise additional equity finance, are discussed.

Preference shares are explained. These shares are hybrid in nature; they are not strictly equity, nor are they strictly debt. Finally, the sources of equity available to unquoted firms are outlined. These sources include venture capitalists, business angels and government initiatives to foster entrepreneurial activity in the business sector. After reading this chapter, it may seem that external sources of equity are the only source of equity. In practice, however, companies will always try to fund their projects using internally generated equity (retained earnings), after which bank debt is the preferred source of finance, followed by tradable debt – with equity being the least preferred source of finance. This ranking is mostly down to the cost of each source and is known as *pecking order theory*. (See chapter 15, 'Capital Structure'.)

Equity as a source of finance

Different types of companies
Equity is the term used to describe an owner's investment in a company. There are many forms of business, with differing types of equity.

Sole traders
A sole trader is an unincorporated business that is owned by one individual. This individual introduces cash, makes profits and withdraws cash. The balance of undrawn profits and cash injections are equity.

Partnerships
Partnerships are unincorporated businesses that are owned by two or more parties. These parties introduce cash, make profits and withdraw cash. The balance of undrawn profits and cash injections are equity.

Limited companies
Limited companies are companies that are incorporated as separate legal entities. They are usually owned by a small number of people who each have a share in the company (these people are usually the directors or are related to the directors). The equity in this type of company will be the initial share issue proceeds, plus any premium made on issue (this is equivalent to capital introduced), plus cumulative profits less dividend distributions made. Limited companies are typically set up by purchasing a 'shell company' from Companies Registry. The company is registered and share certificates are delivered to the equity holders by the individual organising the set-up of the company.

Public limited companies (plcs)
Plcs are companies that are incorporated as separate legal entities. They have a share capital of greater than €/£50,000 and shares are held by the public (persons that are not connected to the directors or major equity holders of the company). The value of equity in a plc at any point in time is the market value of the shares multiplied by the number of shares in issue. Plc equity share issues can be made by either a private issue, wherein a financial intermediary (or accountant) places the shares with a small

number of clients, or a full public issue, wherein the shares are made available on one of the share exchanges.

Equity in financial statements

In the balance sheet of a company a number of different accounts (included in 'equity and reserves') make up the book value of its equity. The main equity account is equity share capital – otherwise known as *ordinary share capital*. This is a monetary value that represents the number of shares a company has issued, multiplied by their nominal value. The nominal value is sometimes referred to as *par value*. The *nominal value* is established by the directors of a company when a company is being incorporated. The nominal value and number of shares authorised for issue are stipulated in a company's articles of association. The directors do not have to issue all the shares that are authorised for issue; they can elect to issue a portion of the shares, leaving a cushion to issue in the future, when the company's finance needs grow. The directors can issue more than the limit laid down in the articles of association; however, they require permission (a special resolution at an appropriately convened meeting) from equity holders to do so. The issued share capital divides the overall value of a company after debt claims into portions (shares), which are then traded. An example of the disclosures required for equity shares (Viridian Group plc) is provided at the end of this chapter.

The nominal value bears no relation to *market value,* which is the price the market places on the equity of a company. The holder of an equity share is a part owner of a company. The holder has a right to vote at equity shareholders' meetings. Decisions that can be influenced by equity shareholders include: the employment of directors, non-executive directors and auditors; the dividend level (equity holders can elect to reduce a dividend, but not increase it); and major strategic decisions.

When a company is initially incorporated and shares are issued, directors usually try to select a nominal value, which they feel represents the market value of the company (they discount it initially to ensure that all shares are taken up by the market). However, they do not always get it right and the shares may be valued at a higher price relative to the nominal value; in this instance, the surplus is regarded as a premium on issue and is accounted for in the *share premium* account. Therefore, the equity share capital and share premium account together represent the net investment by equity holders in a company. Equity holders also make other contributions (indirectly) to the financing of a company. Each year the profits remaining after bond interest, taxation and preference dividends are attributable to equity holders and can be distributed as a dividend. However, to do so would undermine the liquidity of a company and limit the funds available for directors to invest in new projects. Therefore, a portion, if not all, of the yearly *realised earnings* available for distribution may be retained in the company. This is an opportunity cost to the equity holders in terms of it being a dividend forgone. Therefore, it represents an additional supply of finance by the equity holders. Each year the amount not distributed is transferred to the *revenue reserves* account (otherwise known as *retained earnings*). This also forms part of the equity of the company. It is a record of the past dividends foregone by the equity holders. Retained earnings do not equate to cash reserves.

In addition to the realised earnings, a company normally makes other gains each year. These are usually capital gains, which are not realised. Depending on the accounting policies adopted, the financial statements of a company might incorporate these unrealised gains on some assets, for example property. Property values usually increase each year. The increase in value is attributable to the equity holders (debt holders' claims on a company are fixed – so long as these are covered, all other gains accrue to the equity holders) and is posted to a revaluation reserve. The *revaluation reserve* represents the difference between the market value of the property and the historic cost of the property (the price the company paid for the property).

Other types of equity share

Non-voting equity shares: **Non-voting equity shares** have the same rights as ordinary equity shares, except they do not carry a vote. They are not allowed to be issued by companies listed on the London Stock Exchange, but are common in family-run limited companies. This allows a family to retain full control.

Golden shares: **Golden shares** have the same rights as ordinary equity shares, though they also have special decision making powers. They are

Continued

issued to key equity holders (usually founding equity holders/boards) when the company is first incorporated. Their aim is to preserve certain characteristics of a company. For example, a football club may wish that the new owners or management do not change the colour of the strip, or the logo, or the football grounds, or sell players to meet debts. These types of decision may only be agreed by holders of golden shares.

Preferred ordinary shares: The claims of holders of **preferred ordinary shares** are met before the claims of other equity holders (**deferred ordinary**). On the down side, their claim to surplus returns is limited when a company performs well.

Equity: investor's perspective

As investors, equity holders carry the greatest risks: they are last in line (of the financiers) to get yearly distributions and are last when it comes to capital repayment, were a company to go into liquidation. However, they can also reap the highest rewards when a company performs well, benefiting from increases in share price and large dividends. They demand the highest return of all the financiers of a company. If a successful company were to go into voluntary liquidation, the equity holders would get any residual surplus after creditors' and debt holders' fixed claims had been met. They have a right to receive the annual report of the company each year and to be invited to and attend the annual general meeting. At this meeting, they can exercise control by voting on pre-informed decisions that the company directors are proposing. This control is limited, particularly where an equity holder has a minority interest in a company. However, equity holders have the right to sell their shares at any time. If sufficient numbers do so, this will drive down the share price and directors will have to alter their decisions accordingly, or the company will be taken over and the directors removed. The liquidity associated with investing in shares is a key attraction to many equity holders as they can sell their shares at short notice (this advantage only applies to equity holdings that are listed on an exchange – if the equity holding is in an unlisted company, the shares are difficult to liquidise).

Equity: company's perspective

Raising equity is the least-risky form of external finance a company can obtain; dividends can be waived and the issued share capital does not have to be redeemed. A company can buy back its shares (companies usually do this if they feel that their shares are currently under priced). The ability to waive dividend payments is attractive to directors, particularly where there is a possibility of the company experiencing liquidity problems. However, it must be stressed that companies usually do pay a dividend and having a stable dividend policy is considered to influence the value of a company – dividends are interpreted as a means of signalling the future performance of a company to the market (see chapter 19, 'Dividend Policy'). Companies rarely distribute all the available earnings and usually build up retained earnings, which can be used to finance future investments. This is a quick and cheap source of finance, the most popular source of finance to directors.

The main disadvantage of equity finance is the cost of issuing equity shares. Issue costs range from 5% to 10% of funds raised. Indeed, there is usually a minimum fixed level of fees, making this a source of finance that is only appropriate for large companies. Expenses that need to be covered include accountants' fees (additional work may include preparing projections, reports on financing, tax planning, working capital requirements), solicitors' fees (tasks may include updating directors' contracts, registering the company as a plc, underwriting agreements, share options), broker fees (usually 0.5%), sponsor/issuing house fees (this includes the cost of underwriting and sub-underwriting the issue – up to 2%), Company Registrar fees (maintaining a record of the equity holders and issuing certificates) and the costs of preparing a prospectus and advertising the imminent issue.

The 5% to 10% estimate does not include the indirect costs that are incurred, such as administrative costs, transaction costs, managerial time and the burden of having to service this finance in the future. Equity holders will not retain their investment in the company if the company does not provide an annual return, either in the form of a dividend or an increase in share price (or a combination of the two). By increasing the equity of a company, the weighted average cost of capital (WACC) may also increase, resulting in a loss of equity value (see chapter 15, 'Capital Structure' for a discussion of the impact of shifts in a company's WACC on the value of its equity). Another factor that usually influences the decision on whether to raise equity finance is the relationship the directors have with existing dominant equity holders. If the dominant equity holders are supportive of the strategic decisions made by directors, then the directors are less likely to risk a change in the control status of the company. However, if the relationship is poor, the directors are more likely to opt for a new share issue. Finally, dividends are not tax deductible, making them expensive relative to debt finance.

Raising equity finance

Quoted equity: the exchanges
In the UK the main exchange is the **London Stock Exchange**. It has two key markets for equity shares: the **main market,** which is made up of shares in large companies, and the **Alternative Investment Market** (AIM), which caters for smaller companies. Another option is the **PLUS Market**, an independent UK market that has two exchanges: a **primary exchange**, which is aimed at providing a trading platform for medium and small companies wishing to raise equity finance (this competes with the AIM), and a **secondary market**, which provides an additional trading exchange for shares quoted elsewhere in London. In the ROI there is one exchange, the **Irish Stock Exchange**. It has two markets, the **official list** (large companies and government bonds) and the **IEX** (small-to-medium size companies).

The costs of flotation are high (as mentioned in the previous section); however, the London Stock Exchange claims that flotation on one of its markets:

> 'provides a company with access to one of the world's deepest pools of capital and is a proven way to grow a company over the medium and long term.' (Kussan, 2007)

Another advantage was cited by Patrick Smith in a BBC broadcast on 26 May, 2000, when he was discussing the reasons a diamond company from Zimbabwe and Congo was seeking a listing on the London Stock Exchange:

> 'they feel that a listing on the London Stock Exchange is going to give them international respectability'. (Smith, 2000)

Some of the benefits highlighted by the London Stock Exchange (Kussan, 2007) are as follows:

> **Benefits to a company of flotation**
>
> *Access to growth capital:* The opportunity to raise equity finance, both at the time of listing and through further capital raisings at a later stage.
>
> *Access to an acquisitions platform:* Increasing the potential to make acquisitions of other private or quoted companies.
>
> *An exit for equity holders:* Enabling existing investors to exit if they so choose, either on flotation or at a later date.
>
> *Increased credibility:* Reassuring customers and suppliers that the company has undergone a rigorous due diligence process and is appropriately governed.
>
> *Increased public profile:* Including more extensive press coverage and thus a greater awareness of the company and its products.
>
> *Attract, reward and incentivise staff:* Encouraging employee participation in the ownership of the company.
>
> Source: London Stock Exchange: Xenos technical sheet, Mark Kussan, 2007

Current company investors also benefit as the management of a plc has to be more accountable to its equity holders for decisions made, relative to non-public companies. Indeed, it is against stock exchange rules to fail to disclose information that may influence share price, whether good or bad. Information that would influence share price is termed '*price-sensitive information*'. This information need not be financial: for example, Microsoft announced, in the latter part of 2006, that Bill Gates would retire from the company in the next year. A company must have in place a board of non-executive directors to police the activities of the board of directors (see chapter two, 'The Role of Business Finance in Strategic Management and Influences on Business Finance Decision Making').

A government website, which aims to provide businesses with advice on business matters including raising finance, lists several disadvantages associated with flotation.

Disadvantages of flotation

Market risk: The company may become vulnerable to market fluctuations that are beyond its control.

Costs: Issue costs are high and yearly compliance costs are substantial.

Agency theory: When a company is floated, the directors have to consider the interests of the equity holders, not just their own. This may lead to conflict.

Loss of control: There will be a certain amount of loss of control of the company and ultimately the company may be taken over by another company.

Regulatory burden: Having publicly available shares increases the responsibility on directors and the exchange to ensure that appropriate regulatory requirements are adhered to, particularly in respect of corporate governance.

Managerial time tied up: The amount of managerial time required when a company floats is quite high; this means that other areas of the business are deprived of managerial attention.

Employee demotivation: If the company offers share options to some employees, this may cause others to become disgruntled.

> *Source: summarised from the guide 'Floating on a stock market: your options', http://www.businesslink.gov.uk/*

Which exchange?

There are several strategic decisions that will influence the decision on which exchange to issue shares. When a company goes public for the first time, the issue is referred to as an ***Initial Public Offering*** (IPO). Floating is a costly exercise and this effectively prohibits many companies, particularly small or medium-sized companies, from seeking this as a source of finance.

London Stock Exchange: main market
In February 2007, the London Stock Exchange website claimed that it had over 2,800 companies listed on its markets. The main market has:

'around 1,800 companies with a total market capitalisation of over £3,500bn' (London Stock Exchange, 2007)

Only very large companies that are seeking to raise large sums of capital will find that the benefits of a full official listing on the main market outweigh the costs (the sums required should be greater than €/£10 million). The company also has to be suitable from the stock exchange's perspective. To operative effectively, the exchanges need to ensure that companies trading are as their financial statements portray them to be. Indeed, to gain access to the main market of the London Stock Exchange, a company has to have a history and it will only be successful if that history portrays a pattern of secure earnings (which are increasing), with strong prospects for the future and a strong, experienced management team. To protect potential investors, the stock exchange has put in place steps to ensure that funds are not taken from the public, without the public having a voice in the control of a company. To this end, companies floated on the main market cannot issue non-voting shares and at least 25% of the total issued equity shares have to be held by the public. There are additional stringent regulatory requirements (many of which centre around policing the corporate governance of a company) and the initial flotation documents need to be approved by the UK Listing Authority, the Financial Services Authority (FSA). When a company is listed, it has to continue to adhere to high standards. It runs the risk of having trading in its shares suspended if it breaches the rules.

The main information required on flotation is contained in a company's *prospectus*. The aim of this glossy publication is to inform potential investors about a company. It is a key marketing tool, which will influence the success of a flotation and, therefore, runs the risk of being overly optimistic. It is the responsibility of the directors to ensure that the prospectus is not misleading; the UK Listing Authority vets the documentation to provide an independent check on the accuracy of the information being provided. The prospectus normally includes the following:

- details of the directors and the service contracts they have with the company. The directors should be appropriately qualified and have been with the company for over three years;
- details of the current major equity holders and the number of shares being issued relative to the shares already in issue. A listing is not allowed if one equity holder holds 30% or more of the share capital or has a controlling interest over the board of directors;
- a copy of the company's memorandum and articles of association;

- copies of three years' worth of audited financial statements showing the company has its own independent business. The financial statements should be prepared in compliance with legal and regulatory requirements including international accounting standards and should include a summary of key accounting policies;
- a summary of the gearing of the company;
- a statement on the adequacy of working capital;
- expert statements backing up directors' claims in respect of, for example, property values; and
- details of main contracts entered into by the company in the past two years, research and development activity and investments in other companies.

The requirement to have three years trading history is relaxed for scientific research-based companies and companies undertaking major capital investments, for example, *Euro Tunnel plc*.

After a company is listed on the main market, the directors have increased responsibilities towards the equity holders to supply them with any price-sensitive information when it comes to light. This normally means that public statements will have to be made in respect of any major developments affecting the company. Major developments typically include the sale or purchase of any material asset, profit announcements, dividend payout announcements, interim reports, final financial statements (within six months of the year end), changes in directors, share dealings/issues that are planned or directors' dealings with the company (including the purchase and sale of shares). The latter activity is severely restricted by law, so that insider trading cannot take place to benefit directors, who have more information about the company, to the detriment of equity holders.

The London Stock Exchange prepares an index of the weighted average price of its largest 100 companies (called the FTSE 100). It also prepares an index of the top 300 companies (called the FTSE 300). This is used by investors to gauge the performance of the equity market overall and to determine how the market responds to changes in government policy and interest rate changes.

The London Stock Exchange is itself a plc. In February 2007, the equity holders of London Stock Exchange successfully defended a hostile take over bid amounting to $5.1 billion from NASDAQ, the second largest market in the US (Timmons and Kanter, 2006). Indeed, only 0.41% of the equity holders accepted the offer (The Associated Press, 2007). This was NASDAQ's second attempt to take over the exchange. The future of the London Stock Exchange is uncertain at present: its dominance may be affected by the actions of seven leading banks (Merrill Lynch, Goldman Sachs, Deutsche Bank, Citigroup, Morgan Stanley, Credit Suisse and UBS) which are taking steps to set up their own exchange in London, as they believe the London Stock Exchange charges too much for trading. These banks account for about half of the trading activity on the London Stock Exchange (Dey, 2007).

The over-the-counter markets

Several transactions in shares do not go through any exchange; they are orchestrated between dealers who buy and sell to each other electronically. This keeps transaction costs low (though the dealers still have to be paid). Brokers who undertake such activities are termed **market makers** and the market for these types of transactions is referred to as the **over-the-counter** (OTC) market. The AIM and PLUS Markets are examples of OTC markets.

London Stock Exchange: AIM

The AIM was established by the London Stock Exchange in 1995 to replace the Unlisted Securities Market. The London Stock Exchange website claims that the AIM has:

> 'over 1,060 companies listed with a combined market capitalisation of £37bn.' (London Stock Exchange, 2007)

By 15 February 2007, 17 of the 18 IPOs made in 2007 were on the AIM, with only one on the main market (London Stock Exchange, 2007). The AIM is meant to provide a trading exchange for companies that are either too young or small to make flotation on the main market a possibility. It is normally suited to companies wishing to raise amounts up to €/£15 million. The cost of an IPO is usually about 10% to 12% of the total funds being raised. To be accepted on to the exchange, a company must appoint a **nominated adviser**, whose role is to ensure that the company complies with the rules and regulations of the AIM, and a **nominated broker** to assist with share transactions. The nominated adviser has to be retained for the whole period of listing. The regulatory requirements are not as stringent as those required on the main market. Unlike the main market, there is no minimum level of shares that need to be made available to the public and the company does not have to have been in existence for over three years. However, where the company is less than two years old, the existing equity holders must retain their holding for a period of one year after flotation before they start trading.

PLUS Market

The PLUS Market is operated and regulated by PLUS Market plc, a company authorised and regulated by the Financial Services Authority in London. As mentioned earlier, the PLUS Market has two main market services: a primary market and a secondary market. The first of these accepts IPOs mostly from small and medium-sized companies. Its securities are referred to as **PLUS quoted**. It is in direct competition with the AIM. Flotation is suited to companies wishing to raise amounts up to £10 million. The cost of an IPO is usually less than the costs associated with an AIM or main market flotation; however, they may still be up to 10% of the total funds being raised. A formal prospectus is not required, though an **admissions document** is required. It is not required where the sums being raised are below £250,000, or where the public offer: has a restricted distribution; is in connection with a takeover; or is in connection with an employee scheme. The yearly ongoing costs are also less. It is regulated, but the requirements are less stringent than the AIM.

> 'An issuer has to: be lawfully incorporated; ensure that its securities have been allotted and are freely transferable; make appropriate arrangements for the electronic settlement of transactions in its securities; and have a sufficient number of shares in public hands on admission to ensure an orderly market.' (PLUS Market Group plc Rules for Issuers: 23 October 1996)

In addition to this, the market requires that a **corporate adviser** is appointed and retained. A corporate adviser's role is similar to the role of a nominated adviser on the AIM exchange. In some instances, so long as a company has permission from PLUS Markets plc, it can still remain listed, without the services of a corporate adviser.

The Irish Stock Exchange

The Irish Stock Exchange first opened trading in Dublin in 1793. It is the main market for large Irish companies and Irish Government bonds.

According to the Irish Stock Exchange's *'Annual Statistical Review (2006)'*, the exchange has a total market capitalisation of €231,924 million (equity and bonds). The exchange has two markets: the official list and the IEX. The *official list* is similar to the main market of the London Stock Exchange, except on a smaller scale. In 2006, it had 46 companies listed, with a total market capitalisation for equity of €197,048 million (*Annual Statistical Review, 2006*). The entrance requirements are the same as for the London Stock Exchange, as are the regulations and ongoing requirements. The IEX is tailored for small-to-medium size companies. It commenced trading on 12 April, 2005 and took over from the 'Developing Market' and the 'Exploration Market', both of which ceased to exist after this date. All eight companies from the Developing Market and the Exploration Market transferred to it on this date. By the end of 2006, the IEX had 23 companies listed, with a total market capitalisation of €2,464 million. The Irish Stock Exchange prepares an index (*the Irish Stock Exchange Quotation (ISEQ)*) of the weighted average price of all the shares listed on its exchange. This is similar in nature to the FTSE index of the London Stock Exchange. The exchange is regulated by the Financial Regulator (the Irish Financial Services Regulatory Authority), a component of the Central Bank and Financial Services Authority of Ireland (IFSRA, 2007).

Methods of obtaining a listing

There are several approaches to obtaining a public issue, including an offer for sale by prospectus, an issue by tender, a placing, a vendor placing and a stock exchange introduction. These processes all involve a financial adviser/issuing house/sponsor company. The sponsor company not only administers the actual purchase and sale of the shares, but also advises the company on; the price to charge for each share; the contents of the prospectus and how to market, prepare and timetable the issue; and identify the correct type of issue to pursue. This decision will take into account the reputation of the company, stability and growth in its profits, its liquidity, the motives for flotation and, finally, the cost of each option available to the company. The approaches available for raising equity finance in the markets are now considered.

Offer for sale by prospectus

An *offer for sale by prospectus* is the most expensive method of issuing shares to the public and is obligatory if the sums being sought publicly exceed £30 million. There are three main steps to the process, as highlighted in the following diagram:

The offer for sale by prospectus process

1. The company sells the shares it wishes to issue to the sponsor company.
2. The public applies for shares and pays the sponsor.
3. The sponsor company issues the shares to the public at a fixed price; where there has been an oversubscription, the sponsor issues a refund for the shares not allocated.
4. The sponsor pays the company the proceeds of the issue, less an agreed commission.

There are many other parties involved in preparing and guiding the process. A full prospectus and application form will have to be prepared and advertised in the national press. Therefore, the company will require the services of accountants, solicitors, advertisers, graphic designers and a broker, as well as the sponsor company. Some of these parties will help the company to come up with a suitable price at which to offer the shares to the public. Brokers provide specialist advice on the timing of the issue, given that market, hence market price, can be impacted on by many factors that are outside the control of the company.

Getting the price right is a crucial decision. If the price is set too low, the issue will damage the wealth of existing equity holders; if it is set too high, the company runs the risk of the full issue not being taken up. The latter is hedged against as the sponsor company usually *under-writes* the issue. This is a form of insurance, which guarantees the company the full amount of the capital it wishes to raise by contracting with the sponsor company to purchase all the shares that have not been taken up by the public. To reduce its exposure, the sponsor company usually *sub-underwrites* the issue, by contracting with several other intermediaries to take up a portion of the issue, where a residual of shares remain after the issue. This rarely happens in practice. If it were to happen to a company, it would severely damage the company's ability to raise funds by an equity issue in the future. However, some sponsor companies use sta-bilising methods to effectively underwrite an IPO. *Stabilising* happens when the sponsor company, or its sub-underwriters, purchase large quan-tities of the new issue on the market at a price not exceeding the issue price. It is allowed by law, though is seen as a form of price manipulation and reduces the transparency of the market, as the purchaser is not made known. Murdoch (2000) reported that stabilising techniques were used in the IPO of iTouch to maintain its IPO share price of 70p.

Offer for sale by subscription

An *offer for sale by subscription* is similar to an offer for sale by prospectus, except that it is partially underwritten. This method is usually used by new companies which have problems getting a full underwritten agree-ment from their sponsor. If insufficient public demand materialises, the company has the option to abort the issue.

Issue by tender

This method is popular in the US. It is commonly used in the UK if there are no comparable companies listed on the stock exchange to use as a guide when pricing the shares. The process for an *issue by tender* is exactly the same as that outlined above for an offer for sale by subscription, except that the price of the issue is not fixed. The same parties are involved and as a result the costs are also high; however, they are not as high as the costs of an offer for sale by prospectus. In this scenario, members of the public are invited to tender for the shares. They get one shot at it. When the tenders are received by the sponsor company, a strike price is determined. This takes into account the weight of applications at the prices bid. The *strike price* is the price at which the shares will be sold. It is determined by supply and demand and therefore there is less chance of the shares being underpriced (as long as management have produced sufficient information in the prospectus, and application, to reduce any information asymmetry about the future earnings of a company). Any bidders who offered the strike price or above will be awarded shares; any bidders who offered an amount below the strike price do not qualify for any shares on issue and they will have to wait until the shares start trading on the exchange before they can purchase them. Any bidders who offered sums above the strike price will be allocated the number of shares requested at the strike price and given a refund for the surplus.

Placing
An IPO can also be achieved by a *private issue*. This avenue is open to well established, large companies with strong reputations. In these instances, the companies can forgo the large costs of a public issue and go for a *private placing*. A private placing is usually organised by an intermediary (broker firm or an issuing house/sponsor). In these circumstances, an intermediary buys all the shares from the company at a fixed price and places them with selected clients. This is a less expensive method of getting shares quoted on a stock exchange. It usually costs about 5% of the total funds raised. It is commonly used by smaller companies seeking a listing on the AIM. The process is outlined in the following diagram:

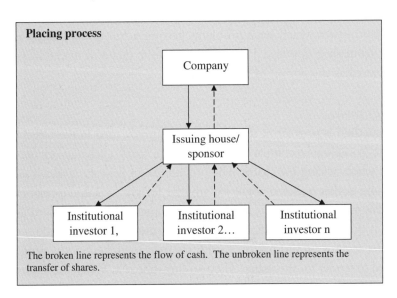

Placing process

The broken line represents the flow of cash. The unbroken line represents the transfer of shares.

The public has to wait until official share trading begins on the stock exchange before they can purchase shares in the company. To ensure marketability of the shares, the stock exchange usually requires that several institutional investors are involved in the initial placing. These large investors are usually pension companies, insurance companies, stock broker companies, merchant banks and commercial banks. The sponsor invites them to take up the shares on issue.

The largest amount of equity issued to date in a private deal in Ireland, happened in October 2006 (reported in *The Irish Times*). Barry O' Callaghan, chief executive in Riverdeep, an educational software firm, was looking to raise $3.33 billion for the purchase of Houghton Mifflin (a Boston publisher). The entrepreneur had already received $3.136 billion from investment-banking institutions (raised privately) and required a further $200 million to close the deal. Dublin's largest stock-broker arranged a private meeting between O'Callaghan and about 150 of its richest clients in the Four Seasons Hotel, Dublin. This was a closed-door meeting and the attendees were required to sign a confidentiality clause. The minimum stake disclosed at the meeting was €1 million. Within a week, Davy Stockbrokers reported that the placing had been:

'significantly oversubscribed'. (Beesley, 2007)

Intermediaries offer

Another variant of the placing method is the ***intermediaries offer***. This approach effectively cuts out the role of the sponsor company and the broker. It is only an option for large, very reputable companies. The issue is not underwritten and hence is less costly. In this instance, the company approaches several large institutional investors and brokers and asks them to tender for shares. The brokers and institutions subsequently sell the shares to their clients. When using this approach, the resultant number of equity holders can be quite low – this undermines the liquidity of the shares. To counteract this, the stock exchange usually insists that a large number of final equity holders should result. The process is shown diagrammatically as follows:

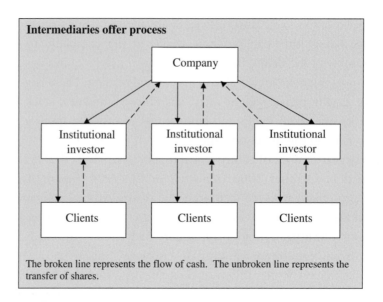

Vendor placing

A **vendor placing** occurs when a company wishes to purchase another company using a share issue, but the other company wants to receive cash for its shares (it does not want to hold the purchasing company's shares on its books). The process is achieved by the following steps. The purchasing company issues shares to the company being purchased, in return for all its shares. The company being purchased then sells the shares to an institutional investor, for cash. Therefore, the purchasing company gains a new subsidiary in return for shares and the subsidiary's equity holders get cash from selling the shares on to an institutional investor. The agreement with the institutional investor is usually pre-arranged.

Stock exchange introduction

A **stock exchange introduction** is usually only available to companies that are already listed, or have over 25% of their shares already held by the public and these equity holders do not wish to sell their holdings. In these instances, the remaining shares are introduced to the market. Investors in the new market will purchase the shares from the existing equity holders. The price will be determined by demand for the shares relative to the willingness of the current equity holders to sell at the price offered. This method is the cheapest as no money changes hands, there are no underwriting fees, there is no need to prepare a prospectus and limited advertising is required. It normally occurs when companies that are quoted on the AIM wish to transfer their holding to the main market to gain access to a wider investor pool. Indeed, some companies make the strategic decision to join the AIM, with the objective of getting an introduction to the main market in the future.

Equity issues after initial listing

After a company is listed on an official exchange, it is easier and not as costly to obtain finance from further share issues. The most common method used to issue further equity shares is a rights issue. A *rights issue* invites the existing equity holders to subscribe for new shares in the same proportions as their existing equity holdings. Therefore, if a company has 2,000,000 issued ordinary shares and decides to issue a further 1,000,000 ordinary shares, every equity holder who holds two shares will be entitled to purchase one additional share in the company. This would be called a 'one for two' rights issue. Companies that are already listed, time the issue carefully to ensure that the market is high when the issue is made, hence maximising the cash the company receives from the issue. To encourage equity holders to take up a new issue, the company normally issues the shares at a discount of 15% to 20% of the current market price.

In the UK, companies have to issue shares using a rights issue as equity holders legally have *pre-emptive rights* to new shares. This allows existing equity holders to retain their relative portion (or control) of a company. Pre-emptive rights can be waived by a special resolution, supported by greater than 75% of the equity holders in attendance at an Annual General Meeting (AGM). Where this agreement is sought, the new shares cannot be issued at a discount of greater than 10% of market price, so that current equity holder wealth is protected to some extent.

Valuing rights/equity holdings

When a company makes a rights issue, the process tries to ensure that no equity holder is disadvantaged, even where they do not take up a rights issue. To make this work, a value is placed on the right to purchase the new shares. The existing equity holders have three options: they can purchase the new shares at a discount, sell the right to purchase the shares at a discount or do nothing, in which case the company sells the right to purchase the shares on behalf of the equity holder, forwarding the proceeds less any costs of sale. The following example is provided to show how the process works and how equity holder value is affected. The market price at which shares are expected to trade after a rights issue is called the *theoretical ex-rights price*.

Worked example 7.1　(Rights issue)

Rojo plc has recently announced a 'one-for-four' rights issue. The price of a share before the announcement was €/£3.00 and the current equity holders will be given pre-emptive rights to purchase new shares at €/£2.00 each.

REQUIRED

a) Calculate the theoretical ex-rights price.

b) Calculate the value of each right (assuming it is attached to an existing share).

c) Calculate the price at which each equity holder can sell their right (i.e. the value of the right, assuming it is attached to a new share).

d) An equity holder owns 1,000 shares. Calculate the value and number of shares in his possession before and after the rights issue assuming that he purchases the new shares.

e) An equity holder owns 1,000 shares. Calculate the value of his holding after the rights issue assuming that the equity holder sells the rights.

f) Assume the equity holder is short of cash. Calculate the number of rights the equity holder has to sell to provide cash to purchase the balance available to him. Show the value and number of shares in his possession after the rights issue.

g) Assume the equity holder does nothing. Calculate the value and number of shares in his possession before and after the rights issue and the monies given to him by the company.

Continued

Solution

a)   Each lot of four shares is currently worth:

(4 × €/£3.00)	€/£12.00
One new issue will be priced at: (1 × €/£2.00)	€/£2.00
The total holding is worth	€/£14.00

Therefore, after the issue the theoretical
ex-rights share price expected will be:

(€/£14.00/5)	€/£2.80

b)   The value of the right attached to each existing share will be:
€/£3.00 − €/£2.80 = €/0.20 per existing share.

c)   The value of the right were it assumed to be attached to the
new share is:
(€/£2.80 − €/£2.00) €/£0.80 per new share.
This can also be found by multiplying the existing shares
required to qualify for a new share by the value of the rights
per current share: (€/£0.20 × 4 = €/£0.80)

d)   *Before:*
The equity holder owned 1,000 shares valued

at €/£3.00 per share: (1,000 × €/£3.00)	€/£3,000

To have received the 250 new shares, the
equity holder will have to pay the company:

(250 × €/£2.00)	€/£500

After: the equity holder will own:
1,250 (1,000 + (1,000/4)) shares valued
at €/£2.80. The total holding will be worth:

(1,250 × €/£2.80)	€/£3,500

Therefore the equity holder's wealth has not increased, but the
company will have €/£500 additional cash to invest in projects.

e)   *Before:* the equity holder owned 1,000
shares valued at €/£3.00 per share:

(1,000 × €/£3,000)	€/£3,000

After: the equity holder decides to sell his
rights. He is issued with 250 rights, which
he can sell for €/£0.80 each, so he gets cash

worth: (250 × €/£0.80)	€/£200

Continued

He still has his 1,000 shares, though they are worth €/£2.80 each after the issue:
(1,000 × €/£2.80)   €/£2,800
Total equity holder value: €/£3,000

f)   The number of shares the equity holder can purchase can be calculated using the following formula:

$$\frac{\text{Rights price} \times \text{number of shares allotted}}{\text{Theoretical ex-rights price}}$$

(€/£0.80 × 250)/€/£2.80 = 71 shares

Therefore, the equity holder will have to sell (250 – 71) 179 rights, providing him with cash of: (179 × €/£0.80)   €/£143.20
He will use this to purchase 71 shares at €/£2.00 each: (71 × €/£2.00)   €/£142.00
(The difference is rounding.)
After the sale, the equity holder will have:
1,071 shares valued at €/£2.80 =   €/£2,998.80

(equivalent to his original investment of €/£3,000 – small rounding difference)

g)   The company will sell the rights at an auction and reimburse the equity holder the proceeds, net of costs incurred in selling the rights: (€/£0.80 × 250 = €/£200)
A cheque for €/£200, less any auction fees, will be issued to the equity holder by the company.

Scrip issue

A ***scrip issue*** involves issuing shares to existing equity holders, in proportion to their existing holding. A scrip issue does not involve the transfer of any cash; it splits the value of equity into smaller portions.

Worked example 7.2   (Scrip issue)

Rojo plc has recently announced a 'one-for-four' bonus issue. The price of shares before the announcement was €/£3.00.

REQUIRED

An equity holder owns 1,000 shares. Calculate the total value, value per share and number of shares in his possession before and after the bonus issue.

Solution

Before: $(1,000 \times €/£3.00)$ €/£3,000

The equity holder is issued with (1,000/4) 250 shares

After: the equity holder will have 1,250 shares worth: €/£3,000

The value per share will fall to: $(€/£3,000/1,250)$ €/£2.40

The main reason for this type of transaction is to reduce the market price of individual shares in order to make them more marketable.

Bonus issues

A **bonus issue** is otherwise known as a **capitalisation issue.** Funds from a company's reserves are converted into shares which are then issued to equity holders. The company is converting past profits not paid out as dividends into equity share capital. This is an accounting adjustment.

Share splits

This is similar to a share issue, except that the nominal value of all the shares in the company is reduced or split. The aim of a share split is to reduce the market price of the share, which should make the shares more marketable and improve the volume of trading in shares.

Worked example 7.3   (Share split)

Rojo plc has recently announced a 'two-for-one' share split. The price of shares before the announcement was €/£3.00. The nominal value of each share before the split was €/£1.00.

Continued

REQUIRED

An equity holder owns 1,000 shares. Calculate the total market value, market value per share, nominal value per share and number of shares in his possession before and after the bonus issue.

Solution

Before: the equity holder has 1,000 €/£1.00 equity
shares valued at €/£3.00: (1,000 × €/£3.00)   €/£3,000

The equity holder is issued with (1,000 × 2) 2,000 new shares and the old shares are cancelled:

After: the equity holder will now have 2,000 50c/p
equity shares valued at: €/£3,000

The market value per share will be: (€/£3,000/2,000)   €/£1.50

Preference shares

Preference shares are part of a company's share capital; however, they are not usually regarded as equity. They have similar characteristics. They may be issued at a premium above their nominal value, the dividend can be waived and they can be traded in the markets. However, they usually carry a fixed dividend (a percentage of the nominal value), do not confer voting rights to their holders (unless the dividend goes into arrears, or the company goes into liquidation, whereupon they have the same voting rights as creditors), may be redeemable or may be convertible. Like any public share issue, raising finance by issuing preference shares is costly and the return required by preference shareholders is quite high (higher than the return required by bond holders, though not as high as the return required by equity holders). This is connected to the risks faced by each type of security holder. Preference shareholders rank after debt and bond holders, but in front of equity holders, when it comes to the payment of interest and dividends and also on the liquidation of a company. Therefore, the risks preference shareholders face is not as great as the risk faced by equity holders – hence the return required is less. Several types of preference shares can be issued (see below). Shares may have more than one characteristic; for example, they can be redeemable, convertible, non-cumulative or participating shares. An example showing the combination of types of preference shares owned by a company is included at the back of this chapter (Viridian Group plc).

Common terms used to describe preference shares

Irredeemable: **Irredeemable preference shares** carry a fixed dividend and are not intended to be redeemed or converted into shares by the company. The shareholders can sell the shares in the markets to liquidate their capital.

Redeemable: **Redeemable preference shares** are issued for a set period of time. When the redemption date arrives, the company pays the holder of the preference shares the nominal value of the shares.

Cumulative: **Cumulative preference shares** afford protection to the shareholder over their yearly claim on the dividend distribution. The dividend becomes a creditor when it is waived. Dividends cannot be paid to equity holders until the total of the cumulative preference dividends outstanding are honoured.

Non-cumulative: When dividends on **non-cumulative preference shares** are waived, the shareholder loses their right to the dividend for that year.

Participating: The holders of **participating preference shares** can 'participate' in the gains of a company, when it performs well. This makes these shares more attractive to potential investors.

Convertible: **Convertible preference shares** may be converted to equity share capital at some specified date in the future or if the company achieves pre-determined performance targets. They are usually converted at a premium so that current equity holders are not disadvantaged.

Classifying preference shares

When it comes to accounting for preference shares, difficulties arise. Under international accounting standards, preference shares have to be categorised as either debt or equity and included in the appropriate section of a company's balance sheet. However, preference shares cannot be categorically classified as either element. In practice, the terms of each preference share issue have to be reviewed and aligned as either more like debt or more like equity. The following figure highlights characteristics that can be used to class preference shares as either debt or equity:

Categorising preference shares as debt or equity instruments

Debt	**Equity**
Cumulative	Non-cumulative
Redeemable	Irredeemable
Non-participating	Participating
Non-convertible	Convertible

Preference shares: investor's perspective

Preference shares are attractive to investors because they provide a fixed yearly return that is in excess of the return earned on bonds. They rank in front of equity when it comes to having their claims met. When preference shares are issued by public issue, a readily available market exists; therefore, investors have an exit avenue at all times. The liquidity makes them attractive. When preference shares are convertible, there is an added attraction: they may be converted into equity share capital, if the company performs well. Thereafter, the investor will be able to share in the fortunes of the successful company. Where the shares are redeemable, the investors are certain of getting a set cash flow on a specified date. So long as the company is not in financial difficulties, this allows investors to plan and manage their cash flows.

On the down side, preference shares are more risky than bond investments. They rank behind bond investments, both in terms of yearly distributions and on liquidation. In addition, preference shareholders do not usually benefit when a company performs well (unless they are participating), as their dividend is fixed.

Preference shares: company's perspective

Companies also find preference shares attractive because dividends can be waived. Even where dividends are cumulative and have to be paid at some point in the future, the fact that they can be waived provides the company with assurance that cash can be retained in the business for operating activity purposes when there are liquidity problems – dividends can be paid at a later stage when the liquidity issues are solved. In addition, preference shares do not confer ownership rights on the holder; therefore, issuing them does not upset the ownership structure of a company. This is particularly important where the current dominant equity holders support management decision making. When the company does well, unlike equity holders, preference shareholders cannot make a claim for a larger return; their dividend is set (unless they hold participating shares). This allows management to retain more funds for investment, resulting in more capital growth and a rise in the share price of equity shares, or allows an even greater dividend to be distributed to equity holders. Where preference shares are convertible, gearing will be improved after the conversion date. This may relax restrictive covenants and allow management the option of raising additional finance, which they can use to take on more investments, resulting in growth. Finally, preference shares are another possible source of finance when the company is highly geared and has problems raising debt finance.

On the down side, preference shares are an expensive source of capital. They cost more than debt to issue, have a higher yearly payout (the cost of which is accentuated by the fact that preference dividends are not tax deductible) and in many cases have to be repaid, or converted, at some point in the future. If they are redeemable, this may cause cash flow problems for the company. If they are convertible, the ownership structure of the company may change, resulting in a change in the control of the company. The next example highlights the difference in cost between preference shares and bonds to a company.

Worked example 7.4   (Preference shares)

A plc has the following capital structure:

	€/£'000
Ordinary shares of 50c/p each	5,200
Reserves	4,850
9% preference shares	4,500
14% debentures	5,000
	19,550

The preference shares are trading at 63c/p and the debentures (irredeemable) at par. Corporation tax is 33%.

REQUIRED

a)   Calculate the cost of the preference shares and the debentures to the company.

b)   Assume that, instead of the 14% debentures, the company raised the €/£5 million by way of preference shares giving the same yield as the existing preference shares. What is the effect on earnings available to the equity holders?

(ICAI, MABF II Autumn 1997, Extract from Question 5(b))

Solution

a)   Cost of preference shares. This is calculated as the yearly dividend divided by the market price per share (see chapter 12, 'Cost of Capital'). In this instance, this is $9c/p/63c/p = 14.29\%$.

The cost of the debentures to the company is the interest (less tax) divided by the market price per debenture (see chapter 12 and the section in this chapter on valuing bonds). In this instance, this is $14c/p(1-0.33)/100c/p = 9.38\%$. This shows that the cost of debt (9.38%) is lower than the cost of the preference shares (14.29%) to the company.

Continued

b)   The current situation means that the equity holders have to forgo the following amount of earnings to service the debentures:

Yearly interest charge: (€/£5,000,000 × 14%)   €/£700,000
Less reduction in tax in the year:
(€/£700,000 × 33%)   €/£231,000
Net earnings cost of the debenture
to the company   €/£469,000

To raise €/£5,000,000 the company would need to issue: €/£5,000,000/€/£0.63 = 7,936,508 preference shares. The yearly cost then would be the dividend payable on these new shares. The dividend is 9c/p per year.

Yearly dividend charge: (7,936,508 × €/£0.09)   €/£714,286
Therefore, the earnings available for distribution to the equity holders will fall by: (€/£714,286 − €/£469,000)
                                                €/£245,286

Equity: unquoted companies

This chapter to date has considered raising equity finance through the markets. This option is really only viable for large, well-established companies. The AIM and the PLUS Market do try to cater for smaller-sized companies; in practice, though, issue costs (even in these markets) are prohibitive to virtually all small companies and many medium-sized companies.

The finance needs of most small companies can be met from capital introduced by the private equity holders' who own the company, retained earnings or bank-sourced debt. A *finance gap* emerges when new companies require a certain scale or small companies start to grow. In these instances, the bank usually does not wish to provide all the finance – the risks are too great. There are usually insufficient retained earnings and the private equity holders do not have the wealth to support a large scale venture; yet the finance requirement is not large enough to substantiate flotation. This finance gap is also referred to as the *equity gap*. In the UK, the finance gap is, to some extent, met by venture capitalists. In NI, the amount of venture capital raised has not been at the levels expected, since the province achieved peace in 1994. Simpson (2001) commented on the surge of:

> 'blow-in pinstripe suits looking for a bargain and grants galore!'

However, noted that:

> 'it didn't happen and I would argue, we are still struggling to make venture capital happen today.'

He suggests that a stumbling block to the growth of venture capital finance in Northern Ireland is the requirement of venture capitalists to get a quick exit. He moots that most entrepreneurs from NI do not emotionally wish to lose control of their venture. By 2001, BCO Technologies, located in West Belfast, was the only start-up venture capital backed (as well as being backed with substantial grants from the Industrial Development Board) company to achieve flotation and subsequent sale (to a large American technologies company). The main terms of the sale were agreed in spring 2000, though it nearly collapsed in June 2000 when the NI political situation reached its annual climax and the rest of the world perceived NI to be at war. It was eventually sold for £101 million. The founders received eight percent of the spoils.

Venture capital

Venture capital is provided by venture capitalists to finance high-risk, high-return projects, with high-growth potential. It is also known as *private equity finance*. The expectation is that a successful investment will yield a 30% annual return, though this depends on the risk of the investment and the type of funding provided.

3i invested £22 million for a 16.2% stake in Petrofac in May 2002. The company was listed on the stock exchange and 3i sold its share in the business for over £120 million: Representing an earnings multiple of 5.6 times on its investment (or an IRR of 67%). The initial funding was used to reinforce the balance sheet during a period of rapid growth and to help Petrofac transform itself from an Engineering Procurement Construction Contractor into a total integrated facilities management solutions provider.

Source: http://3i.com/media/press-release/petrofac_011005.html

---

Two out of ten venture capital deals usually have excellent results, six range from good to poor and two usually fail. In general, venture capitalists will consider offering loans of €/£250,000 or more, though deals ranging from €/£1,000,000 to €/£6,000,000 are becoming more common. Venture capitalists usually require an equity stake in the company in return for their investment, though they may also keep part of their stake as debt, as this is less risky than equity and is more likely to provide a return. Interest has to be paid, whereas dividends can be waived. In addition, debt has to be repaid, whereas equity does not and, finally, equity shares are not marketable.

Venture capital is normally only provided for companies that have a track record, though in some instances capital will be provided based on the strength of the project or idea, the quality of the managerial team (entrepreneurial skills) and the expectation of the project becoming a success. The various types of projects that ventures capitalists are approached with are as follows:

Types of projects seeking venture capital

Seed corn venture capital: **Seed corn venture capital** is difficult to obtain and generally involves funding an idea or the creation of a prototype. Corporate venture capitalists trading in intellectual capital industries are the best source of this type of capital. It is an inexpensive way for them to invest in research and development. The government is also supportive of this type of venture and provides incentives to venture capitalists to invest in them.

Start-up venture capital: **Start-up venture capital** involves developing an idea further and starting to produce the product. This will naturally follow on from a successful seed corn venture and the same venture capitalists will usually support the next stage in the development of the new company. At this stage there are usually no sales and the risk of not receiving a return is high.

Early stage venture capital: **Early stage venture capital** is provided for successful start ups that are starting to trade. The company is usually not yet profitable and is likely to be sourcing markets for its products.

Continued

Growth venture capital: **Growth venture capital** projects are less risky, relative to the earlier types. The company is usually successful, but does not have the capitalisation to fund growth. The growth plan is usually ambitious and may involve expanding sales overseas. The funds are usually used to increase working capital, in support of growth.

Management buy out: This is the venture that is most commonly supported by venture capitalists. A **management buy out** (MBO) usually occurs where a parent company no longer sees a section of its business as being part of its strategic plan. In these instances, the management buy the section, backed by large personal investments (usually placing themselves in debt), large amounts of debt finance and venture capital finance (usually 15–20%). Venture capitalists are interested in this type of venture, as they consider that management are more aware of the future prospects of the company than the parent company (information asymmetry).

Management buy in: A **management buy in** (MBI) is where the management team of one company purchases the shares of a similar company and assumes responsibility for the running of the company. The arguments for financing these ventures are similar to those for an MBO. The value placed on this type of project by venture capitalists depends on the reputation and experience of the management team.

Combination of a **management buy in and buy out** (BIMBO): This is a combination of the latter two types, wherein the management of a company gets together with the management of a similar type of company, to buy a company and run it together.

Venture capitalists usually aim to get a 30–40% share of the company in return for their investment. They like to have a veto on some decisions, such as the raising of additional finance, the distribution of dividends and the sale of the company. In addition, venture capitalists like the company to have a clear exit plan for liquidising the venture capitalists' investment – usually in a five-to-seven-year timescale. The most common **exit strategies** are outlined in the following figure:

Common exit strategies

1. *Flotation:* This is the most attractive option to venture capitalists, however, will only happen if the company is very successful.

2. *Management buy back:* The current management team agrees terms at the outset at which to buy back the shares from the venture capitalists at a specified date in the future.

3. *Sale to an institutional investor:* If the company is successful enough, the venture capitalists may approach an institutional investor to buy out their holding. The institutional investor will usually only be interested if it is likely that the company will eventually float or will be taken over by another company.

4. *Sale of the whole company:* In this instance, the whole company will be sold to another company. This usually happens when smaller research companies strike gold; larger, more established companies will pay a premium to access the new intellectual capital.

The company usually benefits from the relationship with the venture capitalist in more ways than just receiving much needed cash at a low issue price. If the investment is all equity, then dividends can be waived. In addition, the venture capitalist may provide business expertise (financial planning, marketing advice) and trade contacts. Venture capitalists ultimately have the same objective as management – to foster a successful, growing company. They may be prepared to provide future capital injections. On the down side, the current equity holders will experience a loss in control, a loss in earnings and will have to justify their decision making and be accountable to the venture capitalist.

Venture capital providers

There are four main providers of venture capital: venture capital companies; captive firms; financial institutions providing venture capital trusts; corporate venturing; and business angels. These are now explained in turn:

Venture capital companies

Venture capital companies are independent companies that are set up initially by private venture capital individuals to raise funds and invest in venture capital projects. The aim is to invest in projects that are likely to achieve a flotation and to sell the shares in the company when this is achieved. The largest and best known venture capital company in the UK is '*3i*'. It is listed on the main market of the London Stock Exchange. According to the company's website, *3i* considers itself to be a world leader in private equity and venture capital. It focuses on: buyouts; growth capital; and venture capital, and invests in companies across Europe, the US and in Asia Pacific.

Captive firms

Captive firms are usually subsidiaries of large intermediaries such as banks, insurance companies and pension companies. They are created as specialist companies to invest a portion of their parent company's portfolio in riskier ventures, which have the potential to make large returns.

Financial institutions providing Venture Capital Trusts (VCT)

These are similar in nature to captive firms except the financial intermediary offers a VCT direct to their clients, for their investment. To promote investment into entrepreneurial ventures, the government introduced a tax break, in 1995, for all investors who invest in VCT (see below for information on the tax relief available to investors). A *VCT* invests into a range of high-risk, venture capital deals, with several companies. These companies must have less than £10 million in net assets on their balance sheet and cannot be quoted on the main market. Each year a qualifying company can request up to £1 million in finance from a VCT. The VCT is limited to investing a maximum of 15% of its capital in each company. This ensures that there is some diversification of risks. Investors can buy units in this trust, similar to any other investment trust.

Corporate venturing

Corporate venturing occurs when a large company supports a small company in the early stages of its development, or when it undertakes a new venture. The large company usually takes a small equity stake in the company, in return for finance. It is usually a symbiotic relationship with the large company: getting tax relief from the government on the sums invested and on the capital gain made if shares are held for more than three years; gaining access to the small company's intellectual capital; selling products to it; or getting access to a new market. The small company gains: finance; technical resources; help with strategic and financial management; and access to a wider market.

Business angels

Business angels are private equity investors who will invest in high-risk, high-return companies. They typically require an equity investment, though may hold both debt and equity in a company. They are usually wealthy individuals who have surplus cash and wish to use it in an entrepreneurial manner. There is an element of altruism in respect of the motives behind many business angels. They usually invest in local ventures and are keen to see them succeed for the benefit of the community, as well as for their own benefit. Business angels typically invest between €/£10,000 and €/£200,000 and do not push for as early an exit route, as other venture capital providers. They usually require that a company has a trading history, though are more likely to invest in seed corn, or start-up ventures, than other venture capital providers. Many like a hands-on approach and often require the terms of the finance agreement to allow them to sit on the board of directors and have a veto on some decisions. They are usually successful business persons who can contribute to the strategy and financial management of a company. Companies that are looking for business angels are usually put into contact with them by their bank, accountants, solicitors, corporate acquaintances or by searching the World Wide Web. There are dedicated sites set up to assist in this introduction process – some are listed at the end of this chapter.

The Government's invisible hand: solving the financing gap problem

Over the decades the British Government has pursued a policy of encouraging investment in entrepreneurial companies. Aware of the high risks that investors face when they invest in entrepreneurial companies, the British Government started a scheme in 1981 to allow tax relief for qualifying companies (**Business Expansion Scheme** (BES)). Companies could raise up to £500,000 each year under this scheme from private individuals, who each could invest up to £40,000. The private individual would get full income tax relief on the capital invested (40% if a higher rate tax payer), in the year invested and would also qualify for full capital gains tax exemption on the sale of the shares in the company, so long as they are held for longer than five years. In the 1990s the qualifying activities were extended to include investment in residential property on short leasehold terms – the amount that companies could raise under the scheme was raised to £5 million. Investing in residential property is not very risky and many accountants took advantage of the loophole, by setting up investment property companies and selling the shares in those companies to their clients, who benefited from large tax advantages and a positive return on their investment after five years. The government abolished the scheme in December 1993 as they considered it was being used for tax avoidance, not the promotion of entrepreneurial activities.

The Department of Enterprise, Trade and Employment of the Irish Government also supports a BES for qualifying companies (manufacture, tourism, research and development, international services). It undertook a review of companies who have partaken in the scheme (1,391 companies) in 2006. Of the 491 who responded to the survey: 70% classed themselves as start-up, or development companies; 60% employed less than 15 people and 65% had turnover below €1 million with 56% reporting their turnover came from exporting activities. 75% of the companies who responded indicated that they have raised on average €500,000 under the BES. (Source: ICAI website, accessed 14 February 2007).

A tighter type of scheme, the *Enterprise Investment Scheme* (EIS), was introduced by the British Government in January 1994 with the same objectives as the initial BES; however, has less generous tax relief advantages. Under this new scheme, investors can invest up to £100,000 per annum in a qualifying company (not quoted on the main market and undertaking a qualifying activity – not property investment or financial investment activities). This initial investment can benefit from 20% income tax relief and qualifies for capital gains tax relief, if the shares are held for over three years. If capital losses are made, these can be set off against other income, for the purpose of calculating the income tax liability, in the year the shares are sold. Any dividends received on the equity investment are also tax free. Companies can raise up to £1 million each year under this scheme.

A further scheme was introduced in 1995 (mentioned above) *venture capital trusts* (VCT). Investors to this type of company will receive the same tax benefits as are available to investors in EIS companies. The only difference is that the investor must retain the shares for five years, to qualify for the tax relief.

In July 2005 the Government introduced another scheme to help to promote investment in entrepreneurial type companies, the *Enterprise Capital Funds* Scheme (ECFs). £200 million was set aside to match against private funding that is supplied from venture capitalists and business angels. Each company can apply to receive up to £2 million in funding from the ECF. In England the *Regional Venture Capital Fund* (RVCF) also provides risk capital of up to £500,000 per applying company, if matched by investment from a venture capitalist or business angel.

Conclusion

Raising equity capital is time consuming and can be expensive. There are many options available: some are suitable, others are not. What is of importance is the need to get the option correct. It is a complicated decision which requires expert help (particularly where an IPO is being considered). Raising equity finance can take anything from three months to over two years to complete. As it is costly, it is important that a company is ready for it in advance, indeed as the prospectus requires three years' financial information the company should be gearing up for an issue for this period of time. Steps taken can include: preparing financial statements in accordance with international accounting standards and setting up the structures within the company to enable it to comply with the stock exchange regulations; giving a suitably qualified person responsibility for preparing the company for flotation; getting advice from market advisers including the stock exchange's own advisers; and deciding on the best approach to achieving the most beneficial IPO for the company.

Though raising venture capital is cheaper initially; the returns required by venture capitalists over the five-to-seven-year period are high. If a project is successful then venture capitalists stand to gain much financially, for what seems like little effort relative to the entrepreneurs' input. This may cause conflict. A strong personal relationship between a company's management and the venture capitalists needs to be maintained for the full duration of an investment. Companies raising finance in this manner should see the venture capitalists, not only as providers of funds, but as business partners who can provide valuable strategic and business advice and contacts.

Examination standard question

Worked example

REQUIRED

a)   Outline the principal characteristics of the following sources of finance currently used by DOBBIN:
  (i) Venture capital
  (ii) Redeemable debentures
(ICAI, MABF II, Summer 2006, Extract from Question 7)

Solution

a)   (i) Venture capital is capital committed to an unproven venture in return for an equity stake and possible board representation. It is often associated with: business start-ups; development of new products/markets; management buyouts; or the realisation of an investment.

The initial, start-up money is referred to as 'seed money' and entails the greatest risk. If the project gets off the ground it may require additional financing at additional 'rounds', or the 'mezzanine level', before the company is finally brought to the market and the venture capitalist can enjoy handsome rewards.

Experienced investors in venture capital situations typically plan on turning away a minimum of nine out of every ten proposals which are brought to them, and then they expect as many failures as successes from their selected investments.

Continued

Considerations to be made by a venture capital company would include:

- Nature of product.
- Production expertise.
- Management expertise.
- Markets.
- Profit expectation.
- Potential for high rates of return.
- Risk borne by current owners.
- Innovation.
- Ability to outperform competition.

(Other valid points can also be considered)

(ii) A redeemable debenture is a debt instrument, secured on the assets of a company and is repayable at some specified future date, or between specified dates. Interest is fixed for the duration of the debenture. The debenture may be repayable at par (face value) or at a premium. Redeemable debentures are the most common form of debt securities traded in the markets in the UK and the ROI. Their value fluctuates as a result of changes in general interest rates in the economy.

KEY TERMS

Admissions document

Alternative investment market

Bonus issue

Business angel

Business expansion scheme

Capitalisation issue

Captive firms

Convertible preference shares

Corporate venturing

Cumulative preference shares

Deferred equity shares

Early stage venture capital

Enterprise capital funds

Enterprise investment

Equity

Equity gap

Exit strategy

Finance gap

Flotation

Golden shares

Growth venture capital

IEX

Initial public offering

Intermediaries offer

Irish stock exchange
Irish stock exchange quotation
Irredeemable preference shares
Issue by tender
London stock exchange
Main market
Management buy in (MBI)
Management buy out (MBO)
Management buy in and buy out
  (BIMBO)
Market makers
Market value
Nominal value
Nominated adviser
Nominated broker
Non-convertible preference
Non-cumulative preference
Non-participating preference
  shares
Non-voting equity shares
Offer for sale by prospectus
Offer for sale by subscription
Official list
Ordinary share capital
Over-the-counter
Par value
Participating preference shares
Pecking order theory
Placing
PLUS market
PLUS quoted
Pre-emptive rights
Preference shares
Preferred ordinary shares
Price sensitive information
Primary exchange
Private equity finance
Private issue

Private placing
Prospectus
Realised profits
Redeemable preference
Regional venture capital
Retained earnings
Revaluation reserve
Revenue reserves
Rights issue
Scrip issue
Secondary market
Seed corn venture capital
Start-up venture capital
Share premium
Share split
Stabilising
Stock exchange
Strike price
Sub-underwriters
Theoretical ex-rights price
Underwrites
Vendor placing
Venture capital
Venture capital trusts.

WEBSITES THAT MAY BE OF USE

The British Business Angels Association (BBAA):
http://www.bbaa.org.uk/

The British Venture Capital Association (BVCA):
http://www.bvca.co.uk/publications/guide/intro.html

Government advice on raising finance for businesses:
http://www.businesslink.gov.uk/

The European Private Equity and Venture Capital Association (EVCA):
http://www.evca.com/html/home.asp

Information on the Irish Financial Services Regulatory Authority can be found on the following website:
http://wwwfinancialregulator.ie/

Information on the Irish Stock Exchange can be found on the following website:
http://www.ise.ie

Information on the London Stock Exchange (main market or AIM) can be found on the following website:
http://www.londonstockexchange.com/

Information on the PLUS Market can be found on the following website:
http://www.plusmarketsgroup.com/

Advice on raising equity on a company start-up:
http://www.startups.co.uk/

To find out information on stock exchanges all over the world, access the following website:
http://www.123world.com/stockexchanges/

To find out about the Regional Venture Capitalist Funds, access the following website:
http://www.sbs.gov.uk/

To find out information on the largest venture capitalist firm – 3i access its website:
http://www.3i.com/

Extract from the annual report and accounts of Viridian group PLC (2005–06)

29. Share capital

Authorised	2006 £	2005 £
194,400,000 ordinary shares of 27 7/9 each (2005 – 216,000,000 ordinary shares of 25p each)	54,000,000	54,000,000
136,000,000 Redeemable non cumulative non voting shares of 73p each (Redeemable B shares)	99,280,000	–
1 deferred A share of nil value	–	–
	153,280,000	54,000,000

Allotted and fully paid	Ordinary shares Number	Ordinary shares £	Redeemable B shares Number	Redeemable B shares £
At 1 April 2004	133,172,814	33,293,203	–	–
Shares allotted during the year under Executive Share Option/Sharesave schemes	582,292	145,573	–	–
At 1 April 2005	133,755,106	33,437,776	–	–

Shares allotted during the period under Executive Share Option/Sharesave schemes	387,674	96,919	—	—
Share capital cancelled	(134,142,780)	(33,535,695)	—	—
Share capital issued on 15 August 2005	120,728,502	33,535,695	—	—
Shares allotted during the period under Executive Share Option/Sharesave schemes	1,736,985	482,496	—	—
Redeemable B shares issued	—	—	134,142,780	97,924,229
Redeemable B shares redeemed	—	—	(132,971,916)	(97,069,498)
At 31 March 2006	122,465,487	34,018,191	1,170,864	854,731

On 15 August 2005, the ordinary share capital was consolidated on the basis of nine new ordinary shares of 27 7/9p each for every 10 existing ordinary shares of 25p each and one Redeemable B share for every existing ordinary share of 25p each. The Redeemable B shares are redeemable at par. They are unlisted, carry no dividend or voting rights and are not transferable. On winding up of the Company, the Redeemable B shareholders has a right to receive, in priority to any payments to the ordinary shareholders, repayment of the nominal capital paid up or credited as paid up on the Redeemable B shares held by them.

During the year, options in respect of the Sharesave Scheme and Executive Share Option Scheme were exercised for a total consideration of £9.5m (2005 – £3.3m).

REVIEW QUESTIONS

1. Explain the difference between the book value, nominal value and market value of equity.
2. Describe the main stock exchanges in the UK and the ROI, in brief.
3. List the advantages and disadvantages of flotation.
4. Explain the term: 'pre emptive rights'.
5. A company has made yearly profits of €/£2,000,000. It pays corporation tax at 40%. The company is considering raising €/£2,000,000 redeemable preference shares or redeemable debentures to finance its long-term growth needs. To obtain an issue price worth par, the company has to offer a fixed dividend on the preference shares of 9c/p per €/1 share, or a fixed coupon of 14% on each debenture. Calculate which alternative is cheaper to the company in terms of the yearly impact on earnings available for distribution to the equity holders.
6. Amarillo plc has recently announced a 'one-for-two' rights issue. The price of the shares before the announcement was €/£5.00 and the current equity holders will be given pre-emptive rights to purchase new shares at €/£4.00.

REQUIRED

a) Calculate the theoretical ex-rights price.
b) Calculate the value of each right (assuming it is attached to each existing share).
c) Calculate the price at which each equity holder can sell their right (the value of the right assuming it is attached to the new share).
d) An equity holder owns 2,000 shares. Calculate the value and number of shares in his possession before and after the rights issue assuming that he purchases the new shares.
e) Calculate the value of his holding after the rights issue assuming that the equity holder sells the rights.
f) Assume the equity holder is short of cash. Calculate the number of rights the equity holder has to sell to provide cash to purchase

the balance available to him. Show the value and number of shares in his possession after the rights issue.

g) Assume the equity holder does nothing. Calculate the value and number of shares in his possession before and after the rights issue and the monies given to him by the company.

7. What are the key factors a venture capitalist considers when evaluating whether to invest in a company, or not?

CHALLENGING QUESTIONS

1. CAPITAL MARKETS

a) Outline briefly the major functions performed by the capital market and explain the importance of each function in assisting corporate financial management.

7 Marks

(ICAI, MABF II, Autumn 2007, Q6(a))

2. ENAM plc

The Board of ENAM plc ('ENAM') is considering an expansion programme that will require raising €/£79.25 million. The expansion should increase operating profits by €/£15.24 million per annum in the foreseeable future. The expansion apart, operating profit in 2006 is expected to be 3% higher than in 2005. The Board has been presented with three possible options for raising the necessary finance.

Option 1   The company would issue shares at a price of 317c/p each.

Option 2   The company would issue 12% debentures dated 2015.

Option 3   The company would raise a ten-year (9%) loan from a financial institution. If this option is chosen, the institution would require that an interest cover of at least three times is maintained and that the dividend cover is at least 2.5 times.

The Board has also been presented with extracts from the published accounts of the past three years.

INCOME STATEMENT (EXTRACT) FOR THE YEAR ENDED 30 JUNE

	2003	2004	2005
	€/£ million	€/£ million	€/£ million
Operating profit	27.81	54.85	41.77
Interest	9.40	11.94	13.49
Profit before tax	18.41	42.91	28.28
Tax at 30%	5.52	12.87	8.48
Profit after tax	12.89	30.04	19.80
Dividends	8.79	9.23	9.69
Retained profits	4.10	20.81	10.11
Share price (cent/pence) as at 30th June	305c/p	495c/p	413c/p

BALANCE SHEET (EXTRACT) AS AT 30 JUNE

	2003	2004	2005
	€/£ million	€/£ million	€/£ million
Long-term loans	89	114	127
Issued share capital (nominal 50c/p each)	63	63	63
Share premium account	32	32	32
Profit and loss reserve	48.54	69.35	79.49

The Chair of the Board, Jemima Oswald, is concerned about the implications of the various financing options. She and her family hold 48.25 million of the issued shares at the moment. It has been company policy to increase dividends at a rate of 5% per annum and it is intended to continue this policy in the future. Corporation tax is expected to remain at 30%.

REQUIRED

a)   Calculate the current (year ended 30 June 2005) dividend per share in cent/pence.

2 Marks

b) Calculate the number of shares that would need to be issued under Option 1.

1 Mark

c) Draft the projected income statement (in the same format as in the question) for each of the three options outlined for the year ended 30 June 2006. (Assume that taxable profits are the same as accounting profits and ignore deferred tax.)

9 Marks

d) Produce projected balance sheet extracts as at 30 June 2006 under each of the options in the question, showing the following balances only:
  • Long-term loans.
  • Issued share capital.
  • Share premium account.

3 Marks

e) Prepare a brief report to the Chair of the Board outlining which of the financing options you prefer; giving reasons for your decision.

6 Marks

Presentation Mark   **1 Mark**

Total 22 Marks

(ICAI, MABF II, Autumn 2005, Q5)

3.   ENDORPHIN Ltd.

A small company, ENDORPHIN Ltd. ('ENDORPHIN'), has developed a new piece of medical equipment that will considerably reduce the trauma suffered by patients undergoing certain medical procedures. So far, the equipment has been developed using the company's own resources.

Market research indicates the possibility of a large volume of demand and a significant amount of additional capital being needed to finance production.

REQUIRED

Advise the Finance Manager of ENDORPHIN as follows:

a) State the advantages and disadvantages of equity funding from the company's own point of view.

6 Marks

b) Outline FOUR types of finance likely to be available and the sources from which they might be obtained.

6 Marks

c) Of the sources outlined above; state which are likely to be most suitable to ENDORPHIN in the particular circumstances of this company? Give reasons for your answer.

6 Marks

Total 18 Marks

(ICAI, MABF II, Summer 2004, Q6)

4. BANDARAYA plc

BANDARAYA plc ('BANDARAYA') is a Stock Exchange listed business that owns a chain of retailers situated throughout the island of Ireland. It is currently financed principally by equity and has grown organically since its inception.

An opportunity has arisen for BANDARAYA to purchase all of the shares of an unlisted business, SEGAR Ltd. ('SEGAR'), which is in a similar line of business and has many branches in Great Britain, an area into which BANDARAYA is keen to expand. The price being asked by the shareholders of SEGAR equals about 30% of the total market capitalisation of BANDARAYA. Given the price, the perceived strategic fit, and the prospects, the directors of BANDARAYA are anxious to acquire the shares.

The scale of the investment is such that BANDARAYA could not raise the cash from internal sources and will have to either make a rights issue of ordinary shares, an issue of preference shares, or an issue of loan stock. A decision now needs to be made on the method of funding.

The minutes of a recent meeting of the Board of Directors called to discuss the issue record that the following were among the views put forward.

- Director, Mr. Banda 'I'm not keen on loan finance because the interest will inevitably reduce our earnings per share and, therefore, our share price'.

- Director, Mr. Raya 'I don't want a rights issue because inevitably many of our shareholders do not want to increase their investment and will lose out as a result. Irrespective of the direct effects of a rights issue on our share price, this will have an adverse affect on the total market value of our company. An issue of loan stock seems the best idea'.

• Director Mr. Dar   'I favour a preference share issue because it would be neutral as far as the capital gearing question is concerned; it will neither increase nor reduce it'.

The matter is listed for decision at the next board meeting.

REQUIRED

As finance director you are asked to provide a briefing note for the directors to read in preparation for the meeting. Your briefing note should raise all the relevant issues about the raising of finance, and the points expressed by the directors at the recent meeting. This briefing note should be in simple, non-technical language. All relevant factors must be clearly explained and placed in the appropriate context.

18 Marks
(ICAI, MABF II, Autumn 2006, Q7)

5.   YUKI plc

You have just been employed as assistant financial controller in YUKI plc. The capital structure of the company is set out below.

	€/£ Millions
Equity shares of €/£ 100 each........................	20
Retained earnings......................................	10
9% preference shares of €/£ 100 each..............	12
7% debentures...	8
Total...	50

The company earns a pre-tax return on capital of 12%. The corporation tax rate is 25%.

The company requires a sum of €/£ 2,500,000 to finance an expansion programme which will also be required to earn a pre-tax return of 12%. The following funding alternatives are available to the company:

(i)   Issue 20,000 equity shares at a premium of €/£ 25 per share.

(ii)   Issue of 10% preference shares at par

(iii) Issue of 8% debentures

It is estimated that the following price earnings ratios will apply in respect of each of the financing options:

Equity   17.25

Preference   17.00

Debentures   15.07

REQUIRED

a)   Calculate the expected earnings per share and market price per share under each of the three alternatives.

9 Marks

b)   Write a memorandum to the financial controller explaining the impact of each funding alternative on this company's share price, gearing and level of financial risk.

9 Marks
Total 18 Marks
(ICAI, MABF II, Summer 2007, Q6)

SECTION FOUR

INVESTMENT DECISION MAKING: WORKING CAPITAL

WORKING CAPITAL: AN INTRODUCTION

8

LEARNING OBJECTIVES

Upon completing this chapter, readers should be able to:

♣ Define working capital and explain the importance of managing working capital;
♣ Discuss the working capital cycle;
♣ Calculate the net investment by a company in working capital;
♣ Define the operating/cash conversion cycle;
♣ Calculate the operating/cash conversion cycle;
♣ Use ratios to determine the finance required for working capital;
♣ Discuss the symptoms and remedies of over trading;
♣ Discuss the symptoms and remedies of over capitalisation; and
♣ Explain the three main working capital management strategies (aggressive; neutral and conservative).

Introduction

Most plcs have a treasury department that manage global transactions, equity holdings and funding requirements. This department might be called the corporate finance department. Another focus of the treasury/ corporate finance function is the management of a company's working capital. This involves determining the level of inventory to keep in store, the credit period to allow to customers, the credit period to take from suppliers and the cash balance to keep on hand. In most companies the amount held in these current assets and liabilities represents a major investment, tying up funds, which has a cost. Yet, the investment is necessary as otherwise normal trading activities would be disrupted, affecting profits. Another feature of working capital management is determining the type of finance to use. This chapter: defines working capital; explains the purpose of managing working capital; identifies the costs of working capital; and discusses the type of finance to use. The symptoms and dangers of over trading are explained and the three main types of working capital management policy are discussed: aggressive; neutral; and conservative. The information covered in this chapter forms a foundation for the other chapters in this section of the text.

Working capital – definition

Working capital is the net investment by a company in operating current assets (such as trade receivables, inventories, bank and cash) and operating current liabilities (such as trade payables and an overdraft). It is calculated as follows:

$$\text{Working capital} = \text{Inventories} + \text{Trade receivables} + \text{Bank/cash} \\ - \text{Trade payables} - \text{Overdraft}$$

or

$$\text{Working capital} = \text{Current assets} - \text{Current liabilities}$$

A company usually expects its working capital components (i.e. inventories, trade payables, etc.) to be realised within a short period of time, hence are regarded as current at any one point in time. These components are required on an on-going basis and specific items can be turned over many times, in one year. Therefore, a permanent investment in working capital is required to enable an entity to carry on its business.

Other components of working capital
The definition referred to in the previous paragraph captures the material items that make up working capital. However, other funds are tied up in working capital. These are sometimes difficult to quantify (for example,

intellectual capital), or are deemed to be immaterial (accrued employee wages and salaries, where the accrual is for one day). They include VAT, accruals (heat and light) and prepayments (rates). Where material, these items are included as a formal part of the working capital decision making process.

Working capital management

As mentioned earlier in this chapter, a company has to have working capital to carry on its business. Goods are purchased, on credit or by cash, and form inventories. These have to be held before sales can be made. Credit usually has to be given to obtain sales. Working capital management tries to achieve an optimum balance between ensuring that: sufficient levels of working capital are held so as not to negatively impact on a company's operations; adequate liquidity levels are maintained; and costs associated with holding working capital are minimised.

The interrelationship between the first two factors (the working capital elements required to ensure that operational activities are not disrupted) and liquidity are portrayed in the following diagram. This diagrams also highlights the potential impact of working capital on decision making in other areas within a company.

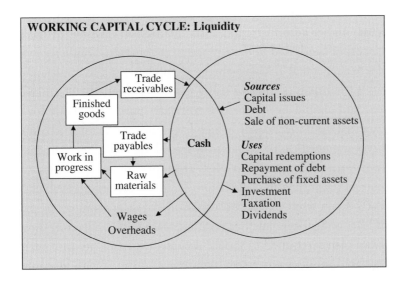

This diagram depicts the dynamic relationship between investment in working capital, cash availability and other uses and sources of cash. When more funds are tied up in the major working capital components (denoted by the white boxes) then the amount of cash available for other business decisions is reduced. This may impact on the future profitability of a company as the company may have less cash available to invest in long-term assets, which earn a higher return.

As highlighted in the diagram cash can be sourced from capital issues, debt or the sale of non-current assets. These sources are usually costly. Cash generated from operating activities that are supported by an optimum investment in working capital, is a more efficient source of cash. This will ensure that optimum levels of cash are available to meet taxation and dividend demands, whilst also providing funds that can be used for long-term objectives (capital redemption, debt repayment, and capital investment). The key to this process is to ensure that the company's activities are profitable and have net cash inflows.

Management of the individual working capital components should ensure that sufficient inventory is available to keep production at a level that ensures there are no stock-outs, resulting in lost sales. Yet the level should not be so high as to increase the overhead costs associated with holding inventory including the cost of the funds tied up (This is examined in chapter nine, 'Inventory Management'). The credit period afforded to customers should be at a level that does not result in customers transferring their custom elsewhere. This should be balanced with the costs that are associated with allowing long credit periods, such as higher levels of bad debts, higher administration costs incurred in chasing up the debts and the cost of funds tied up (examined in chapter ten, 'Trade receivables/payables Management'). Management of purchases is also important. The majority of companies operate using credit facilities, therefore credit is expected and should be taken. If a company purchases goods for cash; funds are tied up unnecessarily, which has implications for the company's liquidity. Care needs to be exercised when taking credit, as payment after an agreed timescale may lead to a loss of supply, interest penalties, or loss of discounts (examined in chapter ten, 'Trade Receivables/Payables Management'). Cash itself needs consideration. Cash is required to pay for certain legal obligations, such as taxation and salaries, therefore a certain amount of cash is required to service running expenses, yet cash sitting in a current account does not earn a high return. A sound cash management policy is required, to identify the optimum level of cash that should be held. This may involve financing the cash requirement where there is a deficit or establishing an investment policy in respect of any surplus (this is considered in detail in Chapter 11, 'Cash Management').

Industry influence

The type and level of working capital a company holds is influenced by the industry within which the company operates. A manufacturing company will purchase raw materials and consumables. Then using inhouse costs such as wages and overheads; work in progress and finished goods are generated. Therefore, at any one point in time a manufacturing company will have four types of inventory: raw materials; work in progress; finished goods and consumables. Its sales and purchases are usually on credit. Manufacturing companies usually hold high levels of raw material and consumable inventory as the cost of a stock-out is high i.e. production is halted and certain costs that are used to generate products are fixed. These costs occur regardless of whether the manufacturing process is active or not, for example, supervisors salaries, rent, rates, etc. Manufacturing entities usually operate with quite high levels of trade receivables and take credit from suppliers. The credit period is influenced by the normal trading terms for each particular manufacturing industry.

In contrast, a retailing entity usually has only one type of inventory-finished goods. Retail companies usually purchase finished goods inventory on credit. Most of their sales are for cash. Inventory levels of finished goods are generally quite high, though some retailers have a just-in-time relationship with their suppliers ensuring prompt delivery of goods straight to the shop floor, reducing the level of inventory that is required to be held in stores.

Even within the retailing sector, differences occur depending on the type and nature of the product being sold. For example, a jeweller will purchase goods infrequently and may hold inventory for over a year. This inventory will not deteriorate and may even gain in value. Whereas a green grocer will purchase inventory every few days, if not daily, and will turn over its inventory every few days (daily) also. A greengrocer's products are prone to deterioration and fall in value over time. Seasonality is also another factor to take into consideration. A jeweller may increase its inventory levels before Christmas and Valentine's Day; whereas a greengrocer will not be subject to the same degree of fluctuation in the demand for its products. Individual items may be seasonal, for example pumpkins at Halloween and brussels sprouts at Christmas.

Working capital: investment and associated finance cost

All the components making up the working capital cycle are considered to be current in nature. However, as mentioned previously, there is never a time when an entity can operate without them and even though the components can turn over quickly; working capital is a permanent requirement that has to be financed. Therefore, a minimum level of working capital should be held as a long-term investment (*permanent working capital*). In some instances the investment can be short term (*temporary working capital*), for example, when an entity trades in a product that has cyclical demand, such as umbrellas, or ice-cream. In these cases the levels of inventory will increase for a few months of the year and the investment requirement will be higher for this period.

Like any investment, working capital has a finance cost. This cost is the *opportunity cost* of not utilising the funds in an alternative project, which will benefit the company. The opportunity cost depends on the circumstances of the company. Where the company has surplus cash; the cost is the return that could be achieved from investing the required funds in other types of investments. Where the company has to seek funding for working capital investment; the cost is the interest that is incurred on the financing. Where both situations exist, i.e. the company is in overdraft and can invest in more profitable projects, then the finance cost of having funds tied up in working capital is the higher of the two rates.

> **Worked example 8.1**   (Operating cost of investing in working capital.)
>
> Verde Ltd. can increase its sales by £/€1,000,000 per annum, if it increases its inventory level by £/€600,000. The company has a contribution margin of 15%. It is expected that the company's average trade receivables will increase by £/€300,000. Trade payables
>
> *Continued*

are also expected to increase. The company has similar credit terms with its suppliers, as it gives to its customers. The company currently receives 12% on its investments.

REQUIRED

Advise Verde Ltd. as to whether it should increase its inventory levels.

Solution

	€/£	€/£
Contribution from additional sales:		
(£/€1,000,000 × 15%)		150,000
Financing requirement		
Additional trade receivables	300,000	
Additional trade payables:		
(£/€300,000 × 85%)	(255,000)	
Additional inventory	600,000	
Total finance requirement	645,000	
Finance cost: (£/€645,000 × 12%)		77,400
Increase in profits		72,600

Verde Ltd. should increase its inventories as the contribution from the increased sales will more than compensate for the finance costs that will be incurred, in having to invest in higher levels of working capital.

As can be seen from the above example an increase in working capital levels within a company has a direct finance requirement (increased by €/£645,000). Alternatively, if working capital were to be managed more efficiently, reducing the investment requirement, then working capital can be seen as a source of finance.

The operating cycle/cash conversion cycle

To this point, the chapter has focused on the absolute amount of working capital that needs to be financed, its potential cost and the finance implications of movements in that requirement. However, this is not useful if comparing the efficiency of working capital management: from year to year where there are changes in operations, sales and purchases; relative to other companies; or relative to the industry average. In particular, focusing on monetary values does not provide an indication of the efficiency of management in relation to working capital. More useful information for assessing the efficiency of management in respect of working capital can be obtained by calculating the company's working capital operating cycle/cash conversion cycle.

The *operating/cash conversion cycle* represents the length of time, in days, that it takes to convert cash payable for net inputs (purchases of raw materials, etc) into cash receivable for outputs (sales). In a manufacturing entity the operating cycle/cash conversion cycle is quite long and will include the number of days that: raw materials are held in inventories; the product is in the manufacturing process; the finished goods remain in inventory before being sold; and the number of days it takes for the customer to pay for the goods. As the purchases of raw materials are rarely for cash, the operating cycle/cash conversion cycle is reduced by the number of days of credit taken from suppliers. The type of product also influences the expected cycle length. For example, a manufacturer who makes safety pins will have a short work-in-progress period, whereas a whiskey manufacturer may have a work-in-progress period of up to ten years, or more.

Operating/cash conversion cycle (manufacturing company)

$$
\begin{array}{c}
\text{Operating/} \\
\text{cash} \\
\text{conversion} \\
\text{cycle}
\end{array}
=
\begin{array}{c}
\text{Raw} \\
\text{materials} \\
\text{conversion} \\
\text{period}
\end{array}
+
\begin{array}{c}
\text{Work-in-} \\
\text{progress} \\
\text{conversion} \\
\text{period}
\end{array}
+
\begin{array}{c}
\text{Finished} \\
\text{goods} \\
\text{conversion} \\
\text{period}
\end{array}
+
\begin{array}{c}
\text{Trade} \\
\text{receivables} \\
\text{conversion} \\
\text{period}
\end{array}
-
\begin{array}{c}
\text{Trade} \\
\text{payables} \\
\text{conversion} \\
\text{period}
\end{array}
$$

In a retail company the cycle is short and is mostly the average number of days purchased items remain in inventory, less the time taken to pay suppliers. Usually sales are in cash. Where credit is given the cycle can be calculated as follows:

Operating/cash conversion cycle (retail company)

$$
\begin{array}{c}
\text{Operating/cash} \\
\text{conversion cycle}
\end{array}
=
\begin{array}{c}
\text{Inventory} \\
\text{conversion} \\
\text{period}
\end{array}
+
\begin{array}{c}
\text{Trade receivables} \\
\text{conversion} \\
\text{period}
\end{array}
-
\begin{array}{c}
\text{Trade payables} \\
\text{conversion} \\
\text{period}
\end{array}
$$

Worked example 8.2   (Cash conversion cycle)

Marron Ltd. is a wholesaler who trades in sports gear. The average inventory holding period is 30 days. Customers usually pay within 40 days, and Marron Ltd. has agreed to pay its suppliers within 20 days.

REQUIRED

Calculate Marron Ltd.'s cash conversion cycle.

Solution

The cash conversion cycle is: 30 days + 40 days − 20 days = 50 days

Marron Ltd. will have to finance the cost of the products for 50 days.

Management have to carefully balance the operating/cash conversion cycle. As mentioned previously, working capital has to be financed, and hence has a cost. If the cycle is too long; this will tie up a company's resources unnecessarily and is a cost to the company, which will reduce company profitability. Tying up funds in working capital unnecessarily is called *over capitalisation*. Over capitalisation can be identified using accounting ratios, such as sales to working capital, liquidity ratios and turnover of the individual working capital components, for example, the trade receivables period, etc. If the cycle is too short, it may affect production, resulting in lost sales, poorer quality products, etc. An insufficient level of working capital is called *under capitalisation*.

The operating/cash conversion cycle is calculated using ratios that convert monetary values into days. The information to do this can be obtained from a company's financial statements. When calculating the cycle in days for a set timeframe, the average monetary value for the year should be used; unless this information is not available, whereupon closing balances should be used. Calculations for the individual components of the operating/cash conversion cycle are as follows:

Total cash conversion cycle (days)

Average number of days raw material is in inventories	$=$	$\dfrac{\text{Average raw material inventory value} \times 365}{\text{Purchases of raw material in period.}}$	Days $= A$
Less: Average number of days credit taken on the purchase of the raw materials	$=$	$\dfrac{\text{Average value of trade payables} \times 365}{\text{Credit purchases of raw material in period}}$	$= (B)$
Plus: Average number of days the product takes in the production process	$=$	$\dfrac{\text{Average value of work in progress} \times 365}{\text{Average cost of goods produced in period}}$	$= C$
Plus: Average number of days finished goods remain in stores before being sold	$=$	$\dfrac{\text{Average value of finished goods} \times 365}{\text{Average cost of goods produced in period}}$	$= D$
Plus: Average number of days credit allowed on sales	$=$	$\dfrac{\text{Average value of trade receivables} \times 365}{\text{Credit sales in period}}$	$= E$

Total operating/cash flow period   A to E

Using the operating/cash conversion cycle for working capital management

The operating/cash conversion cycle can be used to assess the efficiency of an entity in its use of current assets and liabilities. So long as sales are not lost and production is not affected, a lower conversion period would reflect more efficient use of working capital. Indeed, in these circumstances the entity should have a higher return on its assets compared with a similar entity that has a longer operating/cash conversion cycle.

Worked example 8.3   (Cash conversion period)

Two companies: Amarillo Ltd. and Gris Ltd., manufacture shoes which they sell to retailers in Ireland. They are similar entities facing similar competition. Extract information from their income statements and copies of their balance sheets are available. These are as follows:

Extract information from the income statements of each company for the year ended 31 December 20X6

	Amarillo Ltd.	Gris Ltd.
	€/£	€/£
Revenue	2,000,000	4,000,000
Gross profit	400,000	600,000
Net income	100,000	40,000

Both companies provide credit on all sales and obtain credit on all purchases.

Extract information from the balance sheets of each company as at 31 December 20X6

	Amarillo Ltd.	Gris Ltd.
	€/£	€/£
Non-current assets	320,000	420,000
Current assets		
Inventories	120,000	300,000
Trade receivables	128,000	270,000
Bank and cash	2,000	–
	250,000	570,000
Total assets	570,000	990,000
Equity and liabilities		
Equity and reserves		
Equity share capital	100,000	100,000
Revenue reserves	320,000	330,000
	420,000	430,000

Continued

Current liabilities

Overdraft	50,000	160,000
Trade payables	100,000	400,000
	150,000	560,000
Total equity and liabilities	570,000	990,000

REQUIRED

a)   Calculate the cash conversion period for both companies.

b)   Calculate the working capital requirement for both companies.

c)   Using the results from part a) and b) outline which company you believe to be more efficient in the management of their working capital.

Solution

a)   In this question there is insufficient information to calculate separately the raw material conversion period, the production period and the length of time the product remains as finished goods within stores. Therefore an overall inventory conversion period is calculated.

	Amarillo Ltd. €/£	Gris Ltd. €/£
Inventory	120,000	300,000
$\dfrac{\text{Inventory}}{\text{Cost of goods sold}}$	$\dfrac{120,000 \times 365}{2,000,000 - 400,000}$	$\dfrac{300,000 \times 365}{4,000,000 - 600,000}$
Inventory conversion period	27.38 days	32.20 days

Gris Ltd. has its product tied up in the production and inventory holding process for almost five days more than Amarillo Ltd.

Continued

	Amarillo Ltd. €/£	Gris Ltd. €/£
Trade payables	100,000	400,000

	Amarillo Ltd.	Gris Ltd.
$\dfrac{\text{Trade payables}}{\text{Cost of goods sold*}}$	$\dfrac{100{,}000 \times 365}{2{,}000{,}000 - 400{,}000}$	$\dfrac{400{,}000 \times 365}{4{,}000{,}000 - 600{,}000}$
Trade payables conversion period	22.81 days	42.94 days

*A more appropriate denominator is credit purchases: however, this information is not available from the question.

Gris Ltd. takes over 20 days more credit from their suppliers compared to Amarillo Ltd.

	Amarillo Ltd. €/£	Gris Ltd. €/£
Trade receivables	128,000	270,000

	Amarillo Ltd.	Gris Ltd.
$\dfrac{\text{Trade receivables}}{\text{Credit sales}}$	$\dfrac{128{,}000 \times 365}{2{,}000{,}000}$	$\dfrac{270{,}000 \times 365}{4{,}000{,}000}$
Trade receivables conversion period	23.36 days	24.64 days

Gris Ltd. allows one day more credit to its customers than Amarillo Ltd.

Cash conversion cycle

Amarillo Ltd. = 27.38 days − 22.81 days + 23.36 days = 27.93 days
Gris Ltd. = 32.2 days − 42.94 days + 24.64 days = 13.9 days

b)   Working capital requirement

	Amarillo Ltd. €/£	Gris Ltd. €/£
Inventory	120,000	300,000
Trade receivables	128,000	270,000
Trade payables	(100,000)	(400,000)
Working capital requirement	148,000	170,000

Continued

c) From the overall cash conversion period calculation in a) it would appear that Gris Ltd. is more efficient as it has a shorter period. In addition, the calculations in b) show that Gris Ltd.'s net investment in working capital is only €/£22,000 more than that of Amarillo Ltd., yet its sales are double. However, on inspection of the components making up the cash conversion period calculation and the working capital investment, it would seem that Gris Ltd. is using their suppliers to finance their working capital. They are taking nearly 43 days to pay their suppliers, 20 days more than Amarillo Ltd. This may account for the difference in the gross profit return of both companies. Amarillo Ltd. is earning 20% gross profit on its sales (€/£400,000/€/£2,000,000), whereas Gris Ltd. is earning 15% (€/£600,000/€/£4,000,000). Amarillo Ltd. may be availing of discounts or special price deals for their quicker payment, or Gris Ltd. may be paying prices with penalties or finance costs built into them.

Gris Ltd. also has its funds tied up in inventories for almost five days longer than Amarillo Ltd. This may indicate a slower production process, holding higher raw material inventory, or not being able to move finished goods as quickly as Amarillo Ltd. More-detailed information is required to determine exactly where the difference arises.

In terms of trade receivables Gris Ltd. takes one day longer to collect its debts from customers.

Other important information can be obtained from the extracts of financial data that are supplied in the question, which help to form an opinion on the working capital management policy in each company. In particular, it is clear from the balance sheet of Gris Ltd. that the company is reliant on its short-term liabilities (trade payables and overdraft) to finance its current assets. It has a current ratio of 1:1, whereas Amarillo Ltd. has a current ratio of 1.67 to 1. The larger overdraft proportion may contribute to the lower overall net profit of 1% (€/£40,000/€/£4,000,000) being reported by Gris Ltd.,

Continued

> compared to a net profit of 5% (€/£100,000/€/£2,000,000) reported by Amarillo Ltd.
>
> It would seem then from an analysis of the: components making up the operating/cash conversion cycle; profitability; and liquidity of the companies that Amarillo Ltd. has a stronger working capital policy.

Working capital: the finance mix

In the previous example two similar companies are financing their working capital in different ways. Amarillo Ltd. finances its working capital requirement using some current liabilities and some long-term liabilities, as is evident from the current ratio of 1.67 to 1. This ratio reflects that about 60% of the current assets are financed using current liabilities and the remainder are financed from long-term sources. Gris Ltd. finances its current assets almost entirely with its current liabilities. Its current ratio is 1 to 1. The balance sheet data suggests that Gris Ltd. has potential liquidity problems. This example sparks the question: what is the correct finance mix for working capital?

Earlier in this chapter, it is explained that investment in working capital is mostly permanent in nature, though there may be a temporary portion due to seasonal fluctuations in demand for a company's products. A general rule of thumb in respect of financing decisions is that the finance term should match the life of the asset (see chapter four: 'Asset-Mix Decision; Finance-Mix Decision and Short-Term Sources of Finance' for more detail). In the case of working capital the asset requirement is permanent, therefore this portion of working capital should be financed from long-term sources, with temporary fluctuations being financed by short-term means, such as an overdraft. It would seem then that in example 8.3, Amarillo Ltd. is also better at financing its investments than Gris Ltd.

Using the working capital operating/cash conversion cycle to determine the financing requirement

Just as information from the income statement and balance sheet can be used to calculate conversion days, then correspondingly, conversion days can be used with projected sales and cost of sales information, to determine the expected level of working capital, that requires financing.

Worked example 8.4   (Cash conversion period)

Blanco plc expects its annual turnover to increase from €/£500,000 to €/£1,500,000. Its customers currently take 40 days credit.

REQUIRED

Assuming all else remains stable, determine the additional working capital requirement and finance cost of this growth. Blanco plc can invest its surplus cash at 15%.

Solution

Trade receivables before growth: $€/£500,000 \times \dfrac{40}{365} = €/£54,795$

Trade receivables after growth: $€/£1,500,000 \times \dfrac{40}{365} = €/£164,383$

Therefore, the additional finance requirement is: €/£109,588 (€/£164,383 − €/£54,795)

This has an opportunity cost of: €/£16,438 (€/£109,588 × 15%)

Working capital and overtrading

Over trading occurs when a company grows too quickly with insufficient long-term finance to support the increased level of assets that should be held, given the higher level of operational activity. When a company's sales grow, so does the absolute amount of working capital that should be held. Demand is higher; therefore inventory levels need to increase to cater for the increased demand, trade receivables increase in line with the increase in the volume of sales, and the level of trade payables increases also. In the majority of instances the increase in inventories and trade receivables outweighs the increase in trade payables, resulting in a resource requirement that needs to be financed. If no steps are taken to manage this, the company's overdraft will increase, causing liquidity problems. This may result in a situation whereby a profitable, growing company may have to go into liquidation, due to cash shortages. As explained in the prior paragraph, permanent working capital should be financed using long-term finance. Indeed, any company that is planning to expand should take the required long-term investment in working capital into account in the initial decision making process.

Over trading is characterised by increases in turnover, current assets and possibly non-current assets. It is usual that the rate of increase in current assets exceeds the rate of increase in sales. This is characterised by an increase in the trade receivables and inventory cash conversion periods. Current liabilities usually increase to a greater extent than the increase in current assets, resulting in a weakening current ratio. There usually is a large overdraft. Owners' equity or long-term debt does not increase, or increases by a small amount, hence the proportion of total assets that are financed by long-term sources reduces.

Some steps that can be implemented to reduce the impact of over trading are to: continue with the growth policy and take steps to obtain the correct type of long-term financing; sell unwanted non-current assets that are not generating sufficient income and are not critical to the business; examine in detail the working capital policy with a view to reducing the trade receivables and inventory holding periods and increasing the trade payables period, without harming the relationship or the prices/discounts agreed with the suppliers; and finally reconsider the growth plan. If the company is getting itself into financial difficulties, then it may be better to either cancel the growth plan, or pursue it over a longer time period.

Other circumstances can lead to distressful financial situations similar to over trading. For example, when a company repays debt; this may be done too quickly so that the cash outflow is not being adequately generated from day to day operational activities, or from another finance source. A more common situation arises when a company replaces its assets (including non-current assets) from its retained earnings. If the company does not take inflation into consideration it may also result in the company running up an overdraft, or reducing its investment in assets in real terms.

Worked example 8.5   (Assessing company growth)

Amarillo Ltd. appointed a new marketing manager at the start of this accounting year, who has doubled the sales of the company over the past year. To stimulate growth, he reduced sales price, employed more sales staff, rented more office space, purchased additional motor vehicles and focused his attention on meeting sales targets. To this end he demanded that a higher level of inventory be stored, so that sales are not disrupted by stock-outs. Amarillo Ltd. has been renting additional warehouse space to meet this demand. Amarillo Ltd. extended the credit period it receives from suppliers and some of them are now complaining. The overdraft limit agreed with the bank of €/£60,000 has been increased to €/£160,000. Extract information from Amarillo Ltd. company's income statement and copies of its balance sheet are available for the year prior to the marketing manager being appointed, and the subsequent year reflecting the growth he has achieved. These are as follows:

Extract information from the income statements of Amarillo Ltd. for the year ended 31 December 20X5 and 20X6

	20X5	20X6
	€/£	€/£
Revenue	2,000,000	4,000,000
Gross profit	400,000	600,000
Net income	100,000	40,000

The company provides credit on all its sales and obtain credit on all its purchases.

Continued

Extract information from the balance sheets of Amarillo Ltd. as at 31 December 20X5 and 20X6

	20X5 €/£	20X6 €/£
Non-current assets	320,000	420,000
Current assets		
Inventories	120,000	300,000
Trade receivables	128,000	270,000
Bank and cash	2,000	–
	250,000	570,000
Total assets	570,000	990,000
Equity and liabilities		
Equity and reserves		
Equity share capital	100,000	100,000
Revenue reserves	320,000	330,000
	420,000	430,000
Current liabilities		
Overdraft	50,000	160,000
Trade payables	100,000	400,000
	150,000	560,000
Total equity and liabilities	570,000	990,000

REQUIRED

Discuss the impact of the marketing director's policy.

Solution

Profitability
In 20X6 the company's sales doubled from €/£2,000,000 to €/£4,000,000, but the gross profit margin has fallen from 20% to

Continued

15% and the net profit margin has fallen from 5% to 1% (see example 8.3 for the calculations). This reduction in profitability is probably due to the fall in sales price and the increase in overheads resulting from the additional sales and inventory costs. These costs include: sales representative salaries; depreciation on sales representatives motor vehicles; rent of additional office space and warehousing for the additional inventory; and other costs associated with holding inventory (write-offs, storemen's salaries, heat and light, etc). In addition there has probably been increased 'interest and bank charges' costs associated with running a higher overdraft.

Liquidity
At 31 December 20X5 the company had an overdraft of €/£50,000; €/£10,000 under the agreed limit of €/£60,000. By 31 December 20X6 this has increased to €/£160,000 which is the new agreed overdraft limit. In addition, in 20X6 the trade payables balance is 400% of the balance at 20X5, yet turnover has doubled. Inventory levels have more than doubled and inventory turnover is five days longer (see example 8.3). Non-current assets have increased by €/£100,000. There has been no increase in the equity share capital of the company, or no long-term debt sourced.

It is clear from this analysis that Amarillo Ltd. is over trading. In fact, the company is currently at its overdraft limit. As a matter of urgency Amarillo Ltd. needs to extend its overdraft facility. If Amarillo Ltd. does not start to manage its liquidity appropriately and to finance its growth correctly, it may have to go into liquidation.

Other steps that Amarillo Ltd. could take are to perform a cost benefit analysis of the additional costs that were incurred in the year. Though sales have increased, profitability has fallen. Unless costs can be cut, growth does not seem worthwhile. If Amarillo Ltd. can identify efficiencies in its costs and is keen to continue to pursue the growth strategy, then it should consider obtaining long-term finance, either from its equity holders, or long-term debt. In addition, management needs to consider the efficiencies that can be obtained in

Continued

its inventory management and credit management to bring the conversion periods back to their 20X5 levels (see example 8.3 – both increased). Suppliers should be made aware of the steps the company is taking to improve their liquidity and their support requested in the short term. In the longer term, the credit period taken should be reduced to a level that suppliers are happy with.

Targeted working capital management policies

Many factors influence the level of working capital a company chooses to maintain, such as the company's liquidity, ease of sourcing finance, type of business, economic climate and management preferences. Depending on the individual circumstances of a company, the management may choose to finance working capital very differently to what you would expect. Three polar policies are considered to capture the range of strategies that management pursue. These are termed: conservative; neutral; and aggressive. In practice, policies can lie anywhere along a continuum between the extreme conservative and aggressive strategies. The attributes of each policy are explained using the following example:

Example balance sheets showing the three main working policy strategies: conservative; neutral; and aggressive.

	Conservative €/£'m	Neutral €/£'m	Aggressive €/£'m
Non-current assets	1	3	6
Current assets	7	5	2
Total assets	**8**	**8**	**8**
Equity and liabilities			
Equity and reserves	4	3	2
Long-term liabilities	3	2.5	–
Current liabilities	1	2.5	6
Total equity and liabilities	**8**	**8**	**8**
Current ratio	7:1	2:1	0.33:1

Conservative

When a company operates a ***conservative working capital management strategy*** it is over capitalised, holding high levels of current assets including cash, and paying suppliers quickly. It usually has no liquidity problems, reporting high current ratios, as in the aforementioned example. A high current ratio (7 to 1) is indicative of ineffective management of working capital and cash. When working capital is outstanding for long periods, the company is more likely to experience direct costs associated with the timescale, such as increased bad debts within trade receivables and increased obsolescence in inventories. In addition, it is generally considered that higher returns can be obtained by investing in non-current assets. For example, investment in long-term securities provides a higher yield than investment in short-term securities. Investment in plant and machinery secures future yields for a company. Therefore, though a company pursuing a conservative working capital policy is in a strong liquid position and can take action on profitable speculative opportunities that may arise, there usually is an opportunity cost in terms of income foregone from not investing surplus funds correctly.

In terms of how a company is financed, companies that pursue a conservative working capital policy usually finance some of their current assets using short-term liabilities, most though are financed by long-term sources. The level of long-term debt and equity is usually high. As a consequence of the inefficient asset mix, combined with the additional finance costs associated with having long-term debt, the percentage return on assets is usually low. This policy is best suited when an economy is in a recession, as long credit periods are allowed, suppliers are paid quickly (can negotiate high discounts) and all sales can be serviced due to high inventory levels. This will provide an advantage over competitors who have to order in the product.

Neutral

When a company pursues a ***neutral working capital management strategy*** they hold sufficient current assets to cover their current liabilities as they fall due, with a little in reserve. This is reflected by a current ratio of between one and two to one. In the aforementioned example, the ratio is 2 to 1. Pursuing this policy usually ensures that a company keeps an efficient level of working capital with a surplus of cash that may not be sufficient to undertake speculative profitable investments that arise, however, is sufficient to support the daily operational requirements and any planned finance repayments, such as loan repayments.

Under this policy, long-term sources are used to finance some (at least a half) of the current assets and all of the non-current assets. Therefore, the finance term is usually matched to the term of the assets (as explained earlier there is a permanent demand for working capital, hence it is best to finance this using long-term means). This policy is deemed best suited to a stagnant economy. For example, additional inventories are not required as growth is not expected. This approach is also termed *moderate working capital management strategy*.

Aggressive

When a company pursues an *aggressive working capital management strategy* it keeps a minimum level of current assets, with low inventory levels and trade receivables. This results in lower working capital costs. For example, there should be minimal amounts of inventory holding costs and bad debts. Companies pursing this policy usually have high levels of current liabilities as they take credit periods from suppliers and operate with a high overdraft. This may result in increased working capital costs, such as discounts lost and overdraft interest. This policy results in a company reporting a low current ratio – usually lower than 1 to 1. In the aforementioned example, the current ratio shows that for every 33c/p invested in current assets the company has €/£1 of current liabilities i.e. 0.33 to 1. Therefore it cannot meet its current liabilities out of its cash, or near cash. In these circumstances the company usually has liquidity problems and treats its overdraft as though it were a long-term source of finance.

In terms of financing, a company pursuing this strategy usually has low levels of long-term finance and, in particular, does not hold much long-term debt. This ensures that interest costs are minimised. The current liabilities are used to finance current assets and some of the non-current assets. The investment in non-current assets is usually higher relative to the other two policies and return on assets reported is usually high. This policy works best in a boom economic climate, as demand outstrips supply and the company's performance is not adversely impacted on by loosing a sale due to stock-outs. In addition, as a result of the excess demand in the market place, customers are usually happy to settle their accounts quickly in order to secure the supply. A major concern with this policy is liquidity and the reliance on suppliers as a source of finance. It is likely that suppliers may stop supplying if such poor credit terms are maintained.

Conclusion

This chapter highlights the importance of having an appropriate working capital management policy. Working capital has a cost which will directly impact on a company's profitability. In addition, an insufficient investment/strategy in working capital may lead to a loss of profits. For example, in a growth period, increases in working capital will result. If this increase is not funded appropriately, then a company may have liquidity problems, even though it is profitable. The next three chapters lead on from this chapter and focus on working capital management in relation to the individual components of the working capital equation: inventories; trade receivables; trade payables and cash.

Examination standard question

Worked example 8.6

You have been commissioned by the managing director of Amarillo plc to determine the investment in working capital, that will be required if they purchase a small business which manufactures components for motor vehicles. The target company, Violetta plc, has an annual turnover of €/£3 million. Its costs are estimated based on the past three years performance results, as a percentage of its sales price. These costings are expected to be maintained. Direct materials cost about 30 percent of sales price, direct labour 25 percent, variable overheads ten percent, fixed overheads 15 percent and administration is about five percent.

You are also told that similar terms are going to be allowed to customers, and taken from suppliers, and similar inventory levels maintained. These terms are as follows:

(a) Customers take on average three months to pay for goods purchased.
(b) Direct materials are paid for after two months
(c) Direct labour is paid for after one week. The labour force work for 48 weeks of the year.
(d) Variable overheads are paid for within one month
(e) Fixed overheads are paid for within one month

Continued

(f) Administration overheads are paid for within half a month
(g) Three months inventory of raw materials is held
(h) Work in progress (approximately 50% of the finished goods) is held for about two months. Work in progress is valued using the variable production costs. Assume that all of the required direct materials become part of work in progress at the start of the production process.
(i) One month of finished goods inventory is held in store. Finished goods are valued using variable production costs.

REQUIRED

a) Estimate Violetta plc's expected annual profit.

5 Marks

b) Compute the finance that will be required to support operational working capital requirements.

10 Marks

c) Calculate the finance cost associated with the investment in working capital and the adjusted expected profit from the venture. Assume that Amarillo plc has an overdraft of €/£2,000,000, on which it pays interest at the rate of 12% per year.

<u>2 Marks</u>
<u>17 Marks</u>

Solution

a) Violetta plc's expected annual costs are as follows (*excluding finance costs*):

		€/£
Direct materials:	(€/£3,000,000 × 30%)	900,000
Direct labour:	(€/£3,000,000 × 25%)	750,000
Variable overheads:	(€/£3,000,000 × 10%)	300,000
Fixed overheads:	(€/£3,000,000 × 15%)	450,000
Administration costs:	(€/£3,000,000 × 5%)	150,000
Total costs		2,550,000

Therefore expected profit is: €/£450,000 (€/£3,000,000 − €/£2,550,000)

Continued

b)   The working capital requirement is as follows:

Expected current liabilities		€/£
Suppliers for raw materials:	(€/£900,000 × 2/12)	150,000
Direct labour:	(€/£750,000 × 1/48)	15,625
Variable overheads:	(€/£300,000 × 1/12)	25,000
Fixed overheads:	(€/£450,000 × 1/12)	37,500
Administration costs:	(€/£150,000 × 0.5/12)	6,250
Total source of finance		234,375

Expected current assets			
Trade receivables:		(€/£3,000,000 × 3/12)	750,000
Inventory			
Raw materials:		(€/£900,000 × 3/12)	225,000
Work-in-progress:			
Raw materials:	(€/£900,000 × 2/12)	150,000	
Direct labour:	(€/£750,000 × 50% × 2/12)	62,500	
Variable overheads:	(€/£300,000 × 50% × 2/12)	25,000	237,500
Finished goods:			
Raw materials:	(€/£900,000 × 1/12)	75,000	
Direct labour:	(€/£750,000 × 1/12)	62,500	
Variable overheads:	(€/£300,000 × 1/12)	25,000	162,500
Total finance required for current assets			1,375,000

Therefore the total finance requirement is:

$$€/£1,140,625(€/1,375,000 - €/£234,375)$$

c)   The additional finance cost associated with this venture is:

$$€/£136,875(€/£1,140,625 × 12\%)$$

The expected profit from the venture is adjusted to:

$$€/£313,125(€/£450,000 - €/£136,875)$$

KEY TERMS

Aggressive strategy	Over trading
Cash conversion cycle	Permanent working capital
Conservative	Temporary working capital
Moderate strategy	Under capitalisation
Neutral strategy	Working capital
Operating cycle	Working capital cycle
Opportunity cost	Working capital management
Over capitalisation	

REVIEW QUESTIONS

1. What is working capital?
2. What is over trading?
3. What is over capitalisation?
4. Rojo Plc manufactures engines. The market is competitive and profits are being squeezed in many of the other engine manufacturing entities. The company's directors are reviewing its current position, relative to the expected position in the coming year. They are happy to report that profitability will be maintained at the same level. The directors ask you for your comments before they announce the good news in this difficult time, to the equity holders.

REQUIRED

Analyse the following information in light of the above comments. In particular comment on working capital requirements. All purchases and sales are on credit terms.

	Current year €/£'000	Expected next year €/£'000
Sales	500,200	580,000
Cost of goods sold	420,050	500,000
Purchases	280,000	340,000

Working capital

Finished goods inventory	60,000	70,000
Work in progress	45,000	80,000
Raw material inventory	80,000	150,000
Trade receivables	62,500	65,000
Trade payables	42,000	60,000

CHALLENGING QUESTIONS

1.   CELLO plc, FLUTE plc and TRUMPET plc

Three companies, CELLO plc, FLUTE plc and TRUMPET plc have implemented different working capital management policies. Summary balance sheets for the three companies are as follows:

	CELLO plc	FLUTE plc	TRUMPET plc
	€/£	€/£	€/£
Non-current assets	200,000	200,000	200,000
Current assets	150,000	200,000	300,000
Total assets	350,000	400,000	500,000
Equity and reserves	150,000	200,000	250,000
Long-term debt (10%)	–	100,000	200,000
Short-term debt (12%)	100,000	50,000	25,000
Trade payables	100,000	50,000	25,000
Total equity and liabilities	350,000	400,000	500,000
Current ratio	0.75:1	2:1	6:1

The costs of goods sold functions are as follows:

CELLO plc	Cost of goods sold = €/£200,000 + 0.70 (Sales)
FLUTE plc	Cost of goods sold = €/£270,000 + 0.65 (Sales)
TRUMPET plc	Cost of goods sold = €/£385,000 + 0.60 (Sales)

As a consequence of the differences in working capital, expected sales for the three companies will vary under different economic conditions as follows:

	CELLO plc	FLUTE plc	TRUMPET plc
	€/£	€/£	€/£
Expanding economy	1,200,000	1,200,000	1,200,000
Stagnant economy	900,000	1,000,000	1,150,000
Declining economy	700,000	800,000	1,050,000

REQUIRED

a) Discuss the different working capital management policies utilised by the three companies.

6 Marks

b) For each company construct an income statement under each set of economic conditions. Assume that the corporation tax rate is 30%.

9 Marks

c) Examine the implications for working capital management which arise from your results in part b).

7 Marks
Total 22 Marks
(ICAI, MABF II, Autumn 1996, Q5)

2.   ICON plc

ICON plc operates a large chain of supermarkets. The most recent annual report of the company includes the following:

Income statement for the year ended 30 June

	Current year €/£ million	Comparative year €/£ million
Turnover	6,000	5,900
Cost of sales	5,000	4,870
Gross Profit	1,000	1,030
Administration and distribution expenses	584	660
Profit before tax	416	370

Balance sheet extract as at 30th June

	Current year €/£ million	Comparative year €/£ million
Current assets		
Inventories	292	280
Trade receivables	67	64
Short-term investments	98	90
Cash at bank and in hand	15	10
	472	444
Creditors: amounts falling due within one year	1,356	1,200
Net current liabilities	(884)	(756)
Current ratio	0.34:1	0.37:1
Acid test ratio	0.13:1	0.14:1
Cash to current liabilities	0.01:1	0.008:1

An equity holder of ICON plc has expressed concern about the liquidity of the company. He is particularly concerned that the current and acid test ratios are significantly poorer than the theoretical average of 2:1 and 1:1 respectively.

REQUIRED

a) Explain the term 'working capital cycle' and state why this concept is important in the financial management of a business.

5 Marks

b) (i) Calculate the working capital cycle for ICON plc for both the current and the comparative year, based on the information supplied.

(ii) Comment on the results in (i). Include in your comments your opinion as to whether or not the concerns of the equity holder are justified.

9 Marks

c) List THREE ways in which information technology can assist a company in the management of its working capital.

4 Marks
Total 18 Marks
(ICAI, MABF II, Summer 2002, Q7)

3.   BIDOR Ltd.

You work for a commercial bank and you have been asked to examine the draft accounts of BIDOR Ltd. ('BIDOR') whose principal activities are road transport, warehousing services and the repair of commercial vehicles,

You have been provided with the draft accounts for the year ended 31 October 20X6.

Summary income statement

	Draft 20X6	Comparative year
	€/£ '000	€/£ '000
Turnover	10,971	11,560
Cost of sales	(10,203)	(10,474)
Gross Profit	768	1,086
Administrative expenses	(782)	(779)
Interest payable and similar charges	(235)	(185)
Net (loss)/profit	(249)	122

Summary balance sheet as at 31 October

	20X6	20X5
	€/£ '000	€/£ '000
Non-current assets	5,178	4,670
Current assets		
Inventory (parts and consumables)	95	61
Trade receivables	2,975	2,369
	3,070	2,430
Current liabilities	250	–
Bank loan	1,245	913
Overdraft	1,513	1,245
Trade payables	270	–
Lease Obligations	203	149
Other Payables	3,491	2,307
Long-term liabilities		
Bank loan	750	1000
Lease obligations	473	–
	1,223	1,000
Net assets	3,544	3,793

You are also aware of the following facts:

(1)   The decline in turnover is attributable to:

(i) the loss, in July 20X6 of a long-standing customer to a competitor; and

(ii) a decline in trade in the repair of commercial vehicles.

(2)   Due to the reduction in the repairs business, the company has decided to close the workshop and sell the equipment and spares inventory. No entries resulting from this decision are reflected in the draft accounts.

(3)   The draft accounts show a loss for 20%, but forecasts indicate a return to profitability in 20X7 as the directors are optimistic about generating additional revenue from new contracts,

(4)   During the year, the company replaced a number of vehicles, funding them by a combination of leasing and an increased overdraft facility. Your examination forms part of the annual review of BIDOR's facilities,

REQUIRED

Prepare a report on the company's application to extend its financing facilities including the renewal of its overdraft, the limit of which currently stands at €/£1.2 million,

In particular, your report should:

a)   Analyse BIDOR's working capital policies for the two years ended 31 October 20X6.

6 Marks

b)   State the circumstances particular to BIDOR, which may indicate that the company is not a going concern, explain why these circumstances give cause for disquiet.

6 Marks

c)   State what further information you would require before making a final decision on the extension of the overdraft facility.

2 Marks

d)   Suggest some conditions that could be imposed if the facility was to be continued.

2 Marks
Total 18 Marks
(ICAI, MABF II, Autumn 2006, Q6)

4.   DIPPA PUBLISHING

DIPPA PUBLISHING Ltd. ('DIPPA'), a children's book publisher, has approached your bank and wants to borrow €/£250,000 in working capital. The company provides you with the following balance sheet and income statement data:

DIPPA PUBLISHING Ltd.
Balance sheet as at 30 June 20X7

	€/£	€/£
Non-current assets		925,000
Current assets		
Inventory	510,000	
Accounts receivable	375,000	
Cash	50,000	935,000
Less: Amounts falling due within 1 year		
Accounts payable	(166,000)	
Accrued expenses	(37,000)	
Short-term loans	(75,000)	
Current maturity of long-term debt	(25,000)	(303,000)
Long-term debt		(475,000)
		1,082,000
Financed by:		
Equity		1,082,000

DIPPA PUBLISHING Ltd.
Income statement – extracts for year ended 30 June 20X7

	€/£
Sales	4,622,800
Purchases	3,116,000
Cost of goods sold	3,504,100
Operating expenses	893,000

REQUIRED

a) Discuss the implications of adopting a conservative approach, as opposed to an aggressive approach, to working capital management.

8 Marks

b) Assuming a 365-day year, (and rounding to the nearest day), calculate the company's cash operating cycle. Using this information, estimate the company's working capital needs.

6 Marks

c) What general concerns might you have regarding this loan request?

4 Marks

Total 18 Marks

(ICAI, MABF II, Summer 2007, Q7)

INVENTORY MANAGEMENT

9

Debt   10,000,000
Equity   15,000,000
Market Value   25,000,000

LEARNING OBJECTIVES

Upon completing this chapter, readers should be able to:

♣ List the different types of inventory in different industries;

♣ Explain the objective of inventory management;

♣ Discuss influences on inventory levels;

♣ Calculate the optimum inventory reorder level and the inventory costs at this level;

♣ Evaluate the costs and benefits of deviating from the optimum reorder level where a discount is offered for bulk purchasing;

♣ Determine reorder levels under conditions of uncertainty in usage and/or lead times;

♣ Calculate the optimum batch size to produce in manufacturing companies, to minimise holding and set-up costs;

♣ Discuss various inventory management techniques such as: MRP; JIT; ABC inventory classification; periodic; and perpetual inventory systems; and

♣ Discuss other influences on inventory management.

Introduction

Since the first of January 2005, plcs and many large private limited companies in Ireland and GB have started to prepare their financial statements using International Accounting Standards. As a result of this process, business terminology in Ireland and GB has started to change to a global language. A consequence of this globalisation is that stock is now referred to as *inventory*. In any company, the business finance manager will not have direct control over levels of inventory. This will usually be agreed upon as a result of negotiations between the stores/purchasing manager, the production manager and the sales/marketing manager. These individuals are best placed to provide information on: sales demand for products; production requirements; the time it takes to obtain inventory; and the risks and costs associated with holding it. The business finance manager should also be included in the decision making process as he/she can shed light on the financial costs and benefits of various scenarios. This chapter focuses on explaining the importance of inventory management. It also discusses influences on inventory levels, the costs associated with holding inventory and the most common types of inventory management techniques in use.

Types of inventory: industry specific

Manufacturing companies
In manufacturing industries, inventory levels can account for about 15 percent of a company's assets. They are regarded as material assets which require careful management. There are four types of inventory: raw materials, work in progress, finished goods and consumables. Any company that manufactures goods will have varying amounts of each type of inventory. The liquidity risks associated with holding each type of inventory, factors that influence the level to be held and an example of each type of inventory are outlined in the next few paragraphs.

Raw materials can be resold and are considered less risky to hold, relative to other types of inventory. The quantity of raw materials held by a company is dependent on the demand for that material, by the production process. For example, if a manufacturer makes jeans, then an example of raw material inventory is the rolls of denim that are purchased from a cloth manufacturer.

Using the same example, *work-in-progress* would capture the value of those jeans that are partially complete at any one point in time. This value will include raw materials used, labour, and overhead costs attributed to the jeans at their stage of completion. This type of inventory is considered the most risky in terms of liquidity, as it cannot be readily sold. It is most likely that a scrap value amount is all that is recoverable, were the work in progress to be sold. In some instances, where the good being manufactured is specialised, the scrap value may be zero. Demand for work-in-progress is driven by demand for finished goods.

Finished goods are fully complete items that are ready for sale. The liquidity of this type of inventory is dependant on demand for the good. The greater the demand, the lower the risks associated with holding it. Finally, in the context of the manufacturing process, ***consumable inventory*** captures all other, usually immaterial, resources that are required for the production process. An example, might be thread or buttons for use in the production of jeans.

Retail entities

Retail entities typically have two types of inventory: purchased finished goods that are ready for resale and consumables. Consumables in this sector will include items such as price tags, hangers, bags, etc. The liquidity of purchased inventory depends on demand for the products. Retail entities normally have high levels of inventory relative to other industries.

Entities with intangible inventories

Other industries, such as service type sectors, have intangible inventory and consumables. ***Intangible inventory*** is normally work-in-progress. For example, in an accountancy or law firm, at any point in time, there will be a certain level of unbilled work-in-progress. This amount can be obtained from timesheets. Timesheets detail time charged each week to clients for on-going work or advice, provided in the week. This is work-in-progress that will be billed at a later stage.

Assessing inventory management

As highlighted in the previous chapter, a simple means of assessing the efficiency of inventory management is to consider the number of days that items remain in inventory. This is calculated using ratio analysis and can be used to examine separately: raw materials, work in progress and finished goods. However, if comparing different companies/competitors this detail may not be available, though, an overall average inventory days' value can be calculated and is a useful starting point.

$$\text{Average number of days' inventory} = \frac{\text{Inventory value} \times 365}{\text{Cost of sales}} = \text{Days}$$

Industry averages for this ratio are usually available and these can also be used as a guide to assessing the efficiency of a company's inventory management.

Influences on inventory levels

The type of industry, as discussed in the previous section, influences the type of inventory that a company holds. Other factors that influence the *level* of inventory held are now examined.

Potential consequences of stock-outs

The economic impact on the company of a stock-out will influence the level of inventory that a company holds. When a company runs out of inventory (**stock-out**) this may result in a lost sale, directly costing the company the contribution that could have been earned from the sale. Where a company's products are specialised this is less likely to happen, as a customer is more likely to order the product and wait for it. However, if the product is homogenous and the customer can obtain it elsewhere with ease; then the sale will more likely, than not, be lost. Therefore, the state of the economy influences the economic impact of a company experiencing a stock out. When an economy is in boom, a lost sale is more easily replaced by another sale as demand is usually high. However, when an economy is in recession, a lost sale is not easily replaced by another, and hence has greater economic impact for a company.

Where a company is a manufacturing entity, a stock-out of raw materials will affect production. For example, if a jeans factory ran out of denim material, this would result in idle time and overheads not being absorbed into products. This will result in an under-absorption cost adjustment for overheads at the period end.

Finance cost

Holding inventory is a necessity for most companies and deemed to be a good investment. However, as explained in the previous chapter, tying up funds *unnecessarily* in working capital has a cost. This cost is either the interest saving that could be achieved were the monies in the bank (if in an overdraft situation) or the opportunity return that could be achieved if the funds were used for another income generating investment. Therefore, the quality of investment that is available to the company and the company's ability to finance the additional investment will influence the cost associated with tying funds up in inventory. Where a company is experiencing capital rationing (see Chapter 13, 'Capital Investment Decision Making') these costs will be accentuated.

Value of inventory
Related to the previous paragraph the value of individual items of inventory will influence the level held. The opportunity cost of holding expensive items is greater (higher finance cost); and hence, companies are more likely to spend more time managing these items, relative to low cost items that tie up less resources.

Supply and demand factors
Where demand for a company's products is known with reasonable certainty or a predictable pattern is available; then inventory levels can be anticipated in light of the demand requirements and lower levels held.

Relationship with suppliers
The relationship with suppliers can also influence the required inventory holding. Where suppliers have established quick effective distribution channels and the company has built a strong relationship with its suppliers; then lower levels of inventory can be held, as new supplies will be received quickly.

Nature of inventory
The nature of the item being stored also affects the level and length of time an item can remain in stores. For example, highly perishable inventory such as fresh fruit and vegetables might remain in the stores of a fruit and vegetable distributor for a couple of hours (or less) each morning before being distributed to shops. On the other hand, a jeweller's inventory may be held, with its value unscathed, for periods extending beyond one year. Other product specific influences can alter the liquidity and value of inventory. For example, fashion changes can influence demand. If these changes are not anticipated then the liquidity/saleability of inventory reduces, as demand for it slows down. Technological change can also cause a shift in the liquidity/saleability of inventory. This is most evident in the computer hardware industry. New

software, which runs on hardware, usually requires larger memory space. As a result, the hardware industry continually has to develop its products to cater for new higher memory software packages; the result is that hardware becomes obsolete relatively quickly and a computer retailer needs to ensure that they do not hold large quantities of these relatively risky items, as they can date quickly.

Systems and procedures in place

When a company has good systems and procedures in place to keep track of inventory, to highlight potential stock-outs and action the replenishment of inventory quickly, then less inventory needs to be held. An effective integrated computerised system can result in a company having to hold lower levels of inventory relative to a manual system or a stand alone inventory system.

Costs associated with holding inventory and its management

Some of the costs associated with holding inventory have been discussed in the previous section: finance costs, obsolescence, deterioration and stock-out costs. These costs influence the *level* of inventory that a company chooses to maintain. The costs associated with inventory are usually sub-divided into four categories: purchase price, stock-out costs, holding costs and ordering costs. The ***purchase price*** is dependent on competition between suppliers, a company's relationship with the suppliers and the potential to avail of bulk discounts. ***Stock-out costs*** have been explained in the previous section. ***Holding costs*** include finance costs, obsolescence and deterioration (discussed previously) and in addition include other costs that are incidental to holding inventory, such as stores heat and light, stores rent and rates, stores insurance (buildings and inventory), damage, pilferage and the salaries of store men. Finally, ***ordering costs*** are those costs incidental to the ordering of inventory, such as the salaries of purchase staff, telephone and stationery. In manufacturing companies, the ordering costs associated with raw materials are overshadowed by manufacturing set-up costs that are incurred when there is a change in the product being manufactured. In manufacturing companies, set-up costs can include idle time, engineer time, etc.

Inventory management

Inventory management involves determining the *optimum inventory level*. The ***optimum inventory level*** is the level of inventory to keep that optimises the return achievable from the sale of inventory, whilst at the same time minimising the costs associated with holding inventory. There is conflict between these objectives. Holding high levels of inventory will ensure that no stock-outs occur. In addition, the company may benefit from bulk discounts and reduced ordering costs. However, high inventory levels will tie up funds resulting in high holding costs.

Tools to calculate inventory order quantities and reorder levels

The economic order quantity model

The *economic order quantity model* analyses two of the costs associated with the management of inventory (holding costs and ordering costs) at various order quantity amounts. The objective of the model is to find the *Economic Order Quantity (EOQ)*, which is the order quantity that minimises total holding and ordering costs. The relationship between the two costs and reorder quantities is presented in the following graph:

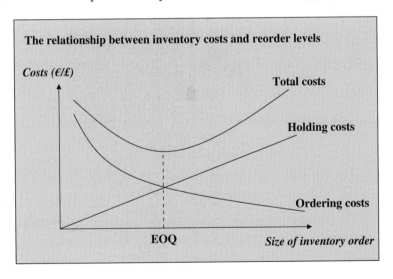

This graph shows that the EOQ is the order size at which ordering costs equal holding costs. This order size can be calculated using the following formula:

$$EOQ = \sqrt{\frac{2FU}{CP}}$$

The EOQ is the quantity that should be ordered. F is the fixed cost per order, U is the total usage (i.e. demand/sales) in units for the period and CP is the holding cost per unit.

Worked example 9.1   (Calculating the EOQ)

Lunes Ltd. sells 2,000 items during a 150 day period. Ordering costs are €/£100 per order and holding costs are £/€10 per unit for each 150 days.

REQUIRED

a)   Calculate Lunes Ltd.'s EOQ.

b)   Using the EOQ calculated in part a) calculate how often Lunes Ltd. has to order the product in each 150-day period (provide the number of times and interval of time between orders being made).

Solution

a)   U for this period is 2,000, F is €/£100 per unit and CP is €/£10.

$$\text{The EOQ is therefore: } \sqrt{\frac{2 \times 2,000 \times 100}{10}} = 200 \text{ units}$$

b)   The order needs to be made ten times in each 150 day period (2000/200 = ten times).

c)   This means that the inventory manager needs to place an order every 15 days (150/10 = 15 days).

Under the basic form of this model it is assumed that demand is known with certainty and is constant in the period. Demand can be ascertained from sales forecasts. Costs are also known with certainty and have a predictable relationship to quantities held and number of orders made in a period. Moreover, holding costs have a variable linear relationship with reorder quantities, wherein the higher the reorder quantities (resulting in higher inventory levels being held) the higher the holding costs. Ordering costs are assumed fixed per order, and hence are variable with the number of orders made. Therefore, total ordering costs per period fall as the size of the inventory order increases. The simple form of the model also assumes that inventory can be delivered immediately when the level in storage reaches zero. The following graph depicts the pattern of inventory usage and replenishment assumed under the simple EOQ model.

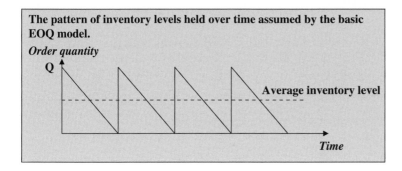

The pattern of inventory levels held over time assumed by the basic EOQ model.

Order quantity

Therefore, the average inventory held by a company will be Q/2 and the total holding costs for a period will be:

Total holding costs = Average inventory × Holding cost per unit

$$= \frac{Q}{2} \times CP$$

Where Q is the quantity ordered and CP is the holding cost per unit. The total ordering costs for a period will be directly related to the number of orders and can be calculated using the following equation:

Total ordering costs = Number of orders × Fixed cost per order

$$= \frac{U}{Q} \times F$$

Where U is the usage or demand level for the period being considered, Q is the reorder number of units and F is the fixed cost per order.

Finally, the total inventory holding costs will be:

Total costs = Holding costs + Ordering costs

These costs are minimised when the quantity reordered (Q) is the EOQ level.

Worked example 9.2   (Calculating inventory costs)

Lunes Ltd. sells 2,000 items during a 150-day period. Ordering costs are €/£100 per order and holding costs are £/€10 per unit for each 150 days.

REQUIRED

a)   Calculate Lunes Ltd.'s: holding costs; ordering costs; and total costs, if it orders at the EOQ level of inventory each time.

b)   Calculate the same information assuming Lunes Ltd. orders 1,000 units each time it makes an order and explain the reason for the difference to the result found in a).

Solution

a)   Total holding costs for the period is as follows: (see example 9.1, the EOQ is calculated as being 200 units and CP is £/€10 per unit)

$$= \frac{EOQ}{2} \times CP$$

$$= \frac{200}{2} \times €/£10 = €/£1,000$$

Total ordering costs for the period are as follows:
(U for the period is 2,000 and F is €/£100 per order)

$$= \frac{U}{EOQ} \times F$$

$$= \frac{2,000}{200} \times €/£100 = €/£1,000$$

Total costs are therefore: €/£2,000 (€/£1,000+€/£1,000).

b)   The quantity ordered (Q) is 1,000 units, therefore the costs will change to:

$$\text{Holding costs} = \frac{1,000}{2} \times €/£10 = €/£5,000$$

Continued

$$\text{Ordering costs} = \frac{2,000}{1,000} \times €/£100 = €/£200$$

Total costs = €/£5,200 (€/£5,000 + €/£200)

The company is worse off by €/£3,200 (€/£5,200 − €/£2,000) if it orders 1,000 units each time, as opposed to ordering the EOQ amount of 200 units, as the inventory holding costs outweigh the benefits obtained from a reduction in ordering costs.

This example uses an extreme variation from the EOQ amount, to highlight the potential additional costs that may be incurred by not taking account of the EOQ recommended level. However, it should be noted that small variations from the EOQ do not really change costs to a great extent. For example, if 250 units are ordered each time instead of the EOQ recommended quantity (200 units, see example 9.1) then the total costs will increase by €/£50 to €/£2,050. The range within with total costs do not vary by material amounts is called the '*Economic Order Range*' (EOR). The implication of this range is that the EOQ model can be successfully used in situations where demand is not completely certain.

Discounts and the EOQ model
One disadvantage of the EOQ model is that it does not incorporate the cost of the unit and how this may be impacted on by order size, in its formula. The only time it will become relevant is when the EOQ lies above a particular minimum quantity which has to be ordered to obtain a discount, as the EOQ can pinpoint the exact quantity to order to minimise costs, whilst obtaining the discount. If the EOQ lies on the underside of the minimum quantity required to qualify for a discount, then the total costs need to be calculated at the minimum order level allowed and compared to the costs at the EOQ level to determine if the discount is worthwhile. In this instance, product cost becomes a relevant cost. If the total costs with the discount are lower, then bulk ordering should take place.

Worked example 9.3   (EOQ and discounts)

Lunes Ltd. has an annual demand for 2000 units. The unit cost price is €/£60 and the cost per order is €/£100. The inventory holding cost per unit is €/£10, of which €/£8 relates to the financing of the purchase price of each unit.

REQUIRED

a)   Calculate the EOQ level and total costs at this level, including the cost of the units.
b)   Recalculate the EOQ level where a 4% discount is available for orders between 300 and 599.
c)   Recalculate the EOQ level where a 10% discount is available for orders of 600 and above.
d)   Recommend the optimal ordering policy for Lunes Ltd. based on the information calculated for requirements a) to c).

Solution

a)   U for this period is 2,000, F is €/£100 per unit and CP is €/£10.

$$\text{The EOQ is therefore: } \sqrt{\frac{2 \times 2,000 \times 100}{10}} = 200 \text{ units}$$

b)   The EOQ changes when a discount of 4% is offered as this impacts on holding costs. As 80% of the holding cost is related to the financing of purchases, the discount will reduce the finance requirements and hence the finance cost by 4%. Therefore, holding costs will now be: €/£9.68 (€/£2 + (€/£8 × 96%)).

$$\text{The new EOQ is therefore: } \sqrt{\frac{2 \times 2,000 \times 100}{9.68}} = 203 \text{ units}$$

Continued

c)   The EOQ changes again when the discount of 10% is offered as the holding cost reduces further. The holding costs will now be: €/£9.20 (€/£2+(€/£8×90%)).

The new EOQ is therefore: $\sqrt{\dfrac{2 \times 2,000 \times 100}{9.20}} = 208$ units

d)   To determine the optimal ordering policy the total costs with ordering at: the EOQ level of 200; the minimum order (300 units) at the 4% discount rate (as this is closest to the EOQ calculated in b)); and the minimum order (600 units) at the 10% discount rate (as this is closest to the EOQ calculated in c)) should be compared, to determine the least costly scenario.

Order quantity €/£	Purchase cost €/£	Order costs €/£	Holding cost €/£	Total cost €/£
200 (W1)	120,000	1,000	1,000	**122,000**
300 (W2)	115,200	667	1,452	**117,319**
600 (W3)	108,000	333	2,760	**111,093**

The optimal order quantity is 600 units. The cost saving in purchase price (€/£12,000) more than outweighs the increase in the total of the ordering and holding costs of €/£1,093 (€/£333+€/£2,760−€/£2,000). Therefore, Lunes Ltd. will be better off by €/£10,907.

W1: *Calculation of costs at the EOQ: order quantity 200*

Purchase cost: (2,000×€/£60)   €/£120,000
Order costs: See example 9.2   €/£1,000
Holding costs: See example 9.2   €/£1,000

Continued

W2: *Calculation of costs at discount one: order quantity 300*

Purchase cost: $(2{,}000 \times (€/£60 \times 96\%))$ €/£115,200

Order costs: $\dfrac{2{,}000}{300} \times €/£100$ €/£667

Holding costs: $\dfrac{300}{2} \times €/£9.68$ €/£1,452

W3: *Calculation of costs at discount two: order quantity 600*

Purchase cost: $(2{,}000 \times (€/£60 \times 90\%))$ €/£108,000

Order costs: $\dfrac{2{,}000}{600} \times €/£100$ €/£333

Holding costs: $\dfrac{600}{2} \times €/£9.20$ €/£2,760

Lead times, uncertainty and the EOQ model.
The EOQ model can still be used even where some of the assumptions underpinning the basic model are relaxed. It can be used where there is uncertainty in respect of demand for the goods and immediate delivery of the goods is not possible. These issues are now considered.

Delivery delay for units: under certainty.
In practice, it is unlikely that a supplier will be able to replenish inventories the minute they run out. Suppliers usually require time to prepare an order and to deliver it. The time taken between placing an order for inventory and receiving the units is called **lead time**. If a inventory manager knows the lead time of a supplier, then a reorder level of inventory can be set. The **reorder level** is the point at which a new order has to be made, to ensure that inventories do not run out. When demand for inventory is known with certainty for a period, the reorder level is:

Reorder level = Lead time in days/weeks × Usage in days/weeks

The average inventory level will not change, the assumption being that if the next order is made at the reorder level; this assures that delivery happens when inventory reaches zero.

> **Worked example 9.4**   (Lead times)
>
> Miercoles Ltd. has an EOQ of 500 units and reorders every 10 days. Its usage is constant per day. The supplier takes three days to deliver the goods.
>
> **REQUIRED**
>
> Under conditions of certainty calculate the reorder level of inventory to be set to ensure there are no stock outs.
>
> **Solution**
>
> The reorder level is: Usage per day × Lead time per day
> (500/10 × 3 = 150 units)

Delivery delay for units: under uncertainty

Where suppliers are located further away, or are unable to guarantee delivery in a set lead time, then a company will have to hold safety stock. *Safety stock* is the minimum level of inventory a company needs to maintain to ensure there are no stock-outs. The level held depends on the uncertainty surrounding lead times and also demand. Where there is uncertainty the average inventory held will be:

$$\text{Average inventory} = \frac{\text{EOQ}}{2} + \text{Safety stock}$$

The reorder level will be the:

Reorder level = (Average usage × Average lead time) + Safety stock

Worked example 9.5 (Reorder levels and uncertainty)

Miercoles Ltd. has an EOQ of 500 units and reorders every ten days. Its usage is constant per day. The supplier takes three days to deliver the goods.

REQUIRED

a) You are informed that the delivery delay on purchases may vary between three and six days. Calculate the new reorder level which should ensure no stock-outs (assume demand is a steady rate per day).

b) You are informed that sales demand for inventory can range from 400 to 600 units every ten days. Calculate the new reorder level, which should ensure no stock-outs (assume the lead time is known with certainty).

c) Assume that both uncertainties outlined in a) and b) exist. Calculate the new reorder level, which should ensure no stock-outs.

Solution

a) As the lead time may vary between three and six days and it is company policy not to run out of inventory, then the worst case scenario (i.e. six-day lead time) is assumed. Therefore, Miercoles Ltd. needs to hold six days of inventory. The daily usage of inventory is 50 (500/10) units per day. Therefore the reorder level should be set at 300 (50×6) units. This means that the company should hold a safety stock of 150 units (300−(50×3)).

b) Usage of inventory can range from 400 to 600 units in the ten day period. The policy is not to run out of inventory, therefore it will be assumed that the worst case scenario exists over the lead time period i.e. demand is at its highest per day. The maximum demand is 600/10=60 units per day. Assuming three days lead time a reorder level of 180 units (60×3) is required. Therefore, the safety stock level is 30 units (180−(50×3)).

Continued

> c) Where the lead time is variable, demand is variable and the company still maintains a policy of ensuring no stock-outs; then the reorder point will be the longest lead time by the highest usage, which is $360\,(6 \times 60)$ units. Therefore, a safety stock of 210 units will have to be held $(360 - (50 \times 3))$.

EOQ in manufacturing entities

Though the basic concepts in manufacturing companies in respect of inventory management is the same as retail companies, (i.e. they do not wish to loose sales, or incur excessive holding costs), there are some subtle differences: manufacturing companies produce inventories for sale rather than purchase them for sale; production can be disrupted by more factors ie raw material shortages, strikes, etc.; and the stockholding pattern is different. This is particularly so where machines used to produce one product have to be used to produce other items. This involves detailed production scheduling. In these circumstances the machines are scheduled to manufacture a certain quantity of an item (called batches), before having their set up changed so that they can be used to manufacture another item. This process should be planned, using the same ethos as the EOQ model, so that the costs of set-up and holding inventories are minimised. The set-up costs for manufacturing inventories include staff idle-time and any other ongoing cost that is normally absorbed into inventory i.e. overheads. The holding costs are similar to those incurred under the EOQ model.

A hybrid of the EOQ model, the ***Economic Batch Order*** (EBQ), is used to identify the optimum number of units that should be produced in each batch. The formula for this model is as follows:

$$\text{EBQ} = \sqrt{\frac{2FU}{CP(1 - d/r)}}$$

Where d is the demand rate per day, r is production per day, F is set up costs, U is demand in the period and CP is the holding cost of one unit. The next example shows how the optimum batch quantity is calculated.

Worked example 9.6   (Calculating the EBQ)

Viernes Ltd. a manufacturing company has customer demand for 2,000 units of item A in a 200-day period. Viernes Ltd. produces three different products and its machines are never idle. Production of item A is at the rate of 50 units per day. Set-up costs are €/£100 per batch and holding costs for item A are €/£20 per unit, for each 200-day period.

REQUIRED

a)   Calculate Viernes Ltd.'s EBQ.
b)   Using the EBQ calculated in part a) calculate how often Viernes Ltd. has to set up its machines to produce item A in each 200-day period (provide the number of times and interval of time between each set up).

Solution

a)   U for this period is 2,000, F is €/£100 per unit and CP is €/£20. The demand rate per day (d) is 2,000/200=10 units and the production rate per day (r) is 50.

$$\text{The EBQ is therefore: } \sqrt{\frac{2 \times 2,000 \times 100}{20(1-10/50)}} = 158 \text{ units}$$

b)   The company should produce quantities of 158 units at a time. Therefore, the machines need to be set up approximately 12 to 13 times in each 200-day period (i.e. 2000/158=12.66 times), or every 15 to 16 days (200/12).

Production is ongoing and will increase inventory levels by a constant amount per day, over the period of production. However, sales are also ongoing on a continuous basis and these deplete inventory. Therefore, when production quantities exceed sale quantities inventory levels will increase and when sales quantities exceed production quantities, inventory levels will fall. See the following graph for a presentation of this relationship:

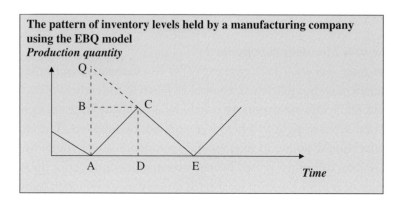

The pattern of inventory levels held by a manufacturing company using the EBQ model
Production quantity

In the above graph the EBQ is the amount of units making up AQ. The period A to E is the consumption period and it is assumed that sales take place at a constant rate over this period. Production of the good takes place in the period between A and D and production stops for the period of time between D and E. In this period the machine can be used to produce different products. Production will start again at time E and the next EBQ will start to be produced, and so on. In the time period A to D the production quantity exceeds sales quantities, hence inventory levels rise from A to C. When production stops at time period D; sales will deplete the inventory from C to E, as there are no additions to the inventory in this period.

Inventory management techniques

Materials Requirement Planning
Materials Requirement Planning (MRP (I)) is an inventory management tool that is used in manufacturing companies. It involves using computer planning software to determine raw material requirements, given a pre-programmed production schedule and known supplier lead times, to achieve a set quantity of finished goods. It is a ***demand driven system*** that identifies the minimum level of inventory that must be held whilst ensuring that production is not affected by stock-outs. The starting point for

management is to correctly determine sales demand; using this, then work back to estimate production and inventory requirements. A more sophisticated computer planning system, *Manufacturing Resources Planning (MRP (II))* extends the MRP system to include labour and machine requirements.

Just-in-time inventory management

Just-in-time inventory management (JIT) is a demand driven inventory management technique, which evolved in Japan in the early 1980's. When it works efficiently, no inventory is held by a company in stores as inventory is delivered straight to where it is required, by suppliers. The amount delivered should equate to the demand requirements of a company. This management technique is used by many companies throughout the world. Evidence of it can be seen in local retail grocery shops, wherein local bakery distributors and fruit and vegetable distributors bring their products straight to the shelves. The benefits of this system are reduced inventory levels (resulting in reduced storage costs and finance costs), reduced damage (retail), reduced defects (manufacturing) and reduced deterioration (retail), as inventory is being managed, to an extent, by suppliers. The supplier takes some responsibility for monitoring and ensuring there are no stock-outs. This should lead to greater productivity.

There are risks associated with this type of inventory management, as the responsibility for stock-outs is moved away from the company, to a certain extent. Though it is a straightforward idea, it usually has hidden costs, in that a company's quality procedures need to be strong and this involves a lot of management time. The company should have strong links, both on a personal basis and an information basis, with its suppliers. This means that suppliers should have access to the inventory monitoring system. Therefore, a computerised system is usually required with real-time information that is accessible by suppliers. To work efficiently suppliers are more likely to be local and have quick efficient distribution channels in place. Deliveries are frequent and cannot be incorrect. JIT is most suited to a manufacturing company that has high volume, steady, repetitive products and processes.

JIT also works well in local retail grocery outlets. Sales do not usually suffer if the supply from one baker runs out, as there is a substitute from another baker on a nearby shelf.

ABC inventory classification

The ***ABC inventory management system*** is a simple approach which involves classifying inventory into three categories: A, B and C. These categories are based on inventory value and/or importance. A items are usually expensive, or important. C items are usually low cost and not important. A typical ABC inventory management system will focus its attention on the management of A items, as these have the highest holding costs, and spend less time managing and monitoring C classified items (lowest holding costs). This means that companies implementing this policy will hold low quantities of item A and high quantities of item C, with medium levels being held for items classified as B. The latter category will typically receive more monitoring than C classified items, though less monitoring than items classified as A type items. A typical profile of the quantity and value of items held by a company adopting this type of inventory management is as follows:

ABC inventory profile

Classification	Quantity of items as a % of total items	Value of items as a % of total value
A	10	75
B	30	20
C	60	5
Total	100	100

The monitoring of A items is typically more sophisticated – forecasting, and scientific methods are used to determine order levels, reorder points and quantities of inventory to be held. Low safety stocks are held. B items would not be subject to the same detailed monitoring, with less frequent forecasting and limited use of scientific methods. C items are most likely consumables. For example, rivets, thread, buttons, etc. in a jeans manufacturing company. Simple techniques such as weighing or visually inspecting the inventory each month, or quarter, may be the extent of monitoring. High levels of safety inventories are held.

Other inventory management and monitoring systems

The two most common types of physical inventory monitoring systems are the periodic inventory control system and the perpetual inventory control system. The latter is sometimes referred to as the *continuous inventory control system*.

Periodic inventory control system

As the name implies, a *periodic inventory control system* involves reviewing inventory levels on a periodic basis. The purpose is to determine the number of items in inventory and to prepare reorder quantities based on the difference between a predetermined minimum inventory level and the actual quantities found. Minimum inventory levels are determined on the basis of sales forecasts for each forthcoming period.

The period between reviews depends on inventory turnover rates, which are affected by the type of inventory (for example more perishable goods require shorter period reviews) and management attitude to tying up funds in inventory. The review period is usually fixed and becomes a routine part of a store manager's duties. As the review period is usually fixed, companies that use this system hold high levels of safety stock. Where forecast sales are incorrectly estimated, the result will have great consequences for a company. On the one extreme it may experience lost sales, whereas on the other it may be left with excess inventory, which cannot be easily sold and is incurring high holding costs.

Companies who utilise this method to manage their inventories usually perform a physical stock count at set times. The count may be yearly, quarterly or monthly. The longer the period between inventory counts, the more likely a company is not to detect theft, damage or obsolescence. These counts may require stores to be closed to ensure an accurate count. In practice, stock counts take place at weekends or overnight so that production or sales are not disrupted.

Perpetual inventory control systems

This system ensures that production or sales are not affected. A *perpetual inventory control system* involves constantly monitoring inventory and reordering items at any time when reorder levels are reached. These systems are usually computerised and use EOQ, minimum reorder levels and safety stocks. Inventory counts are continuous and organised. This system may overlap with the ABC classification model, wherein items classified as A items would be subject to more attention i.e. more frequent inventory counts. It is normal to also undertake a physical count of total inventory once a year for the purpose of preparing the year end accounts/audit. The margin of error between inventory records and physical inventory is expected to be less than the margin expected in a company that uses a periodic inventory control system. This is because errors/differences are noted quickly and fixed throughout the year. This system is more time consuming and expensive to administer relative to a periodic system; however, lower levels of inventory can be held. Before implementing this type of system, a company needs to weigh up the additional costs to be incurred against the benefits to be gained. These systems usually involve tracking inventory from its arrival in the store, to its sale, or use in production. Large retail companies use this form of inventory management system, wherein each item has its own barcode which is scanned when the item is sold, or enters the store.

Other inventory management considerations

Choosing an inventory management technique or strategy is only a starting point in inventory management. There are other practical issues that need to be considered.

Computerisation
Many of the inventory management methods outlined earlier in this chapter are only feasible, if a company has an appropriate computerised system in place. Though computers save costs by reducing staff time. They usually require a large initial capital investment, staff training and ongoing maintenance. Most systems are integrated with the sales and purchases processes, with bar codes being used as a tracking device. The use of bar codes removes the requirement to manually have to record inventory details: as items enter stores; when items are removed from stores; and when items are sold by the company. Having one data entry point reduces the potential for *recording error* and also reduces *input time*. Most systems also have the facility to produce invoices, statements and receipts. In addition, an integrated system can be used for inventory management, as it can be linked to sales forecasts, which can be used to predict inventory demand, calculate

reorder levels, rolling EOQs and prepare exception reports – highlighting those items of inventory that need replenishment. Indeed, some systems can automatically email reorder requirements directly to suppliers.

Sales forecasting/demand management

The quality of inventory management is reliant on having accurate forecasts of demand for inventory. This means that sales forecasting, or production requirements scheduling, needs to be accurately determined. Accuracy is influenced by the sales teams industry awareness (ability to recognise: new trends; changes in preferences) and the reliability of information received from research teams - who are developing new products. Recognising declines in product demand and demand for new products is vital in achieving successful inventory management.

Obsolete/waste management

Sales forecasting is always based on estimates; hence, there is a risk that actual sales will be different to the estimated figures. Therefore, it is important that inventory managers have systems in place to deal with excess inventories that may be obsolete, or going out of date. This should be formulated into an *obsolete inventory management policy*. Regular reviews should assess the potential for inventory becoming obsolete. Computerised systems could be programmed to identify slow moving inventory. If the inventory is still in date and part of the sales plan, then discussions with the sales team should ensue. Perhaps a more aggressive approach could be taken to the sale of items. Techniques used include: placing items in prime sale locations; putting the items on promotion; offering a discount if purchased in bulk (for example *Buy One Get One Free (BOGOF)*); or giving items away free with the purchase of another item. Obsolete inventories do not move fast. Unless action is taken quickly, costs will increase. Obsolete inventories take up store space, which increases holding costs, uses space that could be used for other products and eventually results in wastage costs.

When an obsolete item is no longer part of a company's sales plan, that item is regarded as waste. A company should have a *waste management policy* in place to deal with unsaleable inventory items. This may involve selling the items at a price below cost (as can be noted in the reduced items basket in supermarkets, where for example, bread can be obtained for

20c/p), reworking the product (for example, where a new model of an item comes out, the parts of the old model may be saleable), or even removing the product from stores in the most environmentally friendly and low cost method. Dumping waste has a cost per tonne; therefore, if a company can recycle its inventory. This would be more economical and would give the company better publicity.

Quality maintenance

In today's competitive market, a concern for all management within a company is quality. Poor quality services, or products, can result in lost sales. Therefore inventory management should also consider the quality of products and how customers are treated. When sourcing a supply, an inventory manager should not just be attracted to the cheapest product, but should consider durability, taste, etc. When dealing with customers there should be a target delivery time set (if not immediate), a returns policy and a customer complaints policy.

Conclusion

Managers should try to balance the cost of holding and ordering inventory with the opportunity cost of losing sales, when an item is not in inventory. The objective is to reduce the overall cost to a company and its equity holders. This management process not only involves an acute awareness of the separate inventory costs, but is also reliant on there being sound information in respect of expected demand for inventory items. This can be achieved where there are strong communication channels between the stores manager and: the sales and marketing department; the quality control department; and the research and development department. Inventory management should also have operational procedures in place to identify and manage obsolete and waste inventories. There are many inventory management systems available and an appropriate system should be selected to suit the type of industry a company is in and the type of product a company makes/sells. The choice of system should balance initial costs (capital and training) of a system and its ongoing maintenance, with the benefits to be received from the system (reduction in inventory holding costs, wastage, obsolescence, less stock-outs, etc).

Examination standard question

Worked example 9.7

PAGEANT Ltd. ('PAGEANT') uses the EOQ to determine the optimal quantity of inventory that should be purchased at any time.

The company's product 'Gamma' which is ordered in by PAGEANT as a finished product, is normally consumed at a steady, known rate over the company's planning horizon of one year. However, in recent times demand has fluctuated throughout the year and, in order to protect itself against possible deviations, the company keeps a buffer inventory of 100 units. Further supplies are ordered whenever the inventory falls to this minimum level. The time lag between ordering and delivering is so small it can be ignored.

The costs of ordering Gamma include fixed costs of €/£40 per order plus a variable cost of €/£0.10 per unit ordered. PAGEANT stores its inventories in a warehouse, which it rents on a long lease for €/£6 per square foot per annum. Warehouse space available exceeds current requirements and, as the lease cannot be cancelled, spare capacity is sub-let on annual contracts at €/£8 per square foot per annum. Each unit of product Gamma stored requires 1.5 square foot of space. The company estimates that other holding costs amount to €/£4 per unit of Gamma per annum.

The purchase price of each unit of Gamma is €/£15 and PAGEANT's selling price is €/£25 per unit.

Annual demand for product 'Gamma' is currently 8,000 units.

REQUIRED

a)   (i)   Calculate the EOQ for Gamma.

4 Marks

    (ii) Calculate the annual expected profit on the sale of Gamma.

6 Marks

Continued

b)   Discuss the principal issues to be considered in managing inventories. Include in your answer how information technology can assist in dealing with these issues.

8 Marks

18 Marks

(ICAI, MABF II, Autumn 2002, Q6)

Solution

a)   (i) *EOQ*

Annual demand	8,000 units
Fixed cost per order	€/£40
Holding opportunity cost	€/£12 (€/£8 × 1.5)
Other holding cost per unit	€/£4

EOQ formula = square root of ((2 × order cost × annual demand)/ annual holding cost per unit).

$$EOQ = \sqrt{\frac{2(40)(8000)}{(12+4)}}$$

= 200 units per order

(ii)   *Calculation of annual profit of Gamma*

		€/£	
Sales:	(8,000 × €/£25)	200,000	
Cost of sales (W1)		125,600	
Profit		*74,400*	(37.2%)

W1: Annual costs at the EOQ

		€/£	€/£
Ordering costs:			
Fixed cost:	(€/£40 × (8,000/200))	1,600	
Variable cost:	(€/£0.10 × 8,000)	800	2,400
Holding costs:	(€/£16 × (200/2))	1,600	
(buffer inventory)	(€/£16 × 100)	1,600	3,200
Purchase cost:	(8,000 × €/£15)		120,000
Total costs			*125,600*

Continued

b)   Issues to consider when managing inventory
(the solution should include the following points):

- Type of inventory: raw materials; work-in-progress; finished goods; consumables.
- Variability of demand (The higher the level of uncertainty, the higher the level of finished goods inventory) (MRRP).
- Lead time, cost and reliability of supplies (EOQ assumes lead time is constant).
- Length (or complexity) of the production process.
- Relationship with suppliers (JIT).
- Proximity to customers.
- The physical condition of inventory.
- Special requirements for storage.
- Discounts available for bulk buying of inventories.
- Quantity of inventory.
- Information technology developments in inventory control.
- Value of inventory (ABC classification system).
- Costs of holding inventories versus the cost of a stock-out.
- Financing inventories.
- Obsolete inventory review.
- Quality issues.
- Waste management.

Note: Solution should incorporate the use of information technology in dealing with inventory management (for example, EOQ, EBQ, JIT, MRRP, point of sale systems). Some areas where these systems could be incorporated have been highlighted. A full solution would expand on these explanations.

KEY TERMS

ABC inventory management system

Buy one get one free (BOGOF)

Consumables

Continuous inventory control system

Demand driven system

Economic batch quantity

Economic order quantity

Economic order range

Finished goods

Holding costs

Intangible inventory

Inventory

Just-in-time inventory management

Lead times

Manufacturing resources planning II

Materials requirement planning I

Obsolete inventory management policy

Optimum inventory level

Ordering costs

Periodic inventory control system

Perpetual inventory control system

Purchase price

Raw materials

Reorder level

Safety stock

Stock-outs

Stock-out costs

Waste management policy

Work-in-progress

REVIEW QUESTIONS

1. What are the different types of inventory?
2. What is the purpose of inventory management?
3. What are the possible consequences of having a poor inventory control system in a manufacturing company?
4. Why does a company use the EOQ model?
5. What is JIT inventory management?
6. GREENSIDE
a) GREENSIDE plc has expanded the production of its micro-computer range and now requires 200,000 CD drives each year

which it obtains from an outside supplier. The cost of placing an order for the drives is €/£32 and it has been estimated that the holding cost per drive is 10% of its cost. The CD drives cost £8 each. Demand for the CD drives occurs evenly over the year.

REQUIRED

(i) Estimate the optimal order size and calculate how many orders will be required each year. Calculate the ordering costs and holding costs per annum.

4 Marks

(ii) If actual demand for the drives is 242,000 drives per annum, what is the impact on the cost of retaining the order size estimated in (i) above, instead of using a new order quantity? Comment on your results.

6 Marks

(iii) Are there any situations where the use of the EOQ is not appropriate?

2 Marks

b) Describe and assess the ABC classification approach to inventory management.

6 Marks
Total 18 Marks
(ICAI, MABF II, Autumn 1999, Q6)

CHALLENGING QUESTIONS

1.   MRP (I), MRP (II) and JIT systems

a) Discuss how computer technology can assist in the operation of a MRP (I) system (Materials Requirements Planning).

5 Marks

b) Discuss the essential features of a MRP (II) system (Manufacturing Resources Planning).

5 Marks

c)   It has been stated that the target objectives of Just-in-Time (JIT) are as follows:

(1) Zero inventories.
(2) Zero defects.
(3) Zero breakdowns.
(4) Batch sizes of one.
(5) Elimination of non value added activities.

REQUIRED

Discuss the managerial action that must be taken to try to achieve the target objectives of:

(i) Zero defects.
(ii) Batch sizes of one.

10 Marks
Total 20 Marks
(ICAI, MABF I, Summer 1999, Q3)

2.   **OCTAGON plc**

a)   Discuss and give examples of each of the following inventory management costs:
    (i) Ordering costs.
    (ii) Holding costs.
    (iii) Stock-out costs.

6 Marks

b)   OCTAGON plc utilises an EOQ model to determine optimal levels of raw materials. The following information is available for Material XY:

Current usage:	4,000 units per annum
Holding costs:	€/£15 per unit per annum
Ordering cost:	€/£30 per order

REQUIRED

(i) Estimate the optimal order level of material XY. Ignore the discount referred to below.

6 Marks

(ii) Recently another supplier has offered OCTAGON plc a 2% discount on the current price of €/£24 per unit, if the company orders in excess of 300 units each time.

Assuming that all other costs remain constant, advise OCTAGON plc as to whether it should accept the discount offered by the alternative supplier.

6 Marks
Total 18 Marks
(ICAI, MABF II, Autumn 1997, Q6)

3. **CRYSTAL plc**

a) Outline the main features of each of the following:
    (i) Periodic inventory control systems.
    (ii) Perpetual inventory control systems.
    (iii) ABC classification of inventories.

8 Marks

b) CRYSTAL plc is inviting tenders for the supply of a raw material to be included in a new product. The annual demand for the raw material is expected to be 4,000 units and the purchase price €/£90 per unit. The incremental cost of processing an order is €/£135 and the cost of storage is estimated to be €/£12 per unit.

REQUIRED

(i) Estimate the EOQ and the total relevant cost of that order quantity.

4 Marks

(ii) Assume that the €/£135 estimate of the incremental cost of processing an order proves to be incorrect and that it should have been €/£80, but that all other estimates are correct.

What is the cost of this prediction error, if the solution to part a) is implemented for one year, before the error is discovered.

3 Marks

(iii) One potential supplier has offered to supply all 4,000 units at a price of €/£86 each, if CRYSTAL plc agrees to accept delivery of the entire amount immediately. Assume that the incremental cost of processing this order is zero and that the original estimate of €/£135 for placing an order is correct.

Calculate the relevant cost considerations and, on the basis of your findings, indicate whether the company should accept the offer.

3 Marks
Total 18 Marks
(ICAI, MABF II, Summer 1995, Q6)

4.   PARMENEON

Parmeneon Ltd. uses 10,000 units of raw material per year on a continuous basis. The store manager estimates that it costs 25c/p to hold a unit of inventory in stores for one year. The purchasing department estimates that it costs €/£200 per order to place and process each order.

REQUIRED

a)   As finance manager of Parmeneon Ltd. you have been approached by the managing director to evaluate the cost effectiveness of the current ordering strategy, wherein ten orders are made each year. Outline any changes you would suggest.

9 Marks

b)   Write a brief summary outlining the limitations of the economic order quantity model to the managing director.

6 Marks
Total 15 Marks
(ICAI, CAP 1, Mock 2008, Q5)

TRADE RECEIVABLES/ PAYABLES MANAGEMENT

10

Debt   10,000,000
Equity   15,000,000
Market Value   25,000,000

LEARNING OBJECTIVES

Upon completing this chapter, readers should be able to:

* Explain the importance of trade credit to a company;
* Explain the objective of trade receivables/payables management;
* Measure average credit periods;
* Discuss influences on credit limits and credit periods;
* Discuss the costs and benefits associated with allowing credit sales and receiving credit purchases;
* List and explain the three stages of credit management;
* Evaluate the costs and benefits of reducing/increasing a credit period;
* Determine the annual equivalent cost of a cash discount (sales and purchases);
* Discuss the role of information technology in the management of trade receivables and trade payables; and
* Discuss ethics in relation to the management of trade receivables and trade payables.

Introduction

When a company supplies goods or services to another entity in advance of being paid for the goods or services, they have the option of allowing *trade credit* to their customers. Sales provided on credit are called credit sales, as opposed to cash sales. *Trade receivables* are the total outstanding balances on credit sales, due from customers to a company, at a point in time. Trade receivables are current assets. *Trade debtors* is another term to describe the balance of credit sales outstanding; however, the term *trade receivables* is used internationally.

When a company receives goods from another entity in advance of paying for the goods or services, they may receive *trade credit*. Purchases obtained on credit are called credit purchases, as opposed to cash purchases. The balance of credit purchases owed by a company at any point in time is called its *trade payables*. Trade payables are current liabilities. *Trade creditors* is another term to describe the balance of credit purchases owing; however, the term *trade payables* is used internationally. International phraseology is used in this text.

This chapter evaluates the management of trade receivables, otherwise known as credit management, and trade payables. The two areas are included in one chapter, as they are inherently linked; trade receivables in one company are trade payables in other companies. Therefore, the management policies in relation to both should be similar. There are greater risks associated with a company having trade receivables; therefore, this area receives more attention in companies and, hence, is given prominence in this chapter also. The management of trade payables is considered at the end of the chapter.

Measuring the trade credit period

As highlighted in chapter eight, 'Working Capital: An Introduction', a simple means of evaluating efficiency in the management of trade receivables is by measuring the *trade receivables cash conversion period*. This ratio calculates the number of days that credit sales are outstanding on average. This is calculated using ratio analysis.

$$\frac{\text{Average trade receivables}}{\text{cash conversion period}} = \frac{\text{Trade receivables} \times 365}{\text{Credit sales}} = \text{Days}$$

Industry averages for this ratio are usually available and these can be also used as a benchmark when assessing the efficiency of a company's credit management policies.

Trade credit: cost implications

When a company allows trade credit, it is forgoing a cash inflow. This results in an immediate finance cost to the company. When allowing trade credit is an ongoing policy of a company, the result is a long-term investment in trade receivables, which has an opportunity cost. The funds, if received as cash, could be used to reduce an overdraft, thus reducing interest. They could also be invested in a deposit account, earning interest, or could be used to finance a new project, which could yield a return. In addition, allowing credit creates other costs that would not otherwise occur. First, granting credit creates exposure to payment default (**bad debts**). Second, funds are tied up, resulting in a reduction in liquidity. This may have cost implications in other areas; it might hinder a company's ability to, for example, pay suppliers within a specified timeframe that would enable the company to avail of a discount. Third, credit management and control practices, policies and procedures need to be established and maintained, which will result in incremental administrative costs. The next two examples present methods that are used to estimate the finance requirements associated with granting credit. The first assumes that a constant trade credit policy is adopted for all credit customers; the second incorporates uncertainty into the scenario.

Worked example 10.1   (Finance requirement under certainty)

Cuatro Ltd. has €/£10 million in sales. 20% of these are cash sales. A credit period of 30 days is allowed, although 50% of credit customers take 50 days. Assume there are 360 days in a year.

REQUIRED

a)   Calculate the overdraft facility that Cuatro Ltd. has to arrange to ensure that trade receivables are adequately financed.
b)   What is the cost of the current credit policy, given that the bank overdraft rate is 12%?

Continued

Solution

The company will need to finance the funds that are tied up in average trade receivables.

a)   Credit sales are: €/£8,000,000 (€/£10,000,000 × 80%)

	€/£
Average trade receivables are:	
(€/£8,000,000 × 50% × 30/360)	333,333
(€/£8,000,000 × 50% × 50/360)	555,555
Total trade receivables (finance requirement)	888,888

Cuatro Ltd. will need to arrange a €/£888,888 overdraft facility to finance its trade receivables.

b)   The finance cost of this credit policy is therefore:

$$€/£888,888 × 12\% = €/£106,667$$

In example 10.1, 30 days are allowed; however, customers take on average 40 days to pay for credit sales ((50% × 30) + (50% × 50)). Therefore, the finance requirement could also be calculated using the weighted average trade receivables cash conversion period (i.e. €/£8,000,000 × 40/360 = €/£888,888). Example 10.2 uses this approach and extends it to incorporate risk (the probability that a variety of given outcomes will occur).

Worked example 10.2   (Finance requirement under uncertainty)

Cuatro Ltd. has €/£10 million in sales. 20% of these are cash sales. A credit period of 30 days is allowed. Cuatro Ltd. has analysed the payment pattern of its credit customers and considers that there is a 10% chance that credit customers will take 25 days, a 50% chance that they will take 30 days, a 30% chance that they will take 50 days and a 10% chance of them not paying at all. Assume there are 360 days in a year.

Continued

REQUIRED

a)   Calculate the overdraft facility that Cuatro Ltd. has to arrange
to ensure that its trade receivables are adequately financed.

b)   What is the cost of the current credit policy, given that the
bank overdraft rate is 12%?

Solution

a)   Credit sales are: €/£8,000,000 (€/£10,000,000 × 80%)

Average days credit sales are outstanding:	Expected cash conversion period
(10/90 × 25)	2.78
(50/90 × 30)	16.67
(30/90 × 50)	16.67
	36.12

The trade receivables that need financing are: credit sales less bad
debts, multiplied by the expected trade receivables cash conversion period: €/£722,400 ((€/£8,000,000 × 90%) × 36.12/360).

b)   The finance cost of this credit policy is:

$$€/£722,400 × 12\% = €/£86,688$$

The company also expects to incur €/£800,000 in bad debts:
(€/£8,000,000 × 10%). Therefore, the total cost of the current
credit policy is €/£886,688.

Trade credit: the benefits

Trade credit is used by many companies to attract sales. Indeed, it has
become so enshrined in marketing policies that, in some industries, a normal credit period is expected and if a company chose not to provide trade
credit, this would seriously damage demand for the company's goods or
services as customers would go to a competitor for the good or service.

The objective of trade credit management

The provision of credit is not a productive use of company funds, unless the granting of credit results in a profitable sale that would not otherwise have taken place or in keeping a sale that would otherwise transfer to a competitor. Just as tying funds up in inventory is considered a necessary investment, allowing trade credit should also be regarded as a necessary investment (in most industries). The objective of trade receivables management is to balance the costs of not allowing credit (lost contribution from sales, as customers turn to competitors who provide credit) with the costs of providing credit (holding costs, such as bad debts, the opportunity cost of funds tied up, increased administration costs) to provide the maximum net benefit to equity share holders.

Worked example 10.3 (Special contract/order)

Cero Ltd. is currently evaluating a new contract that will result in annual sales of €/£3 million. The company has a contribution margin of 20%. The average credit period allowed to customers is 80 days. 80 days credit is also received from suppliers. Annual marketing costs amount to €/£170,000, payable on the first day of each year. Cero Ltd. expects 10% of the sales to be uncollectable. Cero Ltd. has a cost of funds of 12%.

REQUIRED

Evaluate whether Cero Ltd. should accept this new contract or not.

Solution

Benefit	€/£
Additional contribution: (€/£3,000,000 × 20%)	600,000
Costs	
Marketing	(170,000)
Bad debts: (€/£3,000,000 × 10%)	(300,000)
Financing (*W1*)	(7,890)
Net annual gain	122,110

Continued

> *W1: Financing*   €/£
>
>   Trade receivables:
>   ((€/£3,000,000 − €/£300,000) × 80/365)   591,781
>   Trade payables:
>   ((€/£3,000,000 × 80%) × 80/365)   (526,028)
>   Net finance required   65,753
>
>   Expected additional finance cost:
>   (€/£65,753 × 12%)   €/£7,890
>
> Based on the above cost benefit calculations, it is expected that the
> company will benefit, to the tune of €/£122,110 each year, from the
> new contract. Therefore, the company should accept the contract.

Most companies have trade receivables. There are some exceptions, such
as food stores, hairdressers or off-licences. In GB and Ireland, trade receivables, on average, account for 25–35% of total business assets. In most
companies, the trade receivables balance is regarded as material. Hence
effective management can impact significantly on company performance.
In the last paragraph, the objective of credit management was explained,
however, a cost benefit analysis is not the only factor influencing trade
credit policy – other influences are now considered.

Trade credit: influences on policy

Marketing strategy and strategic growth

Every company has to market its products to gain sales. Where a company's
products are specialised and there is high demand for its items, then the
marketing strategy can focus on these features. However, in a market where
products are more or less homogenous, terms of sale become very important
and discounts and credit periods are regarded as important marketing tools.
These are used very effectively by, for example, furniture stores that market
their credit period with 'buy now, pay nothing until 2012'. In these circumstances, the cost of financing the item is usually factored into the price
of each item. When a company offers an unusually long credit period, it is
likely to be pursuing more than one agenda. It recognises that trade credit
costs and risks increase when long credit periods are offered; however, it will
balance this with the benefits to be achieved from, for example, breaking

into a market or expanding a market (which will lead to future, more profitable sales). Other situations that increase the attractiveness of allowing long credit periods include allowing credit to get rid of slow-moving inventory or inventory that is subject to obsolescence. The alternative may be to scrap these items.

Industry influence

In most industries, companies try to conform to an industry norm. Therefore, where a company allows a credit period of 40 days, and the industry norm is a credit period of 30 days, then, theoretically, this company can reduce its credit period to 30 days without losing sales, as the competing companies do not offer better terms. A company that allows longer credit terms than the industry norm can usually charge slightly higher prices, resulting in a return on the additional investment. If a company were to reduce its credit period below the industry average, then it is likely that they would lose sales, unless their sales price was lower or they offered discounts. In these instances, the additional costs (discounts or loss in sales price) and benefits (reduction in bad debts, reduced finance costs) would need to be evaluated to determine whether reducing price is worthwhile.

Quality control mechanism

The trade credit period is sometimes used by a customer to assess the quality and effectiveness of a good that has been purchased. If the good is not of the same quality as was advertised, is faulty or not fit for purpose, then the customer is in a much stronger position to reverse the transaction and send the good back, compared with a situation where the good has been paid for, up front.

Effective trade credit management

A company should have a *credit systems and procedures manual* to formally record its policies and practices in respect of the management of its trade receivables. There are three main stages associated with managing trade receivables. The stages follow on from each other, as highlighted in the following diagram:

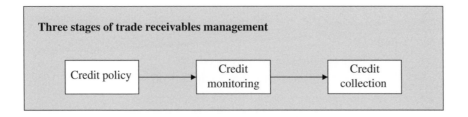

In each of the stages, staff should be appropriately trained and have an awareness of the importance of acting efficiently – 'time is money'.

Credit policy

A company's *credit policy* outlines the conditions underlying the provision of goods or services for credit. This is different to a company's *terms of sale*, which are the conditions underlying the sale of goods or services in cash or credit. Getting the credit policy correct is very important. Allowing longer credit periods usually stimulates more sales, resulting in larger trade receivable balances, with higher holding costs. As long as the contribution from the additional sales exceeds the costs associated with holding larger trade receivables, and liquidity is not jeopardised, then this will be beneficial for a company. A company's credit policy should be flexible, though within boundaries. It should be clear and should answer several questions.

Questions that a credit policy should be able to answer

- What is the strategic objective of the company in respect of credit sales?
- Has it been decided to use the company's credit terms to attract sales?
- Who should be permitted to purchase goods on credit (individuals, businesses, companies)?

Continued

- What should the credit limit for an individual, business or company be?
- How long should the credit period last?
- What is the industry-average credit period?
- How are customers vetted for creditworthiness?
- Are there different credit terms for different risk classes of customers? Is a formalised credit rating score being used?
- Where there are production/supply constraints, is the system capable of changing the credit terms to maximise the company's profitability, without affecting its long-run position?
- Is there a policy for bad debts?
- What are the procedures when a customer breaches its credit period?

Some of these questions are now considered in more depth.

Credit assessment

The decision to allow trade credit to a customer is exactly the same decision a bank has to make when granting a loan. Therefore, each company should have a credit policy, with set credit assessment procedures in place to assess the probability of a credit customer being a slow, or bad, payer. Steps may include:

- Obtaining a *credit rating* or a *special credit report* from a credit bureau. Financial information can be obtained on companies from the likes of Dun and Bradstreet, who source reliable financial information on companies and use this to give them a credit rating. The credit rating awarded is influenced by feedback from a company's suppliers. Other companies, such as Equifax, can provide credit information for individuals also. Care should be taken with credit reports (they should not be used in isolation). For example, a poor credit rating can occur as a result of a customer not being registered on the electoral register (personal experience). To refuse credit in this instance, may upset an otherwise solid credit rated customer, who may take their custom elsewhere.

- Obtaining *trade references* from companies that a customer has traded with in the past. This will outline other companies' experiences when trading with the customer on credit. The quality of this source of information is influenced by the reputation of the company providing the reference. The companies to be approached for a trade reference should be selected by the credit manager, not those recommended by a customer requesting credit. A proforma request form that is quick and easy to complete will improve the chance of another company providing a reference, as will an offer to reciprocate the task in future.

- Obtaining *bank references* in respect of a customer's financial standing. A company can also request information on whether inventories or trade receivables are secured against debt. Customers have to consent to their bank providing this information, before the bank will release the information. The bank charges the customer a fee for providing this service. Bank references may not be as independent as you would initially think. Banks in debt to a potential credit customer may in fact be more interested in the customer obtaining their funding using trade credit, than from an extension to an existing overdraft. A bank's loyalty will always be to its customer, not to an external company making a credit enquiry. Bank references are usually carefully worded proforma letters; therefore, they should be used in conjunction with other evidence on creditworthiness.

- Obtaining information from other departments or individuals within your own company, who have a history or knowledge of the company applying for credit. Where the potential credit account is sufficiently large, a visit to their premises can provide valuable information.

- Obtaining copies of a company's financial statements for the past three years (abridged/abbreviated financial statements) and using these to analyse the company's liquidity and financial position. Financial statements can be obtained from the Company Registrar, for a small fee; alternatively the customer could be asked to supply copies.

Each of the above actions involves time and money; therefore, the extent of investigation required should depend on the size of the credit account requested and the potential profits to be made.

Credit limit

A **credit limit** is the maximum amount of sales that a company will allow on credit to a customer. This is influenced by the credit assessment outcome. There are usually two approaches to setting a credit limit. The first links the credit limit to the sales requirements of a customer. A *factor of customer monthly sales requirements* is usually set as the credit limit. The Better Payment Practice Group (BPPG) recommends that this factor does not exceed two. This policy allows the credit limit to grow, and shrink, in line with customer needs. It needs constant review and is best suited to customers who are regarded as low credit risks. The second method is to set a maximum amount that the company is prepared to be owed by customers as a whole. A common benchmark is the lower of 10% of net worth or 20% of working capital. This approach is easier to implement and needs less revision, though may not be as popular with customers.

Credit period

The **credit period** is the length of time customers are permitted to pay for credit sales. A company's credit policy is sometimes detailed on invoices or credit agreements and may be shortened to, for example, 5/7, net 40. The first part of this (5/7) means that a discount of five percent is permitted if payment is received within seven days; the second part (net 40) means if payment is not made within seven days, the full amount is due within 40 days. Where a customer is a company, a review of their trade receivables period should provide guidance on the maximum period of credit to allow them. Where the length of credit permitted by them is shorter than the period allowed to them, then this is too long and the customer is using the additional credit period to finance other activities. A company's policy in respect of the length of credit period given does not necessarily have to be homogenous, and may be influenced by the individual credit rating of a customer. In addition, the type of industry and normal credit period awarded will influence this decision, as will the type of good (high-turnover goods normally have short credit periods, as do perishable goods or goods with low profit margins), competition for sales and customer type.

Credit agreement

When an initial risk assessment has been completed, a credit agreement should be prepared and signed by all parties involved. The customer should be made fully aware of the rewards for paying within a discount period and the consequences of failing to pay within the credit period permitted. The *credit agreement* should outline all the terms and conditions pertaining to the credit allowed, including discounts, interest penalties and formalised processes adopted by the company to recover overdue debts. The BPPG suggests that each credit agreement should consider about twenty different areas.

Areas which should be covered in a credit agreement (trade receivables and payables)

1. Definitions (e.g. buyer, seller)
2. Quality
3. Price
4. Quotations
5. Delivery/date/arrangements
6. Risk and property/retention of title
7. Terms of payment
8. Time limit for raising disputes
9. Right to interest and compensation for debt-recovery costs
10. Loss or damage in transit
11. Acceptance of goods
12. Variations to contract
13. Patent rights/indemnity
14. Force majeure
15. Jurisdiction/applicable law
16. Assignment and sub-letting contracts
17. Right to inspect goods
18. Warranties and liability
19. Severability
20. Insolvency and bankruptcy

(source: BPPG website)

All companies should prepare a *standard credit agreement* that considers all the above areas, where relevant. This agreement should be tailored for each customer. When agreed, a letter should be sent to the customer confirming key terms. This introduces the person who is managing the account to the customer and reiterates key conditions.

Document processes

A company should also have a ***prompt action code of practice,*** wherein invoices are issued when goods are delivered, highlighting the credit period agreed. Statements are automatically generated for each outstanding customer account and sent either by email or posted to each customer a couple of days before the credit period is breached. Statements should detail the total outstanding balance and should break it down into the periods of time outstanding. This may be split into amounts due in more than one month, within one month, immediately and overdue – with the latter highlighted as being urgent. Statements may include interest on overdue amounts, if this has been agreed in the credit agreement.

Credit monitoring

This is the second phase in credit management. ***Credit monitoring*** involves analysing customers' payment patterns, with the aim of classifying customers according to their credit record. This involves assessing the associated risks based on changes in payment behaviour and determining the likelihood of a debt becoming bad. It may also lead to a renegotiation of the credit limit where it is deemed to impede potential additional sales from a growing customer. The whole process weighs up the cost of monitoring and chasing up a debt, with the benefit to be derived by receiving the debt at all or receiving it earlier than expected.

The BPPG suggests using a 80/20 rule for the management of trade receivables, wherein the few customers (20%) making up the majority of the sales (80%) receive most attention and are prioritised in terms of service and when queries arise.

Reporting

Good credit monitoring can be simplified with the use of an appropriate bookkeeping software package that allows exception reporting. For example, SAGE allows a user to set up default credit limits and periods. When a customer breaches a limit, their account is flagged (the font automatically appears in red). Aged analysis can also be viewed at the touch of a button. This breaks a customer's outstanding balance into those that are due in the current period, within one month, within two months and so on. The use of an aged debtor analysis is vital for highlighting customers who are starting to slow their normal payment pattern, stimulating further investigation. It can also highlight growth and spark renegotiations about a new limit.

Risk rating

On an ongoing basis, credit monitoring should continually classify and code customers according to their perceived credit risk. This will involve, in part, the reports explained in the last paragraph. These should allow a credit manager to quickly assess a customer's payment record and to identify early signs of financial problems. These may include, breaches in the agreed credit period or paying round sums that are below the balance that is in the statement as being due.

If a customer is considered to be becoming higher risk, then this should spark other credit assessment procedures identified earlier, such as meeting with the client to discuss the situation or obtaining fresh credit reports, bank references, trade references or copies of the latest financial statements. These procedures might also include talking to sales people who visit the client and visiting the client. A benchmark risk coding structure might look like the following:

Customer risk-profile code

1. *New:* Customers with short history of trading with the company.
2. *Low risk:* Customers with the best credit history, the strongest references etc.
3. *Average risk:* Customers who have breached their credit terms in the past on an ad hoc basis, but who always pay and whose references are good.
4. *High risk:* Customers who are identified as persistent slow payers and who have poor credit rating.

A company should focus its attention on selling goods or services to those customers coded as risk level two and three; however, they should not rule out selling to customers coded as risk level four when enough business cannot be generated from the risk level two and three customers. Where this happens, the proportion of sales to these customers should not deviate from a set level, the agreed price should reflect the increased risk and the accounts should be monitored closely.

Credit collection

There are many techniques that can be used to assist with credit collection. These range from document design, offering cash discounts for early payment and having clearly agreed overdue account procedures.

Document design

Invoices may be designed to include a detachable bank paying in slip or direct debit slip, to allow customers to process their payment with ease. A direct debit mandate may be agreed at the outset, and the invoice amount automatically transferred from the customer account to the company account within the specified credit period. Each statement should have a detachable part, which should be returned with payment. This will quicken the processing of payments by the credit department. Statements should detail payment address, the person to whom a cheque should be written, a contact name and a contact number for the customer to use, if there is a query. Queries should be appropriately recorded in a queries book or database and there should be a policy of dealing with queries within a pre-determined time frame.

Cash discounts

Cash discounts are used as incentives to encourage customers to pay their accounts within a short period, which is usually shorter than the agreed credit period. Cash discounts are a reduction in the outstanding balance, usually by a set percentage and only apply until a set date.

> **Worked example 10.4** (Cash discounts)
>
> Pero plc offers its customers 30 days credit; however, customers normally take 45 days credit. Pero plc is considering whether to offer a two percent discount for payment within ten days.
>
> *Continued*

REQUIRED

Calculate the effective annual cost for Pero plc of offering a two percent discount for payment within ten days.

Solution

The cost of the discount is: $2/(100-2)=0.0204\%$ for a 35 $(45-10)$ day period
Number of 35-day periods in a year is: $365/35=10.43$ times
Effective annual interest rate is: $(1.0204)^{10.43}-1=23.44\%$

As is highlighted in example 10.4, cash discounts are expensive. Companies usually allow discounts: where they have liquidity problems and no cheaper source of finance is readily available; where competitors provide discounts and failure to join the trend will result in lost sales; where the discount will significantly reduce bad debts; or where the discount will attract new customers.

As discounts are not recoverable, they do not have an opportunity cost of finance; therefore, discounts are deducted from credit sales when determining the finance cost.

Worked example 10.5   (Cost of finance: net of discounts)

Gato plc currently offers 60 days' credit to its customers (i.e. credit terms are net 60). Annual sales amount to €/£500,000 and are spread evenly over the year. The company's cost of funds is 16% per annum. A cash discount of 3% for payment by customers within 30 days is currently being considered (i.e. the revised credit terms would be 3/30, net 60). It is expected that 40% of customers would avail of the discount.

REQUIRED

Determine whether the discount should be offered. Assume that all sales are on credit.

Continued

Solution

This can be assessed by calculating the cost of the current credit policy, relative to the alternative policy of offering the discount.

Current costs

Finance costs	€/£	€/£
Customer balances requiring financing:		
(€/£500,000 × 60/365)	82,192	
Cost of finance: (€/£82,192 × 16%)		13,150

Proposed costs
Discount (40% of customers):
(€/£500,000 × 40% × 3%)   6,000

Finance costs

Customers with no change (60%):		
(€/£300,000 × 60/365)	49,315	
Customers taking discount:		
((€/£200,000 − €/£6,000) × 30/365)	15,945	
Trade receivables balance requiring financing	65,260	
Cost of finance: (€/£65,260 × 16%)		10,442
Total proposed costs		16,442

Incremental cost of new scheme:
(€/£16,442 − €/£13,150)   3,292

Therefore, the discount should not be implemented as this will increase credit costs by €/£3,292.

Late payment procedures

At the outset, customers should be categorised according to a risk assessment of their credit worthiness. This allows the more risky customers to be monitored closely. However, even with close monitoring, customer accounts may become overdue. Therefore, companies who permit credit should implement a set of procedures to deal with overdue accounts. As mentioned previously in the chapter, sales should be invoiced promptly and statements sent out in advance of the payment being due. When accounts become overdue, a series of payment-collection steps should be followed, in order of severity. A timetable may include the following:

- If payment is still overdue a week after the normal time limit has elapsed, write to each customer reminding them of the overdue account. This letter should inform each customer that their account is no longer eligible for the agreed discount (where appropriate) and is now being charged interest at the agreed rate (where this was a condition of the credit agreement). This correspondence could also be faxed or emailed to each customer to quicken the collection process. However, a signed letter has a more personal touch to it; hence, it may have greater chance of success.
- If a customer still has not paid the account within ten days of receiving the letter, or has not made other arrangements, then telephone the customer in respect of the overdue account.
- At this juncture, a customer visit by sales staff or credit control staff may be necessary. When you are at the customers premises, it may be worthwhile offering the customer a payment plan, whereby they can settle their account over a certain period of time (you may charge for this facility; again this would have been agreed in the initial credit agreement), or requesting that the customer obtain a loan to settle the account (in these instances, the company may have a relationship with a finance house to provide loans, which they underwrite).
- If the customer has not paid within a week of the telephone call or visit, send a more forceful letter, possibly threatening to withdraw future supply to the customer, if the account is not paid within a set time frame.
- If payment is still not made, telephone the customer again and write to them threatening legal action if payment is not received within a specified time frame.
- Finally, if the customer still does not settle the account, take legal action or get a debt-collection company involved.

In cases where, at the outset, a customer is categorised as being a credit risk, then the credit policy should be strict in respect of breaches in the credit limit. Where breaches do occur, goods should not be supplied to the customer until earlier supplies are paid for. This will limit the exposure to even greater losses.

Protection against bad debts

Historically, many small businesses in GB and Ireland have failed as a result of late-payment problems. As discussed previously, a strong credit management system will reduce a company's exposure to bad debts. The governments in both regions have a vested interest in increasing the awareness of companies in respect of the importance of having proper cash and credit-management procedures in place. Industry bodies such as the *Confederation of British Industries* promote an overall prompt payment ethos in the business world. Support for companies on credit management policies and practices can be sourced easily on the Web. For example, the BPPG website provides advice and guidance on how to establish and maintain a robust credit-management system, supplies information leaflets and provides information on legislation in respect of late payment.

The authoritative legislation on late payment is the *EC Directive on Late Payment*. The aim of this legislation is to combat late payment in commercial transactions in EC companies. The existence of similar legislation across different countries should provide companies that trade in other EC countries greater payment certainty. This legislation allows companies to charge interest when there is late payment of commercial debt, to claim reasonable compensation of debt-recovery costs incurred as a result of chasing up late payments and to challenge grossly unfair terms and conditions where these undermine the legislation.

Reducing credit risk exposure

There are some steps that can be taken to reduce the risk of bad debts. These are now discussed in turn.

Steps to reduce the risk of bad debts

Discounts: Discounts for early settlement, as discussed earlier.

Percentage rebates for prompt payment: These are similar to discounts, though are usually linked to volume also. Like discounts, **percentage rebates** are expensive and should only be awarded when a customer pays on time.

Special payment terms: Where a customer has been categorised as high risk, then **special payment terms** may be started. These can include stopping supply and renegotiating the current debt or allowing a limited supply of goods, for cash, or a shorter credit period whilst coming to an agreement in respect of the existing debt. When the existing credit balance is recovered, a short special credit period should be maintained, until confidence in the customer's financial position improves.

Part payment: This is usually used where a customer is regarded as being risky. The balance is normally payable within the normal credit period.

Payment protection insurance: Where the sums involved are high and a customer is risky, it may be worthwhile having an arrangement with a finance house, with a link to an insurance company, to provide finance to the customer and to allow them to purchase **payment protection insurance**.

Legal expenses insurance: This may be purchased through a broker. Its aim is to cover the legal costs associated with bringing a customer to court to recover a debt. This can be a deterrent to some customers who might chance not paying their bill, on the premise that it will cost too much to recover the debt.

Stakeholder accounts/secure deposits: The customer lodges funds for the goods or service with an independent intermediary. This type of arrangement is normally used where the customer has requested or purchased an item that has a long-term impact on the company providing credit; for example, a contract to build a building.

Continued

> The sums involved are usually large and intermediaries are normally used as risk-reducing half-way houses to ensure that the company supplying the good knows that funds are available in an account for the sole purpose of paying for the project, and the customer has assurance that the funds will not be released until quality targets and set stages of the build are complete.

The use of technology in credit management

Small, owner-managed companies can sometimes, if an owner is well organised and devotes sufficient time to credit management, operate without a formalised, effective credit-management system. However, the majority of companies need a formal system in place to keep track of transactions. In smaller companies with fewer transactions, this system may be manual; however, the majority of companies would benefit greatly from the use of an appropriate integrated accounting software package. A good customer management system will allow the collection, compilation, storage, analysis and retrieval of information. The main benefits are summarised as follows:

Advantages of information technology for credit management

Saves time: Computerisation usually saves credit control staff time as invoices are entered once by the sales department. In addition, a customer's credit agreement terms can be viewed at the touch of a button.

Monitoring tool: The accounting package can be programmed to monitor overdue accounts by highlighting those that are close to, or in breach of, their predetermined credit limits.

Decision making: The system can be programmed to accept or reject a sale depending on the credit limit. This may be beneficial for front-line sales staff who can blame the system for a refused sale and not have to bear the brunt of customer dissatisfaction being directed at them.

Documentation: The system can be programmed to produce standard invoices, statements and reminder letters and even to produce labels for envelopes.

Continued

Management by exception: This should improve credit managers' decision making as they can manage by exception and, hence, can focus on more risky customers. This is made possible by the use of exception reporting, wherein the system can produce aged analysis reports, payment pattern reports and forecast payment cycles (which are of interest to the treasury department). In addition, if it is set up, the system may generate a report that analyses the payment patterns by, for example, comparing a company's payment patterns with industry averages, analysing payment patterns by region or analysing payment patterns by product type.

In all instances, a cost-benefit analysis should be undertaken to determine whether a technological system should be used. The costs associated with a computerised credit management system include: the substantial capital investment required at the outset; training of credit control and sales staff at the outset and when there are upgrades; and software upgrades and computer maintenance costs.

Credit management system: system controls

Where credit management is supported using technology, two types of controls are required: system procedural controls and computer controls. *System procedural controls* focus on ensuring that the credit management assessment techniques used are appropriate. This involves putting in system checks to ensure that: credit limits are reviewed and considered for amendment on a regular basis; more resources are directed to riskier accounts; invoices and statements are processed quickly, efficiently and accurately; each account is managed in line with the conditions agreed in that customer's formal credit agreement; disputes are adequately dealt with in an appropriate timescale; slow payers are chased up diligently, with all the steps being taken to recover the debts of the company (in line with the slow payment process schedule); and systems are in place to minimise conflict between the sales team (who source the sales), the credit department (who may subsequently refuse credit) and the production team (who have to meet sales demand requirements).

There are two types of *computer controls:* user controls and program controls. *User controls* focus on ensuring that the correct information is entered accurately in the system (for example, the correct price and quantities appear on sales invoices) by putting in controls to ensure that the invoice details are checked to order forms and despatch forms and that the details are input correctly to the system. The treatment of VAT should also be checked. User controls should also ensure that only a credit manager can agree credit limits, credit periods, discount rates, agree interest penalties, and initiate the suspension of supply and start late-payment procedures. The credit payment process should confirm that each payment is matched against the correct invoices and highlight unmatched items for further investigation.

Program controls are concerned with the workings within a computer system after the customer's default settings are established. Default settings comprise customer details and credit agreement details and typically include: credit rating, date account was opened, details of the person who agreed the account, customer address, customer contact name, customer telephone number, customer email address, customer fax number, credit limit, credit period, discount allowed and interest payable when the account is overdue. A good system should be capable of storing and archiving transactions from prior accounting periods. It should have strong links between the information used by the sales department to win sales and the credit department who manages the credit accounts. The sales department should have full knowledge of the credit limit for each customer. The system should be programmed to disallow a sale that causes a customer to breach their limit. This stops an existing problem from increasing and provides an incentive for customers to pay their accounts. The system might also be programmed to require management intervention to match and clear an outstanding invoice, or when a customer pays an invoice amount net of an agreed discount after the agreed time has lapsed. To assist the efficiency of chasing up late payers, the system may be programmed to automatically suggest follow-up action, including producing standard follow-up letters and regular statements.

Overseas trading

Although it is a source of growth, overseas trading brings with it increased risks; in particular, currency exposure and credit risks. Managing these risks is costly and requires specialist knowledge about the foreign country. There may be different payment cultures, attitudes to credit limits and cash discounts that are country specific. A survey by the Credit Management Research Centre (2003) of UK companies that export, reported the following: 69% of the sample surveyed felt that they spend too much time chasing up overseas accounts; 84% are seriously concerned about experiencing overseas bad debts; most felt that overseas credit periods were increasing and 50% use payment protection insurance for their overseas accounts.

Some guidance on the practices and economic climate in different countries can be sourced within the UK from the UK Trade and Investment website and the Trading Safely website *(www.trading-safely.com)*. The latter site provides ratings, insolvency trends, collection methods, a payment incidents index and risk assessment, for different countries. Another useful website is the Credit Services Association website *(www.csa-uk.com)*. It provides information on how to select an overseas collection agent and has a list of registered collection agent members.

Trade receivables and financing

A company's trade receivables are an asset. They represent monies that are due to a company in the short term. As such, they can be used by a company to raise funds. The two most common forms of security on trade receivables are the assignment of debt to specific invoices (such as invoice discounting or acceptance credits) or the sale of all customer accounts or a proportion of the total customer accounts or a collection of specific customer accounts, to a factor for an upfront amount. These sources of finance are discussed in detail in chapter four, 'Asset-Mix Decision, Finance-Mix Decision and Short-Term Sources of Finance'.

Trade payables management

Credit suppliers or creditors supply goods and services to a company in advance of receiving payment from the company. Therefore, they can be considered a source of finance to a company. In most instances, companies would not be able to trade if they did not to receive trade credit from suppliers. Like the other working capital areas (inventory, trade receivables, cash) the aim of sound *trade payables management* is to maximise equity holder wealth. This involves minimising the costs of administering the trade payables function and to maximise the opportunity gain from this low cost form of finance (by maximising the trade payables cash conversion period), while ensuring that supplies are not disrupted and discounts are taken when it is cost beneficial to do so. The policy to be followed by a company in respect of the payment of supplies should not be decided in isolation. The policy has to be viewed in terms of its impact on production, stores costs and sales.

Measuring the trade payables period

As highlighted in chapter eight, 'Working Capital: An Introduction', a simple means of determining a company's policy in respect of trade payables is to measure the length of the trade payables cash conversion period ratio. This ratio calculates the number of days that credit purchases are outstanding on average.

$$\frac{\text{Average trade payables}}{\text{cash conversion period}} = \frac{\text{Trade payables} \times 365}{\text{Credit purchases}} = \text{Days}$$

Industry averages for this ratio are usually available and these can be used as a benchmark when assessing the efficiency of a company's trade payables management policies.

Trade payables management: a cost-benefit analysis

Costs
Every company that operates on a credit basis has a higher administrative burden than a company that operates on a cash-only basis. Purchase ledger clerks need to be employed to manage suppliers' accounts. Most companies also require an appropriate computer software package to record and keep suppliers' account information up to date. The benefits of computerisation are similar to those outlined above for trade receivables.

If a supplier feels that a company is abusing an agreed credit limit, then this will diminish supplier goodwill. The result is that the supplier may withdraw agreed cash discounts, remove trade discounts (pushing up purchase price), charge interest on overdue accounts and place *less* emphasis on getting supplies to a company promptly. The latter will increase the uncertainty of inventory lead time, causing stock-outs initially and subsequently causing the inventory manager to hold a higher level of safety inventories, which will result in higher inventory holding costs.

An additional cost is managerial time. An important aspect of trade payables management is the maintenance of good relations. Time should be scheduled for improving relations with the main suppliers, as this will increase the likelihood of negotiating a better price and will help to smooth over instances where a problem occurs (so long as this is not a frequent occurrence) – for example, where a cheque is not issued within the appropriate agreed timescale.

Benefits

As mentioned in the introduction to the section on the management of trade payables, receiving credit from suppliers is a source of finance. It is the same as receiving a free loan. The benefit can be quantified as it equates to an opportunity saving in finance costs, which equals the amount of credit received multiplied by the relevant finance rate. This rate depends on the circumstances of each company. If a company is operating using an overdraft, then the rate used is the overdraft rate (if suppliers are paid in cash, the company would have a larger overdraft and would be paying additional interest). Alternatively, if the company is cash rich, the rate to be used is either the weighted average cost of capital or the opportunity return that could be received from an investment of the funds, where this is higher than the weighted average cost of capital. Therefore, the longer the trade payables cash conversion period, the greater the benefit to a company.

Availing of discounts receivable is also beneficial. As highlighted earlier in the trade receivables section, discounts allowed are costly to a company; therefore, in a similar vein, availing of cash discounts receivable is an attractive option, as highlighted in the next example.

> **Worked example 10.5** (Trade payables: discounts received)
>
> Late Ltd. normally pays its main supplier after 60 days. The supplier is offering a discount of 3% for payment in ten days. Late Ltd. has a cost of funds of 16%.
>
> **REQUIRED**
>
> Advise whether Late Ltd. should avail of the discount on offer.
>
> **Solution**
>
> The return on the discount is $3/(100-3)=0.03092\%$ for a 50 $(60-10)$ day period
> Number of 50-day periods in a year $=365/50=7.3$ times
> Effective annual interest rate $=(1.03092)^{7.3}-1=24.9\%$
>
> This return is higher than their reported cost of funds (16%); therefore, Late Ltd. should avail of the discount and pay their main supplier within the ten-day limit.

Trade payables management: policy and procedures

Fostering a strong credit reputation and ethical approach
In all instances, a company should negotiate a suitable credit policy with its suppliers. The company allowing credit will be considering all the aspects referred to earlier in the chapter in respect of the management of trade receivables. Therefore, a starting point is to make the credit reputation of the company strong, as this will be used by a supplier to assess the level and length of period to allow credit. Some steps to improve, or create, a good credit reputation include: always paying bills on time; fostering good relationships with suppliers who will then report positively on their experiences of trading with the company; getting listed with a credit rating agency; filing financial statements and the annual return with the Companies Registrar on time (if a limited company); and encouraging key personnel in the company

to have good personal credit practices. The latter is particularly important where a company is very small, as a supplier may request credit references for an owner or for directors.

Where the sums involved are material, the terms of the negotiations can be formalised into a written credit agreement. At this stage, it is up to managers to negotiate the best deal, in terms of purchase price, discounts, credit period and credit limit, with the supplier. This may be achieved by agreeing to direct a significant portion of the company's purchase requirements to the supplier.

Procedural issues

When a credit agreement is finalised, the trade payables function should ensure that the maximum period of credit is taken, but not breached. This will involve checking that invoices are not received, or dated, until the date the goods or services are received. The credit period should start when goods arrive, not when an order is made. Where invoices have an earlier date, the supplier should be informed immediately and asked to reissue a correctly dated invoice. At this stage, the accuracy of the invoice should also be verified, by ensuring that stores have checked the goods received to the purchase order and the invoice. Problems should be alerted immediately to the supplier. It is bad practice to use a minor error as an excuse to delay payment, where there is no issue with the quality of the product or service. If the error is material, or the quality of the product is an issue, then this is a different matter.

Where an invoice has been authorised by a purchases/stores manager for payment, and the dates agreed, it should be input promptly to the system. This will ensure that management are fully aware of their company's financial commitments at all times, that cash flow forecasting is more accurate and that disputes can be settled more efficiently.

When statements arrive from suppliers, only the balance that is due for payment within the agreed credit period should be paid. Statements normally include *all* outstanding amounts. Where a discount is offered by a supplier for payment earlier than that negotiated in the original agreement, this should be referred to the payables manager immediately. The payables manager will undertake a cost-benefit analysis to compare the equivalent annual rate of the discount to the company's weighted average cost of capital. The manager should also consider the company's liquidity position, arrange additional financing through the treasury department, if necessary, and inform creditor ledger staff of the decision in sufficient time to allow them to process the relevant payment earlier.

Payment culture/ethics

In GB, NI and the ROI there is an ethos of taking longer credit periods than in other countries. This culture is seen as a business deterrent by policy makers in each region and steps have been taken to try to change the culture of slow payment.

The first sign of policy being implemented in this respect is evidenced in the ROI, where the *Prompt Payment of Accounts Act* was enacted in 1997. This Act placed a legal obligation on plcs to pay their accounts within agreed time limits, or face interest penalties. The Act also placed a legal obligation on public bodies to publish a yearly report in respect of their payment policies. In 2002 this Act was extended by the *EC (Late Payments in Commercial Transactions) Regulations* to include payments made by all private sector companies and to limit the interest rate that can be charged on late payments to the European Central Bank (ECB) rate plus seven percent. In addition, the Regulations allow suppliers to claim compensation for debt-recovery costs, where applicable.

In GB and NI the *Late Payment of Commercial Debts (Interest) Act* came into force in 1998. It allows small businesses to claim statutory interest (set at the Bank of England Base Rate plus eight percent) for late payments from large companies and most of the public sector. The Act was updated in 2002 to incorporate the features of the *European Directive 2000/35/EC* and, like the legislation in the ROI, allows companies to charge interest on all overdue accounts and gives them the right to claim reasonable debt-recovery costs. Small and medium-sized companies also have a right to ask a representative body to challenge grossly unfair credit-contract terms used by customers.

To change the culture of taking long credit periods the Confederation of British Industry (CBI) issued a *Prompt Payment Code,* which suggests that a responsible company should: have a clear, consistent policy that it pays its bills in accordance with; not extend or alter payment terms without prior agreement from a supplier; provide clear guidance on payment terms to suppliers; and ensure that an appropriate system is implemented for dealing with supplier disputes and complaints quickly. In addition, where a company disputes a supplier invoice, they should inform the supplier of the issues without delay. This Code has been updated by the *Better Payment Practice Code,* which has not changed the underlying ethos, but is administered by the BPPG. Companies are invited to sign up to the code and can use the BPPG logo on their marketing material. Detailed guidance on good management practices for dealing with suppliers and customers can be found by accessing their support website (http://payontime.co.uk).

Conclusion

Credit managers should try to balance the cost of allowing credit with the benefits to be derived from the additional contribution earned because of allowing credit. Purchase managers should try to balance the benefits to be derived from paying for items quickly with the opportunity finance cost of allowing funds to leave the company before necessary.

Underlying good management in both areas is a necessity to have an ethical collection and payment policy, which is clearly defined in a written credit agreement and strictly adhered to by personnel. Each function should have clearly defined procedures and controls to ensure that personnel adopt an appropriate approach to dealing with customers/suppliers. Quality in these processes is vital for the smooth management of collection and payment functions. Information technology can greatly assist the management process within each function, by keeping an up-to-date database of the individual details of customer and supplier companies, providing exception reports, graphical patterns of customer and supplier behaviour, timely documents and letters and up-to-date information on balances. ePurchases and eSales can also save time and improve company profitability. However, the importance of human interaction with suppliers and customers cannot be understated. In addition, the efficiency and accuracy of information that is input to computer systems influences the quality of reporting from the system.

Examination standard question

Worked example 10.6

a) Outline the factors that a company should consider before giving credit to a new customer.

7 Marks

b) SEDLEY plc ('SEDLEY') is a wholesale supplier of office stationery with an annual turnover of €/£1 million. It gives its customers 30 days credit. Credit control has been very relaxed but management has become concerned because customers are now taking an average of 60 days credit and bad debts average 2% of total annual turnover.

Two options to improve the situation have been proposed:

(i) A discount of 2.5% could be offered to all customers who pay their debts within 20 days. It is expected that 60% of customers would pay within the discount period. The costs of administering this scheme are estimated at €/£3,000 per annum, but it is expected that bad debts would be reduced by 50%.

(ii) SEDLEY could use the services of a local credit control company to collect the debts on its behalf. SEDLEY would still be responsible for the debts. However, it is likely that the credit control company would take an aggressive approach to collection and that 70% of the debts would be collected within the official collection period of 30 days. The remaining 30% would continue to take the 60 days.

The fee for this service is 1.5% of annual turnover. However, bad debts are be expected to fall to 30% of their original level and there would be administration savings of €/£7,000 per annum.

Annual turnover is expected to fall by €/£30,000 as a result of the aggressive approach of the credit control company.

The gross profit margin of SEDLEY is 20% and the cost of capital is 10%.

Continued

REQUIRED

Recommend which option would be more profitable for SEDLEY, setting out clearly your reasoning and showing the calculations necessary to support your recommendation.

11 Marks

Total **18** Marks

(ICAI, MABF II, Summer 2003, Q7)

Solution

a)   Factors to consider before giving credit to a new customer.
     The main factors to be considered can generally be discussed under the heading *The Five Cs* as follows:
     1. *Capacity:* Refers to a customer's ability to repay. A credit check with a reputable credit agency, such as Dun and Bradstreet, should be performed.
     2. *Capital:* Refers to the financial soundness of a potential creditor. The overall financial standing can be checked by analysing recent financial statements using ratio analysis.
     3. *Conditions:* Refers to the agreed terms of sale and 'normal' industry conditions.
     4. *Character:* Sources of character references include bank references, trade references, published accounts, credit rating agencies etc. Generally, as a matter of course, references should be sought from a bank and at least two trading customers.
     5. *Collateral:* Refers to the value of security that a customer can offer, if any.

As well as the above, two other major considerations are, the length of the credit period requested and the maximum value of credit allowed at any one time. These depend on the following:

- Credit terms operating in the industry;
- Degree of competition in the industry;

Continued

- Bargaining power of particular customers (average purchase size);
- Risk of non-payment; and
- Marketing strategy.

b) *Option 1: Discount scheme*
    Benefits: €/£
       Bad debts reduction: (€/£1m × 2% × 50%)   10,000
       Release of cash (*W1*)   6,493
    Costs:
       Administration   (3,000)
       Discount: (€/£1m × 2.5% × 60%)   (15,000)
    Net Cost   (1,507)

W1: Finance saving from cash being made available   €/£
Existing investment in trade receivables:
   (€/£1m × 98% × 60/365)   (161,096)
                                                     €/£
New investment in trade: receivables
   (€/£1m × 60% × 97.5 × 20/365)   (32,255)
Plus: (((€/£1m × 40%) −
   €/£10,000) × 60/365)   (64,110)   (95,165)
Release of cash   64,931
Saving of 10% cost of capital: (€/£64,931×10%)   6,493

Option 2: Credit controller
    Benefits: €/£
       Bad debts reduction   14,000
       Administration   7,000
       Release of cash (W1)   5,844
    Costs:
       Fee: (€/£970,000 × 1.5%)   (14,550)
       Loss of turnover: (€/£30,000 × 20% margin)   (6,000)
    Net benefit   6,294

Continued

> W1: *Finance saving from cash*
> *being made available*   €/£   €/£
> Existing investment in trade receivables:
>   (€/£1m × 98% × 60/365)   161,096
>
> New investment in trade receivables:
>   (€/£970,000 × 70% × 30/365)   (55,808)
> Plus: (((€/£970,000 × 30%) −
>   €/£6,000) × 60/365)   (46,849)   (102,657)
> Release of cash   58,439
>
> Saving of 10% cost of capital: (€/£58,439 × 10%)   5,844

KEY TERMS

Bad debts

Bank reference

Cash discounts

Credit agreement

Credit limit

Credit management

Credit monitoring

Credit period

Credit policy

Credit rating

Credit systems and
   procedures manual

Creditor

Customer risk profile codes

Debtors

Legal expense insurance

Part payment

Payment protection

Percentage rebates

Program controls

Prompt action code of practice

Risk rating

Risk profile

Special credit report

Special payment terms

Stakeholder accounts/
   secure deposits

System procedural controls

Terms of sale

Trade credit

Trade credit period

Trade payables

Trade receivables

Trade reference

User controls

WEBSITES THAT MIGHT BE OF USE

Better Payments Practice Group (BPPG) website:
http://payontime.co.uk

Confederation of British Industries (CBI) website for details of the *Prompt Payment Code:*
http://www.cbi.org.uk

Credit Management Research Centre (CMRC) website for reports on credit policies:
http://www.cmrc.co.uk/publications.htm

Credit services association website:
www.cas-uk.com

Debt Collection Ireland for an example of a debt collection agency:
www.eircollect.com/

Irish Business and Employers Confederation (IBEC) website:
http://www.ibec.ie/

Trade Safely website:
www.trade-safely.com

UK Trade and Investment website for information on credit policy when exporting:
https://www.uktradeinvest.gov.uk/

REVIEW QUESTIONS

1.   What is the 80/20 rule?
2.   What steps should be taken when a customer starts to exceed their credit limit?
3.   Explain the term 'credit period'.
4.   Explain the term 'credit quality'.
5.   What are the costs and benefits associated with granting credit?
6.   Ocho Ltd. has been offered an order for 10,000 computers at €/£500 per computer. The following table outlines the probability estimates of repayment terms.

Probability of repayment	*Payment terms*
10%	36 days
60%	45 days
20%	72 days
10%	Bad debt

REQUIRED

Calculate the average level of trade receivables which must be financed were this order to be accepted.

7.   Insight Ltd. is currently considering whether to expand into a new market. Revenues costs are projected as follows:
   - It is estimated that sales in the new market will be €/£10 million per annum
   - 60 days credit would be allowed
   - Insight Ltd. earns a contribution margin of 20% on sales
   - Insight Ltd.'s suppliers give 30 days credit
   - Collection costs are expected to amount to €/£100,000
   - The bad debt risk is estimated at 5% of sales
   - Inventories held by the company will increase by €/£1 million
   - Insight Ltd. has an annual cost of funds of 12%

REQUIRED

Evaluate Insight Ltd.'s proposal to expand into the new market.

10 Marks
(ICAI, CAP 1, Pilot paper, 2007, Q3)

8. a)   In terms of working capital management, describe what is meant by:
   (i) An aggressive working capital policy; and
   (ii) A defensive working capital policy.

6 Marks

b) The directors of WESTON plc are concerned about the level of the company's interest payments. Financial information for two six-month periods is given below:

	January to June 20X6 €/£'000	January to June 20X8 €/£'000
Sales	3,300	3,600
Credit sales as % of total sales	85%	95%
	€/£'000	€/£'000
Average trade receivables	700	1,350
Average inventories:		
Raw materials	95	120
Work-in-progress	210	220
Finished goods	115	80
Average overdraft interest rate (% per year)	8.5%	17%

REQUIRED

(i) The directors have estimated that the interest cost of financing inventories and trade receivables has more than trebled in the period under investigation.

Evaluate WESTON plc's policy in relation to inventories and trade receivables over the period.

6 Marks

(ii) Discuss strategies that the company could implement to reduce the interest cost of trade receivables and inventories.

6 Marks
Total 18 Marks
(ICAI, MABF II, Autumn 1998, Q7)

9. Design a risk assessment checklist to be used in the monitoring of customer balances.

10. What is the key aim in the management of payables and how can a company achieve this?

CHALLENGING QUESTIONS

1.   GULA Ltd.

GULA Ltd. ('GULA') is a recently established company, purchasing electrical equipment for resale to building contractors and retail traders within Ulster and North Leinster.

The terms of sale require payment within a month of invoicing. Customers do not adhere strictly to this and, being new in the marketplace, the company is not in a position to enforce very rigorous credit controls.

However, it is anticipated that the company will have no difficulty in maintaining its current monthly sales at a constant value of about €/£150,000.

At present the average pattern of payment by customers is as follows:

Month 1 -   15%
Month 2 -   35%
Month 3 -   30%
Month 4 -   15%
Month 5 -   5%

The company relies heavily on bank finance at an existing interest rate of 2% per month. The managing director is anxious to reduce the cost of finance, and has suggested a possible alternative scheme:

Alternative Scheme:
To give cash discount of 2.5% for payment within one month. It is believed that this will give a revised payment pattern as follows:

Month 1 -   40%
Month 2 -   30%
Month 3 -   10%
Month 4 -   15%
Month 5 -   5%

The additional cost of implementing improved credit control procedures would be €/£500 per month.

REQUIRED

a) Detail at least FOUR steps that a company should undertake (either before or after the granting of credit), if it wishes to pursue a rigorous policy in relation to the collection of debts. Expand briefly upon the consequences of these steps.

6 Marks

b) State the circumstances under which a customer might decide to take advantage of cash discount terms.

4 Marks

c) Calculate the net present value of the cash flows arising from the sales in perpetuity under each of the following assumptions:

(i) That all customers always pay in full on the last day of the month in which a sale is made.

2 Marks

(ii) That the cash flows are in line with the existing credit terms being taken by customers.

3 Marks

(iii) That the cash flows followed the pattern described in the alternative scheme as proposed above.

3 Marks
Total 18 Marks
(ICAI, MABF II, Autumn 2005, Q7)

N.B. The discount factors for periods in years at annual rates are equally applicable to periods in months at monthly rates.

2.   CURVE Ltd.

CURVE Ltd. ('CURVE') is a small Irish manufacturing company. The following are extracts from the financial statements of the company for each of the three years ended 31 December 20X4.

CURVE Ltd. – Income statement (extracts) for year ended

	Notes	31 Dec. 20X4	31 Dec. 20X3	31 Dec. 20X2
		€/£'000	€/£'000	€/£'000
Sales		2,400	2,160	1,728
Cost of sales	(1)	2,220	1,944	1,512
Gross profit		180	216	216
Profit after tax		120	156	161

CURVE Ltd. – Balance sheet (extracts) as at:

	Notes	31 Dec. 20X4	31 Dec. 20X3	31 Dec. 20X2
		€/£'000	€/£'000	€/£'000
Inventories	(2)	832	745	540
Trade receivables		594	518	546
Trade payables		202	211	173
Bank	(3)	(25)	10	25

Notes

(1)	Purchases	1,440	1,404	1,037
(2)	Raw material inventories	360	292	216
(3)	The current bank overdraft rate is 13%.			

REQUIRED

a)   Analyse the current working capital position of CURVE Ltd. using ratios and such other analysis as you see fit.
List what you think are the principal issues arising from your analysis.

N. B. Assume there are 360 days in a year.

9 Marks

b) The following proposal has been made with a view to reducing the working capital level. Calculate the overall cost/benefit of this proposal using the year ended 31 December 20X4 as the base for your answer.

Decrease the level of credit allowed to customers, to 65 days. This will result in a 20% decrease in sales but is expected to eliminate about €/30,000 of bad debts each year. Annual expenses would increase by €/£15,000 per annum. It is assumed that trade payables and inventory levels will be reduced in proportion to the reduction in sales value.

6 Marks

c) Comment briefly on the performance of CURVE Ltd. over the three-year period. Recommend ways (other than those mentioned in part b) above) in which the working capital investment may be reduced. What are the potential consequences of each alternative you suggest?

7 Marks
Total 22 **Marks**
(ICAI, MABF II, Summer 2005, Q5)

3. **BRENT Ltd.**

a) Explain the term 'working capital investment' and outline the factors that a company should consider when deciding on the level and nature of its working capital investment.

7 Marks

b) The working capital investment can be financed in a number of ways including the use of trade credit.

(i) Discuss the advantages and disadvantages of using trade credit as a source of short-term finance.

4 Marks

(ii) BRENT Ltd. is offered a discount of €/£4,000 on an invoice of €/£200,000 by a major supplier if it settles its account within

15 days rather than taking the normal credit period of 35 days. BRENT Ltd. has no available cash resources to pay the bill early. Calculate the annual percentage cost of not taking the discount on offer.

4 Marks

(iii) If BRENT Ltd. could obtain an overdraft at an interest rate of 2% above the bank's normal lending rate of 10% per annum, calculate whether it should borrow and exploit the discount, or take the full credit period of 35 days.

3 Marks

c)   Outline TWO sources of short-term finance, other than those mentioned above, that might be used to finance the working capital investment.

4 Marks
Total 22 Marks
(ICAI, MABF II, Summer 2000, Q5)

4.   PACKARD plc

a)   Define *'working capital'* and discuss the main factors that determine the amount of investment in working capital.

6 Marks

b)   PACKARD plc wishes to improve the collection of payments from its customers and is considering the introduction of a cash discount scheme to encourage early payment. In the financial year 20X6/X7 the company's sales (which are all on credit) were €/£2 million and its trade receivables at the year end were €/£500,000.

The proposed discount scheme would offer a 4% discount for payment within ten days and a 2.5% discount for payment within 30 days. It has been estimated that customers representing 30% of the sales will take advantage of payment within ten days, and a further 20% will pay within 30 days. The remaining customers will not change their payment policy. The cost of finance for PACKARD is 12% per annum. It can be assumed that sales and payments are spread evenly over the year.

REQUIRED

(i) Calculate the current trade receivables cash conversion period and the trade receivables cash conversion period were the proposed discount scheme implemented.

4 Marks

(ii) Estimate the benefits and costs which would result from the proposed discount scheme and advise whether, on these criteria, the scheme should be implemented.

6 Marks

(iii) Comment on any qualitative factors which should be considered prior to implementation of a discount scheme.

2 Marks
Total 18 Marks
(ICAI, MABF II, Summer 1999, Q6)

N. B. Ignore VAT

5.   WESLEY Ltd.

WESLEY Ltd. is a small company involved in the wholesale supply of office stationery. The company was established ten years ago. Below is an extract from the company's accounts for the year ended 31 December 20X7:

Income statement for the year ended 31 December 20X7

	€/£	€/£	
Sales		320,000	
Cost of sales			
Opening inventory	18,000		
Purchases	240,000		
	258,000		
Closing inventory	20,000	238,000	
Gross profit		82,000	(25.6%)
Overheads		64,000	
Net profit		18,000	(5.6%)

Balance sheet (working capital extract) as at 31 December 20X7

€/£

Current assets

Trade receivables	49,000
Inventories	20,000
	69,000

Current liabilities

Trade payables	18,000
Bank overdraft	5,000
	23,000
Net current assets	46,000

The average trade receivables conversion period and trade payables conversion period for the year 20X7 were 56 and 27 days, respectively. During 20X7, inventories were held for 29 days on average.

The company has forecast the following for the year ended 3l December 20X8:

- Sales will increase by 8% each year for the next two years.
- A discount scheme will be introduced whereby customers will receive a 2% discount if payment is made within 30 days. It is expected that 60% of customers will accept this offer. The remaining customers will take five days more than they currently do.
- The company estimates that, as a result of the changes to the debt collection policies, administration costs will rise by €/£8,000, in 20X8.
- Gross profit margin will increase to 26.4% in 2008 but will remain static after that.
- Closing inventories in 20X8 are estimated to be €/£1,000 plus $1/8^{th}$ of the next period's sales (at cost).
- Suppliers will increase the period of credit by ten days.
- The bank overdraft should be cleared and there is a credit balance expected by 31 December 20X8, of €/£2,800.

REQUIRED

a)   Describe **briefly** the potential consequences of each of the following working capital strategies on the profits of a business.

(i) Aggressive policy   (ii) Relaxed policy

5 Marks

b)   (i) Draft each of the following:
- The budgeted income statement of WESLEY Ltd. for the year ended 31 December 20X8.
- The working capital investment as at 31 December 20X8.

9 Marks

(ii) Comment on the business implications of these figures.

_4 Marks
Total 18 Marks
(ICAI, MABF II, Autumn 2001, Q6)

N. B. Assume there are 360 days in the year.

6.   GREENWELL DISTRIBUTORS Ltd.

a)   _'By its nature, credit management lends itself to the use of computer controls.'_
Prepare a brief report on the use of computer controls in credit management.

6 Marks

b)   GREENWELL DISTRIBUTORS Ltd. makes all its sales on a credit basis and each year carries out a credit worthiness evaluation of all its customers. The evaluation procedure operates by ranking customers on a one-to-five scale of increasing likelihood of defaulting on payment. The company has recently performed its annual evaluation, the results of which are given below:

Customer ranking	Bad debts as a % of customers' purchases	Average collection period	Credit decision	Annual sales lost €/£
1	0 %	10 days	Unlimited credit	0
2	1 %	12 days	Unlimited credit	0
3	3 %	20 days	Limited credit	360,000
4	9 %	60 days	Limited credit	180,000
5	30 %	90 days	No credit	360,000

Variable costs amount to 75% of sales and the opportunity cost of allowing trade credit is 15%.

Assume 360 days in the year.

REQUIRED

Evaluate the effect on profitability, if the company decides to extend unlimited credit to the following:

(i)   Category 3 customers;

4 Marks

(ii) Category 4 customers;

4 Marks

(iii) Category 5 customers.

4 Marks
Total **18 Marks**
(ICAI, MABF II, Summer 1996, Q6)

7.   WESSEX plc

a)   Discuss the main factors which should be taken into consideration when implementing a new collection policy in relation to allowing credit to customers.

8 Marks

b)   WESSEX plc supplies customised machinery to the light engineering industry and has received an order from BARCHESTER Ltd., a private company. BARCHESTER Ltd. has insisted that the order is dependent on receiving two months credit from WESSEX plc. The value of the order is €/£50,000 and the variable costs, which would be incurred by WESSEX plc in manufacturing the machinery, would amount to €/£40,000.

Since BARCHESTER Ltd. is a private company, there is some concern in WESSEX plc as to its credit worthiness and WESSEX plc has made the following estimates:

Probability of BARCHESTER Ltd.
paying in full in two months 0.6

Probability of BARCHESTER Ltd.
completely defaulting 0.4

If the order is accepted and default does not occur, then the management of WESSEX plc believe that there is a high probability (0.7) that a further eight identical orders will be placed in exactly one year's time. Credit statistics suggest that, if a company meets the credit terms on the initial order, then the probability of default decreases to 0.1 for subsequent orders.

WESSEX plc finances all its trade receivables with overdraft finance at a cost of 12% per annum and utilises a discount rate of 15% per annum for longer term decisions.

REQUIRED

Advise WESSEX Plc on whether to accept the order, if:
(i) the current order is likely to be the only order from BARCHESTER Ltd; and

5 Marks

(ii) the current order is expected to lead to the possibility of additional orders, as stated, from BARCHESTER Ltd.

5 Marks
Total 18 Marks
(ICAI, MABF II, Autumn 1995, Q7)

CASH MANAGEMENT

11

Debt 10,000,000
Equity 15,000,000
Market Value 25,000,000

LEARNING OBJECTIVES

Upon completing this chapter, readers should be able to:

* Explain the objective of cash/float management;
* List the main sources and uses of cash in a company;
* Discuss the motives and influences on the amount of cash to hold;
* Outline the costs and benefits associated with holding cash;
* Discuss ways to manage a cash float;
* Calculate the costs to a company of implementing different float-management decisions;
* Calculate the optimal lodgement policy for a company;
* Recommend sources of short-term investment for surplus cash balances;
* Recommend actions to be taken by a company when a deficit of cash is predicted;
* Calculate the most appropriate policy for balancing liquidity and profitability using short-term securities (Baumol model; Miller Orr model);
* Prepare cash budgets; and
* Outline the benefits of cash budgeting.

Introduction

Sound cash management is vital for the survival of a company. A profitable company can fail if it does not maintain liquidity. Though 'cash is king', holding large cash balances may be detrimental to a company; funds held in cash have an opportunity cost as these funds could be invested elsewhere to earn a return. Therefore, cash management is concerned with maintaining a balance between servicing operating needs (liquidity) and earning maximum returns (profitability).

The introductory part of this chapter discusses uses of cash in a company, influences on the level of cash held by a company, underlying motives for holding cash, approaches to cash management and techniques used to manage cash. Then the practical aspects of cash management are discussed in three separate sections: the first considers float management; the second, cash management models (tools to manage the transfer of funds between interest bearing securities and cash so as to optimise the return from the combined cash and securities balances); and the third considers cash budgeting as a management and control tool.

Cash flows

The cash flows of a company are separately analysed for different stakeholders in a company's annual report and financial statements. The information is contained in a primary statement – the **cash flow statement**. This statement shows the sources and uses of cash by a company in its financial year. It breaks cash flow activity into three main categories. The first category analyses **cash flows from operating activities**. This category usually has three main areas. The first deals with adjusting profit from the income statement by removing the effects of all non-cash accounting adjustments, to give a *cash generated from operations*. The second deals with the *cost of servicing finance* within a company (for example – interest paid). The final is *corporation taxation paid* by a company in the year. Any stakeholder interested in the quality of a company's profitability will be interested in the ability of a company to generate cash inflows from normal operating activities.

The second category analyses **cash flows from investing activities**. This separately looks at inflows that may result from the disposal of non-current assets, investing activities of the company (for example – interest received or dividends received from associates) and capital grants received. The outflows might include: payments to acquire property, or plant and equipment; the repayment of capital grants; the purchase of subsidiaries or joint ventures; and investments in and advances to associates.

The final category analyses *cash flows from financing activities*. Inflows usually separately identify proceeds received on an issue of shares or loan stock, increases in interest-bearing loans and borrowings, and increases in finance lease liabilities. Outflows typically include expenses paid in respect of share issues, increases in liquid investments, repayments of interest bearing loans and borrowings, repayments of finance lease liabilities, movements in derivative financial instruments and equity dividends paid.

The objective of cash management

Like the other working capital areas, cash management should focus on maximising equity holder return. This can be achieved by maximising the return that can be obtained from investing cash, with the costs associated with not maintaining an appropriate level of liquidity. The level of cash held by a company is also influenced by many internal and external factors.

Influences on cash balances held

Cash is central to the operational activities of a company. This was highlighted in respect of working capital in chapter eight, 'Working Capital: An Introduction'. However, a standard approach to cash management is not suitable for all companies. Different companies pursue different working capital policies, operate in different markets with different products and may have branches in different countries. Some influences on cash management are now discussed. These have been categorised as internal or external.

Internal influences
Type of business
Though some companies have constant demand for their products throughout a year, other companies have varying levels of demand. Many companies have seasonal or cyclical sales. Polar examples of this pattern of seasonal business are the ice-cream/swimwear/sunglasses industries

and the umbrella/boots/scarf industries. Companies with *cyclical/seasonal cash flows* require strong cash management; they may have a cash demand for most of the year, with immaterial cash inflows, and huge cash surpluses in the remaining months.

Profitability

A company that generates profits each year should have a pattern of increasing cash. The objective of cash management in these circumstances should be to focus on maximising the return that can be generated from this cash (taking all other influences into consideration). In a loss-making company the focus of cash management changes. It becomes more important to balance liquidity, as the survival of the company might be at risk. A loss-making company does not necessarily have to have liquidity issues, so long as cash flows are positive. In these circumstances the reported losses would be as a result of accounting adjustments for non-cash items, such as depreciation or movements in provisions. Liquidity difficulties will arise, however, if losses are prolonged, as extra cash above and beyond the cash needed to cover running costs will be required to purchase capital and repay debt.

Strategy: growth/over trading

As discussed in chapter eight, 'Working Capital: An Introduction', the strategic goals of a company should be assisted by ensuring a company holds an appropriate level of cash. If a company is pursuing a growth strategy, then higher levels of cash need to be available to meet the increased working capital demands. In addition, a growing company usually requires capital investment. Capital investment requires funding, which is likely to have to be redeemed, hence has cash flow implications. Therefore, cash management needs to encapsulate the whole picture, which requires careful prediction and monitoring. When growth is not financed appropriately and liquidity is a real risk, then the company is regarded as over trading.

Strategy: capital investment

Management may pursue a strategic policy of replacing capital items in a cyclical pattern (for example, it may be company policy to replace all sales representative cars every three years), or on a one-off basis (a production machine is starting to break down quite regularly). These decisions have cash implications and will influence the level of cash flow to be maintained by a company.

Strategy: capital structure

A company may have chosen a specific type of capital structure to minimise its cost of capital and subsequently optimise the value of the company (dealt with in chapter 15, 'Capital Structure'). This will have cash flow implications. Debt usually has yearly cash outflows in respect of interest payable and capital redemption payments. The pattern of capital repayments depends on the type of debt used. Bank loans normally require periodic cash outflows, whereas loan stock may be converted to shares or redeemed using the proceeds of another debt issue. Equity share capital does not require repayment. However, equity usually has cash outflows; the majority of companies pay dividends. Dividends can result in one-to-four cash outflows in a year depending on a company's dividend policy.

External influences
The economy

The state of an economy will indirectly influence the level of cash a company should hold. This decision is risk-based and the risk of having a 'cash out' is more costly when an economy is not strong, as short-term funding is not as easily obtained (for example, suppliers will not be happy if the credit payment period is lengthened). In these circumstances a company will have to hold a higher buffer level of cash. When an economy is in boom and the company is mirroring the success of the economy then it is not as risky to have cashouts (suppliers will not be too upset at not having been paid) and lower levels of buffer cash can be held.

Inflation

When there is high inflation the effect is similar to that of growth or overtrading. There is an increased working capital requirement that needs financing from a source beyond normal operating activities. This is even when a company is profitable, as the replacement cost of working capital, expenses and assets may outstrip the income that is profitably obtained from the sale of older items. In these circumstances, cash management is very important as the opportunity cost of getting it incorrect is quite high. This also applies to surplus cash in a high-inflation economy, wherein bulk-buying supplies that are increasing quickly in price is a lucrative investment.

Motives for holding cash

Most text books, when discussing the level of cash to maintain, refer to three motives: transactions motive, precautionary motive and speculative motive. The extent to which these motives influence management will depend on management attitude to risk, the economy and the strategic aim of a company.

Transaction motive
The **transaction motive** is a motive to hold sufficient levels of cash to ensure that the operating activities of a company are not disrupted by the non-payment of transactions. The types of cash outflow covered by this motive include: operating expenses such as wages, heat and light, materials, stationery, consumables; the replacement of capital such as production machinery, cash tills, shelving; tax and payments required by financiers (interest, capital and dividends). A **buffer of cash** is required as cash inflows rarely match cash outflows at any one point in time and cashouts are too costly to risk.

Precautionary motive
A business finance manager will hold cash for **precautionary motives**, where there is a risk that actual cash outflows will exceed expected cash outflows, or actual cash inflows are less than expected cash inflows. The level of risk attributed to cash flows will influence the buffer level of cash a company holds. Companies with unpredictable sales demand, or that are prone to strike action, should hold higher levels of cash as a precaution than companies who do not deviate materially from their predicted cash-flow projections.

Speculative motive
Holding excess cash for **speculative motives** is a strategy whereby management hold sufficient levels of cash above and beyond cash required for transaction and precautionary motives, so that they can act quickly

when profitable opportunities arise. These profitable opportunities are unexpected; hence, cannot be planned for. The speed of access to cash gives management a comparative advantage over other companies. For example, a small supplier in financial difficulties may be open to a takeover bid, or may allow a large discount for cash payment for its goods.

Cash management: the cost implications

There are several costs associated with holding cash. Cash management is all about managing cash so as to minimise the overall cost to a company.

Costs associated with holding too much cash

There are costs associated with holding cash, such as loss of interest were the funds to be invested in a deposit account, or invested in short-term securities and devaluation of the value of the cash as inflation reduces the buying potential of cash.

Costs associated with holding insufficient cash

The costs associated with holding insufficient cash include higher bank interest and fees, where a company has to obtain an overdraft or breach an overdraft limit. Where a company has funds that are invested in short-term securities, penalties associated with having to draw down time-related investments before their maturity date may be incurred. When there is insufficient cash, many companies delay the payment of suppliers: this will result in a loss of cash discount. Indeed, if a company does not pay within an agreed credit period, this may negatively affect the relationship with the supplier, resulting in a reduction or loss of trade discount in the future, or even supply. The overall cost to a company will vary depending on the substitutability of suppliers. An indirect consequence of extending the credit period taken without permission from suppliers may be a reduction in the credit rating and reputation of a company, which will have future ramifications for the company when it tries to obtain credit or finance. When too little cash is held a company could end up in liquidation if something unexpected happens, such as a fire in a store, a strike by the work force or a legal claim against the company. Finally, a company will incur opportunity costs by not holding cash for speculative purposes, as profitable opportunities will be foregone.

Cash management techniques

There are three main areas in relation to cash that require management: *cash float management, cash investment management* and *cash budgeting*.

Cash-float management

The term ***cash float period*** is used to describe the period of time between the point at which payment is initiated (for example, when a customer sends a cheque to clear his balance) and when the cash is cleared for use in the company's bank account. This can be substantial, as shown in the following diagram:

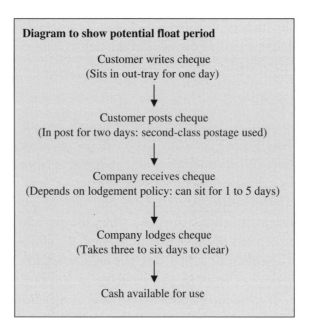

Diagram to show potential float period

Customer writes cheque
(Sits in out-tray for one day)

↓

Customer posts cheque
(In post for two days: second-class postage used)

↓

Company receives cheque
(Depends on lodgement policy: can sit for 1 to 5 days)

↓

Company lodges cheque
(Takes three to six days to clear)

↓

Cash available for use

The total float delay may be up to two weeks long, which will result in a large opportunity cost if the sums involved are material. The reasons for long cash-float periods include:

Inefficient credit procedures
If the inventory, sales and credit-control departments do not have in place a system that allows prompt communication between departments,

then the period of time before cash is usable, is lengthened. Stores need to inform the sales department when goods leave. The sales department should issue an invoice immediately and inform the credit control department, who will start the debt-collection process. This is dealt with in depth in chapter ten, 'Trade Receivables/Payables Management'.

Transmission delay

Transmission delay refers to the period of time that a payment spends travelling between a customer and a supplier. If the payment is by cheque and goes through the post then this may extend the float period by one day if first-class postage is used, or two days if second-class postage is used. In these circumstances a company should consider whether it would be beneficial to have the cheque collected from its customer and banked straight away. A cost-benefit analysis will determine whether this is an appropriate approach. The benefit will be the opportunity income foregone by not having the cash. The cost is the courier charge, or the opportunity loss in revenue that could be earned by an employee if they are sent to collect the cheque – they may also be entitled to expenses.

Worked example 11.1   (Transmission delay)

Overdrawn Ltd. seems to be in a permanent overdraft situation, on which it pays interest at a rate of 10%. Overdrawn Ltd.'s new financial accountant has suggested that if cheques were collected by courier instead of waiting for them to arrive by post, considerable savings on overdraft interest would result. The cost of sending a courier to collect a cheque is approximately €/£10 (averaged over various customers, who are located in various parts of the city).

REQUIRED

Calculate the minimum value at which cheques should be collected assuming:
a)   A one-day delay in the post.
b)   A two-day delay in the post.

Continued

Solution

When the company saves €/£10 in interest, then this will cover the cost of the courier and result in a net benefit to the company. Therefore the cheque should be of sufficient size to earn 10% interest in one day. The cheque amount is represented by y.

a)
$$y = \frac{€/£10}{10\%/365} = €/£36,500$$

Only cheques of €/£36,500 or over should be collected by courier.

b)
$$y = \frac{€/£10}{10\%/(365/2)} = €/£18,250$$

Only cheques of €/£18,250 or over should be collected by courier.

Sending a member of staff to collect a cheque might be more attractive when a customer regularly uses the excuse, 'I'll put the cheque in the post straight away', when experience has dictated that this does not happen.

Lodgement delay
Lodgement delay is the delay in banking payments that have already been physically received by a company. Companies may have a policy in place of banking monies received every day, or every two days, or every week. This delay has a cost as the cash could be used to reduce an overdraft, hence save interest costs, or could be invested in a new project, which could earn a good return. When assessing a company's lodgement pattern, a cost-benefit analysis is required. This will balance the cost of lodging daily (transaction fee, opportunity loss from revenue that could be earned in the time taken to visit the bank, and possibly travel expenses).

Worked example 11.2 (Lodgement delay)

Weekly Ltd. goes to the bank every five days to lodge all the receipts for the week. Sales for the year are €/£2,880,000 and these are received evenly over 360 working days. Weekly is always in overdraft and pays an interest rate of 12% per annum. The company estimates that cash lodgements incur administration costs of €/£10 per lodgement. There are only 360 days in the year. Assume the bank is open every day.

REQUIRED

Calculate the optimal lodgement schedule.

Solution

The way to work out the optimal lodgement schedule is to calculate the costs associated with every possible scenario: lodge daily or lodge every two, three, four, or five days. The objective of this exercise is to find the policy that minimises total costs (administration costs and interest foregone).

$$\text{Daily sales are: } \frac{€/£2,880,000}{360} = €/£8,000$$

Interest paid on each day's takings not lodged is:

$$€/£8,000 \times \frac{12\%}{360} = €/£2.67 \text{ per day}$$

Scenario 1: Lodge daily (total costs)

	€/£
Administration fee*:	
(360 × €/£10)	3,600.00
Interest lost	–
Total cost	3,600.00

*The administration fee is: number of lodgements × cost per lodgement.

Continued

Scenario 2: Lodge every two days (total costs)

	€/£
Administration fee: (360/2 × €/£10)	1,800.00
Interest lost: (360/2 × €/£2.67)	480.60
	2,280.60

Scenario 3: Lodge every three days (total costs)

	€/£
Administration fee: (360/3 × €/£10)	1,200.00
Interest lost: (360/3 × €/£2.67 × 3*)	916.20
	2,161.20

*By lodging every three days, interest will be lost on the first day's takings for two days and on the second day's takings for one day.

Scenario 4: Lodge every four days (total costs)

	€/£
Administration fee: (360/4 × €/£10)	900.00
Interest lost: (360/4 × €/£2.67 × 6*)	1,441.80
	2,341.80

*By lodging every four days, interest will be lost on the first day's takings for three days, on the second day's takings for two days, and on the third day for one day (total six days).

Scenario 5: Lodge every five days (total costs)

	€/£
Administration fee: (360/5 × €/£10)	720.00
Interest lost: (360/5 × €/£2.67 × 10)	1,922.40
	2,642.40

The optimum policy is to lodge the takings every three days. At present the lodgement policy costs the company €/£2,642.40. This will fall by €/£481.20 to €/£2,161.20 if the company starts to lodge every three days instead.

Clearance delay

Clearance delay refers to the time it takes for a bank to clear a cheque. If a customer writes a cheque from the same branch to which the cheque is lodged, then clearance might only take one day. If the lodgement is to the same bank, but the account is in a different branch, then clearance normally takes three days. If the lodgement is to a different bank in the same country, clearance can take five or six days. If the lodgement is to a bank in a different country then clearance can take a minimum of six days. This process can be speeded up by commissioning the bank who receives the cheque to apply through the *Clearing House Automated Payments System (CHAPS)* for immediate clearance. This service normally attracts a fee; therefore should only be pursued if the interest to be saved/ or earned by having the cash cleared more quickly exceeds the fee for the facility. A similar calculation to example 11.1 is required.

Reducing the float time-delay

Some management techniques used to reduce transmission and lodgement delay include:

- Encouraging customers to lodge payments themselves by supplying a bank giro credit slip at the bottom of invoices and/or statements.
- Getting customers to set up a *Bankers' Automated Clearing Services (BACS)* payment for their purchases. Payment using BACS is usually cleared within two days of it being initiated by a company.
- Getting customers to agree to pay their bills using either direct debit or standing orders. Both methods are direct electronic transfers from a customer account to the company account. *Standing orders* are set amounts that are paid at set times. Many utility companies use this as a means of receiving payment promptly (for example, British Telecom and Northern Ireland Electricity). To encourage this form of payment a discount is usually offered. *Direct debits* are variable amounts and can be paid out on variable dates. Many large companies will only supply if the customers agree to this type of payment.

Cash investment management

Cash balances held in a bank's current account earn marginal returns. It makes good cash management sense to invest surplus funds to earn a higher return, whilst maintaining liquidity. Funds that are identified as being long-term surpluses can be invested in long-term projects or investments, which usually earn the highest returns. However, to maintain liquidity, a set amount should be readily available to meet cash demands.

There are several short-term options available to management for this purpose. Some of these are now described.

Bank deposit accounts

There are several types of bank deposit account:

- A ***normal deposit account*** will attract slightly higher interest than a current account. The benefit of this type of account is that funds can be withdrawn and deposited without incurring bank fees. These accounts sometimes have bonuses at the end of each year, when funds have remained intact for the year.

- A ***term deposit account*** attracts a higher interest rate to a normal deposit account. In these accounts, funds are lodged for a fixed period, ranging from one month to several years. The interest rate allowed by a bank is usually related to the length of time funds are locked in for and the bank's base rate. Fixed interest rates can be negotiated for long fixed-term deposits. Variable rates based on the Bank of England base rate (GB and NI) and the European Central Bank base rate (ROI) are the norm for shorter-term deposits. When funds are withdrawn before term there is usually a penalty.

- A bank can also issue ***certificates of deposit*** at a fixed interest rate for a fixed period. These usually cover periods ranging from three months to five years. These can be sold in the money markets.

Treasury bills

Treasury bills are short-term government bonds that have a term of 91 days. They do not attract an interest rate but are issued at a discount, and hence have an implied rate of interest. They can be re-sold in the money markets at any time: This will incur a broker's fee and the price obtained may not be as good as the return that could be earned were the bill held to maturity.

Local authority bonds

Local authority bonds are similar to treasury bills, except they are loans to a local authority. The term can range from as little as one day to over a year.

Money market accounts/finance house deposits

These are offered by most banks and financial intermediaries at variable rates of interest. The timescale of a deposit can range from seven days upward. The rate negotiated usually depends on the size of a deposit and the term required.

Stock market

Stocks can be purchased or sold within the same day. However, this is a risky strategy as the value of the amount deposited (used to purchase shares) can fall as well as rise and there are transaction costs.

Scientific models for cash management

There are two main approaches to the management of surplus cash: a scientific approach, which uses models to predict the liquidisation of investments to provide cash, and cash budgets.

Cash investment management: the EOQ approach

Baumol (1952) formulated the EOQ inventory-management model to determine the optimum policy for releasing monies from fixed-term deposit accounts/securities to service cash requirements for operating activities. This model is termed the **Baumol model**. The objective of the model is to minimise the total costs associated with supplying a predetermined level of cash over a set period (demand for cash). It assumes that there are variable holding costs associated with not keeping the cash in deposits (this is an opportunity cost, which is usually interest foregone) and fixed costs associated with instigating the transaction. Fixed costs may include fixed penalties, and/or administration costs associated with releasing the cash. The costs are as follows:

$$\text{Interest forgone cost} = \text{Average balance} \times \text{Interest rate}$$

$$= \frac{Q}{2} \times i$$

Where Q is the amount to be released from a deposit account, or from securities, each time the company's cash balance reaches zero and i is the interest rate on the deposit account/securities.

Total transaction costs are directly related to the number of withdrawals made and are calculated using the following equation:

$$\text{Total transaction costs} = \text{Number of withdrawls} \times \text{Fixed cost per transaction}$$

$$= \frac{S}{Q} \times F$$

Where S is the cash usage or cash-demand level for the period being considered, Q is the order amount of cash and F is the fixed cost per withdrawal, purchase or sale of each security.

Finally, the total inventory holding costs will be:

Total costs = Opportunity cost of interest forgone + Transaction costs

Total costs are minimised when the amount withdrawn (Q) is:

$$Q = \sqrt{\frac{2FS}{i}}$$

The following diagram shows the assumed pattern of movement in a company's cash balance:

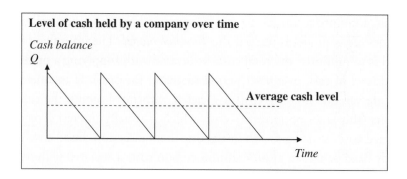

Level of cash held by a company over time

Cash balance
Q

Average cash level

Time

The optimum amount to withdraw from short-term deposits is Q. This will represent the maximum cash that a company should hold under conditions of certainty. The model assumes that cash is used evenly over the period until it runs out and is immediately replenished with the next withdrawal from the deposit account/securities.

Worked example 11.3　(Baumol model)

Cashout Ltd. has an annual cash demand of €/£400,000. The fixed cost of transferring funds from marketable securities to cash is €/£80. The annual yield on marketable securities is 6%, which is forgone if funds are converted to cash.

Continued

REQUIRED

a)   Calculate the amount that should be transferred each time marketable securities are cashed, the number of times this withdrawal will take place, and the total costs at this optimum level.

b)   Calculate the total costs incurred by Cashout Ltd., assuming it were to withdraw €/£100,000 each time.

Solution

a)   The optimum withdrawal amount (Q) is as follows:

$$\sqrt{\frac{2 \times €/£400{,}000 \times €/£80}{6\%}} = €/£32{,}700 \text{ (rounded)}$$

As the company's annual demand is €/£400,000, withdrawals will take place every month (€/£400,000/€/£32,700 = 12 times each year).

Total interest forgone from withdrawing €/£32,700 each time for the period is as follows:

$$= \frac{Q}{2} \times i$$
$$= \frac{€/£32{,}700}{2} \times 6\%$$
$$= €/£981$$

Total transfer costs for the period (S for the period is €/£400,000 and F is €/£80 per transaction) are as follows:

$$= \frac{S}{Q} \times F$$
$$= \frac{€/£400{,}000}{€/£32{,}700} \times €/£80$$
$$= €/£979$$

Therefore, total costs are €/£1,960 per year. (€/£981 + €/£979)

Continued

b)   The quantity cashed (Q) now is €/£100,000 each time the company runs out of cash. This will be required four times each year (€/£400,000/€/£100,000) and will have an annual cost of:

$$\text{Interest forgone} = \frac{€/£100,000}{2} \times 6\%$$

$$\text{Transaction costs} = \frac{€/£400,000}{€/£100,000} \times €/£80$$

$$= €/£3,320$$

$$\text{Total costs} = €/£3,320 \ (€/£3,000 + €/£320)$$

The company is worse off by €/£1,360 (€/£3,320 – €/£1,960) if it cashes €/£100,000 of securities each time, as opposed to the recommended amount of €/£32,700.

Limitations of the Baumol approach

This approach is regarded as providing a good indicator of the optimal policy; however, its assumptions are its limitations. In reality it is unlikely that any company will have a steady demand for cash; it is more likely that demand will vary. The further into the future the predictions are, the more likely they are to be less certain. The model assumes that securities can be cashed in an instant, and notice is usually required for withdrawals. Therefore, a buffer level of cash should be held. There may be other costs associated with holding cash above and beyond interest forgone, such as additional administrative costs involved in managing the cash. The transaction cost of cashing each security may be variable in nature (i.e. a percentage penalty of the amount being released) and/or a fixed amount. Finally, the securities may be in multiples that do not equate to the economic withdrawal amount.

Miller Orr model (stochastic cash flows)

More complicated models have been developed to try to predict more realistic optimum withdrawal/purchase amounts of securities. The **Miller Orr model** is probably the least complicated of these, hence is chosen for discussion in this text. This model operates using predetermined ceiling and floor balances of cash, which are determined at the outside using the Miller Orr model. Securities are not purchased or sold until these levels are reached. Demand and supply for cash within the ceiling and floor level can vary over time and there is no fixed date for withdrawing or purchasing securities. When levels are reached, an amount is bought or sold to return the company's cash balance to a target level. This is shown graphically below:

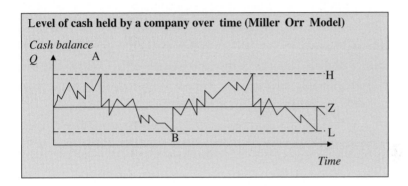

Level of cash held by a company over time (Miller Orr Model)

When the cash balance reaches level A, the company purchases securities to bring the balance back to the target level Z (the target amount). The amount to be purchased is H minus Z. When the cash balance reaches point B, the company has to sell securities, releasing cash, to bring the balance back to target level Z. Miller and Orr argue that the distance between the cap and floor levels is dependent on the variability of cash flows, the extent of transaction costs and interest rates. Where the variability of cash flows is high or transaction costs are high, then the distance between the ceiling and floor level will be high. If interest rates are high the distance between the ceiling and floor level will be less.

The target balance is set at one-third of the distance between H and L and can be calculated using the following formula:

$$\text{Target balance} = \text{Lower limit} + (1/3 \times \text{Spread})$$

Where L is the lower limit and $(H - L)$ is the spread. The lower limit is set by a company and depends on their attitude to risk. Companies who are risk-adverse may set this level to include a safety inventory of cash. The spread is calculated using the following formula:

$$H - L = 3 \times \sqrt[3]{\frac{3FV}{4i}}$$

Where (H−L) is the spread, F is the fixed transaction cost, V is the variability of cash flows as measured by the variance in cash flows, and i is the daily interest rate earned on the securities/deposit account. This can then be used to calculate the target level, ceiling and floor levels, and the amounts to buy and sell each time the cash balance approaches its predetermined limits.

Worked example 11.4   (Miller Orr model)

Gato plc has set its lower cash balance amount at €/£2,000. The variance of daily changes in the cash balance is €/£3,000. The interest on marketable securities is 14% per annum (0.04% per day) and the fixed cost per transaction is €/£40.

REQUIRED

Use the Miller Orr model to calculate the target and upper limit of cash balances for Gato plc and outline the amount that should be purchased and sold when the limits are reached.

Solution

The fixed cost per transaction (F) is €/£40, daily interest (i) is 0.04% and the variability of cash flows is €/£3,000.

$$\text{Spread} = 3 \times \sqrt[3]{\frac{3 \times €/£40 \times €/£3,000}{0.04\% \times 4}} = €/£1,825$$

$$
\begin{aligned}
\text{Target point} &= \text{Lower limit} + (1/3 \times (\text{Spread})) \\
&= €/£2,000 + (1/3 \times €/£1,825) \\
&= €/£2,608 \\
\text{Upper limit} &= \text{Lower limit} + \text{spread} \\
&= €/£2,000 + €/£1,825 \\
&= €/£3,825
\end{aligned}
$$

When the balance in Gato plc's current account reaches €/£3,825, it should purchase €/£1,217 (€/£3,825 − €/£2,608) in marketable securities. If the balance falls to €/£2,000, it should sell €/£608 (€/£2,608 − €/£2,000) of marketable securities.

The Miller Orr model, like all models, is only as accurate as the information that is input to it. Transaction costs may vary and the variability of cash flows may change throughout the year, particularly if a company's products are seasonal.

The Baumol model assumes certainty, hence requires little buffer cash. The Miller Orr model assumes much variation in the daily cash flows, hence requires buffer stock and a wide spread of cash. It is a prudent model, which sets the upper limit at twice the distance from the target balance relative to the lower limit. Therefore, it is more likely that the company will hold a balance of more than the target level. In reality, variation in cash flows can be predicted by a business finance manager with the use of cash budgets and a company will not have to hold such large buffer stocks, nor set its upper cash limit so high.

Cash budgets

A *cash budget* is a monthly/weekly running account of the expected cash income and expenditure of a business. It projects expected cash inflows and outflows into the future. It is seen as a key planning tool, not only for cash management but also for dividend, investment and finance decisions, as it can help predict future liquidity. It is also used as a control tool: the actual cash flows can be compared to budgeted cash flows and questions can be asked, or investigations sparked into areas where there are deviations from the planned. This can be used for *management by exception*, wherein management's attention is directed at problem areas and not wasted managing areas that are performing according to plan.

In terms of cash management, the cash budget can identify whether a deficit/surplus is expected. It can also estimate whether this deficit/surplus is long term or short term. This assists a business finance manager in his decision on the best course of action to deal with the deficit/surplus. For example, if a cash budget predicts a short-term surplus, then the business finance manager might:

- Use it to pay suppliers more quickly, availing of cash discounts;
- Forward-buy supplies that are rising in price;
- Deposit it in an instant-access deposit account with a higher interest rate than the current account;
- Provide a short-term loan to a related company; or

- Purchase tradable securities such as treasury bills, executer bonds, or local authority bonds. This is most likely to occur in two instances. Where the amount is material and the surplus is for a short time and where the business finance manager deems it to be long enough for the additional return from the higher interest to outweigh the cost of initiating the purchase and liquidating the securities in the future.

Where a surplus is regarded as long term, a business finance manager might consider investing in long-term securities, buying additional non-current assets, paying back debt, repurchasing equity, or investing in another business. This puts the business finance manager in a position to suggest changes in the strategic decisions of a company. Decisions might include, for example, changing the dividend policy, changing the capital structure of the company or undertaking a new investment.

If a cash budget predicts a short-term cash deficit, then a business finance manager would put in place actions to alleviate the liquidity problem. Readily available cash is vital for the operational survival of an entity, so it cannot run out of cash. Some expenses cannot be stalled, such as wages or utility bills. Actions taken by a business finance manager might include:

- Selling securities on the money markets;
- Contacting suppliers and requesting a longer credit term, for a short period only;
- Offering a cash discount to entice customers to pay their accounts more quickly;
- Stalling the purchase of inventory, so long as this does not cause stock-outs;
- Arranging an overdraft facility with the bank;
- Arranging a short-term bank loan; and
- Creating an inventory of non-current assets that could be sold, and selling some of these.

Where the deficit is regarded as being long term, then a business finance manager should start negotiations to, for example:

- Raise a long-term loan;
- Sell unwanted non-current assets;
- Sell long-term investments that are not required for operational duties;
- Issue debt securities; or
- Issue equity share capital.

Ethical issues

The above lists assume that a company is profitable, or is loss-making in the short term, but will be profitable in the future. Where a company is loss-making and the cash flows are decreasing a business finance manager should discuss this with the board of directors and possibly suggest that the company apply for voluntary liquidation.

Preparing a cash budget

The cash budget deals only with expected cash flows and not non-cash transactions such as depreciation, bad debts, discounts or movements on provisions. These items are included in the income statement. To provide a check on the accuracy of the master cash budget it should be integrated with the budgeted income statement and balance sheet. The opening balance on the opening balance sheet should form the opening balance of the cash budget, and the closing balance on the cash budget should equate to the closing balance on the expected closing balance sheet.

Preparing a cash budget involves five steps:
1. Find the opening cash balance; (This can be obtained from the opening balance sheet and may not equate exactly to that disclosed by the bank due to outstanding transactions that have not yet been cleared).
2. Identify the expected cash inflows of the company for the period.
3. Identify the expected cash outflows of the company for the period.
4. Calculate the net cash flow for each week/month in the period.
5. Prepare a running total of the balance at the start and end of each week/month of the period, starting with the opening balance and ending up with the predicted closing balance (which should equate to the balance in the predicted balance sheet).

Worked example 11.5   (Cash flows from sales)

In Pajaro Ltd. customers pay within the following timescale:

1 month	30%
2 months	60%
3 months	5%
Bad debts	5%

Continued

You are given the following data in respect of expected sales activity for Pajaro Ltd. for the four months from November to February:

November	€/£90,000
December	€/£120,000
January	€/£150,000
February	€/£100,000

REQUIRED

a) Show the expected cash flows for January and February.
b) What are the income statement sales entries for these two months? Will there be any other entries in the income statement in respect of the above information?
c) What is the balance sheet entry for trade receivables at the end of February?

Solution

a) The cash flows for each month's sales span a three-month period. Therefore, January's total cash flow will include cash received from sales made in November, December and January. Therefore, a spreadsheet showing accounting sales and resultant cash flows should be prepared for the period November to May.

Schedule of sales and resultant cash flows for the period November to May.

	Nov. €/£	Dec. €/£	Jan. €/£	Feb. €/£	Mar. €/£	Apr. €/£	May €/£
Sales	90,000	120,000	**150,000**	**100,000**			
Cash flows							
Within 1 month (30%)	–	27,000	36,000	45,000	30,000		
Within 2 months (60%)			54,000	72,000	90,000	60,000	
Within 3 months (5%)				4,500	6,000	7,500	5,000
Total expected cash		27,000	**90,000**	**121,500**	126,000	67,500	5,000

The pattern of expected cash from November's sales is highlighted by shading in the above schedule.

Continued

> The expected cash inflow from sales in January is €/£90,000, with €/£121,500 expected in February.
>
> b) The budgeted income statement will disclose sales of €/£150,000 for January and €/£100,000 for February. In addition it will also include the expected bad debts for this period that relate to the sales in the period.
> These will amount to €/£12,500 ((€/£150,000 + €/£100,000) × 5%).
>
> c) Trade receivables will amount to the cash outstanding at the end of February. This is €/£198,500 (€/£126,000 + €/£67,500 + €/£5,000).

Advantages of cash budgets

Cash budgets increase the quality of planning within an organisation as they can provide a clear picture of the timing of cash flows. This allows a business finance manager to manipulate cash flows to attain cash flow synchronisation. *Cash flow synchronisation* refers to the matching of cash inflows to cash outflows. A good example of this is the policy of paying suppliers at the end of each month, and insisting on payment from customers by the end of the month.

Cash budgets can also be used to maximise the return receivable from surplus cash by providing information on the amount of cash and period of time that cash is available. Where deficits are predicted, the most cost effective and appropriate finance can be obtained in time, so that the operational activities of a company are not disrupted. One-off cash outflows can be planned for, such as taxation liabilities, dividend payments, repayments of bank loans or capital expenditure. Moreover, cash budgets can help inform the term and pattern of repayments that a company should agree to pay to their financiers.

The management of cheques

Ethics

Many payments in the business world are conducted electronically – direct debits, standing orders, BACS or CHAPS. However, cheques are still regarded as a very important payment method, particularly for small companies. Where cheques are written manually care should be taken to ensure that the cheque is legible and for the correct amount. All parts of a cheque should be completed and if changes are made, these changes should be initialled. The written amount of a cheque should equate to the numbers and any blank spaces on a cheque ruled out with a pen. Cheques should be crossed, account payee only, and dated on the day the cheque is written.

It is bad practice to post-date cheques, as this will only cause problems in the banking system. Indeed the cheque may get processed anyway irrespective of the date, causing a company liquidity problems, or even causing the bank to 'bounce' the cheque. It is bad etiquette to knowingly complete a cheque incorrectly. Though this would allow a company to state that it had written and posted a cheque, it will cause a serious delay for the company waiting for the payment, as the cheque could be returned from their bank and it would have to request a duplicate cheque.

Security

Cheque books should be stored in a secure place, separate from the cheque guarantee card. When payments are made, full details should be recorded in the cheque stubs and this information verified with the bank statement. When a company receives cheques these should be lodged promptly to reduce the risk of loss or theft. A company should not accept a cheque unless they are sure of the credit-worthiness of the issuer. If a cheque is not honoured by the issuer's bank, this will result in a cost to the company in the form of a bank fee. A company should also not accept a cheque where they are unsure of the trust-worthiness of the presenter. Funds can be reclaimed by a cheque-book owner if it is found that a cheque was stolen or counterfeit. When a customer's trust-worthiness is in question a company should seek payment in cash. Electronic payments are less open to fraud than cheques and are also a viable alternative. Other forms of payments, such as bank or building society drafts/cheques, are more secure; however, they will also not be honoured if they have been stolen.

Ethics: money laundering

Businesses that deal mostly in cash are sometimes the target of criminals who wish to legitimise illegal cash. Businesses should not engage in *money laundering* and finance managers are liable to prosecution if they are involved in this activity. Indeed, finance managers will still be liable even if they are not actually involved in money laundering, but know that it is going on. This is commonly known as willful blindness and is an offense. Tipping off a money launderer or giving advice to them is also a criminal offense. Money laundering is commonly considered as the practice of engaging in financial transactions to hide the identity, source and destination of money or money value. Any financial transaction that generates an asset (tangible or intangible), reduces a liability from an illegal act, is tax evasion or false accounting is considered to be money laundering. Money laundering typically has three stages. The first is called either 'placement' or 'hide' and refers to the point of entry of illegal cash to the economy. The second is called 'layering' or 'moving' and refers to the actions taken by a money launderer to obscure the link between the criminal and the money. This can involve the money launderer setting up captive businesses which mostly deal in cash and introducing some of the funds through this, or setting up a network of shell companies, holding companies and offshore accounts to process the cash through. The third and final stage is called 'integration' or 'investing' and refers to the return of the funds through the legitimate economy to the criminal for investment. An individual can be imprisoned for up to 14 years for participating in a money laundering offense.

The United Kingdom

In the UK money laundering is regulated under the Proceeds of Crime Act 2002. This Act covers typical money laundering activity but goes further to include other transactions that may not involve any laundering activity – this act is relevant when a criminal has assets that he/she stole and has in his/her possession. These assets would not have been typically 'laundered', however, are considered to be 'money laundering'. All individuals in the UK are required to report suspicious activities in relation to any asset to the Serious Organised Crime Agency. An individual can be imprisoned for a period of up to five years for failing to report a suspected money laundering offense. There is no lower limit on the amount to be reported. Any involvement with suspected 'dirty money', or 'dirty assets' is an offence.

The Republic of Ireland

In the ROI money laundering is regulated under the Criminal Justice (Theft and Fraud Offences) Act 2001. A new bill is currently under review. The law is as wide as that in force in the UK. It also goes further than dealing with the conversion and concealment of money to include other transactions that may not involve any laundering activity. Possession, acquisition or use of illegal assets are considered to be categories of the crime of money laundering. Tax evasion is also considered to be a form of money laundering. All individuals in the ROI are required to report suspicious activities in relation to any asset to the Garda Siochana. An individual can be imprisoned for a period of up to five years for failing to report a suspected money laundering offense. There is no lower limit on the amount to be reported. Any involvement with suspected 'dirty money', or 'dirty assets' is an offence.

Cash management: group entities and foreign transactions

Where a company has subsidiaries or branches, it makes sense to centralise the cash function. This is possible with relative ease due to the growth in internet banking. A group can have many bank accounts and can undertake transfers between accounts when surpluses and deficits arise. This will reduce the overall banking fees and interest costs. Many banking internet sites provide information on exchange rates, interest rates and short-term deposit rates, making the management of cash easier. A company can make better use of surplus cash, which overall might be a substantial sum, but across individual accounts are of insufficient size to manage on their own.

When receiving cash from or paying cash to another country (for example, when paying a cheque to a customer in the UK from the ROI and vice versa), be aware that the bank clearing system in countries usually only deals with cheques issued in that country; additional time is required to clear cheques from other countries. This is simplified where a company has bank accounts in the country of source. The funds can be lodged in the foreign country and then transferred electronically to the company's own domestic account.

Conclusion

Cash is the lifeblood of any company and its management is crucial to the operational success of a company. Cash management should aim to maximise profitability whilst maintaining adequate liquidity. This can be achieved by good planning and control of cash. A company should have a strong policy for the collection of debt, the minimisation of the float period and an appropriate investment policy for surplus cash. The latter can be assisted by the use of computer technology, which can calculate the optimal amount of high-interest securities to purchase (when in surplus) and to sell (when a deficit is expected). Cash budgets should be prepared on an ongoing basis. These are particularly important to a company that has seasonal activities and one-off flows, such as the purchase or sale of non-current assets, dividend payments, or loan repayments. However, cash budgets can also integrate the impact of growth and inflation on cash flows and can visibly portray the impact of this.

Examination standard example

Worked example 11.6

SATU plc ('SATU') plans to establish a subsidiary to manufacture and sell a new product. The following estimates of sales and production have been made for the first six months of the life of the new company, this being regarded as the critical setting-up period.

Month	Sales units	Production units
	€/£'000s	€/£'000s
1	Nil	15
2	Nil	20
3	10	20
4	20	20
5	30	20
6	30	30

(1) After this time, production will be steady at 30,000 units per month. The sale price will be €/£10 per unit. Half of all sales will be for cash and the other half on one month's credit.

(2) Variable costs of production are expected to be as follows:

	€/£
Material	1
Labour	2
Overhead	3
	6 per unit

Continued

(3)   All materials will be purchased on credit, with one month being taken for payment.

Labour will be paid one week (one quarter month) in arrears and variable overheads will be paid one month after the expense is incurred.

Fixed overheads will amount to €/£300,000 per annum and will be paid quarterly in advance.

In the first month, machinery costing €/£450,000 (payable immediately) will be bought and this is expected to last for five years (ignore depreciation).

Inventories of raw material equal to three months' usage will also be bought at that time and this level of inventory will be maintained by purchases in subsequent months.

(4)   SATU is able to provide €/£500,000 of permanent finance from a subscription of shares in the new subsidiary. It will also source a loan of a further €/£288,240 to be repaid over three years by the subsidiary (capital and interest) in equal monthly instalments, starting at the end of month one. Interest is fixed at 12% per annum.

REQUIRED

a)   Prepare each of the following:

(i) A cash budget for the subsidiary for the first six months of its life.

9 Marks

(ii) A forecast of the balance sheet of the subsidiary at the end of month six.

5 Marks

b)   List two factors likely to influence the level of cash held by a company at any given time.

4 Marks

Total 18 Marks

(ICAI, MABF II, Summer 2004, Q7)

Continued

Solution

SATU plc

a)   (i)   Subsidiary cash budget for first six months of life

Month	Working	1	2	3	4	5	6
		€/£'000	€/£'000	€/£'000	€/£'000	€/£'000	€/£'000
Total cash receipts from sales	1	–	–	50.00	150.00	250.00	300.00
Other cash inflows							
Share issue		500.00	–	–	–	–	–
Loan		288.24	–	–	–	–	–
Total cash inflows		788.24	–	50.00	150.00	250.00	300.00
Costs:							
Materials		–	(55.00)	(20.00)	(20.00)	(30.00)	(30.00)
Labour	2	(22.50)	(37.50)	(40.00)	(40.00)	(40.00)	(55.00)
Variable overhead		–	(45.00)	(60.00)	(60.00)	(60.00)	(60.00)
Total variable cost		(22.50)	(137.50)	(120.00)	(120.00)	(130.00)	(145.50)
Fixed overhead		(75.00)	–	–	(75.00)	–	–
Loan repayments	3	(10.00)	(10.00)	(10.00)	(10.00)	(10.00)	(10.00)
Machinery		(450.00)	–	–	–	–	–
Total cash outgoings		(557.50)	(147.50)	(130.00)	(205.00)	(140.00)	(155.00)
Opening cash position		–	230.74	83.24	3.24	(51.76)	58.24
Monthly cash surplus/(deficit)		230.74	(147.50)	(80.00)	(55.00)	110.00	145.00
Cumulative cash position		230.74	83.24	3.24	(51.76)	58.24	203.24

W1: Sales cash receipts

Month	1	2	3	4	5	6
Sales (in units)	–	–	10	20	30	30
	€/£'000	€/£'000	€/£'000	€/£'000	€/£'000	€/£'000
Sales in money	–	–	100	200	300	300
Cash receipts: cash	–	–	50	100	150	150
Cash receipts from credit sales	–	–	–	50	100	150
Total cash receipts from sales	–	–	50	150	250	300

Continued

W2: Labour cash payments

Month	1	2	3	4	5	6
Production (in units)	15	20	20	20	20	30
	€/£'000	€/£'000	€/£'000	€/£'000	€/£'000	€/£'000
Labour variable costs per unit	2	2	2	2	2	2
Total labour variable costs	30	40	40	40	40	60
Payable in month incurred (3/4)	22.5	30	30	30	30	45
Payable one month in arrears (1/4)	–	7.5	10	10	10	10
Total payable in month	22.5	37.5	40	40	40	55

W3: Loan repayments   €/£

Total principle   288,240
Total interest (12% per annum): (€/£288,240 × 12% × 2.402*)   83,082
Total repayable   371,322
Total repayable per month: (€/£371,322/36)   10,315

*Where 2.402 is the annuity present value factor for three years at 12%.

W4: Balance on long-term loan

Interest portion of repayments in year one   €/£288,240 × 12%
Present value of interest repayments   €/£34,588 × 0.892
Monthly interest portion   = €/£30,882/12
                                                = €/£2,574

Total capital repayment is therefore   €/£10,315 − €/£2,574
Capital repayment for six months   = €/£7,741 × 6
                                                = €/£46,446

Closing balance   €/£288,240 − €/£46,446
                                                = €/£241,794

(ii)   *Forecast balance sheet of subsidiary at the end of month six*

                                                        €/£'000
Non-current assets
Property, plant and machinery   450.00

Current assets
Trade receivables: (€/£900,000 − €/£750,000)   150.00
Inventory of materials: (€/£30,000 × 2)   60.00
Finished goods inventory: (125−90 = 35 units × €/£6)   210.00
Cash   203.24
Total current assets   623.24

Total assets   1,073.24

Continued

Equity and liabilities	
Equity and reserves:	
Equity share capital	500.00
Revenue reserves (balancing figure)	196.45
Total equity and reserves	696.45
Non-current liabilities	
Long-term loan *(W4)*	241.79
Current liabilities	
Trade payables: materials: (€/£30,000 × 1)	30.00
Labour: (€/£250,000 − €/£235,000)	15.00
Overheads: (€/£30,000 × 3)	90.00
	135.00
Total liabilities	376.79
Total equity and liabilities	1,073.24

b)   Two factors likely to influence the level of cash balance held by a company at any given time (any two of the following would be appropriate):

- the predictability of future cash flows;
- the existence of readily realisable securities;
- the availability of short-term finance;
- the period of credit given by suppliers;
- the variation in demand for cash from regular trading transactions; and
- precautionary, 'just-in-case' or speculative reasons.

KEY TERMS

Bankers' Automated
   Clearing Service (BACS)
Baumol model
Buffer of cash
Cash flows from financing activities
Cash flows from investing activities
Cash flows from operating activities
Cash flow statement
Cash flow synchronisation
Certificate of deposit
Clearing House Automated Payments
   System (CHAPS)
Clearance delay
Cyclical cash flow
Direct debits
Float
Local authority bonds

Lodgement delay
Management by exception
Miller Orr model
Money laundering
Normal deposit account
Precautionary motive
Seasonal cash flows
Speculative motive
Standing orders
Stochastic models
Term deposit account
Transmission delay
Transaction motive
Treasury bills

REVIEW QUESTIONS

1.   What are the main motives for holding cash?
2.   List the three main areas of float management.
3.   List five factors that can result in cash shortages.
4.   What are the differences between the Baumol model and the Miller Orr model?
5.   Thomas McKee owns three shops in Belfast. Takings from each shop are brought once a week, on a Saturday night, to the main central shop. There they are collated with the shops own week's takings and banked on the Monday morning. The accountant has suggested that Thomas could save money by lodging more regularly.

Overall sales are €/£3,900,000. These occur evenly over the year. The overdraft rate is 12%. The accountant suggests that Thomas would save interest if lodgements were made at the end of each day. He suggests that Saturday's takings be lodged on the Monday. Assume there are no costs associated with making lodgements and that the shop is open from Monday to Saturday each week of the year.

REQUIRED

Calculate the cost of the current policy and compare this to the cost of the suggested lodgement policy. Advise Thomas on the appropriate course of action.

6.   A company has decided to hold a minimum cash balance of €/£10,000. Its financial director has estimated that the variance in daily cash flows is €/£1,000,000, equivalent to a standard deviation of €/£1,000 per day. The transaction costs for buying and selling marketable securities is €/£50 and the interest rate on the marketable securities is 9.125% per year.

REQUIRED

Calculate a target cash level and a ceiling level for the company using the Miller Orr model.

CHALLENGING QUESTIONS

1.   HAWTHORN plc

a)   HAWTHORN plc is currently attempting to improve the management of its cash and is investigating alternative methods for banking its cash receipts. The annual cash receipts of €/£21 million are spread evenly over each of the 50 weeks of the working year. However, during each week the daily rate of cash received on Mondays and Tuesdays is expected to be twice that for Wednesdays, Thursdays and Fridays. There are no receipts on Saturdays or Sundays.

Current practice is to bank cash receipts only on Friday but two alternatives are being considered.

 (i) Bank cash receipts every day.
(ii) Bank cash receipts on Tuesday and Friday.

The company always operates with a bank overdraft and the current rate charged on its overdraft is 15%. The incremental cost of each banking lodgement is €/£50.

(Assume 360 days in the year.)

REQUIRED

Advise HAWTHORN plc as to whether the company should change from its current practice, and, if so, which alternative it should choose.

10 Marks

b)   *'The cash flow forecast, or cash budget, is the primary tool in short-term financial planning.'* (Pike and Neale)

REQUIRED

Discuss the above statement.

8 Marks
Total 18 Marks
(ICAI, MABF II, Summer 1998, Q6)

2.   MOREAVON Ltd.

MOREAVON Ltd. is a large co-operative whose main business is the distribution of agricultural products. AGRISPRAYS Ltd., a chemical manufacturing company, has developed a new product, Sprayall, which is expected to be successful in the protection of crops from disease if sprayed in July or August. Sprayall will be sold in five-gallon drums and MOREAVON Ltd. has agreed to act as distributor in its area.

From his own general experience and from surveys he has carried out among farm contractors and hardware stores, the manager of the co-operative expects to sell 5,000 drums of Sprayall in 2009. The projected pattern of sales is as follows:

	April	May	June	July	August
Drums	500	1,250	2,000	1,000	250

To meet this sales demand he had originally agreed with AGRISPRAYS Ltd., the following pattern of deliveries of Sprayall for the year – deliveries to be made on the first of each month:

	March	April	May	June
Drums	500	1,500	2,000	1,000

It was agreed that MOREAVON would pay €/£10 per drum for the spray and that payment would be made two months after delivery.

However, the co-operative has now been approached again by the management of AGRISPRAYS Ltd. with an alternative proposal. The company, because of its limited production capacity, finds it necessary to manufacture Sprayall on a year-round basis and, because of the seasonal nature of its sales, this is causing cash and storage problems. The alternative proposal put forward is that a discount of 60c/p per drum off the purchase price would be given if all 5,000 drums are collected and paid for by MOREAVON before 31 December 2008.

450 FINANCE: THEORY AND PRACTICE

The manager of MOREAVON is undecided as to whether he should accept this alternative proposal and has brought you in as financial adviser on the matter. On investigation you ascertain the following:

(1)   The co-operative also has a shortage of storage space but has an arrangement with a local warehouse whereby it is renting space on a monthly basis in blocks of 1,000 square feet at €/£100 per month, payable at the end of each month. Additional facilities are available on similar terms if required. If the drums are collected on 31 December, the additional storage costs would be incurred with effect from 1 January.

(2)   The drums can be stacked in such a way as to store 1,250 in 1,000 square feet of space.

(3)   MOREAVON is running a bank overdraft at an interest charge of 12% per annum. Interest is added to the account at the end of September in each year and is calculated on the basis of the bank balance outstanding at the end of each month. The bank has confirmed that it is willing to make additional finance available on the same terms.

(4)   MOREAVON does not have to pay carriage for collection or delivery of the product from AGRISPRAYS Ltd.

REQUIRED

In your capacity as financial adviser, prepare a report for the manager of MOREAVON advising him as to whether or not the terms of the alternative proposal should be availed of.

Your report should include:

a)   A schedule showing the net effect on the cash flow and bank overdraft balance from 1 June to 30 September inclusive, if the alternative proposal is accepted; and

b)   Your own calculation of the minimum discount per drum that would be required before the alternative proposal should be accepted.

(ICAI, MABF II, Questions and Solutions Manual, 2000/2001)

3. The PINE LOFT company

The PINE LOFT company manufactures a range of pine furniture, which it sells to a number of retail outlets around the country. The company's accounting year-end date is 31 December. The financial accountant has recently prepared estimates of income and expenditure for the first five months of the next accounting period.

These include the following:

(1) Sales (units):

Nov. (act.)	Dec. (act.)	Jan.	Feb.	Mar.	Apr.	May
220	220	260	240	290	320	350

(2) The average unit sales price for the period is expected to be €/£350. This is an increase of €/£20 on current-year prices. It is estimated that 70% of income will be received in the month of sale, and the remainder one month after sale. However, it is expected that 20% of all debts outstanding at the end of the month of sale will be uncollectable.

(3) The company purchases pine wood from one supplier who gives 30 days' credit. The wood is purchased in a treated state and is immediately available for use. The company purchases enough wood each month to meet the current month's sales and to maintain a closing inventory level equal to 10% of the next month's sales. The opening inventory in hand on 1 January is 26 units.

The material cost per unit is forecast at €/£150.

(4) The company employs ten carpenters and three administrative staff. Carpenters work 170 hours per month and will be paid €/£20 per hour, rising to €/£24 in April. Administration and management salaries amount to €/£4,000 per month. All wages and salaries are paid one month in arrears. The wages and salaries bill for December of the current year is €/£30,000.

(5) The company's insurance premium for the forthcoming year is €/£10,000. This will be paid in January.

(6)   Other overheads amount to €/£5,900 per month. These include depreciation of €/£1,500 and provision for bad debts of €/£600. Overheads are paid in the month in which they are incurred.

(7)   Expenditure on non-current assets for the forthcoming period includes the following:

March   Replacement of a delivery van   €/£20,000
April   Computer system upgrade   €/£5,000

(8)   A dividend of €/£10,000 will be paid in March.

(9)   The company upgraded some of its machinery last year. It took out a commercial loan of €/£200,000 to finance this upgrade. The company is repaying the loan (capital and interest) in equal monthly payments over a three-year period. Interest is fixed at 10% per annum.

(10) Overdraft interest is charged on any debit balance on the company's current account at the end of each month at a rate of 14% per annum.

(11) The balance on the company's current account at the start of the forecast period is estimated to be €/£15,000.

REQUIRED

a)   Prepare a cash budget, on a monthly basis, for the months of January, February, March and April.

12 Marks

b)   Comment on the cash budget and advise management on how it might improve its forecast liquidity position.

6 Marks

c)   Discuss briefly how information technology can assist a company in the management of its cash flows.

_4 Marks
Total 22 Marks
(ICAI, MABF II, Summer 2001, Q5)

4.   FLANRA Ltd.

FLANRA Ltd. is a manufacturer of traditional vases and has been in existence for a number of years. The company makes two types of vase.

Version A
This is sold exclusively in the factory shop at a price of €/£80 per unit. The factory shop does not sell on credit.

Version B
This is sold exclusively over the internet for €/£100 per unit. Customers must pay an online deposit on ordering of €/£20 (which goes directly to FLANRA's bank account) and the balance one month after ordering. The product is dispatched in the month of ordering.

FLANRA does not grant any discounts and does not expect to incur any bad debts.

Each vase uses the same materials, but in different quantities. Version A requires two units of material per finished unit, while Version B requires three units of material per finished unit. The materials supplier demands 50% payment in the month of purchase at an agreed total price of €/£20 per unit of material. The remaining 50% is payable in the following month.

All work is carried out by skilled staff who are paid a total of €/£80,000 per month in the month in which the work is performed. From the October sales onwards, staff also receive a bonus, based on sales value, of 3%. This is paid in the month following sale.

A manager is employed to look after the facility and she is paid a salary of €/£3,500 each month. On 1 October 2005 the company purchased a new company car for the manager at a cost of €/£20,000. This car depreciates at a rate of 2% per month on a straight-line basis. On the same day, the company sold the manager's old company car for €/£9,750. The old car had a book value at time of sale of €/£8,000. Both purchase and sale were for cash.

FLANRA rents additional storage space locally at a monthly cost of €/£2,000. This must be paid two months in advance and has been used by FLANRA for the past two years.

Details of the company's unit sales in 2005/2006 are set out below.

August and September are actual sales, while the remaining months are based on forecasts.

	Actual				Forecasted		
Product	Aug.	Sep.	Oct.	Nov.	Dec.	Jan.	Feb.
Version A	3,500	4,000	1,000	1,000	500	1,250	1,500
Version B	1,000	1,500	4,000	3,750	3,250	5,000	4,750

It is company policy to produce enough of each vase to meet the following month's demand. Also, the company purchases materials to ensure that, at the start of the month of production, the entire month's production requirement in terms of materials is on hand.

REQUIRED

a)   Prepare a cash budget for FLANRA for the period October 2005 to December 2005. The opening bank balance at 1 October 2005 was €/£12,300.

14 Marks
(ICAI, MABF II, Autumn 2005, extract from Q3)

5.   A Ltd.

A Ltd has produced a plan for its activities for the forthcoming financial period of six months. This is summarised in the form of a budgeted income statement for the period, as follows:

Budgeted income statement for the forthcoming six months

	€/£	€/£
Sales (50,000 @ €/£10 each)		500,000
Less: Cost of sales		
Material	100,000	
Labour	75,000	
Variable overhead	100,000	275,000
Operating profit		225,000
Less: Fixed overheads	125,000	
Depreciation	20,000	145,000
Net income		80,000

A plc's (summarised) balance sheet immediately prior to the commencement of the six months is as follows:

	€/£	€/£
Non-current assets		99,000
Current assets		
Inventory of raw materials @ €/£2 each	20,000	
Inventory of finished goods @€/£5.50 each	44,000	
Receivables (80% of previous month's sales)	32,000	
Cash	50,000	146,000
Total assets		245,000
Equity and liabilities		
Equity and reserves		200,000
Payables (previous month's supplies)	20,000	
Payables (previous month but one supplies	25,000	45,000
Total equity and liabilities		245,000

Additional information in respect of A plc's cash flows are as follows:

1. A plc's trade is seasonal and its forecast sales for the next full year (of which the current budget is months 1–6) are:

Month	Sales	Month	Sales
	€/£		€/£
1	40,000	7	140,000
2	40,000	8	80,000
3	60,000	9	60,000
4	80,000	10	60,000
5	120,000	11	50,000
6	160,000	12	40,000

2. It is A plc's policy to hold an inventory of finished goods equal to the requirements of the next two months' sales and inventories of raw materials equal to the next one and a half months' production requirements. It pays its suppliers, on average, two months after the goods are delivered.

3. A plc pays for its labour and variable overheads in the month in which they are incurred.

4. Fixed overheads are paid quarterly in advance.

5. 80% of the company's sales are to credit customers (the rest being for cash) and credit customers are allowed one month's credit.

6. Depreciation is a composite figure made up of the appropriate amounts for each of the fixed assets in use.

7. No cash receipts or payments are expected during the six months of the budget period except those referred to above.

REQUIRED

Prepare the cash budget for the six month period.

15 Marks

(ICAI, CAP 1, Mock 2008, Q4)

6.   GARNER

GARNER Ltd. ('GARNER') is a company involved in the construction industry. It has a central depot located in the midlands, into which inventories are received, and from which they are distributed to sites throughout the country. However, local site managers are also empowered to order materials directly from suppliers to be delivered straight to the individual sites. These are referred to as "direct purchases to contract". In such cases the materials are usually consumed almost immediately after receipt on site.

In order to determine the company's ongoing need for working capital, budgets are being prepared as part of the cash management process. You are given the following information:

Monthly profit forecast

	June	July	Aug	Sept	Oct	Nov.	Dec.	Jan/Mar
	€/£'000	€/£'000	€/£'000	€/£'000	€/£'000	€/£'000	€/£'000	€/£'000
								(Note 1)
Contracts invoiced (Note 2)	688	560	1,600	2,000	320	600	720	800
Material ex stock		190	190	180	180	160	210	
Direct purchases to contract		550	626	511	400	330	400	
Direct wages		50	60	60	75	60	72	
Direct input to WIP		790	876	751	655	550	682	
Decrease/(increase) in WIP		(400)	300	610	(395)	(75)	(102)	
Direct cost of sales		390	1,176	1,361	260	475	580	
Factory overhead		60	70	80	75	60	80	
Selling and administration costs		72	72	92	102	82	72	
Royalties		27	80	100	15	30	35	
Premises charges - rent and rates		8	8	8	8	8	8	
Depreciation		5	5	5	5	5	5	
		562	1,411	1,646	465	660	780	
Net profit before tax, subject to commissions (Note 3)		(2)	189	354	(145)	(60)	(60)	
Materials in stock at month end	196	176	200	229	250	240	250	

Notes

(1)   The contracts invoiced are €/£ 800,000 for each of January, February and March.

(2)   There is frequently a large resource commitment from GARNER in making a sale. Accordingly, customers are often required to pay part of the final price, in stages, Research into the pattern of sales shows that, of the total sales invoiced, the amounts are paid in equal instalments as follows:

25 % on signing of sales agreement, three months before invoicing;

25 % on delivery, on average one month before final invoicing,

25 % on the day of final invoicing,

25 % on one month's credit after invoicing.

The scheduled invoiced amounts represent the 'final' invoiced amounts for each month.

(3)   Commissions are payable to staff to the nearest €/£ 1,000 at the rate of 2% on receipts from contracts invoiced, and will be paid one month in arrears.

You are provided with following additional information:

(1)   Of the total purchases for stock and contract, about 1/3rd will attract 2% cash discount, and will be paid for in the month following delivery. The remaining 2/3rds will he paid for, on average, two months after delivery.

(2)   Direct wages, factory, selling and administration overheads are paid in the month in which they are incurred.

(3)   Royalties are paid quarterly at the end of February, May, August and November in respect of the quarters ending on 31 January, 30 April, 31 July and 31st October respectively.

(4)   Rent and rates are paid in arrears at the end of March, June, September and December.

(5)   Outlays on capital purchases in the months given opposite are expected to be as follows.
August......€/£80,000   October.....€/£40,000
December......€/£100,000
No investment grants are expected during the period under review.

(6)   The cash balance at 30 September is €/£120,000.

REQUIRED

a)   Prepare a cash budget for each of the three months October, November, and December.

18 Marks

b)   Comment briefly on the cash position of the company at the end of each of the three months.

4 Marks
Total 22 Marks
(ICAI, MABF II, Autumn 2007, Q5)

SECTION FIVE

CORPORATE VALUE AND RISK

COST OF CAPITAL   12

LEARNING OBJECTIVES

Upon completing this chapter, readers should be able to:

♣ Explain the cost of capital from a company's perspective and separately an investor's perspective;

♣ Describe the link between a company's cost of capital and its value;

♣ Calculate the value and cost of equity capital (dividend valuation model; book value; price earnings ratio; capital asset pricing model);

♣ Calculate the value and cost of untraded debt, redeemable traded debt and irredeemable traded debt;

♣ Calculate the value and cost of preference shares;

♣ Calculate the weighted average cost of capital;

♣ Discuss the assumptions and limitations of the weighted average cost of capital; and

♣ Explain its suitability for project appraisal.

Introduction

Determining a discount rate to use in the evaluation of projects is both a scientific process and an art. This chapter is mostly concerned with the scientific processes used to provide a starting discount rate, the company's *weighted average cost of capital (WACC)*. The WACC provides an estimate of the required return that must be achieved by a company to entice its investors to retain their investment and to provide more finance to the company, when it needs it. The various sources of finance have different required returns; however, if a company consistently achieves the weighted average return required by all its financiers from its investments, then the financiers will be satisfied. Where a company can obtain a return in excess of this minimum threshold then the additional return will add value to the company, which will benefit equity holders. The art (subjective process) of determining an appropriate discount rate for evaluating a specific project/investment starts after the WACC has been determined: for example, a project being evaluated by a company may not have the same business risk as the company; therefore, a premium return above the WACC hurdle rate is required to compensate for this additional risk.

The cost of capital

Every investment undertaken by a company requires financing. This is normally sourced as either debt or equity capital. Each source of finance has a cost.

The cost of capital can be considered from two perspectives: an investor's viewpoint and a company's viewpoint. *Investors* regard the ***cost of capital*** as the ***opportunity cost*** of capital invested in a company. The opportunity cost is the return that can be gained by an investor from reinvesting their funds in the next-best alternative. In considering the opportunity cost, investors will assess whether they are getting an appropriate return from the company, relative to the risks taken, when compared to other investments.

A *company* regards the ***cost of capital*** as the minimum return it has to provide to investors to induce them to retain their investment, or to supply more finance to the company, when additional sources are required. Therefore, when considering whether to invest in a particular project, the returns from that project should at a minimum cover a company's current cost of finance. Getting the cost of capital right is vital for appropriate project appraisal. If the discount rate applied is too high a company is likely to turn down worthy investments, resulting in damage to company profitability. If it is too low it will result in projects being accepted with returns that are not appropriate to investors' expectations, which may cause investors to withdraw their investment.

Therefore, when calculating an appropriate discount rate to apply in investment decision making, the business finance manager has to determine the minimum return required on investments to satisfy all investors. This is usually approximated as the weighted average cost of all the capital invested in the company.

The weighted average cost of capital

The *WACC* is the overall cost of long-term funds invested in a company. When calculating the WACC, the business finance manager has to use up-to-date information, as debt and equity security holders have a freely available market in which they can trade their shares. The required return on investment should reflect the current risk and return pay-off prevalent in the marketplace. Therefore, the WACC is the cost that would be incurred of raising new capital, assuming it is raised in the same proportion as the existing capital structure of a company.

A simple weighting formula may be used to calculate the WACC:

$$\text{WACC} = \frac{E(Ke)}{(D+E)} + \frac{D(Kd(1-t))}{(D+E)}$$

Where E is the market value of equity, D is the market value of debt, Ke is the cost of equity, Kd is the cost of debt and t is the current tax rate.

Worked example 12.1   (Calculating the WACC)

Primavero plc has recently had its capital valued at market rates. Its equity amounted to €/£2 million, as did its debt capital. The cost of equity is 16% and the cost of debt is 12.5%. The current tax rate is 20%.

REQUIRED

a) What is the market value of Primavero plc?
b) What is Primavero plc's WACC?

Solution

a) The market value of Primavero plc's debt capital (D) is €/£2 million and the market value of its equity (E) is €/£2 million. A company's market value is the combined value of its long-term equity and long-term debt. In this instance, that is €/£4 million (€/£2 million+€/£2 million).

Continued

> b) Its cost of equity (Ke) is 16% and its cost of debt (Kd) is 12.5%. The tax rate (ct) is 20%. Therefore Primavero plc's WACC is:
>
> $$\frac{€/£2m\ (16\%)}{(€/£2m + €/£2m)} + \frac{€/£2m\ (12.5\%(1-20\%))}{(€/£2m + €/£2m)} = 13\%$$

The relationship between the WACC, earnings, and the market value of a company

From scrutiny of the WACC formula, it is clear that theoretically there is a direct link between the market value of a company its earnings and the WACC. To remain attractive to its investors, a company will have to have a return equal to or in excess of its current market value multiplied by the required rate of return. So in Primavero plc's case a return of €/£520,000 (€/£4,000,000 × 13%) is required to keep its current investors happy.

Therefore, the WACC is a fundamental determinant of a company's market value. If the earnings and the WACC of a company are known then the theoretical market value of the company can be calculated.

$$\text{Market value of a company} = \frac{\text{Earnings}}{\text{WACC}}$$

The following example is provided to emphasise the importance of managing the WACC in light of the impact of movements in it on the market value of a company.

Worked example 12.2 (Market value and the WACC)

Verano plc has earnings of €/£1 million for the year. Its WACC is 20%. A similar company, Aotono plc, has similar earnings and a WACC of 10%.

Continued

REQUIRED

a)   Calculate the market value of Verano plc.
b)   Calculate the market value of Aotono plc.

Solution

a)   Market value: $\dfrac{€/£1,000,000}{20\%} = €/£5,000,000$

b)   Market value: $\dfrac{€/£1,000,000}{10\%} = €/£10,000,000$

As is highlighted in the above example, the lower the WACC, the higher the market value of a company, and vice versa. Therefore, a business finance manager will strive to minimise the WACC – hence maximise the market value of a company. However, it is not just a simple case of obtaining the cheapest form of finance each time a company requires to finance an investment. There are differing views as to how changes in the capital structure impact on the cost of each source of finance and the resultant WACC. This is considered in chapter 15, 'Capital Structure'.

Investors and the risk/return relationship

There is a general risk/return trade-off. The more risk associated with an investment, the higher the expected return and vice versa. Different investors will be attracted to differing risk levels. Risk adverse investors will wish to invest in more or less risk-free investments, such as government bonds. Speculative investors will be attracted to junk bonds that are very risky, but will yield high returns if they reach maturity. It is assumed for the purpose of this chapter that investors hold well-diversified portfolios of investments with a variety of complementary investments of differing risk levels. Hence, they will be happy to take on more risk, so long as sufficient return is offered.

Debt and equity capital returns

Holders of debt capital are usually guaranteed a set distribution each year, with a lump sum guaranteed on the maturity of the capital. They value this stream of future cash payments based on the alternatives available in the marketplace and the credit risk associated with investing in a company. On the other hand, equity holders are not actually offered any specific income stream. Dividends can be waived and there is no requirement on companies to buy back equity shares. However, as mentioned at the start of this chapter, equity holders will expect a certain return, which can be either in the form of a dividend or a share-price increase. This return is related to the level of risk taken and will be compared to the alternatives available in the marketplace.

Equity

Equity is the owners' investment in a company. On a company's balance sheet, it is reflected in the equity (ordinary) share capital and equity reserve accounts. One of these reserve accounts is retained earnings. As discussed in chapter seven, 'Long-Term Sources of Finance: Equity', a misconception held by some managers is that retained earnings are a free source of finance. This is not the case. Retained earnings are the opportunity cost of dividends forgone by equity holders. If equity holders had these funds they could invest them elsewhere, hence they have an opportunity cost. Therefore, the cost of retained earnings is the same as the cost of equity except there are no issue costs. Put differently, retained earnings are like making a fresh equity distribution to current equity holders, except they receive the benefit in the form of an increase in their share price, not the number of shares. The market value of a company's equity share capital reflects the value placed on retained earning by equity holders.

Value of equity

As mentioned previously, a company's equity should be valued as though it were being sourced from the market now. This means that the market value should not include any premium to reflect a declared dividend payment and should be reduced to reflect costs associated with issuing the shares. The market value of equity (E or P_0) is calculated as follows:

$$P_0 = \text{Share issue price} \times \text{Number of shares currently in use}$$

The *share issue price* is the current long-run market price for each equity share (ex-dividend) less issue costs. Companies usually distribute dividends twice a year. A dividend payout transfers value from a company to its equity holders. This value cannot be recouped from equity holders. Therefore, the long-run equilibrium share price will exclude a declared dividend that is about to be paid. The market value of equity shares in the period up to payment of the dividend is inflated by the amount of the dividend and is called trading cum-dividend (with the dividend right attached to it). When the dividend is paid, the share price falls to its perceived equilibrium level again. This is known as trading ex-dividend (without the dividend right).

Worked example 12.3   (Calculating the market value of equity)

Invierno plc has two million issued equity shares. The current market price (cum-dividend) is 240c/p per share. The accrued dividend is 22c/p per share. A discount of 10% would be allowed on a new issue of equity shares.

REQUIRED

Calculate the market value of Invierno plc's shares that should be used in the calculation of its WACC.

Solution

The market value of Invierno plc's equity shares (P_0) is:
€/£3,924,000 (((€/£2.40 − €/£0.22) × 90%) × 2,000,000).

Cost of equity
There are variant methods of valuing a company's cost of equity. It could be considered in terms of: returns currently received by equity holders, or returns required to compensate for risks associated with investing in a company relative to other investments. These two approaches are now considered.

Dividend valuation model

The return made to equity holders should maximise their wealth. Returns can either be a cash distribution (dividend) or capital growth (retention in equity reserves). The dividend valuation model uses the pattern of dividends paid historically to work out the return on/(cost of) a company's equity, when the market value of the company's equity shares is known. A key assumption of the dividend valuation model is that the market value placed on an equity share by equity holders is the present value of the expected future stream of dividends (to infinity) paid by a company. Therefore, the dividend valuation model is the value of a company's dividends in perpetuity. When a company distributes all its earnings each year, its dividends are constant (there is no growth in earnings or dividends, hence there will be no increase in share price). The equity market will value the future stream of dividends as:

$$P_0 = \frac{D_1}{Ke}$$

Where P_0 is the market value of equity, D_1 is the annual dividend and Ke is the equity holders' required return (company's cost of equity). This formula can be rearranged to work out the return provided by a company on its equity shares (so long as the market price of the equity shares and the constant dividend amount is known).

$$Ke = \frac{D_1}{P_0}$$

Investors can use this model to decide whether or not to invest in equity shares, which provide a set dividend. By working out the return on offer, they can compare it to the expected return, (given the level of risk associated with investing in the particular company). Companies can use this model to work out the current cost of their equity capital (given the dividend policy and share price are known).

Worked example 12.4 (Cost of equity capital: dividend valuation model)

Febrero plc pays an annual dividend of 16c/p per share. The shares are currently trading at 188c/p. An interim dividend of 8c/p is about to be paid. The flotation cost of issuing new shares is 5%.

Continued

REQUIRED

Calculate the cost of equity capital for Febrero plc.

Solution

The first step is to calculate the market price that Febrero plc would expect to receive on a new share issue.

$$P_0 = ((188c/p - 8c/p) \times 95\%) = 171c/p$$

The question states the Febrero plc pays an annual dividend of 16c/p. Therefore dividends are constant. Therefore the cost of equity (Ke) is:

$$\frac{16c/p}{171c/p} = 9.36\%$$

Growth
The majority of companies retain some of their earnings, which they invest for future growth. Two different methods are used to calculate the expected growth of dividends in a company. The first assumes there is a linear relationship between retentions and growth: the more a company retains, the higher the growth levels. Higher growth leads to larger future earnings; hence higher future dividends. This relationship is expressed as follows:

$$g = br$$

Where g is growth in dividends, b is the percentage of earnings that are retained for investment and r is the return on the company's investments i.e. the ROCE.

The second method estimates growth based on the historic pattern of dividends paid. The assumption is that growth in dividends is more or less constant from one year to the next. There will be slight variation from the mean growth rate each year depending on the performance of a company; however, over time a constant pattern emerges.

This assumption is not too unrealistic, as managers manage dividends so that they grow in line with equity holders' expectations of how they should. These expectations are formulated by equity holders based on projected earning forecasts made by managers. Many companies distribute dividends that are slightly higher than those distributed in the previous year, irrespective of fluctuations in performance. For example, when a company is very profitable, a small increase in dividends usually results. When a company makes losses, the dividends level is usually maintained (see chapter 19, 'Dividend Policy', for more detail on dividend policies and their impact on equity holder wealth). The formula for calculating growth using this method is as follows:

$$g = \sqrt[y]{\frac{D_{t0}}{D_{t0-y}}} - 1$$

Where g is the growth rate, D_{t0} is the dividend that has just been paid and D_{t0-y} is dividend that was paid y years ago.

These models provide an estimate for growth. However, other factors should be considered. For example, a full evaluation of a company's performance using ratio analysis would provide insight into the operational performance, efficiency, liquidity and risk of a company relative to other companies in the industry. An evaluation of the management team would provide some evidence to substantiate the appropriateness of the growth rate calculated using the above formulae.

When a growth rate is estimated, this is then factored into the dividend valuation model to provide a cost of equity that takes future increases in dividends into consideration. Therefore, the dividend valuation model takes the capital appreciation of equity shares into consideration. The adjusted model is as follows:

$$Ke = \frac{D_0(1+g)}{P_0} + g$$

In this formula D_0 is the last dividend paid, P_0 is the market value of equity on issue, g is the constant growth rate and Ke is the cost of equity capital.

Worked example 12.5 (Calculating growth)

Junio plc has made the following earnings and dividends over the past five years.

Year	Earnings €/£	Dividends €/£
2002	520,000	195,000
2003	663,000	249,600
2004	715,000	267,800
2005	845,000	318,500
2006	910,000	341,055

Junio plc has an authorised equity share capital of 2,000,000 shares, of which 50% are allotted and fully paid up. The balance sheet of Junio plc shows €/£3.8 million in equity capital and reserves and no long-term debt. The shares are currently trading at €/£5.00. Issue costs associated with a new allotment of shares amount to 64.5c/p.

REQUIRED

a) Calculate the growth in Junio plc's dividends using two different methods.

b) Calculate the resultant cost of equity capital for Junio plc using both growth rates.

Solution

a) The first method adopted is to calculate growth using the *retentions return* formula ($g=br$). There is sufficient information provided in the question to allow the calculation of b (retentions) and r (return on capital invested).

Continued

The retentions percentage (b) is now calculated:

Year	Earnings €/£	Dividends €/£	Ratio €/£	Retentions (b) %
2002	520,000	195,000	325,000*/520,000	62.5
2003	663,000	249,600	413,400/663,000	62.4
2004	715,000	267,800	447,200/715,000	62.5
2005	845,000	318,500	526,500/845,000	62.3
2006	910,000	341,055	568,945/910,000	62.5

*Retentions are earnings less dividends paid in the year (€/£520,000 − €/£195,000).

The return earned by a company is the earnings divided by the capital employed in the company (r).

$$r = €/£910,000/€/£3,800,000$$
$$r = 23.95\%$$

Therefore growth is $62.5\% \times 23.95\% = 14.97\%$

The second method of calculating growth uses the pattern of historic growth as an indicator of future growth.

$$\sqrt[4]{\frac{€/£341,055}{€/£195,000}} - 1 = 15\%$$

In this example growth is similar using both methods.

b)   The market value of the shares to be used in the dividend valuation model has to be net of issue costs. Therefore in Junio plc's case the market value is: €/£4,355,000 ((€/£5.00 − €/£0.645) × 1,000,000). The cost of equity is:

$$Ke = \frac{€/£341,055\ (1+0.147)}{€/£4,355,000} + 0.147 = 0.2368\ (23.68\%)$$

$$Ke = \frac{€/£341,055\ (1+0.15)}{€/£4,355,000} + 0.15 = 0.24\ (24.00\%)$$

As expected, equity holders who invest in a company that achieves a return of 24% will pay an amount that ensures they receive that return. Therefore, the market price of the shares, hence the value of the company, in this instance depends on the returns achieved and the resultant growth.

Limitations with using the dividend valuation model

As with most models, the limitations with using the dividend valuation model are the assumptions that underlie the model. In particular, the proxies for growth and return are open to much variation. It could be argued that dividends do not grow smoothly and that the growth calculations are only possible when a company's dividend payout increases over time. Indeed, some companies pay zero dividends, arguing that they are better-placed to invest the earnings than equity holders are. The return they provide to equity holders is solely by capital appreciation. Dividend valuation models cannot be used to calculate the cost of equity in these circumstances.

The return variable is also open to debate. The financial statements of an enterprise disclose one return. Yet, when assessing projects, discounted cash flows are taken as the ultimate performance measure and it is argued that cash flows are a better proxy for return (Rappaport, 1986). Another view taken is that a charge for the opportunity cost of capital employed should be deduced from operating profit; this return is known as the *economic profit* (Solomons, 1965). More recently, some large financial consultants (Stern Stewart and Co.) have been calculating return using a technique called *economic value added (EVA)*, wherein the earnings reported by a company are adjusted (there can be over 150 different adjustments) and a 'true' return calculated using the company's adjusted capital at the company's WACC.

Capital asset pricing model

A second method of determining the cost of equity capital expected on a company's shares is to evaluate the risks associated with investing in a company relative to other capital market investments. The risk associated with investing in a particular share is that the return received will be different to the return expected. There are two types of influence that lead to variations from expected return. These influences are categorised as being either specific to a company (or industry), or affecting the whole market.

Unsystematic risk captures the exposure of a company's returns to all events that are unique or company specific (these events are likely to result in a variation of the actual returns from expected returns). Examples of events that affect an industry or company include strike action by employees or a merger with another company. These events will impact on a particular company's expected return, but will not affect the whole market. Unsystematic risk is sometimes referred to as *business risk*.

Systematic risk captures events that impact on a large number of companies' expected returns. For this reason, systematic risk is sometimes referred to as *market risk*. In general, macroeconomic influences such as inflation, interest base rate changes or GDP are considered to be examples of systematic risk. On average, all market-share returns will vary from expected returns, with the whole market either performing better or worse.

Portfolio theory suggests that an investor can diversify away unsystematic risk by holding a *well-diversified portfolio of shares*. The larger the number of differing types of shares held, the more likely that unsystematic risk will be reduced. It is thought that holding eight to ten carefully chosen shares is sufficient to diversity away unsystematic risk. The relationship between the number of different shares held and risk is shown in the following graph.

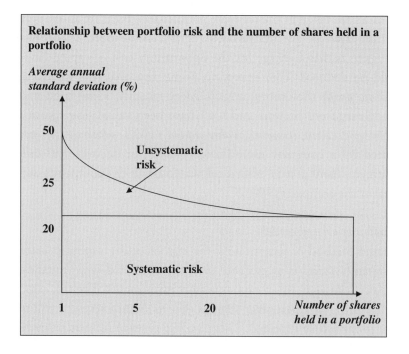

An investor who holds a portfolio with a small number of shares will be exposed to systematic risk and some unsystematic risk. Risk is measured as the average standard deviation (average fluctuation) of actual returns from the expected mean return. Investors who hold a balanced portfolio of shares that reflect the market will only be exposed to systematic risk. Systematic risk cannot be diversified away, as shown in the above graph. It remains constant, regardless of the number of differing types of share held.

As unsystematic risk can be diversified away, it is not taken into account when determining the required return on a share. Therefore, the only risk to impact on the expected return from a share is systematic risk.

Though an average level of systematic risk is used to reflect overall market risk, each individual company has a different sensitivity to systematic risk. Some are more sensitive than others. For example, the return of manufacturing companies with high wage costs that are sourced within the UK or the ROI will be particularly sensitive to an increase in inflation rates in these countries, relative to a company that imports goods for sale manufactured abroad. Therefore systematic risk is a key influence on the expected return from an equity share. Systematic risk is commonly measured by a beta coefficient.

Beta (β)

Beta is a measure of the systematic risk of an individual equity share relative to the systematic risk experienced by the market. It is obtained by plotting the returns of a company against the returns of the market over time and estimating a line of best fit from the pattern that emerges. Beta represents the gradient of this line. A key assumption of this measurement is that the volatility in an individual share's returns over time will consistently be more or less risky than market volatility to the same external influence, hence is predictable. The market beta is always pegged at 1.0 (regardless of the influence of systematic risk on the expected market return). The assumed linear relationship between the expected rate of return of the market (r_m) and systematic risk (beta) is called the *security market line.*

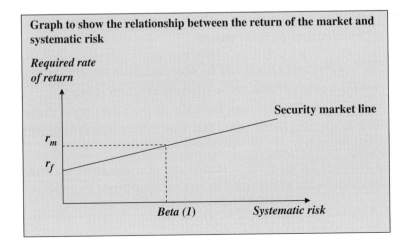

Graph to show the relationship between the return of the market and systematic risk

Required rate of return

Security market line

r_m

r_f

Beta (1)   *Systematic risk*

A company with a beta value of 1.0 experiences the same movement in its returns as the market when factors that affect systematic risk come into play. For example, if market returns increase by 5% then it is expected that the increase in the return on that company's shares will also increase by 5%. This company's expected return will lie on the security market line. A company with a beta factor greater than 1.0 is more sensitive to factors that affect the market. Hence, when an external stimulus causes the expected market return to increase, the returns experienced by this type of company will increase by a greater amount, and vice versa. For example, if market returns increase by 5% and a company has a beta value of 2.0, then the expected increase in the return from that company's shares is 10%. This company's equivalent security market line will be steeper to that presented in the above graph.

A company with a beta factor of less than 1.0 is not as sensitive as the market to factors that influence systematic risk. This type of company may have its systematic risk diversified by spreading its operations across countries. It will not benefit from the same level of return as the market when there is a market-wide influence that increases the expected market return, nor will it experience the same reduction in return when a market-wide influence reduces the expected market return. For example, where the average market return falls by 5%, a company whose beta has been calculated at 0.5 should expect the return on its shares to fall by 2.5%. This company's equivalent security market line will have a smaller gradient to the security market line in the previous graph.

The securities market line is the graphical representation of the capital asset pricing model (CAPM). It shows the expected rate of return for an overall market as a function of systematic risk. The expected return on a share (r_j) is dependent on three factors:

1. *The risk-free rate (r_f):* It can be observed from the previous graph that for zero systematic risk a guaranteed return is available. This is known as the risk-free rate. Investors do have the option of putting their funds into investments that have guaranteed returns, such as government bonds.

2. *A premium for accepting systematic risk ($r_m - r_f$):* Investors require a return in excess of the risk-free rate to compensate them for accept-

ing systematic risk. This is expressed as the difference between the average expected market return (r_m) and the risk-free rate (r_f), and is referred to as the ***market-risk premium.***

3.   *The level of systematic risk (β):* This represents the sensitivity of a particular company's returns to systematic risk, relative to the market.

The model is expressed as:

$$r_j = r_f + \beta(r_m - r_f)$$

Where r_j is the return expected from company j, r_f is the risk-free rate of return, β is the level of systematic risk and $(r_m - r_f)$ is the market-risk premium.

Worked example 12.6   (CAPM)

Julio plc has a beta factor of 1.2. The yield on government bonds is 6% and the market-risk premium is 5%.

REQUIRED

Calculate Julio plc's equity cost of capital.

Solution

$$r_j = 6\% + 1.2(5\%)$$
$$r_j = 12\%$$

In this example you are given the market-risk premium, which is $(r_m - r_f)$. The return on the market is different. In this instance r_m is: 11% (5%+6%).

Unquoted companies
Unquoted companies do not have a market value for their equity. Three methods can be used to obtain an equity value. Firstly, the

accounting-equity book value can be ascertained from the balance sheet. However, this may not represent the true value of a company as assets may be recorded at historic cost, which may be less than their market value, or not recorded at all, i.e. goodwill. Consequently equity will be undervalued, whereas debt will reflect the actual balance owed. Equity usually costs more than debt, hence underestimating the proportion of the company financed by equity will understate the WACC, which may lead to a company accepting projects it shouldn't.

Worked example 12.7   (Unquoted companies: book value of equity)

Agosto Ltd. has the following entries in its balance sheet.

	€/£m
Equity share capital	50
Share premium account	40
Preference shares	100
Loan stock	50
Irredeemable loan stock	50
Long-term bank loan	10
Retained earnings	100
	400

REQUIRED

Calculate the book value of Agosto Ltd.'s equity capital.

Solution

The equity share capital, share premium and retained earnings are equity accounts; all the others are debt. The book value of equity is therefore €/£190 million.

The second method is to use *earnings per share* of an unquoted company and apply the *price-earnings ratio* of a similar quoted company (adjusted to reflect the lack of marketability) to estimate the equity value.

Worked example 12.8 (Unquoted companies: valuing equity using the price-earnings ratio)

Septiembre Ltd. has 2,000,000 issued equity shares. Its earnings per share are 28c/p. The price earnings ratio of Enero plc, a similar quoted company, is ten. It is estimated that this should be reduced by 20% to allow for the fact that Septiembre Ltd.'s shares are not readily marketable.

REQUIRED

Estimate Septiembre Ltd.'s equity cost of capital.

Solution

$$P_0 = 2,000,000 \times (€/£0.28 \times (10 \times 80\%))$$
$$P_0 = €/£4,480,000$$

Finally, as long as the cost of equity is known, the dividend valuation model can be used to determine the expected share price, hence the value of equity of an unquoted company. The dividend valuation model is rearranged to:

$$P_0 = \frac{D_0(1+g)}{Ke - g}$$

Worked example 12.9 (Unquoted companies: valuing equity using the dividend valuation model)

Noviembre Ltd. has one million authorised ordinary shares, of which 50% are issued. The dividend to be paid in the next period is 18c/p. The equity holders' required return is 15% and growth is estimated at 5%.

REQUIRED

Calculate the cost of equity capital for Noviembre Ltd.

Continued

Solution

The dividend of the next period (18c/p) is D_1, which is the equivalent of $D_0(1+g)$. The equity holders' cost of equity is 15%. Therefore, the current market price (P_0) of the shares at present is:

$$= \frac{18c/p}{0.15-0.05} = €/£1.80$$

The expected market value of equity is: €/£900,000 (500,000 × €/£1.80).

Debt

Debt capital is part of the long-term funding of a company, which can be traded or untraded. The same principles are used to value debt as are used to value equity: i.e. the current market value and opportunity cost should be sought for input to the WACC model. The main difference is that the yearly distribution (interest) on debt capital is usually pre-arranged, non-negotiable and tax deductible. In addition, debt capital is usually repayable in either cash or equity.

Untraded debt capital

When long-term debt is untraded, such as a bank loan, the market value equates to the book value and the cost is the after-tax market interest rate charged. This is usually the current market rate, which is the opportunity cost to a lender. If lenders do not get the current market rate, they may either not issue funds or withdraw their funds for investment elsewhere. The after-tax rate is:

$$K_{dt} = i(1 - t)$$

Where K_{dt} is the cost of debt after taxation, i is the interest rate and t is the taxation rate.

Traded debt capital

There are two main types of traded debt capital: irredeemable and redeemable. When a company opts for raising traded debt capital, it issues bonds that are traded in the stock markets. In the UK these 'bonds' have a nominal value of £100, in the ROI the equivalent is €100. The most common type of bond is the plain vanilla bond, which carries an annual fixed interest rate. Traders will value the bond based on the coupon (interest) on offer, compared to the returns offered by other similar types of investment.

Irredeemable

When a bond is irredeemable, its interest is paid for into infinity and the bond nominal amount will not be redeemed by a company. Therefore, this is valued as the present value of a future stream of coupon cash inflows into infinity, i.e. in perpetuity.

$$D = \frac{i(1-t)}{K_d}$$

Where D is the market value of the bond, i is the yearly coupon rate, t is the current tax rate and K_d is the bond holders' required return, or the cost of debt.

This calculation is usually required when bonds are first issued – when bonds are already in issue the market will dictate the bonds' market value. When this is the case the formula can be rearranged to determine the current return expected by debt holders based on the price they are willing to pay for the future stream of income. This is the cost of debt. It is calculated by rearranging the above formula, as follows:

$$K_d = \frac{i(1-t)}{D}$$

Worked example 12.10   (Irredeemable debt capital)

Octubre plc has €/£500,000 10% debentures issued that are currently trading at €/£90.00. The half-yearly interest has just been paid. The company is profitable and is paying tax at 40%.

Continued

REQUIRED

Calculate the value and cost of debt capital for Octubre plc for inclusion in its WACC.

Solution

There are €/£500,000/€/£100=5,000 bonds in issue, which are currently valued at €/£90 each.

Therefore the total market value of the company's debt capital is €/£450,000 (5,000 × €/£90).

Octubre plc's cost of debt (K_d) is:

$$\frac{€/£10(1-0.40)}{€/£90} = 6.67\%$$

When valuing debt to include in the WACC model, market value should be adjusted to reflect cash inflows that would be receivable by a company were it to issue new debt. Therefore, it should be valued ex-interest and less issue costs. The market price of traded debt leading up to a coupon payment date reacts in a similar manner to the market price of equity in the lead-up to a dividend distribution. The price of debt will include the value of the coupon that is about to be received by the holder; this is called the cum-interest price. This is not the equilibrium long-term value of the debt. To find a better representation of the long-term value of debt, the coupon that is about to be paid should be deducted from current price; this will give the ex-interest price. In the market, prices are quoted as being either cum-interest or ex-interest.

Worked example 12.11   (Debt: calculating market value for use in the WACC)

Noviembre plc has €/£200,000 10% irredeemable loan stock in issue. The loan stock is currently trading at par. This includes six months' accrued interest. The company pays tax at 40%. Issue costs for loan stock are €/£5.

Continued

REQUIRED

Calculate the value and cost of debt capital for Noviembre plc for inclusion in its WACC.

Solution

There are €/£200,000/€/£100=2,000 bonds in issue, which are currently valued at €/£100 each. However, this value includes six months' interest, which is €/£5 (€/£100×10%×6/12) per bond. Therefore the equilibrium market value of the bonds is €/£95 and Noviembre plc would expect to get €/£95 less the €/£5 issue costs if it were to raise new debt. Therefore the total market value of the company's debt capital is €/£180,000 (2,000×€/£90).

Noviembre plc's cost of debt (K_d) is as follows:

$$= \frac{€/£10(1-0.40)}{€/£90} = 6.67\%$$

Redeemable

A similar approach is used to ascertain the cost of redeemable debt except the coupon is an annuity for a set number of years. At the end of the annuity period the nominal value (£100 in the UK and €100 in the ROI) is redeemed (sometimes at a premium). The coupon is tax deductible by the company but the debt capital repayment is not. The calculation of the cost of redeemable debt can be split into three steps:

1. Calculate the current market value to be received by a company were it to issue the debt now;
2. Calculate the cash outflows, net of tax, expected by a company; and
3. Use the internal rate of return to find the rate that bond holders are willing to pay for this stream of cash payments.

> ### Worked example 12.12   (Calculating the cost of redeemable debt)
>
> Diciembre plc has €/£5,000,000 8% debentures (2012) that are trading at €/£90. The interest payment for 2007 has just been made. The company is profitable and is paying tax at 50%.
>
> **REQUIRED**
>
> Calculate the value and cost of Diciembre plc's debentures. Assume it is 31 December 2007 and the tax cash outflow occurs in the same year as the interest cash outflow.
>
> **Solution**
>
> The market value of the debentures is €/£90.00 for each €/£100.00 block. There is no mention of issue costs and the debentures are trading ex-interest. Therefore, the market value of the debt to be included in the WACC is €/£4,500,000 (€/£5,000,000/€/£100 × €/£90).
>
> *The cost of the debentures is as follows:*
>
> | Year | Cash flows | Discount Try 5% | PV | Discount Try 7% | PV |
> |------|-----------|-----------------|------|-----------------|------|
> | | €/£ | | €/£ | | €/£ |
> | 0 | 90 | 1.000 | 90.00 | 1.000 | 90.00 |
> | 1–5 | (8(1−0.5)) | 4.329 | (17.32) | 4.100 | (16.40) |
> | 5 | (100) | 0.784 | (78.40) | 0.713 | (71.30) |
> | | | | (5.72) | | 2.30 |
>
> $$K_d = 5\% + \frac{-€/£5.72\ (2\%)}{-€/£5.72 - €/£2.30} = 6.43\%$$

Preference share capital

Preference share capital is similar to irredeemable traded debt capital in that both require a yearly distribution of a set amount. However, the payout on preference share capital is dividends, which are not tax deductible and the nominal value can be any amount (though typically is denominated in values of under €/£1). The cost of preference share capital can be found using the formula:

$$K_p = \frac{D_1}{P_p}$$

Where K_p is the cost of the preference shares, D_1 is the annual dividend and P_p is the market value of the shares. Preference shares should be valued at the amount the company would expect to receive in a new distribution.

Worked example 12.13   (Calculating the value and cost of preference shares)

Sol plc has issued 11% irredeemable preference shares. Their nominal value is €/£300,000 and they were issued at €/£1 each. They are currently trading at €/£1.04 and the dividend has recently been paid.

REQUIRED

Calculate the value and cost of the preference share capital for Sol plc.

Solution

There are €/£300,000/€/£1 = 300,000 shares in issue, which are currently valued at €/£1.04 each. Therefore the total market value of Sol plc's preference share capital is €/£312,000 (300,000 × €/£1.04).

Sol plc's cost of preference shares (K_p) is as follows:

$$\frac{11c/p}{104c/p} = 10.57\%$$

Weighted average cost of capital

The WACC model provided at the start of the chapter can be adapted to include various different types of debt:

$$WACC = \frac{E(Ke)}{(E + D1 + D2\ldots)} + \frac{D1(Kd(1-t))}{(E + D1 + D2\ldots)} + \frac{D2(Kd(1-t))}{(E + D1 + D2\ldots)}\ldots\ldots$$

When the tax benefit is adjusted for in the workings to find the cost of debt do not include the $(1-t)$ again in the WACC model. This would result in a double deduction for tax.

Worked example 12.14   (Calculating the WACC and its elements)

Balance sheet for Llueva plc at 31 December 2006

Assets	*€/£'000*
Non-current assets	
Tangible assets	2,100
	2,100
Current assets	
Inventories	1,200
Trade receivables	1,500
Bank and cash	500
	3,200
Total assets	5,300
Equity and liabilities	
Equity and reserves	
Equity share capital	900
Share premium	500
Revenue reserves	1,100
	2,500
Non-current liabilities	
Loan stock (8%)	1,000
	1,000
Current liabilities	
Trade payables	1,170
Dividend	180
Taxation	450
	1,800
Total equity and liabilities	5,300

Additional information:
The equity share capital has a nominal value of 25c/p per share and is currently trading at €/£1.40. A dividend of 5c/p per share will

Continued

be paid shortly. It is expected that this dividend will increase by 7% each year.

The current market value of the loan stock is 98%. The half yearly interest coupon has just been paid.

The current corporation tax rate is 40%.

REQUIRED

Calculate the WACC for Llueva plc.

SOLUTION

Llueva plc has two sources of finance: equity and traded debt. To work out the WACC, five steps are required:

1. Work out the total market value of the equity share capital.
2. Work out the cost of equity.
3. Work out the total market value of the debt capital.
4. Work out the cost of the debt capital.
5. Use the data obtained from steps one to four to calculate the WACC.

1. The equity is currently trading at €/£1.40 (cum-dividend). Therefore, the value to be used in the WACC is €/£1.35 (€/£1.40−€/£0.05). Multiply this by the number of shares in issue: 3,600,000 shares (€/£900,000×€/£1.00/€/£0.25) to give the market value of equity of €/£4,860,000 (3,600,000×€/£1.35).

2. In this question, the information is directing the reader to use the dividend valuation model. You are told that g is 7%, D_0 is 5c/p and the market value (P_0) is €/£1.35. Therefore the cost of equity (Ke) is:

$$\frac{5c/p(1+0.07)}{135c/p} + 0.07 = 0.1096 \ (10.96\%)$$

Continued

3. The market value of the loan stock is €/£980,000 (((€/£1,000,000/€/£100) × (€/£100 × 98%)).

4. The loan stock is assumed to be irredeemable as there is no information to indicate that it is redeemable. The yearly interest is €/£100 × 8% = €/£8, taxation is 40% and the loan stock is trading at €/£98. Therefore the cost of debt (K_d) is:

$$\frac{€/£8(1-0.4)}{€/£98} = 0.0489 \ (4.89\%)$$

5. The WACC for Llueva plc is (in 000's):

$$\text{WACC} = \frac{€/£4,860 \ (10.96\%)}{€/£4,860 + €/£980} + \frac{€/£980 \ (4.89\%)}{€/£4,860 + €/£980} = 9.94\%$$

Limitations of using the WACC for investment appraisal

The WACC is an appropriate discount rate when: the rate reflects the marginal cost of new capital; the company's capital structure is at its optimal level; the project being evaluated is of the same business risk as the company; and the finance raised is in similar proportions to the existing capital structure. Any theory based on assumptions is limited by those assumptions. Other limitations of using the WACC are that sometimes companies raise floating-rate debt capital, the cost of which fluctuates, impacting on the WACC, and sometimes the variables used are not so easily determined. For example, some forms of debt capital are quite complicated and at some stage in the future may even convert to equity.

However, regardless of its limitations, the WACC is a good approximation for a discount rate to use in the evaluation of projects. An appreciation of its limitations will allow a business finance manager to adjust the WACC rate in light of knowledge about the current capital structure of the company and the riskiness of any project being evaluated. Higher-risk projects should require a larger return to compensate a company for the increased risk, hence should be discounted using the WACC plus a premium for additional risk. The premium to be added is a matter of judgement.

Conclusion

Finding an appropriate discount rate for evaluating investments for a company is more difficult than just using the WACC, which applies theoretical formulae to calculate the cost and value of a company's debt and equity capital, which are then combined to provide an overall WACC. This rigorous process does provide a framework upon which a business finance manager can estimate an appropriate discount rate for project evaluation. However, it should be regarded as a starting point. Calculating the WACC has another advantage in that it keeps business finance managers ever-conscious of the return required by financiers in current terms. However, business finance managers have to be careful: if the discount rate estimated is too high, projects will be turned down that would satisfy equity holders and provide wealth for them; if too low, the resources of a company will be depleted and equity holders will lose wealth.

KEY TERMS

Beta
Beta factor/coefficient
Business risk
Capital asset pricing model
  (CAPM)
Cost of capital
Coupon rate
Diversified portfolio
Dividend valuation model
Economic profit
Economic value added
Equity
Marginal cost of capital
Market return

Market-risk premium
Opportunity cost
Portfolio theory
Risk-free rate
Risk premium
Security market line
Systematic risk
Unsystematic risk
Weighted average cost of capital
  (WACC)

REVIEW QUESTIONS

1. Enero plc has one million authorised equity shares, of which 50% are issued. Issue costs amount to 10c/p per share. Its shares are currently trading at €/£2.05. A dividend of 15c/p will be paid shortly.

REQUIRED

Calculate the value of Enero plc's equity shares, which should be used in the calculation of its WACC.

2. The ordinary share capital of Marzo plc is currently trading at €/£2.50 (ex-dividend). Issue costs are 20c/p per share. The company pays a fixed dividend each year of 46c/p.

REQUIRED

Calculate the cost of equity for Marzo plc.

3. The equity share capital of Abril plc is currently trading at 90c/p. A dividend of 8c/p has recently been paid. Dividends grow at 6% per year.

REQUIRED

Calculate the cost of equity for Abril plc.

4. Mayo plc has an ROCE of 20%. Each year it retains 50% of its earnings to invest in projects.

REQUIRED

Calculate the expected growth in Mayo plc's dividends.

5. Octubre Ltd. has one million authorised equity shares, of which 50% are issued. Its earnings per share are 20c/p. A similar quoted company, Febrero plc, has a *price-earnings ratio* of ten.

REQUIRED

Estimate the market value of Octobre Ltd. to be used in the calculation of its WACC. Assume a reduction of 10% for lack of marketability.

6.   Frio plc has €/£1 million of 10% debentures, which are redeemable after eight years. The debentures are currently trading at €/£112 and a full year's interest is about to be paid by the company. The tax rate is currently 30%.

REQUIRED

Calculate the value and cost of Frio plc's debentures.

7.   When can the WACC be used as an appropriate discount rate for capital investment appraisal?

8.   **CRYSTAL plc**
The following figures have been extracted from the most recent accounts of CRYSTAL plc.

Balance sheet as at 30 June 2009

	€/£'000	€/£'000
Assets		
Non-current assets		
Tangible assets		10,115
Financial assets		821
		10,936
Current assets		3,658
Total assets		14,594
Equity and liabilities		
Equity and reserves		
Equity share capital		
Authorised: 4,000,000 shares of €/£1		
Issued: 3,000,000 shares of €/£1		3,000
Reserves		6,542
Total equity and reserves		9,542
Nong-current liabilities		
7% debentures		1,300
Deferred taxation		583
		1,883

Current liabilities

Trade and other payables	1,735
Corporation tax	1,434
	3,169
Total equity and liabilities	14,594

Summary of profits and dividends

Year ended 30 June	2005 €/£'000	2006 €/£'000	2007 €/£'000	2008 €/£'000	2009 €/£'000
Profit after interest					
and before tax	1,737	2,090	1,940	1,866	2,179
Less tax	573	690	640	616	719
Profit after interest					
and tax	1,164	1,400	1,300	1,250	1,460
Less dividends	620	680	740	740	810
Added to reserves	544	720	560	510	650

The current (1 July 2009) market value of CRYSTAL plc's equity shares is €/£3.27 per share cum-dividend. An annual dividend of €/£810,000 is due for payment shortly. The debentures are redeemable at par in ten years time. Their current market value is €/£77.10. Annual interest has just been paid on the debentures. There have been no issues or redemptions of equity shares or debentures during the past five years. The current rate of corporation tax is 33%, and the current basic rate of income tax is 25%. Assume that there have been no changes in the system, or rates of taxation, during the last five years.

REQUIRED

a) Estimate the cost of capital CRYSTAL plc should use as a discount rate when appraising new investment opportunities.

17 Marks

b) Discuss any difficulties and uncertainties in your estimates.

8 Marks

25 Marks

(ICAI, MABF II, Questions and Solutions Manual, 2000/2001)

CHALLENGING QUESTIONS

1.   VIENTO plc

a)   VIENTO plc has the following capital structure:

	€/£'000
Equity shares of 50c/p each	5,200
Reserves	4,850
9% preference shares	4,500
14% debenture shares	5,000
	19,550

The market price of the equity shares is currently 80c/p and the most recent dividend was 4c/p. Dividends will increase by 12% per annum. The preference shares are trading at 72c/p (cum-dividend) and the debentures (irredeemable) at par. Corporation tax is 33%.

REQUIRED

Calculate the WACC for VIENTO plc.

8 Marks

(ICAI, MABF II, Autumn 1997, Q5 a)

2.   MARCO and POLO Ltd.

You are given the following information about two companies, which are both financed entirely by equity capital:

	MARCO Ltd.	POLO Ltd.
Number of equity shares of €/£1 ('000)	150,000	500,000
Market value per share, ex-dividend (€/£)	3.42	0.65
Current earnings (total) (€/£'000)	62,858	63,952
Current dividend (total) (€/£'000)	6,158	48,130
Balance sheet value of capital employed (€/£'000)	315,000	293,000
Dividend five years ago (total) (€/£'000)	2,473	37,600

Both companies are in the same line of business and sell similar products.

REQUIRED

a)   Estimate the cost of capital for both companies, using two growth models.

10 Marks

b)   Describe, giving your reasons, any additional evidence you would refer to, in order to increase your confidence in the estimates of the cost of capital in practice.

5 Marks

(ICAI, MABF II, Questions and Solutions Manual, 2000/2001)

3.   PAVLOVA plc

The directors of PAVLOVA plc wish to calculate the cost of the company's equity capital for various decision making purposes. In order to investigate the sensitivity of their calculations, they have decided to utilise both the dividend valuation model and the capital asset pricing model (CAPM) for their calculations.

A dividend of €/£0.10 per share has been paid recently by the company and the current market price of the equity shares is €/£1.00.

The dividend growth rate is expected to continue at its current level of 10% per annum.

Market analysts have forecast the expected return on the stock market in the near future will be 15% per annum. The return on three-month government stock, regarded as risk-free assets, is expected to be 5% per annum.

The relevant beta factor for this company is 1.1.

REQUIRED

a)   Estimate the cost of equity capital for PAVLOVA plc, using both the dividend valuation model and the CAPM.

8 Marks

b)   Comment on your results.

5 Marks

c)   Evaluate the two methods used from both a theoretical and a practical viewpoint.

12 Marks
Total **25 Marks**
(ICAI, MABF II, Autumn 1994, Q1)

4.   STRETFORD plc

STRETFORD plc and TRAFFORD plc are two companies that operate in the same industrial sector. The following information regarding their financial structure and profitability is available:

	STRETFORD plc	TRAFFORD plc
Number of equity shares (€/£1)	2,000,000	1,000,000
	€/£	€/£
Net profits attributable to equity holders	600,000	250,000
Gross dividends	500,000	200,000
Market value per share	3	2
Market value of debt	3,000,000	1,500,000
Gross interest yield on debt	10%	12%
Expected annual growth rate of dividends	12%	10%

Assume that the rate of corporation tax is 50%.

REQUIRED

a)   Estimate the weighted average cost of capital (WACC) of each company.

12 Marks

b)   Discuss any limitations you consider relevant when using the WACC for the evaluation of investment projects.

10 Marks
Total **22 Marks**
(ICAI, MABF II, Autumn 1995, Q7)

5.   EQUITAS plc

c)   EQUITAS plc currently earns an annual profit before interest and tax of €/£8 million. Profits are expected to remain at this level. The company operates a policy of distributing all available profits to its equity holders as dividends. Recently, an interim dividend of 3.3c/p has been declared and the company's shares are currently trading at €/£0.56 cum-dividend. The market price of the company's debentures is €/£103.25 ex-interest.

The capital structure of the company is as follows:

	€/£'000
Equity shares (€/£0.25 par value)	6,500
Reserves	12,350
	18,850
15% debentures 31 December, 2008	
(€/£100 par value)	12,600
	31,450

The rate of corporate taxation is 35%.

REQUIRED

Calculate the cost of capital of EQUITAS plc, assuming that it is now 31 December 2005.

8 Marks

(ICAI, MABF II, Autumn 1996, extract from Q7)

6.   BINDAROO plc

BINDAROO plc had the following balance sheet at 31 March 2007:

	€/£m
Equity share capital (€/£1 nominal value)	
Authorised	1,000
Issued and fully paid...	500
8% cumulative irredeemable	100
preference share capital	
9% non-cumulative irredeemable	80
preference share capital	
Capital redemption reserve fund	90
Revaluation reserve...	150
Revenue reserves...	448
Equity holders' funds..	1,368
6% irredeemable loan stock..	156
4% debentures (redeemable on	
31 March 2011 at €/£115)	300
Total capital employed..	1,824
Represented by	
Sundry net assets	1,824

The following information is also available:

(1) The equity shares are trading at €/£3.60 ex-dividend.

(2) The 8% preference shares are quoted at €/£1.09.

(3) The 9% preference shares are quoted at €/£1.14.

(4) The current price of the 6% loan stock is €/£105.

(5) The current price of the 4% debentures is €/£104.

(6) In the year to 31 March 2007, a dividend of €/£0.06 was paid on the equity share capital of the company. Recent trends indicate that BINDAROO increases its dividend payment on average by 3% per annum.

(7) The risk-free rate of interest is 2.5%. The market rate of return is 6%.

(8) The beta factor applicable to the equity of BINDAROO is 1.04.

(9) Profit before interest and tax for the year ended 31 March 2007 was €/£650,000.

(10)   Assume that the taxable profit is identical to the accounting profit. Ignore deferred tax.

(11)   The corporation tax rate applicable to BINDAROO is 12.5%.

REQUIRED

a)   Calculate, in respect of BINDAROO, as at 31 March 2007, each of the following:

(i) The profit retained for the year ended 31 March 2007.

4 Marks

(ii) The capital gearing and the income gearing (times interest earned) ratios.

3 Marks

(iii) The cost of equity using both the CAPM and the dividend valuation model (Gordon's growth model).

3 Marks

(iv) The cost of redeemable debentures.
The cost of irredeemable debentures.

4 Marks

(v) The WACC, using either of the figures for cost of equity in part (iii) above.

5 Marks

b)   Explain why the two different methods of calculating the cost of equity noted above give different results. State which method is superior in your opinion, and why.

3 Marks
Total 22 Marks
(ICAI, MABF II, Summer 2004, Q5)

7.   LUBOK plc

a)   It is commonly accepted that a crucial factor in the financial decisions of a company, including the evaluation of capital investment proposals, is the cost of capital.

Explain in simple terms what is meant by the 'cost of equity capital' for a particular company. Specifically, what is the difference between the 'cost of equity capital' and the 'weighted average cost of capital'?

5 Marks

b) Calculate the cost of equity capital for LUBOK plc, as at the beginning of 2006, from the data given below, using the following two alternative methods:

(i) The dividend growth model;

4 Marks

(ii) The capital asset pricing model.

3 Marks

LUBOK plc - data

(1) Price per share on the Stock Exchange at 1 January 2006 €/£1.20, ex div.

(2) Annual dividend per share

Year	c/p per share
2001	7.63
2002	8.31
2003	8.88
2004	9.35
2005	10.00

(3) Beta coefficient for LUBOK plc shares   0.7

(4) Expected rate of return on risk-free securities   8%

(5) Expected return on the market portfolio   12%

c) State, for each model separately, the main simplifying assumptions made, and express your opinion as to whether, in view of these assumptions, the models yield results that can be safely used in practice.

6 Marks
Total 18 Marks
(ICAI, MABF II, Summer 2006, Q6)

8   MILO plc

a)   Define the 'cost of capital' and explain its significance in financial decision making.

6 Marks

b)   The following information is available for your perusal:
The capital structure (book value) of MILO plc is:

	€/£
Redeemable debentures (€/£100 per debenture)	800,000
Redeemable preference shares (€/£100 per share)	200,000
Equity shares (€/£10 per share)	1,000,000
Retained reserves	800,000
	2,800,000

All these securities are traded in the capital markets. Recent prices are as follows:

Debentures at €/£110 per debenture
Preference shares at €/£120 per share
Equity shares at €/£22 per share

Anticipated external financing opportunities are as follows:

(1)   €/£100 per debenture redeemable at par; 14-year maturity, 8% coupon rate, 4% issue costs, sale price €/£100.

(2)   €/£100 preference share redeemable at par; 15-year maturity, 10% dividend rate, 5% flotation costs, sale price €/£100.

(3)   Equity shares: €/£2 share flotation costs, issue price €/£22.

In addition, the dividend expected on the equity share at the end of the current year is €/£2 per share; the anticipated growth rate in dividends is 5% per annum, and the company has the practice of paying all its earnings in the form of dividends. The Corporate tax rate is 12.5%.

REQUIRED

Determine the weighted average cost of capital of MILO plc using:
(i)   Book value weightings; and
(ii)   Market value weightings.

12 Marks
Total 18 Marks
(ICAI, MABF II, Autumn 2007, Q7)

CAPITAL INVESTMENT DECISION MAKING

13

Debt   10,000,000
Equity   15,000,000
Market Value 25,000,000

LEARNING OBJECTIVES

....

Upon completing the chapter, readers should be able to:

* Identify the relevant cash flows for investment appraisal (including the effects of taxation, working capital and inflation);
* List the limitations of investment appraisal;
* Evaluate different investments using the annual rate of return, the payback period, the discounted payback period, the internal rate of return, the net present value and the incremental cash flow approaches;
* List the advantages and disadvantages of each investment appraisal method;
* Explain the difference between hard and soft capital rationing;
* Evaluate single period investment decisions under conditions of capital rationing (when investment projects are divisible, non-divisible and mutually exclusive); and
* Evaluate asset replacement decisions, including when and how often, to replace assets.

Introduction

There are two main types of investment decision: external investment and internal investment. *External investment* involves making decisions in respect of the acquisition of, or merger with, other companies or ventures. This falls outside the scope of this chapter. *Internal investment* involves investment in assets within a company. This can fall into two categories, the purchase of speculative investments (such as shares in the stock market), or the purchase of capital items that are used to enhance a company's operational worth. These capital investments may be similar to the current activities of a company, or may be new. This chapter is only concerned with capital investment decisions. Capital investments normally involve an initial outlay, or series of cash outlays, followed by a stream of cash inflows over a longer period of time.

As mentioned in the introductory chapters to this book the investment decision is the most important decision facing a business finance manager. Investment decisions determine the future cash flows of a company and expected future cash flows determine company value. As is consistent with the rest of this text, it is assumed when making investment decisions that the ultimate objective from each decision is the maximisation of equity holder wealth. Regardless of how a company is financed, or the level of dividend it pays out, if investment decisions are not successful, a company will not be able to service its finance or pay dividends to its equity holders.

Investment decisions are usually material and wrong decisions can be costly to a company: capital investments are usually expensive to terminate, as they are usually tailor made for a particular company. This reduces the investment's marketability. An example of a capital appraisal failure is the ISIS project that was commissioned by the Irish League of Credit Unions in Ireland (ILCU). The ILCU, a trade body representing the majority of credit unions in the island of Ireland, decided to embark on an investment in computer software to modernise credit unions and allow them to provide banking services not too dissimilar to banks (internet banking, integrated banking and cash machine networks). The estimated project cost was €60 million. Within a couple of years of the project commencing, this estimate increased to €100 million. The project was eventually scrapped, after running out of funds (McKillop, Goth, Hyndman, 2006). The resultant product was not completed and could not be resold as it was bespoke. An enquiry into the debacle found that: the initial appraisal figures had errors (including a VAT error of €7 million), were understated; and that the ILCU used funds to finance the overrun in costs that it should not have (from insurance reserves). As a result, 19 of the strongest credit unions left the ILCU, reducing the ILCU's revenue and undermining their strong position as the voice for credit unions in Ireland.

This chapter outlines the major difficulties underlying project appraisal (the time value of money, taxation, working capital, inflation, capital rationing, mutually exclusive projects, multi-period projects and risk). The most commonly utilised appraisal methods are explained (accounting rate of return; payback period method; net present value method; and the internal rate of return method) and the chapter concludes by identifying the most appropriate technique to be used and compares this to research findings on the use of the various techniques, by companies.

Difficulties facing project appraisal

Strategic issues: goal congruence

When a manager is assessing a project, it is of utmost importance that the decision is made with the big picture in mind. The outcomes should be congruent with the goals of a company. This may mean sacrificing a project that makes strong short-term gains, in favour of a project which will have strong long-term implications for a company. For example, Viridian Group plc sold their software and IT subsidiary, S×3, in 2005–06, for £155 million (http://www.ukbusinesspark.co.uk/viridian.html). Though the subsidiary was profitable, Viridian Group plc is streamlining its operations to their long-term strategies:

> 'We remain strongly focused on our energy businesses in Ireland: Northern Ireland Electricity (NIE) – maximising the efficiency of our regulated assets, which remain the mainstay of our business; and VP&E – growing a profitable integrated energy business in competitive markets across Ireland. Our goal remains to deliver shareholder value through consistent performance and sustainable dividend growth' (Viridian Group plc, Annual Report 2005–06).

Relevant cash flows

Some of the theoretical rules pertaining to management accounting decision making, are equally relevant for project appraisal. Project appraisal should only consider relevant cash flows. *Relevant cash flows* are incremental cash flows and opportunity cash flows. *Incremental cash flows* are those that will occur only as a consequence of a project being undertaken.

Cash flows that occur as a result of decisions made in the past, which cannot be changed are deemed to be *sunk cash flows* and should not influence decision making in respect of potential projects. This will include any management time and marketing costs already spent gaining information on the specific projects to be appraised and it also includes fixed costs that will occur regardless, such as overheads. These should be excluded even if a project cannot proceed without these costs being occurred. However, any additional overhead costs would be deemed relevant. *Opportunity cash flows* are cash flows forgone from other investments, or actions that have been changed, as a result of the project being implemented. For example, in a decision on whether to sell a machine, or use it to process a new product; the opportunity cash flow being lost if the machine were to be utilised further, is the resale value that the company could obtain now. Therefore, this is a relevant cost, which will form part of the project's appraisal. Where a project impacts on cash flows from other areas, these should be taken into account in the assessment, for example, a project may lead to a reduction in the sales of another product.

The time value of money

Cash v profit

In finance, cash is king and cash is very different to profit. Management performance is usually assessed using accounting ratios, which are calculated using profit figures. This may cause agency problems when project appraisal is being undertaken, as the pattern of cash is more important in project appraisal, than profits made. For example, when calculating profit, a project that takes five years and yields £5 million at the end of the period will have similar yearly profit figures (assuming that costs are evenly spread across the five years and the contract is certain), to a project that takes five years and has five £1 million yearly instalments for the five years ending in year five. In profit terms both projects will result in the same overall performance. However, if this project were to be viewed with a finance cap on, then the latter project would be valued much higher, relative to the former project. This is due to the impact of the time value of money. The value of money declines in line with the length of time a company has to wait to receive the money. This means that matching and accrual entries such as: trade receivables; trade payables; provisions; and depreciation (to name a few) are not important in the investment appraisal process and have to be removed to ascertain expected cash flows.

Discount rates

As mentioned in the previous paragraph a company benefits from receiving money now rather than later. This money can be used to either: earn a return from another investment (another project, or just sitting in a deposit account); or to reduce costs (such as interest on an overdraft). To evaluate the correct worth of future cash flows, it is important to determine their current or present value. *Present value* (PV) is a term used to depict the current value of funds received in the future. The present value of cash flows will always be less than the *future value* of cash flows. The differential between the present value and the future value of cash flows depends on the return a company can expect to get by utilising the funds in the intervening period. For example, a company could use the funds to pay back its financiers, or to invest in a project.

A starting point when evaluating the present value of a future expected cash flow is to determine a company's required rate of return. In most instances the starting point is to use a company's WACC (the current cost of a company's finance). The thinking behind this is that a company should earn a sufficient return to at least pay its financiers. The WACC is an average yield, say 10%. When a company expects to get a cash flow in the future; it should consider the opportunity cost of not having the cash now – assuming it can invest the cash to earn a return. The future cash flow is *discounted* by 10%; this means that the current equivalent of the future cash flow will be a smaller sum, which if invested for the period of time up to the date of the future cash flow would earn a return of 10%, bringing the total value of the present cash flow to the expected future cash flow value.

Therefore receiving €/£1 in one year's time is deemed to be the equivalent of receiving 90.9c/p now. If the company had 90.9c/p now, it could earn a return of 9.1c/p on the funds (90.9c/p × 10%) over the year. The relationship between the present value of funds and their future value is as follows:

$$PV(1+r)^n = FV$$

Where PV is the present value, r is the *discount rate* (the rate at which the funds can be invested), n is the number of years the cash flows will be received in the future, and FV is the future value of the cash flow. The PV of a future cash flow of €/£1 discounted at 10% is 90.9c/p

$(PV(1+10\%)^1 = €/£1$; hence the PV is: $(€/£1/1.1))$. The above formula can be expressed in PV terms. This is as follows:

$$PV = FV \times \frac{1}{(1+r)^n}$$

The component on the right had side $(1/(1+r)^n)$ is called the **discount rate factor**. It can be used for any amount of FV cash flow being analysed.

Worked example 13.1   (Present value)

Frank Ltd. expects to receive cash from an investment of €/£50,000 in each year, for three years starting on the last day of the first year. Frank Ltd. has a weighted average cost of capital of 12%.

REQUIRED

What is the present value of these future cash flows?

Solution

Year	Cash flow €/£	Discount factor		Present value €/£
1	50,000	$1/(1.12)^1$	0.893	44,650
2	50,000	$1/(1.12)^2$	0.797	39,850
3	50,000	$1/(1.12)^3$	0.712	35,600
				120,100

The present value of the three €/£50,000 cash inflows received at the end of year 1, 2 and 3, discounted at 12%, is €/£120,100. This means that Frank Ltd. would have to invest €/£120,100 now at 12%, to receive €/£50,000 at the end of each of the next three years.

To have to calculate discount rate factors every time a future stream of cash flows requires discounting is time consuming, therefore tables of *discount factors* (pre-calculated discount rates per year (for 15 years) for each rate) have been prepared. These tables are provided in appendix three, 'Present Value Discount Factors'.

Another short cut to reduce calculation time is to use annuity tables. An *annuity* is a constant stream of cash flows over a set period of consecutive time. An example is a pension. As the cash flow amount does not change the discount factors can be added together and the sum of these applied to the constant periodic cash flow to calculate their present value. In the previous example a constant cash flow was received for three consecutive years starting in year one. Therefore an *annuity factor* equals the sum of the yearly individual discount factors, which is: 2.402 (0.893+0.797+0.712). The present value of the €/£50,000 annuity is €/£120,100 (€/£50,000×2.402). Annuity factors remain constant for given rates and given numbers of years, therefore pre-calculated annuity factors for a range of rates and years are presented in a table in appendix four, 'Annuity Factor Tables'.

For most companies cash flows from projects will occur continuously throughout a year. However, to undertake daily discount calculations would be very time consuming (it could be performed using computer technology); therefore, for the purpose of this text it is assumed that all cash flows, in a year, occur on the last day of the year, unless a question specifies different. For example, a question might state that the company will acquire a machine on the first day of year two. This would be treated as the last day of year one and discounted by one year only, as it better reflects reality.

Project appraisal methods

There are four main methods of project appraisal: the accounting rate of return method, the payback period method, the net present value method and the internal rate of return method. These methods are now discussed using a common example to highlight differences between the methods.

The Accounting Rate of Return (ARR)

The *accounting rate of return* estimates the rate of accounting profit that a project will generate over its entire life. It compares the average annual profit of a project with the cost (book value) of the project. This is the only investment appraisal method not to focus on cash flows. Two equations can be utilised:

$$\text{ARR (total investment)} = \frac{\text{Average annual profit}}{\text{Initial capital invested}} \times 100$$

$$\text{ARR (average investment)} = \frac{\text{Average annual profit}}{\text{Average capital invested}} \times 100$$

Where the *average annual profit* is the total profit for the whole period (typically cash less depreciation) divided by the life of the investment in years; and the *average capital invested* is the initial capital cost plus the expected disposal value divided by two.

The accounting rate of return is used in practice; however, is deemed inappropriate as the main technique to be used, due to the importance of the timing of cash flows to the success of a project (see the earlier discussion on cash versus profit). In practice, companies usually set a target accounting rate of return and consider projects that meet or exceed this target. This method is shown using the following example:

Worked example 13.2   (Accounting rate of return)

Cow Ltd. is considering three projects (each costing €/£240,000). The following profits before depreciation are predicted:

Yearly profits before depreciation	Friesian €/£	Aberdeen €/£	Saler €/£
Year 1	160,000	120,000	238,000
Year 2	60,000	120,000	2,000
Year 3	120,000	40,000	35,000
Year 4	140,000		
Year 5	20,000		
Year 6	10,000		

REQUIRED

a)   Given that Cow Ltd. has a target average accounting rate of return of 10% per annum (averaged over the investment period), which of the above projects should be accepted, if any? (Assume

Continued

that the asset is specialised and cannot be sold at the end of the project).

b) How would the results be affected were you informed that the asset could be sold after three years for €/£60,000 and after six years for €/£30,000.

Solution

a) The first step is to calculate the average profit of each project after depreciation. Therefore, the depreciation charge has to be deducted from the reported profit figures.

$$\text{Depreciation will equal } \frac{€/£240,000}{6} = €/£40,000 \text{ per year for Friesian}$$

$$\text{Depreciation will equal } \frac{€/£240,000}{3} = €/£80,000 \text{ per year for Aberdeen and Saler}$$

Yearly profits/(losses) after depreciation	Friesian €/£'000	Aberdeen €/£'000	Saler €/£'000
Year 1	120	40	158
Year 2	20	40	(78)
Year 3	80	(40)	(45)
Year 4	100		
Year 5	(20)		
Year 6	(30)		
Total profits	270	40	35
Average profits ratio	$\dfrac{€/£270,000}{6}$	$\dfrac{€/£40,000}{3}$	$\dfrac{€/£35,000}{3}$
Average profits	€/£45,000	€/£13,333	€/£11,667
ARR ratio	$\dfrac{€/£45,000}{€/£120,000}$	$\dfrac{€/£13,333}{€/£120,000}$	$\dfrac{€/£11,667}{€/£120,000}$
ARR	37.5%	11.11%	9.72%

The company has a target ARR of 10%. The 'Friesian' and 'Aberdeen' projects exceed the target, with reported ARRs of

Continued

37.5% and 11.11%, hence should be accepted. Saler should not be accepted, as its ARR is marginally below the target.

b)   In this instance the depreciation charge will change and is different for the 'Friesian' project, which lasts six years, relative to the other two projects (they last three years). In addition, the average capital investment will change as the asset has a residual value, which differs depending on the length of project.

Friesian (depreciation calculation):
   $(€/£240,000 − €/£30,000)/6 = €/£35,000$
Aberdeen and Saler (depreciation calculation):
   $(€/£240,000 − €/£60,000)/3 = €/£60,000$

Yearly profits/ (losses) After depreciation	Friesian €/£'000	Aberdeen €/£'000	Saler €/£'000
Year 1	125	60	178
Year 2	25	60	(58)
Year 3	85	(20)	(25)
Year 4	105		
Year 5	(15)		
Year 6	(25)		
Total profits	300	100	95
Average profits ratio	$\dfrac{€/£300,000}{6}$	$\dfrac{€/£100,000}{3}$	$\dfrac{€/£95,000}{3}$
Average profits	€/£50,000	€/£33,333	€/£31,667
Average investment	$\dfrac{€/£240,000+€/£30,000}{2}$	$\dfrac{€/£240,000+€/£60,000}{2}$	$\dfrac{€/£240,000+€/£60,000}{2}$
Average investment	€/£135,000	€/£150,00	€/£150,000
ARR ratio	$\dfrac{€/£50,000}{€/£135,000}$	$\dfrac{€/£33,333}{€/£150,000}$	$\dfrac{€/£31,667}{€/£150,000}$
ARR	37.03%	22.22%	21.11%

In this instance all three projects would be accepted as they all provide a return in excess of the 10% benchmark.

An advantage cited for using the ARR method of investment appraisal, is that it is understandable and closely correlates with accounting ratios that are used to assess a company's performance, for example the ROCE. However, it does not take into account the size of a project, the duration of a project, the cash flows and more importantly the time value of money. It can also be distorted by the pattern of profits; causing managers to make incorrect conclusions. For example, if in example 13.2, an extra year of use yields an extra €/£500 profits to 'Friesian' company, this may be beneficial causing total profits to rise to €/£300,500; however, it will mean that the average profits will fall as the total profits will be divisible by seven, hence will fall from €/£50,000 to €/£42,928 and the ARR will consequently fall from 37.03% to 31.8%. Therefore, when comparing projects, care needs to be taken as inappropriate use of the ARR may lead the decision maker to make incorrect decisions.

The payback period

The *payback period method* ranks investments in order of the speed at which the initial cash outflow is paid back by subsequent cash inflows. Under this method the most attractive investment would be the one that pays back the initial outlay in the quickest time. This method focuses on cash flows not profits, therefore depreciation and accrual accounting is ignored. This method calculates the number of years it takes for cumulative cash flows to achieve breakeven point.

Worked example 13.3   (Payback period method)

Cow Ltd. is considering three projects (each costing €/£240,000). The following cash flows are predicted:

Yearly cash flows	Friesian	Aberdeen	Saler
	€/£	€/£	€/£
Year 1	160,000	120,000	238,000
Year 2	60,000	120,000	1,000
Year 3	120,000	40,000	36,000
Year 4	140,000		
Year 5	20,000		
Year 6	10,000		

Continued

REQUIRED

Using the payback method, advise Cow Ltd. as to the investment to undertake.

Solution

The investment in 'Friesian' takes two years and two months to pay back the initial outlay: (€/£160,000 (first year) + €/£60,000 (second year) + €/£20,000/€120,000 (which is one sixth or two months of the third year)).

The 'Aberdeen' investment takes two years exactly to pay back the initial outlay: (€/£120,000 + €/£120,000).

The 'Saler' investment takes two years and ten days to pay back the initial outlay: (€/£238,000 (first year) + €/£1,000 (second year) + ((€/£1,000/€/£36,000) × 365) (ten days)).

Therefore using the payback period method – 'Aberdeen' is the highest ranking investment opportunity of the three on offer.

The above example highlights the shortcomings of the payback period method. The first major disadvantage is that it focuses on cash flows and ignores profitability. Both elements should be considered for project appraisal. In addition it ignores cash flows received after the payback period, which in the case of 'Friesian' is material. It also ignores the time value of money. The cash flows of 'Saler' are more attractive relative to those of 'Aberdeen' as most of the funds are received in the first year, yet this is not taken into account in the calculations. Were 'Saler' to have a €/£2,000 cash inflow in year two instead of the €/£1,000, it would have been ranked the same as 'Aberdeen', yet would be deemed to be much more superior, if the time value of money were to be considered. In addition, the payback method does not take into account the size or relative impact of an investment. In this example the investment cash outflow in each case was the same; however, this is unlikely to be the case in practice. Use of the payback period method might lead to a small project with a short payback period being ranked in front of a large project that has a slightly longer payback period, but a much larger impact on the organisation and potentially larger net cash inflows in subsequent periods. Many companies set an initial hurdle payback period for their investment projects. Setting a period limit is regarded as subjective. It might eliminate more profitable projects that have a longer life.

On a positive note, the payback period method is a quick and simple investment appraisal technique that is particularly useful for companies who have liquidity issues and who need to recoup their cash outlay quickly. It can also be used to help decide between two projects that have similar annual accounting rates of return. Another advantage of the payback method is that it can be regarded as a risk screening technique. There is a correlation between risk and the length of time that cash flows are estimated for; in that cash flows predicted in the first couple of years are inherently less risky than cash flows that are estimated for say, ten years time. Therefore the payback method focuses managers' attention on projects that have more reliable estimates.

Research has shown that companies do use the payback period, though mostly as an initial screening device in their overall investment appraisal programme.

Discounted payback method

The *discounted payback period method* overcomes one of the weaknesses of the payback period method, as it takes the time value of money into consideration. This method ranks investments according to the speed at which the cumulative *discounted cash flows (DCF)* of an investment cover the initial cash outlay. An appropriate discount rate needs to be utilised. The factors affecting the discount rate to be used in investment appraisal were discussed earlier in this chapter and should be taken into account when using the discounted payback period method.

Worked example 13.4 (Discounted payback method)
Cow Ltd. is considering three projects (each costing €/£240,000). The following cash flows before depreciation are predicted:
Continued

Yearly cash flows before depreciation	Friesian €/£	Aberdeen €/£	Saler €/£
Year 1	160,000	120,000	238,000
Year 2	60,000	120,000	1,000
Year 3	120,000	40,000	36,000
Year 4	140,000		
Year 5	20,000		
Year 6	10,000		

REQUIRED

Which of the above projects should Cow Ltd. invest in? Cow Ltd. has to borrow funds at 10%. Management decide that this is an appropriate discount rate to use and it is company policy to use the discounted payback period method for capital investment appraisal.

Solution

Yearly cash flows	Discount factor	Friesian €/£	Aberdeen €/£	Saler €/£
Year 0	1.000	(240,000)	(240,000)	(240,000)
Year 1	0.909	145,440	109,080	216,342
Year 2	0.826	49,560	99,120	826
Year 3	0.751	90,120	30,040	27,036
Year 4	0.683	95,620		
Year 5	0.621	12,420		
Year 6	0.564	5,640		

The investment 'Friesian' has a total discounted payback period of two years and six months. (€/£145,440 (one year) + €/£49,560 (one year) + (€/£45,000*/€/£90,120 × 12) (six months)).
*Where €/£45,000 is: (€/£240,000 – (€£145,440 + €/£49,560)).

The investment 'Aberdeen' does not recover its initial outlay when the time value of money is taken into account. The project costs €/£240,000 and the discounted cash inflows total: €/£238,240 (€/£109,080 + €/£99,120 + €/£30,040).

Continued

> The investment 'Saler' has a total discounted payback period of two years and ten months.
> (€/£216,342 (one year) + €/£826 (one year) + (€/£22,832*/ €/£27,036) × 12) (ten months)).
> *Where €/£22,832 is: (€/£240,000 – (€/£216,342 + €/£826)).*
>
> Therefore, 'Friesian' is the highest ranking project using the discounted payback period method.

The highest ranking investment from the straight payback period analysis ('Aberdeen') would be totally eliminated from the appraisal process were the discounted payback period method to be used; as its discounted cash inflows are insufficient to cover the initial outlay. Though this method of investment appraisal does remove one of the disadvantages associated with using the payback method, all the other disadvantages remain.

Internal Rate of Return (IRR)

The *IRR*, sometimes referred to as the ***discounted cash flow yield method*** also involves discounting future cash flows to their present value. It could be considered a type of *break-even analysis,* which focuses on trying to find the discount rate at which the present value of the future cash flows (inflows and outflows combined) equals the initial investment cash outlay. It basically tries to find the return received from an investment opportunity. This is the rate which gives a NPV of zero. It is usually used by management to rank investment projects, or to provide a cut-off rate for determining which projects to investigate further.

The predetermined return rate should be at least the company's project discount rate for this type of project. If the IRR is greater than the target rate, then the project is expected to provide a return that is higher than the minimum return expected by management; hence should be pursued further. When the IRR equals the target rate the project can be accepted. When the IRR is lower than the predetermined target rate, the project should not be accepted. Where a company has to decide between a number of projects that have an IRR in excess of the target rate, then the project with the highest IRR should be accepted.

> ## Advantages of using the IRR for investment appraisal
>
> *Time value of money:* The time value of money is taken into consideration.
>
> *All cash flows:* All cash flows are considered in the appraisal process.

Calculating the IRR

The approach to calculating the IRR is to use trial and error and then to interpolate between two rates to find the best estimate of the IRR. The process of interpolation is described using the following graph. In the first instance cash flows are discounted using a ten percent discount rate[1]. The result is a positive net present value of €/£10 million, as this is positive, a higher discount rate is selected for the second trial – 15 percent. This is again selected subjectively. The result is a negative net present value of €/£8 million. Therefore, the true rate lies between ten percent and 15 percent. Interpolation works by assuming that the returns received from the project have a linear relationship to the rate of return. The true IRR rate is the point X; however, interpolation will use a simple mathematical equation to find the point Y, which is a close approximation to X, though not exact.

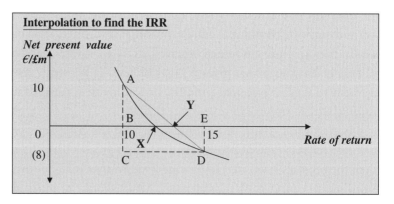

The calculation is based on the assumption that the triangle ABY is a smaller version of the triangle ACD. As the rates and NPV's are known

---

[1] This rate is selected subjectively.

for the larger triangle, this relationship can be used to find Y. The key is to find the proportion that BY is of the difference between C and D (i.e. the proportion of 5% (15% − 10%)). This proportion is then used to find the additional rate of return that is added to the lower value (B) to give an overall approximation for the IRR (Y). The proportion that BY is, relative to CD, can be calculated as follows:

$$\frac{BY}{AB} = \frac{CD}{AC}$$

Where BY is unknown. BY represents the distance between B and Y (in terms of rates of return). AB is the distance between A and B (in terms of NPV) and so on.

> **Using the above graph, the IRR is:**
>
> $$\frac{Y - 10\%}{€/£10m - €/£0} = \frac{15\% - 10\%}{€/£10m - (-€/£8m)}$$
>
> $$\frac{Y - 10\%}{€/£10m} = \frac{5\%}{€/£18m}$$
>
> $$€/£18(Y - 10\%) = €/£10 \,(5\%)$$
>
> $$€/£18Y - €/£1.8 = €/£0.5m$$
> $$€/£18Y = €/£0.5m + €/£1.8m$$
> $$€/£18Y = €/£2.3m$$
> $$Y = €/£2.3m / €/£18m$$
> $$Y = 12.78\%$$

This process is simplified into the following formula:

$$IRR = Rate\ 1 + \frac{NPV\ 1\ (Rate\ 2 - Rate\ 1)}{NPV\ 1 - NPV\ 2}$$

This is the correct formula to use where the first trial discount rate lies below the IRR (positive NPV) and the second lies above the IRR (negative NPV). In this instance Rate 1 will be the lower rate used and NPV 1 will be its associated positive NPV. Rate 2 is the second trial rate that is used (higher rate) and NPV 2 is its corresponding negative NPV. This is shown using the following example:

Worked example 13.5   (IRR: interpolation)

Cow Ltd. is considering a project (costing €/£240,000). The following cash flows before depreciation, are predicted:

Yearly cash flows before depreciation	Friesian €/£
Year 1	160,000
Year 2	60,000
Year 3	120,000
Year 4	40,000
Year 5	30,000

REQUIRED

Calculate the IRR of the above named project using interpolation.

Solution

For the first trial a discount rate of 10% is selected. At this rate the investment has a NPV of €/£91,070 (see table below).

Therefore, a higher rate (30%) is selected for the second trial. At this discount rate a negative NPV of €/£4,770 results (see table below).

Yearly cash flows	Discount factor (10%)	Present value (€/£)	Discount factor (30%)	Present value (€/£)
Year 0	1.000	(240,000)	1.000	(240,000)
Year 1	0.909	145,440	0.769	123,040
Year 2	0.826	49,560	0.592	35,520
Year 3	0.751	90,120	0.455	54,600
Year 4	0.683	27,320	0.350	14,000
Year 5	0.621	18,630	0.269	8,070
NPV		91,070		(4,770)

Continued

Therefore the IRR lies between 10% and 30% and can be found using interpolation:

$$IRR = Rate\ 1 + \frac{NPV\ 1\ (Rate\ 2 - Rate\ 1)}{NPV\ 1 - NPV\ 2}$$

$$IRR = 10\% + \frac{€/£91,070(30\% - 10\%)}{€/£91,070 - (- €/£4,770)}$$

$$IRR = 10\% + 19\% = 29\%$$

Interpolation can also be used when two trial runs result in two positive or two negative NPV's. The same example is utilised again to provide an example of this:

Worked example 13.6   (Interpolation)

Cow Ltd. is considering one project (costing €/£240,000). The following cash flows before depreciation are predicted:

Yearly cash flows before depreciation	Friesian €/£
Year 1	160,000
Year 2	60,000
Year 3	120,000
Year 4	40,000
Year 5	30,000

REQUIRED

Calculate the IRR of the above named project using interpolation.

Solution

For the first trial a discount rate of 10% is selected. At this rate the investment has a positive NPV of €/£91,070 (see table below).

Continued

Therefore, a higher rate (20%) is selected for the second trial. At this discount rate a positive NPV of €/£35,740 results (see table below).

Yearly cash flows	Discount factor (10%)	Present value (€/£)	Discount factor (20%)	Present value (€/£)
Year 0	1.000	(240,000)	1.000	(240,000)
Year 1	0.909	145,440	0.833	133,280
Year 2	0.826	49,560	0.694	41,640
Year 3	0.751	90,120	0.579	69,480
Year 4	0.683	27,320	0.482	19,280
Year 5	0.621	18,630	0.402	12,060
NPV		91,070		35,740

Therefore the IRR is a rate above 20% and can be found using interpolation:

$$\text{IRR} = \text{Rate } 1 + \frac{\text{NPV 1(Rate 2 − Rate 1)}}{\text{NPV 1 − NPV 2}}$$

$$\text{IRR} = 10\% + \frac{\text{€/£}91{,}070(20\% − 10\%)}{\text{€/£}91{,}070 − \text{€/£}35{,}740}$$

$$\text{IRR} = 10\% + 16.45\% = 26.45\%$$

The estimation is different to the first example due to the fact that the two chosen trial percentages are further away from the true IRR figure. This is an estimation error that increases in line with the distance the trial rates are from the true rate. The use of a linear calculation is not strictly correct, though does provide a reasonable approximation, provided the trial rates are not too far away, as they were in the previous two examples.

The IRR cannot capture benefits to be received by projects that have unconventional cash flows – for example some projects may have negative cash flows in the future. Use of the IRR will result in two possible return outcomes. However, projects with unconventional cash flows are rare in practice. Another problem is that the IRR does not take into account the absolute cash flows to be earned, enticing the decision maker to choose an investment based on a single rate. For example, if one project had an IRR of 15%, it would be rated higher than a project with an IRR of 14%, yet it may have less of an impact on equity holder wealth as the scale of the investment is not taken into consideration. In absolute money terms the project with the IRR of 14% may provide twice as much cash; relative to the project with the 15% IRR. For example, one million invested at 14% will increase equity holder value by more; than €/£100,000 invested at 15%.

Summary of the main disadvantages of using the IRR for investment appraisal

1. Time consuming calculations (though this is now normally compiled by a computer).

2. The linearity assumption that underlies the interpolation process.

3. It ignores the scale of projects, which may lead to sub-optimal decision making.

4. It is difficult to utilise when investments have unconventional cash flows, as more than one IRR will result.

5. It cannot be used when projects are mutually exclusive.

Worked example 13.7   (IRR for choosing projects)

Cow Ltd. is considering three projects (each costing €/£240,000). The following cash flows before depreciation are predicted.
(Note: the cash flows for 'Friesian' and 'Aberdeen' have changed from those used in previous examples)

Yearly cash flows	Friesian €/£	Aberdeen €/£	Saler €/£
Year 0	(24,000)	(240,000)	(240,000)
Year 1	6,000	120,000	238,000
Year 2	6,000	120,000	1,000
Year 3	10,000	40,000	36,000
Year 4	13,000	3,000	
Year 5	2,000		
Year 6	1,000		

Continued

REQUIRED

Calculate each project's IRR and rank the resulting information for reporting to management.

Solution

Friesian investment

Yearly cash flows	Discount factor (10%)	Present value (€/£)	Discount factor (20%)	Present value (€/£)
Year 0	1.000	(24,000)	1.000	(24,000)
Year 1	0.909	5,454	0.833	4,998
Year 2	0.826	4,956	0.694	4,164
Year 3	0.751	7,510	0.579	5,790
Year 4	0.683	8,879	0.482	6,266
Year 5	0.621	1,242	0.402	804
Year 6	0.564	564	0.335	335
NPV		4,605		(1,643)

$$IRR = 10\% + \frac{€/£4,605(20\% - 10\%)}{€/£4,605 - (-€/£1,643)}$$

$$IRR = 17.37\%$$

Aberdeen investment

Yearly cash flows	Discount factor (10%)	Present value (€/£)	Discount factor (12%)	Present value (€/£)
Year 0	1.000	(240,000)	1.000	(240,000)
Year 1	0.909	109,080	0.893	107,160
Year 2	0.826	99,120	0.797	95,640
Year 3	0.751	30,040	0.712	28,480
Year 4	0.683	2,049	0.635	1,905
NPV		289		(6,815)

Continued

$$IRR = 10\% + \frac{€/£289(12\% - 10\%)}{€/£289 - (-€/£6,815)}$$

$$IRR = 10.08\%$$

Saler investment

Yearly cash flows	Discount factor (10%)	Present value (€/£)	Discount factor (15%)	Present value (€/£)
Year 0	1.000	(240,000)	1.000	(240,000)
Year 1	0.909	216,342	0.870	207,060
Year 2	0.826	826	0.756	756
Year 3	0.751	27,036	0.657	23,652
NPV		4,204		(8,532)

$$IRR = 10\% + \frac{€/£4,204(15\% - 10\%)}{€/£4,204 - (-€/£8,532)}$$

$$IRR = 11.65\%$$

In this instance the investment ranked first is 'Friesian' with a yield of 17.37%, followed by 'Saler' (Yield of 11.65%). 'Aberdeen' is ranked third with a yield of 10.08%.

Net Present Value (NPV)

Due to the limitations outlined above, the IRR should be utilised with caution. A more appropriate project appraisal method to use is the NPV method. The *NPV* method of project appraisal, discounts the cash inflows and outflows of an investment, to their present value. Use of the correct discount rate is very important: different rates may be required for different projects depending on their risk profile (discussed earlier and in the next chapter). If the NPV is positive then the project should be accepted as the positive amount will increase equity holder value. If the NPV is negative then the project should be rejected as acceptance will damage equity holder value.

Worked example 13.8 (NPV for choosing projects)

Cow Ltd. is considering three projects (each costing €/£240,000). The following cash flows before depreciation are predicted:

Yearly cash flows	Friesian €/£	Aberdeen €/£	Saler €/£
Year 0	(240,000)	(240,000)	(240,000)
Year 1	60,000	120,000	238,000
Year 2	60,000	120,000	1,000
Year 3	100,000	40,000	36,000
Year 4	130,000	3,000	
Year 5	20,000		
Year 6	10,000		

REQUIRED

Calculate each project's NPV and rank the resulting information for reporting to management. The company has a WACC of 16% and all the projects being considered are of similar risk to the current operating activities of the company.

Solution

Friesian investment

Time	Cash flows (€/£)	Discount factor (16%)	Present value (€/£)
Year 0	(240,000)	1.000	(240,000)
Year 1	60,000	0.862	51,720
Year 2	60,000	0.743	44,580
Year 3	100,000	0.641	64,100
Year 4	130,000	0.552	71,760
Year 5	20,000	0.476	9,520
Year 6	10,000	0.410	4,100
NPV			5,780

Continued

Aberdeen investment

Time	Cash flows (€/£)	Discount factor (16%)	Present value (€/£)
Year 0	(240,000)	1.000	(240,000)
Year 1	120,000	0.862	103,440
Year 2	120,000	0.743	89,160
Year 3	40,000	0.641	25,640
Year 4	3,000	0.552	1,656
NPV			(20,104)

Saler investment

Time	Cash flows (€/£)	Discount factor (16%)	Present value (€/£)
Year 0	(240,000)	1.000	(240,000)
Year 1	238,000	0.862	205,156
Year 2	1,000	0.743	743
Year 3	36,000	0.641	23,076
NPV			(11,025)

When the discount rate used is 16%; the only investment that should be accepted by the company is 'Friesian', as it covers the cost of finance and provides an excess return of €/£5,780. The other two projects have negative NPVs and if accepted, would result in a loss of equity holder value, as they are not covering the current cost of the company's capital.

Advantages of using the NPV for investment appraisal

Time value of money: The time value of money is taken into consideration.

All cash flows: All relevant cash flows are considered in the appraisal process.

Adjusted for risk: The discount rate can be adjusted for risk.

Continued

> *Choosing amongst alternatives:* When there are several alternatives the alternative with the largest NPV will maximise equity holder value.
>
> *Variant cash flows:* Unlike the IRR, when cash flows are not conventional, the NPV will provide one answer.

The main disadvantage of using the NPV for investment appraisal is that it does not provide a method of deciding which investment provides the best value for money. It considers the absolute money value that a company will end up with by the end of an investment's life; however, an investment with a small outlay and small net cash inflows may give the same NPV as an investment with a large outlay and larger inflows. The latter investment would be more risky as the amounts are larger, but using the NPV on its own as a means of selecting a project does not take this into account. For example, in example 13.7, the investment in 'Friesian' is €/£24,000 and the resultant NPV when the cash flows are discounted at 10% is €/£4,605. The investment in 'Saler' is ten times more (€/£240,000). When the cash flows are discounted at 10%, their NPV is €/£4,204 (only marginally higher than 'Friesian's' NPV). It is clear that the Saler project is much more risky – yet had it returned a NPV of €/£4,650; it would have been the preferred project, if the decision was based purely on the NPV.

Taxation

When appraising a project, it is important to consider all material relevant cash flows. Tax is a cash flow which is usually material. The relevance of this to the value of a capital asset is depicted by the next example.

Worked example 13.9   (Taxation)

ABC Ltd. is considering an investment which would require the immediate purchase of a capital asset costing €/£200,000. The company pays corporation tax at the rate of 30%, one year in arrears. The equipment is not expected to have a residual value. Capital allowances for the period of the investment are expected to be allowed at a rate of 25%, on a straight line basis. The cost of capital for investment appraisal purposes, is 15%.

Continued

REQUIRED

Calculate the NPV of the cash flows relating to the capital asset only.

Solution

The impact of purchasing a capital asset on cash flows will be an initial cash outlay followed by annual cash savings due to the tax shield on the capital allowances.

The capital allowances will be: €/£50,000 (€/£200,000 × 25%) per year for four years. This will result in a tax saving of: €/£15,000 (€/£50,000 × 30%). As tax is payable in the year following the year in which profits are made, this cash flow advantage will have a time delay of one year. Therefore the total present value of the cash flows that relate to the asset cost alone are as follows:

Time	Cash flows (€/£)	Discount factor (15%)	Present value (€/£)
Year 0	(200,000)	1.000	(200,000)
Year 1	–	0.870	–
Year 2	15,000	0.756	11,340
Year 3	15,000	0.657	9,855
Year 4	15,000	0.572	8,580
Year 5	15,000	0.497	7,455
	NPV		(162,770)

In year 1 the company will have been able to claim capital allowances. However, the cash benefit will not occur until the next year and is assumed to occur at the end of the year. The net cost of the asset is €/£162,770.

Capital projects normally have two influences on tax cash flows: tax on profits made by the project and tax relief on capital expenditure. As tax payable is dependent on profits made, not cash flows, a separate working based on profits needs to be prepared to determine the tax cash flows. Depreciation is always deducted when profits are calculated. However, this expense is not allowable by the tax authorities, who have their own allowable deductions for capital investment, called *capital allowances*. Capital allowances are sometimes referred to as *written down allowances*. These allowances are normally 25% per annum, calculated using the reducing balance method, though in some instances the tax authorities allow a *first year allowance*, which is usually up to 100% of the capital cost of an asset, though can be as much as 110% of the capital investment (by giving an allowance of more than 100%, the UK government support some industries and types of expenditure: for example research and development expenditure). Therefore, to work out the tax cash flow, profits have to be adjusted – depreciation has to be added back to profit, and capital allowances/first year allowances/balancing allowances have to be deducted and balancing charges added back. A balancing charge results when an asset is disposed of for a sum that exceeds the written down allowance on the date of the sale. Balancing charges increase the tax charge. A balancing allowance results when the asset is disposed of for a sum that is less than the written down value of the asset on the date of the sale. The balancing allowance reduces the tax charge. The tax cash flow will be the remaining profit multiplied by the tax rate relevant for the company (assuming the company is profitable).

The other important attribute of tax cash flows, is that they do not occur in the year profits are made, but in the subsequent year. This should be assumed unless a question directs otherwise.

Worked example 13.10 (Advanced taxation)

ABC Ltd. is considering purchasing one of two capital assets for use in a particular project. The first ('Fresco') costs €/£200,000 the second ('Tempera') costs €/£220,000. The following information is available about the project.

- The net yearly profits expected from the use of the Fresco asset are €/£100,000 (Year 1), €/£120,000 (Year 2), €/£140,000 (Year 3) and €/£50,000 (Year 4).
- The net yearly profits expected from the use of the Tempera asset are €/£120,000 (Year 1), €/£110,000 (Year 2), €/£120,000 (Year 3) and €/£60,000 (Year 4).
- The company's depreciation policy for this type of equipment is to depreciate it over three years using the straight-line basis. A blanket company policy in respect of determining the residual value of machines is followed by the company, whereby from past experience machines on average realise 25% of their purchase value.

Continued

- Capital allowances are 25% calculated using the reducing balance method.
- Corporation tax is 30%.
- The company's cost of capital is 15%.

REQUIRED

Calculate the NPV of both options assuming that:
a) Fresco is expected to be sold at the end of year four for €/£40,000; and
b) Tempera is expected to be sold at the end of year four for €/£100,000.

Solution

Before preparing the NPV schedule four workings are required. The first calculates depreciation. The second uses the information from the first step to decipher the cash flows from the project. The third calculates capital allowances and the fourth uses the information from the latter two workings to determine the tax cash flow expected.

a) Fresco

Working 1: Depreciation

The residual value is €/£50,000 (25% × €/£200,000)

Straight-line method

$$\text{Depreciation} = \frac{\text{Cost} - \text{residual value}}{\text{Useful economic life}}$$

$$\text{Depreciation} = \frac{€/£200,000 - €/£50,000}{3}$$

$$\text{Depreciation} = €/£50,000 \text{ per year}$$

In year four there will be a loss on the sale of the asset. It will have been written down to its residual value of €/£50,000, but will have been sold for €/£40,000. Therefore, this is treated as an accounting loss on the sale of the asset of €/£10,000. This will have been deduced to find the profit, hence will have to be added back to determine the cash flows in year 4.

Continued

Working 2: Cash flows from the project

Year	Profits (€/£)	Depreciation/ loss on sale (€/£)	Cash flows (€/£)
Year 0	–	–	–
Year 1	100,000	50,000	150,000
Year 2	120,000	50,000	170,000
Year 3	140,000	50,000	190,000
Year 4	50,000	10,000	60,000

Working 3: Capital allowances

Year	Opening written down value €/£	Workings €/£	Capital allowances €/£
Year 1	200,000	(200,000 × 25%)	50,000
Year 2	150,000*	(150,000 × 25%)	37,500
Year 3	112,500	(112,500 × 25%)	28,125
			Balancing allowance
Year 4	84,375	(84,375 – 40,000)	44,375

*The opening written down value in year 2 is the opening written down value in year 1 less the capital allowances in that period (€/£200,000 – €/£50,000)

Working 4: Tax cash flows

Year	Cash flows (€/£)	Capital allowances (€/£)	Taxable cash flows (€/£)	Taxation charge @ 30% (€/£)	Taxation cash flow (€/£)
Year 0	–	–	–	–	–
Year 1	150,000	(50,000)	100,000	(30,000)	–
Year 2	170,000	(37,500)	132,500	(39,750)	(30,000)
Year 3	190,000	(28,125)	161,875	(48,562)	(39,750)
Year 4	60,000	(44,375)	15,625	(4,688)	(48,562)
Year 5	–	–	–	–	(4,688)

continued

Fresco: Net present value calculation

Year	Machine	Operating activities	Taxation	Total cash flow	Discount factor (15%)	Present value (€/£)
Year 0	(200,000)	–	–	(200,000)	1.000	(200,000)
Year 1	–	150,000	–	150,000	0.870	130,500
Year 2	–	170,000	(30,000)	140,000	0.756	105,840
Year 3	–	190,000	(39,750)	150,250	0.657	98,714
Year 4	40,000	60,000	(48,562)	51,438	0.572	23,702
Year 5	–	–	(4,688)	(4,688)	0.497	(2,330)
NPV						_156,918_

b) Tempera

Working 1: Depreciation

The residual value is €/£55,000 (25% × €/£220,000)

Straight-line method

$$\text{Depreciation} = \frac{\text{Cost} - \text{residual value}}{\text{Useful economic life}}$$

$$\text{Depreciation} = \frac{€/£220,000 - €/£55,000}{3}$$

$$\text{Depreciation} = €/£55,000 \text{ per year}$$

In year 4 then there will be a profit on the sale of the asset. It will have been written down to its residual value of €/£55,000, but will have been sold for €/£100,000. Therefore, this is treated as an accounting profit on the sale of the asset of €/£45,000. This will have been added to the operating profits to find the overall profit, hence will have to be deducted to determine the cash flows from the project in year 4.

Working 2: Cash flows from the project

Year	Profits (€/£)	Depreciation/ (profit on sale) (€/£)	Cash flows (€/£)
Year 0	–	–	–
Year 1	120,000	55,000	175,000
Year 2	110,000	55,000	165,000
Year 3	120,000	55,000	175,000
Year 4	60,000	(45,000)	15,000

Working 3: Capital allowances

Year	Opening written down value €/£	Workings €/£	Capital allowances €/£
Year 1	220,000	(220,000 × 25%)	55,000
Year 2	165,000*	(165,000 × 25%)	41,250
Year 3	123,750	(123,750 × 25%)	30,938
			Balancing charge
Year 4	92,812	(92,812 – 100,000)	(7,188)

*The opening written down value in year 2 is the opening written down value in year 1 less the capital allowances in that period (€/£220,000 – €/£55,000)

Working 4: Tax cash flows

Year	Cash flows (€/£)	Capital allowances (€/£)	Taxable cash flows (€/£)	Taxation charge @ 30% (€/£)	Taxation cash flow (€/£)
Year 0	–	–	–	–	–
Year 1	175,000	(55,000)	120,000	(36,000)	–
Year 2	165,000	(41,250)	123,750	(37,125)	(36,000)
Year 3	175,000	(30,938)	144,062	(43,219)	(37,125)
Year 4	15,000	7,188	22,188	(6,656)	(43,219)
Year 5	–	–	–	–	(6,656)

continued

Tempera: Net present value calculation

Year	Machine	Operating activities	Taxation	Total cash flow	Discount factor (15%)	Present value (€/£)
Year 0	(220,000)	–	–	(220,000)	1.000	(220,000)
Year 1	–	175,000	–	175,000	0.870	152,250
Year 2	–	165,000	(36,000)	129,000	0.756	97,524
Year 3	–	175,000	(37,125)	137,875	0.657	90,584
Year 4	100,000	15,000	(43,219)	71,781	0.572	41,059
Year 5	–	–	(6,656)	(6,656)	0.497	(3,308)
NPV						158,109

Based on the results of these workings, ABC Ltd. should invest in Tempera as it is expected to return a higher NPV of €/£158,109 relative to the NPV reported for Fresco (€/£156,918).

Working Capital

As mentioned in earlier chapters, working capital is both an investment and a source and use of finance. It has cash flow implications and where a project requires increases in working capital, this should be factored into the calculations. Likewise, when a project ends and the working capital reduces again, then the cash inflow from that process should be factored into the appraisal process. The implications of working capital investment are highlighted in the following example:

Worked example 13.11   (Working capital)

ABC Ltd. is considering an investment which would require the immediate purchase of a capital asset costing €/£400,000 and working capital of €/£120,000. Net inflows will be €/£180,000, €/£160,000 and €/£140,000 for year one, year two and year three. The working capital requirement will increase by 20% per year in each of the first two years. All of the working capital will be turned into cash at the end of year three. The company's cost of capital is 15%.

Continued

REQUIRED

Calculate the NPV of the investment (ignore taxation).

Solution

The impact of increasing the investment in working capital on cash flows is as follows:

Time	Cash flows (€/£)	Working capital (€/£)	Net cash flows (€/£)	Discount factor (15%)	Present value (€/£)
Year 0	(400,000)	(120,000)	(520,000)	1.000	(520,000)
Year 1	180,000	(24,000)[1]	156,000	0.870	135,720
Year 2	160,000	(28,800)[2]	131,200	0.756	99,187
Year 3	140,000	172,800[3]	312,800	0.658	205,822
				NPV	(79,271)

1. This represents an increase in the working capital requirement: (€/£120,000 × 20%),
2. This represents an increase on the working capital requirement from year one: ((€/£120,000 + €/£24,000) × 20%).
3. This is the total working capital that has been built up over the life of the investment, now released.

Inflation

Inflation is a term used to describe the percentage increase in the cost of goods. It reflects a reduction in the purchasing power of money. Inflation has a major influence in capital investment appraisal. It impacts on the return required by a company's investors, hence the discount rate. Inflation will also impact on expected cash flows. In most countries inflation is positive hence the expectation is that prices will increase in the future. This would not cause a problem, were all the variables included in an investment increasing at the same general inflation rate. In this instance inflation could be ignored. However, inflation may impact on different variables, in different ways. For example, wages may increase by a factor that is higher than inflation, sales price may remain static due to cheap imports and rents may remain static due to a legal rental agreement covering several years. These issues cause complications for investment appraisal; particularly where cash flows extend over several years.

Two approaches are utilised to deal with the problem of inflation. The first involves adjusting the annual cash flows of a project by the expected rate of inflation and using a discount rate that is also adjusted for inflation. This rate is usually called the *money/market discount rate* or the *nominal discount rate* (in some instances it is also referred to as the *basic discount rate*, particularly when bank rates are utilised as they reflect the banks prediction for expected inflation). The nominal discount rate is calculated using the following formula:

$$\text{Nominal discount rate} = ((1 + \text{Real rate}) \times (1 + \text{Inflation rate})) - 1$$

Worked example 13.12   (Calculating nominal interest rates)

Frank Ltd. is evaluating a project where projected cash flows are estimated at future prices. Frank Ltd. has a real cost of capital of 12% and inflation is expected to be 4% per annum.

REQUIRED

What is the nominal discount rate to be used when appraising this project?

Solution

$$\text{Nominal rate} = ((1 + \text{Real rate}) \times (1 + \text{Inflation rate})) - 1$$
$$\text{Nominal rate} = (1.12 \times 1.04) - 1$$
$$\text{Nominal rate} = 16.48\%$$

As mentioned previously, in many instances different variables are affected in different ways when inflation changes. Some costs may include imported goods that are not subject to the same level of inflation, other costs such as wages may rise by more than inflation. In these circumstances the best approach is to convert all cash flows, to actual expected cash flows and to discount them using the nominal/money rate, as the discount factor. This approach is reflected in the next example:

Worked example 13.13   (NPV including variant inflation)

Z Ltd. is considering an investment that will cost €/£500,000 now. The annual benefits, for four years, would be a fixed income of €/£250,000 per annum, plus savings of €/£50,000 in year one, rising by 5% each year due to inflation. Running costs will be €/£100,000 in the first year, but would increase at 10% each year due to inflating labour costs. The general rate of inflation is expected to be 5% and the company's required nominal/money rate of return is 20%.

REQUIRED

Should the company invest in the project (ignore taxation)?

Solution

Some of the cash flows are expressed in terms of the actual amounts that will be received whereas others will increase by a set percentage over the period. In these circumstances the cash flows will be inflated and the combined actual expected amounts calculated. When the actual expected cash flows are known, the nominal/money rate can be used as the discount rate.

Time	Fixed income (€/£)	Other savings (€/£)	Running costs (€/£)	Capital cost (€/£)	Net cash flows (€/£)
0	250,000	50,000	(100,000)	(500,000)	(300,000)
1	250,000	52,500	(110,000)	–	192,500
2	250,000	55,125	(121,000)	–	184,125
3	250,000	57,881	(133,100)	–	174,781

Time	Cash flow (€/£)	Discount factor (20%)	PV (€/£)
0	(300,000)	1.000	(300,000)
1	192,500	0.833	160,352
2	184,125	0.694	127,782
3	174,781	0.579	101,198
		NPV	89,332

This project should be undertaken as it has a positive NPV of €/£89,332.

Question four and five of the review questions, deal with a situation where a company has not incorporated inflationary effects into its cost of capital.

The alternative is to exclude inflation from the calculations by adjusting cash flows accordingly to find the real cash flows, and by using a discount rate which is net of inflation. This rate is usually called the *real discount rate.* The real discount rate is found by deflating the nominal discount rate by the general rate of inflation.

Real cash flows reflect the current general purchasing power of cash flows. To obtain real cash flows, the expected monetary cash flows for each variable should be calculated (inflate using the various expected inflation rates) and then deflated using the general rate of inflation for the period in question.

Worked example 13.14   (NPV including general inflation)

X Ltd. is considering investing in a project with the following cash flows:

	€/£ (actual cash flows)
Year 0	(300,000)
Year 1	180,000
Year 2	160,000
Year 3	140,000

Inflation is currently 10% per year, and this rate is not expected to change in the lifetime of this project. The company requires a minimum return of 20% under the present and anticipated conditions.

REQUIRED

Should the company invest in the project?

Continued

Solution

The cash flows are expressed in terms of the actual monies that are expected to be received or paid, at the given dates. Therefore, the correct discount rate to use is the nominal/money rate of return. This equates to the cost of capital.

Time	Cash flow (€/£)	Discount factor (20%)	PV (€/£)
0	(300,000)	1.000	(300,000)
1	180,000	0.833	149,940
2	160,000	0.694	111,040
3	140,000	0.579	81,060
		NPV	42,040

As the investment has a positive NPV; the company should make the investment.

Approach to take when assessing a project in respect of inflation

Cash flows utilised in calculations	Discount rate utilised
Expressed in present prices	Real discount rate
Expressed in future prices	Nominal discount rate

Incremental cash flow approach

The *incremental cash flow approach* can be used to choose between two mutually exclusive alternatives. The cash flows from one project are subtracted from the cash flows of another project: these are then discounted to present value using a company's current cost of capital. The sign of the resultant NPV is then interpreted to determine the course of action to take. This process is highlighted in the next example:

Worked example 13.15   (Incremental cash flows)

X Ltd. is considering whether to replace or repair a current asset. The company has a cost of capital of 15% and the following cash flows for each scenario have been estimated:

	Replace €/£	Repair €/£
Year 0	(50,000)	(20,000)
Year 1	(4,000)	(14,000)
Year 2	(6,000)	(16,000)
Year 3	(8,000)	(18,000)
Year 4	(10,000)	(20,000)
Year 5 (Realisable value)	22,000	6,000

REQUIRED

Should the company replace the asset?

Solution

The present value of the incremental cash flows are as follows:

Time	Calculation	Cash flow (€/£)	Discount factor (15%)	PV (€/£)
0	(50,000) – (20,000)	(30,000)	1.000	(30,000)
1	(4,000) – (14,000)	10,000	0.870	8,700
2	(6,000) – (16,000)	10,000	0.756	7,560
3	(8,000) – (18,000)	10,000	0.658	6,580
4	(10,000) – (20,000)	10,000	0.572	5,720
5	22,000 – 6,000	16,000	0.497	7,952
			NPV	6,512

As the investment has a positive NPV; the company should replace the asset.

Capital Rationing

The general rule when deciding on whether or not to invest in capital projects, is that it is in equity holders' best interests, to select all projects with a positive NPV; however, this is not always possible. *Capital rationing* occurs when a company has a restricted supply of cash available for investment purposes. In these circumstances a business finance manager has to decide which capital projects, from a pool of possibilities, to invest in. There are two types of capital rationing: hard capital rationing; and soft capital rationing.

Hard capital rationing

Hard capital rationing occurs when the market places a restriction on the funds available for investment. External restrictions may be as a result of a company being too heavily geared. High gearing makes it difficult to raise more debt and will also make an equity issue prohibitively costly. Another influence may be the condition of the stock market. If it is low, a share issue would be undervalued; the result is that current equity holder value would be damaged. In addition, the size of the finance requirement may negate equity as an option: equity distributions are costly and need to be of significant size to make them worth while (the same applies for market bond finance). Lastly, the project itself may limit funding: if it is deemed to be very risky, potential financiers may be put off.

Soft capital rationing

Soft capital rationing occurs when internal management decide to place a restriction on the level of funds that should be invested in capital projects. The most common reason for placing a limit on the amount that can be invested each year is the wish of management to maintain the capital structure of the company as it is. Management may not want to raise more capital from the stock market or bond markets. Raising funds is expensive, time consuming and may have consequences on the value of a company, due to changes in capital structure and risk profile. There is also the need to have controlled growth – ensuring that a project's objectives are congruent with the company as a whole and are undertaken without over trading or overstretching a company's resources and organisational structure.

Restrictions may also be put in place by parent companies in an attempt to maintain a portfolio of balanced projects, which can be more easily managed.

Choosing among alternative projects

A common approach cannot be adopted when evaluating capital projects under conditions of capital rationing. Three different scenarios may influence the method of evaluation adopted. In the first instance projects may be *divisible*, in that it is possible to invest in a whole capital project and part of another, or they may *not be divisible*, in which case two smaller projects with a higher combined NPV will provide more added value for equity holders, relative to one large project, which has the highest NPV for each unit of scarce resource. Finally, projects may be *mutually exclusive*. This means that a manager has the option to invest in one project OR another project, but not both.

Divisible projects that are independent of each other
It might seem that the most appropriate approach is to rank projects according to the size of their NPVs. However, this does not result in the most efficient use of limited funds. A more appropriate method is to maximise the NPV per scarce resource (euro/pound). This is represented by the following formula:

$$\text{PV per euro/pound of scarce resource} = \frac{\text{NPV of inflows}}{\text{Initial outlay}}$$

This ratio is calculated for each project with a positive NPV and ranked into a *profitability index*. The projects with the highest value in the index should be accepted, to the point at which the funds available for investment are exhausted.

The calculation is straightforward when appraising investments that are divisible. This is portrayed in the following example:

Worked example 13.16   (Capital rationing – divisible investments)

Enero Ltd. has a maximum of €/£800,000 available to invest in new projects. Three possibilities have emerged and the business finance
Continued

manager has calculated NPV's for each of them, as follows (you are informed that the projects are divisible):

Investment	Initial cash outlay	NPV
	(€/£)	(€/£)
X	540,000	100,000
Y	600,000	150,000
Z	260,000	58,000

REQUIRED

Which investments/combination of investments should the company invest in?

Solution

As the funds are restricted the normal NPV rule of accepting investments with the highest NPV's first, cannot be adopted. As the projects are divisible, a profitability index can be utilised, to provide the most beneficial mix of investment for the company.

Project	Profitability index	PV per (€/£)	Calculation
X	3	1.185	(€/£640,000/€/£540,000)
Y	1	1.250	(€/£750,000/€/£600,000)
Z	2	1.223	(€/£318,000/€/£260,000)

Therefore Enero Ltd. should invest €/£600,000 into investment Y earning €/£150,000 and €/£200,000 into investment Z earning €/£44,615 ((€/£200,000/€/£260,000) × €/£58,000), resulting in a total NPV of €/£194,615, from the €/£800,000 investment.

Non-divisible projects

When projects are not divisible the profitability index approach should not be adopted. Projects should be ranked in order of the size of their NPV and the combination of projects resulting in the highest overall NPV, for the limited finance that is available, should be selected. The above example is utilised again to show the result, were this condition to hold.

Worked example 13.17   (Capital rationing – non-divisible investments)

Enero Ltd. has a maximum of €/£800,000 available to invest in new projects. Three possibilities have emerged and the business finance manager has calculated NPV's for each of them, as follows (you are informed that the projects are not divisible):

Investment	Initial cash outlay (€/£)	NPV (€/£)
X	540,000	100,000
Y	600,000	150,000
Z	260,000	58,000

REQUIRED

Which investments/combination of investments should the company invest in?

Solution

In this instance the absolute maximum amount of NPV that can be achieved from an investment, or combination of investments, should determine which investments to invest in. Two possibilities arise: either to invest in project Y costing €/£600,000 or in both project X and Z costing €/£800,000. The total NPVs resulting from each possibility are detailed below.

Project	Total NPV (€/£)
Y	150,000
X and Z	158,000

Therefore Enero Ltd. should invest the full €/£800,000 into investments X and Z as this will provide them with a total NPV of €/£158,000, whereas investment in project Y will yield a NPV of €/£8,000 less.

Mutually exclusive projects

When projects are ***mutually exclusive***, they are competing with each other, for the funds available. For example, there may be two different machines from different suppliers that are suitable for manufacturing one product. A company seeking the investment is only interested in one machine. This company may have a budget of available investment funds for capital projects, some of which have to be used to purchase one of the two machines; the remainder to be invested in other projects. So the decision will be based on an evaluation of the mutually exclusive projects combined with the non-divisible projects. The approach to take is to compare the various combinations available and to select the combination resulting in the greatest NPV. For example, four possible projects may be available, but three of these are considered mutually exclusive. In this instance the NPV of the fourth project should be combined with each of the other three and the combination with the highest resulting NPV selected.

Worked example 13.18   (Capital rationing – mutually exclusive investments that are non-divisible)

Enero Ltd. has a maximum of €/£800,000 available to invest in new projects. Five possibilities have emerged and the business finance manager has calculated NPV's for each of them, as follows (you are informed that the projects are non-divisible):

Investment	Initial cash outlay (€/£)	NPV (€/£)
V	260,000	54,000
W	260,000	49,000
X	540,000	100,000
Y	600,000	150,000
Z	260,000	58,000

REQUIRED

Which investments/combination of investments, should the company invest in, given that investment V, W and Z are mutually exclusive?

Solution

In this instance the absolute maximum amount of NPV that can be achieved from an investment, or combination of investments, should determine which investments to invest in; given the €/£800,000

Continued

capital limit. In addition, the decision is complicated further by the fact that the company can only invest in V; W or Z.

There are four possibilities. Enero Ltd. can invest in Y, in X and Z, in X and V, or in X and W. The combination that results in the largest NPV should be selected.

Project	Amount invested (€/£)	Total NPV (€/£)
Y	600,000	150,000
X and Z	800,000	158,000
X and V	800,000	154,000
X and W	800,000	149,000

Therefore Enero Ltd. should invest the full €/£800,000 into investments X and Z as this will provide them with a total NPV of €/£158,000.

Projects with unequal lives

Assessing capital projects that are ***multi-period*** requires a special approach as an incorrect decision may be made when deciding on two projects; where one has a long life, the other a short life. In these instances, the project with the long life is likely to have a higher NPV and be accepted; however, it is likely that another project will be started when the short-term project has completed. If this future project has a positive NPV then it should influence the decision, at the outset. Therefore, the approach taken is to assume that future similar projects can be commenced on completion of the first project. There are two approaches, the first is called the shortest common period approach (a similar approach the *'finite horizon'* approach can also be utilised to assess a project), the second the equivalent annual annuity approach.

Shortest common period approach
Under the **shortest common period approach** the project should be analysed according to the shortest common period of time. If one project has cash flows that last two years and the other has cash flows that last three years, then the analysis should cover a period of six years $(2 \times 3 = 6)$. The NPV of each project would be calculated and the NPV of the projects started in the future, would be discounted back to the present value now. The approach is considered in the next example:

Worked example 13.19   (Unequal lives – shortest common period)

Enero Ltd. can invest in one of two competing projects. Its current cost of capital is 10%. The cash flows relating to each project are detailed as follows:

Year	Investment X Cash flows (€/£)	Investment Y Cash flows (€/£)
0	(50,000)	(70,000)
1	25,000	30,000
2	35,000	40,000
3		15,500

REQUIRED

Which of the two projects should Enero Ltd. invest in (ignore inflation and tax)?

Solution

In this instance the shortest common period approach will be used to compare the two outcomes. The shortest common period is six years (2×3). It is assumed that project X will be invested in three times during the six-year period and project Y, twice. The NPV of each project is as follows:

	Investment X			Investment Y		
Time	Cash flows (€/£)	Discount factor (10%)	Present value	Cash flows (€/£)	Discount factor (10%)	Present value
0	(50,000)	1.000	(50,000)	(70,000)	1.000	(70,000)
1	25,000	0.909	22,725	30,000	0.909	27,270
2	35,000	0.826	28,910	40,000	0.826	33,040
				15,500	0.751	11,640
		NPV	1,635		NPV	1,950

If the timeframe for each project is not taken into consideration, investment Y would be selected as it has the highest NPV. However, the NPV for each investment over a six-year period needs to be determined. In respect of investment X this will mean that two more NPV's (of the same amount) are assumed to accrue to Enero Ltd. within the six-year period,

Continued

one at the end of year two (day one of year three) the other at the end of year four (day one of year five). These need to be discounted to their present value at time 0 using the 10% discount rate. The total NPV for the six years for investment X will be:

$$NPV = €/£1,635 + (€/£1,635/1.10^2) + (€/£1,635/1.10^4)$$
$$NPV = €/£4,103$$

Investment Y will occur twice in the six-year period; therefore, the total NPV for the whole period will be:

$$NPV = €/£1,950 + (€/£1,950/1.10^3)$$
$$NPV = €/£3,415$$

When the projects are considered over a common time frame, the selection is reversed. In this instance the two-year project is deemed to provide the best value for the company, as it has a higher NPV for the six-year period.

Finite horizon approach

The *finite horizon approach* is similar to the shortest common period approach, except it considers a much longer time period, for example it might assume that identical projects are to be continued for 18 years, not the shortest common period of six years.

These two methods are time consuming and cumbersome, particularly where the life span of the project is quite large – for example, when one project has a life of five years and the other a life of seven years – the shortest common period will be 35 years. Another method can be utilised which overcomes this problem, by using the annuity concept. An annuity is the receipt or payment of a fixed cash return for a set period. This approach is now discussed.

Equivalent annual annuity approach

The *equivalent annual annuity approach* converts the NPV of a project into an annual cash annuity that extends for the expected duration of a project. This is calculated for each project and the project with the highest annual annuity is selected. The annual annuity equivalent of the NPV of a project can be determined using the following formula:

$$\text{Annual annuity equivalent of the NPV} = NPV \times \frac{i}{1 - (1+i)^{-n}}$$

Where i is the discount rate and n is the number of years the investment lasts for. This approach can be utilised to assess projects with unequal lives as highlighted in the next example.

Worked example 13.20   (Unequal lives–equivalent annual annuity approach)

Enero Ltd. can invest in one of two competing projects. Its current cost of capital is 10%. The cash flows relating to each project are detailed as follows:

Year	Investment X Cash flows (€/£)	Investment Y Cash flows (€/£)
0	(50,000)	(70,000)
1	25,000	30,000
2	35,000	40,000
3		15,500

REQUIRED

Which of the two projects should Enero Ltd. invest in (ignore inflation and tax)?

Solution

In this instance the equivalent annuity approach will be utilised to choose the most appropriate investment:

	Investment X			Investment Y		
Time	Cash flows (€/£)	Discount factor (10%)	Present value	Cash flows (€/£)	Discount factor (10%)	Present value
0	(50,000)	1.000	(50,000)	(70,000)	1.000	(70,000)
1	25,000	0.909	22,725	30,000	0.909	27,270
2	35,000	0.826	28,910	40,000	0.826	33,040
				15,500	0.751	11,640
		NPV	1,635		NPV	1,950

The annuity equivalent factor for investment X is: $0.576\ (0.10/(1-1.1^{-2}))$

Continued

> The equivalent annual annuity is: €/£942 (€/£1,635 × 0.576)
>
> The annuity equivalent factor for investment Y is: 0.402 $(0.10/(1-1.1^{-3}))$
>
> The equivalent annual annuity is: €/£784 (€/£1,950 × 0.402)
>
> Consistent with the shortest period approach, the equivalent annual annuity approach would suggest that investment X is the best option.

Asset replacement decisions

The replacement of company assets is a more complicated decision than it would initially seem. Certain assets have a cost and revenue life cycle pattern; in the early years an asset is likely to be more productive, contributing more to revenue; whereas in later years the asset is more likely to require maintenance and repair, resulting in increased costs, including down time. In addition, as an asset ages, its resale value reduces. Therefore, these increasing costs have to be balanced with the cost associated with buying a new asset. An asset should be replaced when:

$$(b) + (c) < (a)$$

Where (a) is the running costs associated with owning the current asset; (b) is the replacement cost of the asset; and (c) is the running costs associated with owning the new asset.

Identical assets

When assets are being replaced with identical assets, the approach should be to identify the replacement cycle. A ***replacement cycle*** is the period of time an asset should be kept, before being replaced by a new asset. This can be determined using the equivalent annual cost. The ***equivalent annual cost*** focuses on the present value of the costs of operating the asset in yearly terms, which can be obtained using the following equation:

$$\text{Equivalent annual cost} = \frac{\text{NPV}}{\text{Annuity factor}}$$

When the equivalent annual cost is minimised – this is the optimum replacement cycle. This method is simple; however, cannot be used where there is inflation. In these instances the shortest common period approach or the finite horizon approach should be adopted (discussed earlier).

The following example shows the calculation of a replacement cycle using the equivalent annual cost.

Worked example 13.21 (Asset replacement cycle)

Enero Ltd. has a machine which produces widgets. The machine costs €/£600,000. The following yearly costs and possible re-sale values have been provided in respect of the machine for the next four years:

Year	Realisable value (€/£)	Repair costs (€/£)
1	360,000	24,000
2	300,000	34,000
3	260,000	50,000
4	200,000	62,000

Enero Ltd.'s current cost of capital is 14%.

REQUIRED

When should Enero Ltd. replace its machine (ignore inflation and tax)?

Solution

The first step is to calculate the alternative replacement cycles ranging from one year to four years and then to compare the outcomes using the equivalent annual cost.

Year	Replace yearly Cash flow €/£'000	Replace yearly NPV (14%) €/£'000	Replace every two years Cash flow €/£'000	Replace every two years NPV (14%) €/£'000	Replace every three years Cash flow €/£'000	Replace every three years NPV (14%) €/£'000	Replace every four years Cash flow €/£'000	Replace every four years NPV (14%) €/£'000
0	(600)	(600)	(600)	(600)	(600)	(600)	(600)	(600)
1	336	294	(24)	(21)	(24)	(21)	(24)	(21)
2			266	205	(34)	(26)	(34)	(26)
3					210	142	(50)	(34)
4							138	82
NPV		(306)		(416)		(505)		(599)
Annuity factor	0.877		1.647		2.322		2.914	

Continued

Equivalent cost	€/£306,000 / 0.877	€/£416,000 / 1.647	€/£505,000 / 2.322	€/£599,000 / 2.914
Annual equivalent cost	*(€/£349,000)*	*(€/£253,000)*	*(€/£217,000)*	*(€/£205,000)*

The equivalent annual cost is lowest for a four year cycle (€/£205,000). Therefore, the machine should be replaced every four years.

The 'shortest common period approach' and the 'finite horizon approach' can also be used, wherein the four scenarios are treated as different options with the option providing the best NPV for the whole period being selected.

Different assets

In some situations an asset will be replaced by a different asset. In these circumstances the focus is on when to replace the asset, not on how often to replace it. The first step in this decision making process is to determine the replacement cycle period. Then using the minimum cost identified, calculate the present value in perpetuity (this should reflect the cost of owning the machine). Finally, compare the present value of the costs and benefits for each time period. The asset should be replaced in the year where the present value represents the lowest cost. This is portrayed using the following example.

Worked example 13.22   (Replacement with a different asset)

In the last example the optimum replacement cycle for a machine was determined for Enero Ltd. as being four years with an equivalent annual cost of €/£205,000. This machine is now assumed to be brand new and is considered to be the replacement for an existing machine, which is quite different. The realisable value and repair costs for the existing machine are as follows:

Year	Realisable value (€/£)	Repair costs (€/£)
0	15,000	–
1	13,000	6,950
2	10,000	7,700
3	6,500	8,900

Enero Ltd.'s current cost of capital is 14%.

Continued

REQUIRED

When should Enero Ltd. replace its existing machine with the new machine (ignore inflation and tax)?

Solution

This involves comparing the present value cost of replacing the old machine in each of the four years with the new machine and selecting the option with the lowest overall present value cost. The equivalent annual cost of the new machine was calculated in the last example (13.21) as being €/£205,000. This is the starting point for assessing each scenario.

Scenario	Year	Cash flows (€/£'000)	Discount factor (14%)	PV Cost (€/£'000)
Replace immediately	0	(205)	1.000	(205)
		15	1.000	15
				(190)
Replace in one year	1	(205)	0.877	(179.78)
	1	13	0.877	11.40
	1	(6.95)	0.877	(6.10)
				(174.48)
Replace in two years	1	(6.95)	0.877	(6.10)
	2	(205)	0.769	(157.65)
	2	10	0.769	7.69
	2	(7.7)	0.769	(5.92)
				(161.98)
Replace in three years	1	(6.95)	0.877	(6.10)
	2	(7.7)	0.769	(5.92)
	3	(205)	0.675	(138.38)
	3	6.5	0.675	4.39
	3	(8.9)	0.675	(6.01)
				(152.02)

> The existing machine should be replaced with the new machine, in three years time, as this results in the lowest present value for the cash flows, even though the costs of maintaining the machine in year three exceed the realisable value of the machine in that year.

Conclusion

The investment decisions a company undertakes are vital to its overall value. Investment decisions are the source of future income streams to a company. Evaluating each investment correctly is very important, as incorrect decisions can damage company value and are usually costly to rescind. This chapter outlines a number of techniques that can be utilised to assess different investments. The ARR ranks projects in terms of the average accounting profits generated relative to average investment. The payback period approach ranks projects in terms of the shortest period taken to recoup the initial cash outlay from future cash inflows. The discounted payback period approach is the same as the payback period approach, except it takes the time value of money into consideration. The IRR approach determines the overall return that a project makes from its discounted cash flows, relative to the initial investment cash outflow. It ranks projects according to the size of their return. Finally, the NPV approach ranks projects in terms of their overall absolute return in present value terms. The latter method is deemed to be the most appropriate by academics; however, the payback method (Lefley, 1994) and the IRR methods are commonly used by manufacturing companies in practice (see Arnold and Hatzopoulos, 2000; Pike, 1996; Drury, Braund, Osborne and Tayles, 1993) with the payback method being the most popular. Many companies use the payback period approach as an initial screening device and then use more sophisticated methods thereafter to differentiate between the screened projects.

It would be easy to get carried away by the techniques on offer and to assume that the investment decision is a black or white affair. However, this is not the case. The techniques should be used in conjunction with other information. The following questions might stimulate other factors that need to be considered: Are the selected projects consistent with the overall objectives of the company? What are the absolute values of the projects? Are any so large that they cause an imbalance in the diversification of projects within the company? If so, is risk affected? What is the payback period? – This may be important if a company has liquidity issues.

In addition to these more strategic issues, there are limitations with the appraisal process. Expected cash flows are estimates and the discount rate – though calculated scientifically – is subjective. Gut feeling, though completely unscientific, may play a larger role in practice than is documented. This may also be quite dangerous, as gut feeling might lead to bias in estimates that are used in project appraisal.

Examination standard question

Worked example 13.23

a) LAYTOWN plc is considering the purchase of a machine which could fulfil the company's future expansion plans. In this context the company is currently appraising two machines but only one machine may be purchased.

The *Standard* machine costs €/£50,000 and the *Deluxe* machine costs €/£88,000, payable immediately. Both machines require €/£10,000 of working capital throughout their working lives, which would be recoverable when both machines are scrapped at the end of their working lives (viz. four years for the *Standard* machine and six years for the *Deluxe* machine).

The forecast pre-tax net cash inflows associated with the two machines are as follows:

	Year 1 €/£	Year 2 €/£	Year 3 €/£	Year 4 €/£	Year 5 €/£	Year 6 €/£
Standard	20,500	22,860	24,210	23,410	–	–
Deluxe	32,030	26,110	25,380	25,940	38,560	35,100

The discount rate for the *Standard* machine is 12%.

The *Deluxe* machine has only recently been introduced to the market and has not been fully tested in operating conditions. Because of the higher risk involved, the appropriate discount

Continued

rate for the *Deluxe* machine is believed to be 2% higher than the discount rate for the *Standard* machine.

If it decides to purchase one or other of these machines, the company is proposing to finance the purchase with a term loan at a fixed interest rate of 11%.

Taxation at 35% is payable on operating cash flows one year in arrears, and capital allowances are available at 25% per annum on a reducing balance basis.

REQUIRED

For both the *Standard* and *Deluxe* machines, calculate:
(i) The payback period; and
(ii) The net present value.

Advise the company as to which machine, if either, it should purchase.

14 Marks

b) A recent survey (Pike 1992) investigating the capital investment methods of large UK companies yielded the following results:

Firms using:	%
Payback	94
Accounting rate of return	50
Internal rate of return	81
Net present value	74

REQUIRED

Suggest reasons for the continuing widespread use of traditional techniques in the investment decision process.

8 Marks
Total 22 Marks
(ICAI, MABF II, Summer 1997, Q5)
Continued

Solution

a)   (i)   The payback period for the *Standard* machine is approximately three years: The cash flows in the first three years amount to €/£60,050 (€/£20,500+€/£20,060+€/£19,490). The initial cost of the investment is: €/£60,000.

The payback period for the *Deluxe* machine is approximately four years.

The cash flows in the first four years amount to €/£98,033 (€/£32,030+€/£22,599+€/£22,016+€/£21,388). The initial investment is: €/£98,000.

   (ii)   The NPV for the *Standard* machine is €/£5,136.
The NPV for the *Deluxe* machine is €/£5,510.
(see below for workings.)

Recommendation:
The NPV of the *Deluxe* machine is greater than that of the *Standard* machine; initial considerations would suggest that the *Deluxe* machine should be preferred for this reason. However, the difference in NPV is not great and the uncertainty involved in the estimates for a five to seven-year period is such that a small difference in NPV may not be the weightiest consideration. In favour of the *Standard* machine is its shorter payback period and its established reliability. Although the higher discount rate applied in the case of the *Deluxe* machine, is intended to compensate for its greater risk, a risk averse management board may still prefer the *Standard* model.

a)   *Discounted cash flow analysis of relevant cash flows – Standard machine*

Year	Non-current assets	Working capital	Cash inflows	Taxation W1	Net cash flow	Discount factor	NPV
	€/£	€/£	€/£	€/£	€/£		€/£
0	(50,000)	(10,000)	–	–	(60,000)	1.000	(60,000)
1	–	–	20,500	–	20,500	0.893	18,307
2	–	–	22,860	(2,800)	20,060	0.797	15,988
3	–	–	24,210	(4,720)	19,490	0.712	13,877
4	–	10,000	23,410	(6,013)	27,397	0.636	17,424
5	–	–	–	(811)	(811)	0.567	(460)
						NPV	5,136

Continued

NOTE: re interest payable:

The cash profits are assumed to be net of the interest payable of 11% on the term loans of €/£50,000 and €/£88,000 required for capital outlay on the *Standard* and the *Deluxe* machines respectively. As this interest is allowable for corporation tax purposes, no adjustment has to be made to the accounting cash profit figures to arrive at the taxable profits (assuming all other expenses charged against these cash profits are allowable for tax purposes).

*Discounted cash flow analysis of relevant cash flows – **Deluxe machine***

Year	Non-current assets €/£	Working capital €/£	Cash inflows €/£	Taxation W2 €/£	Net cash flow €/£	Discount factor	NPV €/£
0	(88,000)	(10,000)	–	–	(98,000)	1.000	(98,000)
1	–	–	32,030	–	32,030	0.877	28,090
2	–	–	26,110	(3,511)	22,599	0.769	17,379
3	–	–	25,380	(3,364)	22,016	0.675	14,861
4	–	–	25,940	(4,552)	21,388	0.592	12,662
5	–	–	38,560	(5,831)	32,729	0.519	16,986
6	–	10,000	35,100	(11,060)	34,040	0.456	15,522
7	–	–	–	(4,976)	(4,976)	0.400	(1,990)
						NPV	5,510

W1: Workings on taxation cash flows:

Standard machine

	Capital allowances tax effect (€/£)	Tax on net cash inflows (€/£)	Taxation cash flows (€/£)
0	–	–	–
1	–	–	–
2	4,375	(7,175)	(2,800)
3	3,281	(8,001)	(4,270)
4	2,461	(8,474)	(6,013)
5	1,846+5,537	(8,194)	(811)

Continued

Capital expenditure on Standard machine qualifying for capital allowances:

	€/£		€/£
Cost	50,000		*Reduction in tax cash flow*

Year 1

$$\begin{array}{l}25\% \\ \text{WDV}\end{array} \quad \dfrac{(12,500)}{37,500} \times 35\% \qquad\qquad 4,375$$

Year 2

$$\begin{array}{l}25\% \\ \text{WDV}\end{array} \quad \dfrac{(9,375)}{28,125} \times 35\% \qquad\qquad 3,281$$

Year 3

$$\begin{array}{l}25\% \\ \text{WDV}\end{array} \quad \dfrac{(7,031)}{21,094} \times 35\% \qquad\qquad 2,461$$

Year 4

$$\begin{array}{l}25\% \\ \text{WDV}\end{array} \quad \dfrac{(5,274)}{15,820^*} \times 35\% \qquad\qquad 1,846 \qquad 5,537^*$$

*It is assumed that the machine was scrapped and so there is a balancing allowance of €/£15,820 (€/£NIL−€/£15,820).

The tax impact of this is €/£5,537 (€/£15,820×35%).

W2: Calculation on taxation cash flows:

Deluxe machine

	Capital allowances tax effect (€/£)	Inflows (€/£)	Taxation cash flows (€/£)
0	–	–	–
1	–	–	–
2	7,700	(11,211)	(3,511)
3	5,775	(9,139)	(3,364)
4	4,331	(8,883)	(4,552)
5	3,248	(9,079)	(5,831)
6	2,436	(13,496)	(11,060)
7	1,827+5,482*	(12,285)	(4,976)

Continued

Capital expenditure on Deluxe machine qualifying for capital allowances:

	€/£		€/£
Cost	88,000		Reduction in tax cash flow
Year 1			
25% WDV	$\dfrac{(22,000)}{66,000} \times 35\%$		(7,700)
Year 2			
25% WDV	$\dfrac{(16,500)}{49,500} \times 35\%$		(5,775)
Year 3			
25% WDV	$\dfrac{(12,375)}{37,125} \times 35\%$		(4,331)
Year 4			
25% WDV	$\dfrac{(9,281)}{27,844} \times 35\%$		(3,248)
Year 5			
25% WDV	$\dfrac{(6,961)}{20,883} \times 35\%$		(2,436)
Year 6			
25% WDV	$\dfrac{(5,221)}{15,662} \times 35\%$		(1,827) (5,482)*

*It is assumed that the machine is scrapped, so there is a balancing allowance of: €/£15,662 (€/£662 – NIL).

The tax impact of this is: €/£5,482 (€/£15,662 × 35%).

Comment on the choice of machine using the NPV approach:

The application of the NPV method is complicated when a choice must be made between two or more projects, where the projects have unequal lives. It is important to consider what will happen at the end of year four, when the *Standard* machine is scrapped. Some methods assume continual replacement and then perform an analysis of the relevant cash flows of the two machines over a common time horizon, which thus renders the two machines comparable. To identify the common time horizon, one must compute the lowest common multiple of the lives of the two alternative machines under consideration. In this example, it is 12 years. However, this would be a tedious calculation and therefore the more usual method is the equivalent annual cost method.

The present value of net cash flows for the *Standard* machine is the equivalent annual net cash flow × annuity factor for four years at 12%.

€/£5,136 is equal to the: equivalent annual net cash flow × 3.037 (using cumulative present value factors).

So the equivalent annual net cash flow is €/£1,691.

Similarly, for the *Deluxe* machine:

€/£5,110 is equal to the equivalent annual net cash flow × 3.889.

So the equivalent annual net cash flow is €/£1,313.

Using this method, the decision rule is to choose the machine with the lower annual equivalent cost or the greater annual net cash inflow. So on this basis, the *Standard* machine would be selected.

The final method is to restrict the analysis to an evaluation interval equal to the shortest lived alternative. Applying this approach, an estimate is made of the terminal value for the *Deluxe* machine at the end of year four and this is then shown as a cash inflow for the *Deluxe* alternative, which then is curtailed to just a four-year analysis, instead of six years as shown above. The disadvantage of this method is that the estimate of the disposal value is likely to be highly uncertain and the cash flows in years five and six are ignored.

b)   The survey by Pike (1980) supports the importance of unquantifiable aspects in decisions involving capital budgeting. The survey shows that 63% of respondents ranked qualitative factors as important or very important in investment decisions, while only 55% gave such ratings to sophisticated investment methods and systematic procedures.

(1) Discounting may also be questioned in terms of relevance. A fundamental assumption underlying DCF methods is that decision makers pursue the primary goal of maximising equity holder value. Empirically, this is questionable with equity holder goals often given a lower priority.

Continued

(2) The literature generally assumes that DCF methods are appropriate for all companies regardless of context. The employment of sophisticated tools and formal approaches to decision making does not suit all companies. This process will vary with a company's external environment and internal characteristics. For example, DCF methods and formal risk analysis may well be appropriate in large, capital intensive, decentralised companies operating in high technology industries and with a management which feels comfortable with analytical decision methods. But smaller companies may prefer a more interpersonal approach to management and so may find sophisticated techniques unhelpful. Puxty and Dodds (1991) report that the tendency to use DCF techniques becomes less pronounced in small and medium-sized enterprises.

(3) The relevance of DCF methods is also questioned on pragmatic grounds. Management remain sceptical that the adoption of such techniques actually results in a discernible improvement in performance. Indeed, a major reason for the slow acceptance of DCF methods appears to be the paucity of evidence to show that it improves performance. In fact, empirical studies appear to show that the more profitable companies tend to implement less sophisticated techniques.

(4) Another reason for disenchantment arises more from errors in application of the model than from the model itself. Frequently, there are critical errors in the way theory is applied and generally, these errors are biased against investment.

(5) Drury, C. (1996) notes that most companies employ a combination of evaluation methods, and international surveys of capital budgeting methods bear this out. For example, Horngren, Foster and Datar (1997) tabulates an international comparison of various capital budgeting surveys carried out by a number of authors and notes that for all the countries surveyed ranging from the US, the UK, Australia, Canada, Ireland, Japan, Scotland and a host of other countries, that with the exception of Japan and

Continued

Poland, the remaining countries in the tabulation used more than one method to evaluate capital investments. The payback method remains a very popular method in all countries, particularly in Japan and Poland where the use of DCF techniques is recorded at very low percentages. Payback method is used along with, for example, the IRR in the US and Canada, and with DCF methods (IRR or NPV) in Ireland and with the IRR in Scotland.

The question must be asked as to whether the continuing use of traditional techniques is in any way a reflection of the tendency in a wide variety of countries to avoid relying on just one method. The traditional techniques are retained along with the newer DCF techniques, simply because no single appraisal technique can embody all the relationships and aspects of the capital budgeting decision (risk, reward, financial constraint, competing alternatives etc.)

(6) The question must also be asked as to whether the *particular type of capital investment decision faced by a company* may affect the relative popularity of DCF and non-DCF techniques of appraisal. In regard to this point, Puxty and Dodds (1991) report on a survey by Klammer and Walker (1984) of the principal capital budgeting techniques used by large US companies. The study is unusual, as it distinguishes among different types of capital investment (for example, expansion of operations, foreign operations, abandonment and social expenditures). *For capital investment decisions involving the expansion into new operations, this survey suggests that ARR and payback are disappearing into very low percentage figures, such as 10% and 5%, down from 28% and 15% respectively.*

Surveys by Pike and Woulfe (1981) and by Pike (1988) and Drury (1993), all point to growth in the use of DCF techniques alongside the continuing popularity of payback and Accounting rate of return (ARR).

However, the results are not analysed by industry or by type of product. Further analysis might shed more light in

Continued

this area. Drury (2000) categorised the *type of investment decisions* faced by companies and then examines the popularity of DCF versus non-DCF techniques across such categories.

(7) Behavioural commentators suggest that a manager, who believes that a particular project should be accepted, will select the technique that reflects the project in the best possible light (Drury, 1996). Thus, human factors may confound scientific interpretations of the DCF/non-DCF debate.

KEY TERMS

Accounting rate of return (ARR)
Annuity
Annuity factor
Asset replacement decision
Basic discount rate
Capital allowances
Capital rationing
Discount rate
Discount rate factor
Discounted cash flow yield
Discounted cash flows
Discounted payback period
Divisible projects
Equivalent annual annuity approach
Equivalent annual cost
External investment
Finite horizon approach
First year allowances
Future value
Hard capital rationing
Incremental cash flows
Inflation
Internal investment

Internal rate of return (IRR)
Market discount rate
Money discount rate
Multi-period projects
Mutually exclusive projects
Net present value (NPV)
Nominal discount rate
Opportunity cash flow
Payback period
Present value (PV)
Profitability Index
Real cash flows
Real discount rate
Relevant cash flows
Replacement cycle
Shortest common period approach
Soft capital rationing
Sunk cash flows

REVIEW QUESTIONS

1. Outline the difficulties inherent in the evaluation of projects.
2. List briefly the advantages and disadvantages of using the ARR method for project appraisal.
3. List the advantages and disadvantages of using the payback period method for project appraisal.
4. YZ Ltd. is considering investing in a new machine costing €/£200,000. The machine will produce 10,000 products each year for the next five years. The company has a contract for the next five years for the sale of the products. This contract fixes the price of the product at €/£20 per item. Production will cost €/£12 per item in the first year. This is expected to increase by 10% each year due to competition for supply. YZ's cost of capital is 12% per annum.

REQUIRED

Should the company undertake the project (assume no inflation)?

5. YZ Ltd. faces the same situation as outlined in 4; however, in this instance they are informed that inflation of 5% is expected each year and the real cost of capital is 12%. The cost of capital has not been adjusted to take account of the expected inflation.

REQUIRED

Given this additional information – should YZ accept the project?

6. What is the difference between the nominal/money discount rate and the real discount rate?
7. CASSANOVA Ltd.
a) The selection of a discount rate for project appraisal can be a difficult issue. Various methods have been put forward, as follows:

    (1) A single company cut-off rate based on the company's overall WACC; or
    (2) A system of multiple cut-off rates that reflect the risk of each particular investment; or
    (3) A rate that reflects the specific cost of funding each project.

REQUIRED

Comment on the suitability of each of the methods above and recommend which method would, in your opinion, be most suitable for appraising a new project.

7 Marks

b) The directors of CASSANOVA Ltd. are considering a new project. Their company policy is to select a discount rate that reflects the risk of each individual project.

The financial details of the project are as follows:
Project R123
Initial cost

	€/£
Plant and machinery	1,500,000
Equipment	500,000
Working capital	40,000
Market research	200,000

Annual pre-tax cash flows:

Year 1	Year 2	Year 3	Year 4
€/£400,000	€/£620,000	€/£960,000	€/£1,000,000

Additional information:

(1) The fee for market research has already been paid but the company intends spreading the cost over the four-year life of the project.

(2) Capital allowances are allowed at a rate of 25% per annum (straight-line basis) on all plant, machinery and equipment.

(3) Corporation tax is 10% per annum and is paid one year in arrears.

(4) Included in the annual cash flows is a figure of €/£15,000 per annum, which is the interest charge on the loan for financing the project.

(5)   The level of working capital investment is not expected to change for the duration of the project. The plant, machinery and equipment purchased for the project will be sold in year five for €/£40,000.

(6)   The WACC of the company is 12%, but this new project is considered to be significantly more risky. A more appropriate discount rate is considered to be 18%. The project is being financed by a 9% long-term loan.

REQUIRED

Calculate the NPV and IRR of the new project and recommend whether the company should proceed with the project, or not.

11 Marks
Total 18 Marks
(ICAI, MABF II, Summer 2000, Q6)

CHALLENGING QUESTIONS

1.   INDIGO plc

a)   Describe and discuss briefly the main stages to be followed when a company wishes to implement a new programme of capital investment.

10 Marks

b)   INDIGO plc is considering the production of a new product, *Beta*, which would necessitate the purchase of a new machine costing €/£600,000. The machine would be capable of producing 10,000 units of *Beta* per annum and would have an economic life of four years, after which it would be scrapped at zero value.

To enable a target selling price per unit to be established, the following standard cost figures (per unit of *Beta*) have been prepared, based on the capacity of the machine:

		€/£
Materials		50.00
Labour		
Skilled:	10 hours @ €/£6 per hour	60.00
Semi-skilled:	10 hours @ €/£5 per hour	50.00
Variable overheads	20 hours @ €/£2 per hour	40.00
Fixed overheads		
General overheads	20 hours @ €/£0.75 per hour	15.00
Specific overheads	20 hours @ €/£0.75 per hour	15.00
Total		230.00
Total profit margin (30%)		69.00
Target selling price per unit		299.00

The Marketing Department has identified a wholesale distributor who is prepared to sign a four-year contract to take all of the budgeted production of *Beta* at the target selling price. Under the terms of the contract, the wholesale distributor would pay for the product yearly in arrears.

Additional information:

(1) The machine would be financed by a loan at the current rate of interest of 10% and the company would, therefore, incur annual interest costs of €/£60,000.

(2) The company policy is to allocate fixed overheads on the basis of labour hours. The general fixed overheads represent an allocation of the company's existing fixed overheads to the new product. The specific fixed overheads charge is an allocation of the depreciation of the new machine over its economic life.

(3) There is currently a shortage of skilled labour. Consequently, during the first year of production of *Beta*, skilled labour would be diverted from the company's existing products. Skilled labour could be made available for the remaining three years of the

project by implementing a recruitment and training programme during the first year, which would entail a one-off cost of €/£1 million. This would enable the diverted labour to return to its normal work after the first year. Currently each skilled labour hour generates an average contribution of €/£3.50.

REQUIRED

Estimate the project's:

(i) Payback period.

(ii) Net present value.

and make a recommendation based on your results.

15 Marks

Total 25 Marks

(ICAI, MABF II, Summer 1994, Q1)

2. **SPHERE plc**

a) Describe and distinguish between each of the following:

   (i) Soft capital rationing.

   (ii) Hard capital rationing.

6 Marks

b) A small conglomerate, SPHERE plc, has recently undertaken an investigation to identify suitable investment projects in an attempt to further diversify its operations.

As a result of the investigation, five projects have been selected for further consideration and an initial evaluation has yielded the following results:

Project	Net present value (NPV) €/£	Initial outlay €/£
A.........	150,000	500,000
B.........	40,000	100,000
C.........	40,000	400,000
D.........	100,000	200,000
E.........	90,000	150,000

The company does not wish to access external financial markets and has identified €/£750,000 available from within its internal cash resources.

All the projects are completely divisible.

REQUIRED

(i) Identify the projects which should be selected to maximise NPV.

5 Marks

(ii) State the NPV figure which results from the optimal selection of projects.

4 Marks

(iii) Indicate how your recommendation and figure would be affected, if projects C and D were mutually exclusive.

3 Marks
Total 18 Marks
(ICAI, MABF II, Summer 1995, Q7)

3. **CLIFTON plc**

a) Write a report to your managing director explaining the benefits that information technology has brought to the investment decision process.

6 Marks

b) CLIFTON plc utilises an item of capital equipment which has a useful life of four years. Recently, a new model has been launched and the company is deciding when to replace the existing equipment. To assist this decision, the following information regarding costs and residual values has been ascertained:

	Current model		
Year	*Operating costs*	*maintenance costs*	*Residual value*
	€/£'000	*€/£'000*	*€/£'000*
0	–	–	1,500
1	2,500	500	1,000
2	3,000	1,000	600
3	3,500	1,500	100
4	4,000	1,700	–

New model

Year	Outlay	Operating costs	Maintenance costs	Residual value
	€/£'000	€/£'000	€/£'000	€/£'000
0	7,000	–	–	–
1	–	1,800	200	4,000
2	–	2,200	500	3,000
3	–	2,600	900	2,000
4	–	2,800	1,200	1,000

The company's current cost of capital is 8%.

REQUIRED

Advise CLIFTON plc as to when it should replace the existing equipment.

12 Marks

Total 18 Marks

(ICAI, MABF II, Summer 1996, Q7)

4.   **JASPER plc**

a)   JASPER plc is currently experiencing a shortage of finance available for investment projects, but cannot postpone any of the four projects which it is currently considering. There is a limit of €/£60,000 available at present but no capital rationing is expected in future periods. The expected cash flows of the four projects are as follows:

Project	Year 0	Year 1	Year 2	Year 3	Year 4
	€/£	€/£	€/£	€/£	€/£
A........	(50,000)	(20,000)	20,000	40,000	40,000
B........	(28,000)	(50,000)	40,000	40,000	20,000
C	(30,000)	(30,000)	30,000	40,000	10,000
D	(30,000)	(20,000)	25,000	40,000	10,000

The cost of capital is 10%.

REQUIRED

In view of the capital rationing and assuming that the projects are divisible:

   (i)   Advise the company as to which projects should be undertaken; and

8 Marks

   (ii) Advise the company as to which projects should be undertaken, if projects C and D, were mutually exclusive.

4 Marks

b)   The Business Finance Director has suggested that using the company's normal cost of capital might not be appropriate in a capital rationing situation.

State, with reasons, whether you agree with the Business Finance Director's viewpoint.

6 Marks

Total 18 Marks

(ICAI, MABF II, Summer 1998, Q7)

5.   MADDEN Ltd.

MADDEN Ltd. is a company involved in a wide range of activities. It is now considering a new project which has been proposed. The estimated revenues and costs of the proposed project are as follows:

Investment period:	Five years
Initial outlay:	€/£1.2 million on machinery and production equipment
	€/£30,000 on working capital
Annual sales units:	Year (1) 15,000
	(2) 20,000
	(3) 25,000
	(4) 40,000
	(5) 28,000

Unit prices (at year '0' prices)		€/£	€/£
Sales price per unit			87.00
Cost per unit:			
Materials	31.30		
Direct labour	30.70		
Overheads	11.50		73.50
Profit			13.50

Additional information:

(1)   The scrap value on machinery and production equipment at the end of year five is expected to be €/£120,000.

(2)   It is expected that the level of working capital investment will increase by €/£1,000 at the beginning of each year for the duration of the project.

(3)   The selling price of the product is expected to increase by the average annual retail price index rate of 2.5%, while the material costs, labour and overheads are expected to increase by 1.5% per annum.

(4)   Overheads of €/£11.50 per unit include depreciation of €/£2.00 per unit.

(5)   The project is to be financed by 8% debentures redeemable at a premium of 20% after ten years.

(6)   The company's nominal cost of capital is 12%. This is deemed to be a suitable discount rate for this project. In addition, the company has a required payback period on all its investments of three years.

(7)   The rate of corporation tax is 22% per annum and is payable one year in arrears.

NOTE: Ignore capital allowances.

REQUIRED

a)   Calculate the payback period and NPV of the project.

13 Marks

b)   Write a report to the Board of Directors in which you should explain:

(i)   Your recommendations on whether the company should proceed with the proposed project;

(ii)   Your treatment of each of the following.
- Working capital investment.
- Interest on debenture capital.

7 Marks

(iii)   Why payback continues to be the most popular method of investment appraisal.

2 Marks
Total 22 Marks
(ICAI, MABF II, Autumn 2000, Q5)

6.   JENNA Ltd.

The directors of JENNA Ltd. are contemplating the replacement of one of the company's machines. The machine cost the company €/£200,000 two years ago. A new improved model has come on to the market which, it is claimed, can improve output by up to 50%. The new model will cost €/£400,000.

Both machines are considered to have a useful life of five years from now.

The new machine is expected to have a significant impact on operating costs and, as a result, the company plans to reduce the selling price of its product by 5%. Market research has indicated that this will have a significant impact on sales.

Details of the selling price and related costs are as follows:

	Current machine per unit (€/£)	Proposed machine per unit (€/£)
Sales	12.00	11.40
Materials	(3.00)	(2.50)
Labors	(4.00)	(3.20)
Variable overhead	(1.20)	(1.00)
Fixed overheads (Note 1)	(1.50)	(1.70)
Profit	2.30	3.00
Number of units per annum	50,000	75,000

Additional information:

(1)   The only change to fixed overheads is in relation to increased depreciation on the new machine.

(2)   If the existing machine is not replaced, it will require an immediate maintenance overhaul, costing €/£5,000.

(3)   If the proposal goes ahead, the company could sell the existing machine for €/£30,000 immediately.

(4)   If the new machine is acquired, it will lead to an immediate working capital reduction of €/£5,000. This reduction will last for the duration of the project.

(5)   Taxation is 20% and is paid one year in arrears. (For the purpose of this question, candidates should ignore capital allowances.)

(6)   The discount rate for appraising this project is 15%.

REQUIRED

a)   Calculate the IRR of the replacement decision.

8 Marks

b)   Write a report to the Board of Directors outlining:
  (i)   Your recommendation (with reasons) as to whether or not the company should replace its machine; and
  (ii)   The principal assumptions upon which your analysis is based.

4 Marks
(ICAI, MABF II, Summer 2001, extract from Q6)

7.   MAGENTA Ltd.

MAGENTA Ltd. ('MAGENTA') has spent the last two years developing a new type of domestic thermometer.

The company has incurred expenditure of over €/£3 million to date in researching the product. The thermometer is ready for commercial production.

MAGENTA is now trying to decide between two mutually exclusive options for the company. The options are to both manufacture and sell the product itself or to licence out the manufacture and sale to a large multinational company. In each case the product will have an estimated useful life of three years.

The financial details of each option are as follows:

Option 1: Manufacture and sell the product.

Sales	Year 2003	Year 2004	Year 2005
Units (000's)	50	90	160
Price per unit (€/£s)	40	40	30

Materials

The estimated material cost for one thermometer is €/£10. However, this is expected to fall to €/£6 in year three. MAGENTA has some existing inventory on hand that will cover 80% of the first year's production. This inventory had originally cost €/£300,000, has a replacement cost of €/£400,000 and could be sold immediately to another company for €£325,000. If MAGENTA does not proceed with this venture, this material could not be used in any other project undertaken by the company.

Labour

The labour force required to produce the thermometer will comprise six employees who are currently working on another project. If MAGENTA proceeds with the manufacturing option, this other project will be postponed and the estimated loss in contribution from postponement would be €/£50,000 per annum. The six employees are currently paid €/£28,000 each per annum. If transferred to this project, they will be awarded a pay increase of 10% per annum for each of the three years.

Capital outlay

A special machine costing €/£1.2 million will be required to produce the thermometer. It will be purchased immediately but will not be paid for until the end of year one. The machine is expected to be worth €/£250,000 at the end of the three years.

Working capital
The total working capital investment for the period at the beginning of each year of the investment is as follows:

2003 – €/£50,000   2004 – €/£70,000   2005 – €/£100,000

All working capital can be realised at the end of the life of the project.

Other costs
Additional overheads (excluding depreciation) are estimated to be €/£0.5 million per annum. In addition, the marketing costs will be €/£500,000 per annum. There will be no money spent on marketing in year three. The project should also be allocated a 'fair share' (€/£20,000 per annum) of the company's general fixed administration costs, although these would not increase as a result of accepting the contract.

Capital allowances and taxation
The machine will attract annual capital allowances of 20% on a straight line basis. Corporation tax is 15% per annum and is payable one year in arrears. Corporation tax is charged on all profits.

Research and development costs
It is the policy of the company to write-off research and development expenditure to the income statement in the year in which it is incurred.

MAGENTA could agree to another company manufacturing and marketing the product under licence. A multinational company has offered to enter into a licensing agreement with MAGENTA in return for a royalty fee of €/£4.50 per unit payable at the end of each year. It is estimated that the annual number of units sold will be 10% higher if the multinational company manufactures and markets the product.

MAGENTA's cost of capital is 15%.

REQUIRED

a)   (i) Calculate the NPV for each option.
      (ii) Explain, with reasons, which option should be selected by MAGENTA Ltd.

17 Marks

b)   Outline the principal advantages and disadvantages of using finance
     leases as a source of medium-term finance.

5 Marks
Total 22 Marks
(ICAI, MABF II, Summer 2002, Q5)

8.   TROLAK Ltd.

TROLAK Town ('TROLAK'), a club playing in a professional football
league in Ireland, is considering signing the talented but eccentric goal-
keeper, Pablo Goodsavo, from a club in Spain. It is now the start of the
new season and you have been asked to advise on the financial aspects of
the transfer negotiations. At present the club, in common with many others in the same league, barely manages to break-even after expenses, in an
average year. You have ascertained the following information:

Cost of existing players
The existing players cost €/£1,450,000 in transfer fees.

'Gate' receipts, television rights and sponsorship
The average home gate for the team is 15,000 people, 21 times a season
and the entrance price is €/£12 per head. There is an existing squad of
22 players (some full time and some part time) and they earn on average
€/£750 per week each. (Assume a 52-week year).

Five of the games are normally televised live each season earning €/£50,000
for the club on each occasion. The rights to show the delayed transmission
highlights of the other games have been sold to a satellite broadcaster at
€/£8,000 per game.

The directors now consider that, if an additional once-off €/£200,000
is spent immediately on promotional activity, and with Goodsavo on the
team, it will be possible to increase the number of spectators to 17,000 on
average and to raise the entrance price to €/£14 per head.

If Goodsavo joins the club, a new sponsorship deal, to be agreed with
a local company, would bring an additional €/£110,000 per annum in
sponsorship revenue. In addition, the number of games televised live

would increase from five to eight but the revenue from the delayed transmission of highlights of these matches would no longer be available.

Ground improvements

To cope with the increased attendance if Goodsavo joins, it will be necessary to spend €/£324,000 improving facilities at the ground. This amount would be contracted for and paid immediately and capital allowances would be available on it at the rate of 25% per annum reducing balance.

Personal terms and further implications

Goodsavo is now 33 years old and the club proposes to offer him a three-year contract after which he will again be a free agent, allowed to walk away from the club if he so wishes. It has been agreed with the Spanish club that the transfer fee will be paid immediately. Personal terms are yet to be agreed with Goodsavo but his agent has indicated that he will require to be paid €/£78,000 in the first year increasing at 5% per year compound, for each of the years of his contract, plus a 'golden hello' of €/£100,000, payable immediately. The directors also estimate that the rest of the team will require a pay increase of 20% because more will now be expected of all of them.

Cost of capital and corporation tax

The cost of capital for TROLAK is 13% and the rate of corporation tax (payable one year in arrears) is 34%.

Other assumptions

You may assume that, unless otherwise stated, all costs are to be paid in full and all revenues are received at the end of each year. Ignore the effect of capital allowances after year three. The 'golden hello' and the additional promotional expenditure are not tax deductible.

REQUIRED

a) Assuming that the Spanish club will not accept less than €/£2,000,000 for Goodsavo, should TROLAK sign him given that the decision is based on an incremental net present value analysis? Show your workings clearly.

16 Marks

b)   It is widely accepted that the payback period method of invest-
     ment appraisal has little or no theoretical or academic justification
     as a means of investment appraisal. Yet in practice it seems that it is
     widely used by many companies.

     List briefly THREE reasons why the payback method is so popular
     as a method of investment appraisal, in spite of the lack of theoreti-
     cal justification for its use.

6 Marks

Total 22 Marks

(ICAI, MABF II, Autumn 2003, Q5)

9.   BRISK plc

You have recently been appointed Business Finance Director of BRISK
plc ('BRISK'). The company is considering investing in the production
of an electronic security device with an expected market life of four years.
The previous Business Finance Director had undertaken an analysis of
the proposed project. The main features of his analysis are shown below.

	Year 0 €/£'000	Year 1 €/£'000	Year 2 €/£'000	Year 3 €/£'000	Year 4 €/£'000
Investment in depreciable assets	4,500	–	–	–	–
Investment in working capital	300	–	–	–	–
Sales		3,500	4,900	5,320	5,740
Materials		535	750	900	1,050
Labour		1,070	1,500	1,800	2,100
Overheads		50	100	100	100
Interest		576	576	576	576
Research costs		300	300	300	300
Depreciation		900	900	900	900
Total costs		3,431	4,126	4,576	5,026
Profit before tax		69	774	744	714
Taxation		24	271	260	250
Profit after tax		45	503	484	464

Additional information:

(1) All of the above projected profits have been computed in terms of present day costs and prices. However, due to inflation, overhead expenses and selling prices are expected to increase at a rate of 2% per annum, and material costs and labour are expected to increase by 5% per annum.

(2) Capital allowances are allowed at a rate of 25% per annum on the reducing balance basis on all depreciable assets.

(3) Corporation tax is 18% per annum and is paid one year in arrears.

(4) The estimated scrap value of the assets at the end of year four is nil.

(5) The company has already incurred costs of €/£1.2 million in researching the product. The payment for this research is due in year one. It is the policy of the company to write off research costs to the income statement over a four-year period.

(6) The company's (nominal) required rate of return on all projects is 20%.

REQUIRED

a) Calculate the relevant inflated net cash flows that would arise from this proposal for each of the four years.

12 Marks

b) Calculate the NPV and the payback period for the investment and recommend, with reasons, whether the company should proceed with this investment.

5 Marks

c) Outline briefly some of the limitations of the appraisal you have prepared above.

5 Marks
Total 22 Marks
(ICAI, MABF II, Autumn 2004, Q5)

10.   CAPITAL RATIONING

a)   Describe how the following factors can impact on a capital investment decision:
   (i)   inflation;
   (ii)   tax;
   (iii)   residual value; and
   (iv)   the treatment of working capital.

8 Marks

b)   A company has limited access to funds and is considering investing in the following projects, none of which can delayed:

Project	Now €/£m	Year 1 €/£m	Year 2 €/£m	NPV €/£m	IRR %	Payback years
X	(25)	21	12	3.32	23%	1.33
Y	(20)	20	6	2.64	24%	1.00
Z	(10)	10	4	2.12	31%	1.00

The company's cost of capital is 12% and it has €/£30 million of funds available to invest now.

(i)   Assuming the projects are indivisible, (i.e. it is not possible to undertake a fraction of a project), which project(s) should the company invest in, and why?

2 Marks

(ii)   If the projects are divisible (i.e. it is possible to invest a fraction of the initial outlay now and, receive a corresponding fraction of the NPV), which project(s) should the company invest in, and why?

4 Marks

c)   In perfect capital markets, the condition known as capital rationing should not arise. Explain briefly why capital rationing is nevertheless experienced by many companies.

4 Marks
Total 18 Marks
(ICAI, MABF II, Summer 2003, Q6)

11.   LAZER

LAZER plc. ('LAZER') is a large, entirely equity financed, engineering company whose financial year ends on 31 December. The company's objective is to maximise equity shareholders' wealth, and it generates sufficient taxable profits to relieve all capital allowances at the earliest opportunity. Currently, one of the company's divisional managers has to fulfil a particular contract, and he can do this in one of two ways. Under the first (Proposal 1), he can purchase plant and machinery; while under the second (Proposal 2), he can use a machine already owned by the company.

The year-end operating net cash inflows in nominal (i.e. money) terms, and before Corporation Tax, are as follows:

	2008	2009	2010
	€/£	€/£	€/£
Proposal 1.....................	40,000	55,000	70,000
Proposal 2.....................	70,000	70,000	NIL

Proposal 1
Under this proposal the company will incur an outlay of €/£62,500 on 31 December 2007 for the purchase of plant and machinery.

The labour force required under this proposal will have to be recruited locally, and budgeted wages have been taken into account in preparing the estimates of the future nominal net cash inflow given above.

The plant and machinery is expected to be scrapped on 31 December 2010, with the nominal cash proceeds at that date being projected as €/£5,000. This has not been included in the nominal net cash inflows given above.

Proposal 2
This second proposal covers a two-year period from 31 December 2007. It will require the company to use a machine which was purchased for €/£150,000 a number of years ago when 100% first year capital allowances were available and which is therefore fully written down for tax

purposes. The company has no current use for the machine, and its net realisable value at 31 December 2007 is €/£50,000.

However, if the machine were retained unused, there would be no incremental costs of keeping it, and it would be sold on 31 December 2008 for an estimated €/£60,000 in nominal money terms. If used under this proposal, the expected residual value of the machine would be zero at the end of the two-year period.

The labour force required under this proposal would be recruited from elsewhere within the company and, in end-year nominal cash flow terms, would be paid, in total, €/£20,000 and €/£21,600 respectively for 2008 and 2009. However, the staff that would have to be taken on in other divisions to replace those switched over to the new project would, in corresponding year-end nominal cash flow terms, cost in total – €/£22,000 for 2008 and €/£23,760 for 2009.

The end-year nominal net cash inflows of €/£70,000 for both 2008 and 2009 which are associated with this proposal are after deducting the remuneration of the work force actually employed on the project.

Working capital requirements

For both proposals, working capital requirements, in nominal money terms, at the beginning of each year are estimated at 10% of the year-end operating net cash inflows referred to in the table above. The working capital funds will be released when a proposal is completed. There are no tax effects associated with changes in working capital.

The corporation tax rate is expected to be 30% over the planning period, tax being payable 12 months after the accounting year-end to which it relates.

The annual writing down allowance for plant and machinery is 20% straight-line. A full writing down allowance is given in the year in which the asset is first put into use, and a balancing charge or balancing allowance may occur in the year of disposal. Any balancing charges or allowances are calculated for individual assets (i.e. they are not part of the general pool for tax purposes).

The company's nominal cost of capital is 6%.

REQUIRED

a)   Calculate the net present value at 31 December 2007 of each of the two mutually exclusive proposals.

18 Marks

b)   Indicate briefly any reservations you might have about basing an investment decision on these figures.

4 Marks
Total 22 Marks
(ICAI, MABF, Summer 2007, Q5)

NOTE: *Calculate to the nearest €/£. Show all calculations clearly. Repetition of a project is not possible.*

CAPITAL INVESTMENT DECISION MAKING: INCORPORATING RISK 14

Debt   10,000,000
Equity   15,000,000
Market Value   25,000,000

LEARNING OBJECTIVES

Upon completing the chapter, readers should be able to:

* Explain the difference between risk and uncertainty in the context of capital appraisal decisions;
* Discuss factors that cause risk and uncertainty;
* Explain the additional risks that are associated with investing in projects in foreign countries;
* Evaluate projects that are subject to risk using sensitivity analysis, scenario analysis, certainty equivalents and probability theory;
* List the advantages and disadvantages of each of these evaluation techniques; and
* Discuss simulation analysis, including the use of information technology in assessing risk in capital projects.

Introduction

Capital investment appraisal techniques should play a small part in an overall strategic investment plan. The techniques are mechanical and should only be used as aids that inform management decision making, not make decision for managers. They should not lead directly to an 'accept' or 'reject' decision. A lot of background work has to be undertaken in the stages prior to a project's financial evaluation. For example, the investment ideas have to be generated and formulated into a plan. Data has to be collected about cash flows etc. At this stage, the ideas and plan should be reviewed for viability, before more formal capital investment appraisal takes place. It is at this stage also, that the risks or uncertainties in respect of estimated cash flows of a project are assessed and projects are screened before being submitted for authorisation.

Future cash flows in respect of an investment are rarely known with certainty; one example might be the placement of monies in a fixed-term, fixed-rate deposit account. Virtually all capital investment projects have cash flows that are not known with certainty. Where cash flows are totally uncertain, the project should not proceed. When cash flows are *totally uncertain*, they cannot be assigned probabilities of occurrence, even subjective ones. Totally uncertain cash flows are different to risky cash flows. When cash flows are risky, they can be assigned probabilities related to their expected occurrence. The probabilities assigned can be *objective* (predetermined using historical patterns from the outcomes of similar projects) or *subjective* (given best estimates by management). The latter introduces an amount of uncertainty into the risk assessment of a project, but not total uncertainty.

This chapter introduces the concept of risk into capital investment appraisals. It explains risk and its relationship to return. The main body of the chapter deals with techniques that are used to account for risk in the appraisal process. The approaches used include manipulation of the input variables (sensitivity analysis, scenario analysis, simulation analysis and certainty equivalent approach) and the use of statistics in the evaluation of various projects with differing predicted outcomes, given the chance of the occurrence of that cash flow being known. The latter part of the chapter provides an overview of other factors that can cause risk, particularly risk associated with foreign-based capital investments.

Risk

In investment appraisal, *risk* is the likelihood that any estimates or assumptions made will differ to what actually occurs. The possibilities of actual cash flows being different from those predicted, are formulated into various probable outcomes, each with an assigned probability. Capital projects involve a range of estimated cash flows that can occur over a number of years. The further away the estimates (in time terms), the greater the risk

that actual cash flows will be different; therefore the range of possible outcomes will be greater for estimates far into the future.

Capital investment appraisal is subject to many forms of risk, including risks that are inherent in any economy. Cash flow estimates may be
based on the expectation that the current economic climate will continue
into the future; however, the economy can be volatile and when a downturn occurs, it has the potential to occur quickly. In addition, cash flow
projections can be influenced by competition from other countries. This
has been exacerbated over recent decades by the globalisation of product
markets. Predicting product prices, and hence cash outflows, is now more
difficult as they may be impacted upon by inflation rates in other countries (affecting sale or supply prices).

There is risk involved in determining estimated cash flows. For example, a project's estimated costs may not have captured all the indirect costs;
the purchase of a machine may involve carriage costs, duty charges, fitting
and installation charges, downtime in the factory while a machine is fitted, training of staff etc. Capturing all costs accurately may be difficult.
Cash inflows are also subjective. Sales prices are affected by market forces
including the actions of competitors, the economy and technological
change. In addition, the rates of taxation and capital allowances may be
changed by government.

There is also risk associated with predicting the discount rate to be
used in the capital appraisal process. The discount rate is usually based on
a company's WACC, which encapsulates the returns required by a company's financiers. However, the WACC is in constant flux. For instance,
interest rates change, stock market prices rise and fall, a company's capital
structure may alter and the company may change its business, impacting on the financier's assessment of the risks involved in investing in the
company.

The risk of obsolescence will also impact on the investment appraisal
process. At the outset, an assessment has to be made in respect of the
period of time that a company will derive economic benefits from an
asset or project, and this will be influenced by expected advances made
by other companies. For example, a new computer system may reasonably
be expected to last a company for ten years; however, advances in software
development, web programs and complementary hardware may cause the
hardware to become obsolete within three years. Therefore, a point in time

may come when the current project, though still capable of generating products, will no longer be viable and a new project should be pursued. This risk is more evident in high technology types of capital projects, as these are developed in a highly competitive and fast changing environment. If a company does not keep abreast of current developments, it may lose market share.

Project appraisal methods used to consider the impact of risk

Some companies set a limit on the payback period that has to be met before a project goes ahead; others use conservative cash flows. The advantages of these methods are that they are quick and easy; however, they use arbitrary assumptions.

Another commonly used technique is to leave the cash flow predictions as they are and to build in a risk factor (margin of safety) to the discount rate. This is called a *risk-adjusted discount rate*. This technique is based on the theory that there is a relationship between expected risk and expected return; the higher the risk of an investment, the higher the required return. Therefore, if a project is deemed to be risky, a *risk premium* will be added to the normal discount rate to compensate for additional risks. The more risky a project, the higher the risk premium required. The relationship is depicted in the following graph and is based on the theory underlying the CAPM.

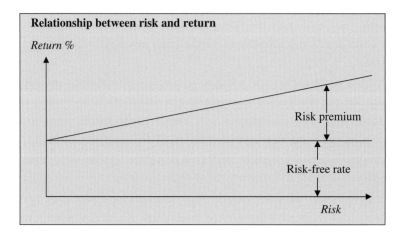

The risk premium may be determined arbitrarily or may be based on the return required for similar projects, by other companies. Some companies classify projects into risk categories and have predetermined required return rates for each risk category. Again, the categorisation process is subjective, as is the premium that is required. The required rates and risk classifications may be influenced by an individual manager's views, which may not reflect the views of the equity holders (agency theory). Where the project is similar in risk to the operational activities of a company, then the WACC can be used, though it may need to be adjusted if the capital structure of the company is expected to change due to a change in the method of financing. In this instance, the ***adjusted present value*** may also be utilised to provide a more realistic outcome (see chapter 15, 'Capital Structure').

Other more scientific methods, though time consuming to obtain, provide better insight into variables that might be deemed to be most risky and the resultant outcome from variations in their estimates. This information can be obtained using sensitivity analysis. Sensitivity analysis only considers variations in one variable at a time; another method, scenario analysis, can be used to consider variations in all the variables, given likely outcomes (usually three or four) and simulation analysis extends scenario analysis to consider hundreds of potential outcomes. These three methods are now discussed.

Sensitivity analysis

Sensitivity analysis involves examining the impact of variations in key input variables on the outcome of a project. This type of analysis strives to determine the margin of safety for each key input variable, holding all else constant. There are two approaches to using sensitivity analysis. The first considers variations in cash flows; the second considers variations in rates used.

Sensitivity analysis: cash flows
There are two approaches to calculating the sensitivity of a project to changes in input cash flows. The first uses a ratio of the *NPV of a project to the PV of a variable*. Therefore, the first step is to determine the total PV of the variable for which sensitivity is being tested and then to express

the NPV of the project as a percentage of the PV of the variable (see example 14.1).

The *margin of safety* approach results in exactly the same outcome. It determines the extent of change in a variable required before a project starts to make a negative NPV. It is calculated in the same manner as the margin of safety in break-even analysis. The margin of safety in absolute terms is calculated as:

$$\text{Margin of safety} = \text{Worst value} - \text{Estimated value}$$

The margin of safety is sometimes expressed in percentage terms. For example, *'the variable can change by x% before the project becomes unviable'*. This can be determined using the following formula:

$$\text{Margin of safety} = \frac{\text{Worst value} - \text{Estimated value}}{\text{Estimated value}}$$

Worked example 14.1 (Sensitivity analysis: cash flows)

The business finance manager in Johnny Ltd. is appraising a five-year project that has a positive NPV of €/£1 million. Wages of €/£250,000 per annum have been charged in arriving at the NPV of €/£1 million.

The company's WACC is 15% and this was deemed an appropriate discount rate to use for this project.

REQUIRED

How sensitive is the outcome of the project to wage levels?

Solution

Step 1 Calculate the total present value (PV) of wages
$$PV = FV \times \text{discount rate}$$

Continued

Where the future value (FV) of the expected wages cash flows is €/£250,000 per year for five years (assumed to be incurred at the end of each year) and the discount rate is an annuity factor representing discount rates for five years at 15%.

PV (wages): €/£838,000 (€/£250,000 × 3.352)

Step 2 Express the NPV of the project as a percentage of the PV of the cost of wages.

The NPV of the project is €/£1 million and the present value of the wage cost is €/£838,000. Therefore the NPV of the project is 119% of the PV of the wage cost (€/£1,000,000/€/£838,000).

This means that wages can rise by 119% before the project's NPV would fall to zero.

This information can also be obtained using the margin of safety approach. In this instance, the margin of safety in money terms is €/£1,162,000 (€/£1,000,000+(€/£1,000,000−€/£838,000)). The annual wages can increase from €/£250,000 to €/£547,500 calculated as €/£250,000+(€/£250,000×119%)). This has a PV of €/£1,835,220(€/£547,000×3.352). The margin of safety in percentage terms is 119% ((€/£1,835,220− €/£838,000)/(€/£1,000,000−€/£162,000)). The same result as that obtained when the NPV to PV percentage is utilised.

Sensitivity analysis: rate changes
This approach considers the sensitivity of a project's NPV to changes in input rates, such as the discount factor, the tax rate or price per unit. This requires an IRR approach and is best explained with the use of an example.

Worked example 14.2   (Sensitivity analysis: rate changes)

A manufacturing company is considering the purchase of a new machine to manufacture beach balls. The machine costs €/£550,000. It is anticipated that the machine will be used for ten years and then scrapped. The company expects to sell the balls at 25c/p each and to sell 900,000 balls per annum. Variable costs per ball are

Continued

expected to be 5c/p per ball and fixed costs are predicted to be €/£50,000 per annum. The manufacturing company has a WACC of 15%. It is considered appropriate to use this rate when assessing this project.

REQUIRED

Calculate the NPV of this project.
How sensitive is the outcome of the project to the selling price of the balls?

Solution

	€/£
Cost of machine	(550,000)
Cash inflows from sales:	
(900,000 × 25c/p × 5.019)*	1,129,275
Cash outflows for variable costs:	
(900,000 × 5c/p × 5.019)	(225,855)
Fixed overheads: (€/£50,000 × 5.019)	(250,950)
NPV	102,470

*Annuity factor representing discount rates of 15% for ten years.

To assess the sensitivity of the project outcome to a change in sales price, a rate of 22c/p is selected (arbitrary selection – as the NPV is positive, the cash inflows need to fall so a lower amount is selected).

	€/£
Cost of machine	(550,000)
Cash inflows from sales:	
(900,000 × 22c/p × 5.019)*	993,762
Cash outflows for variable costs:	
(900,000 × 5c/p × 5.019)	(225,855)
Fixed overheads: (€/£50,000 × 5.019)	(250,950)
NPV	(33,043)

*Annuity factor representing discount rates of 15% for ten years.

Continued

Interpolation is now utilised to find the selling price, which will result in a zero NPV.

$$\text{Sales price} = 22\,c/p + \frac{\text{€}/\text{£}33{,}043 \times (25c/p - 22c/p)}{-\text{€}/\text{£}33{,}043 - \text{€}/\text{£}102{,}450} = 22.73c/p$$

Therefore, so long as the other variables are accurately estimated this project will be viable – unless the sales price for each beach ball falls below 22.73c/p.

Sensitivity analysis involves numerous calculations (depending on the number of variables in an appraisal) that are mechanic in nature. Information technology is usually utilised to speed up the process. Spreadsheets with preprogrammed formulae can easily determine the margin of safety percentage and perform IRR calculations for rate changes.

Sensitivity analysis: advantages

Increases awareness: Sensitivity analysis provides management with an insight into the potential impact of changes in variables on a project – it makes them aware of the risks inherent in a project.

Critical variables: Management can identify those variables that have the smallest margin of safety.

Efficient use of management time: As critical variables are identified, management can direct their attention to ensuring that estimates of these variables are more valid.

Other alternatives: Where the margin of safety is small, management may decide to utilise a substitute, if possible, or to change the project.

Management by exception: If, and when, a project has started, management can focus their attention on ensuring that the critical variables remain close to their estimates.

Sensitivity analysis: disadvantages

Subjective: Sensitivity analysis does not result in clear decision rules when trying to decide whether to 'accept' or 'reject' a project.

Restricted: Only one input is varied at a time.

Scenario analysis

As mentioned in the previous section the main disadvantage with sensitivity analysis is that it only considers the impact of a change in one input variable, whilst holding all others constant. Though informative, it is more likely that several variables will be impacted upon when there is, for example, a change in the economic climate. *Scenario analysis* involves changing a number of variables to provide a particular view. The most common type views presented are optimistic (best case), most likely and pessimistic (worse case) scenarios. The advantages and disadvantages of scenario analysis are now outlined.

Scenario analysis: advantage

Risk assessment: Management can get a broad sense of the impact of a down turn in the economy and conversely, an upturn.

Scenario analysis: disadvantages

Subjective: This method does not indicate the likelihood of each scenario occurring.

Restricted: It usually only presents three or four different outcomes.

Ease of choice: Though providing some indication of the vulnerability of a project, it does not provide a definite answer to the question of whether to invest in a project or not.

Continued

> *Wood and tree syndrome:* Sensitivity analysis highlights the most risky variables; in scenario analysis, the risks associated with critical variables might be masked by the overall approach.

Simulation analysis

Simulation analysis is performed using computer models. It is formally known as *'Monte Carlo Simulation'* and involves organising the variables and the influences on the variables into models and determining the various outcomes predicted for each variable, and the resultant influence of that on a project's NPV. The package runs many different scenarios, resulting in different NPVs. These are plotted to form an overall probability distribution, which can be used to determine the most likely outcomes and the risk associated with these outcomes for each project.

Though this technique is more sophisticated than scenario analysis and provides a wider range of potential overall outcomes, it is still subjective. The project appraisal manager still has to determine the probabilities of various variable changes in light of external influences and to model these into the program application. In addition, creating the initial model can be very time consuming and the relationships between variables may be difficult to model, particularly if variables are correlated or impact on existing project outcomes.

Certainty equivalent approach

The *certainty equivalent approach* technique alters variables to take account of risk. Cash flows are converted to *'risk less'* or *'certain equivalent values'*. This technique is regarded as subjective and does not provide as useful information in respect of risk, as can be obtained using sensitivity analysis or scenario analysis. The technique uses a *certainty equivalent coefficient* (Z) to translate expected cash flows to certain cash flows. Calculation of the certainty equivalent coefficient is outlined in the next example:

> **Worked example 14.3** (Certain equivalent cash flows)
>
> Junio plc is considering a project that has a one-year life. A cash inflow, estimated at €/£10,000, is expected at the end of year one.
> *Continued*

Junio plc has used a 15% discount rate for similar project appraisals in the past. The risk-free rate of return is currently 5%.

REQUIRED

a)   Calculate the certainty equivalent coefficient.
b)   How low can the actual cash flow fall before management are unhappy with the outcome?

Solution

a)   The present value of the project using the normal discount rate is: €/£8,695 (€/£10,000/1.15).

The certainty equivalent coefficient can then be calculated as: €/£8,695 ((Z×€/£10,000)/1.05).

Therefore, Z is: 0.91298 ((€/£8,695 (1.05))/€/£10,000).

b)   Therefore, management will be indifferent about the actual cash flow if it falls from €/£10,000 to €/£9,130 (€/£10,000 × 0.91298) as the project will return the same PV, were it to be discounted at the risk-free rate of return.

The previous approaches consider changes to the variables that underlie the calculation of a project's NPV. Another approach is to consider the possibility of the project having a series of different NPVs (probability theory approach). This technique is now outlined.

Probability theory approach

The *probability theory approach* calculates the *Expected Net Present Value (ENPV)* of the cash flows of a project, given a range of possibilities and their probable outcomes. This can be used to examine the risk associated with a project by determining the probability that the project will fail to generate a positive NPV. It can also be used to examine the worst case scenario and to determine the probability of that outcome. Statistics are used to provide an overall average or mean, or ENPV (Y in the following equation). All NPV outcomes are weighted by the probability of their occurrence. This calculation is denoted by the following formula:

$$Y = \sum_{i=1}^{n} p_i X_i$$

Where Y is the expected value of Event X, X_i is the outcome i from event X and p_i is the probability (p) of outcome i occurring and n is the number of possible outcomes. This process is shown in the next example:

Worked example 14.4   (Probability theory approach)

A manufacturing company is considering three new projects. The project appraisal team has investigated the projects and come up with a range of possible NPV outcomes and the probability of those outcomes occurring.

Project	Likelihood	NPV €/£'000
Project 1	Certain	4,400
Project 2	30% chance	(2,000)
	50% chance	7,000
	20% chance	8,000
Project 3	20% chance	25,000
	30% chance	16,000
	50% chance	(10,000)

REQUIRED

Which project should be selected if risk is ignored?

Continued

Solution

Project	Probability	NPV €/£'000	ENPV €/£'000
Project 1	1.000	4,400	4,400
Project 2	0.30	(2,000)	(600)
	0.50	7,000	3,500
	0.20	8,000	1,600
			4,500
Project 3	0.20	25,000	5,000
	0.30	16,000	4,800
	0.50	(10,000)	(5,000)
			4,800

When risk is ignored, the project with the highest ENPV should be accepted, which in this case is Project 3.

The standard deviation of the resultant ENPV can be calculated for each project and used as an indication of the risk of each project: the larger the standard deviation, the riskier the project. The standard deviation (σ) is a statistical measure of the dispersion of outcomes (NPVs) around the mean value (ENVP). It is calculated as the square root of the variance σ^2. The variance is calculated as follows:

$$\sigma^2 = (X_1 - Y)^2 p_1 + (X_2 - Y)^2 p_2 \cdots\cdots (X_n - Y)^2 p_n$$

Where $X_1 - Y$ is the variation of outcome one (X_1) from the mean value (Y). This is then squared, to remove the sign problem, and multiplied by the probability of that outcome occurring. The standard deviation is calculated to allow a meaningful interpretation of the variance. This process produces an outcome that is denominated in the same scale as the expected/mean value. For example, if the mean was €/£5 and the standard deviation was €/£2, this would mean that the average dispersal of all outcomes from the expected/mean value is €/£2. Therefore, most outcomes lie between €/£3 and €/£7. The smaller a standard deviation, the closer most values are to the mean, the more likely that the actual outcome will be close to the expected outcome, hence the less risky the project. The calculation of the standard deviation is provided in the following example.

Worked example 14.5   (Probability theory approach)

A manufacturing company is considering three new projects. The project appraisal team has investigated the projects and come up with a range of possible NPV outcomes and the probability of those outcomes occurring.

Project	Likelihood	NPV €/£'000
Project 1	Certain	4,400
Project 2	30% chance	(2,000)
	50% chance	7,000
	20% chance	8,000
Project 3	20% chance	25,000
	30% chance	16,000
	50% chance	(10,000)

REQUIRED

Calculate the standard deviation of the projects and recommend one project for investment, given that management are risk adverse.

Solution

Project	NPV (X) €/£'000	Proba-bility	Y €/£'000	X - Y €/£'000	$(X - Y)^2$ €/£'000	$P(X - Y)^2$ €/£'000
1	4,400	1.00	4,400	–	–	–
2	(2,000)	0.30	(600)	(6,500)	42,250,000	12,675,000
	7,000	0.50	3,500	2,500	6,250,000	3,125,000
	8,000	0.20	1,600	3,500	12,250,000	2,450,000
			4,500			18,250,000

Continued

$$\text{Standard deviation} = \sqrt{18,250,000,000} = \text{€/£4.272 million}$$

€/£'000		€/£'000	€/£'000	€/£'000	€/£'000
3	25,000	0.20	5,000	20,200	408,040,000	81,608,000
	16,000	0.30	4,800	11,200	125,440,000	37,632,000
	(10,000)	0.50	(5,000)	(14,800)	219,040,000	109,520,000
			4,800			228,760,000

$$\text{Standard deviation} = \sqrt{228,760,000,000} = \text{€/£15.125 millon}$$

The three projects offer expected returns of €/£4.4 million, €/£4.5 million and €/£4.8 million.

Project 3 offers the largest expected return, though it has the highest level of risk, with a standard deviation of €/£15.125 million. This deviation is very large, at three times the mean size. It is unlikely that management will find this project attractive.

Project 2 has the next largest mean value (€/£4.5 million) and reports a standard deviation of €/£4.272 million. Unlike the last project, there is a far greater chance of this project returning net cash inflows, as the standard deviation is smaller than the mean value, though it cannot be guaranteed that the project will not turn a net cash outflow of €/£2 million.

In Project 1, the expected cash inflow is certain and there is no risk involved. Though the expected value is €/£100,000 lower than that reported for Project 2, there is no risk, therefore it is recommended that management opt for this project.

Influences on the risk associated with an investment

Risk: strategic issues

When analysing a project, management cannot just rely on the financials; there are so many other influences that may impact on the success of a project. As mentioned earlier, a starting point in the process is to ensure that the project outcomes are congruent with the company's overall objectives. Management also have to consider the impact of the new project on the company. Will the new project have any impact on its current resources? Is there the expertise required for the new project? Will there be economies of scale/dis-economies of scale? Will the new project displace current sales?

Risk: foreign issues

Many companies try to diversify country risk by starting projects or investing in other countries. In addition to hedging themselves against losses that may result from a downturn in the local economy, a company can tap into cheaper resources in other countries. For example, many labour-intensive companies have opened or relocated branches in countries with low labour costs, for example China, Bangladesh or India. When a project is being considered for a foreign country, there are additional risks that need to be factored into the assessment; these risks are now briefly outlined.

Country risk

Country risk is the risk associated with a particular country. Factors that may heighten this risk include the policies of the local government in respect of foreign investment. Some governments encourage investment by providing grants or tax incentives; others have policies that are deemed to be discouraging. For example, they may place an additional tax on profits repatriated out of the country and in extreme instances may freeze bank accounts and/or expropriate assets. There are specialist agencies that advise on levels of country risk. In addition, there are a number of steps that can be taken to reduce these risks. A commonly used strategy is to form a joint venture with a local company or the government in the country being considered. Other steps include sourcing materials and labour from local companies and investing in the local communities by building schools, making donations and building hospitals.

Business environment risk

As well as country-specific risks, there are risks associated with trading in a different business environment. These risks are termed ***business environment risks***. These risks include cultural differences and common practices in trading deals. For example, in some countries, considerable offers of hospitality are part and parcel of normal business activity, whereas in other countries this is deemed to be unethical. In 2006 the media started to question the ethics of the British government during the Thatcher era, when it emerged that a large amount of hospitality expenditure was incurred when government officials were seeking a military sales order for aircraft from the Saudi Arabian military. This sort of expenditure is expected, and received, in transactions of such a nature in Saudi Arabia; however, it is deemed unethical within GB – hence the publicity. In addition to cultural and common practices being different, the law is also usually different. Expert advice is recommended at the planning stage of a project to determine the impact of legal and cultural differences. Consistent with country risk, business environment risk can be reduced by forging links with a local company or the government, or simply by taking on a local businessman as a director of the foreign investment. These sources will provide expert local knowledge.

Foreign exchange rate risk

Foreign exchange rate risk refers to the risk that the exchange rate in the future will be different to that used in the initial projections. A change in exchange rates will lead to a change in cash flows: a rise in the value of the currency of the foreign country will have a beneficial impact[1] (each unit of foreign currency will be converted to more euros/pounds – a strong dollar will mean that less is required to buy euros/pounds, for example €/£1 = $0.70), whereas a fall (each unit of foreign currency will be converted to less euros/pounds – a weak dollar will mean that more is required to buy euros/pounds, for example: €/£1 = $0.90) may alter the feasibility of a project. There are a number of techniques to manage currency exchange rate risk – for example, opening a bank account in a foreign country and using hedging products such as swap contracts, forward contracts and futures contracts.

Credit risk

There is additional exposure to credit risk when dealing with customers from other countries. This is discussed fully in chapter nine, 'Trade Receivables/Payables Management'.

---

[1] Assuming a net cash inflow situation.

Conclusion

Risk is inherent in cash flow prediction for any capital investment. Where this risk can be quantified, several techniques may be utilised to analyse the impact of the risk on the decision making outcome. Some of the techniques utilised are quite mathematical, iterative and time consuming and lend themselves well to being handled by a pre-modelled computer package. This should help to speed up the analysis stage of the overall investment decision making process. However, in all instances it should be remembered that computers only do what they are being told to do and the resultant NPV is still not risk free: the actual outcome is unlikely to be exactly as was expected. In all instances, capital appraisal projects should be subjected to a post-completion audit. A *post-completion audit* monitors and evaluates the actual project's cash flows, relative to the expected cash flows. This highlights deviations inciting corrective action, informs future investment appraisal decision making processes and provides an incentive for the preparers of the appraisal cash flows to strive for accuracy in their estimates.

A survey by Cranfield School of Management in 2003 on the effectiveness of the information technology investment appraisal process found that:

'the quality of information technology appraisal was poor, bureaucratic, inconsistent and greatly influenced by personal or political aspirations'.

The respondents regarded that the assessment of cash flows relating to project appraisal was also poor. This is a significant issue, as the approving board place great emphasis on the figures they are provided with (Financial times, 2005). The Cranfield study commented on the lack of overall vision recognised by each company that responded to their survey. Investment appraisal is the most important issue facing a company. Investment should be made into projects that achieve outcomes that are consistent with the overall company mission. Alkaraan and Northcott (2006), in a study of the use of both conventional financial analysis tools and more sophisticated risk adjusting approaches to the capital investment decision making within large UK manufacturing companies, found little evidence of integration between strategic approaches and financial approaches, with risk-adjusting analysis tools being rarely used in practice. The authors concluded that the 'sentiment' of directors seems to be that 'simple is best' and that analysis techniques should not replace intuition and judgement.

In large companies, a separate committee or board should be established to approve projects. It could include the head of the project appraisal team, representatives of customers who will be using the products resulting from the investment process, the finance director and a director who represents the strategic views of the overall board of directors. The latter's role should be to ensure that project outcomes are consistent with the company vision. This does not mean that innovation should be stifled, but that innovation should be consistent with the ongoing change that a company wishes to pursue.

Examination standard question

Worked example 14.6

a) Describe briefly some methods and techniques that can be used to analyse uncertainty and risk for assisting decision making.

6 Marks

b) MARTA plc has a cost of capital of 10%. The company is considering an investment with the following expected cash flows:

Year	Cash flow (€/£'000)	Discount factor (10%)	Present value (€/£'000)
0	(4,500)	1.000	(4,500)
1	3,500	0.909	3,181
2	2,500	0.826	2,065
3	2,500	0.751	1,877
	NPV		2,623

The project seems to be worthwhile. However, a certain amount of uncertainty exists in respect of the future cash flows. Management decide to reduce them to certainty equivalents by taking only 70%, 60% and 50% of the expected cash flows in years one, two, and three respectively.

Continued

REQUIRED

Advise MARTA plc on whether the project is worthwhile or not.

6 Marks

c)   What is the main disadvantage of this approach?

2 Marks

Solution

a)   Methods and techniques that can be used to analyse uncertainty and risk, which can be informative to a capital investment appraisal process, include the following:

(i)   Conservative estimates of cash inflows can be made. Outcomes will then be estimated in a conservative manner as a built-in safety factor is included. This is known as the *certainty equivalent approach*, wherein the cash flows are converted to certain equivalents. This method, though simple and quick, does not explicitly consider a range of possible outcomes, and hence is likely miss the most likely outcome, which may lead to incorrect decision making, with projects being rejected that might actually have increased company value.

(ii) *Sensitivity analysis:* This considers the influence of changes in one variable on the overall NPV of a project. It determines the percentage move possible in a variable before a project makes a negative NPV. This allows an analyser to identify the most risky variables, which may need extra management during the project, or may cause the project planners to consider a different source. A disadvantage of this approach is that it only considers the impact of movements in one variable, whereas external influences usually influence several variables – possibly in the same direction. This is considered by the next approach.

Continued

(iii) *Scenario analysis:* This involves assigning values to the project's variables, assuming different outcomes. The norm is to consider three possibilities. The first is the 'worst case' scenario. This involves, for example, determining the minimum number of units that might be sold at a low price (given the price elasticity of demand analysis) and determining the highest cost cash flows that might result. Then, the other extreme, the 'best case' scenario, is considered, wherein the cheapest costs are recorded and the highest expected demand (and price, given the demand) is determined. The third scenario to be considered is the 'most likely' outcome. This is the scenario that is given the most weight in the decision making process, with the other two examples being used to indicate the risk associated with the project. The further away from the most likely NPV the other two outcomes are, the more risky a project.

(iv) *Probability theory:* Management have to assess and assign probabilities to a range of possible outcomes. This involves determining the expected value of costs and benefits, given the probability of their occurrence and calculating the risk associated with a project, by calculating the standard deviation of the possible outcomes. A probability distribution of the possible outcomes can be plotted to give visual information on the risk associated with the project.

(v) Finally, information that would allow uncertain events/ or variables to be analysed using risk techniques, such as assigning probabilities to various outcomes in an objective manner, can be identified. The costs and benefits associated with obtaining this information should be considered to determine whether it is worthwhile seeking further information.

Continued

b)   The risk-adjusted NPV is as follows:

Year	Cash flow (€/£'000)	Discount factor (10%)	Present value (€/£'000)
0	(4,500)	1.000	(4,500)
1	2,450	0.909	2,227
2	1,500	0.826	1,239
3	1,250	0.751	939
		NPV	(95)

Using this approach, this project would be deemed too risky and would be rejected.

c)   The main disadvantage of the certainty equivalent approach is that the adjustment to each cash flow is determined subjectively, increasing the uncertainty within the decision making process.

KEY TERMS

Business environment risk
Certainty equivalent approach
Certainty equivalent coefficient
Certainty equivalent value
Country risk
Expected net present value (ENPV)
Expected net present value approach
Foreign exchange rate risk
Margin of safety
Monte Carlo simulation
Objective probabilities
Post-completion audit

Probability theory approach
Risk
Risk-adjusted discount rate
Risk premium
Subjective probabilities
Scenario analysis
Sensitivity analysis
Simulation analysis
Uncertainty

REVIEW QUESTIONS

1. Explain the difference between the term 'risk' and the term 'uncertainty'. Why are these two terms sometimes used interchangeably, even though they have different meanings?
2. Explain the term 'margin of safety' in the context of sensitivity analysis.
3. Why have information technology advances increased the use of simulation analysis in capital investment decision making?
4. Briefly suggest two steps that can be taken to reduce, or hedge, a company's exposure to country risk, when a capital project is being considered in a foreign country.
5. Explain the term 'foreign exchange risk'.
6. Perro plc is considering a project that is deemed to be risky. An initial investment of €/£200,000 will be followed by three years, with the following 'most likely' annual cash flows:

	€/£	€/£
Annual sales:		
(100,000 units × €/£4.20 per unit)		420,000
Annual costs		
Labour	210,000	
Materials	80,000	
Other direct costs	20,000	310,000
Net cash flows		110,000

The initial investment includes €/£150,000 for machines, that have a zero scrap value at the end of the three-year period, and €/£50,000 in working capital, which is recoverable in full at the end of the three-year period. The company's discount rate is 10%. Ignore inflation and taxation.

REQUIRED

a) Calculate the NPV of the *most likely* outcome from the project being considered.
b) State the break-even point and the percentage deviation from the *most likely* levels before break-even NPV is reached for each of the following variables: sales price, labour costs, material

costs and the discount rate (assuming all other variables remain constant).

c) Recalculate the NPV given the following information in respect of the best possible scenario and the worst case scenario.

	Best case scenario	Worst case scenario
Project cost	€/£200,000	€/£200,000
Project life	3 years	3 years
Discount rate	10%	13%
Sales volume	130,000	80,000
Sales price	€/£4.25	€/£3.80
Labour costs	€/£200,000	€/£230,000
Material costs	€/£76,000	€/£50,000
Other costs	€/£18,000	€/£22,000

CHALLENGING QUESTIONS

1.   BRAYSHAW plc

a)   Discuss TWO methods of adjusting for investment risk.

8 Marks

b)   BRAYSHAW plc is currently considering a project with the following cash flows:

	Year 0 €/£'000	Year 1 €/£'000	Year 2 €/£'000
Initial investment	(7,000)	–	–
Variable costs	–	(2,000)	(2,000)
Cash inflows			
(650,000 units at €/£10 per unit)		6,500	6,500
Net cash flows	(7,000)	4,500	4,500

The company's cost of capital is 8%.

REQUIRED

Calculate the margin of safety of the project with respect to changes in the following variables:

(i) Initial investment.
(ii) Sales volume.
(iii) Selling price.
(iv) Variable costs.
(v) Cost of capital.

14 Marks
Total 22 Marks
(ICAI, MABF II, Autumn 1998, Q5)

2.   RINGROSE Ltd.

RINGROSE Ltd. is a company that operates multi-storey car parks. The company's Head Office is in Dublin, but it operates car parks in various locations throughout Ireland.

The company is now considering the construction of a large car park adjacent to a new shopping centre, in a large town in the North West of Ireland. The car park will provide space for a maximum of 500 cars.

The Financial Accountant of the company has produced the following financial projections for the proposal. The figures are based on a life of five years:

Initial costs

Construction costs	€/£5 million
Other set-up costs	€/£1.5 million

Sales

It is estimated that the daily income from each car parking space will be €/£12 in year one, rising thereafter by 2% per annum.

It is estimated that the car park will be open for 300 days in the year and, on average, there will be 70% occupancy of the available spaces.

Costs

Variable and fixed costs of operating the car park are estimated to be €/£450,000 and €/£810,000 respectively in year one. Fixed costs include annual depreciation of €/£250,000 and overheads allocated from Head Office of €/£100,000.

Fixed and variable costs are expected to rise by 2.3% annually.

Capital allowances
Expenditure on the construction of multi-storey car parks that are developed in accordance with criteria laid down by government, attracts capital allowances at enhanced rates.

It is expected that the costs of constructing this car park, will attract an initial allowance of 50% and an annual allowance of 4% of cost thereafter.

Capital allowances on other capital outlays will be 15% per annum, on a straight-line basis.

Corporation tax
Corporation tax is expected to be 20% per annum for the foreseeable future. You may assume that corporation tax is paid in the year in which profits are earned.

Residual value
It is estimated that the car park could be sold for €/£10 million at the end of the five-year period.

Discount rate
The project is to be discounted at the company's current WACC of 12%.

Uncertainty
One of the equity holders of RINGROSE Ltd. has voiced concern over the projections. He considers that they are too optimistic given the national economic forecasts for the next five years. He is concerned that, if the economy goes into recession, it could have a serious effect on the profitability of the project.

REQUIRED

a)   Calculate, on the basis of the figures provided, the NPV of the proposed investment.

Make your recommendations, based on your calculations, as to whether or not RINGROSE Ltd. should proceed with the project.

12 Marks

b) In order to provide some comfort to the concerned equity holder, the Financial Accountant has decided to carry out some sensitivity analysis on the project. Assuming that none of the other inputs deviate from the estimates provided – calculate by how much each of the following inputs would need to change before the project would cease to become worthwhile.

(i) The discount rate.

(ii) The residual value.

Comment on your results

6 Marks

c) Outline TWO weaknesses in the sensitivity analysis approach to measuring risk.

_4 Marks
Total 22 Marks
(ICAI, MABF II, Autumn 2002)

3.   PROJECT X and PROJECT Y

A company is manufacturing a consumer product, the demand for which at current price levels is in excess of its ability to produce. The limiting factor on production is the capacity of a particular machine, which is now due for replacement.

The possibilities exist either of replacing it with a similar machine (Project X) or acquiring a more expensive machine with greater throughput capacity (Project Y). The pre-tax cash flows under each alternative have been estimated and are given below. The company's opportunity cost of capital is 10% after tax.

Tax is payable at the rate of 12.5% one year in arrears. Assume that tax is payable on all the cash inflows, but that capital allowances are available at a rate of 25% reducing balance per annum on the cost of either machine from the accounting period in which the machine is first put into use. There are currently, and will continue to be, sufficient surplus profits in the company to absorb any excess of capital allowances or balancing allowances that may arise. Whichever machine is purchased it will be put into use at the end of 2006. The Project X machine will be sold for €/£1,000 before the end of

December 2011, whereas the Project Y machine will have no sales value at the end of its useful life, and will be scrapped in early 2012.

The pertinent data is as follows:

Projected pre-tax cash flow	Project X €/£'000	Project Y €/£'000
2006 (cost of machine)	(27)	(40)
2007 (cash flows generated)	–	10
2008	5	14
2009	22	16
2010	14	17
2011	14	15

REQUIRED

a) Using the information above and taking into account tax information, calculate the following:

(i) Net present value.

8 Marks

(ii) Profitability index.

2 Marks

(iii) Discounted payback period.

2 Marks

b) Discuss the relevance of these calculations to the decision to be taken.

5 Marks

c) The variables used in calculating the cash inflows on Project X are as follows:

Year	Sales/production quantity Units	Production cost per unit €/£	Sales price per unit €/£
2007	9,000	1.5	1.5
2008	10,000	1.5	2
2009	40,000	1.45	2
2010	28,000	1.4	1.9
2011	28,000	1.4	1.9

The managing director has doubts about the accuracy of these estimates, and would like to concentrate his attention on that variable for which an error in estimating, would have the most significant effect on the DCF rate of return for the project as a whole.

Calculate, in respect of Project X only, the impact of each of the following (independently) on the total pre-tax undiscounted cash flows. In this part of the question, you may ignore taxation and capital allowances.

(i)   A 5% increase in the production cost per unit.
(ii)   A 5% decrease in the selling price of the product.

5 Marks
Total 22 Marks
(ICAI, MABF II, Autumn 2006, Q5)

CAPITAL STRUCTURE

15

Debt 10,000,000
Equity 15,000,000
Market Value 25,000,000

LEARNING OBJECTIVES

Upon completing this chapter, readers should be able to:

- Discuss the link between a company's capital structure, its WACC and company value;
- Discuss the link between gearing, financial risk and bankruptcy;
- Evaluate the traditional theory of capital structure;
- Evaluate Modigliani and Miller's theory of capital structure, with and without taxation;
- Discuss the assumptions and limitations of each theory;
- Calculate the cost of equity and the subsequent WACC under each theory;
- Use Modigliani and Miller's propositions to work out the value and cost of equity of similar companies that have different capital structures;
- Discuss the arbitrage process and use the arbitrage steps to evaluate whether an equity holder should sell shares in one company and buy shares in another similar company;
- Use the adjusted present value to evaluate an investment; and
- Discuss other issues deemed to impact on the level of gearing in a company's capital structure.

Introduction

One of the key financial decisions that a business finance manager has to be concerned with is how should a company finance its long-term investments.

A company's *capital structure* is the mixture of long-term debt and equity the company has used to finance its projects and operations. The value of a company is regarded as the market value of its capital structure, i.e. its debt and equity.

$$MV = D + E$$

Where MV is the total value of a company, D is the market value of its debt and E is the market value of its equity.

Debt is regarded as a cheaper form of finance than equity, hence would appear to be the best alternative; however, the level of gearing in a company's capital structure is argued to impact on the required return by existing equity and debt holders due to increased levels of financial risk. A financial manager has to strive to obtain the level of debt and equity that minimises a company's WACC, as this will maximise company value (this was discussed in chapter 12, 'Cost of Capital'). The capital structure that minimises the WACC is called the *optimum capital structure*.

Debt, gearing and financial risk

From a company's perspective the costs of issuing debt are usually less than the costs associated with issuing equity; moreover, the annual cost to a company is cheaper than debt's observed coupon/interest rate, as it is tax deductible. Therefore, so long as a company is profitable, the cost of debt is reduced by the rate of tax payable. Debt holders require a lower rate of return than equity holders because they face less risk. Debt holders have claim to a company's profits in front of equity holders, and in the event of a company winding up, they have to be settled before equity holders. Indeed, many trading debt instruments are secured on the assets of a company and may impose covenants on the actions of management.

Though there are benefits to having debt in a company's capital structure, there are practical limitations that can restrict the level of debt used.

Practical limitations on the level of debt used by a company

Management preferences: Management may prefer not to gear a company to high levels, due to the increased risk attached to borrowing. In addition, management like to keep a borrowing facility in reserve

Continued

so that when they do require finance, they do not have to justify their requirement to equity holders.

Industry norms: Industry norms impact on debt levels. The market usually reacts negatively to companies that veer away from industry norms.

Constitution: A company's articles of association may contain borrowing restrictions.

Covenants: Prior debenture trust deeds may have covenants that restrict further borrowing.

Security: Security for long-term debt may run out.

Financial risk: Lenders may feel a company has saturated its debt levels and are unwilling to provide more debt. Alternatively, to compensate for the increased risk of default, they may increase the cost of borrowing to the extent that it is no longer a viable alternative.

Liquidity: Liquidity levels also influence the ability of a company to source debt. Most debt finance has a compulsory fixed interest coupon that has to be paid yearly; in addition, the nominal value of debt capital has to be repaid on its maturity (sometimes with a premium). Floating-rate debt is sensitive to market interest rates and the capital element is usually repaid over the term of the debt.

When the proportion of long-term debt to equity capital reaches a certain level, the benefits (debt is cheaper and easier to obtain) are outweighed by the financial risk associated with holding debt. *Gearing* is the proportion of a company's capital structure financed by long-term debt and is calculated as follows:

$$\frac{D}{D+E}$$

Where D is the market value of debt (including preference shares) and E is the market value of equity.

In practice, many financial advisors and analysts use book values in their calculation. However, in finance theory, market values are substituted.

Worked example 15.1   (Gearing)

Bastante plc has 40,000 ordinary shares in issue. They are currently trading at €/£3.00 each. Bastante plc also has 400 debentures, trading at par.

REQUIRED

a)   Calculate the gearing ratio for Bastante plc.
b)   Explain the outcome.

Solution

a)   The market value of Bastante plc's equity is €/£120,000 (40,000 × €/£3.00).
      The market value of its debt is €/£40,000 (400 × €/£100). Therefore the gearing level is 25% (€/£40,000/(€/£40,000 + €/£120,000)).
b)   25% of Bastante plc is financed by debt; the remaining 75% is financed by equity. This is a low level of gearing for a plc.

The level of gearing provides an indication of the financial risks associated with investing in a company. Financial risk occurs because debt has a fixed yearly return that has to be paid, whereas the distribution to equity holders (dividends) can be waived when cash flows are insufficient. From equity holders' perspectives, debt has a fixed cost element: this is a constant drain on a company's liquidity and, beyond a certain point, may even lead to bankruptcy risks. Equity holders will regard companies with higher levels of gearing as being riskier due to the sensitivity of net income available. This risk is termed financial risk. *Financial risk* is the additional sensitivity in returns to equity holders that arise due to the level of debt in a company's financial structure. The impact of gearing to equity holders is highlighted in the following example.

Worked example 15.2   (Financial risk)

The directors of Atono plc were informed at a golf outing by fellow directors that it is more valuable to have debt in a company's capital structure than equity, as debt is cheaper than equity. Atono plc currently has no debt in its capital structure, though it is considering borrowing funds, which it will use to buy back the more expensive equity capital. The capital structure of Atono plc is as follows:

	Current €/£'000	Suggested €/£'000
Assets	10,000	10,000
Equity and reserves	10,000	5,000
Long-term debt	–	5,000
Total equity and liabilities	10,000	10,000
Shares outstanding	500,000	250,000

Additional information:
- The company's equity shares are currently trading at €/£20 each and it is assumed that this value does not change when the suggested capital structure change takes place.
- The long-term debt attracts an interest rate of 8%.
- Taxation is 30%.

REQUIRED

a) Calculate the gearing ratio for Atono plc under both scenarios.
b) Assume the company faces three differing external environment scenarios: boom, steady state and recession. Each scenario has different income potentials: if there is a boom economy, earnings before interest and taxation (EBIT) of €/£1 million are expected; if the economy stays steady, EBIT are expected to remain at €/£660,000; whereas if the economy goes into recession, EBIT are expected to fall to €/£450,000. Calculate the impact of the change in gearing on the *return on equity* and the *earnings per share* for each scenario.

Continued

Solution

a)   At the present time Atono plc has no debt, therefore its gearing ratio is zero. When Atono plc raises €/£5 million in debt capital to purchase back 50,000 shares at €/£20 each, the gearing ratio becomes €/£5m/(€/£5m+€/£5m)=50%.

b)   The impact of the economy on the *return on equity* and the *earnings per share* is evaluated, assuming capital structure does not change:

Current

	Recession	*Steady*	*Boom*
	€/£'000	*€/£'000*	*€/£'000*
EBIT	450	660	1,000
Interest	0	0	0
Taxation	(135)	(198)	(300)
Net income	315	462	700

Return on equity ratio	$\dfrac{€/£315,000}{€/£10,000,000}$	$\dfrac{€/£462,000}{€/£10,000,000}$	$\dfrac{€/£700,000}{€/£10,000,000}$
Return on equity	*3.15%*	*4.62%*	*7%*
Earnings per share ratio	$\dfrac{€/£315,000}{500,000}$	$\dfrac{€/£462,000}{500,000}$	$\dfrac{€/£700,000}{500,000}$
Earnings per share	*63c/p*	*92.4c/p*	*140c/p*

Suggested

	Recession	*Steady*	*Boom*
	€/£'000	*€/£'000*	*€/£'000*
EBIT	450	660	1,000
Interest	(400)	(400)	(400)
EBT	50	260	600
Taxation	(15)	(78)	(180)
Net income	35	182	420

Return on equity ratio	$\dfrac{€/£35,000}{€/£5,000,000}$	$\dfrac{€/£182,000}{€/£5,000,000}$	$\dfrac{€/£420,000}{€/£5,000,000}$
Return on equity	*0.7%*	*3.6%*	*8.4%*

Continued

Earnings per	€/£35,000	€/£182,000	€/£420,000
share ratio	250,000	250,000	250,000
Earnings per share	14c/p	72.8c/p	168c/p

The increased gearing has exposed equity holders to higher risk, as captured by the higher spread in the potential *return on equity* and the *earnings per share*.

The impact of gearing on equity holder return can be better assessed in light of the evidence from example 15.2. Under the three different scenarios the *return on equity* and the *earnings per share* are more variable, when there is debt in the capital structure. When a geared company makes lower EBIT, the return to equity holders is markedly lower compared to a similar ungeared company. Similarly, the return to equity holders is increased when a company performs well, at a larger margin relative to the return received by a similar ungeared company.

The impact of gearing on the cost of equity

The most debated topic in capital structure theory is the likely behaviour of equity holders in response to increased levels of gearing. Four outcomes are possible:

Increased gearing and the reactions of equity holders

Scenario 1: Changes in the capital structure will not impact on equity holders' required return.

Scenario 2: The required return by equity holders increases due to increased financial risk by an amount that exactly offsets the benefits derived from having more debt, a cheaper source of funds.

Scenario 3: The required return by equity holders increases due to increased financial risk, though by a smaller amount to that in the second scenario.

Scenario 4: The required return by equity holders increases due to increased financial risk by a larger amount to that in the second scenario.

Capital structure and the value of a company

The relationship between the cost of capital and the value of a company was explained in chapter 12, 'Cost of Capital'. In brief, the lower a company's cost of capital, the higher the value of a company (assuming earnings/cash flows remain constant).

$$\text{Market value of a company} = \frac{\text{Earnings}}{\text{WACC}}$$

Given this relationship, the impact of the four scenarios outlined above can be interpreted in light of the expected shift in company value. As previously explained, debt is a cheaper source of funds than equity. Therefore, in the first scenario (wherein the cost of equity does not change), when debt is introduced the overall WACC falls, resulting in an increase in company value. However, this first possibility is not considered realistic, as debt exposes equity holders to financial risk; in consequence, they require a higher return to compensate for it.

In the second scenario (wherein the cost of equity increases by an amount to exactly offset the reduction in the WACC, caused by having a greater proportion of cheaper debt), when debt is introduced the overall WACC remains unchanged, as does the market value of a company. In the third scenario (wherein the cost of equity increases by a smaller amount), when debt levels increase the overall WACC falls, resulting in an increase in company value. In the fourth scenario (wherein the cost of equity increases by a larger amount), when debt levels increase the overall WACC increases, resulting in a fall in company value.

Capital structure theories

Introduction
The latter three scenarios form the basis of two schools of thought on how changes in capital structure impact on both the WACC and the resulting market value of a company. The two schools of thought can be categorised as the *relevancy theory* (*traditional theory*) and the *Modigliani and Miller irrelevancy theory* on capital structure.

Relevancy theory (traditional theory)

The traditionalists consider that equity holders' behaviour changes from the third scenario, through the second scenario to the fourth scenario as the level of gearing increases. Indeed, they also argue that the premium required by debt holders also increases when financial risks exceed a certain point. The exact point differs between companies depending on their business risk and operating risks. Therefore to a certain level of gearing, additional debt is actually beneficial to a company and increases company value. The relationship is illustrated the following graph.

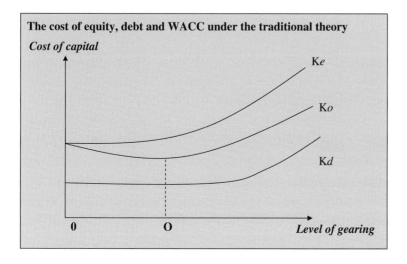

Where Ke is the cost of equity capital, Kd is the cost of debt capital and Ko is the WACC. At a certain level of gearing, point O, the WACC is minimised. Point O represents the **optimum capital structure**. At this level of gearing the value of a company is maximised. As is illustrated in the above graph, the traditionalists assume that the cost of debt (Kd) remains constant up to a certain level of gearing, beyond this, the financial risks associated with having more debt cause debt holders to require a premium for increased financial risk. When there are low levels of gearing, equity holders will require a small increase in their return; however, when gearing levels increase beyond a certain threshold, equity holders will command a much higher return to compensate them for increased financial risk. The impact of the behaviour of debt and equity holders on the WACC is to cause it to fall when there are low levels of gearing. However, beyond a certain threshold, (O), the premium required by equity holders, is greater than the benefit to be derived from obtaining cheaper debt capital. Moreover, at certain levels of gearing, this increase in the WACC will be accentuated by an increase in debt holders' required return. The expected behaviour of investors and the resultant impact on the WACC at increasing levels of gearing might be similar to that presented in example 15.3.

Worked example 15.3   (Traditional theory: changes in gearing)

The required return of debt and equity holders was recorded for a company as it increased its gearing levels.

Debt (%)	Required return (Kd) (%)	Equity (%)	Required return (Ke) (%)	WACC (Ko) (%)
0	5	100	15	15*
20	5	80	16	?
40	5	60	18	?
60	10	40	23	?
80	15	20	35	?

*0%(5%)+100%(15%)=15%

REQUIRED

Assume the traditional theory on capital structure is relevant. Complete the table and identify which capital structure is most beneficial for this company.

Solution

As the traditional theory on capital structure is relevant, it is assumed that the cost of equity is at its equilibrium level for each gearing level.

Debt (%)	Required return (Kd) (%)	Equity (%)	Required return (Ke) (%)	WACC (Ko) (%)
0	5	100	15	15*
20	5	80	16	13.8^1
40	5	60	18	12.8^2
60	10	40	23	15.2^3
80	15	20	35	19^4

1. 20%(5%)+80%(16%)
2. 40%(5%)+60%(18%)
3. 60%(10%)+40%(23%)
4. 80%(15%)+20%(35%)

The optimum gearing level is to hold 40% debt and 60% equity, as this results in the lowest WACC value (12.8%).

In example 15.3, debt holders require a constant return (5%) until debt reaches a certain level of gearing (60% in this instance); at this stage, their required return has increased to 10% and increases further as the company becomes more geared. Equity has a higher cost than debt at all levels of gearing, though the increases in the required return are marginal until gearing reaches 60%, when the required return increases by large amounts due to financial risk.

The result of the behaviour of both debt and equity holders to increases in financial risk is that, to a certain level of gearing (in this case 40%), more debt is actually beneficial to company. The cost savings from obtaining a cheaper source of capital (debt at 5%), outweighs the increased return required by equity holders (increases from 15% to 18% – for a shift in gearing from 0% to 40%); the consequence of this is a fall in the WACC from 15% to 12.8%. This will increase company value. Any increases in gearing beyond this level are damaging to company value.

Worked example 15.4   (Traditional theory)

Calor plc is partly financed by equity (cost 19%) and partly financed by debt (cost 12%). Its current WACC is 16.5%. The company pays all its profits as dividends. These amount to €/£3.8 million each year. The company wishes to invest in a new project, which would return €/£1.12 million each year before interest charges. This project would cost €/£6 million and will be financed using debt capital, which can be obtained at 12%. As a result of the increased financial risks the cost of equity is expected to increase to 20%. (Taxation is to be ignored.)

REQUIRED

Assuming a traditional perspective:
a)   Show the impact on the value of equity of Calor plc undertaking the project.
b)   Analyse the change in the value of Calor plc's equity into returns expected from the new project (i.e. its NPV) and the resultant change in capital structure.

Continued

Solution

a)   The current market value of equity can be calculated using the dividend valuation model. As all earnings are paid out in dividends, there is no growth. The current dividend is €/£3.8 million and the required return by the equity holders is 19%. Therefore the current market value of equity is:

$$P_0 = \frac{D_1}{Ke}$$

$$= \frac{€/£3,800,000}{0.19}$$

$$= €/£20,000,000$$

The new market value can be ascertained in the same manner. The first step is to calculate the new dividend.

	€/£'000
Current dividend	3,800
Additional dividend:	
(€/£1,120,000 − (€/£6,000,000 × 12%)	400
New dividend	4,200

The market value of equity is expected to increase from €/£20,000,000 to:

$$\frac{€/£4,200,000}{0.20} = €/£21,000,000$$

b)   The project is evaluated at the original WACC to determine what the NPV would have been had the capital structure not changed. The difference between the project's NPV and the €/£1,000,000 gain is the change in the value of equity that is attributable to the change in capital structure.

Continued

The NPV of the project is:

$$\frac{€/£1,120,000}{0.165} = €/£6,787,878 - €6,000,000 = €/£787,878$$

Therefore the remaining increase in equity value, €/£212,122 (€/£1,000,000 − €/£787,878), is due to the inclusion of additional debt. It must reduce the WACC; hence, increase company value.

Modigliani and Miller theory (M&M theory)

Franco Modigliani and Merton Miller, two Nobel laureates, formulated their capital structure theory in 1958. They argued that, in a simplified world where the assumptions hold true (listed on the next page), the value of a company will not be influenced by its capital structure. The reasoning for this is that equity holders will require a premium on their return equating to the amount that keeps the WACC constant. Therefore, a company's capital structure is irrelevant, as changes to it do not impact on its WACC, which remains constant. As the WACC remains constant, capital structure does not influence company value. It is for this reason that M&M's theory is sometimes referred to as the *irrelevancy theory*. M&M argue that market value is solely determined by the quality of a company's past investment record, which is evidenced by its operating profits/cash flows, before distributions to stakeholders. Due to this view, it is also sometimes referred to as the *net operating income theory*.

The assumed behaviour of debt and equity holders is illustrated in the following graph. The cost of debt (Kd) remains constant regardless of the level of gearing. The cost of equity (Ke) rises in such a manner as to keep the WACC (Ko) constant. (See example 15.8 for changes in the required returns of debt and equity holders as gearing increases.)

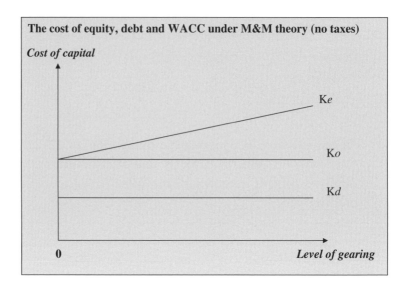

The cost of equity, debt and WACC under M&M theory (no taxes)

Cost of capital

Ke

Ko

Kd

0

Level of gearing

Assumptions

To examine the impact of changes in capital structure, M&M assume certain restrictions to the operating and business environment of a company. These are summarised as follows:

Assumptions underlying M&M capital structure theory

Growth: There is no growth, as companies pay out all their earnings in dividends. Therefore earnings are constant and equity holders' expectations regarding future earnings are constant.

Business risk: Business risk is constant. Where a company raises capital for investment, it is assumed that the investment is into similar projects that do not alter the company's risk profile. When comparing two similar companies, it can be assumed that they have identical business risks.

No transaction costs/or delay: The capital structure of a company can be changed quickly, i.e. debt securities can be redeemed by the proceeds of an equity issue and vice versa. This process does not involve any costs, i.e. no issue costs.

Continued

Perfect capital markets: The capital markets are perfect. There is no information asymmetry or insider trading and market participants act rationally.

Individuals are similar to companies: Individuals can borrow funds at the same rate as companies and are happy with similar levels of gearing.

Taxation and bankruptcy: At the earlier phase of the theoretical debate on capital structure, taxation and bankruptcy risks were ignored.

As the relationships between the cost of debt, the cost of equity, the WACC and their required return is linear, M&M theory has been formulated into three propositions. The first proposition considers the relationship between company value and gearing levels; the second captures the change in return required by equity holders as a company becomes more geared; and the third considers the change in the investment appraisal discount rate to use for investment appraisal (i.e. the WACC), as a company becomes more geared. These propositions are now discussed assuming a world with no tax.

Proposition I (Company value – no taxation)
M&M's proposition I states that capital structure is irrelevant to the value of a company; therefore, the value of a geared company (Vg) is the same as the value of a *similar* ungeared company (Vu).

$$Vg = Vu$$

The value of a geared company is the market value of its equity and debt (Vg = D + E). The value of an ungeared company will be the market value of its equity.

Worked example 15.5   (M&M proposition I)

Blanco plc is similar in every respect to Negro plc, except that it is financed by equity only. It has one million ordinary shares that are currently trading at €/£1.00 each (their equilibrium share price). Negro plc has 5,000 debentures trading at par and 250,000 ordinary shares. These are currently trading at €/£1.80. The finance manager of Negro plc does not think that the market is aware of the value of Negro plc's recent projects. He has been reliably informed that Negro plc's debt capital is at its equilibrium value. An investor, Azul, has approached you seeking advice on whether or not to purchase shares in Negro plc.

REQUIRED

Advise Azul as to whether he should purchase shares in Negro plc. Assume M&M theory applies, with no taxes.

Solution

As both companies are the same, M&M argue that they should have the same value.

At present Blanco plc (Vu) is valued by the market at: €/£1,000,000 (1,000,000 × €/£1.00).

Negro plc is valued at the market value of its debt: €/£500,000 (5,000 × €/£100), plus its equity: €/£450,000 (250,000 × €/£1.80).

Therefore, the market value is: €/£950,000 (€/£500,000 + €/£450,000)

Under M&M proposition I, Negro plc's equity is undervalued by: €/£50,000 (€/£1,000,000 − €/£950,000).

As the market value of Negro plc's debt is in equilibrium, as is the market value of Blanco plc's equity, then the difference in market value between the companies must be due to mispricing in Negro plc's equity shares. They must be undervalued by €/£50,000.

Therefore, Azul would be advised to purchase shares in Negro plc as a speculative gain of 20c/p per share (€/£50,000/250,000) can be achieved.

Arbitrage

In example 15.5, the shares of one of the two companies (Blanco plc and Negro plc) are regarded as being mispriced under M&M's theory. A key assumption underpinning their theory is that equity price differences between two similar companies that have different capital structures are short term, and that a process of arbitrage will ensue until an equilibrium price is achieved. The ***arbitrage process*** is the cumulative action of equity investors selling and purchasing shares in mispriced, similar companies across markets, until equilibrium prices are reached. At this point, the earnings and WACC of the similar companies will be the same. Investors will compare the return they are receiving from the company they hold equity shares in, to the return they could receive from the other company (with a different capital structure).

If, for example, an investor is investing in a geared company and he considers that he could earn a higher return in a similar ungeared company, then it is assumed that he will act rationally and sell his portion of the geared company, gear himself to the same level as the geared company using personal borrowings, and purchase a greater number of shares (greater proportion) in the ungeared company; hence earning a higher return (see example 15.6). For arbitrage to work successfully it is assumed: that capital markets are perfect (i.e. there are no transaction costs, no information asymmetry and investors act rationally); that companies can be categorised as being similar in all respects, except for capital structure; and that individuals are indifferent about corporate and personal borrowing.

Worked example 15.6   (M&M arbitrage)

EXE plc and WYE plc are two companies in the engineering industry. Both companies have identical business risk but are financed by different capital structures, which are summarised below:

EXE plc

	€/£'000
Equity shares (€/£0.25 par value)....	20,000
Share premium account...................	45,000
Retained earnings	36,500
Equity holders' funds.......................	101,500

Continued

The equity shares are currently trading at €/£1.40. This is considered to be their equilibrium price.

WYE plc

	€/£'000
Equity shares (€/£1.00 par value)....	25,000
Share premium account..................	8,000
Retained earnings	44,000
Equity holders' funds......................	77,000
12% debentures (newly issued)........	25,000
	102,000

The equity shares are currently trading at €/£4.00 and the debentures at €/£100.

Each company has annual earnings of €/£25 million before interest (assume a world with no taxes).

REQUIRED

a) An investor currently owns 4% of the ordinary shares of WYE plc. Explain how that investor may take action to improve his financial position.

6 Marks

b) Calculate the amount of the potential improvement in the investor's financial position if he follows the course of action suggested in part a).

6 Marks

c) Critically evaluate the assumptions upon which the arbitrage process is based.

3 Marks

(ICAI, MABF II, Summer 1996, Q5)

Solution

a) Despite having different capital structures, EXE plc and WYE plc should have the same market value.

Continued

Market value of EXE plc (Ungeared)

20,000,000/0.25=80 million ordinary shares of €/£0.25 par value

Share price   =€/£1.40

Market value of equity (Vu) is: €/£112,000,000 (80 million × €/£1.40)

Market value of WYE plc (Geared)

Equity: (25,000,000 × €/£4.00)	€/£100,000,000
Debt: (25,000,000/100 × €/£100)	€/£25,000,000
Total market value (Vg)	€/£125,000,000

M&M state that: Vg=Vu

Therefore, WYE plc is overvalued, as EXE plc and WYE plc should have the same valuation and EXE plc's shares are at their equilibrium value.

An investor in WYE plc can improve his financial position by:

1. Selling his shares in WYE plc, i.e. 4% of 25m=1,000,000 shares for €/£4 each, realising €/£4,000,000.
   Then, gearing himself to achieve the same gearing level he was exposed to when investing in WYE plc (WYE plc has a debt/equity ratio of €/£25m/€/£100m or 25%), so he borrows an equivalent amount to leave himself with a debt/equity ratio of 25%, i.e. €/£1,000,000 (25% of €/£4,000,000).

2. With this cash in hand, €/£5,000,000 (€/£4,000,000 + €/£1,000,000), he can invest the total proceeds in EXE plc, whose shares currently cost €/£1.40, so he can buy 3,571,429 (€/£5,000,000/€/£1.40) shares, or 4.4643% (€/£5,000,000/€/£112,000,000) of EXE plc's equity. By taking these steps, he hopes to increase his income.

Continued

b) Increase in income is calculated as follows:
Investor income is dividend paid by the companies (all earnings are paid out as dividends, so there is no capital growth). This is calculated as follows:

Dividend calculation	WYE plc €/£'000	EXE plc €/£'000
Earnings before interest and tax	25,000	25,000
Less: interest on debentures	(3,000)	–
Available for dividend	22,000	25,000

Investor's income	Holding 4%	Holding 4.4643%
Before: (4% × €/£22,000,000)	880,000	
After: (4.4643% × €/£25,000,000)		1,116,075
Less: interest on personal debt:		
(12% × €/£1,000,000*)		120,000
Net income for the investor	880,000	996,075

*M&M assume that equity holders can obtain debt funding at the same rate as is available to companies.

So, by switching from the overvalued to the undervalued company, an investor can increase his income by €/£116,075 (€/£996,075 − €/£880,000).

c) Assumptions upon which arbitrage is based:
Personal gearing is equivalent to corporate gearing, which implies:

- Individuals can borrow at the same rate as companies and are happy to borrow to the same gearing levels as the companies they invest in.
- Individuals have limited liability.
- Individuals have the same tax shields as corporate enterprises.

Continued

Critical appraisal of these assumptions:

Individuals cannot borrow at the same rate as companies; banks issue loans using the base rate as a benchmark and add premiums to it for different classes of borrowers. Individuals do not have unlimited liability. Therefore, individuals have higher borrowing costs than companies. In addition, individuals are not happy to take on personal debt to the same levels as is held by companies they invest in. Personal debt has greater financial risk implications for an investor. These imperfections limit the arbitrage process; however, this does not destroy the essential message of the M&M argument – an arbitrage mechanism can exist. Whether it works fully depends on the degree of market imperfection.

Proposition II (Cost of equity, without taxation)
M&M proposition II describes the behaviour of equity holders when the capital structure of a company changes. M&M proposition II assumes that a company's cost of equity has a positive linear relationship to gearing levels and that equity holders will require a premium to compensate them for any additional financial risk faced. The linear relationship is represented by the following formula:

$$Keg = Keu + \frac{D}{E}(Keu - Kd)$$

Where Keg is the cost of equity in a geared company, Keu is the cost of equity in an ungeared company, Kd is the cost of debt, D is the market value of debt and E is the market value of equity in a geared company.

This formula shows that the expected cost of equity in a geared company is equal to the expected cost of equity in a similar but ungeared company, plus a premium for financial risk. The latter part of the formula is the premium. In all eventualities:

$$Keg > Keu$$

The relationship between the cost of equity, the cost of debt and the WACC is highlighted in examples 15.7 and 15.8.

Worked example 15.7   (M&M proposition II)

The WACC of Rojo plc, a geared company, is 20% and the cost of its debt, is 6%. Debt amounts to 50% of Rojo plc's capital structure. Verde plc is similar in every aspect, except it is financed totally by equity shares. There are no taxes.

REQUIRED

a)   Assuming M&M theory, calculate the cost of equity required by the equity holders of Rojo plc and Verde plc.

b)   What is Verde plc's expected WACC?

Solution

a)   There are two approaches to working out the cost of equity (Ke) in Rojo plc. The first uses the WACC model:

$$20\% = \frac{50\%(Ke)}{100\%} + \frac{50\%(6\%)}{100\%}$$

$$20\% = 0.5Ke + 3\%$$

$$17\% = 0.5Ke$$

$$34\% = Ke$$

The second uses M&M's proposition II formula, by which the cost of equity in Rojo plc (Keg) can be estimated.

$$Keg = 20\% + \frac{50\%}{50\%}(20\% - 6\%)$$

$$Keg = 34\%$$

b)   Under proposition III (see below), M&M argue that the WACC of a geared company is the same as the WACC of a similar ungeared company. In an ungeared company the WACC is its Keu.

Therefore, the WACC and cost of equity in Verde plc is 20%.

Proposition III (WACC, without taxation)

The third proposition is related to the first proposition. *M&M proposition III* suggests that the WACC of a geared company is the same as the WACC of an ungeared company.

$$WACCg = WACCu$$

Therefore, the cost of equity in an ungeared company can be used to discount capital appraisal projects in a similar geared company. All investments, or projects undertaken by a company, should have a return equal to or exceeding its WACC. As the WACC is unaffected by capital structure, it can be the cost of equity of a similar ungeared company.

Worked example 15.8   (M&M proposition II)

A company is ungeared and has a cost of equity of 15%. The following table highlights the expected return required by debt holders (under M&M theory), were the company to alter its capital structure and become more geared.

Debt value (%)	Required return (Kd) (%)	Equity value (%)	Required return (Ke) (%)	WACC (Ko) (%)
0	10	100	15	15
20	10	80	?	?
40	10	60	?	?
60	10	40	?	?
80	10	20	?	?

REQUIRED

a)   Complete the table and identify which capital structure is most beneficial for the company (assuming M&M theory, without taxation).

b)   Explain the behaviour of the equity holders (assuming M&M theory, without taxation).

Continued

Solution

a)

Debt value (%)	Required return (Kd) (%)	Equity value (%)	Required return (Ke) (%)	WACC (Ko) (%)
0	10	100	15.00	15
20	10	80	16.251	15*
40	10	60	18.332	15*
60	10	40	22.503	15*
80	10	20	35.004	15*

*Under M&M theory the WACC of a company does not change regardless of changes in capital structure. Therefore, when debt is introduced, the WACC remains at 15%.

There are two approaches to working out the required return on equity. The first is to use the WACC formula and work back (assume no tax).

$$WACC = \frac{K(Ke)}{(D+E)} + \frac{D(Kd)}{(D+E)}$$

1. $$15\% = \frac{80\%(Ke)}{100\%} + \frac{20\%(10\%)}{100\%}$$

$$15\% - 2\% = 0.8\,(Ke)$$

$$16.25\% = Ke$$

Or, M&M proposition II formula could be used, where Keu is the cost of equity when the company was not geared (15%), the market value of debt (D) equates to 20%, the market value of equity (E) is 80% and the cost of debt (Kd) is 10%.

1. $$Keg = 15\% + \frac{20\%}{80\%}(15\% - 10\%)$$
$$Keg = 16.25\%$$

2. $$Keg = 15\% + \frac{40\%}{60\%}(15\% - 10\%)$$
$$Keg = 18.33\%$$

Continued

$$3. \quad Keg = 15\% + \frac{60\%}{40\%}(15\% - 10\%)$$

$$Keg = 22.50\%$$

$$4. \quad Keg = 15\% + \frac{80\%}{20\%}(15\% - 10\%)$$

$$Keg = 35.00\%$$

b)   Equity holders require an additional return to compensate them for additional financial risk, which is sufficient to keep the overall WACC constant. Therefore at very high levels of gearing, say 80%, their required return has increased from 15%, when the company was ungeared, to 35%.

Limitations of the M&M theory on capital structure

As with all theories, the underlying assumptions are its main weakness. In the case of the M&M irrelevancy theory, the assumptions are considered to be unrealistic. For instance: capital markets are not perfect (for example, there are issue costs with every transaction); individuals do face different financial risks compared to companies and their costs of borrowing are usually higher; it is almost impossible to find two companies that are exactly the same, except for their capital structures; most companies retain earnings each year for investment; and investors do not act rationally. The two most-criticised assumptions of M&M's earliest theory was that tax should not be ignored, as the effect of taxation makes debt cheaper, which directly impacts on a company's WACC and market value. The second is that gearing levels beyond a certain point do impact on returns required by debt holders, particularly as a company reaches bankruptcy levels. In 1963, M&M adjusted their theory to take account of tax. These amended views are now presented.

M&M theory (with taxation)

Interest on debt is tax deductible, whereas dividend distributions are not. This makes the cost of debt to a company cheaper than the coupon rate or cash flow that is paid, so long as a company is profitable. For example, in a profitable company that pays interest at 8% and tax at 50% (assume the debt is trading at par), the net cost of debt to the company will actually be 4% (8%(1 − 0.50)). M&M argue that the behaviour of equity and debt holders will be as in the model without tax, except the cost of debt is lower. The impact of this is that as gearing increases, the premium required by equity holders reduces, and the WACC reduces, by the impact of the tax benefit gained. The relationship between the cost of equity, debt and the WACC is illustrated in the next graph.

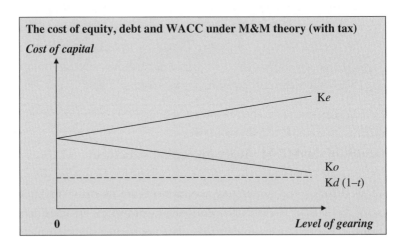

After relaxing this assumption, M&M's theory would suggest that companies should aim to increase their gearing levels and that the optimum capital structure is now 100% debt, as the WACC falls when debt levels increase. However, in the real world this would not be recommended. Debt has another consequence, in that failure to meet debt obligations as they fall due will eventually result in bankruptcy. This is likely to occur when gearing levels are very high. This section of the chapter considers the impact of taxation on M&M's two propositions. It is considered that the propositions have merit to a certain level of gearing, beyond this, the risk of bankruptcy becomes so great as to make the assumptions totally unrealistic.

Proposition I (revisited with taxation)

An example is used to explain the impact of tax on the value of a company. The example considers two identical companies: Gris plc, an all-equity company, and Blanco plc, a geared company.

Worked example 15.9   (M&M proposition I, with taxation)

Gris plc, an all-equity company, and Blanco plc, a geared company, earn €/£2,000,000 each year from their operations. Blanco plc holds €/£1,000,000 (10%) bonds. The current rate of tax is 40%.

REQUIRED

What is the difference in value between Gris plc and Blanco plc? Assume M&M capital structure theory with taxes.

Solution

The market value of either company is not known. However, the earnings are. Under M&M theory, companies are valued at the present value of their cash flows from earnings (discounted at the WACC). Therefore, the difference in their value will be the difference in their cash flows. (It is assumed that the operating earnings equate to cash flows, i.e. no depreciation, accruals, etc.)

	Gris plc (Ungeared) €/£'000	Blanco plc (Geared) €/£'000
Earnings	2,000	2,000
Interest	–	100
Earnings before tax	2,000	1,900
Taxation (40%)	800	760
Net income/dividend	1,200	1,140

The cash flows for distribution to financiers, who are both debt and equity holders, are operating earnings less taxation:

	€/£'000	€/£'000
Earnings	2,000	2,000
Taxation	800	760
Net cash for distribution	1,200	1,240

Continued

This €/£1,200,000 goes to the equity holders of Gris plc. In Blanco plc €/£100,000 is distributed to the debt holders, with the remainder, €/£1,140,000 (€/£1,240,000−€/£100,000), going to the equity holders.

The difference in the total net distribution represents the difference in the value of the two companies. Blanco plc is worth more as its total net cash flows are higher (€/£1,240,000) compared to €/£1,200,000 by Gris plc. The difference between the two companies' net cash flows is the difference in the tax paid by the companies.

The difference in the market value between the two companies is the present value of this tax saving discounted at the cost of debt, assuming it will be received in perpetuity:

$$\frac{€/£40,000}{0.1} = €/£400,000$$

This is the total tax saving expected and amounts to the value of the debt (D) by the tax rate (t), Dt:

$$€/£1,000,000 \times 40\% = €/£400,000$$

Therefore, the difference between an ungeared company (Vu) and a similar geared company (Vg) is the present value of the tax saving on the interest differential. This is known as the *interest tax shield* and is calculated as Dt, where D is the market value of debt and t is the tax rate. Proposition I (with taxes) becomes:

$$Vg = Vu + Dt$$

Therefore, a geared company will always be valued higher than a similar ungeared company.

Worked example 15.10   (Example 15.5 revisited with taxation)

Blanco plc is similar in every respect to Negro plc, except it is financed by equity only. It has one million ordinary shares currently trading
Continued

at €/£1.80 each (equilibrium value). Negro plc has 5,000 debentures trading at par and 250,000 equity shares. These are currently trading at €/£1.80. The finance manager of Negro plc does not think the market is aware of the value of Negro plc's recent projects. He has been reliably informed that Negro plc's debt capital is at its equilibrium value. An investor, Azul, has approached you seeking advice on whether or not to purchase shares in Negro plc.

REQUIRED

Advise Azul as to whether he should purchase shares in Negro plc. Assume M&M theory with taxes and the tax rate is 30%.

Solution

As both companies are the same, M&M argue that the only difference in the market value of each company is the interest tax shield (Dt).

At present Blanco plc (Vu) is valued by the market at €/£1,000,000.

Negro plc is valued at the market value of its debt plus its equity, which is €/£950,000 (€/£500,000+€/£450,000).

Under M&M proposition I the equity of Negro plc should be:

$$Vg = Vu + Dt$$
$$Vg = €/£1,000,000 + €/£500,000(30\%)$$
$$Vg = €/£1,150,000$$

As €/£1,150,000 is the value of Negro plc's debt and equity combined, and given that the debt is at its equilibrium value, then Negro plc's equity is undervalued by €/£200,000 (€/£1,150,000 − €/£950,000).

Per M&M proposition I, Negro plc's equity should be €/£650,000 (€/£1,150,000 − €/£500,000); it is currently trading at €/£450,000.

Azul would be advised to purchase the shares in Negro plc as a speculative gain of 80c/p per share (€/£200,000/250,000) can be achieved.

Arbitrage (revisited with taxation)

Worked example 15.11   (Example 15.6 revisited)

EXE plc and WYE plc are two companies in the engineering industry. Both companies have identical business risk but are financed by different capital structures, which are summarised below:

EXE plc

	€/£'000
Equity shares (€/£0.25 par value)	20,000
Share premium account..	45,000
Retained earnings...	36,500
Equity holders' funds...	101,500

The equity shares are currently trading at €/£1.40. This is considered to be the equilibrium price.

WYE plc

	€/£'000
Equity shares (€/£1.00 par value)	25,000
Share premium account..	8,000
Retained earnings...	44,000
Equity holders' funds...	77,000
12% debentures (newly issued)	25,000
	102,000

The equity shares are currently trading at €/£4.00 and the debentures at €/£100.

Each company has annual earnings of €/£25 million before interest and tax and pays corporation tax at 35%.

REQUIRED

a)   An investor currently owns 4% of the ordinary shares of WYE plc. Explain how that investor may take action to improve his financial position.

6 Marks

Continued

b) Calculate the amount of the potential improvement in the investor's financial position if he follows the course of action suggested in part a).

6 Marks
(ICAI, MABF II, Summer 1996, Q5)

Solution

a) The current market value of each company has not changed (see example 15.6). In the presence of taxation, M&M argue that the value of a geared company will always be greater than an ungeared company, but only by the value of the tax savings of the geared company.

> Vg = Vu + PV of tax shield (Dt)
> Vg = Value of geared company
> Vu = Value of ungeared company

If we assume that the value of the ungeared company (EXE plc) is correct, then the actual market value of the geared company (WYE plc) should be higher by the amount of the tax savings. It the actual market value of WYE plc is not the same as this, then it has been incorrectly valued by the market; hence, its equity holders would exercise arbitrage until the equilibrium price is reached.

	€/£'000
Market value of EXE plc (Vu):	
(80m shares × €/£1.40)	112,000
Tax savings of WYE plc (Dt): (€/£25m × 0.35)*	8,750
Market value of WYE plc,	
as per above formula (Vg)	120,750
Actual market value of WYE plc,	
as computed before	125,000

Using the above formula, the market value of WYE plc should be €/£120,750,000. However, the actual market value is €/£125,000,000.

Continued

Therefore, WYE plc is overvalued by €/£4,250,000 (€/£125,000,000 − €/£120,750,000). As the value of debt is in equilibrium, equity must be overvalued by this amount. Equity value should be €/£95,750,000 (€/£100,000,000 − €/£4,250,000).

The annual tax saving is €/£1,050,000 (€/£25,000,000 × 12% × 35%).
The value of the tax savings in perpetuity is €/£8,750,000 (€/£1,050,000/12%).

An investor in WYE plc can improve his financial position by:

1. Selling his shares in WYE plc for €/£4 each, realising €/£4,000,000 (€/£4 × 1,000,000 shares).
2. Gearing himself to achieve the same gearing as WYE plc, (debt/equity ratio of €/£25m/€/£100m or 25%). He borrows €/£1,000,000, as before. However, this is reduced for tax relief, so he need only borrow €/£650,000 (€/£1,000,000 × (1 − 0.35).
3. With this cash in hand, €/£4,650,000, he can invest the total proceeds in EXE plc, whose shares currently cost €/£1.40, so he can buy 3,321,428.60 (€/£4,650,000/€/£1.40) shares, or 4.1518% (€/£4,650,000 /€/£112,000,000) of EXE plc's equity.

b) The increase in income is calculated as follows:
The dividend distributed to equity holders (after tax) changes to:

	WYE plc €/£'000	EXE plc €/£'000
Earnings before interest and tax	25,000	25,000
Less: interest on debentures	(3,000)	–
Earnings after interest	22,000	25,000
Less: corporation tax @ 35%	(7,700)	(8,750)
Available for dividend	14,300	16,250

Continued

Investor's income:	Holding 4%	Holding 4.1518%
Before: 4%×€/£14,300,000	572,000	
After: 4.1518%×€/£16,250,000		674,668
Less: interest on personal debt:		
12%×€/£650,000		78,000
Net income for the investor	572,000	596,668

So, by switching from the overvalued to the undervalued company, an investor can increase his income by €/£24,668 (€/£596,668 − €/£572,000).

Proposition II (revisited with taxation)

M&M argue that when tax is taken into account, equity holders behave in a similar manner as when it was assumed there was no tax; however, they recognise the benefit of having debt in the capital structure. The tax deduction reduces the risk associated with having debt. Therefore the risk premium required is reduced by $(1-t)$. A linear relationship is assumed as before:

$$Keg = Keu + \frac{D}{E}(Keu - Kd)(1-t)$$

Proposition III (revisited with taxation)

The market value of a geared company is always larger than the market value of a similar ungeared company. As such, the WACC of a geared company is always smaller than the WACC of an ungeared company. The difference is related to the difference in their market value and is represented by the following formula:

$$WACCg = WACCu \times \frac{Vu}{Vg}$$

The WACC of an ungeared company has not changed; it is still its cost of equity (Keu). Another equation can be used to decipher the WACC of a geared company when the WACC or cost of equity of a similar ungeared company is known. This formula is as follows:

$$WACCg = Keu\left(1 - \frac{Dt}{E+D}\right)$$

These formulae are derivations of propositions I and II. The prior examples used to illustrate M&M theory *without tax* are now revisited.

Worked example 15.12   (example 15.7 revisited)

The WACC of Rojo plc, a geared company, is 20% and the cost of its debt is 6%. Debt amounts to 50% of Rojo plc's capital structure. Verde plc is similar in every aspect, except it is financed totally by equity shares. Tax is payable at 30%.

REQUIRED

a)   Assuming M&M theory, calculate the cost of equity required by the equity holders of Rojo plc and Verde plc.
b)   What is Verde plc's expected WACC?

Solution

a)   The first step is to work out the cost of equity in Rojo plc by using the WACC model:

$$20\% = \frac{50\%(Ke)}{100\%} + \frac{50\%(6\%)(1-0.30)}{100\%}$$

$$20\% = 0.5Ke + 2.1\%$$

$$17.9\% = 0.5Ke$$

$$35.8\% = Ke$$

Continued

b)   The outcome from a) can then be slotted into M&M proposition II formula (with taxes), to find the cost of equity in the ungeared company, Verde plc (Keu).

$$35.8\% = \text{Keu} + \frac{50\%}{50\%}(\text{Keu} - 6\%)(1 - 0.30)$$

$$35.8\% = \text{Keu} + 0.7\text{Keu} - 4.2\%$$

$$40\% = 1.7\text{Keu}$$

$$23.53\% = \text{Keu}$$

This also represents the WACC of Verde plc.

Check
Under proposition III, M&M argue that the WACC of a geared company will be smaller than the WACC of a similar ungeared company by an amount that represents the tax saving on the debt capital. In an ungeared company the WACC is its Keu.

$$\text{WACCg} = 23.53\%\left(1 - \frac{50\%(30\%)}{100\%}\right)$$

$$= 20\%$$

Capital appraisal and investment appraisal

As discussed in chapter 13, 'Capital Investment Decision Making', a business finance manager should aim to invest in all projects that have a positive NPV, and to finance them in a manner that does not change a company's WACC. This chapter highlights the dangers that may result from financing projects incorrectly. A change in capital structure might be harmful to equity holders. In circumstances where the capital structure is changing, the WACC is not an appropriate discount rate. A technique based on the M&M ideals, called the adjusted present value, should be used.

Adjusted present value

The *adjusted present value (APV)* approach to investment appraisal, discounts a project's cash flows using an ungeared cost of equity (adjusted to reflect the systematic risks associated with the project) and then adds the impact of any other specific side effects, such as financing, i.e. the present value of any tax benefit resulting from the specific financing being used, issue costs, etc. The side effects are discounted at a rate appropriate to their cash streams. The most common example is the tax-shield benefit. This should be discounted at the debt interest rate (before tax).

Each project is evaluated as if it were a mini-company. The approach adopts M&M proposition I i.e. Vg=Vu+Dt, where Vu is the present value of the cash flows from a project discounted using an ungeared cost of equity and Dt is the present value of the interest tax shield, for the debt being used to finance that particular project. Another relevant side effect is issue costs. Therefore, a formula to find the APV might be as follows:

$$APV = Vu + Dt - PV \text{ of issue costs}$$

Worked example 15.13   (APV)

Quien plc has a capital structure of 20% debt and 80% equity. Que plc is similar in every respect except it is financed entirely with equity, which has a cost of 15%. The risk-free rate is 9% and tax is payable at 30%. Quien plc is considering investing in a project that costs €/£5 million and is expected to yield an annual cash flow return of €/£700,000. This project will be financed entirely by debt capital. The project has the same systematic risk as the company's current projects.

REQUIRED

a)   Using NPV, determine whether Quien plc should undertake the project.

b)   Reassess the project using APV.

Continued

Solution

a)   When evaluating a project using NPV and it is assumed that the systematic risk of the company is not going to change, then it is normal to use the WACC as the discount rate. As the cost of equity is not provided, M&M proposition II can be used to calculate this, given that gearing levels are known and the cost of equity in Que plc, a similar geared company, is 15%. Therefore the cost of equity (Keg) in Quien plc is 16.05%:

$$Keg = 15\% + \frac{20\%}{80\%}(15\% - 9\%)(1 - 0.30)$$

The WACC is 14.1%:

$$WACCg = \frac{80\%(16.05)}{100\%} + \frac{20\%(9\%)(1 - 0.30)}{100\%}$$

The NPV of the project is (€/£35,461):

$$\frac{€/£700,000}{14.1\%} - €/£5,000,000$$

Therefore, using the NPV, this project would be rejected.

b)   This project is being financed using debt, which is cheaper than equity. This will cause a change in the capital structure of the company; hence the project should be evaluated using the APV.

The first step is to find the present value of the cash flows when discounted at an ungeared cost of equity rate. (This rate is given as 15%.) Therefore, the present value of the project discounted at the ungeared cost of equity capital is (€/£333,333):

Continued

$$\frac{€/£700,000}{15\%} - €/£5,000,000$$

Then adjust for the method of financing, i.e. find the present value of the tax benefit (Dt):

$$€/£450,000 \ (€/£5,000,000 \times 9\%).$$

Therefore the APV of the project is €/£116,667 ((€/£333,333) + €/£450,000).
The project is now acceptable.

M&M: other issues?

Financial distress/bankruptcy

M&M's theory with taxation suggests that the value of a company increases by the present value of the tax shield; however, there comes a point when the company starts to incur costs associated with financial distress. At a certain level of gearing it will no longer be advantageous for a company to seek more debt finance as the benefit of the tax shield becomes outweighed by the additional costs associated with financial distress. *Financial distress* increases in line with gearing and is related to the probability of a company not being able to pay its debt holders. Assets are used to pay a company's debts; therefore, theoretically when a company's assets equal its debts, equity has no value. When this happens, ownership of a company's assets becomes the debt holders', as they have first claim to the assets in the event of bankruptcy. In addition, there are liquidity risks associated with debt capital. It has a guaranteed yearly interest cash outflow, whereas dividends can be waived. M&M proposition I can be adjusted to reflect the costs associated with financial distress.

M&M proposition I (with financial distress)

$$Vg = Vu + Dt - PV \text{ (financial distress costs)}$$

These costs are also known as bankruptcy costs and can be categorised into *indirect* and *direct* costs. **Indirect costs** are difficult to measure.

When a company is experiencing financial distress, management may direct their attention to trying to avoid bankruptcy, instead of properly running the business. It is in this climate that indirect costs are more likely to occur. They encapsulate: lost sales to customers who are concerned about the security of supply; the inability to source supplies at competitive rates, as suppliers become aware of the additional default risk associated with trading with the company; the loss of valuable employees, who become aware of the situation; and sub-optimal decision making, resulting in lost profits. *Direct costs* are the actual costs incurred when a company goes bankrupt. At this stage the assets of a company are legally distributed to its debt holders. The process includes direct costs such as solicitor's fees, insolvency practitioner's fees and general administrative costs associated with the bankruptcy, including managerial time.

In reality no two companies are alike. The have different business risks and cost structures. This will impact on the capital structure their financial managers choose to pursue. Companies with high levels of tangible assets, strong operating income and cash flows that are not sensitive to changes in the economic environment are better placed to adopt higher geared capital structures, as they can benefit from the tax shield. Companies with intangible assets and fluctuating income that are affected by changes in the economic environment are more likely to pursue more equity funding in their capital structures. In addition, there are the actions of management. Under M&M, it is assumed that business finance managers act in a manner to maximise company value, even if this means pursuing a capital structure with 100% debt and awarding a 100% dividend payout policy. Several research studies suggest that this does not take place, with two key theories regarding the behaviour of management in respect of their use of earnings and the resultant impact on the capital structure of a company.

Pecking order theory

Pecking order theory suggests that when managers source finance, they do not seek an optimal capital structure, instead have a preference for using retained earnings over external funds, and a preference for sourcing debt capital in front of equity capital. This theory emerged in 1961 (Donaldson). An explanation for this behaviour is effort and cost. Internally generated funds can be sourced with no effort and have no issue costs. At the other extreme, it takes a considerable amount of management effort to raise equity, and equity issues are costly. Another reason for this ranking is provided by Myers and Majluf (1984); they suggest that asymmetric information provides an explanation, that the issue of equity is perceived by stock markets to indicate that shares are overvalued, and internal management is cashing in on the potential gains to be made. This means it is unattractive to issue shares as the issue of shares may signal that current shares are overpriced, resulting in the current equity holders requiring a larger return. In support of the latter, Asquith and Mullins (1983) found that equity issues result in large declines in the value of equity. Circumstantial evidence in support of pecking order theory is put forward by Baskin (1989). He found a negative relationship between the level of gearing and profitability and also reported that equity issues were not common amongst well-established profitable companies which retain funds for investment. They are more common amongst less-profitable companies without internal reserves built up for investment. These companies also tended to have more debt.

Agency costs
In conflict with M&M theory, it is argued that the level of debt capital raised by a company is influenced by agency costs built into, for example, debt capital trust deeds. Agency costs are direct or indirect costs that strive to ensure that agents (company managers) act in the interest of the principals (equity and debt holders) (Jensen and Meckling, 1976). When a company is geared, debt holders usually introduce agency costs to ensure that their interests are protected. The most obvious agency cost is *covenants*. These can be written into debt contracts and usually restrict management decision making in a manner that protects debt holders' positions. Examples of typical covenants include: restrictions on dividend payouts, restrictions on asset disposals, restriction on the type of projects invested in or restrictions on further gearing.

Other practical issues considered to influence a company's capital structure

Level of tangible assets
Most lenders require security for loans provided. This can restrict gearing levels, as only some types of asset are considered appropriate as security; for example, property is more attractive to lenders than other tangible assets.

The reason for this is that other tangible assets, such as plant and machinery, may have restricted external sale markets. This results in uncertainty in respect of the recoverability of capital for lenders, making these tangible asses less attractive as security than property which is likely to increase in value. Hence the level of gearing in a company's capital structure may actually be determined by lenders and not be the result of managerial policy.

Managerial conservatism

All investors (equity and debt) lose when a company goes into liquidation. The parties to suffer the greatest loss are management and employees. Investors usually have portfolios made up of several investments. If one fails, then the loss to the investor is restricted, as there will be income from other parts of their portfolio. However, a manager or employee will lose their main source of income. This may cause managers to restrict gearing, as higher levels of gearing increase the likelihood of liquidation. Ross (1977) argues that the decision to increase gearing levels is in fact an indication of managerial confidence in the future of a company. The reason for this is that, as management are naturally conservative, they are more likely to raise debt if they are confident about a company's ability to repay the cash flows; therefore this can be interpreted as a signal to the market about the strength of expected cash flows and should lead to an increase in share price.

Investment opportunities

When there are many profitable investment opportunities it is more likely for a company to change its capital structure and increase the level of gearing, particularly if there is a shortage of available funds. Indeed, it can be argued that management prefer to hold on to a certain level of liquid funds than to invest them, as this provides flexibility for future decision making. When possible investment opportunities are not as profitable, management are more likely to build up reserves and increase the equity proportion of capital.

Control

When there are dominant equity holders, they are more likely to oppose raising equity finance, particularly if the balance of control might be shifted. In these circumstances, the current equity holders are more likely to support raising debt finance.

Conclusion

This chapter explains the relationship between capital structure, the WACC and company value. In the latter part of the chapter a new investment appraisal technique, the APV, is introduced. This technique can be used when the capital structure of a company is not in equilibrium or is changing.

The bulk of the chapter explains the theoretical views regarding whether an optimum capital structure exists. The traditional argument, M&M theory, and M&M theory with tax, are outlined. The latter theory suggests that an optimum capital structure has very high levels of debt. High levels of debt result in financial risk, which has many repercussions on a company, the most severe of which is bankruptcy. The chapter discusses financial risk and outlines the assumptions regarding the behaviour of equity holders under each of the capital structure theories.

Finally, practical considerations that affect a company's capital structure are presented. For example, as a company gears, it starts to incur financial distress costs; at some stage these costs outweigh the benefit of having lower cost debt. Also, some types of company are more suited to having debt in their capital structures. These companies are likely to have: higher levels of tangible assets, such as property; steady operating cash flows; and low levels of fixed costs. Then there are the influences of the decision makers: the managers and equity holders. Managers' salaries usually provide the bulk of their personal income; therefore, their actions are likely to be risk adverse. Indeed, it is considered that managers use a pecking order when selecting the type of finance they source; having a preference for retained earnings, followed by debt issues, and lastly equity capital issues. This is because of cost issues and the fact that equity holders have to approve any approaches to the market for more finance. Dominant equity holders are unlikely to support any action, which reduces their control within a company.

Examination standard question

> **Worked example 15.14**
>
> A plc has an annual operating income of €/£1 million in perpetuity, and a market value of €/£15 million. The market value of A plc's debt is €/£5m, at a cost of 3% (ignore taxes).
>
> *Continued*

REQUIRED

a) Estimate the company's WACC.

3 Marks

b) Calculate the market value using the traditional method – assuming the gearing ratio increases to 0.5. (You are informed that the equity holders do not consider that the change in gearing impacts on the overall risks of investing in the company.)

c) Calculate the market value and the WACC using M&M theory, assuming the gearing ratio increases to 0.5 (ignore taxation). What implications does this have for the cost of equity?

5 Marks

d) Compare and contrast the traditional and M&M theories of the cost of capital and discuss how useful they may be in the determination of an appropriate capital structure for a company.

10 Marks

22 Marks

(ICAI, MABF II, Summer, 1998, Q5)

Solution

a) To estimate the company's WACC, it is necessary to find the value and cost of the company's debt and equity.

The question states that the market value of the company is €/£15 million and the market value of its debt is €/£5 million. Therefore, the market value of equity can be obtained by working back from company value a (MV=D+E).

Market value of equity

Total market value	€/£15m
Market value of perpetual debt (D)	(€/£5m)
Market value of equity (E)	€/£10m

Continued

Cost of equity (Ke)

$$Ke = \frac{\text{Dividend}(D_1)}{\text{Market value }(P_0)}$$

Dividend $(D_1) = $€$/£1m - $interest charge on debt

$$= $€$/£1m - (3\% \times $€$/£5m)$$

$$= $€$/£1m - $€$/£0.15m$$

Dividends $= $€$/£0.85m$

Therefore the cost of equity is: $Ke = \dfrac{€/£0.85m}{€/£10m} = 8.5\%$

Cost of debt (K*d*) is given in the question as 3%.

Market value of debt (D) is given in the question as €/£5m.

$$\text{WACC} = \frac{Kd(D)}{(D+E)} + \frac{Ke(E)}{(E+D)}$$

$$= 3\% \,(€/£5m/€/£15m) + 8.5\% \,(€/£10m/€/£15m)$$

$$= 6.667\%$$

Check: market value $= \dfrac{€/£1m}{0.0667} = €/£15m$

b)   Current gearing ratio $= \dfrac{€/£5m \text{ debt}}{€/£15m \text{ (debt + equity)}}$

$$= 0.333 \,(33.3\%)$$

Continued

If the gearing ratio increases to 50% under the traditionalist approach, the cost of debt and the cost of equity remain constant.

Note: The cost of equity is likely to rise, but not by a large margin, so unless an increased rate is given in a question, the cost of equity is assumed to remain constant.

$$WACC = 3\% \ (0.5) + 8.5\% \ (0.5)$$
$$= 5.75\%$$

$$\text{Market value} = \frac{€/£1m}{0.0575} = €/£17.4m \ (\text{rounded})$$

c) Under the M&M approach, a change in capital structure does not affect market value or the WACC, which remains at 6.6667%.

By implication, the cost of equity rises to exactly offset the benefits of the cheaper debt. M&M propositions II and III (without taxes) can be used, as M&M assumes that the WACC of a geared company equals that of an ungeared company; hence the cost of equity in an ungeared company (Keu) is 6.67%. This rate can be used to find the cost of equity (Keg) in a similar geared company.

$$Keg = Keu + \frac{D}{E}(Keu - Kd)$$

$$= 0.0667 + (^{0.5}/_{0.5})(0.0667 - 0.03)$$

$$= 0.1034$$

$$= 10.34\%$$

The cost of equity (Ke) rises from 8.5% to 10.34% because of the increase in financial risks associated with having more debt in the capital structure.

Continued

d)   The traditional approach to cost of capital theory would suggest that the amount of debt within a company's capital structure can affect both the cost of capital and, in turn, the market
value of a company. By introducing small amounts of debt into
an equity-financed company, this use of a cheaper source of
finance can provide benefits to the existing equity holders by
reducing the overall cost of capital and hence increasing market
value. Increasing the proportion of debt capital will continue to
be favourably viewed by equity holders up to a point, where the
increased financial risk associated with increases in debt capital
will just be compensated for by the enhanced returns available
to the equity holders. After this point, the cost of capital will
begin to rise again and market value will start to fall. Therefore,
there is an optimum level of gearing, which will minimise the
cost of capital and maximise the value of a company.

By contrast, the M&M theory or the net operating income
approach concludes that in a world of certain assumptions
(listed below), the level of gearing is irrelevant to an investor
because it does not affect the overall cost of capital of a company, the market value of the company, or the market value of
an individual share.

M&M theory purports that as the level of gearing rises, the
cost of debt remains unchanged, but the cost of equity rises in
such a way as to keep both the WACC and the market value of
the company's equity shares constant. Companies are classified
into equivalent risk classes and, within these classes, are perfect
substitutes for each other. If the values of these equity shares
diverge, then arbitrage will subsequently equate the prices.

However, upon introducing taxation into their model, M&M
admit that gearing does affect the cost of capital due to the tax
deductibility of debt interest. In fact, they suggest that in this
instance the optimal capital structure would be 100% debt
finance. In subsequent amendments they incorporated bankruptcy
costs, which they claim will deter a very highly geared structure.
Therefore, they argue that their theory applies for a company up
to a high level of gearing. (This will be less than 100%.)

Continued

Assumptions of M&M theory (no taxes)

- Companies pay out all their earnings as dividends.
- The gearing of a company can be changed immediately by issuing debt to repurchase shares, or by issuing shares to repurchase debt. There are no transaction costs for issues.
- The earnings of a company are expected to remain constant in perpetuity and all investors share the same expectations about these future earnings.
- Business risk is also constant, regardless of how a company invests its funds.
- Tax implications and the possibility of bankruptcy can be ignored (in the original theory).
- Investors are assumed to act rationally.
- The cost of borrowing for an individual is the same as for corporate borrowers.

Conclusion

The theory of the capital structure decision, be it the traditional theory or M&M, does not give company management clear advice. M&M's theory with tax concludes that companies should gear up as much as possible, due to debt being cheap and tax deductible. The traditional view concludes that some gearing will be advantageous, but not too much and, for each company, the optimal gearing ratio will be a matter of trial and error. Finally, M&M's assumptions on arbitrage (that a person can obtain debt at the same cost as a company and is happy to gear to the same levels) may not be valid.

In the real world, business finance managers will review average gearing ratios for their industry group and will endeavour to keep the ratio of their own company in line with industry average (for example, the property industry has very high levels of gearing). In the theory of capital structure, gearing has always been measured in terms of market values, but in reality, gearing tends to be measured in terms of accounting balance sheet values. For a quoted company, it is easy to calculate the total market value of equity; this is not the case with the total market value of debt. The vast majority of corporate debt capital is issued privately and so is unquoted. Therefore, it does not have a market value that can be observed. If the balance sheet value

Continued

of debt is to be used, it would be inconsistent to use market values of equity, so accounting balance sheet values for both debt and equity are used.

In making the capital structure decision in practice, business finance managers are aware of the relationship between risk and return. If a company's gearing is increased, this will in turn lead to an increase in the amount of financial risk borne by equity holders. As a result, equity holders will require some additional reward in compensation. An immediate and direct measure of the reward for increased risk taking, due to a proposed increase in gearing, would be to assess whether the company will be able to generate sufficient extra return to compensate the equity holders for an increased level of financial risk. The business finance manager will estimate the impact of the proposed gearing on the *earnings per share* of the company.

In practice, business finance managers tend to make capital structure decisions on the basis of the gearing ratio measured in terms of accounting balance sheet values and the subsequent impact on *earnings per share*; the final decision being, of course, a matter of judgement guided by intuition and industry average gearing ratios.

KEY TERMS

Adjusted present value (APV)
Agency cost theory
Arbitrage process
Bankruptcy
Capital structure
Direct costs of bankruptcy
Financial distress
Financial risk
Gearing
Indirect costs of bankruptcy
Interest tax shield

Irrelevancy theory
Modigliani and Miller theory
Modigliani and Miller theory
   (with taxes)
Net operating income theory
Optimum capital structure
Pecking order theory
Traditional theory

REVIEW QUESTIONS

1. What is a company's capital structure?
2. Explain the relationship between a company's capital structure and its WACC.
3. What is financial risk?
4. Pero plc and Gato plc are two identical companies. They have similar business risks, similar operating risks and identical operating profits (€/£300,000), which are distributed in full every year, after interest is deducted.

   Pero plc is financed entirely by equity; having 1,600,000 50c/p ordinary shares that are currently trading at €/£1.40. Pero plc has just paid a dividend.

   Gato plc has 800,000 50c/p ordinary shares that are currently trading at €/£1.60. They have also just paid a dividend. In addition to equity shares, Gato plc has €/£1.2 million (10%) irredeemable loan stock that is currently trading at par value. Assume traditional capital structure theory applies.

   a) Calculate the cost of equity for each company (ignore taxation).
   b) Calculate the WACC for each company (ignore taxation).
   c) Provide explanations for any differences between the rates reported for both companies, arising from your calculations in a) and b).
   d) What would M&M say about the results in a) and b)?

5. Discuss M&M's propositions concerning the cost of capital and the value of a company, under different levels of gearing (assume a world of no taxation).

   7 Marks
   (ICAI, MABF II, Summer 1996, Q5 a)

6. The cost of equity in Naranja plc, an all-equity company, is 18%. Another company, Marron plc, is identical in every respect, except for its capital structure. It has a debt equity ratio of 20:80. The cost of debt is 8% and this is regarded as a risk-free rate. Assume there are no taxes.

REQUIRED

    a) Assuming M&M theory, calculate Marron plc's WACC.

    b) Calculate Marron plc's expected cost of equity, when in equilibrium.

7.   Rosa plc has a capital structure with 40% debt capital. The cost of this debt is 10%. (This is regarded as the risk-free rate.) A similar ungeared company has a WACC of 12%. Assume M&M theory on the capital structure of a company applies.

REQUIRED

    a) What is Rosa plc's WACC?

    b) Calculate the cost of equity capital required by the equity holders of Rosa plc.

8.   Violeta plc is financed entirely by equity with a cost of 12%. Amarillo plc is similar in all respects, except it is financed with €/£2 million of 4% debentures that are currently trading at 50% of their par value, and one million ordinary shares that are currently trading at €/£3.00 each. A dividend of 20c/p has just been paid. Assume M&M's capital structure theory with no tax.

REQUIRED

Calculate Amarillo plc's cost of equity and WACC.

9.   (Question 6 revisited) The cost of equity in Naranja plc, an all-equity company, is 18%. Another company, Marron plc, is identical in every respect, except for its capital structure. It has a debt equity ratio of 20:80. The cost of its debt is 8% and this is regarded as a risk-free rate. Assume a tax rate of 30%.

REQUIRED

    a) Assuming M&M theory, calculate Marron plc's WACC.

    b) Calculate Marron plc's expected cost of equity, when in equilibrium.

10. (Question 7 revisited) Rosa plc has a capital structure with 40% debt capital. The cost of this debt is 10% (regarded as the risk-free rate). A similar ungeared company has a WACC of 12%. Assume M&M theory on the capital structure of a company applies and the tax rate is 40%.

REQUIRED

a) What is Rosa plc's WACC?
b) Calculate the cost of equity capital required by the equity holders of Rosa plc.

11. (Question 8 revisited) Violeta plc is financed entirely by equity with a cost of 12%. Amarillo plc is similar in all respects, except it is financed with €/£2 million of 4% debentures that are currently trading at 50% of their par value, and one million ordinary shares that are currently trading at €/£3.00 each. A dividend of 20c/p has just been paid. Assume M&M's theory and a tax rate of 30%.

REQUIRED

Calculate Amarillo plc's cost of equity and WACC.

CHALLENGING QUESTIONS

1. NOTNIL plc AND NEWBEGIN plc

Notnil plc and Newbegin plc are companies in the same industry. They have the same business risk and operating characteristics, but Notnil plc is geared, whereas Newbegin plc is ungeared. Notnil plc earns three times as much profit as Newbegin plc. Both companies pursue a policy of paying out all their earnings each year as dividends. The market value of each company is as follows:

		Notnil plc €/£m	Newbegin plc €/£m
Equity	(10m shares)	36 (20 m shares)	15
Debt	(€/£12m of 12% loan stock)	14	
		50	15

The annual profit before interest of Notnil plc is €/£9 million and that of Newbegin plc is €/£3 million. The tax rate is 28%.

It is thought that the current market value per equity share in Newbegin plc is at the equilibrium level, and that the market value of Notnil plc's debt capital is also at its equilibrium level. There is some doubt, however, about whether the value of Notnil plc's shares are at their equilibrium level.

REQUIRED

a) Apply the M&M formula to establish the equilibrium price of Notnil plc's shares.

4 Marks

b) Calculate the cost of debt, equity and the WACC for Notnil plc and the cost of equity and WACC for Newbegin plc (using M&M theory).

5 Marks

c) Calculate the cost of debt, equity and the WACC for Notnil plc and the cost of equity and WACC for Newbegin plc (using traditionalist theory).

<u>5</u> **Marks**
Total <u>14</u> **Marks**
(ICAI, MABF II, Questions and Solutions Manual, 2000/2001)

2.   GATE plc AND HEDGE plc (Proposition I)

a) Distinguish between the traditional view and the M&M view on the relevance of a company's capital structure to valuation and briefly explain the M&M arbitrage process.

4 Marks

b) Gate plc and Hedge plc are two companies that operate in the same industry and are considered to have identical risks and operating characteristics. Both have a policy of paying out 100% of their earnings and the capital markets expect this to continue. Gate plc is five times the size of Hedge plc in terms of turnover, profits, capacity, employees, etc. The only difference in the two companies is in respect of size and capital structure. Details of capital structure are as follows:

	Nominal value €/£m	Market value €/£m
Gate plc		
€/£1 equity share capital	25	75
12% irredeemable debentures	50	50
	75	125
Hedge plc		
€/£1 equity share capital	5	20

Gate plc is currently earning (before interest) €/£17.5 million per year and no growth is expected in these earnings. Hedge plc is currently earning €/£3.5 million and again earnings are expected to remain at this level for the foreseeable future.

REQUIRED

(i) Prepare calculations (ignoring tax) assuming that the price of Gate plc's debt and Hedge plc's equity remains stable, which would show the equilibrium price of Gate plc's equity.

4 Marks

(ii) State, assuming both companies pay tax at 50%, what the expected equilibrium price of Hedge plc's equity will be, assuming the prices of Gate plc's debt and equity remain constant.

4 Marks

(iii) Explain in what circumstances the M&M view on capital structure is unlikely to hold for Gate plc and Hedge plc.

4 Marks

Total 16 Marks

(ICAI, MABF II, Questions and Solutions Manual, 2000/2001)

3. GATE plc AND HEDGE plc (Arbitrage)

The question is the same as question 2 above. However, this question requests the reader prepare the answer using the mechanics of arbitrage theory. To this end you are provided with the following additional information.

Samuel Murphy holds 250,000 shares in Gate plc and has approached you for advice. He is considering selling some or all of his holding in Gate plc and investing the proceeds in Hedge plc. He also tells you that his bank manager is willing to lend him funds at 12% per annum and in light of this he feels he could improve his position by borrowing personally in the same ratio (in market value terms) as Gate plc and investing in Hedge plc.

REQUIRED

a) Prepare calculations (ignoring tax) that would show whether Samuel Murphy can improve his position as he suggests.

6 Marks

b) Prepare calculations (ignoring tax) assuming that the price of Gate plc's debt and Hedge plc's equity remains stable, which would show the equilibrium price of Gate plc's equity if all investors were to act in a similar manner to Samuel Murphy.

4 Marks

c) State, assuming both companies pay tax at 50%, what the expected equilibrium price of Hedge plc's equity will be, assuming the prices of Gate plc's debt and equity remain constant. Assume that the investor can get the same tax deductions for investments as a company can.

6 Marks
Total 16 Marks
(ICAI, MABF II, Questions and Solutions Manual, 2001)

4.   EQUITAS plc

a) Define financial gearing and explain its significance for corporate financial management.

4 Marks

b) Discuss the factors that may limit the amount of debt finance a company may utilise.

6 Marks
(ICAI, MABF II, Autumn 1996, Extract from Q7)

5.   M&M

a)   *'Capital structure can have no influence on the value of the firm.'*
(M&M)

REQUIRED

Discuss this statement and comment briefly on the main factors a
company should consider when determining capital structure.

8 Marks
(ICAI, MABF II, Autumn 1997, Extract from Q5)

6.   SKAROK plc

Skarok plc plans to raise finance some time within the next few months.
Skarok's managing director is acutely aware of the recent stock market
downturn and is worried about the possible effects on the company's cost
of capital.

The managing director has asked for your advice and has provided you
with the following information:

Skarok plc
Summarised balance sheet as at 31 March 2007

	€/£m
Non-current assets at net book value	619.51
Current assets	
Inventories	163.03
Trade receivables	195.63
Bank	65.21
	423.87
Total assets	1,043.38
Equity and liabilities	
Equity and reserves	
Equity shares (€/£1 par value)	163.03
Reserves	293.46
	456.49

Non-current liabilities	
11% debentures, redeemable in 2022 at par	326.05
Current liabilities	
Trade payables	177.93
Dividend	21.24
Taxation	61.67
	260.84
Total liabilities	586.89
Total equity and liabilities	1,043.38

Five-year summarised income statements:

Year ended 31 March	Turnover	Profit before tax	Tax	Profit after tax	Dividend
	€/£m	€/£m	€/£m	€/£m	€/£m
2003	1,379.10	117.26	46.90	70.36	23.30
2004	1,522.98	138.03	48.32	89.71	25.85
2005	1,610.94	140.84	49.29	91.55	28.75
2006	1,753.83	147.50	51.62	95.88	31.85
2007	1,915.20	176.19	61.67	114.52	35.39

The company's current share price is €/£12.90 ex-dividend, and the debenture price is €/£93. No new share or debenture capital has been issued since 2000. Corporation tax is at the rate of 35%.

REQUIRED

a) Calculate the existing cost of equity for Skarok.

4 Marks

b) Calculate the existing cost of debt for Skarok.

4 Marks

c) Calculate the existing WACC for Skarok.

4 Marks

d) Academic papers concerning cost of capital and capital structure often appear highly theoretical and seem to have little practical relevance. Discuss the significance of the theories of capital structure, especially those of M&M.

4 Marks

e)   Describe briefly two weaknesses of sensitivity analysis in capital budgeting.

5 Marks

Presentation mark

1 Mark
Total 22 Marks
(ICAI, MABF II, Summer 2003, Q5)

7.   FAZE plc

a)   Explain the terms *business risk* and *financial risk* and outline what effect these may have on the discount rate used to appraise a long-term investment.

8 Marks

b) (i) Faze plc is currently expanding its business. It is considering a venture that would require an investment of €/£20 million and would last five years. Details are as follows:

(1) The investment consists of €/£16.5 million in non-current assets and €/£3.5 million in working capital. 60% of total initial cost will be paid immediately, while the remaining 40% will be paid evenly over the following two years.

(2) The estimated pre-tax cash flows for the project are as follows:

Years	€/£m
1	3.5
2	5.0
3	6.2
4	7.5
5	7.0

(3) Corporation tax is estimated to be 20% per annum for the duration of the venture. You may assume that corporation tax is paid in the year in which profits are made.

(4) Residual values at the end of the five-year period are estimated to be as follows:

Non-current assets (including goodwill)	€/£3 million
Working capital	In full

(5) The company is 100% equity financed and has a cost of capital of 15%. This project is considered to have the same level of business risk as the company's existing operations.

REQUIRED

Calculate the NPV of the project using the current cost of capital of Faze plc.

8 Marks

(ii) The company now decides to issue a €/£6 million 10% debenture to help finance the project (with the remainder coming from a combination of retained earnings and new equity).

REQUIRED

Calculate the APV of the project and comment on the results. You can assume that there are issue costs on the debt capital of €/£100,000 (which are tax deductible) and the debt would be repayable at par after five years.

<u>6 Marks</u>
Total 22 Marks
(ICAI, MABF II, Autumn 2001, Q5)

VALUING COMPANIES

16

Debt   10,000,000
Equity   15,000,000
Market Value   25,000,000

LEARNING OBJECTIVES

Upon completing this chapter, readers should be able to:

- ♣ Summarise why valuations of entities or equity are needed;
- ♣ Outline the inherent problems with valuing companies;
- ♣ Describe the valuation process and economic rationale for such activities;
- ♣ Calculate a company's value using asset values, earnings, dividend payout policy, discounted cash flows and market values;
- ♣ Explain the advantages and limitations of each of the methods; and
- ♣ Outline typical steps taken by an analyst when valuing an entity.

Introduction

The majority of businesses, whether private or publicly listed, have to be valued at some point in their existence. Even small private businesses are likely to be valued, with the valuation usually required to assist an individual's decision making with personal financial wealth management in mind. For example, partners/sole traders may wish to have a valuation undertaken if they are considering succession planning, when refinancing the business or when an individual offers to purchase a share in the business. The tax authorities may require a valuation when the business is being transferred on the death of a sole trader to their next of kin, or when there is a change in a partnership. The courts may require a valuation if a partner/sole trader gets divorced and their partner is claiming a portion of the individual's assets.

Many businesses are not valued by the markets. For example, sole traders, partnerships and private companies will not have a market value for their equity or debt, therefore they require a formal company valuation if the owners are trying to determine company value. When a company's shares are publicly traded a market value for that company's equity already exists. However, even in these circumstances a formal valuation is normally required. The reason for this is now explained. If stock markets are strong-form efficient (discussed in chapter 2, 'The Role of Business Finance in Strategic Management') then equity share values would correctly value the equity stake in a company. Research has shown that the UK, ROI and US stock markets are weak to semi-strong-form efficient, this suggests that equity value does not always reflect the underlying value of a company. Therefore, a company valuation has to be undertaken to determine if the stock market is correctly valuing a particular company, when the company is faced with a variety of strategic decisions that require knowledge of the company's valuation.

Companies usually obtain a valuation for strategic purposes. The valuation may be for the purpose of purchasing or selling a business, for investing in a company, for raising capital on the stock exchange (an initial public offering (IPO)), for considering a joint venture or merger with another company, for assessing a management buyout, for raising debt by using the business as security, for pricing services, for securing control of another company, or simply to benchmark the company's business value with that of its competitors. In addition, a company may find itself the target of a predator company that is trying to take over its business. In these circumstances management might have their company valued independently to determine the attractiveness of the purchase offer. All plc's have to consider any offer made, as they are obliged (by stock exchange regulations) to make decisions with their equity holders' best interests in mind.

Valuing companies is regarded as both a 'science' and an 'art'. It is considered a science as most of the approaches involve a technical approach. It is considered an art because most of the techniques use estimated data and assumptions and are also amended subjectively to take account of factors that are difficult to measure accurately such as business risk and financial risk. Indeed, each of the techniques used will provide different valuations, though some of the techniques are considered to be more appropriate in some situations than others. The process is not black and white either.

When valuations are being used to fix a value for the sale or purchase of a company, various techniques provide a range of values. These values inform both sides of the contract and contribute to a bartering process.

There are three main types of approach used to value companies. The first analyses the specific asset values of the company, the second derives company value using multiples obtained from comparable companies, comparable transactions or from past experience and the final approach uses the time value of money theories to determine the present value of the future stream of cash flows expected from the company. The main techniques are discussed under the three types of approaches to company valuation. An example is used to identify the type of adjustments or calculations that are required. The philosophy underlying each technique is explained and the most appropriate conditions to use that particular technique are highlighted. In addition, the advantages and limitations of that approach are outlined.

Asset-based approaches

In general *asset-based approaches* use accounting data – net book value, net realisable value or replacement value to value a company's assets. The philosophy behind this approach is that the company is considered to be a collection of individual assets that can be sold and company value is the sum of the individual specific assets. This approach would not be suitable if the valuation was for the purposes of buying a company as a going-concern as this technique does not consider the earnings potential of the assets. It is also of limited use where the company being valued is a service type company, as this type of company will likely have a small proportion of tangible assets making up its value. Most of its value will be intangible intellectual capital, such as employee skills, networks or brand names. This approach is most suited when a predator company is determining whether it is worth purchasing a target company with the view to dismantling the company and selling off its assets for a quick gain. The predator company will not be interested in the future earnings potential of the current assets, it will only be interested in the net realisable value of the company's assets and will only be willing to pay an amount which ensures that the net realisable value of the assets exceeds the purchase price and the costs.

Asset-based approach: advantages

Easy to obtain, simple and understandable: On the face of it this approach is simple to calculate and is understandable by all parties involved.

Asset stripping: If the purpose of the valuation is to determine whether to purchase a company to make a quick profit by selling its assets, then this approach will provide the best indication of how profitable the purchase may be to the predator company's shareholders.

Minimum value: This approach can provide a value which represents the minimum amount that the company should accept if it is being purchased by an external entity. It can be used to set a floor value for negotiation purposes.

Asset-based approach: disadvantages

Conservative value: This valuation is the lowest valuation that should be accepted by any equity holder. It does not take into account the future earnings potential of the company.

Valuations: Valuing assets can be complicated and a variety of approaches to asset valuation is possible (discussed below).

Incomplete: Several assets are not reflected in a company's financial statements, such as brand value or intellectual capital.

Accounting treatments: There is a variety of accounting treatments which impact on the book value of assets such as depreciation and inventory valuation techniques. These accounting treatments involve the use of formulae and do not consider economic reality.

Technology: This approach will seriously understate a company's value, when the company is technology or intellectual capital based.

Asset valuation: some issues

There are two main valuation issues that affect company valuation using asset-based techniques. The first is that, as mentioned above, some assets are not recorded in the financial statements. These are typically intangible assets, such as goodwill, employee skills, synergies between assets working together and brands. Purchased intangible assets are capitalised in the financial statements, but home-grown intangible assets are not (the only exception is development costs and these can only be capitalised if they meet stringent preconditions as laid down in *International Accounting Standard 38: Intangible assets.* **Intangible assets** are difficult to identify separately from other assets because they are inert, changeable and difficult to value. In most cases there is no readily available market for the sale, hence valuation, of intangible assets (there are some exceptions such as quota or franchise licences). Therefore, in most instances these assets are ignored when a valuation is being prepared, or a subjective value is placed on them.

Tangible assets can also be omitted under accounting rules. For example, depending on the content of a leasing agreement, some leased assets and corresponding debt end up capitalised on a company's balance sheet (those that are classified as finance leases) and other assets and corresponding debt do not (those that are classified as operating leases).

The second valuation problem concerns the bases used to value tangible and intangible assets that are recorded in the financial statements of a company. Intangible assets are usually recorded at purchase value and amortised over their useful economic life, unless it is considered that they have an infinite life, wherein they remain valued at historic cost and are not subject to amortisation. The main concern here is that this value is unlikely to reflect the economic value of the asset. The value will be impaired where a permanent diminution in value occurs but cannot be re-valued upwards to reflect increases in value. Therefore, it is likely that the balance sheet value is understating the true value of intangible assets.

Tangible assets in audited financial statements may not reflect economic reality either, as they are typically based on historic cost and are depreciated over the useful economic life of the asset. **Depreciation** is not an attempt by accountants to measure the reduction in the value of an asset. Depreciation is the application of the matching concept wherein the costs of an asset are matched against the revenue generated by the asset, over the life of the asset. Depreciation tries to measure the reduction in the economic life of an asset to the company in a period. The balance remaining (the net book value) is just the economic life of the asset that has not been allocated yet. When inflation rates are high the gap between market value and historic net book value is likely to be accentuated.

The alternative accounting method available under *International Accounting Standard 16: Property, Plant and Equipment* is to value tangible assets at their fair value, which equates to market value and to then depreciate this figure. Even if the assets have been re-valued to fair value, this is the value at the balance sheet date, and hence does not reflect current value. Valuations are costly and most companies will only adopt this approach if it is deemed to be beneficial by the management of a company and companies that adopt this approach usually only revalue property and land. Other tangible fixed assets typically remain valued at historic cost. This is a problem for the individual who is valuing the company as there may not be a readily available market for second hand plant and machinery, fixtures and fittings or tools. Their market value may only be properly determined if they are put up for sale, which is not feasible. Different accounting bases can also result in different valuations for inventories and trade receivables which will affect overall company value.

Net book value

There are three common types of company valuation that are based on permutation of asset values. The first is the **net book value approach**. This approach assumes that the company's value is the value of its total assets as portrayed by the audited balance sheet:

Company value (total assets) = Non current assets + Current assets

The equity holder's value is therefore the **net assets**, which is total assets less total liabilities, and the value per equity share is:

$$\text{Value of an equity share} = \frac{\text{Total assets} - \text{total liabilities}}{\text{Number of equity shares in issue}}$$

Note: Preference shares are considered to be debt and are therefore taken away from total assets in the above formula.

Net Realisable Value (NRV)

A more informative approach is to substitute market value for book values where possible. There are two approaches. Assets can be valued at net realisable value or at replacement cost. The **net realisable value**, otherwise known as the **liquidation value**, is the value that the company would expect to achieve were the assets to be sold, less the costs of sale. As mentioned above the net realisable value can be difficult to determine if a readily available liquid market does not exist and can vary depending on the circumstances of the sale. A quick sale will realise a lower price than a managed sale. The value of the company will now change to:

Company value = Non current assets at NRV + Current assets at NRV

The equity holder's value is therefore the **net realisable assets**, which is total assets at realisable value less total liabilities at their realisable value, and the value per equity share is:

$$\text{Value of an equity share} = \frac{\text{Total assets at NRV} - \text{total liabilities at NRV}}{\text{Number of equity shares in issue}}$$

Replacement cost approach

The final valuation approach sometimes adopted by companies that are considering setting up a business themselves or buying an already established business, is the replacement cost approach. This approach provides a higher company value than the latter two techniques as it assumes that each asset will be replaced and intangible assets will be purchased. The same valuation problems outlined earlier apply. The company is now valued as:

Company value = Replacement value of + Replacement value of
non-current assets   current assets

The equity holder's value is therefore the **net replacement value**, which is total assets at replacement cost less total liabilities at their replacement value, and the value per equity share is:

$$\text{Value of an equity share} = \frac{\text{Total assets at replacement value} - \text{total liabilities at replacement value}}{\text{Number of equity shares in issue}}$$

Worked example 16.1 (Calculating company value using the net assets approach)

The balance sheet of Tipex Ltd. on the 30 June 20X8 was as follows:

Non-current assets	€/£'000
Land and buildings	500
Plant and equipment	200
Motor vehicles	50
Investments	100
	850
Goodwill	100
Current assets	
Inventories	150
Trade receivables	150
Short-term investments	20
Bank	15
	335
Total assets	1,285
Equity and liabilities	
Equity and reserves	
Equity share capital (50c/p shares)	400
Reserves	305
	705
Non-current liabilities	
Debentures	200
Preference shares	100
Loan	100
	400
Current liabilities	
Trade payables	130
Taxation	30
Dividends	20
	180
Total equity and liabilities	1,285

Continued

The directors inform you that the land and premises were valued at €/£750,000, the plant and equipment at €/£140,000, the motor vehicles at €/£35,000 and the investments at €/£120,000. The plant and equipment can be replaced for €/£280,000 and the motor vehicles can be replaced for €/£85,000. The directors also inform you that circa €/£20,000 of the inventory is slow moving and is only expected to realise 50% of its carrying value and 10% of trade receivables usually end up as bad debts.

REQUIRED

Prepare valuations per share for Tipex Ltd. using the:
a)   Net assets valuation approach
b)   The net realisable value approach and
c)   The replacement cost approach

Solution

a)   *Net assets valuation approach*

	€/£'000
Total assets	1,285
Less: intangible assets	(100)
Tangible assets	1,185
Less:	
Debentures	(200)
Preference shares	(100)
Loan	(100)
Current liabilities	(180)
Net asset value of equity	605
Number of equity shares	800
Value per share (€/£605,000/800,000)	75.625c/p

Continued

b)   *Share valuation using the net realisable value approach:*

	(adjustments to determine NRV)	€/£'000
Total assets		1,285
Intangible assets		(100)
Revaluation of land and buildings	(€/£750,000 − €/£500,000)	250
Revaluation of plant and equipment	(€/£140,000 − €/£200,000)	(60)
Revaluation of motor vehicles	(€/£35,000 − €/£50,000)	(15)
Revaluation of investments	(€£120,000 − €/£100,000)	20
Revaluation of inventories	((€/£20,000 × 50%) − €/£20,000)	(10)
Revaluation of trade receivables	€/£150,000 × 10%	(15)
Tangible assets		1,355
Less:		
Debentures		(200)
Preference shares		(100)
Loan		(100)
Current liabilities		(180)
Net asset value of equity		775
Number of equity shares		800
Value per share	(€/£775,000/800,000)	96.875c/p

c)   *Share valuation using the replacement value approach:*

		€/£'000
Total assets		1,285
Intangible assets		(100)
Revaluation of land and buildings	(€/£750,000 − €/£500,000)	250
Revaluation of plant and equipment	(€/£280,000 − €/£200,000)	80
Revaluation of motor vehicles	(€/£85,000 − €/£50,000)	35
Revaluation of investments	(€£120,000 − €/£100,000)	20
Revaluation of inventories	((€/£20,000 × 50%) − €/£20,000)	(10)
Revaluation of trade receivables	€/£150,000 × 10%	(15)
Tangible assets		1,545
Less:		
Debentures		(200)
Preference shares		(100)
Loan		(100)
Current liabilities		(180)
Net asset value of equity		965
Number of equity shares		800
Value per share	(€/£965,000/800,000)	120.625c/p

Using market-based multiples

The philosophy under the ***multiples approach*** is to value companies by benchmarking them against similar companies that have publicly available data. The analyst tries to determine a common denominator which applies to both the company being valued and a similar company. The common denominator is called the *'multiple'*. The advantage of this approach to company valuation is that it captures valuation information that is already available in the marketplace. A commonly used multiple is the price-earnings ratio (P/E ratio). The approach is to use the P/E ratio, which is publicly available for another similar company in the same industry and then apply this to the earnings/revenue of the company being valued. If this similar company has a P/E multiple of eight then this reflects the market's view about risk and return for this type of company.

In some instances, when earnings are not considered to be meaningful, revenue is utilised instead. The multiples approach is usually used when a private company is being valued or when a publicly traded company wishes to benchmark their market value against the market value of its competitors. The multiple chosen by an analyst who is valuing a company is usually based on recent similar transactions (sales of similar companies/equity holdings), current information available for similar plcs and the analyst's experience and judgement. Apart from the P/E ratio, other commonly used multiples include the dividend yield ratio, the CAPM approach and the use of a multiple of adjusted EBIT. The most commonly used multiples are now discussed.

The P/E ratio

As noted in chapter three, 'Financial Statement Analysis', the P/E ratio is calculated as:

$$\text{P/E ratio} = \frac{\text{Market value}}{\text{Earnings per share}}$$

This can be rearranged to find the company's equity market value:

$$\text{Market value of a share} = \text{Earnings per share} \times \text{P/E ratio}$$

Note: The ***earnings per share*** is earnings after interest, tax and preference dividends divided by the number of shares in issue. To find the total value of the company's equity, the market value of a share is multiplied by the number of shares in issue.

Public limited companies (plcs)

Though the UK, ROI and US markets are regarded as being efficient, researchers have noted that they are not strong-form efficient. A company's share price may therefore not reflect economic reality, though it may be argued to reflect most of the information that is available publicly on the company about the past and the future. In addition, investors may not act rationally: investors hold shares in companies that they support because of their environmental policies, or because they have held the shares for a considerable period in the past and are loyal to the company, or because they like the products being traded in by the company. Alternatively, investors may not like the ethical policies of a company. This will impact on the demand for a company's shares in the marketplace and its subsequent equity value. The result is that the market price of a company may be different to the company's true economic value. Therefore, the management of a plc may use this approach to try and determine if their company is undervalued or overvalued by the market.

Private companies

When valuing a private company using the P/E multiple approach it is normal to discount the P/E ratio of a similar quoted company by between 30% and 50% (Bishopgate Corporate Finance, 2008) as in the next example.

Worked example 16.2   (Calculating company value using the P/E ratio)

In advance of the board of directors meeting of Pero plc, the finance manager was asked to provide a valuation for two target companies, one public (Gato plc) and one private (Pajaro Ltd.), using the P/E ratio approach. The companies being targeted are similar in nature to Pero plc. Pero plc's shares are currently trading at €/£6.40 and the company's EPS is 40c/p.

Continued

REQUIRED

a)   What market value is the finance manager likely to suggest for the public limited company Gato plc? Gato plc has 500,000 equity shares and currently earns €/£300,000 per year (after interest and tax). A preference dividend of €/£50,000 was also paid in the year.

b)   What market value is the finance manager likely to suggest for the private company, Pajaro Ltd.? Ten shares are in issue, each share is held by members from two families. Pajaro Ltd. has earnings of €/£75,000 per year after interest and tax.

c)   What other issues should the finance manager inform the board about in respect of these valuations?

Solution

a)   Given the information supplied above the finance manager can calculate the P/E ratio of Pero plc and apply this to the EPS of Gato plc to determine a starting value for Gato plc.

The P/E ratio of Pero plc is:

$$\text{P/E ratio} = \frac{\text{Market value}}{\text{Earnings per share}}$$

$$\text{P/E ratio} = \frac{\text{€/£6.40}}{\text{€/£0.40}}$$

$$\text{P/E ratio} = 16$$

The EPS ratio of Gato plc is:

$$\frac{\text{Earnings after tax and preference dividends}}{\text{Number of ordinary shares in issue}} = \text{EPS}$$

Continued

$$\frac{€/£300,000 - €/£50,000}{500,000} = 50c/p \text{ per share}$$

Therefore an estimated market value for Gato plc is:
Market value $= 16 \times 0.50$
Market value $= €/£8.00$ per share
Total market value $= €/£8.00 \times 500,000 = €/£4,000,000$

b) A similar approach is utilised when the finance manager values the equity of Pajaro Ltd.; however, Gato plc's P/E ratio would be discounted to take into account the lack of marketability of Pajaro Ltd.'s shares. Selecting the discount factor is subjective – in this instance a discount of 40% is assumed. Therefore the P/E ratio to be applied is now:
P/E ratio $= 16 \times 60\%$
P/E ratio $= 9.6$

The EPS for Pajaro Ltd. is:

$$\frac{€/£75,000}{10} = €/£7,500 \text{ per share}$$

Therefore an estimated market value for Pajaro Ltd. is:
Market value $= 9.6 \times €/£7,500$
Market value $= €/£72,000$ per share
Total market value $= €/£72,000 \times 10 = €/£720,000$

c) These P/E ratios are only a starting point. They may have to be adjusted when other factors come to light. Some other factors that may influence the value to be placed on these two companies include the following:

The market value of Gato plc's shares will be available. This would allow the finance manager to calculate the current total value of the company as determined by the market. This value could then be compared to the €/£4 million valuation calculated in a).

Continued

Other factors will influence the decision. Size is important – large sized companies usually command a higher P/E ratio relative to a small sized company. This would influence any adjustment that would be required to the P/E ratios in a) and b). Gato plc and Pajaro Ltd. are very different sizes – Pero Plc would need to determine if Gato plc was too large for their needs, or if Pajaro Ltd. was too small. This would influence the P/E ratio adjustment.

Growth potential is also an influencing factor. It is likely that the smaller private company Pajaro Ltd. has higher growth potential relative to the larger company Gato plc (though this needs to be determined); therefore, the discount applied may be considered to be too low. Where it is considered that Gato plc has high growth potential a premium may be added to the P/E ratio to account for this.

Potential synergies will also impact on the valuations. If there are synergies to be made by Pero plc from investing in either company (increased profitability, increased growth, or the achievement of a strategic objective), then this will mean that Pero plc should be willing to pay a premium over their reported P/E ratio. This will raise the value that Pero plc is willing to give for the companies.

A full review of the accounting policies and management policies of both companies should be undertaken before a valuation using the P/E ratio is relied upon. In particular, Pajaro Ltd. may have very different policies in respect of directors' remuneration. Where this is the case, there should be an adjustment to Pajaro Ltd.'s directors' payment policy to bring it into line with Pero plc's payment policy before the EPS is calculated.

Finally, it is assumed that Gato plc and Pajaro Ltd. are two similar companies in the same industry as Pero plc. If they were not, then a P/E ratio of a company in the same industry as the two companies would be more appropriate to use than Pero plc's ratio.

P/E approach: advantages

Straightforward calculations: This approach is simple to calculate.

Market view: Quoted companies are being valued by the market according to the economic conditions at the time of valuation.

Future economic value: The market price of a company will include investors' views about future cash flows expected. Investors are experts at analysing company value (it is their job to notice discrepancies in company value and to act in order to make abnormal gains when a discrepancy is noted – only in this way can they beat market returns).

P/E ratio approach: disadvantages

Similar company: This approach is dependent on finding a similar company to the one that is being valued. This is not likely in practice. Companies in the same industry are likely to have different cost structures, sizes, management teams, dividend policies and different capital structures.

Accounting adjustments: Even if a similar company is located, it is very likely that this company will be using different accounting policies and may possibly have a different accounting year end.

P/E ratio: See chapter three, 'Financial Statement Analysis' – the P/E ratio itself has a number of factors that influence its value, including the risk associated with expected earnings.

Marketability: The P/E ratio of a quoted company will always be larger than that which would result for a private company as the ratio will be affected by the marketability of shares. Private company shares have a restricted market (usually family members). This impacts on their value which impacts on the P/E ratio.

Subjective adjustments: The P/E ratio of a quoted company is usually reduced to take account of the lack of marketability of an unlisted company's shares. The discount used is subjectively determined (usually 30% to 50%).

Dividend yield ratio approach

Another multiple that can be utilised is the ***dividend yield method***. This ratio is discussed in chapter three, 'Financial Statement Analysis'. Under this approach the dividend yield of a similar quoted company can be utilised to determine the market value of an unquoted company, given its expected maintainable annual dividend. The dividend yield ratio is calculated as follows:

$$\frac{\text{Dividend per equity share}}{\text{Market price per equity share}} \times 100 = \text{dividend yield}$$

The above ratio can be rearranged to find the market value of a private company.

$$\frac{\text{Dividend per equity share}}{\text{Dividend yield (similary company)}} \times 100 = \text{Market value of one share}$$

The dividend per equity share is the maintainable dividend level of the private company. The maintainable dividend level is calculated by multiplying the earnings of the private company by the dividend payout ratio of a similar quoted company.

Dividend yield ratio approach: advantages

Straight forward to calculate: On the face of it this approach is simple to calculate.

Constant dividend policy: This approach works best when companies pursue a constant dividend policy. It values the company's shares according to the cash flow benefit expected to be received by shareholders, in the form of dividends. This is argued to be the most relevant value to minority shareholders.

> **Dividend yield ratio approach: disadvantages**
>
> *Sourcing a similar quoted company:* As mentioned previously, under the P/E ratio approach to company valuation, it is not likely that a similar company exists.
>
> *Dividend policies:* Different companies will have different dividend policies. Some companies do not pay a dividend at all and private companies typically have lower payout policies when compared to Plcs.
>
> *Dividends:* Dividends represent a portion of a company's earnings and a valuation based on dividends only may not represent the full value of a company, particularly if the company does not adopt a steady dividend payout policy.

The dividend yield ratio approach is deemed to be more suitable to use when a minority shareholding is being valued, as it is considered that these equityholders do not have control over company decision making and have to make do with the dividend that the company decides to pay-out. Therefore, they are considered to have purchased their share on the strength of the company's dividend policy and will value the share on this basis.

Earnings before interest and tax multiples
In some instances EBIT multiples are used to value a company. Bishop-gate Corporate Finance disclosed that they have used multiples of EBIT that range from 4.5 to nine times. They report that the multiple selected is influenced by the level of interest shown from prospective buyers. After the multiple is applied to the EBIT, debt and surplus cash are deducted to provide a value for the equity portion of the company.

Valuing future potential earnings/cash flows
The other commonly used approach is to estimate the future stream of benefits that an equity holder will expect to receive and to discount these to their net present value to determine equity value. There are several versions of this approach. The two most common versions are considered

in this chapter. The first focuses on dividend cash flows expected and the second forecasts a company's expected free cash flows into the future and discounts these back to find their present value. This present value is the maximum price that should be paid for a company. These two methods are discussed in turn.

The dividend valuation model approach

In some instances the expected future dividends can be determined and discounted back to their present value to give an equity valuation. This would involve using straightforward discounting and/or the dividend valuation model (discussed under Chapter 12, 'Cost of Capital'). The dividend valuation model is rearranged to determine the market value of an unquoted company's equity shares using the cost of equity of a similar quoted company. The formula is as follows:

$$P_0 = \frac{D_0(1+g)}{Ke - g}$$

Where D_0 is the last dividend paid, P_0 is the estimated market value of equity, g is a constant growth rate and Ke is an appropriate cost of equity capital. The use of this approach is highlighted in the next example.

Worked example 16.3   (Calculating market value using the dividend yield method)

Verano Ltd. expects to break-even in the next two years, therefore is not going to pay a dividend in year one or in year two. In year three the finance manager predicts that the company will pay a dividend of 5c/p. It is then expected that the dividend will increase to 8c/p in year four and to grow at the rate of 5% each year thereafter.

REQUIRED

Verano Ltd. is considering floating on the AIM/IEX and the board of directors have asked you to calculate a market value for Verano

Continued

Ltd.'s equity. An analysis of equity holders' required returns in the industry, suggests that a return of 14% would be required by equity holders to entice them to buy or sell these shares, were the company to go public.

Solution

Given the information supplied in the question, the only approach that can be utilised to determine a value for Verano Ltd.'s equity is to calculate the present value of the future stream of dividends that will accrue to an equity holder. As the cash flows are uneven, straight-forward discounting will be applied to the expected dividends from years one to three. Then from year three on, the dividend amount is set and will grow at a constant rate into perpetuity. The dividend valuation model can be used to determine the expected share price, though the resultant figure will represent the value in four years time, so it will also have to be discounted to the present day value. The dividend valuation model is:

$$P_0 = \frac{D_0(1+g)}{Ke - g}$$

Where D_0 is the last dividend paid, P_0 is the maximum market value that the equity should be issued at, g is the constant growth rate and Ke is the return expected by shareholders.

In year four the present value of the future stream of constantly increasing dividends will be worth:

$$P_0 = \frac{8c/p(1+0.05)}{0.14-0.05}$$
$$P_0 = €/£0.93$$

This is then discounted to determine its value now, along with the present value of the earlier dividends. As this formula provides the value of the future stream of dividends on the first day of year four, it is discounted as if it were received on the last day of year three.

Continued

Year	Cash flow €/£	Discount factor (14%)	Present value €/£
1	0.00	0.877	0.000
2	0.00	0.769	0.000
3	0.05	0.675	0.034
3	0.93	0.675	0.628
		Net present value	0.662

Verano Ltd. should expect to receive 66.2c/p for each share it intends to issue. To ensure a 100% uptake of shares by the market on an IPO, a discount of 10% is allowed off the issue price. Therefore Verona Ltd. should be advised to issue its shares at 59.56c/p.

Dividend valuation model approach: advantages

Economic sense: From an equity holder's perspective, it makes economic sense to value shares based on the present value of the future stream of cash flows that the equity holder should expect to receive from holding the share.

Dividend valuation model approach: disadvantages

Determining the cost of equity: It is difficult in practice to find companies that are similar to the company being valued. Therefore, finding a reliable cost of equity can be problematic.

Dividend policies: Different companies will have different dividend policies. Some companies do not pay a dividend at all, hence this approach cannot be utilised.

Continued

Estimating future dividends: Dividends are unlikely to grow at a constant rate into infinity. Estimates of dividends for a period of three or four years may be reliable, but estimates beyond this time period are subject to more risk.

Determining the growth rate: This is difficult to calculate. In some instances growth in historical dividend payments are utilised as a proxy for growth in prospective dividends.

High growth: If the growth rate exceeds the cost of equity, the model cannot be used as the denominator becomes negative and the outcome is infinite. However, this phenomenon would be rare.

Like the dividend yield approach, the dividend model approach is more appropriate to use when an analyst is trying to value a minority interest in a company. When a minority interest changes hands, this will have little impact on dividend policy. However, when a whole company is taken over, dividend policy is likely to change to align with the new owners' views; therefore, future expected dividends are unknown. The stage the company is at within its lifecycle will also influence the relevance of this method. An emerging (fast-growth) company with many growth opportunities is likely to have a fluctuating dividend policy and is also likely to offer high growth rates in dividends that are unsustainable into infinity. Whereas a mature company in a mature industry will be more likely to have a steady dividend policy, wherein dividends grow in line with company earnings, and the business finance manager pursues a policy of smoothing dividend payouts to achieve a constant growth pattern.

Determining an appropriate cost of equity: Capital Asset Pricing Model (CAPM)

In some instances the CAPM is utilised to determine a company specific cost of equity. As is explained in chapter 12, 'Cost of Capital', the CAPM determines a company's cost of equity by measuring the relationship between the risk and return of a company relative to that of the market over time. Historical prices are analysed to determine how the return on a company's shares react when there are changes in market returns. The parameter utilised to capture the difference in reaction between the company and the market (the risk) is beta (β). It is then assumed that the equity holders will require a return (r_j) over and above a risk-free investment's return (r_f) to compensate them for the specific risk attached to this particular company. The additional return to be gained from investing in the market is the average market return (r_m) less the risk-free return (r_f). This additional return is then adjusted to take account of the specific company's risk, in that the market premium (r_m-r_f) is multiplied by the beta factor. When a company is not as risky as the market, beta will be a number below one; hence the return required by an equity holder above the risk-free rate will be less than the premium to be gained were the company to have the same risk profile as the market. When a company is riskier than the market, the beta factor will be a number above one; hence the premium required by the equity holder above the risk-free rate will be greater than that of the market. The CAPM formula is as follows:

$$r_j = r_f + \beta(r_m - r_f)$$

The cost of equity can be determined quite easily using the CAPM for any plc as historical data on returns is readily available. The problem arises when trying to determine the cost of equity for a private company, for use in the dividend valuation model to determine the market value of the company. A similar approach to those mentioned previously is followed. The first step is to find a comparable quoted company with historical data. The company being used as a benchmark should be in the same industry, in the same type of business and in particular, should be affected by the same economic forces that impact on the private company. Next, the beta for the selected plc should be determined. Then this beta should be adjusted for financial risk. The adjusted beta should be utilised in the CAPM to determine the equity holders required return (cost of equity) and finally, the value of equity should be determined (dividend valuation model) using the calculated cost of equity.

Worked example 16.4   (Equity value calculated using the CAPM)

Julio Ltd. is a private company with an issued share capital of 1,000,000 equity shares. Half of its financing comes from debt sources. It is planning an IPO wherein 45% of its existing shares will be offered to the public. No new shares will be issued. At present Julio Ltd. pays 40% of its earnings as dividends and reinvests the remainder. Growth in earnings is expected to be maintained at 7%. Earnings in the year just past amounted to €/£800,000.

REQUIRED

You have been asked to suggest an equity share price to the board of directors, which will ensure that current equity holders' wealth is maximised and to ensure that the whole issue is taken up in the IPO. The board of directors informs you that the current return on Gilts is 6% and the average market return on equity shares is double this.

You have investigated the listed companies that operate in the same industry as Julio Ltd. and have identified three that have very similar operations: Mala plc has an equity beta of 3.5 and his highly geared – 80% of its funding comes from debt sources. Cocina plc has an equity beta of 1.6 and is geared to 50%; Lampa plc has an equity beta of 1.1 and 10% of its funding is sourced as debt.

Solution

The first step in the process has already been completed, with companies that have comparable operations already identified. The next step involves looking at financial risk as portrayed by the gearing ratio. Julio Ltd. has a gearing level of around 50%; therefore, it would seem that Cocina plc is the most suitable company to benchmark against as it has similar business risk and similar financial risk. Cocina plc's beta value will be used to determine a cost of equity for Julio Ltd., using the CAPM.

$$r_j = r_f + \beta(r_m - r_f)$$

In this instance r_f is 6%, β is 1.6 and r_m is 12% (6% × 2). Therefore, the cost of equity (r_j) is:

Continued

$$r_j = 6\% + 1.6(12\% - 6\%)$$

$$r_j = 15.6\%$$

And the market value of each share (P_0), before discount, is calculated using the dividend valuation model:

$$P_0 = \frac{D_0(1+g)}{Ke - g}$$

In this instance D_0 is 32c/p ($€/£800,000/1,000,000 \times 40\%$), g is 7% and Ke is 15.6%.

$$P_0 = \frac{32c/p(1+0.07)}{0.156 - 0.07}$$
$$P_0 = 398c/p$$

You recommend that the maximum value to offer shares at is $€/£3.98$ per share. However, to ensure a 100% uptake of shares a discount of between 10% and 20% should be offered which means that the share should be issued at a price of between $€/£3.18$ and $€/£3.58$.

Free cash flow approach
Free cash flows are cash flows that are available to lenders and equity holders after tax and after investment cash outflows. Interest and dividends are not deducted. The estimated free cash flows may be as follows:

Year	20×8	20×9
Cash flows	$€/£$	$€/£$
Revenue	6,000,000	6,500,000
Cash paid for operating activities	(4,000,000)	(4,100,000)
Taxation paid	(500,000)	(480,000)
Decreases/(increases) in working capital	100,000	(150,000)
Cash invested in projects	(300,000)	(200,000)
Free cash flows	1,300,000	1,570,000

These free cash flows are estimated into the future and discounted using either the cost of equity (calculated using the CAPM where the purpose of the valuation is to offer a price for a share repurchase/buyout) or the WACC (suitable for project valuation or valuing an entire company for a takeover bid) to provide a valuation for the whole company. Then debt is deducted to find the equity value. The following formula can be used to determine the market price to offer for each equity share:

$$\text{Value of an equity share} = \frac{\text{NPV of the estimated free cash flows minus debt}}{\text{Number of equity shares in issue}}$$

This approach is best suited when the company or project has a finite life. When the company being valued has an infinite life the above approach combined with an adjusted dividend valuation model can be adopted to provide a valuation for the whole company. In this instance the free cash flows for the initial years are determined as above and a terminal value is given to the value of the company after this period. This **terminal value** is considered to be the present value of a future stream of free cash flows in perpetuity, which increase at a steady growth rate each year in the same manner as dividends are assumed to increase by a steady rate under the dividend valuation model. The formula for determining this terminal value is:

$$\text{Terminal value}_0 = \frac{\text{Free cash flows}_0 (1+g)}{r-g}$$

Where r can either be the company's cost of equity or its WACC and g is the constant rate of growth in free cash flows. The estimated free cash flows for the early period and this terminal value at the end of this period are discounted to determine the total value of the company. As before, debt should be deducted to find the appropriate value for equity.

Worked example 16.5   (Calculating the market value of equity using the free cash flow approach)

Gato plc is considering purchasing a private company called Pero Ltd. Up to this point Pero Ltd. earns about €/£50,000 per year after tax. Its investment in working capital at the end of the year is €/£120,000. Pero Ltd. is financed by equity only and has 5,000 shares in issue. Gato plc estimates that a sustained investment policy would increase the future profits after tax by the following amounts:

Continued

Year	Capital investment in year	Working capital balance	Cash flow after tax from operating activities
0	€/£180,000	€/£120,000	€/£70,000
1	€/£150,000	€/£140,000	€/£100,000
2	€/£80,000	€/£150,000	€/£130,000
3	€/£60,000	€/£160,000	€/£150,000
4	€/£50,000	€/£150,000	€/£160,000
5	€/£50,000	€/£140,000	€/£170,000

It is Gato plc's policy that all investments payback the initial cost, in discounted terms, within five years. Gato plc's WACC is 12%.

REQUIRED

As finance manager, you have been asked to determine a bid amount to be tabled at the next board of directors meeting. This bid should reflect Gato plc's investment policy.

Solution

Gato plc's hurdle condition is that investments should be paid back, in discounted terms, within five years (using a discount rate of 12%). Therefore, the maximum that can be offered for Pero Ltd. will be the present value of the free cash flows over the five-year period.

The first step is to determine the free cash flows:

Year	Cash flow after tax from operating activities (€/£)	Capital investment in year (€/£)	Changes in working capital (€/£)	Free cash flows (€/£)
0	70,000	(180,000)	–	(110,000)
1	100,000	(150,000)	(20,000)	(70,000)
2	130,000	(80,000)	(10,000)	40,000
3	150,000	(60,000)	(10,000)	80,000
4	160,000	(50,000)	10,000	120,000
5	170,000	(50,000)	10,000	130,000

Continued

These are then discounted using the company's cost of capital to find the NPV as follows:

Year	Free cash flows (€/£)	Discount Rate (12%)	Present value (€/£)
0	(110,000)	1.000	(110,000)
1	(70,000)	0.893	(62,510)
2	40,000	0.797	31,880
3	80,000	0.712	56,960
4	120,000	0.636	76,320
5	130,000	0.567	73,710
		NPV	66,360

Therefore, Gato plc should offer a maximum of €/£1.3272 (€/£66,360/50,000) per share for the equity of Pero Ltd.

Free cash flow approach: advantages

Theoretical justification: The NPV approach to investment appraisal is regarded as the most appropriate technique to use in investment appraisal. This argument can also be extended to company valuations.

Straightforward: This approach does away with the problems associated with obtaining information from a similar company, as it focuses on the cash returns from the company being valued.

Free cash flow approach: disadvantages

Determining the cash flows: This involves subjectivity. It is difficult to estimate future cash flows. The further away the cash flow being estimated, the greater the risk that the actual cash flow will be different.

Continued

Determining the discount rate to use: There are weaknesses underlying the models used to obtain a discount rate.

Amount of investment: It is difficult to determine in advance the amount that will be invested each period.

Determining the terminal value: The model used to determine the terminal value assumes that earnings grow at a constant rate. This is not likely to happen in practice as there is less incentive for management to smooth cash flows (management bonuses are usually linked to earnings and they are more likely to try to manipulate these figures).

Shareholder value analysis

The free cash flow approach has been repackaged as '**shareholder value analysis**' by Rappapport (1986) and is widely used by large plcs. The shareholder value analysis approach strives to link management decision making and strategy to value creation. It assumes that the primary corporate objective is equity holder wealth maximisation and that this can be achieved by focusing management attention on **value drivers** such as, sales growth and gross profit, internal investment, the cost of capital (capital structure) and taxation. Under shareholder value analysis an analyst has to consider the cash flows of the entity being valued over a set time horizon, normally five to ten years. Once the time period has been set, shareholder value analysis involves four more steps. Firstly, the cash flows for each of the value drivers (sales, investment, cost of capital and taxation) are determined for each year within the specified period. Secondly, discount rates are calculated. Then a terminal value reflecting the value of the resultant company at the end of the specified period is calculated. Finally, the resultant cash flows are discounted to the net present value. This provides an indication of the company's value. The difference between the value based on shareholder value analysis and a free cash flow approach is due to the focus on strategic value drivers.

The accounting rate of return (ARR) method of share valuation
This approach uses accounting data to determine equity value.

$$\text{Equity value} = \frac{\text{Estimated future profits}}{\text{Required return on capital employed}}$$

In many instances the profits of the company being valued may have to be adjusted to reflect the expected profits of the company in the future after the sale/transaction takes place. For example, the company may become a plc. In these circumstances the directors' wages would be expected to increase, so this should be adjusted for. Where the sale involves any changes to gearing, the resultant expected interest changes should be adjusted for. If the company is going to purchase or sell a property, a rent/interest adjustment may be required and any economies/dis-economies of scale expected should be adjusted for. The resultant profit figure should be the expected equilibrium amount.

Worked example 16.6   (Calculating equity value using the ARR method)

The directors of Leonardo group plc are considering purchasing Bottecilli Ltd. Bottecilli Ltd. has returned a profit after taxation of €/£650,000 per year. The directors of Leonardo group plc reckon that, using their own marketing channels that are already well established, they can increase profits by about €/£150,000 (after tax). At present the owner/manager of Bottecilli Ltd. receives a dividend of €/£70,000 each year instead of taking a regular salary. The directors of Leonardo group plc reckon that they can either replace him with a suitable manager, or encourage him to remain. They think that a salary of €/£80,000 would be required in either case.

REQUIRED

What value should Leonardo group plc place on Bottecilli Ltd.? You are informed that all the subsidiaries within Leonardo group plc have to yield an after tax accounting rate of return of 16% of capital employed.

Solution

The market value should be:

$$\text{Equity value} = \frac{\text{Estimated future profits}}{\text{Required return on capital employed}}$$

Continued

Where the estimated future profits are €/£720,000 (€/£650,000 + €/£150,000 − €/£80,000) and the required return on capital employed is 16%.

$$\text{Equity value} = \frac{€/£720,000}{16\%}$$

$$\text{Equity value} = €/£4,500,000$$

This figure should represent the maximum that Leonardo group plc should pay for Bottecilli Ltd. This valuation should be compared with valuations prepared using other methods to determine the correct offer amount.

Some practical issues to consider

Regardless of the approach taken, there are some issues that will influence the value of a company and the value of its equity.

Control premium

A premium over the normal price to be paid for equity is usually offered when purchasing equity in an entity, when the intention is to obtain a controlling interest. Some corporate finance houses recommend a **control premium** of 20% (InterFinancial Limited, 2002).

Size discount

In most instances large companies are valued higher than their smaller counterparts. Large companies are usually regarded as less risky. In general, a **size discount** of 20% is applied to large company shares where they are being used as a benchmark to value a smaller similar company (20% is the average discount rate used over the period 1993 to 2001 by InterFinancial Limited (2002)).

Liquidity discount

When an entity's equity shares are not tradable, or have limited marketability then this will impact on the valuation that should be placed on the shares. Normally a **liquidity discount** of between 10% and 40% is applied, particularly if the entity is not a plc and is smaller in size to a similar plc that is being used to provide a benchmark for the smaller non-quoted company's share price.

Maintainable earnings

In all instances where earnings are being utilised to determine the market value of equity (and the market value of an entity), it is important that the earnings figure represents normal earnings. Hence any exceptional profits or losses need to be removed. In many instances a multiple calculated from a plc that has a market value is applied to the earnings of an unquoted entity to determine the unquoted company's value. In these circumstances adjustments may need to be made to the unquoted company's earnings to reflect expenditure that is normal for a plc, but not for the unquoted company. The most common example is directors' salaries. In many private companies, the directors are the equity holders and for taxation reasons they may take their yearly earnings from the company in two ways: as a salary and/or as dividends. In addition, directors in plcs normally command a higher salary and were the valuation to be used to value the unquoted company for the purposes of obtaining a listing on the stock exchange then the directors salaries should be added back to earnings and an equivalent salary, which would be payable to the directors were the company a plc, should be deducted. The multiple can then be applied to the adjusted **maintainable earnings**, when determining equity value.

Terminal value

In most instances it is assumed that earnings will occur in perpetuity. When earnings forecasts involve specific estimates in the initial years, with more general forecasts beyond a certain point, it is common practice to calculate the exact estimated cash flow forecasts for the initial years and to value the remainder as though they are in perpetuity. This means allocating a residual value to the company/project. This residual value should be accounted for in the cash flows of the final year.

Risk premium

In all instances when determining the market value of a company's equity, hence their total market value, it is important to consider risk. Even when a similar plc is being used to benchmark the value of the company under scrutiny, the analyst should always ask the question 'is the resultant return on equity suitable for the risk that the company being valued is exposed to?' A *risk premium* may be required if the company being valued is located in a different country to take account of country risk (volatility of that country's economy, risk of war, etc), political risk, structure of the market where the entity is quoted and foreign exchange risk. Risk associated with the structure of a company's markets differs across countries. In some countries only stable, large diversified companies are listed. The shares in companies quoted on these markets are likely to command a lower premium to shares quoted in markets that allow more risky companies to raise funds on. A risk adjustment may also be required if the target company has a different capital structure and different levels of business risk.

Rules of thumb
In some industries, the sale of entities is quite common and rules of thumb about company valuation emerge. The valuation methods may involve applying a typical multiple to historical sales (service firms), or price per tonne of annual production (mining industries). These common practices should be taken into consideration.

Comparative transactions
In many industries, where the sale of entities is quite common, a good guide to determining the value of equity - hence the value of the company - is to review the prices that were paid in the past to purchase similar entities (review takeovers, merger deals, IPOs and acquisitions).

Other more general factors that may impact on company valuation include the following:

General factors that may impact on company valuations

Exchange rate movements: This becomes important when a company's operations are spread over several countries.

Interest rate changes: When a company is highly geared and some of the long-term financing is variable rate interest, then changes in interest rates will increase the financial risk associated with the company. Changes in interest rates will also impact on the required return by equity shareholders.

Continued

Legislation changes: Most entities are impacted on by legislation changes but some are more susceptible than others. For example, if the company being valued has high emissions and legislation changes mean that future expenditure is required to change operations to make them greener, then this will impact on equity value.

The state of the economy: When the economy is in boom, growth is assumed to be maintainable and may even be assumed to increase. This will impact on earnings and cash flow projections. When the economy goes into recession much lower growth rates will be estimated – impacting on share valuation.

Takeover speculation: When there is demand for the equity of a company from a variety of sources, this will have a positive impact on expected share price and should be factored into the valuation.

Announcements of results: When the announcements indicate a change in the pattern of the performance of a company, then this will impact on share price. In particular, the growth variable will most likely be affected, resulting in a different expected share price valuation.

Other information: Any information that is regarded as being **value relevant** (ie impacts on share price) such as information on management recruitment, on retirement, new products and new strategic decisions, will impact on expected future earnings and growth; hence will impact on share valuation.

Industry information: Information on an industry will also impact on equity valuation. For example, the manufacturing industry in the UK and in the ROI has been in decline and this will impact on the valuation of a company's shares within that industry.

In addition to all the above underlying factors, the final price agreed when a company is being valued is usually the product of intense negotiation, whereupon the purchasing entity/individuals and the selling entity/equityholders come to an agreement in respect of the price that will ensure the trade takes place and keeps most parties to the transaction happy.

Valuation process summarised

As a general approach to company/equity valuation an analyst normally considers all the methodologies and decides upon the methodology/methodologies that best suit the situation. For example, if the valuation is to obtain a majority shareholding, or control, then an assets basis, cash flow or earnings basis might be most appropriate; whereas if the valuation is for the purposes of obtaining a minority shareholding, then a dividend yield basis might be considered to be more appropriate. The next step will involve the analyst reviewing prior IPOs, takeovers, mergers and company sales to determine if a similar company went through this process in the past and then using the corresponding value agreed as guidance for the current valuation. At this stage the analyst usually tries to identify a number of similar companies that have publicly available data for the purposes of benchmarking. The aim here is to identify multiples (such as the P/E ratio or the dividend yield ratio) that can be applied to the company being valued. These companies should be in the same line of business, of similar size and affected by similar economic forces. After the most appropriate companies have been identified and suitable multiples noted, the multiples are adjusted to take into consideration the difference in size and marketability/liquidity of the shares between the company being valued and the company being used as a benchmark. In addition, the earnings that the multiples will be applied to should be adjusted to determine the expected future long-run earnings. Therefore, exceptional items should be removed, economies of scale should be predicted and additional expenditure factored in (particularly if the company being valued is a private company). When all the adjustments have been undertaken, it is usual for a number of the approaches to be adopted and a value selected with these in mind. Regardless of the scientific approach, the value of the company will be affected by market demand, market sentiment and other similar transactions.

Conclusion

Valuing companies is both a science and an art. There is a variety of quantitative techniques available to help an analyst come up with a variety of different values for a company. Even though these techniques are very black and white, there is much subjectivity involved in estimating cash flows, discount rates and multiples to be utilised in the models. Indeed, many analysts will use more than one technique when deciding on a final valuation. In most instances the valuation process involves benchmarking the company being valued to a similar quoted company. Quite a bit of knowledge of the stock market is required if a benchmarking approach is adopted. Benchmarking can provide valuable information, although it comes with the caveat that no two companies are the same and adjustments always need to be made – either to the multiples or to the figure the multiple is being applied to (such as earnings, sales, etc.). These adjustments are usually subjective.

Examination standard question

Worked example 16.7   (Calculating company value using the net assets approach)

Background
HIGHTECH Ltd. ('HIGHTECH') was established in 20X2 by its owner and managing director, Mr. Guage. HIGHTECH manufactures calibration equipment for use in the healthcare industry. The company has grown quickly to date and its success has been largely attributable to the quality of its products to which Mr. Guage, an engineer, has devoted considerable time and capital in the area of research and development. Extracts from the recently completed management accounts for the year ended 31 December 20X6 appear in APPENDIX I. Administration expenses in 20X6 include non-recurring research costs of €/£0.1 million. Retained earnings are budgeted to be €/£0.72 million in 20X7.

Technological developments

The high growth rate of the laboratory equipment industry has resulted in an increasing emphasis on quality. Mr. Guage has recently been researching Ultra Precision Calibration ('UPC'), the latest computer assisted assembly equipment, and its potential impact on production efficiency and quality. Initial research has suggested that the following costs and benefits would accrue to HIGHTECH as a result of investing in such a system:

Continued

Costs: (i) Capital costs of the equipment would be €/£4 million. The equipment would have a useful life of six years, after which its disposal value would be €/£0.4 million.

(ii) Incremental annual maintenance costs of €/£0.2 million would be incurred.

(iii) Changes in the existing plant and production process of HIGHTECH to accommodate the new equipment would mean that both production and sales would be lost in the first two years at an estimated cost (in terms of lost contribution) of €/£0.35 million in Year 1, and €/£0.25 million in Year 2.

Benefits: (i) UPC would result in shorter lead times and thus a permanent reduction in existing working capital levels from €/£3.0 million to €/£1.8 million.

(ii) The improvement in quality and efficiency would reduce re-work levels and generate production cost savings of €/£1.0 million per annum.

(iii) The UPC equipment requires less floor space than the existing machinery. It is anticipated that one of the existing warehouses could be let at an annual rental of €/£0.15 million commencing in Year 2.

Mr. Guage believes that all investments should generate a minimum return of 15% per annum.

Acquisition offer

BIGLAB plc ('BIGLAB'), HIGHTECH's largest UK customer, has recently approached Mr. Guage, expressing an interest in acquiring the entire share capital of HIGHTECH. Public information indicates that BIGLAB has the capacity to complete a purchase from its existing cash balances. Mr. Guage has little experience as to methods of valuing companies, and would like some guidance on the matter. Recent publicly available information on BIGLAB and MEDICAID plc, a competitor of HIGHTECH, is as follows:

Continued

	EPS : Year ended 31 December 20X6	Dividend Net	Cover	P/E Ratio
BIGLAB plc	15.8 pence	2.4 pence	6.6 times	10.5
MEDICAID plc	12.4 pence	1.8 pence	6.9 times	10.0

The market value of HIGHTECH's premises is estimated to be €/£0.3 million in excess of its carrying value in the company's books.

REQUIRED

a) (1) Determine whether HIGHTECH should invest in the UPC equipment.
        (*N.B.   Ignore taxation in making the assessment.*)

12 Marks

   (2) Discuss FOUR additional factors which HIGHTECH should consider when deciding to invest in the UPC equipment.

8 Marks

b) (1) Advise Mr. Guage on the probable valuation range of HIGHTECH, both on an earnings and on an assets basis, and comment briefly on FIVE factors which may impact on the valuation.
        (*N.B.   Ignore the UPC investment proposal in advising on the valuation range for HIGHTECH.*)

16 Marks

   (2) Outline TWO benefits/synergies that could accrue to BIGLAB if it were successful in its acquisition of HIGHTECH and outline the nature of their impact on the bid price.

4 Marks

c) Mr. Lance, the Finance Director of BIGLAB, has phoned you privately to say that, in the event of a successful acquisition, you would be the natural choice for Finance Director of HIGHTECH, at a considerably enhanced remuneration

Continued

level. In the light of Mr. Lance's phone call, discuss briefly the ethical implications, if any, of advising Mr. Guage in relation to item **(b)(1)**.

10 Marks
Total 50 Marks
(ICAI, FAE, MABF, Extract from Autumn 1997)

APPENDIX I

HIGHTECH Ltd. Income statement

For the year ended 31 DECEMBER 20X6

	€/£'000
Turnover	12,000
Cost of production	(8,000)
Gross profit	4,000
Selling and distribution expenses	(2,300)
Administration expenses	(1,000)
Interest	(200)
Net income before tax	500
Tax	(50)
Net income after tax	450
Dividends	(60)
Net income retained for the year	390
Revenue reserves brought forward	1,210
Revenue reserves carried forward	1,600

HIGHTECH Ltd. Balance sheet as at 31 December 20X6

	€/£'000
Non-current assets	2,600
Net working capital	3,000
Net debt	(2,400)
	3,200

Continued

Financed by

Share capital...1,000

Revenue reserves...<u>1,600</u>

2,600

Capital grants..<u> 600</u>

<u>3,200</u>

Solution
HIGHTECH Ltd.

To: Mr Guage

From: _____, Company Accountant

Date: XX January, 20X7

Subject

  (a)   UPC equipment investment

  (b)   BIGLAB acquisition offer

(a)   **UPC equipment investment evaluation**

(i) Net present value - (€/£'million)

Year	Capital €/£	Working capital €/£	Maintenance €/£	Re-org costs €/£	Savings €/£	Rent €/£	Net flow €/£
0	(4.0)	–	–	–	–	–	*(4.00)*
1	–	1.2	(0.2)	(0.35)	1.0	–	*1.65*
2	–	–	(0.2)	(0.25)	1.0	0.15	*0.70*
3	–	–	(0.2)	–	1.0	0.15	*0.95*
4	–	–	(0.2)	–	1.0	0.15	*0.95*
5	–	–	(0.2)	–	1.0	0.15	*0.95*
6	0.4	–	(0.2)	–	1.0	0.15	*1.35*

Continued

NPV @ 15%

Year	Net flow €/£	Present value factor	Present value €/£
0	(4.00)	1.000	(4.00)
1	1.65	0.870	1.44
2	0.70	0.756	0.53
3	0.95	0.658	0.63
4	0.95	0.572	0.54
5	0.95	0.497	0.47
6	1.35	0.432	0.58
		NPV	0.19

The investment yields a positive net present value of €/£0.19 million when discounted at the required minimum return of 15% per annum. This should be assessed further in the context of (ii) below:

(ii)   Additional factors to be considered:

(1)   All investment decisions should be subject to sensitivity analysis of its key variables, given the inherent uncertainty associated with forecasts, and the fact that this investment only yields a positive NPV in year six.

(2)   The impact on balance sheet gearing may be prohibitive given the existing debt position of HIGHTECH. The funding of the initial investment thus needs to be carefully assessed with the availability of grants investigated and the possibility of leasing.

(3)   The risk of not adopting the new technology should also be considered i.e. what if HIGHTECH's competitors take on UPC, relative quality decline may adversely impact on sales.

(4)   Other benefits - no allowance has been made for increases in sales due to quality improvements.

(5)   Other costs - HIGHTECH should consider that loss of sales for two years may make it difficult to recover market share.

(6)   Labour relations - UPC may lead to redundancies and higher wage costs due to a smaller yet more skilled workforce.

Continued

(7)   Time horizon - with the rapid change in technology the new machinery could well be obsolete in six years thus impacting on its disposal value.

(8)   Several suppliers should be contacted to quote and report on the technology. The quality and reliability of the new equipment should be thoroughly investigated and references taken wherever possible. Any warranties on the system should be carefully evaluated.

(9)   Any potential tax benefits should be considered.

(b)   (i)   HIGHTECH Valuation:

Asset valuation

Asset-based valuations see the value of the business as being the value of the underlying assets. Net realisable value is the most common approach used with allowances to be made for disposal costs, including redundancy, if relevant.

20X6

	€/£'000
Non-current assets	2,600
Net working capital	3,000
Net debt	(2,400)
Market value (property uplift)	300
Asset valuation	3,500

Earnings valuation

Earnings-based valuations see the value of the business as the present value of its future cash flows. Therefore the results will only be as good as the estimates of future earnings and the capitalisation rate.

	Historic 20X6 €/£'000	Budget 20X7 €/£'000
Retained profit	390	720
Dividends declared	60	–
Exceptional charge	100	–
Earnings	550	720

Continued

Private companies are normally valued at a discount to public companies in the same sector. Therefore, applying a discount of between 15% and 30% of Medicaid plc's earnings valuation yields the following:

		Profits Historic 20X6	Budgeted 20X7
15% Discount	P/E: 8.5	Value: €/£4,675	€/£6,120
30% Discount	P/E: 7.0	Value: €/£3,850	€/£5,040

In determining maximum and minimum prices for a company, the figures are only as good as the techniques employed and the data provided. The final price will be agreed by negotiation and other factors need to be taken into account, such as:

(1) The high growth nature of the laboratory equipment industry and the relatively good margins.

(2) General economic and financial conditions.

(3) The size of the undertaking and its status within its industry. HIGHTECH, although a young company, has grown quickly and established a good reputation for quality.

(4) An unquoted company is normally valued at a discount to that of a quoted company, due to the lack of a liquid market for its shares.

(5) The lack of intention to sell by Mr. Guage, the sole equity holder, may cause any approach to be described as hostile, which is likely to put upward pressure on price. This is referred to as a control premium.

(6) The reliability of profit estimates and the strong past trading record.

(7) The relatively high level of asset backing.

(8) The highly specialised nature of the assets may indicate a specialised nature which would detract from their break-up value.

(9) HIGHTECH currently has a relatively high level of gearing. The higher the ratio, the greater the financial risk for equity shareholders, which in turn demands a higher rate of return on equity.

(10) The extent to which the business is dependent on the technical skills of one or more individuals/key personnel (i.e. Mr. Guage).

Continued

Conclusion:

An offer range of €/£5 million (+/– €/£0.25 million) would appear appropriate. This represents a premium of 43% over existing assets, a relatively high multiple of 9.1 times current earnings, but only a multiple of 6.9 times budgeted current year earnings, possibly a more appropriate multiple given the high-growth history and positive trading outlook.

(ii)   Possible benefits/synergies to BIGLAB:

(1)   HIGHTECH's reputation for quality inputs should enhance the quality of BIGLAB's outputs, thus increasing the revenue potential for BIGLAB.

(2)   Vertical integration by BIGLAB should achieve cost savings on the inputs to its business. This is most likely to occur by way of reduced selling and distribution costs incurred by HIGHTECH.

(3)   The acquisition of HIGHTECH may broaden the target markets of BIGLAB and thus reduce the risk associated with its chosen industry. This may in turn favourably impact on its share price and the rating attached thereto.

(4)   BIGLAB's substantial cash balances should enable the acquisition to be funded at a low cost of finance, eliminate HIGHTECH's annual interest charge and result in a higher return on capital employed for itself.

(5)   BIGLAB's UK operations may offer opportunities to reduce foreign exchange risk in HIGHTECH's existing operations.

Each or any of the above increase the value of HIGHTECH to BIGLAB. Earnings synergies of €/£0.1m per annum, where achievable, in theory will add value of €/£1.05m to the market value of BIGLAB at its current P/E of 10.5 (ignoring the financing impact of the acquisition on BIGLAB).

c)   Ethical considerations

The concept of independence has no direct relevance to a chartered accountant employed in industry. However, the requirement for objec-

Continued

tivity and thus professional integrity is of equal application to all members. Without the capacity of being fully independent of an employer, it is even more important that the employed member should strive constantly to maintain objectivity in every aspect of his/her work.

An employed member should recognise the problems which may be created by financial involvements or personal relationships which, whether sanctioned by his/her contract of employment or not, could nevertheless by reason of their nature or degree threaten his/her objectivity. Where any doubt exists, the involvement or relationship should be disclosed to the employer.

An employed member should be aware of the difficulties which may arise from the offer of any gift or favour which may be intended to influence the recipient or which could be interpreted by a reasonable person in full possession of the facts as likely to have that effect.

Any report for which an employed member is responsible should be prepared with integrity and objectivity. This means, for example, that while a report prepared by an employed member may properly present only one side of the case and may present that case to its best advantage or in the worst light, the report should be accurate, truthful and, within its scope, both complete and balanced. It should not rely on ambiguities or half truths, but should be objectively justifiable and should not be based on unreasonable assumptions.

(ICAI, FAE, MABF, Extract from Autumn 1997)

KEY TERMS

Asset-based approach	Net realisable assets
Control premium	Net realisable value approach
Dividend valuation model approach	Net replacement value
Dividend yield approach	Price-earnings approach
Free cash flows approach	Replacement cost approach
Liquidation value	Risk premium
Liquidity discount	Shareholder value analysis
Maintainable earnings	Size discount
Multiple	Terminal value
Multiples approach	Value drivers
Net book value approach	

WEBSITES THAT MAY BE OF USE

For a quick business valuation visit the site:
http://www.valueourcompany.com/

For further reading on the methods used in practice to calculate the value of companies, visit
http://www.natweststockbrokers.co.uk/learn/learn_choosing_company.cfm

For information on the approaches to company valuations visit:
http://www.infinancials.com

REVIEW QUESTIONS

1. Explain the difference between determining company value and determining the value of a company's equity.

2. Carmon plc has operating profit (after depreciation of €/£7m) of €/£50m. It paid €/£3m in interest, invested €/£6m in capital expenditure and increased its working capital by €/£1m.

    REQUIRED

    Calculate the free cash flow for Carmon plc. Assume that the tax rate is 25% and tax is paid in the year it becomes due *(ignore capital allowances)*.

3. Greenan plc has EPS of 25c/p. It retains 80% of its profits for internal investment. It earns about 16% from this reinvestment. The current equity holders have a required return of 14%.

    REQUIRED

    a) Calculate the value of Greenan plc's equity shares.
    b) Determine the impact on the value of Greenan plc's equity shares if the company's risk profile changes such that the equity holders now require a return of 16%.

4. List the advantages and disadvantages of the dividend yield method of valuing equity shares.

5. McKee plc is an agricultural company. Its equity holders require a
    return of 14%. An excerpt from its estimated income statement for
    the forthcoming year is as follows:

	€/£'000
Revenue	1,500
Operating costs*	1,000
Gross profit	500
Tax	200
Operating income after tax	300

    *Operating costs include depreciation of €/£180,000

    You are also informed that McKee plc plans to purchase new agricultural
    equipment worth €/£220,000 in the coming year and will increase its
    working capital from €/£900,000 to €/£1,000,000. This will give McKee
    a competitive advantage for the next five years and will increase its free
    cash flow as follows:

    In year two the free cash flows expected is €/£200,000, in year
    three it is €/£220,000, in year four it's €/£250,000 and in year five it's
    €/£280,000. At that stage the net assets of McKee plc are considered to
    be worth €/£350,000 and terminal value for McKee plc is predicted to be
    €/£3,000,000.

    REQUIRED

    a) Calculate the free cash flows for year one from the information
        provided above. Highlight the value drivers in your calculation.
    b) Calculate the value of McKee plc now, assuming a shareholder
        value analysis approach is adopted.
    c) Determine the impact on the valuation if it is assumed that
        McKee plc invests €/£500,000 now in order to extend its
        competitive advantage to nine years. Assume that the free cash
        flows for years six to ten is expected to be €/£290,000 per year
        and the terminal value is predicted to be €/£5,000,000.

6. List the valuation stages that an analyst normally takes when valuing
    a company/share holding.

CHALLENGING QUESTIONS

1. REDBRICK plc

Background

You have recently been appointed Financial Director of REDBRICK plc ('REDBRICK'), a company that manufactures a traditional range of red brick products for use in the construction industry. The company operates from factory premises located just outside a major urban centre, which allows easy access to the large number of construction sites located in the area. The company sources its raw materials (mainly sand and mineral supplies) from a variety of local quarry operators.

REDBRICK's main customers include major local residential housebuilders and property development companies. However, the company has traditionally found it difficult to break into the cross border market, due to the strong competition from local manufacturers. One of REDBRICK's main competitors across the border is TARRAGH Ltd. ('TARRAGH') which, although smaller in size to REDBRICK, has experienced significant sales growth due to the success of its unique range of sandstone brick products. TARRAGH's main manufacturing plant is located beside its own quarry, from which it is able to extract the unique local sandstone that is the main raw material used in the manufacture of its bricks.

Mike Ryan, REDBRICK's Chief Executive, has long admired TARRAGH's growth record and its complementary product range, and has asked you to prepare a report commenting on the benefits or otherwise of a possible acquisition of TARRAGH. He also asked you to give an indication of the likely price that REDBRICK should consider paying for the acquisition.

TARRAGH also has a small roof tile distribution operation that is located in separate premises. It is envisaged that this Division would be disposed of post acquistion. This could potentially free up space that, with a small capital investment, could be potentially used to create additional production capacity, should this be required at a future date.

On the assumption that the acquisition will proceed, Mike Ryan has also asked you to detail those matters which you would wish to be included in a due diligence report on TARRAGH, and to comment on any potential impact on the company's valuation.

Financial information on TARRAGH is provided in APPENDIX 1

Oldestyle Brick

After a long period of product research and development REDBRICK has recently introduced a new range of brick products called 'Oldestyle'. This product gives the appearance of an aged and rougher brick surface, more associated with older houses. The distressed appearance of the Oldestyle range has recently become fashionable again, particularly in the construction of inner city houses and pubs, and this product is now seen as a way to diversify into a distinct niche market.

The unique texture of the Oldestyle brick is achieved by using a rougher grade of material (which actually costs less than that used in the manufacture of the company's other red brick ranges), and increasing the baking time in the kiln.

REDBRICK's full product range now includes the following.

- *Rustic* (standard red brick range/smooth surface texture)
- *Mellow* (same finish as rustic/slightly lighter colour)
- *Oldestyle* (more weathered appearance/rougher surface texture).

REQUIRED

Draft a report to the Chief Executive detailing each of the following matters:

a) Calculate an estimated valuation range for TARRAGH using both an earnings and an asset-based valuation technique.

26 Marks

b) Detail THREE specific matters which you would want to be included within a due diligence report on TARRAGH (other than standard due diligence procedures), and comment on their possible impact on the valuation of the company. Outline two specific matters on which you would seek directors' warranties.

12 Marks

c) List THREE potential benefits that could arise from the proposed acquisition of TARRAGH and list THREE potential difficulties that may arise with the enlarged group (excluding those matters to be examined under the due diligence procedures).

N. B. Ignore any foreign exchange issues.

<u>12</u> Marks
Total <u>50</u> Marks
(ICAI, MABF, FAE, Extract from Autumn 2000)

APPENDIX 1

Financial information on TARRAGH Ltd.

Balance sheet as at 31 December 20X7

	Notes	€/£'000
Non-current assets		
Tangible assets		
Premises	(1)	1,300
Quarry reserves	(2)	700
Plant and machinery		1,000
		3,000
Intangible assets		
Goodwill		200
Current assets		
Inventories		300
Trade receivables	(3)	700
Cash		50
		1,050
Total assets		4,250
Equity, reserves and liabilities		
Equity and reserves		
Equity share capital		300
Revenue reserves		2,450
		2,750

Non-current liabilities

Long-term bank loan		400
3% debentures	(4)	300
		700

Current liabilities

Overdraft	500
Trade payables	300
	800
Total equity reserves and liabilities	4,250

Income statement extracts – year ended 31 December 20X7

	€/£'000
Net income before tax	300
Taxation	75
Net income after tax	225
Dividend	75
Retained income	150

Financial information on TARRAGH Ltd.
Notes

(1) Premises includes €/£500,000 relating to a small office block that houses the company's accounting department. It has been established that the accounts function could be managed from REDBRICK's existing accounts function, thereby saving salaries of €/£250,000 per annum. In addition, TARRAGH's office building could be sold or let post acquisition. This property has a current rental value of €/£70,000 per annum and could be readily sold to reflect a 10% yield to a prospective purchaser.

   In addition, it is estimated that the remaining TARRAGH premises are under valued by €/£150,000.

(2) Quarry reserves are stated at the historical cost of the sandstone quarry purchased in 20W7. At the time of purchase it was estimated

that the reserves were the equivalent of 25 years production. No revised valuation survey has since been undertaken to estimate the depth of reserves under ground.

(3) Trade receivables includes €/£25,000 owing from a small construction company that has now gone into liquidation.

It is thought that this amount is likely to be unrecoverable. It would appear that there are potentially a number of other similar debtors whose financial position is known to be precarious.

(4) The debenture stock holders have agreed to redeem their debentures for a total consideration of €/£200,000.

(5) The non-core Roof Tiling division has a net asset value of €/£400,000. It is estimated that this division, which generates annual pre-tax profits of €/£100,000, could be readily sold off for €/£600,000.

(6) If the acquisition proceeds, Mike Ryan has indicated that he would undertake a €/£600,000 capital expenditure programme that would result in other cost savings of €/£120,000 per annum.

(7) TARRAGH's long-standing Managing Director and its Sales Director have both indicated their wish to retire if the acquisition is successfully completed. This would save a further €/£130,000 per annum.

(8) The employee pension fund was last subject to an actuarial valuation in 2004 and, at that time, required no adjustments to annual contributions. The directors of TARRAGH now estimate that the fund is currently under-funded to the extent of €/£150,000. It is proposed that this short-fall should be met by increased employer's contributions over the next three years.

(9) The directors have made reference to on-going legal action by a former employee who was injured whilst working in the quarry. They are of the opinion that their case is strong and consequently they have not provided for any contingent liability in the audited accounts.

(10) TARRAGH is under legal obligation to operate the quarry in accordance with the latest EU Environmental Directives.

(11) Both REDBRICK and TARRAGH have effective tax rates of 25% which should be assumed to remain unchanged. Some years ago TARRAGH was the subject of an investigation by the tax authorities, which resulted in a payment of €/£75,000 to cover unpaid tax and resultant penalties.

(12) Ignore any foreign exchange issues.

Financial information on REDBRICK plc

The following information is available in respect of shares in REDBRICK as at 31 December 20X7:

Share price	€/£2.20
Earnings per share	22c/p

2. ACA CORPORATE FINANCE

Background

You have just been appointed Manager in a firm of specialist corporate financiers, 'ACA CORPORATE FINANCE'. As part of your new role, you specialise in providing recommendations to clients who are considering acquisitions and disposals, as well as other corporate finance activities.

TIMBER plc

One of your most important clients is TIMBER plc (TIMBER), a company that has three sawmills, one each in Dublin, Belfast and Sligo, from which it supplies timber to builders merchants around Ireland. The business is notoriously cyclical and closely follows trends in the construction industry, which uses a lot of timber, particularly for house building.

The directors of TIMBER are currently considering a number of new investment projects and the directors have asked you to calculate an appropriate discount rate that could be used to appraise these projects. You have received information on the current financing structure of TIMBER (see APPENDIX 1).

New saw mill

One of the new projects being considered involves the replacement of an old sawmill, which is causing production problems due to continued breakdowns, etc. A new sawmill would cost €/£25 million and would deliver 25% more efficiency, as well as reduced electricity consumption.

FINEFURNITURE Ltd.

Another potential investment project involves the acquisition of a furniture manufacturing company called FINEFURNITURE Ltd. (FINE-FURNITURE). The rationale behind this acquisition is that it would provide TIMBER with a new market for its wood, offering diversification into a new industry and thereby reducing the risk of any downturn within the core timber business. Furniture manufacturing is considered to have a lower level of systematic risk than the timber industry (see Note 5 in APPENDIX 1). Demand for furniture is growing steadily and seems to avoid the peaks and troughs associated with the timber industry.

Potential disposal

While in the process of considering the above expansion options, the directors of TIMBER have recently received, from its largest competitor, BIGWOOD plc (BIGWOOD), an unsolicited offer to buy the company. Should the acquisition proceed, the enlarged group would be the largest timber company in Ireland and there would be significant cost and buying power synergies, which would have a very positive impact on profits.

BIGWOOD's offer includes a substantial takeover premium, which is conditional on the directors of TIMBER leaving the company, i.e. they would not become directors in the enlarged group, going forward. As part of the cost synergies identified by BIGWOOD, the directors of TIMBER would be made redundant and would receive termination payments in line with their individual contracts of employment.

Given the imminent prospect of redundancy, the directors of TIMBER are extremely reluctant to contemplate a sale of the company to BIG-WOOD and are proposing to reject the offer outright. Before rejecting the offer they have asked for your advice as to their responsibilities to the equity holders, under the Stock Exchange rules, in respect of the offer. They have also asked for your views on what potential valuation should be placed on TIMBER.

REQUIRED

Prepare a report to the board of directors of TIMBER outlining the following:

a)   Calculate TIMBER's cost of equity using the dividend growth model and subsequently calculate the discount rate which should be used to assess the new sawmill project, outlining clearly any assumptions you make.

20 Marks

b) Calculate the most appropriate discount rate which TIMBER should use to assess the acquisition of FINEFURNITURE, outlining clearly your reasons.

10 Marks

Note: Assume the company finances the acquisition so that its existing capital structure remains unchanged.

c) Compare and contrast the Beta factors and P/E ratios associated with the timber and furniture industries, outlining your views as to why they differ so much between these two industries.

8 Marks

d) Advise the directors of TIMBER as to their responsibilities to the shareholders, under the Stock Exchange rules, in respect of the offer from BIGWOOD.

8 Marks

e) Calculate TWO valuations of TIMBER, one based on earnings, and the other based on a valuation of assets.

8 Marks

f) Outline THREE factors which should be taken into account in the valuation when considering the price being offered by BIGWOOD.

8 Marks
Total 60 Marks
(ICAI, MABF, FAE, Extract from Autumn 2005)

APPENDIX 1

TIMBER plc
Income statement extracts for the year ended 31 December 20X7

	€/£ million
Net income before interest and tax	125
Interest	25
Net income before tax	100
Taxation	20
Net income after tax	80

Balance sheet extracts as at 31 December 20X7

	€/£ million
Non-current assets	325
Current assets	
Inventories	120
Trade receivables	52
Cash	3
	175
Total assets	500
Equity, reserves and liabilities	
Equity and reserves	
Equity share capital	25
Revenue reserves	175
	200
Non-current liabilities	
Long-term bank debt	150
9% debentures	100
	250
Current liabilities	
Trade payables	25
Taxation	25
	50
Total equity and liabilities	500

(1) The current P/E ratio of TIMBER is seven while the standard P/E ratio of companies in the furniture sector is ten.

(2) Ordinary share capital comprises 25 million shares at €/£1 each.

(3) The company is about to pay a dividend which will result in a dividend yield of 3.5% on its ordinary shares.

(4) Dividends are expected to increase at 5% per annum.

(5) Companies in the timber industry have a Beta coefficient of 1.2, while companies in the furniture industry have a Beta coefficient of 0.8.

(6) The 9% debentures are currently trading at 110%. A full year's interest is due immediately and has been provided for in the financial statements.

(7) The bank debt carries an interest rate of 6%.

(8) The interest rate on Government securities is 7% and, historically, the stock market has given a return of about 5% above the risk-free rate of return.

(9) Corporation Tax is currently 20%,

(10) Non-current assets have a book value of €/£325 million. However, the market value of the company's property has been independently valued at €/£100 million more than the book value.

(11) At the beginning of 20X4 the company purchased a new computer system costing €/£20 million, which is being depreciated on a straight-line basis over a four year period. The net recoverable amount of this asset is currently 50% of its purchase price.

3. MEDICON plc

Background

You are a partner in a Big 4 firm of Chartered Accountants who specialises in offering advice to high growth companies, mainly in the pharmaceutical and technology sectors. One of your clients is MEDICON plc ('MEDICON'), a pharmaceutical company formed ten years ago by a bio-chemistry graduate, Gerard Smith, who pioneered research into new techniques for diagnosing liver diseases. Smith subsequently patented a diagnostic kit which could be used to test for a variety of common liver complaints.

MEDICON commenced trading in 20X8 (with Gerard Smith as Managing Director), when its testing kit received approval from the relevant health authorities in Ireland and the UK. The company grew quickly as local hospitals realised the convenience and simplicity of MEDICON's product. The testing kit effectively replaced the need to send blood samples to hospital laboratories to diagnose liver illnesses, which consequently saved substantial amounts of hospital time, and resulted in significant cost savings.

Smith's ambition and enthusiasm were instrumental in driving the company forward. In 20Y5 you were heavily involved in the decision to float MEDICON on the Stock Exchange. Since then Smith has continued to aggressively target new markets for the company's key product whilst maintaining a tight grasp on overhead costs. MEDICON now provides liver testing kits to most of the main hospitals throughout Ireland and the UK. However, the company has recently become aware of plans by a foreign competitor to launch a similar liver testing kit in the Irish and UK markets within the next year.

Smith had foreseen this eventuality and, in recent years, MEDICON has invested considerable resources in Research and Development ('R & D') in an attempt to expand its innovative testing kit idea to the diagnosis of other ailments. The company will shortly introduce a new testing kit that can be used to diagnose kidney complaints. This new product is seen as a major growth area that will provide a platform for future expansion of the company.

MEDICON is also considering investing in an additional new product that will be used to measure cholesterol levels. Details are now provided.

Investment projects

Gerard Smith has advised you that MEDICON is currently considering investing in two separate projects, as follows:

(i)   New cholesterol testing kit
MEDICON is considering commencing a new R & D project to develop a new testing kit to measure cholesterol levels. This would involve expenditure of €/£1 million per annum for two years, with a grant of €/£0.5 million to be received in the second year. The project is then estimated to generate additional after-tax profits of €/£0.75 million per annum for the following four years. This investment is considered to have the same level of business risk as the company's existing liver testing product. Additional information in respect of MEDICON is provided in APPENDIX I.

(ii)   SCHOOLWEB Ltd.
Smith has recently held discussions with a friend, Michael Jones, who owns SCHOOLWEB Ltd. (SCHOOLWEB), an e-commerce company that sells a wide selection of children's schoolbooks via the internet. SCHOOLWEB's turnover has grown rapidly since its formation in early 20Y6, and Jones is keen to raise additional finance to fund a marketing campaign aimed at further increasing the awareness of its website which

in turn, should yield additional turnover. Consequently, he has offered MEDICON the opportunity to invest in SCHOOLWEB in return for an agreed shareholding in the company.

SCHOOLWEB is considered to operate in a higher risk industry than the pharmaceutical sector and like many similar e-commerce companies, is currently making losses. However, revenues are projected to continue to grow significantly over the next three years, with profitability likely to be achieved within that period. Jones has undertaken to provide a Business Plan showing projected earnings and cash flow over the next three years, which can be used by Smith to determine if MEDICON should consider investing in SCHOOLWEB.

Given the high-risk sector in which SCHOOLWEB operates, Smith has asked you for advice on how to appraise the investment. In particular, he is keen to know what rate should be used to discount any projected cash flows. Additional financial information in relation to SCHOOLWEB Ltd is set out in APPENDIX I.

Flotation

Michael Jones has indicated to Smith that he is keen to float SCHOOL-WEB at some point within the next couple of years. This would provide the long-term finance necessary to fund the increased size of operations that are projected over the coming years. However, given that the company is currently making losses and has only been incorporated for two years, Jones considers that SCHOOLWEB currently does not have the necessary track record to contemplate undertaking a flotation. Given your experience of the flotation of MEDICON and of the technology sector in general, Smith has asked you to prepare a brief report on the feasibility of floating SCHOOLWEB.

REQUIRED

Prepare a Report to the Managing Director addressing each of the following issues:

a) Calculate MEDICON's Weighted Average Cost of Capital (WACC) and then advise on whether the company should proceed with the new R & D project to develop the cholestoral testing kit. Outline any limitations arising from the use of the WACC for the evaluation of investment projects.

23 Marks

b) Outline briefly any significant qualitative issues that should be considered in the decision to undertake the cholesterol testing kit project.

8 Marks

c) Determine a suitable discount rate which could be used to appraise the cashflows (to be provided by Michael Jones) relating to the investment in SCHOOLWEB, outlining clearly the rationale for your approach.

9 Marks

Note.   Assume that both projects could be financed in such a way as to leave MEDICON's existing financial risk unchanged, and that SCHOOL-WEB carries a similar level of gearing to MEDICON.

d) Given Michael Jones' decision to float SCHOOLWEB within the next couple of years, advise on whether you consider flotation feasible, outlining the specific reasons for your answer.

10 Marks
Total 50 Marks
(ICAI, MABF, FAE, Extract from Autumn 2001)

APPENDIX I

Financial information on MEDICON plc

Extracts from MEDICON plc's balance sheet as at 31 July 20Y8

	Notes	€/£'000
Non-current assets		20,000
Net working capital		6,500
Total assets		26,500

Equity, reserves and liabilities

Equity and reserves

Equity shares (3 million €/£1 shares)		3,000
Share premium		1,500
Revenue reserves		10,500
		15,000

Non current liabilities

10% irredeemable debenture stock	(3)	3,000
Long-term bank loan	(4)	5,000
11% preference shares	(5)	2,000
		10,000

Current liabilities

Bank overdraft		1,500
Total equity, reserves and liabilities		26,500

The following information is also available in respect of MEDICON:

Notes

(1) New equity could be issued in MEDICON at a discount of 40c/p to the current share price of €/£5.75 (cum. div.).

(2) MEDICON has declared a dividend of 50c/p per equity share for the year ended 31 July 20Y8, and dividends are expected to increase at an annual rate of 3%.

(3) Debenture interest has just been paid and the debenture stock has a current market value of 85%.

(4) MEDICON currently has a ten-year bank loan of €/£2 million at a fixed interest rate of 8% per annum. Interest on any additional long-term debt would be payable at an interest rate of 9% per annum.

(5) The preference shares have a current market value of 105%.

(6) MEDICON's overdraft is used for short-term working capital requirements and is not considered to be a long-term source of funds. It should therefore be ignored in any calculation of the company's WACC.

(7) Corporation tax is expected to remain at the current rate of 25% for the foreseeable future.

Financial information on SCHOOLWEB Ltd.

(1) SCHOOLWEB is considered to operate in the internet sector with a Beta risk factor of 1.7, compared to 1.2 for the pharmaceutical sector in which MEDICON operates.

(2) The average level of gearing in the internet industry may be assumed to be the same as MEDICON's level of gearing.

(3) The risk-free rate of return is currently 3% and the average market rate of return is 10%.

COMPANY RECONSTRUCTIONS 17

Debt 10,000,000
Equity 15,000,000
Market Value 25,000,000

LEARNING OBJECTIVES

Upon completing this chapter, readers should be able to:

♣ Explain the difference between a merger and a takeover;

♣ Describe the different types of merger/takeover;

♣ Explain the motives for mergers/takeovers;

♣ Describe the different methods used by a bidding company to finance a merger/takeover;

♣ Explain the advantages and limitations of each of the finance methods and outline situations where these would be most appropriate;

♣ Distinguish between minority and controlling interests, in the context of a takeover situation;

♣ Summarise common defence tactics and comment on their appropriateness;

♣ Describe potential ethical issues that may arise in takeover/merger situations;

♣ Outline the various steps that a bidding company might follow, which are likely to improve the chance of making a takeover successful (including post-acquisition measures);

♣ List and explain the various due diligence work that a bidding company may request when negotiating a takeover;

♣ Outline the various types of company restructuring techniques that are used when a company elects to restructure its strategic operations; and

♣ Describe the results of research into the success of mergers/takeovers in the past, outlining the stakeholders who have most to benefit from this type of investment activity.

Introduction

Company reconstruction can take many forms. The most common types are where companies merge with another company, are taken over by another company, are formed by a spin-off from a parent company, or are purchased by parties who are not equity holders.

The first two types of company reconstructions to be considered in this text, mergers and acquisitions, are examples of external growth investment decisions that involve the *amalgamation* (coming together) of two or more independent companies. A *merger* usually occurs when two companies come together amicably to form a new larger company. Both sets of equity holder receive shares in the new entity in exchange for the equity shares they held in the original entities. The assets of both companies are transferred to the new company. A *takeover* is different, one company, the *'target company'* is absorbed into the other company, the *'bidding company'*. In general, the bidding company is larger, though this is not always the case. When a small company merges with a large company this is called a *'reverse takeover'*, though is sometimes referred to as a *'reverse merger'*. When a takeover occurs, the target company's assets are transferred to the bidding company and all the shares of the target company are purchased using cash, equity, debt, or a combination of these three forms of consideration. Takeovers can occur amicably, or can be contested by the management of the target company. In the latter scenario, they are referred to as *'hostile takeover bids'*.

Mergers/takeovers are usually classified according to the relationship that exists between the two companies who are parties to the transaction. When the two companies are in the same industry involved in the same type of activity, for example both refine crude oil; this is known as *'horizontal integration'*. When the two companies are in the same industry, but are involved in different activities, for example one refines crude oil, the other owns a network of filling stations; this is known as *'vertical integration'*. When a bidding company takes over an entity which supplies goods to it, this is termed *'backward vertical integration'*, when a bidding company takes over an entity which it supplies goods to, this is called *'forward vertical integration'*. When the two companies are in unrelated industries, for example one refines crude oil, the other is in pharmaceuticals; this is referred to as a *'conglomerate merger'*.

Many companies also restructure to downsize for a variety of reasons, which will be covered later in this chapter. The three main methods used to downsize are a *leveraged buy-out* (LBO), the sale of a portion of the company to another company (a sell-off), or a spin-off. A leveraged buy-out describes a variety of methods that are used to explain the sale of a portion of a company to others, wherein the main financing used by the purchasing parties is debt. Examples of LBO's include a management buy-out (MBO), a management buy-in (MBI) and sales to private equity investors. A *spin-off* occurs when a large company with more than one business activity, separates one or more of the business activities and their assets into a separate company. The parent company provides its current equity holders with shares in the new entity.

The next section explains the motives for restructuring a company, then the methods that are commonly used to finance company mergers/takeovers are discussed and the steps that are usually required during and after this process are outlined. The final part of this chapter links the theory into practice by considering the research on the success of company mergers/takeovers.

Motives for takeovers/mergers

As mentioned, mergers and takeovers are investment decisions – hence, the principles and approaches to capital investment appraisal, covered in chapter 13, 'Capital Investment Decision Making' apply. In brief, the net present value of the expected future *incremental* cash flows of the company (including those specific to the target company) less the cost of the target company, should be positive, when discounted at the company's required rate of return (adjusted for risk if necessary). The underlying objective of the decision on whether to amalgamate with another business is the same as that for normal capital appraisal decision making, to maximise equity holder wealth.

As seen in earlier chapters, each investment undertaken by a company should be aligned with the strategic objectives of the company, maximising equity holder value. This means that takeovers/mergers are likely to be undertaken for a number of reasons, which might include: speculative investment, cost reduction, increasing market share, gaining access to markets, increasing production capacity, expanding to achieve critical mass so that 'costly' developments can be pursued, and achieving synergies. Other reasons for mergers and takeovers, which may not be consistent with maximising equity holder value, include amalgamating with another company to utilise surplus funds or to diversify risk. The motives are now discussed in more detail.

Speculative investment

A company may launch a bid to takeover another company when they perceive that the other company is undervalued. Where the target company is a public limited company, then the bidding company might be of the opinion that the market is not valuing the target company correctly. The intention of the bidding company in a speculative takeover would be to purchase the target company and sell off its components for an overall premium, a process termed *'asset stripping'*. The total revenues received for the component parts are expected to exceed the initial purchase consideration, hence increasing the wealth of the equity holders of the bidding company.

Cost reductions

Economies of scale are cited in many instances as being motivations for amalgamating with another company. Economies of scale might include, for example: the ability to purchase larger quantities, hence negotiate cheaper purchase prices; the ability to reduce costs that are duplicated (typically central costs such as administrative costs, marketing costs, or research and development costs); the ability to reduce production costs where the company is a manufacturing entity; and/or the ability to negotiate cheaper finance fees when accessing finance from financial institutions, and the markets.

Synergies

The term *synergy* is used to describe gains that are not associated with scale economies. Synergies are commonly explained using a mathematical example; assume that the two companies that are merging have earnings of €/£2 each. However, after the amalgamation the combined earnings amount to €/£5. The €/£1 is considered to reflect synergies gained from the amalgamation. Examples of synergies include gains from using similar distribution channels. When Belleek Pottery purchased Galway Crystal in 1993, Donegal Parian China in 1996 and Aynsley China in 1997 a strategic incentive was to use the company's established worldwide distribution systems and retail outlet network to reduce the overall costs of distribution and to increase the sales of the aforementioned products. Several banks have also amalgamated to take advantage of their complementary resources. For example, Lloyds bank merged with the TSB Group and Barclays merged with the Woolwich.

Increasing market share

When a company operates in a competitive industry where margins are tight and the products are homogenous, it may be possible to gain more earnings by eliminating competition by taking other companies over. This can allow the company to raise prices which will result in more earnings. Unchecked, horizontal mergers can actually be damaging for the general public who purchase the end products. Therefore, horizontal mergers are policed by governments in both the UK and in the ROI (discussed later in this chapter). Examples of horizontal mergers/possible mergers, which attracted much attention because of the perceived impact on competition included: the proposed takeover of Safeways by Morrisons, Asda, Sainsbury's and Tesco in the UK in 2005; and the proposed takeover of Aer Lingus by Ryanair in the ROI in 2007. In the UK, the competition commission blocked the Asda, Sainsbury and Tesco bid, but gave the go-ahead to Morrisons. This they felt would actually increase competition between the one-stop-shop retail entities as it would produce four large players instead of three. In the ROI, the Irish Government (a large equity holder in Aer Lingus) publicly rejected Michael O' Leary's bid for Aer Lingus on the grounds that *'it would not be in the best interests of the company, the country, passengers and staff'*.

Gaining access to markets

In some instances a company will make a takeover bid for another established entity to gain access to its market. The target market may be geographically different, or have a totally different customer base. For example, in 2007 CRH acquired companies in Spain, Denmark, the Netherlands and in the US. This provided them with access to wider geographical markets. In March 2008, Tata (an Indian conglomerate) purchased Jaguar and Land Rover from Ford. Tata had been trying to expand its product range. It currently produces four-wheel drives in India as well as the world's cheapest car, the 1 Lakh car, which is expected to sell for little over £1,000. Tata is expecting the purchase of Jaguar and Land Rover to provide access to the luxury vehicle market worldwide. At the time of writing the Dutch insurance giant 'Eureko' is reported to be in negotiations with FBD Holdings plc. One of Eureko's strategic aims is to *build an integrated, pan-European group consisting of market leaders in the territories in which it operates*. Eureko currently owns an Irish-based insurance firm called Friends First. This firm wrote €246 million of insurance premiums in 2006. Friends First is not one of the main providers of insurance in Ireland, whereas FBD holdings has about 11% of the market share.

Recognising underutilisation of resources

In some instances a bidding company will approach a target company when they perceive that the target company is not utilising its resources to the full potential. An example of an area where underutilisation may be found is managerial effectiveness; wherein the bidding company considers that the target company's management team are not utilising the resources of the company to their full potential. When a company reorganisation occurs primarily to change the management team, this is commonly referred to as the *'market for corporate control'*. This theory suggests that a motivation for mergers/takeovers comes from management who compete to control company resources. In some instances mergers are agreed to by target companies and used as a tool to selectively remove inefficient staff. The threat of takeover is argued to improve the effectiveness of management teams, and hence will benefit equity holders. Takeovers are considered by some to be a necessary market control which will ultimately benefit equity holders by routing out ineffective management teams, which are normally replaced after the takeover.

Another example of underutilisation might be where a manufacturing company has excess production capacity. This sort of company may be attractive to a bidding company, when it has constraints on its production facility. It may believe that a takeover/merger provides a quicker and better mode of growth, relative to purchasing more factories and more plant and equipment.

Obtaining critical mass

In some industries, companies have to undertake extensive research and development to survive – for example the pharmaceuticals industry, high-tech industries, and the aerospace, weapons and motor industries. Research and development is typically very expensive and in some instances is actually a barrier to entry. Companies in these industries grow either internally or using external means to obtain a critical mass which can then support a significant annual investment in research and development. An example is the Glaxo Wellcome takeover of Smith Kline Beecham in 2000.

Obtaining intellectual capital
In many instances a large company will purchase a smaller company to obtain rights to their intellectual capital. This approach is used by some entities as part of their research and development strategy. Ireland has seen a number of its home-grown tech companies being purchased by overseas companies just as they reach a certain stage of development as noted by Shane Dempsey of the Irish Software Association (ISA). *"That's almost become a natural trajectory for Irish software companies: they start up, develop a product, then get to a certain stage and are sold or acquired."* Examples include the purchase of Xiam, a Dublin-based software developer (for mobile phones) by Qualcomm a US wireless communications company for $32 million and the purchase of Havok, a software company (creates games) by Intel for $110 million[1]. At the time of writing a number of other Irish companies (Iona Technologies, Norkom, Curam Software, Qumas and Zamona) are reported to be in negotiations with bidding entities, though details of the proposed offers were not available.

Growth
In some instances, older companies in mature industries target younger companies in industries that have growth potential to increase their sales/growth figures. Over the last decade a number of companies in mature industries have acquired high-tech companies, in the hope that their overall growth performance continues to improve. For example, the Belfast-based company – W&R Barnett (trades grain, animal feed ingredients and vegetable oils internationally) purchased the Belfast computer software firm ICS computing in 1999.

---

[1] Other acquisitions in the recent past include the purchase of Cape Clear by Workday for an undisclosed sum, the purchase of FotoNation by Tessera for $29 million, the purchase of Allfinanz by Munich Re for €48 million, the purchase of Datacare by Computershare for $12 million and the purchase of Serve cast by Level 3 for €33 million.

To obtain a cost effective listing

A motivation for merging with another company can be to obtain a listing in a cost effective manner. This is usually achieved with a reverse merger, wherein a large private company merges with a small listed company. This circumvents the listing process; there is no need to file a prospectus, or to pay the expenses that are required for an IPO. The normal approach in this type of takeover is for the equity holders of the private company to sell their shares to the bidding company (listed company) in exchange for shares in the listed company. This is also known as obtaining a *'back door listing'*. A practical example of this happened in May 2007 when the UK based mobile video company – ROK Entertainment Group merged with Cyberfund, a US based shell company. ROK's equity holders received 57 million common shares in Cyberfund in exchange for their equity holdings in ROK. After the merger, Cyberfund changed its name to ROK Entertaining Group.

Investment strategy

In some instances a company will takeover another company as part of their investment strategy. When a company has surplus funds they have two options, both of which should lead to the maximisation of equity holders funds: distribute it to the equity holders, who can subsequently invest the funds to earn their required rate of return; or invest it in an investment which earns a return in excess of the company's costs of capital (adjusted for the risk of the project, etc.). It is under the latter option that a company may elect to purchase a target company for investment.

Taking over another company is a quick way to get an investment up and running. However, additional issues have to be considered when an external investment is being evaluated. Agency theory may apply in this type of decision as managers' lives are usually severely affected by a merger/takeover. Because of the potential personal consequences, directors may pursue sub-optimal decision making that has their own interests at the forefront. Another problem usually arises due to the sheer size of these external investments, which makes the whole investment appraisal process very difficult and additional steps using external experts are usually required (for example, due diligence reports are typically required).

Possible dysfunctional motivations for business combinations

In the 1960s 'bootstrapping' was used by some company managers to boost their earnings per share and growth performance measures. The **bootstrap effect** is a phrase used to describe a merger/takeover which provides no real economic benefit to a company's equity holders. It is best explained using an example:

Worked example 17.1   (The bootstrap effect)

Financial information for Bidding Group plc (a fast growing ungeared company) and Target Company plc (a slow growing ungeared company), are as follows:

	Bidding Group plc	Target Company plc
	€/£'000	€/£'000
Total net earnings	400	400
Total market value	6,000	3,000
Number of shares in issue	200	200

Bidding can acquire the share capital of Target in exchange for 100,000 shares in Bidding. Therefore each share of Bidding is regarded as being worth two shares in Target – Bidding's market value being twice that of Target. There are no synergies, economies of scale or any other benefit to be gained from this business combination.

REQUIRED

a)   Calculate the current market price per share, earnings per share, price-earnings ratio and earnings per euro/pound for both companies.

b)   Calculate total earnings, total market value, total shares in issue, the new market price per share, earnings per share, price-earnings ratio and the earnings per euro/pound invested, for Bidding Group plc, post acquisition.

c)   Why might this be regarded as an example of financial manipulation? Who stands to gain or loose from this deal?

Continued

Solution

a) *Current ratios*

	Bidding Group plc	Target Company plc
Market price per share	€/£6,000,000	€/£3,000,000
	200,000	200,000
=	€/£30.00	€/£15.00
Earnings per share	€/£400,000	€/£400,000
	200,000	200,000
=	€/£2.00	€/£2.00
Price-earnings ratio	€/£30.00	€15.00
	€/£2.00	€/£2.00
=	15 times	7.5 times
Earnings per €/£ invested	€/£2.00	€/£2.00
	€/£30.00	€/£15.00
=	6.67%	13.33%

b) *Resultant performance and ratios*

	Bidding Group plc €/£'000	Target Company plc €/£'000	Bidding (after acquisition) €/£'000
Total net earnings	400	400	800
Total market value	6,000	3,000	9,000
Number of shares in issue	200	200	300
Market price per share	€/£30.00	€/£15.00	€/£30.00
Earnings per share	€/£2.00	€/£2.00	€/£2.67
Price-earnings ratio	15 times	7.5 times	11.24 times
Earnings per €/£ invested	6.67%	13.33%	8.9%

Workings

	Bidding Group plc
Market price per share	€/£9,000,000
	300,000
=	€/£30.00

Continued

Earnings per share   €/£800,000

                                  300,000

                    =   €/£2.67

                                  €/£30.00
Price-earnings ratio   ─────────
                                   €/£2.67

                    =   11.24 times

Earnings per €/£ invested   €/£2.67
                                  ─────────
                                  €/£30.00

                    =   8.9%

c) Research has found little evidence to suggest that capital mar-
    kets are strong-form efficient. Indeed, it has been questioned
    whether they can be regarded as being semi-strong-form effi-
    cient. In a nutshell, it would seem that market price does not
    reflect the true value of a company because there is informa-
    tion asymmetry, and irrational behaviour, etc. in the markets.
    Therefore, it is possible that market participants do not fully
    understand the implications of, for example, the above acquisi-
    tion. It might be interpreted that the growth in earnings per
    share from €/£2.00 to €/£2.67 (a rise of 33.5%) is sustaina-
    ble, but it is not. It might be perceived that Bidding Group plc
    will improve the performance of Target Company plc to obtain
    similar growth as is currently being experienced by Bidding
    Group plc as reflected in its high price-earnings ratio. If this
    sentiment spreads, the share price of Bidding Group plc will
    rise in the near future and equity holders will make gains based
    on their interpretation of the expectations of the performance
    of Bidding Group plc. This will fall later as actual results will
    confirm that this is not the case.

    There will be no winners or losers, provided the equity holders
    of both Bidding Group plc and Target Group plc understand
    the deal.

Companies with high price-earnings ratios can actually increase their earnings per share by acquiring companies with a lower price-earnings ratio, as
in the above example. All things being equal, this should not impact on

share price and should bring down the price-earnings ratio as the increase in value caused by the short-term growth in earnings will be offset by reduced long-term expected growth. However, if the transaction is interpreted incorrectly by investors, such that they believe the growth prospects of the new company to be higher than it actually is, then this will drive up share price and the resultant price-earnings ratio, in the short term.

Diversification

The motivation between many conglomerate integrations is the wish of the management team of the bidding company to diversify their activities. This is a highly suspect reason for acquiring other businesses. It is argued that management teams who diversify to reduce risk (portfolio theory) are not acting in the best interests of their equity holders. Indeed, it could be suggested that this strategy is an example of agency theory, wherein the management are taking action to diversify the risk associated with losing their main source of income – their salary. Purchasing another company is a costly exercise. The bidding company normally has to pay a premium for the target company's shares and has to pay substantial costs to consultants and advisers, whereas equity holders can diversify their portfolios at a lower cost. The shares they purchase will include a premium and they just incur broker fees on each transaction.

Agency theory

As mentioned earlier in the text, managers act as agents for equity holders. They are employed by equity holders to run the company for the benefit of its equity holders. To recap, agency theory is a term to describe actions taken by management that are in their own interests, not those of the equity holders. For example, it is argued that some managers pursue acquisitions for self-interest/egotistic reasons. There is a certain amount of status and esteem in being the manager of a large-sized company. Getting a managerial position in a large company is difficult for an individual who only has managerial experience in small-sized entities. One way to open the career door to a large company may be to grow the company the manager works in. In addition to curriculum vitae building, managers of large-sized companies might get satisfaction from the power that they hold over so many resources. Further dysfunctional managerial behaviour may arise if a bidding company gets into competition with other bidding companies. The winners in this scenario are the equity holders of the target company.

Purchase consideration and the evaluation of business combinations

There are three main sources of finance that are used by a bidding company to purchase a target company - cash, shares, or debt securities. The cash offered by a bidding company can be obtained by an issue of shares to its current equity holders, by issuing debt and/or using cash reserves that have been built up in the bidding company. When the purchase consideration is by share exchange, the bidding company issues equity shares and exchanges these for the target company's equity shares. Finally, the bidding company can issue debt securities to the equity holders in the target company in exchange for their equity shares in that company. Any combination of these is also a possibility, for example, on 7 June 2007, the Board of Medical Solutions plc (a diagnostics and healthcare business) announced that it conditionally agreed to acquire the entire share capital of Geneservice Limited for a total consideration of £3.86 million, payable in cash and loan notes. In some instances the bidding company may give the equity holders of the target company an option, shares only, cash only or a combination of shares and cash.

Cash consideration

Cash consideration: advantages

Easy to understand: Every party involved in the transaction understands where they stand when the offer is in cash.

Reduces price movement risk: When the offer is in cash, the price is not exposed to the risk of an adverse movement in equity share price impacting on the cost of the acquisition. This risk is prevalent when an offer is made on the basis of an exchange of equity shares.

Receiving equity holders have more flexibility: The equity holders in the target company can easily adjust their portfolio to what suits them best, using the cash received. If they receive shares instead of cash they would then incur transaction costs liquidating these for re-investment. If they want to retain their investment in the company they can purchase shares in the new larger entity in the market.

Continued

Bidding company equity holders do not lose control: As no shares are issued the current equity holder mix remains unchanged by this transaction; hence there are no shifts in control. This may suit management, where they have a strong positive relationship with their current equity holders.

Bidding company equity holders reap future rewards: Where the business combination is a success and reaps rewards in excess of that originally anticipated, then the equity holders of the bidding company stand to gain the total reward.

Cash consideration: disadvantages

Financing cash: Most bidding companies have to source the cash required for the purchase. They may have some built up in reserves, but it is more likely than not that the bidding company will have to issue debt securities, obtain large bank loans, sell assets, or undertake a rights issue to allow them to finance the purchase of a target company. The bidding company's equity holders may not like this.

Deferred payments make the offer unattractive: One way to spread the cash burden on the bidding company is to spread the purchase payments over a period of time. Though attractive to the bidding company's equity holders, this will not be attractive to the target company's equity holders.

Transactions costs: The equity holders who are receiving cash are going to incur transaction costs when they invest the cash in alternative investments.

Taxation: When shares are sold for cash, the equity holder will be liable to capital gains tax.

Evaluating an acquisition where the purchase consideration is cash
When a business finance manager is evaluating the acquisition of an external entity, two key questions need to be positively answered to justify the acquisition in light of the key objective of public companies – to maximise equity holder wealth. Firstly, will the acquisition of the target company result in a net gain, in present value terms, to the bidding company?

Secondly, how much of the overall gain will be attributed to the equity holders of the bidding company, and how much goes to the equity holders of the target company? Though difficult to answer, projections can be utilised to determine answers to these questions. These projections will be used to help justify the proposed acquisition to the equity holders of a bidding company. The following simple example highlights how to approach the calculation of gains and their subsequent split between the two sets of equity holder.

Worked example 17.2   (Evaluating a business acquisition – cash)

Pike plc is considering acquiring all of Minnow plc's share capital for €/£22 per share. Minnow plc is a similar company to Pike plc: they both sell similar items and have no gearing. Relevant details on both companies are as follows:

	Pike plc €/£'m	Minnow plc €/£'m
Extracts from the balance sheet		
Total assets	260	23
Of which:		
Cash	70	4
Other assets (book value)	190	19
Extracts from the income statement		
Revenues	170	25
Costs	125	20
Market value of company	550	48
Number of shares in issue	11	3

After an extensive review on the potential impact of the merger on the future financial performance of the company it is considered that the combination will lead to some synergies. Revenues are expected to increase by €/£3 million and costs are expected to fall by €/£2 million. These are the only synergies expected. Pike plc's cost of capital is 18%.

REQUIRED
a)   Explain why synergies occur.
b)   Calculate the economic gain to be made from this merger.

Continued

c) Detail out who is going to benefit from this gain, the equity holders of Pike plc, or Minnow plc?

d) What are the expected market value, cash balance, other assets and earnings of Pike plc post-acquisition?

Solution

a) Synergies occur when two companies that come together are worth more than they are when on their own. In this example, the increase in revenues may be due to the fact that both companies have complementary products, and the combination may result in the products of, for example, Pike plc being sold alongside the products of Minnow plc, when this did not happen in the past. Perhaps a competitor offered a similar product to that being sold by Minnow plc. Cost savings may be experienced where the company has similar distribution channels, savings can be made on complementary marketing and administration costs may be reduced.

b) The economic gains to be made from the business combination are the excess benefits to be made by having one larger company, over the sum of the gains to be made by having two individual companies. The synergies are expected to amount to €/£5 million (an increase in revenues of €/£3 million and a reduction in operating costs of €/£2 million). If it is assumed that these synergies can be maintained into the future (a perpetuity) then the additional economic value resulting from the synergies amounts to €/£27,777,778 (€/£5,000,000/0.18).

c) The current market price of an equity share in Minnow plc is €/£16.00 (€/£48,000,000/3,000,000). The offer price is €/£22.00. Therefore, the equity holders of Minnow plc stand to gain €/£6.00 per share, or €/£18,000,000 (3,000,000 × €/£6) in total.

The remaining economic gains will benefit the equity holders of Pike plc. The expected benefit amounts to €/£9,777,778 (€/£27,777,778 − €/£18,000,000). Assuming perfect capital markets, this will result in an increase in share price by about 89c/p (€/£9,777,778/11,000,000), bringing an individual share's price up to €/£50.89 ((€/£550,000,000/11,000,000) + 0.89c/p).

Continued

On paper, both sets of equity holder benefit from this business combination. However, the equity holders of Minnow plc end up with the greatest proportion of the economic gains to be made. In addition, there is no risk associated with their gain, whereas the equity holders of Pike plc are exposed to the risk that the projected synergy benefits do not materialise, which could mean that the merger makes them worse off.

d)   The expected market value, earnings, cash balance and balance in other assets of Pike plc after the merger (assuming perfect capital markets) are as follows:

Expected market value of Pike plc[1].	€/£559,800,000
Number of equity shares in issue.	11,000,000
Expected market value of an equity share	€/£50.89
Expected earnings[2].	€/£55,000,000
Expected cash balance[3].	€/£8,000,000
Expected value of other assets[4].	€/£209,000,000
Expected total assets	€/£217,000,000

Workings

1.   *Expected market value of Pike plc post-acquisition*

	€/£m
Market value of Pike plc prior to business combination	550
Market value of Minnow plc prior to business combination	48
Present value of synergies expected	27.8
Cash paid to the equity holders of Minnow plc[a]	(66)
Expected market value of new larger company	559.8

a. The total cash offer is €/£66,000,000 (€/£22.00 × 3,000,000)

2.   *Expected earnings of Pike plc post-acquisition*

	Pike plc	Minnow plc		Pike plc post-acquisition
	€/£m	€/£m		€/£m
Extracts from the income statement				
Revenues	170	25	(+3)	198
Costs	125	20	(−2)	143
Net earnings	45	5	(+5)	55

Note: the synergies are shown in brackets.

Continued

3. *Expected cash balance of Pike plc post-acquisition*

	€/£'m
Cash balance in Pike plc prior to business combination	70
Cash balance in Minnow plc prior to business combination	4
Cash paid to the equity holders of Minnow plc	(66)
Expected cash balance in the amalgamated company	8

4. *Expected other asset values of Pike plc post-acquisition*

	€/£'m
Other assets in Pike plc prior to business combination (book value)	190
Other assets in Minnow plc prior to business combination (book value)	19
Expected other assets (book value) balance in the new larger company	209

The economic gain to be made from a business combination by the equity holders of the bidding company can be calculated using a number of different approaches. The gain to the equity holders of the bidding company is expressed using the following formula:

$$\text{Gain on business combination} = V_{i+j} - V_i - \text{Purchase consideration}$$

wherein V_i is the value of company i, V_j is the value of company j and V_{i+j} is the expected value of the combined entity post acquisition. Therefore, the gain on the business combination for the equity holders of Pike plc post-acquisition is €/£9,800,000 ((€/£550,000,000 + €/£48,000,000 + €/£27,800,000) − €/£550,000,000 − €/£66,000,000). Alternatively, an incremental approach to working out the gain attributable to a bidding company's equity holders is possible:

$$\text{Gain on business combination} = \text{Incremental gain from synergies} - \text{cost of target company}$$

Wherein the cost of the target company is calculated using the following equation:

$$\text{Cost of target company} = \text{Cash consideration paid} - \text{market value of target company}$$

Therefore, using the information from the previous example, the cost of purchasing Minnow plc is €/£18,000,000 (€/£66,000,000 − €/£48,000,000) to Pike plc and the gain on the business combination to the equity holders of Pike plc is €/£9,800,000 being the incremental gains from synergies (€/£27,800,000) less the cost of purchasing Minnow plc (€/£18,000,000).

Share exchanges

The second type of purchase consideration considered in this text, a *share exchange*, is where a bidding company issues additional equity shares and uses these as currency to exchange for the equity shares of the target company.

Share exchanges: advantages

Liquidity: The bidding company's liquidity is not impacted on by the acquisition, except for the costs associated with the transaction (for example, consultancy fees and administration fees).

Taxation: The target company equity holders, who receive shares in the bidding company in exchange for their equity shares in the target company, will not be subject to capital gains tax, as the gain will be rolled over until the equity holder decides the sell their shares.

Retain an interest in the company: The target company equity holders retain an interest in the original company. They may have an attachment/interest in the company and may want to keep their investment in the company. They also have the ability to reap any additional gains/synergies made by the new combined company.

Reduced costs: Where the cash offer involves having to issue debt securities to raise the funds, then a share-for-share exchange may be more cost effective, with less of an impact on gearing, relative to a cash offer that is financed using debt.

Share exchanges: disadvantages

Costly: Equity is the most expensive source of finance. A company has to earn higher returns to keep the equity holders happy, relative to the returns required by debt holders.

Continued

Control: There is a dilution in control within the bidding company and possibly a reduction in the earnings per share available for equity holders, if the new larger number of shares is not matched by an equivalent increase in the earnings of the company.

Articles of association: The bidding company may have to approach its equity holders to approve an extension in the number of authorised shares that can be issued (if the company has already issued all those that were authorised within the articles of association).

Price risk: The attractiveness of the offer to the target company is affected by the movements in the share price of the bidding company's shares. If the equity holders are not happy about the proposed business combination then the bidding company's share price may fall, making the offer unattractive to the equity holders in the target company. In addition, if the price of the target company's shares rise, the offer will also be less attractive.

Difficulty in evaluating the offer: Connected to the previous point, where the share prices of both companies fluctuate, it is difficult for the equity holders in the target company to accurately evaluate the offer on hand.

Evaluating an acquisition where the purchase consideration is a share exchange

The next (simple) example follows on from the previous example. It is the same in every respect, except assumes that the purchase consideration is in the form of equity shares in the bidding company.

Worked example 17.3   (Evaluating a business acquisition – share exchange)

Pike plc is considering acquiring all of Minnow plc's share capital in a share-for-share exchange, as it wants to conserve its cash for future investments. Pike plc is offering one share in Pike plc for three shares in Minnow Plc. Minnow plc is a similar company to Pike plc. They both sell similar items and have no long-term debt. Relevant details on both companies are as follows:

Continued

Extracts from the balance sheet	Pike plc €/£'m	Minnow plc €/£'m
Total assets	260	23
Of which:		
Cash	70	4
Other assets (book value)	190	19
Extracts from the income statement		
Revenues	170	25
Costs	125	20
Market value of company	550	48
Number of equity shares in issue	11	3

After an extensive review on the potential impact of the merger on the future financial performance of the company it is considered that the combination will lead to some synergies. Revenues are expected to increase by €/£3 million and costs are expected to fall by €/£2 million. These are the only synergies expected. Pike plc's cost of capital is 18%.

REQUIRED

a) Calculate the number of shares that Pike plc will have to issue to purchase the shares of Minnow plc.

b) What are the expected market value, cash balance, total assets and earnings of Pike plc post-acquisition?

c) Calculate the consideration that the equity holders of Minnow plc will receive, compare this to the consideration received if the offer were a cash offer of €/£22.00 per share, as in the previous example.

d) Detail out who is going to benefit from this gain, the equity holders of Pike plc, or Minnow plc? Compare this to the balance of benefit received, when the offer was a cash offer, as covered in the previous example.

Continued

Solution

a) Minnow plc has 3,000,000 shares in issue. Pike plc will be issuing one share for every three held by Minnow plc. This means Pike plc will have to issue an additional 1,000,000 shares (3,000,000/3), bringing its total issue share capital up to 12,000,000 (11,000,000 + 1,000,000).

b) The expected market value, earnings, cash balance and balance in other assets of Pike plc after the merger (assuming perfect capital markets) are as follows:

Expected market value of Pike plc[1.]	€/£625,800,000
Number of shares in issue	12,000,000
Expected market value of an equity share	€/£52.15
Expected earnings[2.]	€/£55,000,000
Expected cash balance[3.]	€/£74,000,000
Expected value of other assets[4.]	€/£209,000,000
Expected total assets	€/£283,000,000

Workings

1. *Expected market value of Pike plc post-acquisition*

	€/£m
Market value of Pike plc prior to business combination	550
Market value of Minnow plc prior to business combination	48
Present value of the synergies expected	27.8
Expected market value of new larger company	625.8

2. *Expected earnings of Pike plc post-acquisition*

	Pike plc	Minnow plc	Pike plc post-acquisition	
	€/£m	€/£m		€/£m
Extracts from the income statement				
Revenues	170	25	(+3)	198
Costs	125	20	(-2)	143
Net earnings	45	5	(+5)	55

The synergies are shown in brackets.

Continued

3. *Expected cash balance of Pike plc post-acquisition*

	€/£'m
Cash balance in Pike plc prior to business combination	70
Cash balance in Minnow plc prior to business combination	4
Expected cash balance in the new larger company	74

4. *Expected other asset values of Pike plc post-acquisition*

	€/£'m
Other assets in Pike plc prior to business combination (book value)	190
Other assets in Minnow plc prior to business combination (book value)	19
Expected other assets (book value) balance in the new larger company	209

c) Given Pike plc's expected share price movement (calculated in b) above), the total value received for one share is €/£17.38. This is calculated as follows:

The total consideration for the whole of Minnow plc is €/£52,150,000 (1,000,000 × €/£52.15), this is then divided by the number of shares held by the equity holders in Minnow plc pre-acquisition to give an individual price of each share of €/£17.38 (€/£52,150,000/3,000,000). The total premium on offer to the equity holders of Minnow plc is therefore €/£4,140,000 ((€/£17.38 − €/£16.00) × 3,000,000).

The cash offer was allowing the equity holders of Minnow plc a premium of €/£6.00 per share (€/£22.00 − €/£16.00). This amounted to a total premium of €/£18,000,000 (€/£6.00 × 3,000,000). Therefore, the equity holders of Minnow plc are worse off by €/£13,860,000 (€/£18,000,000 − €/£4,140,000).

d) As was calculated in the previous example, the total economic gain expected is €/£27,800,000. In this example, the equity holders of Minnow plc stand to benefit from a premium on the transfer of €/£4,140,000.

The current equity holders of Pike plc stand to gain an increase in their share value from €/£50.00 (€/£550,000,000/11,000,000) to

Continued

€/£52.15 (calculated in a)). Therefore the gain to be made per share is €/£2.15 (€/£52.15 − €/£50.00), which equates to a total value of €/£23,650,000 (€/£2.15 × 11,000,000). So in this instance the bulk of the benefit to be gained from this business combination will go to the equity holders of Pike plc.

On paper, both sets of equity holder benefit from this business combination, but the equity holders to Pike plc end up with the greatest proportion of the economic gains to be made. In this instance both sets of equity holder are exposed to the risk that the projected synergy benefits do not materialise.

To summarise, the total economic gain remains the same regardless of the consideration type, at €/£27,800,000, but the balance of gain in this instance has shifted to the equity holders of the bidding company, Pike plc, as they will now receive 85.11% (€/£23,660,000/€/£27,800,000) of the gain, whereas the equity holders of Minnow plc will receive 14.89% (€/£4,140,000/€/£27,800,000) of the gain.

Debt securities

Sometimes the purchase consideration is an exchange of debt for equity, wherein the bidding company exchanges loan stock for shares in the target company. The advantages and disadvantages of this form of purchase consideration are now outlined:

Debt securities: disadvantages

Liquidity: Each year from the date of the acquisition until the maturity of the debt securities, the bidding company will be obliged to make coupon payments, and on maturity of the securities, the capital will have to be repaid.

Gearing: The gearing ratio of the bidding company may increase by an amount which increases the financial risk in the company to levels that the equity holders are not happy with. This will increase their required return, resulting in a reduction in share price.

Debt securities: advantages

Liquidity: The bidding company's liquidity is not immediately impacted on by the acquisition, except for the costs associated with the transaction (for example, consultancy fees and administration fees).

Control: The issue of debt securities will not involve any changes in the control of the company, unless the interest, or repayment of the debt falls into arrears, then the debt holders have voting rights.

Capital structure/cost of capital: Where the bidding company is low geared, the increase in gearing may actually increase the value of the bidding company as equity holders may react positively to this cheaper form of finance, which is tax deductible, being available. They stand to make higher returns in the future, if the business combination is successful, as the debt holders' return is fixed, all the excess return being attributable to the equity holders.

Lower risk for target company equity holders: When the target company's equity holders are unsure about the viability of the combined entity, they may be more attracted by a debt for share exchange, relative to a share-for-share exchange, as the debt option provides them with guaranteed yearly coupon income and the knowledge that they rank in front of the equity holders, were the company to go into liquidation.

The choice of purchase consideration is impacted on by a number of factors. Research suggests that the bidding company is more likely to offer a share-for-share exchange when the stock markets are performing well (bullish). The gearing levels of the bidding company will influence the preferred source of finance to use to fund the acquisition – high geared companies are more likely to opt for a share-for-share exchange, and low geared companies with strong cash flows are likely to opt for a bond-for-share exchange. Companies with high-growth performance are also found to be more likely to use a share-for-share exchange. High-growth companies have a constant funding requirement, as growth itself requires investment. Any surplus cash made by the company on a yearly basis will be needed to fund this growth. In addition, the company is likely to be less keen to tie itself into the fixed cash outflows that would be required if debt securities were issued in exchange for the target company's shares.

A further reason to explain the preference of high-growth companies for share-for-share exchanges over the use of debt is management's wish to keep a future source of funding in reserve (debt). This is less costly to obtain than additional equity. Finally, bidding companies that have low-growth potential are less likely to opt for a share-for-share exchange as this form of consideration is less attractive to the equity holders of the target company, who may have invested in the target company primarily for its high growth potential.

Difficulties that arise when evaluating a bid

In the last section two acquisition offers were evaluated. In these simple examples everything that could impact on share price was known with certainty. In the real world, things are not so clear cut. Some of the main issues facing stakeholders who try to evaluate an offer, or who try to come up with an offer price, are now outlined. The examples discussed in this section are by no means exhaustive.

Very few acquisitions take place without there being public knowledge of the event. Therefore, the equity share prices of both parties to the transaction usually change in anticipation of the acquisition happening. For example, when Ryanair made it known that it was interested in purchasing the equity shares of Aer Lingus there was an immediate response in the markets. Aer Lingus's shares rose by 15%, whereas the value of Ryanair's equity shares fell by one percent. This may be because the bid price disclosed was €2.80, whereas the market was valuing Aer Lingus at €2.20. The immediate 15% increase in the price of Aer Lingus's shares reflects the premium expected from the takeover and does not reflect the market's view of the long-term equilibrium value of Aer Lingus. Therefore, determining the equilibrium price of a target company may be quite difficult, especially if the market becomes aware of the impending offer; indeed, the market may overestimate the expected premium, which may scupper the acquisition as the equity holders in the target company expect too much for their shares.

Deciding on the extent of synergies or economies of scale that will result from a business combination is very difficult. An analyst usually estimates expected future revenues and costs from the amalgamated company and then discounts these back to their present value to determine the expected economic value of the new larger entity. The current market value of the target company and the consideration are then taken away from this to determine the gains to be made from the business combination. However, any gain that results from this exercise may be due to errors being made in the estimation of the potential additional revenues and reduced costs. These may not be as good as estimated. Conversely, pessimistic estimations of future cash flows may lead to a company not pursuing an acquisition, when in fact gains would arise.

Regulation of takeovers and mergers

Regulation in the UK
The regulation of business combinations in the UK comes from three sources: under UK legislation, under European direction and by the City (the Takeover Panel). The first two sources have legal backing; the third provides a framework of good practice.

1. UK competition regulation
The main concern of this first form of regulation is to ensure that the merger or takeover is in the public interest. The Fair Trading Act (1973) and the Competition Act (1998) put responsibility for the control of the regulation of takeovers and mergers in the UK into three entities: the Secretary of State for Trade and Industry; the Office of Fair Trading and the Competition Commission (formerly the Monopoly and Mergers Commission).

Office of Fair Trading (OFT)
At present, the Director General of the Office of Fair Trading is responsible for monitoring mergers and acquisition in the UK, whether notified about them, or not. The OFT will be interested in business combinations that are in the public interest. The OFT use an asset size measure and a market dominance measure to determine if the merger is of public interest. Mergers are deemed to be in the public interest when the value of the assets of the target company exceed £70 million, or the combined entities together supply, or receive, a minimum of one quarter of the goods or services, of a particular good or service supplied in the UK (or a substantial part of it). In addition, the OFT will assess smaller mergers/takeovers

that are brought to their attention, either by complaint, or by one of the companies that are party to the merger/takeover. The OFT will investigate the proposed merger/takeover and hear the views of the main interested parties. Where the OFT is happy that the merger/takeover does not harm competition and is in the public's interest, then that is the matter ended. However, if they feel that there are competition concerns, they will then refer the proposed merger/takeover to the Secretary of State for Trade and Industry and provide their opinion as to whether the proposed merger/takeover be referred to the Competition Commission. They may advise actions to be taken to make the merger/takeover more in the public interest and will monitor these actions. The OFT can also refer a proposed merger/takeover to the European Commission (see below).

Secretary of State for Trade and Industry

The main role of the Secretary for State is to determine whether a proposed merger/takeover is to be referred to the Competition Commission. In the main, the Secretary of State will follow the advice of the OFT. The Competition Commission is a department under the control of the Secretary of State and it will provide its findings to the Secretary of State who will then publish the resultant report and take action (as is recommended by the Competition Commission).

The Competition Commission

The **Competition Commission** investigates any proposed merger/takeover that is referred to it by the Secretary of State for Trade and Industry. They will hear evidence from the main parties and will assess the public's reaction to the proposed business combination. If they think that steps can be taken to make the proposed merger/takeover in the public interests, they will outline these and provide their final opinion in a report to the Secretary of State.

2. European competition regulation

The second form of regulation considers competition within a European context and comes under the jurisdiction of the European Union. Article 82 of the Treaty of Rome prohibits the abuse of a dominant company where it may affect trade between different member states. The European Directive on Takeover Bids was adopted on 21 April 2004 by the European

Commission and had to be implemented by member states by 20 May 2006. It was enacted in the UK initially by the Takeovers Directive (Interim Implementation) Regulations 2006, and subsequently incorporated into part 28 of the Companies Act 2006. The main issues covered in the directive are concerned with: providing general principles for the conduct of the stakeholders in a takeover/merger; providing a regulatory framework to guide bodies that supervise takeovers/mergers in EU countries; providing basic rules to follow during a takeover/merger; outlining restrictions to barriers that can be placed in the way of takeovers/mergers; requiring minimum disclosure requirements for companies whose shares are traded on regulated markets; and providing guidance on the treatment of minority interests who have not accepted the bidding company's offer (squeeze-outs and sell-outs).

The underlying issue that is considered under the European Directive is whether the merger/takeover will result in a company that has a dominant position, such that it will impede competition across member states. If this is deemed to be the case, then this merger/takeover will be considered to be incompatible with the common market. The recent proposed merger between Ryanair and Aer Lingus was ruled to be incompatible under the European Directive.

3. Conduct of a takeover

The first two forms of regulation are more concerned with protecting the public/competition. The third form of regulation, the *'City Code'* is not concerned with this issue, and focuses on ensuring that all parties to the takeover/merger act in a manner which is in all the equity holders' best interests. This regulation is not enshrined in law. It is a framework that has been accepted and promoted by the market as guidance on good practice on how the engagement process of a takeover/merger should take place. The City Code is enforced by the *Takeover Panel*; a team of representatives from the main associations who are involved in most takeovers. The panel typically includes a representative from the regulators (for example, the Confederation of British Industry (CBI)), equity holders (the Stock Exchange) and advisers (the ICAEW). Though the panel does not have any legal force, it can publicise its findings, which may damage the reputation of those parties that did not comply with the City Code. The panel can ask its members (advisers, the stock exchange and regulators) to withdraw their services publicly from the perpetuators. The bidding company can appeal to the FSA if they disagree with the panel's decision.

The Takeover Panel and City Code on Takeovers and Mergers

This code is sometimes referred to as the *Takeover Code*, or as is used in this text the 'City Code'. The purpose of the code is to ensure that '*equity holders are treated fairly and are not denied an opportunity to decide on the merits of a takeover. The code also provides an orderly framework within which takeovers are conducted. In addition, it is designed to promote, in conjunction with other regulatory regimes, the integrity of the financial markets. The code is not concerned with the financial or commercial advantages or disadvantages of a takeover*' (City Code, page 26).

The City Code: general principles

Unbiased: The equity holders of the target company should be treated similarly. One offer should be given to all equity holders who hold shares of a similar class.

Sufficient time and information: The equity holders of the target company should be given relevant and adequate information to enable them to reach a properly informed decision on the bid (no information should be withheld).

Maximise equity holder value: Directors should act in the best interests of the whole equity holder body, not in their own interests.

Behaviour of directors: Directors should not encourage or frustrate a bid, without first obtaining the approval of the equity holders.

False market: A false market in the shares of either the bidding company or the target company should not be created. Both companies will not be allowed to offer inducements to increase the demand for their equity share capital.

The City Code: detailed rules

Making a bid: There are specific rules on the approach a bidder has to take when making a bid for a target company.

Going public: The bidding company has to declare its intent to make a takeover bid for the target company publicly.

Conduct: The conduct of both parties is restricted under the City Code. For example, all holdings in the target company of over three percent must be declared to the company, no 'dawn raids' are allowed (the bidding company cannot acquire equity shares, in any seven-day period, that will bring their holding to above 15 percent) and when a company amasses over 30 percent of the shares in a company they are obliged under the City Code to make a formal bid for the remaining shares in the company (the price offered must be at least the maximum price paid for any of the shares acquired in the previous 12 months).

Independent advice: Once an offer comes in, the directors of a target company must seek independent advice from a financial adviser, such as a merchant bank. This serves to protect the interests of the equity holders.

Time limits: There are time limits throughout the whole process, which should be completed within 60 days (more detail is given later). In addition, a bidding company cannot make a further takeover bid for the target company within one calendar year of the first offer.

Regulation in the ROI

The regulation in the ROI is similar. Competition and public interest are controlled by government departments and the European Parliament and a framework for proper conduct during a takeover is regulated by the Irish Takeover Panel. The details provided for the ROI are in brief as they are similar in many respects to those in the UK.

ROI legislation on competition

The relevant legislation is the Mergers and Takeovers (Control) Acts, 1978 to 1996. When a takeover comes within the scope of these acts, the parties to the business combination must inform the Minister of the Department of Enterprise, Trade and Employment (DETE) in writing, within one month of an offer being made. It is the Minister's responsibility to monitor takeovers/mergers in the ROI. The report to the Minister must include full details of the proposal. The takeover/merger cannot proceed without the Minister stating that it will not be objected to, or stating it can go ahead, with conditions. If the Minister does not respond within three months, the business combination may proceed. If the Minister feels that the proposed takeover/merger is not in the public's interest then they can refer it to the *Competition Authority* for investigation (the Minister must do this within 30 days of receiving the proposal).

The Competition Authority will advise the Minister as to whether the merger/takeover is in the public interest, or not. Alternatively, it may recommend steps that the bidding company can take to make the proposal in the public's interest.

On 20 May 2006, the Minister for DETE introduced the European Communities (Takeover Bids (Directive 2004/25/EC)) Regulations 2006. The terms of this legislation are similar to that outlined above for the UK. The one difference that has made Irish companies more attractive as potential targets relative to UK companies is the rules surrounding minority interests – though it is pointed out that these regulations have narrowed the historic difference between the treatment of minority interests in the two regions. Up until these regulations were enacted, a *statutory compulsory acquisition* (otherwise known as *a squeeze-out* or *a sell-out*) came into play when a bidding company acquired 80% of the shares in a target company. As mentioned previously, in the UK this condition comes into play when equity holders in the target company who together hold 90% of the remaining equity shares in the target company accept the offer (the remaining equity holders, the minority interest, have to sell their shares). With the new legislation, the threshold for takeovers in the ROI has been raised to 90%, though only applies when the target company is a listed company and (unlike in the UK) the bidding company can count the proportion it already holds as going towards this 90%. The 80% rule still applies to all mergers/takeovers that do not fall within the remit of the European Directive (all non-listed companies).

Conduct of a takeover

The European Communities (Takeover Bids (Directive 2004/25/EC)) Regulations 2006 assigned responsibility for the proper conduct of takeovers to the Irish Takeover Panel (ITP)(the government's designated competent authority). The panel is responsible for making rules to ensure that takeovers, mergers and substantial acquisitions comply with the general principles that are set out in the Irish Takeover Panel Act. The most recent version of this act was introduced on 19 December 2007; the Irish Takeover Panel Act, 1997, Takeover Rules, 2007. The rules provide an orderly framework within which takeovers are conducted. They are not concerned with the advantages, disadvantages, or the financial or commercial implications of a proposed business combination. This they consider to be a concern of the relevant companies and their equity holders. The ITP is not concerned with competition as this is regulated by the legislation outlined in the previous paragraphs. Like the UK takeover panel, they are concerned with the rules of engagement between the parties. Unlike the UK takeover panel, their rules and framework are set out in legislation (the aforementioned Act).

The process

As mentioned previously, the City Code is a document, prepared by the Takeover Panel, which gives guidance (non-statutory rules) on what is good practice for participants to follow during a takeover process. The City Code suggests that a bidding company should prepare an *offer document*. It recommends that this document be made available to all the equity holders of the target company within 28 days of the announcement of an intention to make an offer for the target company.

Contents of an offer document might include the following:

- The offer price (type of consideration)
- How it is financed
- The identity of the bidding company
- The purpose of the acquisition

Continued

> - The future plans of the bidding company, in respect of the target company
> - The changes to the management/control of the target company
> - How to accept the offer, if interested
> - The period of time for which the offer is open

The Takeover Panel recommend that the offer remain open for 21 days following the date on which the offer document is made available to the equity holders of the target company.

The City Code recommends that the board of the target company publish a circular containing its opinion of the offer to its equity holders and employees within 14 days of the offer document being available. This circular should ideally have the views of the employees' representatives on the proposed offer attached (this may not be available). If the board of directors are not happy with the offer they usually publish a *defence document*. This document states reasons for rejecting the offer.

It is possible that the whole process ends within 21 days. The City Code recommends that the bidding company disclose the quantity of the target company's equity holders who have voted to support the takeover. If this is over 50% then the takeover will go ahead. If less than 50% support is obtained, the bidder may decide to drop the attempt.

If 50% has not been achieved, the bidding company may extend the offer period. The offer period can be set (full details of the new closing date must be given), or can be open. Where the offer date is open, a minimum of 14 days notice must be given to the equity holders who have not accepted the offer, before it can be closed. In this period the board of the target company can produce new circulars in support of or against the takeover bid. However, there is a time limit on the ability to do this of 39 days, from when the initial offer document was made available (unless permission is obtained from the panel). At this stage, the bidding company has only four days to up its offer – 43 days from the initial offer document being issued. The bidding company cannot purchase equity in the target company, if the new holdings take its overall equity holdings in the target company to more than 30% of its issued equity share capital. The bidding company must disclose the quantity of the target company's equity holders who have elected to support the takeover. As before, if the proportion is now over 50%, the takeover goes ahead. If it is below 50%, then the target company is not taken over and the bidding company cannot make a further bid to gain control for a full year (from this date, which is usually 60 days from the offer document was issued).

When the takeover consideration is accepted and the takeover goes ahead, the City Code recommends that the bidding company provide the purchase consideration to the equity holders of the target company within 14 days.

Key documents supporting an acquisition

Heads of agreement stage

When a bidding company has identified a target company and justified it as a suitable investment to its equity holders, who accept that the approach should be made, then a 'heads of agreement' is prepared. The *heads of agreement* sets out the proposed terms of purchase/sale between the bidding and target companies and is usually 'subject to contract'. It typically requires that certain conditions are fulfilled (normally in respect of providing information for the due diligence stage). It is not a legally binding agreement, more of a moral agreement.

Due diligence stage

In the context of acquisitions and mergers, *due diligence* is the performance of a voluntary investigation commissioned by the bidding company into the target company. This investigation is performed with a duty of care towards the equity holders of the bidding company. It is defined in the Oxford Dictionary as '*the responsibilities of a person, or business, to exercise proper care and caution prior to any business decision, or entering into any business relationship.*' Due diligence emerged in the US after the introduction of the Securities Act of 1933. Due diligence was a term used to describe a defence that could be used by dealers when they sold equity shares to investors. So long as dealers undertook a due diligence investigation and disclosed their findings to investors (and the investigation was conducted properly), then they could not be held liable for not knowing about facts that became evident thereafter.

A due diligence audit usually starts with the team obtaining information on the background (history and development) of the company as well as the structure of the company (group, subsidiaries, branches, etc.). It should detail out the organisational chart, main people, lines of communication, etc. In terms of financial information, as a minimum the due diligence audit will verify the information provided by the target company to the bidding company directors. The verification will consider the accuracy and integrity of actual information provided. Most target companies provide estimates of future investments and project earnings into the future. The due diligence audit will evaluate the reasonableness of the assumptions used.

Accounting

A due diligence audit will typically cover normal audit practices on accounting information, though it is likely to go deeper. Indeed, the normal audit work will probably help to inform the due diligence report, and may even highlight weak areas that the due diligence team may wish to focus in on. The due diligence team will usually request the past three years financial statements (this will detail the company's accounting policies), the management accounts, projections, copies of trading arrangements with stakeholders (customers, suppliers), details of the strategic policy in respect of working capital, accounting systems, taxation (foreign taxation, tax bills, deferred tax). In addition, the team will pay particular attention to unrecorded items, such as the value of tangible assets, particularly land and property (when last re-valued, etc.) and the value of intangible assets held (including patents, trademarks, software, quota, intellectual capital, customer databases). On the potential liability side, any contingent liabilities should be evaluated, and contracts reviewed that may result in an economic outflow from the target company. Risk should also be assessed. Details of the company's perceived risk exposure may be outlined in the annual report (attached to the published financial statements). Due diligence work should focus on determining whether the company's risk assessment is appropriate. Other risk areas will also be investigated, including insurance cover, proper recording of intellectual capital, key employee insurance, reliance on a small number of employees, reliance of a couple of large customers, or suppliers, reliance on software systems (how up-to-date are these), etc.

Legal documentation

The due diligence team will also review the memorandum and articles of association of the company, any trust deeds for loans issued, loan agreements, contracts with employees (particularly where there are golden parachutes and tin parachutes (discussed later in the chapter)) and contracts with suppliers and customers.

Business compatibility

The due diligence team are likely to investigate the compatibility of various operational aspects of the target company in light of the practices and ethos being followed by the bidding company. The software system in the target company should be assessed to see if it can interface with that in use in the bidding company. The production process, sales, credit control (terms and conditions, etc.), marketing, advertising and management information systems should be investigated to determine how they will integrate within the larger amalgamated company.

Friendly/hostile

The amount of information that can be captured and verified under the due diligence process is dependent on how the target company reacts to the takeover bid. If the board of directors are happy with the interest, then it is likely that they will provide most, if not all, of the information required by the due diligence team. However, if they consider the takeover interest to be unwelcome they will only allow the minimum amount of information permissible under the City Code to be made available to the due diligence team. In this instance the due diligence report will only have limited value.

Sale and purchase agreement

The *sale and purchase agreement* will form the legal sale agreement. Its contents will be influenced by the earlier stages. The original offer detailed on the head of agreement stage, may be accepted, though the due diligence work may highlight a few uncertainties that the bidding company will want clarification on, or compensation for, if they turn out to be different, or more costly for the bidding company. Any additional warranties or conditions of sale will be included in a disclosure letter.

Equity holders' perspective

Bidding company's equity holders

Large takeovers cannot proceed without the permission of a company's equity holders at a general meeting. When the equity holders in the bidding company are happy with a proposed takeover, this will be reflected in an increase in the bidding company's share price. If they are unhappy with the takeover, the bidding company's share price will fall. This is most likely to happen when the bidding company's equity holders expect their earnings per share to fall, when they expect the risk profile of the company to change (possibly due to a reduction in liquidity or a reduction in the proportion of tangible assets held in the company), or if they feel that the offer price is too high.

Target company's equity holders

When a company comes under the scrutiny of other companies then this can be taken as a signal that the company is undervalued, or is not utilising its resources correctly. Either way the equity holders of the target company stand to gain. If the offer provides the equity holders with a good return, then they are likely to support it. In addition, if they are unhappy with the current management, they are likely to welcome the offer.

The directors of a target company are supposed to act in the interests of their equity holders and should investigate every offer and determine if the company's equity holders would be better off remaining as they are, or accepting the offer. When the target company is unquoted, the directors may also be the dominant equity holders. They simply will not proceed with the takeover unless they are happy with the deal. There is nothing the bidding company can do.

When the target company is a quoted company the situation is different. Sometimes directors resist takeovers, for reasons that may be in their own interests, not in their equity holders' interests. This is costly for equity holders as defending a takeover is expensive. The target company will need to hire professional advisers, advertising and marketing specialists, undertake underwriting costs, interest costs, loss of management time, and possibly cause a downturn in the company's share price (or a rise). In most instances, directors will act in the best interests of the equity holders and resist the attempted takeover by adopting defensive tactics to ward off the predator company. In addition, equity holders can refuse to sell their shares. The City Code puts in place certain rules of engagement to allow fairness to all parties to the transaction. It makes it difficult for directors not to act in their equity holders' interests and protects the bidding company, once the takeover process has been agreed. As mentioned beforehand, the bidding company must mount a takeover bid once they purchase 30% of the target company's equity capital. If the takeover is agreed and 90% of the equity holders sell their shares to the bidding company, then legally the remaining 10% (minority interest) must sell their shares to the target company at the price agreed in the offer. This is called a **statutory compulsory acquisition (sell-out)**.

Defensive tactics

Several defensive tactics have been utilised in the past to fend off a takeover bid. Some of these are no longer allowed by the City Code as they are considered to negatively impact on equity holder value.

General defences

As a strategic issue, a company should always consider whether they are susceptible to a takeover bid. Research has shown that an analysis of certain ratios, which record the return earned on shares by equity holders and which monitor a company's growth and resources relationship, can be used to provide an indication of the likelihood of being targeted for a takeover bid. In particular, when the return on shares by equity holders starts to decline steadily over a four or five year period or where a company has high growth, but low resources, or low growth and high resources, then this can be seen as a sign of managerial inefficiency and bidding companies may see gains to be made by the takeover. Other ratios which focus on profitability and liquidity are also considered to be predictive.

Efficient management

The first line of defence for the directors of any company is to maximise the return possible from a company's resources. The fact that there is an active takeover market in the UK and in the ROI, means that company managers always have to 'be on their toes' as inefficiencies/opportunities will be spotted by others.

Employee share ownership schemes

Employees are more likely to resist a takeover bid as successful takeovers usually start with the rationalisation of costs – which normally means cutting jobs. If the company can build up the proportion of the equity holders who are employees then this provides some protection.

Convert to an unquoted company/purchase own shares

When a company feels vulnerable, becoming unquoted will make it more difficult for the bidding firm to obtain a takeover. Another option is for the company to repurchase its own shares. This will drive up demand for the company's shares and hence make the takeover more expensive. This step cannot be taken once the takeover offer is made public.

Create a poison pill, which will only be triggered if a takeover is threatened

A **poison pill** is an anti-takeover measure that can be introduced by a company. An example of a poison pill might be to give existing equity holders rights to buy additional shares, at a discount, if an individual holding exceeds beyond a certain percentage (typically around 15%), or issuing large quantities of convertible debt securities. This tactic was used by Time Warner in 1994 (to fend of the growing interest of Seagram, a Canadian drinks company) and by AMP to resist a takeover offer made by AlliedSignal in 1998 (both companies produce computer equipment – cables, etc.). Another form of poison pill is *'golden parachutes'*. This is where agreements are reached to pay management (white collar workers) large sums of money in the event of the company being taken over. *Tin parachutes* are similar, except they are directed at 'blue collar' workers. This is unattractive to bidding companies. These sort of tactics are not supported under the City Code and a bidding company can possibly have them removed with the intervention of the takeover panel and the support of the target company's equity holders.

Aggressive defences – usually undertaken after an offer is made

Provide information to equity holders

In many instances the equity holders of a company are not fully aware of all of a company's future plans. Management manage the supply of information to their equity holders and normally do not release every investment option that is being considered, until it is more or less certain, or if they feel the market is not valuing the equity shares of the company correctly. When a takeover is being proposed and the directors feel that the offer is not in the equity holders' interests, the directors may prepare and distribute a circular to the equity holders. This circular will outline their opinion of the offer and may provide the equity holders with information that they did not have beforehand. The price sensitive information they disclose typically includes profit forecasts, dividend forecasts, investment plans, asset valuations, changes in the management team, etc.

The directors have to be careful with their disclosures. If they issue profit forecasts which cause the takeover to fail and then do not live up to their projections, then equity holder confidence in the directors will fall and in addition, the company will be likely to be the target of another takeover attempt, possibly at a lower rate than beforehand. It is normal for this circularisation to include increased dividend forecasts. However, the impact of this is limited as this is something which is usually offered by the bidding company. The bidding company can also respond to this circular publicly.

Lobby against the takeover
The directors of the target company may advertise reasons for staying independent, calling on the loyalty of equity holders and may even attack the bidding company's proposal, or their track record (their management and financial statements). The bidding company are likely to respond to this.

Competition authorities/Takeover panel
The bidding company may petition the competition authorities to get involved if they feel that competition may be severely impacted upon (detailed earlier in the chapter). This technique was successfully used by Aer Lingus to fend of Ryanair's takeover bid. The target company may also petition the takeover panel if they feel any aspect of the City Code has not been adhered to.

Seek a White Knight
Sometimes the management of a company may make it publicly known that they are open to offers from other parties and may enter into friendly takeover talks with another entity, a so called *'White Knight'*. Sometimes the white knight is the management themselves and the process is called a *Management Buy-Out (MBO)*. In a similar theme an individual, called

a *'White Squire'*, may purchase sufficient shares in the target company to deter the takeover.

Pacman defence

Pacman defence is where the target company launches a counter-offer to take over the bidding company. This is not common, as the target company is usually much smaller than the bidding company and cannot realistically finance the deal. Related to this, the target company may start to takeover another company. This will drive up its value, making it too costly for the bidding company to afford.

Crown Jewels

Another possible defence is to break up the company and to sell off its most valuable portions, its *'Crown Jewels'*. This approach may be resisted under the City Code, particularly if it is felt that this will damage the target company's equity holders' wealth.

Leveraged Buy-Outs (LBO)

A *leveraged buy-out (LBO)* is the US term for debt-backed company buy-outs. The most common type of LBO is when the management team from a company backed by external investors (who usually supply some form of mezzanine finance – discussed in chapter six, 'Long-Term Sources of Finance: Debt') purchase a business from its equity holders. This is called a *MBO*. The company becomes a private company after the buyout, hence is no longer listed. The term LBO also captures MBIs, BIMBOs (also discussed in chapter six) and purchases by consortiums of private equity investors. An example of a large LBO was the purchase by Grupo Ferrovial (equity investors from Spain) of BAA for £10.1 billion on 6 June 2006. This purchase by Grupo Ferrovial was financed by a consortium of banks and financial institutions from Spain. As discussed in Chapter six, most MBO's are financed using management's personal funds, bank finance and venture capital finance.

Management of the combined company post-merger

This is seen as the most important part of a business combination. If this is not given sufficient attention, then the whole exercise may end up being a failure. When a large company takes over a small company that has its own pecking order, organisational structure and communication systems in place, then care has to be taken to ensure that the target company's employees and management team are made to feel that they are an important part of the larger entity and to integrate them into the larger company, in a quick and pain-free manner. A major flaw highlighted in prior studies on the process of mergers is that once the combination has taken place, the management of the large company move their attention on to the next issue and assume the takeover/acquisition has been a success. Meanwhile the directors and employees of the target company become disillusioned and morale and performance drop.

The integration process which takes place after a business combination is agreed is regarded as the most difficult part of the whole process, particularly where the takeover was not welcomed by the board of directors, or employees of the target firm. In these circumstances the bidding company will have less information about the target firm, which would have been forthcoming from a due diligence report that had received the full support of the target company. Jones (1982, 1986) suggests that the level of integration between the two combining businesses depends on the type of business combination: if it is a conglomerate type acquisition then there will be less integration (usually just the financials) with both companies operating more or less independently of each other. When it is a vertical acquisition, the levels of integration increase (usually include financials, marketing and some elements of manufacturing). When the combination is horizontal in nature, full integration is likely. Several approaches to successful integration have been suggested by a number of academics. The first of these is known as Druker's five golden rules for the successful integration of two businesses. These rules are more concerned with conduct and attitude towards a business combination, than actual steps that need to be taken.

Druker's – five golden rules for successful post-acquisition integration

Common core of unity - Both the bidding company and the target company should share a 'common core of unity' including shared technology and markets, not just financial links.

Symbiotic relationship: The bidding company should ask 'What can we offer them?' as well as 'What's in it for us?'

Continued

Be respectful: The acquirer should treat the products, customers, etc., of the acquired company with respect, not disparagingly.

Tailored skills for management: The acquirer should provide top management with relevant skills for the acquired company within a year.

Recognition to employees: Cross-company promotions of staff should happen within one year.

Adapted from http://www.globusz.com/ebooks/Mergers/00000018.htm

Jones (1986) considers that corporate strategy, management accounting and applied psychology all have a role to play in the successful integration of two businesses. He developed an integration sequence which has five key stages. He suggests that these be done in turn.

Jones' integration sequence

Set up initial reporting relationships – Decide upon and communicate initial reporting relationships (even if temporary). Jones suggests that it is important to do this before managers establish their own informal relationships.

Control of key factors: It is important to quickly gain control of the information flows within the new company. Information assists management to gain control. Financial control should be one of the first areas integrated. At an early stage agree expenditure limits, investment limits, overdraft limits, etc. and assess the quality of the system supporting the financial decision-making within the acquired company. The system may be good, or it may not. If it is the latter then implementing a more appropriate system should be a priority.

Resource audit: Investigate the quantity and quality of tangible and intangible assets (including human capital) and gain a clear picture of the quality of management at all levels within the acquired company.

Continued

Corporate objectives and plans: Review the corporate objectives and strategic plans of the acquired company and harmonise these with those of the parent company. When the company is in the same industry, harmonisation is easier. When the company is in a different sector, then its objectives may be deemed acceptable and the focus may be on integrating the financing and accountability of the acquired company, to the parent company.

Revising the organisational structure

Attention should be afforded to the human capital side of the business combination. The aim should be to keep morale high. This may be achieved, in part, by deciding on any factors that impact on the workforce and communicating these to the workforce promptly and clearly. Employees will be particularly interested in finding out about job security, redundancies, pensions, career progression possibilities, performance pay, changes in their role, employment contract, etc.

Finally, Schuler (2003) outlined five best practices that a parent company should implement in their approach to integrating a newly acquired company. These are listed (in brief) as follows:

Schuler – five best practices for integrating a new company

1. Start planning early.

2. Pay careful attention to leadership selection.

3. Get an insider's view of knowledge networks and information flow.

4. Develop clear, coherent and timely communication strategies.

5. Dedicate adequate resources to the transition management team.

Post-audit procedures

Every company should undertake a post-audit of the acquisition process and the success of the integration afterwards. This allows management to learn lessons from the acquisition process and to adjust their approach and behaviour in future acquisitions. The audit should compare the actual integration with the planned integration. Like any capital investment project, the performance of the combined group after the amalgamation should be compared to what has been predicted at the bidding stage. This will highlight management's investment performance, or lack of performance.

Other forms of company restructuring

Company restructuring is a strategic decision that should be taken if it is expected to lead to an increase in equity holder value.

Types of restructuring

Company restructuring is commonly categorised into three types: corporate, business and asset restructuring. At corporate level/strategic level, corporate restructuring takes place. *Corporate restructuring* refers to changes in the ownership structure of a corporation. Examples of this include: when a company amalgamates with another company, or splits into two or more companies; when a company issues more shares causing a change in control; when it repurchases its own shares; or when it goes into liquidation.

Changes in the ownership structure of business units (a lower level relative to corporate restructuring) are called *business restructuring*. Examples of this include when a company acquires another business unit, when a company lets a business unit be taken over by its management (MBO), or by another company's management team (MBI), or simply sells the business unit, franchises it, or forms a spin-off company, or when the company forms a strategic alliance or a joint venture with another entity. A strategic alliance/joint venture allows the individual companies in the agreement to retain their separate identities. This form of partnership is more common between companies in industries that are reliant on research, exploration and development and where the costs and risks are high. In particular companies come together to invest in emerging economies, where the economic and political climate is unstable.

The third main type of restructuring *'asset restructuring'* is concerned with restructuring the legal ownership of a company's assets. Examples of this include, encumbering assets with debt, entering into sale and lease-back agreements, purchasing assets using leases/hire purchase contracts, divestments (sell-offs and spin-offs) and factoring debts.

Divestures

Divestment is term used to describe the sale of an investment. Divestures can occur at corporate level, through a demerger; at business level when a business is separated and sold, or at asset level when an asset/product line, etc. is sold. Two forms of demerger are possible, a sell-off and a spin-off. A *sell-off* is the straightforward sale of a separate demerged business from the parent to a third party, usually for cash. A MBO, MBI and MIMBO are examples of business sell-offs to management teams. A *spin-off* is where the business is demerged from the parent into a separate independent unit and shares are issued in it to the parent company's equity holders, in the same proportion to the holdings they have in the parent. Therefore, in a spin-off, the ownership structure stays the same.

Group motives for divestment

Reverse synergies

Some managers believe that reverse synergies can be obtained from splitting a business. This can be explained using a simple mathematical example. Assume a company is worth €/£7 million. This includes a business unit which is valued at €/£2 million. Management may feel that the other parts of the company will be worth more than €/£5 million if this business unit is hived off to form a separate company.

Strategic decision

In some instances a company may demerge a business unit where it feels that that unit is no longer part of the company's corporate plan. In many cases it is not that this unit is unprofitable, just that the management team want to focus on core activities. It may be considered that the business is a *'poor fit'* within the overall group. For example, Viridian Group undertook a restructuring of their activities over the past decade, so that they could streamline their attention to developing power generation and supply in the whole island of Ireland. In 2001 they sold VCL, a Leeds-based power generation unit. In 2002 they sold Open and Direct Finance Services to Alchemy partners for £111 million. At this point they invested in a £100 million power station near Dublin. They also sold (for a nominal sum) their 50% stake in Nevada tele.com (a provider of telecoms and internet services in Ireland) to their joint venture partner Energis (which they now own). In 2003 they sold the Moyle Interconnector between NI and Scotland to Moyle Holdings for £122 million and in 2006 they sold SX3, their IT services subsidiary, to Northgate Information Systems for £155 million. At this time they started to develop a £120 million electricity connector which they hoped would double cross-border capacity between NI and the ROI. In addition to reinvesting the funds from these divestments, Viridian also returned funds to their equity holders. Viridian plc was taken over in 2006 by Electricinvest (a division of a Bahrain-based private equity company called Arcapita) for £1.62bn (€3bn). This was a friendly takeover, which was welcomed by Viridian's equity holders - share price rose by 9% on the day the initial offer was made (the initial offer was £1.5bn).

Improved efficiencies

The most commonly cited motive for undertaking a spin-off in a business entity is to improve efficiency. When a company's various businesses are integrated, it is difficult to identify which parts are efficient and which parts are not. Indeed some businesses may be supporting others. When the main businesses are separated and tailored strategic objectives which suit the business are set, the management and organisational structure can be clearly defined and costs controlled. Efficiency and effectiveness can be improved. Consequently investors will be in a better position to value the constituent parts of the company and can decide to remain an investor, or to sell their shares.

Reduce the risk of a takeover bid

When management believe that reverse synergies can be made, they should demerge the business unit, otherwise they are not taking steps to maximise their equity holders' wealth. Third parties will see the financial gain to be made from splitting the company and are likely to be attracted to launching a takeover bid.

> **Disinvestment – advantages**
>
> 1. A business can be sold at a profit for the benefit of its equity holders.
>
> 2. A risky business can be sold to reduce a group's overall business risk.
>
> 3. The business can be sold for cash, which can be used to reduce gearing and financial risk.
>
> 4. A business can be sold and the funds used for investment in an alternative which has a higher expected return.
>
> 5. A business can be sold that is not a core activity, freeing up management time to devote elsewhere.
>
> 6. An unprofitable business can be sold, reducing the burden on the group's management and on the group's resources.
>
> 7. A spin-off will allow investors to clearly see the performance of different parts of the company.

Divestments can also have consequences. The following table summarises potential consequences (in brief).

> **Disinvestment – disadvantages**
>
> 1. There may be loss of economies of scale where the demerged business shared overheads (marketing, advertising, finance functions).
>
> 2. Both demerged entities may find it more difficult to raise capital in the future, as some forms of capital (particularly market-based sources of finance) are really only practical for large entities.
>
> 3. The individual demerged companies are more likely to be targeted for takeover by a predator company.

Conclusion

Takeovers and mergers have been popular amongst UK and ROI companies for a number of decades (both by home and by overseas bidders). Company acquisitions are complicated. There will be a certain amount of information asymmetry between the quantity of, and interpretation of knowledge that the advisers to the bidding company have of the target company, relative to what is known by the management of the target company. When a takeover is deemed to be hostile, this problem is accentuated. Most takeovers are large and require additional financing. If a takeover is financed using debt, the capital structure and financial risk of the bidding company may be changed. Then integration of the acquired entity is complicated. If this is not carefully managed, the amalgamation may fail.

Research has shown that takeover activity amongst companies in the marketplace happens in waves. There was an increase in the number of takeovers in the early 1970s and in the late 1980s and an increase in the size of the companies being taken over in the period 1995 to 2000. Several research studies have suggested reasons for the peaks in amalgamation activity in the 1970s and 1980s including: growth in company profitability, increasing the ability of companies to finance large-scale investments of this type – this growth in profitability being accompanied by increases in a company's share price making it attractive for companies to offer share-for-share exchanges or to raise cash by issuing equity; deregulation of the financial services markets making debt more accessible – it is argued that the rising markets at this time led to larger firms being overvalued relative to smaller companies, making it easier for them to acquire small companies cheaply (in a share-for-share exchange they will be getting a bargain as the larger company's shares are overvalued); in the mid-to-late 1980s the regulatory environment was considered to be relaxed (the UK government relaxed the Monopolies and Mergers Commission recommendation on the proposed takeover of Anderson Strathclyde by the Standard Chartered Bank).

The large amalgamations in the late 1990s are considered to be companies' responses to the globalisation of the economy. In some countries, governments are hostile to foreign companies entering and utilising their resources; a merger with a local-based company reduces this hostility. In addition, the advances in telecommunications (the internet) and transportation has meant that many companies that are located far apart, can now effectively work together.

For a takeover to be successful the price range suggested by the buyer must overlap with the price range deemed to be acceptable by the vendor. Both companies are likely to use a range of the methods outlined in chapter 16, 'Company Valuation' and to come up with a price range at which they are willing do deal.

For example, assume the following information.

Vendor perspective: *Minimum price (€/£2.00 per share)*
                         Maximum price (limitless)

Buyer perspective: *Minimum price (€/£1.80 per share)*
                         Maximum price (€/£1.95 per share)

The buyer usually sets a lower value; otherwise the vendor company may take offence and as a consequence will not take the offer bid seriously. The buyer usually starts with a bid closer to their minimum price as it is common practice for the selling company to renegotiate for a higher price for their equity holders. In this scenario, no deal will result. Assume the following price ranges:

Vendor perspective: *Minimum price (€/£2.00 per share)*
                         Maximum price (limitless)

Buyer perspective: *Minimum price (€/£1.80 per share)*
                         Maximum price (€/£2.40 per share)

In this instance it is likely that the takeover bid will be successful as the price range between the two entities overlaps.

In terms of who benefits, research suggests that the winners are the equity holders of target companies. When an offer is made, it typically includes a premium over the market price of the shares. The expectation is that the premium is only part of the overall gains expected from the amalgamation; however, research suggests that in most instances the premium reflects the full gains, if not more. Indeed, in some instances it is thought that the equity holders of the bidding company may even be worse off afterwards. Gregory (1997) reported that the performance of amalgamated companies after a large *domestic* acquisition is typically negative, on average, in the longer term. He also noted that takeovers that were financed using share exchanges, adversely impacted on the bidding company's equity holders' value, to a greater extent than cash takeovers, as did agreed bids and companies that had not undertaken an amalgamation before. Conversely, he concluded that hostile bids and companies that had experienced an amalgamation before created more wealth for their equity holders. In addition, he found that conglomerate integrations were the least successful for creating equity holder wealth and horizontal integrations were the most successful. KPMG researched the success of 700 international takeovers that occurred between 1996 and 1998 and reported that 17% created value, 30% had no significant difference in value and the remaining 53% actually damaged value.

Therefore, research would question the rationality of takeovers as an appropriate investment, given the history of failures in this area. It would also seem that boards of directors who object to bids, should be made to justify their actions, as it is typically the equity holders of the target company who benefit from a takeover.

Examination standard question

Worked example 17.4 (Evaluating the purchase of a target company)

You are the financial adviser to Cushion plc, and in that capacity you have been asked to assess and report on a proposal that Cushion plc should acquire Pin plc (a similar company).

The proposal is to acquire the entire issued share capital of Pin plc at a valuation of 90c/p per share to be satisfied by a cash payment of 50c/p per share and the balance in shares of Cushion plc valued at €/£1.60 per share. The following are summarised balance sheets and income statements of Cushion plc and Pin plc as on 31 December 20X7:

Continued

Balance sheets

	Cushion plc €/£'000	Pin plc €/£'000
Non-current assets	3,200	3,650
Current assets		
Inventory	1,900	960
Trade receivables	1,720	1,280
Cash	520	20
	4,140	2,260
Total assets	7,340	5,910
Equity and liabilities		
Equity and reserves		
Equity shares of 25c/p each	1,200	900
Capital reserves	1,200	1,500
Revenue reserves	1,520	1,030
	3,920	3,430
Non-current liabilities		
Deferred taxation	–	250
Term loans	660	700
	660	950
Current liabilities		
Trade payables	2,270	920
Hire purchase commitments	50	-
Short-term loans	200	480
Taxation	240	130
	2,760	1,530
Total equity and liabilities	7,340	5,910

Continued

Income statements

	Cushion plc €/£'000	Pin plc €/£'000
Net income before taxation and interest	1,350	740
Interest	(55)	(120)
Taxation	(495)	(270)
Net income attributable to equity holders	800	350

The following information is or may be relevant:

1. Both companies are quoted on the stock exchange and have a wide spread of equity holders.
2. The equity share prices of Cushion plc and Pin plc were 170c/p and 75c/p respectively on 17 April 20X8.
3. Due to a reduction in the demand for the products of Pin plc in the home market, it is expected that profits in the year to 31 December 20X8, will be the same as in the year to 31 December 20X7.
4. The strength of the export markets for the products of Cushion plc means that the profit of Cushion plc in the year to 31 December 20X8 will be 30% higher than in the year to 31 December 20X7.
5. The rate of taxation is 50%.
6. Cushion plc can borrow funds at 15% per annum.

The managing director of Cushion plc believes that with tighter management control and more aggressive marketing, the profit of Pin plc could be increased by at least 15% in a full year. He is also satisfied that, although there would be overlapping in some product areas, in the event of an acquisition of Pin plc by Cushion plc, this would be compensated for by other benefits.

REQUIRED

You are required to prepare a report for your Board, in which you should:

Continued

a)   Indicate whether, on the basis of the information available to you, it would, in your view, make financial sense for Cushion plc to purchase Pin plc; (you are expected to show earnings per share and net assets per share calculations); and

b)   Comment on the suitability of the proposed cash and share issue and discuss possible alternatives.

N. B. You should make whatever assumptions you consider necessary but the assumptions which you do make should be clearly indicated in your report.

Total 50 Marks
(FAE handbook, ICAI, 2007/08)

Solution
Cushion plc

To: Managing Director
From: Financial Adviser
Date: 30/03/08

Acquisition of Pin plc

Introduction

1.   In accordance with your instructions I have examined the proposed acquisition of Pin plc.

2.   It is proposed that we acquire the issued share capital of Pin plc at a valuation of 90c/p a share, satisfied by a cash payment of 50c/p per share and an exchange of four equity shares of Pin plc for one equity share of Cushion plc. The valuation of 90c/p per share represents a premium of 15c/p over the current market price of the Pin plc shares.

3.   The financing of the acquisition on the proposed terms would require us to borrow €/£1,800,000, which at a rate of interest of 15% would increase our annual interest charges by €/£270,000. In addition, a further 900,000 equity shares will have to be issued which will result in an increase in the issued share capital to 5,700,000 equity shares of 25c/p each.

4.   The principal factors influencing my assessment of the financial viability of the proposed acquisition include the effect on the net assets and earnings per share of Cushion plc, the calculations of which are outlined at Appendices A and B respectively.

Continued

NET ASSETS PER SHARE

5. The valuation of 90c/p attached to the Pin plc shares compares with their present asset value of 95.3c/p per share. The poor trading performance of the company is illustrated by a comparison of the net asset value per share with the market price of 75c/p.

6. The book value of the assets of Pin plc may not be of particular significance in view of the limited scope for improvement in the company's trading results. However, I have calculated that the proposed acquisition terms would result in an increase in the net assets per share of Cushion plc from 81.6c/p to 97.4c/p per share. This increase results from the significant variation between the current book value of each company's equity share capital in relation to valuations used in the formulation of the offer terms.

EARNINGS PER SHARE

7. On the basis of the 20X7 earnings after tax of Cushion plc and Pin plc of €/£800,000 and €/£350,000 the current earnings per share in each company amount to 16.7c/p and 9.7c/p respectively. The market's view of the poor future trading prospects for Pin plc is reflected in its present price-earnings ratio of 7.7, as compared to Cushion plc's price-earnings ratio of 10.2.

8. On the basis of our budgeted results for 20X8, I have calculated that the present strength of our export markets may result in an increase in earnings per share to 17.7c/p from the present level of 16.7c/p (Appendix B).

    In addition, I have calculated that the effect of the acquisition of Pin plc on the proposed terms may be to further increase the earnings per share of Cushion plc to up to 18.9c/p.

9. The effect of the acquisition of Pin plc on the market valuation of Cushion is difficult to forecast. However, the maintenance of our present price earnings ratio would result in an increase in the market price of Cushion plc shares in proportion to the projected increase in earnings per share.

Continued

Conclusion and recommendation

10.   On the basis of the offer terms and projected earnings outlined above, the acquisition of Pin plc may be expected to lead to an increase in earnings per share of Cushion plc from 17.7c/p to 18.9c/p and an increase in net assets per share from 81.6c/p to 97.4c/p.

11.   On the assumption that the market maintains our current price-earnings ratio of 10.2 times after the acquisition of Pin plc, the projected increase in earnings per share will result in an increase in our equity share price from 180.5c/p to 193.0c/p with the resulting benefit to our existing equity holders. However, the projected increase in our market valuation may be considered to be marginal in view of the degree of uncertainty in respect of the market reaction to the takeover and to the increased quantity of share capital on the market.

12.   The effect of an increase in the cash element of the offer terms will be to further increase the projected gearing of the company with a possible adverse effect on our credit rating from the viewpoint of future sources of loan finance. However, it will be noted that a lower proportion of the bid price accounted for by the share capital of Cushion plc will result in an increase in the anticipated improvement in our earnings per share and market capitalisation.

13.   An alternative which we should consider is the inclusion in the offer terms of an element of unsecured loan stock at, for example, a rate of interest of 12%, convertible into equity share capital after five years at a discount against the expected market value of our equity share capital at that date. This rate of interest is lower than the present rate at which we can obtain loan finance, and, in substitution for the equity share capital of Cushion plc offered to the Pin plc equity holders, would result in an increase in earnings per share accruing to our present equity holders. In addition, such an issue would have a less disadvantageous effect on our capital structure as a result of the fact that the borrowed capital will not eventually have to be directly repaid by the company.

Appendix A

ASSETS PER SHARE

i) Present assets per share

	Cushion plc	*Pin plc*
	€/£'000	*€/£'000*
Equity capital	1,200	900
Capital reserves	1,200	1,500
Revenue reserves	1,520	1,030
Total net assets	3,920	3,430
Equity shares of 25c/p	4,800,000	3,600,000
Net assets per share	81.6p	95.3p

(ii)Projected assets per share (Cushion plc, post acquisition)

	€/£'000
Net assets	
- Cushion plc	3,920
- Pin plc	3,430
	7,350
Less cash paid to equity holders of Pin plc	1,800
Projected total net assets	5,550
Equity shares of 25p	5,700,000
Projected net assets per share	97.4p

Appendix B

EARNINGS PER SHARE

(i) Present earnings per share

	Cushion plc	Pin plc
Earnings per share	€/£800,000	€/£350,000
	4,800,000	3,600,000
=	16.7c/p	9.7c/p
Price-earnings ratio	170c/p	75
	16.7c/p	9.7c/p
=	10.2 times	7.7 times

(ii) Projected earnings per share of cushion plc in 20X8

	€/£'000
Trading profits before tax and interest (+30%)	1,755
Less interest	(55)
	1,700
Less Taxation (50%)	(850)
	850
Equity shares of 25p	4,800,000
Earnings per share	17.7c/p

(ii) Projected earnings per share of Cushion plc in 20X8 (post acquisition)

	€/£'000
Trading profit before tax and interest	
- Cushion plc	1,755
- Pin plc (+15%)	851
	2,606
Less interest - Cushion plc (+€/£270,000)	(325)
Pin plc	(120)
	2,161
Less Taxation (50%)	(1,080)
	1,081
Equity shares of 25c/p	5,700,000
Earnings per share	18.9c/p

(FAE handbook, ICAI, 2007/08)

KEY TERMS

Amalgamation	Management buy-out
Asset restructuring	Merger
Asset stripping	Offer document
Back door listing	Pacman defence
Backwards vertical integration	Poison pill
Bidding company	Post audit procedures
Bootstrap effect	Reverse mergers
Business restructuring	Reverse takeovers
City Code	Sale and purchase agreement
Competition Authority	Sell-off
Competition Commission	Sell-out
Conglomerate merger	Share-for-share exchange
Corporate restructuring	Spin-off
Crown jewels	Squeeze out
Defence document	Statutory compulsory acquisition
Due diligence	Synergy
Golden parachute	Takeover
Heads of agreement	Takeover code
Horizontal Integration	Target company
Hostile takeover	Tin parachute
Integration	Vertical integration
Leveraged buy-out	White knight
Market for corporate control	White squire
Management buy-in	

Websites that may be of use

For details on the Irish takeover panel visit:
http://www.irishtakeoverpanel.ie/

For details of the UK takeover panel visit:
http://www.thetakeoverpanel.org.uk/new/

For advice on how to grow a business (including a report detailing the pros
and cons of mergers/takeovers visit:
http://www.businesslink.gov.uk/

See the following website for a copy of a proposed acquisition in June 2007, including the purchase consideration and expected benefits: *http://miranda.hemscott.com/servlet/HsPublic?context=ir.access&ir_option=RNS_NEWS&item=44770739346217&ir_client_id=676&leftnav=ir*

To access the May 2006 takeover code, visit: *http://www.thetakeoverpanel.org.uk/new/codesars/DATA/code.pdf*

REVIEW QUESTIONS

1. Outline the steps that a company should take when it decides to take over another company.
2. A plc has 1,000,000 shares in issue. They are currently trading at €/£20 per share. A smaller company in the same industry B plc has 400,000 shares in issue that are currently trading at €/£10 per share. A plc is considering offering €/£11.25 per share to the equity holders in B plc for their shares. A plc has a cost of capital of 20%. It expects a yearly increase in net earnings arising from synergies of €/£140,000.

   REQUIRED

   a) Calculate the NPV of the bid by A plc for B plc.
   b) Determine who will get the value of the synergies (i.e. the proportion of the synergies going to the equity holders in A plc and the proportion going to B plc).

3. Explain the difference between a MBO and a MBI.
4. Financial information for Bidding Group plc (a fast-growing ungeared company) and Target Company plc (a slow-growing ungeared company), are as follows:

	Bidding Group plc	*Target Company plc*	*Bidding (after acquisition) – estimate*
	€/£'000	€/£'000	€/£'000
Total net earnings	400	400	800
Total market value	6,000	3,000	9,000
Number of shares in issue	200	200	300
Market price per share	€/£30.00	€/£15.00	€/£30.00
Earnings per share	€/£2.00	€/£2.00	€/£2.67
Price-earnings ratio	15 times	7.5 times	11.24 times
Earnings per €/£ invested	6.67%	13.33%	8.9%

The above information was calculated in example 17.1 and assumed that Bidding acquires the share capital of Target in exchange for 100,000 shares in Bidding. Therefore, each share of Bidding is regarded as being worth two shares in Target (Bidding's market value is twice that of Target). There are no synergies, economies of scale or any other benefit to be gained from this business combination. However, there have been concerns in respect of the potential earnings of Target Company plc and the directors of Bidding Group plc have commissioned a due diligence audit of Target Company plc. The results of this audit will be made public and are expected to impact on the share price of 'Target Company plc' immediately.

The due diligence report predicts that the growth of 'Target Company plc' is not as strong as was first anticipated and that the equilibrium market price of Target Company plc should in fact be €/£7.50.

REQUIRED

Recalculate the impact of the acquisition on the number of shares to be issued by Bidding Group plc and on the performance ratios of both 'Target Company plc' and the combined company thereafter, in light of the revised information emanating from the due diligence audit.

5.   Fox plc makes a cash offer of €/£20.00 per share for the equity shares of Hen plc. Hen plc has 500,000 shares in issue and they are currently trading at €/£15.00 per share.

REQUIRED

a)   In terms of the economic gain to be made from this takeover, what must the directors believe the value of the minimum synergies to be?

b)   Given that Fox plc has a cost of capital of 20%, what is the expected yearly increase in earnings (from synergies only)?

6.   Explain how synergy gains impact on the cost of the acquisition to a bidding company, assuming the company elects to offer cash. Compare this to the cost of the acquisition, were the company to offer a share-for-share exchange.

7.   List the reasons why a MBO might result in a demerged business being more successful that it had been when it was part of the group.

8.   List potential reasons for the failure of a MBO.

9.   What questions might an investor ask when assessing whether to back a buyout, or not?

CHALLENGING QUESTIONS

1. Pike plc and Minnow plc

Pike plc is considering acquiring all of Minnow plc's share capital. Two options are being proposed by the management of Pike plc to its equity holders. The equity holders have to vote on the option to select in a meeting in two weeks time.

- The first option is to offer €/£20.00 for each share in Minnow plc.

- The second is to offer one share in Pike plc for two shares in Minnow Plc.

Minnow plc is a similar company to Pike plc. They both sell similar items and have no long-term debt. The management have informed the equity holders that, after an extensive review of the potential impact of the merger on the future financial performance of the company, they believe that the acquisition will lead to synergies; revenues are expected to increase by €/£4 million and costs are expected to fall by €/£3 million. These are the only synergies expected. Pike plc's cost of capital is 20%.

Relevant details on both companies are as follows:

	Pike plc	*Minnow plc*
Extracts from the balance sheet	*€/£m*	*€/£m*
Total assets	260	23
Of which:		
Cash	70	4
Other assets (book value)	190	19
Extracts from the income statement		
Revenues	170	25
Costs	125	20
Market value of company	550	48
Number of equity shares in issue	11	3

REQUIRED

You are a financial adviser to the equity holders of Pike plc. You have been asked to write a report explaining the economic consequences of both options and advising the equity holders in respect of both options. You will meet the equity holders next week to discuss the finding of your report. The report should cover the following areas and should:

a)   Calculate the value of the synergies expected.

b)   Evaluate the cash offer. This will involve:

   i)   Determining the purchase consideration of the acquisition

   ii) Determining the expected new market value, cash balance, total assets and earnings of Pike plc post-acquisition?

iii) Advise the equity holders of Pike plc on how the synergy gains will be split between the equity holders of Pike plc and Minnow plc under the cash offer.

iv) Highlight which set of equity holders are exposed to the risk that the synergy calculations may be incorrect.

c) Evaluate the share exchange offer. This will involve:

i) Calculating the number of shares that Pike plc will have to issue to purchase the shares of Minnow plc.

ii) Determining the expected new market value, cash balance, total assets and earnings of Pike plc post-acquisition.

iii) Determining the purchase consideration of the acquisition.

iv) Advise the equity holders of Pike plc on how the synergy gains will be split between the equity holders of Pike plc and Minnow plc under the cash offer.

v) Highlight which set of equity holders are exposed to the risk that the synergy calculations may be incorrect.

d) Advise the equity holders of Pike plc of which option to support in the forthcoming meeting.

60 Marks

2. EAST-WEST

PURCHASE OF SUPPLIER

At the recent board meeting, the divisional director informed the board that the main supplier of raw materials, SIL Co Ltd. ('SILCO'), has been offered for sale. The divisional director expressed the view that the purchase of SILCO would not only be a good investment, because it would improve control of the supply line, but it would enable EAST-WEST to reduce the cost of materials within its product. The board asked you to investigate the possibility of purchasing SILCO and the financial impact the purchase could have on EAST-WEST.

REQUIRED

Write a report to the board of EAST-WEST setting out the following:

c)   State what information the board of EAST-WEST would need to enable it to evaluate the purchase of SILCO. Indicate what factors the Board should consider.

10 Marks
(ICAI, MABF, FAE, Extract from Autumn 2007)

3. DRAINCO

FLOTATION

The current equity holders of DRAINCO have suggested that in three years time they would like to sell their equity holdings and dispose of the company. This would likely occur by either a trade sale (i.e. sale to a competitor), or a flotation of the company on a recognised stock exchange. They have asked you for your advice on the merits of each type of disposal.

REQUIRED

Prepare an Internal Memorandum to the board setting out the following:

c)   Advise on the relative merits of both a trade sale and a flotation of the business, as a means of disposing of the equity holders' ownership of DRAINCO.

14 Marks
(ICAI, MABF, FAE, Extract from Autumn 2006)

4. INTERGLAZE plc

BOTTLING DIVISION

Several years ago INTERGLAZE set up a Bottling Division, which sells a range of glass bottles manufactured from recycled glass wastage produced by the core Windows Division. At the time, it was thought that the Bottling Division would be a useful means of utilising the significant wastage produced by the Windows Division, which would otherwise incur cost in having its waste transported and safely dumped in the local council dump. It was felt that if the Bottling Division broke even, the company would, in effect, save the cost of disposing of the waste.

As the Bottling Division was relatively small in comparison to the core Windows Division, a rudimentary management information system was installed. Recent financial information (shown in APPENDIX III) would seem to suggest that the Bottling Division is now loss-making and should therefore be closed.

INTERGLAZE has received an offer from INSULATE Ltd. ('INSULATE'), a local company that uses ground glass in the manufacture of insulation materials, to purchase its waste glass. The directors have requested that an exercise be carried out to ascertain whether the Bottling Division should now be closed, and whether the offer from INSULATE should be accepted.

REQUIRED

Draft a report to the managing director setting out your advice on the following matters:

b) (i)   Based on the information provided, advise the directors on whether or not the Bottling Division should now be closed, outlining clearly reasons in support of your advice.
(Note: ignore the impact of the proposed offer from INSULATE Ltd.)

20 Marks

(ii)   Advise the Directors on whether they should accept the offer from INSULATE. Advise on any qualitative factors that should be taken into account in this decision.

16 Marks

(ICAI, MABF, FAE, Extract from Autumn 2002)

Appendix III

BOTTLING DIVISION
Estimated product costs/revenues per tonne of waste:

	Notes	Per tonne of waste €/£
Selling price		4,000
Less:		
Direct materials		
A	*(1)*	(500)
B	*(2)*	(750)
Direct labour		
Glass cutters	*(3)*	(500)
Contract staff	*(4)*	(1,000)
Variable overhead	*(5)*	(500)
Fixed overhead	*(6)*	(750)
Depreciation		
Cutting machine	*(7)*	(250)
Blow line	*(7)*	(500)
Loss		(750)

Notes

1. Material A is a stock item that is also used in INTERGLAZE's core glazing business. This material is in inventory at a cost of €/£500 per tonne. However, following a price increase by the manufacturers, replacement orders will now be priced at €/£750.
2. Material B is a specialist material that is used solely in the Bottling Division.
3. Glass cutters are specialist workers who are also used in the core glazing business. Each tonne of waste glass in the Bottling Division requires 10 hours work at a cost of €/£50 per hour. These workers are operating at full capacity, and a contribution of €/£25 per hour is lost in the core Windows Division when these workers are re-deployed in the Bottling Division.
4. Contract staff refers to casual labour employed on an hourly basis.

5.   Variable overhead refers to light and power and other variable costs associated with the Bottling Division.

6.   Fixed overheads have been apportioned to the Bottling Division on the basis of €/£75 per machine hour.

7.   Depreciation relates to two different machines used in the production process. Both Divisions use the glass-cutting machine, with the Bottling Division's cost being allocated on the basis of direct machine hours. The blow line is used solely in the Bottling Division. This plant has a net book value of €/£50,000. However, because of its age, its open market value is likely to be negligible.

8.   If the Bottling Division was closed, and no other alternative was available for the sale of waste glass, INTERGLAZE would incur a cost of €/£300 per tonne in disposing of the waste glass in the local council dump.

9.   INSULATE has offered INTERGLAZE an initial three-year contract to purchase all waste glass at a price of €/£400 per tonne. INTERGLAZE produces approximately 100 tonnes of waste glass per month.

RISK MANAGEMENT

18

Debt   10,000,000
Equity   15,000,000
Market Value   25,000,000

LEARNING OBJECTIVES

Upon completing this chapter, readers should be able to:

♣ Describe the functions performed by a typical treasury department;
♣ Outline the advantages and disadvantages of a centralised and decentralised treasury function;
♣ Identify and describe the key financial risks facing a business;
♣ Summarise how key financial risks can be managed and measured;
♣ Outline how a risk management policy may be set and monitored;
♣ Outline the basic relationships between currencies;
♣ Explain different methods of managing currency risk using hedging products;
♣ Select an appropriate hedging product for use in hedging currency exposure in different circumstances;
♣ Explain different methods of managing interest rate exposure;
♣ Select an appropriate hedging product for use in hedging interest rate exposure in different circumstances;
♣ Perform simple calculations to determine the cost of a hedge; and
♣ Determine the financial implications of a derivative position.

Introduction

In terms of business finance, *risk* is the expectation that actual outcomes (input and output prices, cash flows, interest rates, foreign exchange rates, etc.) will differ from expected outcomes. The greater the variability in cash flows, the greater the risk and vice versa. In business, it is difficult to manage cash flows, where there are high levels of uncertainty in respect of costs, revenues and cash flows. To reduce this uncertainty, managers take steps to manage their risk exposures, preferring stable certain outcomes to gains that may occur when interest rates/commodity prices/exchange rates move in the company's favour. The process of transferring a risky cash flow to a risk-free/risk-reduced cash flow is called *'hedging'*. Hedging has become more important for most large companies as the globalisation of the economic market over the past two to three decades has resulted in companies being exposed to greater types and as a result greater aggregate levels of risk. The financial services sector has responded by developing a sweep of products which are designed to hedge against risk. In the main, these products are paper securities (contracts) which are attached to underlying assets, such as cash, commodities, or currencies. These paper securities are called ***derivatives*** because they derive value from movements in the value of the underlying asset.

A network of financial institutions and exchanges has developed over time to provide derivative products that enable managers to manage their risk exposures. Some managers do not purchase derivatives to manage risks. Instead they purchase derivatives for speculative purposes. In these circumstances managers make an assumption as to the direction of the possible fluctuation in the underlying asset values, whilst not actually owning the underlying assets. This leaves them exposed to losses if their assumptions do not hold, but also provides them with profits if their assumptions do hold. In general, risk management in large companies is undertaken by a specialist department called the treasury department.

This chapter starts off by describing the typical activities undertaken within a treasury function and outlines the advantages and disadvantages of a company having a centralised or a decentralised treasury function. Then the economic environment is examined, with particular emphasis being placed on the globalisation of markets and products and the interaction between microeconomic factors across countries. This sets the scene for introducing the variety of financial risks that a business faces and examining the way in which these risks can be managed. The management techniques used to manage risks include internal structuring and derivative products. In addition, the financial implications of a derivative position are explained.

The global economy

Many large companies are ***multinationals***. This means that they own or control a business unit outside the country in which the head office is located. Multinationals usually position some of their activities in 'Tax Havens' so as to minimise their worldwide taxation bill. ***Tax haven*** is a term used to describe a country that has lenient taxation rules which are designed to attract foreign direct investment (FDI). Another reason for locating business units in foreign countries is to gain access to resources, such as lower labour costs, lower oil costs, etc. (raw material seeking), products (by purchasing an already established company), intellectual capital (purchasing research/technology based entities), or to move closer to customers reducing transportation costs (market seeking).

Possible benefits of being a multinational company

Cost efficiencies from economies of scale: Multinationals are usually massive companies. Therefore, they can locate certain parts of their processes in countries that have comparative benefits over other countries. For example, the manual parts of production might be located in business units in India or China where labour is cheap, whereas the technical parts of production might be located in a country that has a highly educated workforce, such as Sweden.

Treasury economies: Multinationals can reduce their overall interest fees by facilitating the ability of business units to loan to each other. In addition, they can hedge their interest and currency exposures by pooling debt and currencies centrally and managing them from one pot. They may source funds in one country were debt is cheaper for use in another country where debt is more expensive (discussed later).

Technology/intellectual capital: Most multinationals invest heavily in research and development. It is argued that this makes them attractive to countries that are trying to increase their FDI. Many countries are welcoming to multinationals because they expect multinationals to bring superior technology and expertise into their country.

The global economic conditions at present make it easier and more attractive for companies to become a multinational, or to expand their foreign-based activities. The advances made in telecommunications (world wide web) have resulted in multinationals being better able to control a wider dispersed range of business units. In addition, capital markets worldwide are easier to access and have more sophisticated telecommunications systems that report real-time information. The financial environment in many countries has experienced much deregulation, therefore, the financial markets have similar rules and over the last decade many of the exchanges have signed up to International Accounting Standards. This makes it easier and more cost effective for an entity to raise funds around the world as one set of financial statements is appropriate for most exchanges. In addition, securities from different counties can be traded on a variety of exchanges. Companies also can access cash in the Eurocurrency markets. This is where local banks do business in foreign currencies; for example, a UK bank may loan US dollars to its UK client company.

The treasury function

Treasury is defined as *'a place in which treasure is kept'* or *'a place in which private or public funds are received, kept, managed, and disbursed'*. **Treasury management** is concerned with the management of cash flows (liquidity) and the financial risks surrounding these cash flows. In smaller companies treasury management comes under the remit of the accounting department. In these instances the head of this department is commonly referred to as the chief financial officer (CFO). The CFO's duties usually include risk management, funding management, strategic planning, financial reporting and investor relations. However, most large companies have a separate treasury function, manned by suitably qualified individuals who have a strong knowledge of derivative products. The head of a treasury department is usually called the corporate treasurer. The corporate treasurer's responsibilities may involve managing the capital structure of the company, managing risk and managing relationships with investors/providers of finance. When the treasury department is separate from the accounting department, a close relationship must exist if the two departments are to maximise their potential.

The importance of having a treasury function is dependent on the size of the organisation, the extent of its globalisation, the risk surrounding the value of its inputs and outputs and the attitude of the company's board of directors to risk. For example, most large oil companies have fluctuating oil prices and supply oil all around the world. Commodity price risk and exchange rate risk are real concerns for this type of company. Therefore, the majority of large oil companies have sophisticated treasury functions which are managed by an appropriately qualified corporate treasurer.

Most treasury departments in very large companies have four distinct roles. The first deals with *equity management* including mergers and acquisitions, the markets, issuing equity and maintaining relationships with investors. The second role usually focuses on *global financial transactions*, including managing currency transactions, hedging interest rate exposures and insurance management. These two roles are sometimes referred to as *treasury management*. The third deals with *cash handling* (for example, determining the optimum lodgement policy, managing the flow of cash between short-term deposits and the current account to ensure sufficient liquidity is maintained and cash forecasting for operational needs). A fourth role is usually concerned with *corporate finance*. This entails maintaining strong banking relationships, dealing with the bond markets, managing the company's financing, liquidity and working capital. The latter two roles are sometimes referred to as *funding* management. These topics are covered specifically in other chapters in this text.

Treasury function: strategic policy
The organisational structure, aims and policies of the treasury department (including the working capital and liquidity stance to take) are decided upon at board of director level. The board should set out strict controls, such as limiting involvement in derivatives for hedging purposes only (limiting risk), setting authorisation levels on transactions beyond which the board has to be informed of a transaction, and preparing and reviewing control procedures. Trading in derivatives is highly specialised and in many instances dealers working within treasury departments have accumulated huge losses over time unnoticed by others, an example being Nick Leeson. Nick Leeson, on his own, caused the demise of Barings Bank, by using high-risk strategies whilst trading in derivatives[1]. He was not using derivatives for

---

[1] He is now CEO of Galway United.

hedging purposes but for speculative purposes. Barings Bank ended up being purchased by the Dutch Bank Internationale Nederlandes Group (ING) for £1. Though Nick Leeson is famously blamed for bringing down this bank and this debacle gave derivatives a bad image, the fact of the matter is that Nick Leeson was not controlled. The board of directors must shoulder a portion of the blame. They were aware that Nick Leeson's strategy was risky — in prior years they reaped the rewards from his trading strategies (in the first seven months of 1994, Nick Leeson's department generated profits of US$30.7 million) and allowed him to continue without check.

A similar scenario unfolded during the next year (13 July 1995) when Toshihide Iguchi the executive vice president of Daiwa's New York branch[2] wrote to the president of his bank in Japan informing him that he had lost about $1.1 billion of the bank's funds over the past 11 years, whilst dealing in US Treasury bonds. The bank then proceeded to cover up this problem for a further two months, which caused problems with the US Federal Reserve Board. The board subsequently kicked Daiwa out of the US markets. Daiwa changed its strategic objectives and focused its attention on the home market in Japan and Southeast Asia. In addition, the company's equity holders took legal action against the management at that time, and on 20 September 2000, a Japanese court told 11 current and former board members to pay the bank $775 million in damages. The court considered that the management failed to oversee the branch correctly. The court made reference to the fact that the board attempted to cover up the problem and did not have appropriate risk management policies in place in the New York branch.

The reason this fraud was able to continue unnoticed by others was because of a lack of segregation of duties in the New York securities branch. Toshihide Iguchi was the back office manager, as well as a trader. This meant that he had access to the recording of transactions in relation to trades he and others had made on behalf of the bank and on behalf of customers. When he made losses, he simply sold securities to cover the losses, and falsified the bankers trust account statements to make it seem that the bank still owned the securities. He had full access to, and was in control of every transaction that took place in the branch in relation to securities. The internal auditors never independently confirmed the *custody account statements* (statements issued by the bank detailing securities held by the bank on behalf of the company).

---

[2] Daiwa is a large Japanese bank that had an international network of branches, $200 billion in assets and $8 billion in reserves.

Treasury department functions

Cash management: This involves controlling cash within the group, determining a cash management policy and implementing a supporting information system (perhaps integrating it with the banks' systems, etc.). This also involves considering risk and the willingness of the group to expose cash flows/liquidity to risk.

Bank relationships: This involves selecting a bank and the types of account to operate and in general meeting the information needs of banks.

Cash investment policy: This involves identifying cash investment opportunities and fostering relationships with brokers and dealers.

Risk management: This involves credit management, managing contingencies including possible legal actions, creating business disaster recovery policies, identifying and managing employee risks, and identifying and managing economic risks (competition, customers, etc.).

Insurance management: Treasury management should make sure that all a firm's risk exposures are covered in some form or other. This involves considering all a company's insurance needs and selecting appropriate policies to reduce risk.

Hedging: This is considered to be a form of insurance, which is normally utilised to reduce currency risk, interest rate risk and commodity price risk.

Accounts receivable management: This involves creating policies and systems for controlling cash receipts within the company, setting up facilities for credit card and debit card receipting, etc., enhancing relationships between customers and the group, and dealing with disputes.

Accounts payable management: This involves creating policies and systems for controlling cash payments from the company, including maintaining a balance between maintaining liquidity, keeping suppliers happy and availing of discounts (if profitable to do so).

Continued

It also involves enhancing relationships between suppliers and the group and dealing with disputes.

Investor relations: This involves ensuring the company has a competent equity holder service provider. The service provider should manage the flow of information from the company to its equity holder body so as not to breach any listings rules.

Structure of the treasury function

The structure of the treasury department should be decided upon by the board of directors. The main issues are whether the treasury department should be centralised or decentralised and whether the treasury department operates as a profit centre or a cost centre.

A **centralised treasury department** is where one central treasury department serves the needs of all the companies in a group, regardless of their size and location. The advantages of having a centralised treasury department are as follows:

Centralised treasury department: advantages

Easy to manage: The corporate treasurer will find it easier to manage the funding and treasury needs of the group as the information will be readily available.

Hedging: Internal hedging is easier. When a group has companies located in different countries, and sources and supplies to different companies, then a centralised treasury department can operate with a variety of accounts in the different currencies. This will reduce both transaction costs and currency risk exposure.

Taxation: The corporate treasurer can expatriate/supply cash from/to foreign countries in the most tax efficient manner, from the group's perspective.

Scale economies: It is argued that a centralised department will result in the group achieving economies of scale. Overhead and staff costs are likely to be more efficient as costs will not be duplicated.

Continued

Expertise/human capital risk: Treasury management is a highly specialised topic. Having one department enables the group-wide policy to be shared amongst several employees. It also promotes the spread of intellectual capital in respect of dealing with treasury and funding management issues amongst the employees of the department. This reduces a company's exposure to the loss of intellectual capital when a key employee leaves, as others should be knowledgeable enough to continue their work.

When a group has a decentralised treasury function, each subsidiary, or division may have their own treasury function, either separately or within the accounts department. The individual treasury functions usually follow group-wide policies and aims, which are set by the board of directors. The advantages of having a decentralised treasury function are as follows:

Decentralised treasury function: advantages

Cost control and responsibility: When the treasury function is decentralised the cost centre managers (subsidiaries/branches/divisions/business units) are in control of the cost of running the treasury department. When the treasury function is centralised its costs are either charged out or allocated to the various business units. The centre manager has no control over these costs, yet the performance of his/her unit is impacted on by the allocation.

Comparative advantage: A decentralised treasury function is more aware of the local opportunities and threats in respect of funding, finance and treasury issues.

Speed of action: A decentralised treasury function can take action quickly to reap rewards, maintain liquidity, or reduce costs (resulting from local opportunities or threats).

Treasury functions can be operated as either cost or profit centres. When they operate as a cost centre they do not have profit targets, nor do they charge business units for their services at commercial rates. Instead their costs are allocated to business units. Their aim should be to service the group's needs in the most cost effective manner. Profit centres tend to charge the business units market rates for their services, indeed, they could also provide services to outside entities. They are more likely to have profit-related performance targets; however, cost minimisation will be a major factor. Most companies operate their treasury function as a cost centre with strict controls on the type of derivative transactions that they can enter into.

Finally, a treasury department has usually the same underlying goal as every other department within an organisation — to maximise equity holder value by providing a quality service/product at minimum cost. Teigen (2001) suggests that a successful treasury function should have the following attributes:

Attributes of a successful treasury department

- Teamwork
- Respect for the organisation
- Forward thinking
- Global thinking
- Technologically advanced
- Customer focused
- Finance/accounting knowledge
- Legal knowledge
- Reliability

As a Director of a Corporate Treasury, Teigen (2001) suggests that the other departments within an organisation should regard the treasury department as *an internal consultant, with expertise in risk and finance*.

Managing risk

Most companies will have policies that specifically relate to risk management. Credit, cash and liquidity management have been covered in other chapters in this text. This chapter focuses on the specific policies and techniques that a treasury department may take to manage market risk. The three main categories of *market risk* are currency risk, interest rate risk and commodity price risk. Risk can rarely be eliminated fully and most treasury departments aim to minimise the exposure, whilst maximising the return expected from a transaction, though this is not always the case. Recognising, evaluating, measuring and balancing the risk and return associated with trading internationally using a variety of different currencies, loan products and commodities are part of a treasury department's risk management function.

Recognising risk

Most companies have improved their risk recognising procedures in the wake of the Turnbull Report (1999), wherein it was suggested that the board of directors of a company should focus on identifying their company's risks and should direct their attention to managing the riskier areas. This means that risk is a corporate problem, with corporate level responsibility over identifying and managing it. The treasury department will be particularly interested in identifying financial and business risk exposures (imports and exports). *Exposure* is a term used to describe being vulnerable to risk.

Risk can be categorised into two types: contractual and non-contractual. *Contractual risks* are risks that are caused by movements in exchange rates/interest rates/commodity process from the time a contract is agreed to the time of delivery of the required currency/funds/goods. For example, assume a ROI company purchases supplies on credit (90 days) from a company in the UK for a set sterling price. This is a non-negotiable contract and the ROI company will be exposed to contractual risk, as the euro/sterling exchange rate may change over the 90-day period making the produce either cheaper or more expensive. *Non-contractual risks* occur when no specific contract has been entered but exchange rate/interest rate/ commodity price movements have caused the competitive position of the company, overall, to change. For example, at the present time (June 2008) UK-based companies that export to European countries are experiencing a competitive advantage over their position one year ago, because sterling has weakened against the euro (one euro is worth 77p sterling, whereas in the same period one year earlier, one euro was worth 68p sterling).

Evaluating and measuring risk

Once risk has been identified the next stage is to determine the extent of the risk. This should be evaluated in light of the impact that the risk might have on the profitability, liquidity and indeed, the survival of the company. Risk and return are related and a company which accepts a high level of risk exposure can make huge profits; however, they can also make huge losses. At strategic level, the board must decide whether the company should be a risk taker (speculator), or a risk avoider (hedger), or agree some level of risk taking activity that reflects corporate attitude. Cost is also an influencing factor. Hedging has its costs and a company will weigh up whether the cost of hedging outweighs the benefits received from hedging (opportunity losses possible and the likelihood of these happening).

Nick Leeson was a speculator. His risky strategy is an example of the benefits and pitfalls that can arise when risk is taken. As mentioned previously, in the early 1990s Nick Leeson's department reaped large rewards from accepting risk, his department generated profits of US$30.7 million in the first seven months of 1994. Then these gains were reversed and huge losses made which resulted in the collapse of Barings Bank.

Managing risks
Several approaches can be taken in respect of the management of market risk. These are now outlined briefly.

Choosing to do nothing about risk

A large company may elect to stay exposed to risk. They may be risk takers and may have attracted equity holders who support this approach, in the hope of making excess gains over normal trading activities. Other large companies may not hedge because they feel that the cost of hedging outweighs the benefits. They may take the view that profits and losses associated with changes in interest rates, currency rates and commodity prices even out in the long term and the company will be no better, or no worse off. If a company has a strategy of not hedging, then they need to ensure that they hold sufficient cash to cover unexpected changes in trading and finance cash flows. This strategy might not be appropriate in companies that have high levels of business and financial risk, as there is less cash flexibility in these types of entities.

Avoiding risk totally

Companies that avoid risk might only enter into contracts that are risk free. They may have a policy of only supplying to reputable customers in countries with stable economies and may demand payment in their own currency. Likewise they may purchase locally or from reputable companies in countries that have stable economies. They might only purchase goods if the supplier agrees a price which is denominated in their own currency. This effectively means that currency risk is transferred fully to the third parties in each transaction. Companies with this approach are likely to miss many profit-making opportunities. Suppliers are going to factor the risks accepted into the price they quote for the supplies and customers will be willing to purchase the product, only when the exchange rate makes the price favourable.

A totally risk-adverse company is likely to be conservative in its approach to entrepreneurial activities, hence may find itself left behind its competitors in the long term in terms of product, etc.

Policy of reducing exposure

A company can adopt a policy of reducing the risk exposures identified, or some of the exposures identified. Non-contractual exposures are difficult to manage; however, a large company may diversify its interests globally in an attempt to diversify away some of the risks associated with currencies and indeed countries. For example, a company may relocate a factory close to the sales marketplace for a particular product and may start to source supplies locally. This will reduce currency risk, which would arise if the product was being manufactured in one country and sold in another. Another example is where a company that is selling goods to one country may start to source supplies in that country. When the sales and the purchases cash flows are the same, the exposure to movements in the exchange rate between the two countries is reduced.

Some companies diversify their product range (becoming conglomerates) in an attempt to diversify their risk. This is discussed in chapter 17, 'Business Combinations'.

Contractual exposures are easier to manage. There are two approaches. The first is to pay a premium to transfer downside risks to another entity (an insurance company/bank) which specialises in diversifying risk exposures. In return for a premium an insurance company will reimburse the premium holder for losses made if the underlying factor (interest rate/currency rate/commodity price) moves in such a manner as to cause the company to make losses on a contract. In these instances, the policy holding company is able to reap the rewards from gains made if the factor price moves in such a way as to benefit the company.

The second approach involves transferring the full risk of the contract to a third party for a fee. The practice of transferring risks is called *hedging*. There are always investors, companies or financial institutions that want to take risks in the hope that they can make a good return. In addition, there may be companies on the opposite end of a similar transaction who wish to reduce their risk and who will enter into a contract to hedge (eliminate) their risk exposure. A simple example of a hedged transaction is where one company sells to another company in a foreign land at an agreed price and an agreed exchange rate. In this example, both companies have hedged their positions. Though one will lose and one will gain from this agreement, both will be happy that they are not exposed to the risk of loss, which might occur, if the market price of the product or the exchange rate were to change.

Hedging

Several standard *financial instruments* (paper agreements) are utilised to hedge risks. These are commonly called *derivatives* (short for derivative financial instruments). Though they are primarily designed to reduce risks, some investors/companies/financial institutions use them for speculative purposes. Speculators do not have the underlying asset. They buy and sell paper assets in an attempt to make a premium on the spread values of the underlying assets each time the derivative contracts mature.

Hedging: advantages

Risk reduction: Hedging reduces risk. Currency fluctuations can cut profitability overnight. Changes in interest rates can push fixed costs up, and so hedging can avert bankruptcy risks and can control financial risk.

Planning made easier: Hedging reduces the uncertainty associated with financial planning as future cash flows are more certain.

> ## Hedging: disadvantages
>
> *Speculative profits missed:* A company cannot claim speculative gains when the value of the underlying hedged asset moves in such a manner as would favour the company.
>
> *Costly:* Hedging is not free. It is costly to set up a hedging agreement. This agreement is usually a legally binding agreement between two or more parties.
>
> *Additional controls:* Given the scandals that have occurred in the past in respect of derivative financial instruments, most treasury departments have strong controls in place to ensure that one person does not have full control of derivative transactions.
>
> *Expertise:* To effectively hedge transactions, business finance managers require specialist training in derivatives and in risk management.

Derivatives

Derivatives are commonly used to manage the contractual risks that arise in a company's normal business activities, such as currency risk, interest rate risk and commodity price risk (all discussed later). The most commonly used derivatives are futures contracts, forward contracts, swaps and options. These are now explained in turn.

Futures contracts

A *futures contract* is an agreement between two parties wherein a specified asset will be bought, or sold, at a predefined price on a specified date in the future. The underlying asset is typically money, currency or commodities. However, anything of value is possible. For example, there are futures contracts which have equity shares, stock market indices, gold or bonds as the underlying asset. Indeed, futures contracts are also used to trade EU carbon allowances (EUAs) on the European Climate Exchange. These contracts are a standard size: 1,000 EUAs. Financial futures are traded on financial exchanges and are traded in standard sizes (in the UK this is £62,500 a contract), have standard delivery dates, terms and conditions.

The mechanics of trading in futures contracts

All futures contracts are traded on a futures exchange. As mentioned, EUAs are traded on the European Climate Exchange. Corn is traded on the Chicago Board of Trade, the first ever futures exchange (a standard corn futures contract size is 5,000 bushels). In the UK, financial futures were traded on the London International Financial Futures and Options Exchange (LIFFE) until its takeover by Euronext in January 2002. This expanded LIFFE by joining it with exchanges in Amsterdam, Brussels, Paris and Lisbon. The new larger exchange became known as Euronext. liffe (a subsidiary of Euronext). The exchange experienced a further strategic change in April 2007, when it merged with the New York Stock Exchange.

When a finance manager starts trading in futures they **'open'** a futures position by either buying or selling a future contract. To **'close'** the contract the opposite occurs, the company then sells or buys a similar future contract. Most futures contracts are 'closed' before their maturity date. When a finance manager believes that the price of the underlying asset will increase, they usually buy futures 'long'. This means the finance manager is going to buy the underlying asset at the agreed price on an agreed date. When a finance manager believes that the price of the underlying asset will fall, they usually sell futures 'short'. This means the finance manager will sell the underlying asset at the agreed price on the agreed date.

Exchanges normally disclose two prices for each future contract. The **bid price** is the price at which the trader is willing to buy futures contracts. The **offer price** is the price at which the market-maker is willing to sell a futures contract. The difference between the bid price and the offer price is called the **spread**. Anyone wishing to deal in futures usually approaches a broker (member of an exchange), who subsequently instructs a market-maker. At the outset the parties to a futures contract have to give an initial margin to the exchange. This is a liquidity deposit for the exchange, which is refunded when the futures contract is closed. No money changes hands in respect of the futures contract. Futures contracts are usually **marked-to-market** daily. This means that the parties to a futures contract must make good any loss, or can withdraw any benefit from movements in the price of the underlying asset from the exchange. They have to keep the margin at an agreed level. Futures are described in terms of ticks. A **tick** is one hundredth of a percent (0.01%) and this is the smallest movement allowed by the market in the value of a future. They are traded at a percentage value i.e. 90.00 means that the future is worth 90% of its nominal value.

How a futures contract can be utilised to hedge risk exposure

The price of a futures contract is normally the current price of the underlying asset plus a premium for financing costs and holding costs less any income receivable from the asset during the futures period. Therefore, to hedge against an asset falling in value, the holder of the asset should sell futures (short), then before the maturity of the futures contract, buy back 'close' the futures contract. The losses made on the underlying asset, will be compensated for by the profit made on the futures contract.

Worked example 18.1   (Futures contracts for hedging)

In April 2008 the futures market for corn was quoting a bid price of €/£2.00 a bushel. A co-operative decides to lock into this price for the benefit of its members, so it sells 100 futures contracts (there are 5,000 bushels in each contract). The futures are due to mature when the harvest season is over in September. The co-operative is hedging against a fall in the potential sale price of corn.

REQUIRED

(a) Calculate the profit/loss made by the co-operative assuming the market value of each bushel falls to €/£1.20 each.

(b) Calculate the profit/loss made by the co-operative assuming the market value of each bushel rises to €/£2.40 each.

Solution

The actual cash flows are now detailed.

In April 2008 the co-operative considers that it will have to sell 500,000 bushels of corn for its members at harvest time (September) and considers that €/£2.00 (the current market price) is a fair price. Therefore, to hedge against price movements the co-operative sells

Continued

100 corn futures contracts at €/£2.00 for each bushel (€/£1,000,000 in total). The only money to change hands at this stage is the margin which the co-operative will have to post with the relevant exchange. This is refundable at a later stage.

a)   By September the market price has fallen to €/£1.20.

The co-operative now has to take two steps. They will sell the 500,000 bushels of corn in the market place for €/£1.20 each (€/£600,000) and will buy 100 futures contracts at €/£1.20 each (commodity futures contracts usually reflect current market price of the underlying assets). This closes out their initial futures contract. Therefore, they will make a margin of 80c/p (€/£2.00 − €/£1.20) on each bushel under the futures contract, which amounts to €/£400,000 overall.

Therefore, the co-operative has secured a net sale price of €/£2.00, made up of a cash price of €/£1.20 (€/£600,000) and a profit on the futures contract of 80c/p a bushel (€/£400,000).

This profit on the futures contract will have been received by the co-operative throughout the life of the futures contract as it will have been marked-to-market at the close of business every day and any surplus made over the initial margin withdrawn by the co-operative.

b)   The approach is similar to that in a). In April 2008 the co-operative considers that it will have to sell 500,000 bushels of corn for its members at harvest time (September) and considers that €/£2.00 (the current market price) is a fair price. Therefore, to hedge against price movements the co-operative sells 100 corn futures contracts at €/£2.00 for each bushel (€/£1,000,000 in total). The only money to change hands at this stage is the margin which the co-operative will have to post with the relevant exchange.

By September the market price has risen to €/£2.40.

Continued

The co-operative now has to take two steps. They will sell the 500,000 bushels of corn in the market place for €/£2.40 each (€/£1,200,000) and will buy 100 futures contracts at €/£2.40 each (commodity futures contracts usually reflect current market price of the underlying assets). This closes out their initial futures contract. Therefore, they will make a loss of 40c/p (€/£2.00 − €/£2.40) on each bushel under the futures contract, which amounts to a loss of €/£200,000 overall.

Therefore, the co-operative has secured a net sale price of €/£2.00 (€/£1,000,000) as intended. It is now made up of a cash price of €/£2.40 (€/£1,200,000) and a loss on the futures contract of 40c/p a bushel (€/£200,000).

The €/£200,000 loss will already have been paid by the co-operative to the exchange over the life of the futures contract as the contracts are marked-to-market every day. With every increase in price, the corresponding opportunity revenue lost will be paid to the exchange to maintain the margin.

How to speculate using a futures contract

Futures contracts can also be utilised for speculative purposes. In these circumstances the investor does not own the underlying asset. He/she is gambling on the suspected movement in the value of the underlying asset. This is best explained using the above example amended.

Worked example 18.2 (Futures contracts for speculative profits)

In April 2008 the futures market for corn was quoting a bid price of €/£2.00 a bushel. An investor is diversifying his portfolio of investments and decides that he will put a portion of his wealth into the futures markets. He thinks that the price of corn will rise, therefore he buys 100 futures contracts long (there are 5,000 bushels in each contract). The futures are due to mature when the harvest season is over in September. The investor has no corn and has no intention of ever owning the underlying corn!

Continued

REQUIRED

a) Calculate the profit/loss made by the investor assuming the market value of each bushel rises to €/£2.40 each.

b) Calculate the profit/loss made by the investor assuming the market value of each bushel falls to €/£1.20 each.

Solution

The actual cash flows are now detailed.

In April 2008 the investor decides to buy 100 corn futures contracts (the underlying price of the corn is €/£2.00 a bushel). The only money to change hands at this stage is the margin which the investor will have to post with the relevant exchange. This is refundable at a later stage.

a) By September the market price has risen to €/£2.40.

   In September the investor will sell 100 futures contracts at €/£2.40 each (commodity futures contracts usually reflect current market price of the underlying assets). This closes out their initial futures contract. Therefore, they will make a margin of 40c/p (€/£2.40 − €/£2.00) on each bushel, which amounts to a profit of €/£200,000 overall.

   This profit on the futures contract will have been received by the investor throughout the life of the futures contract as it will have been marked-to-market at the close of business every day and any surplus made over the initial margin withdrawn by the investor, or the broker acting on the investor's behalf.

b) The approach is similar to that in a). In April 2008 the investor decides to buy 100 corn futures contracts (the underlying price of the corn is €/£2.00 a bushel). The only money to change hands at this stage is the margin which the investor will have to post with the relevant exchange. This is refundable at a later stage.

Continued

By September the market price has fallen to €/£1.20 per bushel

In September the investor will sell 100 futures contracts at €/£1.20 each. This closes out their initial futures contract. Therefore, the investor will loose 80c/p (€/£2.00 − €/£1.20) on each bushel, which amounts to a loss of €/£400,000 overall.

This deficit on the futures contract will have been paid to the exchange by the investor throughout the life of the futures contract as it will have been marked-to-market at the close of business every day and any deficit made over the initial margin lodged by the investor, or the broker acting on the investor's behalf.

This example shows just how rewarding and penalising futures contracts can be when used for speculative purposes. Many investors see the potential for profit and siphon a proportion of their portfolio into hedging markets in an attempt to reap higher rewards. Where this goes wrong is when an investor places too large a proportion of his portfolio in these instruments and the market goes against them. The current oil price surge is reportedly being fuelled, in part, by demand in the futures markets for oil futures contracts. However, it is also considered that this view is a political scapegoat argument and is not based on economic fact. Visit the following website for a discussion of this.
(http://www.economist.com/opinion/displaystory.cjm?story_id=11670357)

Forward contracts

Futures contracts are standardised, with set sizes, terms and conditions and maturity dates. This may not suit some companies that are trying to hedge a value that is different to the standard sizes, or has a delivery date that does not correspond to the standard dates. In these circumstances, a company can buy or sell a forward contract. ***Forward contracts*** are bespoke futures contracts. Like a futures contract, no cash exchanges hands on inception; however, a margin may be posted by both parties to the contract as collateral. The price agreed for the asset on maturity is calculated in the same way as the price under a futures contract. There are two major differences. Firstly, forward contracts are not traded on an exchange – they are usually administered OTC by a bank on behalf of their customer. Secondly, they are not marked-to-market. The overall difference between the spot price and the forward price is determined and settled at maturity. The difference is called the ***forward premium*** (profit) or ***forward discount*** (loss).

Worked example 18.3   (Forward contracts for hedging purposes)

Ringo plc wishes to sell a building. Star plc wishes to purchase the property in two years time. The current market value of the property is €/£750,000. Ringo plc has a cost of capital of 10%. Star plc has a cost of capital of 12%. It costs Ringo plc £10,000 each year to insure and maintain the building, payable at the start of each year.

REQUIRED

(a) Calculate the minimum forward price that Ringo plc will accept before signing up to a forward rate contract with Star plc.
(b) Calculate the profit/loss made by Ringo plc and Star plc if the market value of the property:
   i)   Rises to €/£1,000,000
   ii) Rises to €/£850,000

Solution

(a) The minimum forward price that Ringo plc will agree to must cover the market value of the building plus the opportunity cost of holding the building for a further two years. This opportunity cost will include the revenue forgone from not investing the funds that the company could receive now.

Therefore Ringo plc will only sign up if the forward price agreed is equal to, or greater than €/£930,600 made up as follows.

Continued

	Costs	*Cumulative*
Spot price	€/£750,000	€/£750,000
Costs in year 1	€/£10,000	€/£760,000
Return forgone in year 1		
(€/£760,000 × 10%)	€/£76,000	€/£836,000
Costs in year 2	€/£10,000	€/£846,000
Return forgone in year 2		
(€/£846,000 × 10%)	€/£84,600	€/£930,600

b)   (i) If the market value of the property in two years time is €/£1,000,000 then Ringo plc will have made a loss on the contract of €/£69,400 (€/£1,000,000 − €/£930,600). Star plc will have made a profit on the contract of the same amount.

(ii) If the market value of the property in two years time is €/£850,000, then Ringo plc will make a profit of €/£80,600 (€/£930,600 − €/£850,000) and Star plc will make a loss on the forward contract of the same amount.

Forwards versus futures

Advantages of forwards over hedges
Bespoke: The dates and amounts in a forward contract can be tailored to suit the needs of the investor, while futures contracts are standardised.

Perfect hedge: In a forward contract the amount and timing of the contract can be changed to form a perfect hedge, or as near to a perfect hedge as is possible.

Assets: Forward contracts can be written in respect of any asset. Futures contracts usually cover set assets. For example, futures are not available for every currency, nor for individual properties.

Disadvantages of forwards over futures
Cost: Forward contracts are usually more costly to set up because they are bespoke.

Continued

> *Less flexible:* The futures contract can be closed out at any time up until the maturity of the future, and is usually closed out after the sale/purchase of the underlying asset. The futures contract is therefore like an option, which must be exercised by a set date. The forward contract does not have this option period.

Swap contracts

A *swap* is a written contractual agreement between two counterparties to exchange one stream of cash flows for another stream of cash flows. The two cash flow streams are called the *legs* of the swap. Like both futures and forward contracts, the underlying asset – called the principal amount – is normally not exchanged between counterparties. The five main types of swaps are interest rate swaps, currency swaps, credit swaps, commodity swaps and equity swaps. Most swaps are bespoke and are traded OTC, usually through banks, though some can be obtained in the derivatives markets. The Bank for International Settlements reported that swaps with notional principal amounts of $692 trillion were outstanding in the quarter to June 2008[3].

Swaps are typically used to hedge risk exposures (usually interest rate risk or currency risk), though they can be used for speculative purposes. Normally, one leg is variable in nature, the other is fixed. The party with the variable cash flows wants fixed cash flows (hedging their position); the party with the fixed cash flows wants variable cash flows (speculating on changes in the rate to be applied to the underlying asset value). This is normally called a *fixed-to-floating rate swap*. The party that pays floating and receives fixed is said to be *short* in the swap and the party that pays fixed and receives floating is said to be *long* in the swap. The variable rate is usually pegged to an independent source, such as LIBOR, the European Bank's base rate, or the FTSE 100 index.

---

[3] The enormity of this investment is only realised when compared to world GDP. In 2006, the Central Intelligence Agency of the US reported this at $65.95 trillion. Therefore, swap contracts are outstanding which amount to about ten times the world's GDP!

Valuation

A swap is valued as the net present value (NPV) of the expected future cash flows. At the outset, the NPV of a swap agreement is zero as the initial set-up fee that transfers between the counterparties will equal the expected benefit to be derived, otherwise the party with the better expected stream of cash flows will not agree to the swap. It is only when the actual cash flows differ (due to changes in the underlying variable rate) from expected cash flows, that either party make profits or losses on the swap.

Worked example 18.4   (Swap contracts for hedging purposes)

John plc has €/£2,000,000 of debt on which it pays interest at the rate of 5%. Paul plc also has €/£2,000,000 of debt on which it pays interest at the rate of LIBOR plus 100 basis points (equivalent to 1%). LIBOR is currently 5%. In both instances, the principal amount has to be repaid to the lenders in five years time.

John plc expects interest rates to fall and therefore wants to speculate a little by converting his interest payments to floating rate. Paul plc is quite heavily geared and wants to reduce its financial risk by locking-in interest rates to a fixed rate. Both parties are introduced to each other by their perspective banks, who agree to administer the contract.

REQUIRED

(a) Calculate the fee that Paul plc will have to pay John plc to get it to sign up to the swap, at the above rates. John plc's cost of capital is 7%.

(b) Calculate the profit/loss made by John plc and Paul plc if LIBOR:
   (i) Rises to 7%
   (ii) Falls to 3%

Solution

(a) The minimum fee that John plc will accept to enter into the swap agreement (given the differential in the interest rates) must cover the cost of the additional interest that John plc expects to

Continued

pay over the life of the swap. At the present time John plc is paying 5%, Paul plc is paying 6%. Therefore, John plc will not enter this agreement unless Paul plc pays it an initial premium to cover the present value of the interest differential, assuming the differential remains for five years. Therefore, the initial fee payable by Paul plc to John is the present value of a five-year annuity of €/£20,000 (€/£2,000,000 × 1%) at 7%.

Which is €/£20,000 × 4.10 = €/£82,000

(b) i)   Assume that interest rates rise to 7%
         In this instance:
         John plc's interest charge before the deal is €/£100,000 (€/£2,000,000 × 5%).
         Paul plc's interest charge before the deal is €/£160,000 (€/£2,000,000 × 8%).

         Because both parties have signed up to a swap agreement, John plc will have to pay Paul plc €/£60,000 being the difference between the variable rate interest (€/£160,000) that the company wanted and the fixed rate that the company currently pays (€/£100,000). In the first year Paul plc will have to pay John plc the agreement fee of €/£82,000; therefore a net payment from Paul plc to John plc of €/£22,000 (€/£82,000 − €/£60,000) will result.

     (ii) Assume that interest rates fall to 3%
         In this instance:
         John plc's interest charge before the deal is €/£100,000 (€/£2,000,000 × 5%).
         Paul plc's interest charge before the deal is €/£80,000 (€/£2,000,000 × 3%).

     In this instance Paul plc will have to pay John plc the interest differential of €/£20,000 (€/£100,000 − €/£80,000) each year plus the initial fee of €/£82,000.

As is noted in the above example, the underlying notional amount does not change hands. Indeed, only the interest and fee differential changes hands on pre-agreed dates.

Types of swap contract

Total return swap: In a total return swap, one party to the contract (A) swaps the total return on a notional asset (capital gain/loss plus any interest/dividend received) with the other party (B) for periodic interest payments on the capital value of the notional asset, which can be fixed or floating. Therefore, B can get access to the return on the asset, without owning it; whereas A (has the asset on their balance sheet) has hedged their exposure to a loss in the asset value and income from the notional asset.

Equity swap: An equity swap is a total return swap. Therefore, much of the previous paragraph applies. As the name suggests, the notional principal asset in an equity swap is a particular type of equity share, a basket of equity shares, or an equity share index.

Credit default swap: This is like an insurance agreement. In a credit default swap, one party pays the other party a stream of payments (buyer) in return for credit protection from the swap seller, for a particular debt from a third party. If the third party defaults, the seller has to make good the difference between the amount received (recoverable amount) from the third party and the notional amount noted in the swap agreement.

Plain vanilla swap: A plain vanilla swap is a straight exchange of the right to pay a fixed rate of interest on a notional principal amount for the right to pay a variable rate of interest on the notional principal amount.

Currency swap: Involves exchanging both the principal and the repayments (capital and interest) in one currency with the principal and repayments (capital and interest) in another currency.

Swaps are normally arranged by a dealer who usually takes a cut on the cash flows that are being exchanged. For example, if a company wishes to change floating for fixed rate debt, and they agree to pay a fixed rate of 7.5%, then a broker may agree the exchange, but charge them 7.6% for the swap. The dealer will then close out this swap with another company who is looking for variable rate payments, and will also take a margin on the cash flow agreed with that party.

Options

Options are derivative finanancial instruments that convey the right, but not the obligation, to undertake a transaction at a specified *exercise price* (also known as the *strike price*) on or before a specified date, which is referred to as the *exercise date*. A *call option* is a term used to describe an option that conveys the right to buy a certain quantity of an asset at a set price (the exercise price), on or before the exercise date. The holder of a call option will only exercise it on, or before the exercise date, if the market value of the underlying asset to be purchased is worth more than the preagreed exercise price. Indeed, the price of the share would need to move to the exercise price plus the option price before the holder makes a gain. The value of a call option is the difference between the market value of the underlying asset and the exercise price. When the market value of the underlying asset is less than the exercise price, the call option is worthless. For example, when the call option specifies that the exercise price that the holder can buy at is €/£2.00 per share and the option was purchased for 10c/p. Then the transaction will be worthless if the market value of the share price falls below €/£2.00, as the holder will not exercise the option but will just buy the shares at the lower price. If the market value is €/£2.00 the holder may, or may not exercise the option – in this instance, the holder will make a loss which is equal to the price of the option (10c/p). The holder starts to make money when the market value of the share rises above €/£2.10 (€/£2.00 + €/£0.10).

A *put option* is a term used to describe an option that conveys the right to sell a certain quantity of an asset at a predetermined exercise price on, or before, the exercise date. The holder of a put option will only sell on the exercise date if the exercise price of the asset is higher than the market value of the underlying asset. The value of a put option will be the exercise price less the market value of the underlying asset. When the market value of the underlying asset is worth more then the exercise price, the put option is worthless as the holder of the asset can sell the asset for a higher price in the marketplace. The holder of a put option will make money when the market value of the asset is less than the exercise price, net of the option price. For example, when the put option specifies that the exercise price that the holder can sell at is €/£2.00 per share and the option was purchased for 10c/p. Then the transaction will be worthless if the market value of the share price moves above €/£2.00, as the holder will not exercise the option but will just sell the shares at the higher price. If the market value is €/£2.00 the holder may, or may not exercise the option — in this instance, the holder will make a loss which is equal to the price of the option (10c/p). The holder starts to make money when the market value of the share falls below €/£1.90 (€/£2.00 − €/£0.10).

Sometimes the holder of equity shares may hedge their position against both upward and downward price movements. To do this they will hold both a call and a put option with the same exercise date and price. This is called a **straddle**. A variety of other combinations are also possible depending on the holder's perception of how share price will move; a **strip** is created when two puts are combined with one call option, a **strap** is combining two calls and one put option. Finally, another commonly used strategy is a **covered call**. This is where a holder buys a stock and sells a call option. If the share price rises, the trader exercised his option, if it falls, the trader's loss is reduced by the amount received from the sale of the call option. In all instances, the writer of an option will hold an equal, but opposite position and will make an gain/(loss) that will be equivalent to the (loss)/gain being made by the holder. Trading in options for speculative purposes is risky, with the trader likely to make high returns, or to suffer high losses. This is highlighted in the following example.

> ### Worked example 18.5   (Trading in options versus buying shares)
>
> Pero plc has €/£500,000 to invest. The company have decided to invest this into either options, or equity shares. The company is strong, has steady returns and has pigeonholed this €/£500,000 for investment in risky type investments, in the hope that premium returns can be made. This strategy has been agreed at board level.
>
> Assume that the finance manager has decided to invest in one particular company, Zena plc. At present Zena plc's share price is €/£2.50 per share and its call options are 40c/p per share with an exercise price of €/£2.40.
>
> *Continued*

REQUIRED

Prepare calculations to show the profits/ (losses) that will result if the finance manager elects to purchase shares in Zena plc, or call options in Zena plc. In your answer assume two outcomes. The share price will either:

(i)   rise to €/£3.10 or
(ii) fall to €/£2.00
by the exercise date.

Solution

The finance manager can either decide to purchase shares or call options.

(i)   Share price rises to €/£3.10
      Assume the finance manager purchases shares in Zena plc.

Purchase 200,000 shares (€/£500,000/€/£2.50)	(€/£500,000)
Sale value on exercise date (200,000 × €/£3.10)	€/£620,000
Profit on sale	€/£120,000
Return on investment (€/£120,000/€/£500,000)	24%

Assume the finance manager purchases call options in Zena plc.

Purchase 1,250,000 options (€/£500,000/€/£0.40)	(€/£500,000)
Exercise price (1,250,000 × €/£2.40)	(€/£3,000,000)
Sale at market value (1,250,000 × €/£3.10)	€/£3,875,000
Profit on sale	€/£375,000
Return on investment (€/£375,000/€/£500,000)	75%

(ii) Share price falls to €/£2.00
      Assume the finance manager purchases shares in Zena plc.

Purchase 200,000 shares (€/£500,000/€/£2.50)	(€/£500,000)
Sale value on exercise date (200,000 × €/£2.00)	€/£400,000
Loss on investment	(€/£100,000)

Continued

> *Assume the finance manager purchases call options in Zena plc.*
> Purchase 1,250,000 options
> (€/£500,000/€/£0.40)   (€/£500,000)
> Loss on investment   (€/£500,000)*
>
> *In this instance, the finance manager will not exercise the option; therefore his loss is restricted to the cost of the options.

Options are traded separtely on equity exchanges; however, they can also be arranged OTC usually through a financial intermediary. **Exchange traded options (listed options)** are standardised agreements which are administered by a clearing house. Exchange traded options include commodity options, bond options, interest rate options, index options (equity), options on futures contracts and employee share options. **Employee share options** are options that are issued to employees by a company as a form of compensation. Options can be written into any contract, including mortgages (the right but not the obligation to repay capital each year in lump sums up to a certain amount) and real estate deals (the right to purchase adjoining land in three years time at a set price) and bespoke option agreements, or **over-the-counter options** (also called **dealer options**) can be brokered through a dealer. These are not listed on any exchange and typically include interest rate options, currency options and **swaptions** (options on swap agreements).

There are a variety of mathematical models that are used to predict how the value of an option will change in response to changes to the variables that will impact on an options value. Two models are considered in this chapter. The binomial model and the Black-Scholes model.

Binomial model
The **binomial model** values an option based on the assumption that share price will be one of two options, one a low value, the other a high value. A call option is valued using the following formula:

$$C_0 = \frac{H(P - P_L)}{(1 + r)}$$

Where C_0 is the value of the call option with one period to the exercise date, P is the current share price, P_L is the lower value of the share expected at the end of the period, r is the risk-free rate of return and H is the hedging ratio. The hedging ratio is calculated as:

$$H = \frac{(C_u - C_L)}{(P_u - P_L)}$$

Where C_u is the upper value on the option at the end of the period, C_L is the lower value on the option at the end of the period and P_u is the upper value of the share at the end of the period.

Worked example 18.6   (Valuing an option – binomial model)

The current price of a share is €/£7.50 and the exercise price of the call option is €/£7.50. The risk-free interest rate is 10%.

REQUIRED

Assuming that the share price will either rise to €/£10.00, or fall to €/£5.00 by the exercise date, calculate the value of the call option one period before the exercise date using the binomial model.

Solution

$$C_0 = \frac{H(P - P_L)}{(1 + r)}$$

Where:
C_0 is the value of the call option with one period to the exercise date (to find)
P is the current share price (€/£7.50)
P_L is the lower value of the share expected at the end of the period (€/£5.00)
r is the risk-free rate of return (10%) and
H is the hedging ratio:

$$H = \frac{(C_u - C_L)}{(P_u - P_L)}$$

P_u (€/£10.00) and P_L are given in the question. However, C_u and C_L need to be calculated. The maximum value of the option C_u will

Continued

be the maximum market value less the exercise value, which in this case is €/£2.50 (€/£10.00 − €/£7.50), the lowest option value C_L will be zero as the option will not be exercised if the share price falls below €/£7.50. Therefore:

$$H = \frac{(€/£2.50 − €/£0)}{(€/£10.00 − €/£5.00)}$$

$$H = 0.5$$

And the value of the option is:

$$C_0 = 0.5(€/£7.50 − €/£5.00/(1 + 0.1))$$

$$C_0 = €/£1.477$$

Though the binomial model approach is straightforward, it is constrained by the unrealistic assumption that the share price has only two possible outcomes. This constraint is eliminated by the Black-Sholes model which assumes that the share price return between the period of valuation and exercise date is normally distributed. This is considered to be a more realistic assumption.

Black-Scholes model

The **Black-Scholes model** is named after its founders – Fischer Black and Myron Scholes[4]. The model assumes that capital markets are in equilibrium and a portfolio of shares and call options can be created which is risk-free (the options hedge the holder against risk). Therefore, the option is priced assuming that the rate of return on the underlying equity assets is equal to the risk-free rate of return. The model assumes that the value of the option is dependent, not on the expected return on the share, but on the current market price of the asset, the exercise price, the cost of holding the underlying asset (for example, interest and dividends), the time to the exercise date, restrictions on exercise dates and an estimate of the future volatility of market returns of the asset over the term of the option. The first four of these variables are relatively easy to determine. The last

---

[4] Robert Merton and Myron Scholes were awarded a Nobel Prize in Economics in 1997 for their ground-breaking work in relation to this model (Fischer Black passed away in 1995).

is estimated. A typical approach is to view the variability of returns of the asset in the past and to use this as a proxy for the expected variability of returns in the future.

The Black-Scholes model to value a call option is as follows:

$$P_0 = PN(d_1) - \frac{E}{e^{rt}} N(d_2)$$

Where P_0 is the current value of the option, P is the current value of the asset, E is the exercise price, e is the exponential constant (2.7183), r is the risk-free rate of interest for the period and t is the time (in years) remaining in the option contract. $N(d_1)$ and $N(d_2)$ are values of the cumulative normal distribution, defined as:

$$d_1 = \frac{Ln(P/E) + (r + \sigma^2/2)t}{\sigma t^{1/2}}$$

and

$$d_2 = \frac{Ln(P/E) + (r - \sigma^2/2)t}{\sigma t^{1/2}}$$

Where Ln is the natural logarithm, σ^2 is the variance of the return on the share (i.e. the changes in market value and income) and σ is the standard deviation of the return on the share.

Worked example 18.7   (Valuing an option)

Sherry plc is offered 100 options by one of the companies that they invest in (Gallagher plc). The current market price of Gallagher plc's shares is €/£2.00. The exercise price written into the option agreement is €/£2.40. At the present time, the continuously compound rate of interest is 6%. The option is open for three years.

REQUIRED

Calculate the price that Sherry plc should pay for the options given that the return on Gallagher's shares over the past year has a standard deviation of 25%.

Continued

Solution

$$P_0 = PN(d_1) - \frac{E}{e^{rt}} N(d_2)$$

P_0 is the current value of the option (?)
P is the current value of the asset (€/£2.00)
E is the exercise price (€/£2.40)
e is the exponential constant (2.7183)
r is the risk-free rate of interest for the period 6%
t is the time (in years) remaining in the option contract (3 years)

$$d_1 = \frac{Ln(P/E) + (r + \sigma^2/2)t}{\sigma t^{1/2}}$$

$$d_1 = \frac{Ln(200/240) + (0.06 + 0.25^2/2)3}{0.25 \times 3^{1/2}}$$

$$d_1 = 0.2111$$

$$N(d_1) = 0.5832^*$$

This value is obtained from Appendix six 'Area under the normal curve up to t standard deviations above the mean.

$$d_2 = \frac{Ln(P/E) + (r - \sigma^2/2)t}{\sigma t^{1/2}}$$

$$d_2 = \frac{Ln(200/240) + (0.06 - 0.25^2/2)3}{0.25 \times 3^{1/2}}$$

$$d_2 = -0.2218$$

$$N(d_2) = 1 - 0.5871^* = 0.4129$$

This value is obtained from Appendix six 'Area under the normal curve up to t standard deviations above the mean.

Therefore the value of the option is:

$$P_0 = 200(0.58332) - \frac{240}{2.7183^{0.06 \times 3}} \times 0.4129$$

Continued

$$P_0 = 116.64 - 82.77$$

$$P_0 = 33.86 \ (\text{€}/\pounds 0.34)$$

Sherry plc should offer €/£34 for the 100 options (€/£0.34 × 100).

Though the above Black-Scholes model is used in practice, it is academic. As such it has a number of assumptions which are also regarded as limitations.

The assumptions of the Black-Scholes model:

1. The option being priced is European in nature.

2. There are no transaction costs, or tax implications.

3. There are no penalties, or restrictions on short-selling.

4. The underlying asset does not pay a return (no dividend).

5. The value of the underlying asset is continuous.

6. The market operates continuously.

7. The asset price is 'log normally' distributed.

8. The risk-free interest rate is known and is constant.

Regardless of the model that is used to value options, two variables are regarded to influence the price of an option, both are risk related; the length of time to the exercise date and the variability in the returns of the asset. Options with longer exercise times and greater variability in expected returns will be valued higher than options that have short life spans and lower variability in expected returns.

Options applied to financing and investment decision making

It has been argued that managers should apply the principles laid down in the Black-Scholes model to other decisions, such as deciding on whether to invest in a particular venture that may have an option to expand/grow in the future. By using the Black-Scholes model and data for the five key variables, a value can be placed on the option to expand/grow, which should be taken into consideration at the outset. In other instances finance managers may purchase call options on the ability to purchase. For example, land in the future which may be required for expansion. A variety of financial assets also have options (usually call options) written into them. For example, warrants may be issued with equity, or debt as a sweetener to entice investors to invest in the company. A **warrant** gives the holder the right to purchase equity shares from the company at a set price before a specified future date. A **convertible bond** is similar. It gives the holder the right to exchange their bond for a specified number of shares on or before a specified future date. A **callable bond** puts flexibility into the hands of the issuer, by allowing them to repurchase the bond back in any period up to the maturity date. These financial products have been discussed in more depth in chapter six, 'Long-Term Sources of Finance: Debt'.

Specific risks: exchange rate risk

Exchange rates

Any company that trades with overseas suppliers, customers or is a multinational will have to have a good knowledge of exchange rates and the influences on exchange rates. This is vital to determine with accuracy the cash flows expected by the company. An **exchange rate** is the rate at which one country's currency can be traded in exchange for another country's currency. Currency which is traded and is immediately exchanged is traded at the **spot rate** (current rate) and currency which is purchased now at an agreed rate, but which will be exchanged at some time in the future is regarded as being traded at a **forward rate**. Banking institutions form the backbone of the foreign exchange markets and most companies buy and sell currencies through banks. The bank makes money on these transactions by buying currency at one rate and selling it at another rate. The difference between the buying and selling rate is called the **spread**. The spread is the bank's premium. They may also charge an administration fee. For example, if you went to purchase sterling, it may cost €1.30 for every £1.00 required (plus a set transaction fee). However, if you wanted to exchange sterling for euro then the bank may give €1.22 for every £1.00 exchanged (plus a transaction fee). Exchange rates fluctuate between countries in response to supply and demand for the respective currencies within foreign exchange markets. Both supply and demand are influenced by a variety of factors which include the following:

> *Exchange rates are influenced by:*
> - Inflation rate differentials between countries.
> - Interest rate differentials between countries.
> - Government policy on intervening to influence exchange rates.
> - Gross Domestic Product.
> - A country's balance of payments.
> - Levels of speculation.
> - The sentiment of the market participants in respect of the future economic prospects.
> - Political stability within a country.
> - Government policy on holding currency reserves (the weak US exchange rate in 2008 is partially caused by investors shifting their reserves from US dollars to euro).
> - Natural resources within a country – a country with high levels of natural resources is more likely to have a strong currency relative to a country that has limited natural resources.

Two of these influences are considered to have a linear relationship to each other and to the currency exchange rate and are discussed next in more detail.

The relationship between interest rates, exchange rates and inflation rates
As mentioned earlier in the chapter, a multinational might be tempted to borrow funds in one country, which has low interest rates, for use in another country which has high interest rates. Though this seems like a smart idea, in practice it is not straightforward. It would make sense if interest rates were the only factor impacting on this type of transaction, however, demand for the cheaper debt will actually drive up the price of the currency in that country (causing a shift in the exchange rate). A process of arbitrage will occur until it is no longer beneficial to purchase currency (obtain debt) in the country with the low interest rate. As there

is a readily available market of investors and companies who are looking to obtain debt/currency cheaply, it will not be possible to obtain debt cheaper in another country as demand will cause the currency rate to change to eliminate the interest rate differential quite quickly. This is known as *interest rate parity* — the difference between the interest rates will equal the difference between the forward and spot rates for the currencies. The spot rate is the exchange rate at present, the forward is the exchange rate the currency is expected to move to in the future, given the difference in the interest rates. This is expressed by the following equation

$$\frac{1 + r_{euro}}{1 + r_{stg}} = \frac{Forward_{euro/stg}}{Spot_{euro/stg}}$$

This equation can be rearranged to determine the expected forward rate, given the spot rate and the interest rates in the two different countries.

$$Forward_{euro/stg} = Spot_{euro/stg} \times \frac{1 + r_{euro}}{1 + r_{stg}}$$

This relationship is best explained with an example:

Worked example 18.8   (Interest rate parity)

A company in NI can borrow funds at 9% in NI and can also get access to funds at 7% in the ROI. The current exchange rate between the euro and stg is 1.298. Wherein one pound of sterling will purchase 1.298 euro, conversely one euro will purchase 77p sterling.

REQUIRED

a)   What is the expected one-year forward rate (assume the interest rate parity theory holds)? Explain the impact of this on sterling and on the euro.

b)   If a company borrows the equivalent of £500,000, how much euro will it have to borrow now and to repay in one year's time? What is the sterling equivalent of this repayment (given the movement in the exchange rate predicted in a) happens)?

c)   What would this debt have cost if it were sourced in NI?

Continued

Solution

a)   The forward rate can be calculated as follows:

$$\frac{1+0.07}{1+0.09} = \frac{\text{Forward}_{\text{euro/stg}}}{1.298}$$

$$1.274 = \text{Forward euro/stg}$$

Sterling will weaken against the euro: one euro will buy 78p sterling. £1 sterling will buy €1.274.

b)   It will borrow £500,000 × 1.298 = €649,000. The bank in the ROI will charge 7% interest: €649,000 × 7% = €45,430. At the end of one year the company will have to pay back: €694,430 (€649,000 + €45,430).

In one year's time the company will have to convert £545,078 sterling (€649,430/1.274) into euro to pay the loan back.

c)   Had the debt been sourced in NI then it would have cost the company: £545,000 (£500,000 + (£500,000 × 9%)).

The difference between the answer given in b) and the answer given in c) is rounding. This question does not take into account set-up fees, which may make borrowing in a different currency more expensive.

A company can forward buy a currency to enable them to pay back debt, or to pay for supplies that are denominated in another currency. It is argued that buying forwards forces the spot rate to equate towards the forward rate, therefore, speculators will not be able to make consistent gains on currency speculation about forward rates. This is called the **expectations theory of exchange rates** — the expected spot exchange rate will equal the forward rate and the difference between the forward and spot rate will equal the expected change in the spot rate. This is portrayed by the following formula:

$$\frac{\text{Forward}_{\text{euro/stg}}}{\text{Spot}_{\text{euro/stg}}} = \frac{\text{Expected spot}_{\text{euro/stg}}}{\text{Spot}_{\text{euro/stg}}}$$

So the: $\text{Forward}_{\text{euro/stg}} = \text{Expected}_{\text{spot euro/stg}}$

If this theory applies then a business finance manager can take comfort from the fact that any currency he/she forward buys will reflect the spot exchange rate on the maturity of the forward contract. In the above example the spot exchange rate between sterling and the euro is 1.298 and the forward rate is 1.274. This means that the current spot rate is trading at a discount. Any entity holding sterling now would be tempted to sell their sterling for euro to obtain the larger quantity. The cumulative impact of companies/investors selling sterling would eventually drive down sterling's value until it was no longer economically viable to exchange sterling (i.e. this value would be the rate 1.274) – so the forward rate becomes the expected spot rate.

Given these theories, why then do countries have different interest rates and why do governments/central banks change interest rates? The answer lies with inflation (increases in the cost of goods which erodes the purchasing value of a currency). Governments/central banks use interest rates to control inflation. When inflation is high interest rates are high and vice versa. Investors are interested in the real rate of return to be earned on a currency; this is the return after inflation is stripped out of the gross reported return. The *'International Fisher Effect'* theory, otherwise known as the *'Open Fisher'* theory suggests that real interest rates in all countries are the same. Where differences arise, then this is due to expectations about inflation. This is portrayed by the following formula (which depicts that differences in the interest rates between two countries equals the expected differences in the two countries inflation rates):

$$\frac{1 + r_{\text{euro}}}{1 + r_{\text{stg}}} = \frac{1 + i_{\text{euro}}}{1 + i_{\text{stg}}}$$

Where r is the interest rate and i is the inflation rate. When this is linked to the interest rate parity equation the follow relationship results:

$$\frac{1 + r_{\text{euro}}}{1 + r_{\text{stg}}} \times \text{Spot}_{\text{euro/stg}} = \text{Forward}_{\text{euro/stg}} = \text{Spot}_{\text{euro/stg}} \times \frac{1 + r_{\text{euro}}}{1 + r_{\text{stg}}}$$

Worked example 18.9   (International fisher effect theory)

The base rate charged in the UK in June is 5% and the most recent inflation figure (May 2008) was 3.3%. This has increased from 2.2% in March. The UK government has set an inflation rate target of 2%. The economy had remained within this target for part of 2007, when the bank of England base rate was 5.75%; however, has seen a steady increase in inflation rates caused by the impact of increases in the price of oil, and all products that are made using energy.

The inflation rate in the ROI was 5% in April, up from 4.2% in January and the European Central Bank (ECB) base rate is currently 4%. The European Parliament has set itself an inflation target of 2%. The inflation rate in the ROI is being affected by oil in a similar manner to the UK market.

REQUIRED

(a)   Which governing body is likely to be more concerned about inflation and why?

(b)   Which governing body is likely to change interest rates?

(c)   Assume that the equilibrium inflation rate is 2% and that an interest rate of 5.5% captures the equilibrium real return required by the international markets. Assume that inflation in the UK and in the ROI cannot be controlled because the price of oil cannot be influenced by the governments. What should the interest rates move to, assuming the International Fisher Effect is evident?

(d)   The ROI is a member of the European Monetary Union (EMU). What does this mean?

(e)   List the arguments for and against becoming part of the EMU.

Solution

(a)   The Irish Government is more likely to be more concerned about inflation. Inflation in Ireland (5%) is higher than the

Continued

overall European rate of 3.3% in the same period and the government in Ireland does not have control of interest rates, hence cannot raise them to curb inflation. The high inflation rate suggests that there may be future problems with the Irish economy as research has shown that high inflation rates usually cause a slow down in a country's economy.

(b)   Though the European Union should be the first to raise interest rates, they have to take action that is in the interest of Europe as a whole, not to benefit individual countries like Ireland. Several countries have inflation rates that are below the 2% target, though several others (new entrants) have inflation rates that are very high (double figures). Raising the interest rate may damage growth in those countries with low inflation. At the time of writing it is predicted that the ECB base rate might rise to 4.75% by the end of 2008. Time will tell.

The UK central bank (Bank of England) is concerned about the downturn that has occurred in the housing market. An increase in interest rates now may slow down the economy even further. They would like to increase interest rates to reduce inflation; however, they are concerned about the impact of this on demand in the housing market and the economy. It is likely that the UK central bank will hold interest rates steady for a couple of months to see if inflation starts to come down. It may then even reduce interest rates, in an attempt at kick-starting the housing market again. Alternatively, the Bank of England may react if inflation does not start to fall, raising rates. This may slow growth in the economy. Time will tell.

(c)   Given this information, the interest rate in the UK (r) should move to:

$$\frac{1+0.05.5}{1+r_{euro}} = \frac{1.02}{1.033}$$

$$1 + r_{euro} = 1.0684$$

$$r_{euro} = 6.84\%$$

Continued

Wherein 5.5% is the equilibrium interest rate given 2% inflation and 3.3% is the underlying inflation rate in the UK that cannot be changed.

The interest rate in the ROI (r) should move to:

$$\frac{1+0.05.5}{1+r_{euro}}=\frac{1.02}{1.05}$$

$$1+r_{euro}=1.086$$

$$r_{euro}=8.6\%$$

Wherein 5.5% is the equilibrium interest rate given 2% inflation and 5% is the underlying inflation rate in the UK that cannot be changed.

The interest rates being offered by several of the finance houses/banks on investment products are likely to be higher than the underlying base rate and more reflective of the rate reflected by the International Fisher Effect model.

(c)   The point of the European Union (EU), in general, is to provide an unrestricted common market that promotes free trade between member states. To this end, the EU introduced the EMU which provides for a unified monetary policy for all member states who signed up to the EMU and introduced a single currency, the euro (not all member states signed up to the EMU, the UK is one example). The ECB was established to issue euro, to establish the monetary policy for the EU, to act as a lender of last resorts for member states and to manage the currency exchange rate for the euro.

(d)   The arguments in favour of joining the EMU may include the following:

Economic stability: To remain a member of the EMU a country must adhere to strict economic criteria. For example, the interest rate is set centrally and the member state government cannot raise it to control inflation.

Continued

Reduces short-term political policies: Many governments change economic variables as election ploys in the run-up to election time. Though the changes may be popular with the electorate, they may have long-term ramifications for the economy. When a country is a member of the EMU, monetary policy is out of the country's government's hands.

Lower interest rates: The interest rates set by the ECB have been consistently low, indeed they are currently at their highest level, a respectable 4% (June, 2008).

Free trade: Having a single currency eliminates currency risk in transactions between companies, individuals and governments from different countries. This should save transaction and hedging costs.

The arguments against joining the EMU might include the following:

Loss of control: The government loses control over economic policy, this is now within the hands of the ECB. Governments are unable to raise interest rates to control inflation.

Weaker countries: The stronger countries usually have to loan funds to weaker countries to support them as they try to remain within the EMU.

Loss of national pride: Some individuals feel that joining with the EU and merging everything takes away from a country's identity.

As noted, inflation is considered to impact on interest rates, and vice versa. It is also considered to impact on exchange rates. When a country's inflation rate increases relative to the inflation rate in other countries, then the value of its currency will fall relative to the value of the currencies in the other countries. This is because inflation impacts on the price of goods within a country and price differentials will cause shifts in demand for that country's produce, which will cause a shift in the demand for that country's currency, resulting in a shift in the value of the currency (i.e. a movement in the exchange rate). This theory is termed the **Purchasing Power Parity** (PPP). The PPP theory assumes that the overall cost of living in different countries is the same, because exchange rates adjust to offset inflation differences between countries. A numerical example is best to explain this theory. Suppose inflation in the ROI was such that the price of a Mars bar increased from 50c to €1.00. If PPP were to hold then the value of the euro would fall by a half. So say a euro is currently worth 78p (sterling). At present a Mars bar in the ROI costs 39p (sterling). After the period of high inflation, PPP theory suggests that the high inflation rate will be counteracted by a fall in the value of the euro, such that a euro will now be worth 39p, hence the Mars bar will cost the same to someone in the UK. This relationship is reflected in the following equation:

$$\frac{1+i_{euro}}{1+i_{stg}} = \frac{\text{Expected spot}_{euro/stg}}{\text{Spot}_{euro/stg}}$$

The expected difference in the inflation rate (i) between two countries equals the expected change in the spot rate between the two countries.

This section has highlighted the relationships that exist between inflation rates, interest rates and exchange rates between countries. Supporters of the theories outlined in this section would argue that the world economy is relatively efficient and that price differentials (i.e. potential to make abnormal profits on currency, interest, and product prices) are eventually eroded by arbitrage. They suggest that treasury managers need to be very careful when they source debt, even though a source in a different country may have a lower interest rate tag. The exchange rate and inflation rate movements may actually make the debt more expensive in the long term.

Identifying currency risks

Exchange rate risk is also known as *currency risk*. Exchange rate risk is prevalent in every company that either transacts with a third party (such as a customer/supplier) in a different country, or has assets, or debt, denominated in a foreign currency. There are two main types of short-term currency risk: transaction risk and translation risk. A third type of risk *'economic risk'* occurs when exchange rate uncertainty prolongs for a long period of time.

Transaction risk affects the cash flows and profitability of a company. It is another name for contractual risk and is prevalent in every credit transaction that involves the conversion of one currency into another currency. For example, a ROI company may agree to purchase 1,000 cars from Charles Hurst in Belfast at £10,000 each car. If it is assumed that the spot rate when the transaction takes place is €1.22:£1, then this will cost the ROI company €12,200,000. However, three months credit is agreed. If in this three-month period the euro weakens against sterling so that the exchange rate is €1.45:£1, then the cost of these vehicles increases significantly to €14,500,000. This is a significant difference which will impact on the profitability and cash flows of the ROI company. Transactions reported in a company's income statement and cash flow statement are subject to transaction risk.

Translation risk does not impact on a company's cash flows. It affects the reported value of assets that are located in a different country or are denominated in a different currency. When currency rates change, these assets will be translated at different values to those previously reported. The result is that balance sheet values can change significantly, not because the underlying assets have changed, but because their reported value has changed. This can impact on a company's overall perceived performance as ratios such as the return on capital employed, or the return on assets will be affected.

Economic risk occurs when the exchange rate movements are long-term. This can be caused by a change in country risk, or political risk. Where the exchange rate of a foreign country weakens, more of it is required to buy a similar amount of a company's core currency. This means that any assets held in that country will be worth less and any sales made that are translated will produce lower profits. This will be a long-term issue which may impact on the underlying value of the whole company.

Managing currency risk

Managing currency risk was a more common problem amongst companies in the ROI before the introduction of the euro. In the UK the problems are still widespread as all companies who export will encounter currency issues.

As mentioned previously, a company should have a set policy on risk and the management of risk. Currency risk will fall within this policy. If it were assumed that the interlocking theories on inflation rates, interest rates, commodity prices and exchange rates (discussed earlier) held true and moved in line with the efficient market hypothesis then currency risk would not be a concern as the price of products in every country would be the same when converted into one currency. However, these theories do not operate in a totally free market. Government intervention in many countries strives to control inflation rates, interest rates and exchange rates and responses to shifts in inflation and interest rates take time. The result is differences between currency rates that do not conform to the predicted equation's results. This means that speculators can reap rewards from dealing in currencies and companies can gain profits, or hedge against losses by managing their finances effectively.

Budgeting for currencies

A starting point in currency management is to forecast the company's need for, and surplus of, different kinds of currencies. Then the finance manager should try to forecast expected exchange rates for each currency. This approach will allow a finance manager to determine the steps to take to manage cash flows that are expected to originate and to be paid in other currencies. This enables more accurate cash flow and profit forecasts to be made, which allows better decision making in respect of pricing goods, working capital management and project appraisal in foreign countries. It also allows a finance manager to determine the impact of exchange rate movements on the value of the company.

When determining the change in expected exchange rates a finance manager usually takes two approaches. The first, called *fundamental analysis*, considers how the balance of payments on a country's current account will change. It is assumed that the balance of payments impacts on a country's exchange rate. When a country imports more than it exports, then the current account will be in deficit. This will reduce the value of the country's currency as there is less demand for its currency. Changes in inflation rates and interest rates impact on the balance of payments as these factors impact on the demand for exports and imports. Therefore, the finance manager will try to predict prospective inflation and interest rates and then determine how these will impact on the exchange rate (the finance manager is likely to consider the impact of the International Fisher Effect, expectations, PPP and the interest rate parity theories). A further factor to impact on a country's currency demand is the level of investment in the country by foreign entities/individuals. This equates to exporting when the balance of payments is considered. When foreign entities/individuals purchase government bonds and equity shares on domestic markets, they are not only buying the underlying asset but are also purchasing the local currency. The second approach, called ***technical analysis***, is a chartist approach. To determine future changes in foreign currency exchange rates, the finance manager considers patterns in the movement of exchange rates in the past and uses these to predict into the future.

Hedging

Once currency exposures have been identified, the next step is to determine if they should be hedged, or not. It may be that the finance manager believes that exchange rate movements will benefit the company and may decide exposures should not be hedged. However, this is speculation which, as an approach, would need to be agreed strategically. In many instances currency exposures are hedged internally: for example by arranging for the company to export and import from the same country. Only expected net differences require hedging. Another internal hedge is when a company finances foreign investment using debt denominated in the currency of the foreign investment. Long-term non-monetary investments are not usually hedged either because PPP is argued to hold in the long-term but not in the short-term. To recap, PPP suggests that the value of the asset/liability denominated in a foreign currency will rise or fall in value to exactly offset the fall or rise in the value of the foreign currency. Assets that are held for short periods of time are exposed to exchange rate risk as the links between the assets value (inflation) and the exchange rate take time to move to equilibrium. It is also argued that short-term loans do not require hedging as the interest rate is pegged at such a level so as to take currency differences into account. Therefore, the currency issues that a finance manager will focus on to manage will be monetary assets denominated in another currency and transactions that are not hedged internally but are subject to translation risk (when converting from the foreign currency to the domestic currency).

Hedging techniques

Centralise the currency management function – This means that currency netting can take place centrally and hedging requirements are reduced. Netting will not only reduce the exposure of the company to exchange rate risks but will also reduce transaction costs.

Leading and lagging currency payments – This is cash flow management and involves paying early when exchange rates are favourable and paying late when they are not (in the hope that they reverse), or offering a discount for payment to encourage customers to pay their accounts when the exchange rate is favourable and allowing longer credit periods when it is not. All the principles covered in respect of the management of trade receivables and trade payables are still relevant. For example, it may make sense to delay payment for supplies as this will result in cheaper supplies due to expected exchange rate movements. However, discounts may be lost and suppliers may get annoyed with the company (impacting on future price and even supply).

Factoring – An international factor will absorb exchange rate risk, paying up to 80% of the credit receivable up front. However, as noted in chapter ten, 'Trade Receivables/Payables Management', international factoring is more expensive than domestic factoring because of the transfer of risk from the company to the factor company.

Bills of exchange – Many exporting companies use bills of exchange when dealing with customers in foreign companies. This allows them to sell the bill at the spot rate, hence passing the exchange rate risk to the holder of the bill.

Matching currency flows – this involves being proactive in approach and ensuring that there is both demand and supply for a particular currency. This may be achieved by sourcing supplies from a country that is a customer of the company, or investing in a project in that country. In some instances the match can be achieved by investing or supplying to a country that is closely connected economically with the foreign country. Countries that are closely linked economically will experience similar movements in their prospective exchange rates. The most commonly cited example is the US and the Canadian dollar.

Adjusting price – A company might anticipate exchange rate movements and may, for example, factor the additional expected cost into the price of the good. This effectively transfers a portion of the risk to the customer. However, if exchange rates move beyond what was expected, then the company's profits will be affected, in addition, the increase in price may result in a loss of the sale.

Invoicing in the domestic currency – A company might transfer all the risks to customers by denominating its sales prices in the domestic currency and insisting on purchasing goods at prices that are denominated in the domestic currency. However, this may impact on the demand for the company's goods and the price of goods being supplied to the company, as customers and suppliers will prefer to deal with companies who absorb the exchange rate risk.

Risk sharing – In some instances, a company may be able to enter into an agreement with a customer/supplier in respect of exchange rate movements, which shares the risk between the parties to the transaction.

Forward contracts - Currency forward contracts are bespoke agreements which specify that a set amount of currency will be bought/or sold at a pre-agreed exchange rate on a specified date. This is a contractual agreement which has to be fulfilled on the specified date. Both buyer and seller to this contract agree with the terms. The exchange rate agreed is usually influenced by the forward rates being quoted by the markets. When exchange rates on the exercise date are different, one party suffers a loss relative to the market, the other makes a profit.

Futures contracts – Currency futures are agreements to buy, or sell, a specific amount of a specified currency on a set date. Unlike bespoke currency forward contracts, currency futures are standardised and traded in the futures markets. They can be closed before maturity by entering into an opposite agreement. The have all the attributes of a general futures contract, as discussed earlier, i.e. marked-to-market, margin, set maturity dates, set size, market prices, etc. They can be used for example when a company knows that they are going to receive a foreign currency in three months time. They can contract to sell that currency at future rates agreed now, in three months time. This means that any loss on the currency exchange will be offset to an extent, by profits on the futures contract.

Options – Currency options give the holder the right, but not the obligation, to buy or sell a predefined amount of a particular currency at or before a specified date at a pre-agreed exchange rate. This exchange rate is the exercise price. Options can be traded through exchanges. In these instances the contracts are for specific amounts, specific currencies and have specific exercise dates and exercise prices. Options can also be traded OTC, usually through banks. As these are bespoke they are more expensive. There are two types of options **'European options'**, which restrict exercise of the contract to the exercise date only, or **'American options'**, which can be exercised at any time up to, and on, the exercise date. The greatest loss that can be incurred in both instances is the cost of the option.

Swap agreements – Foreign currency swaps involve the exchange of cash flows in one currency for cash flows in another currency. For example, if

A plc (a UK company) purchases goods that cost €100,000 from B plc (a ROI company) every month and C plc (a ROI company) purchases goods from D plc (a UK company) for £82,000 every month and assuming the exchange rate is €1:£0.82 (i.e. the two cash flows are worth the same) then a swap contract can be agreed whereby A plc (a UK company) agrees to pay D plc (a UK company) £82,000 and C plc agrees to pay B plc €100,000 (both ROI companies) each month. This agreement means that exchange rate risk for the four companies is totally hedged. This is a simplified version of a swap. In practice, the stronger, more dominant companies that are involved in the transaction may demand commission. Banks who have branches in different countries may take the place of two of the companies. They will charge a fee for this service. Currency swaps are more likely to be used to hedge debt transactions than operating transactions.

Interest rate risk

Interest rate risk arises when market rates change in a manner that was not expected. When a finance manager considers that interest rates will rise, it is likely that they will arrange debt that has a fixed rate of interest attached to it. When a finance manager considers that interest rates will fall, they are more likely to tie the company into floating rate debt. The problem arises when market rates turn out to be different to what the treasurer predicted. If market rates fall and the company's debt is on fixed interest rate terms, then the company will not benefit from the reduction in interest rates. Alternatively when market rates rise and the company's debt is variable in nature, then the company is exposed to potential increases in cash outflows. Therefore, a finance manager can take several steps to hedge against these unexpected interest rate movements, or to speculate for financial gain, if it is the company's policy to do so. The following products can be obtained either from banks, or in some instances the financial exchanges to hedge interest rate exposures.

Caps, collars and floors

A *cap* is a pre-agreed ceiling interest rate that can be written into variable interest loan agreements. The interest rate charged floats with the base rate (Euribor or LIBOR), but only to a certain level, the cap rate. When the rates increase beyond the cap level, the bank suffers a loss. Because the bank takes over this risk, they will charge a set-up fee for this facility, the size of the fee being dependent on how likely the rates are to exceed the stated cap rate. A benefit of a cap is that it reduces a company's downside risk, whilst allowing the company to reap all the benefits were interest rates to fall. A *floor* is a pre-agreed lower interest rate, which the interest that is charged will not fall below. It can be written into variable interest loan agreements. Like a cap the interest rate charged floats with the base rate, but does not fall below the floor level. The company absorbs the loss when market rates fall below the floor level, as the company has to pay interest to the bank at the floor level. Because of this the bank is unlikely to charge a fee to set up this type of agreement. A *collar* is a combination of a cap and a floor. The interest rate charged by the bank will not exceed the cap level, nor will it fall below the floor level. The fee charged by the bank in a collar transaction will be less than that charged for a cap agreement, because the bank has a chance of making excess returns if rates fall below floor level.

Swap agreements

Swap agreements are commonly utilised to manage interest rate risk. Companies wanting to stabilise their cash flows, arrange to exchange variable rate debt interest payments for fixed rate debt interest payments. This can be achieved using a fixed-for-floating rate swap agreement. An example of this was provided earlier in the chapter. The principal amounts do not change hands, just the net difference in the interest rates, less commission. These swap agreements are straightforward. Swap agreements are also commonly used to hedge both interest rate and currency rate risk in one contract. This typically happens when a company issues bonds, or obtains bank debt in a foreign country and wants to convert the whole transaction into the domestic currency, or when a company wants foreign currency for business reasons (to pay for an investment in that country, or to pay for supplies that are being received from that country). The whole currency/interest swap agreement is usually arranged through a bank and typically has three stages. In the first instance the principal amounts are exchanged usually at spot rate, then the interest payments are exchanged (this can be fixed-for-variable, fixed-for-fixed, or variable-for-variable). Finally, the original principal amounts are re-exchanged at an exchange rate that is agreed at the outset. The patterns of cash flows are best explained using an example. Assume that A plc (a ROI company) requires £40 million and B plc (a UK company) requires €50 million. The two companies enter into a currency and interest rate swap agreement through their bank. The three steps to this agreement are outlined in the following three diagrams.

Currency and interest rate swap (step 1)

Exchange of principal amounts

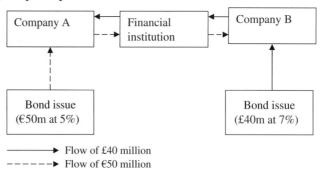

A plc receives €50m from a bond issue which it transfers through the financial institution to B plc, in return for B plc transferring £40m in sterling to it. Both parties will pay the financial institution a premium for arranging the swap.

Currency and interest rate swap (step 2)

Interest payments during the life of a swap contract

The lines represent the flow of cash which will occur each year for the duration of the swap contract. Company A can then use the euro received from B to pay the coupon to the debt holders each year and company B can use the sterling received from company A to pay its debt holders.

The financial intermediary who set up this transaction and who administers it will receive a commission on every currency transfer. This makes the swap expensive. The cash flows in relation to the principal amount are fully hedged from the perspective of both company A and company B. However, the interest payments are not. For example, company A, which is located in the ROI will need to find £280,000 sterling each year to honour their side of the swap agreement. This will probably be obtained using transactions which are exchanged at the spot rate in existence each time the payment is required. The companies can opt to hedge these cash flows also using for example, forward rate contracts.

Currency and interest rate swap (step 3)

Repayment of the principal sum

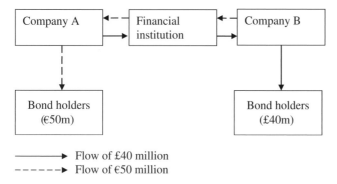

At the end of the swap contract Company A will return the £40 sterling to company B who will use it to redeem its debentures and company B will return the €50 million to company A, who will also use it to redeem its debentures.

As in all hedging transactions, one of the parties will make a loss, the other a profit when currency rates and exchange rates differ to those built into the swap agreement. Most companies are happy to accept the possibility of making a loss on the agreemsent, so long as cash flows are certain. Indeed, some companies and financial institutions will enter into these agreements for speculative purposes, not to hedge risk exposures.

Swaptions

A *swaption* is an option to buy an interest rate swap agreement. It gives a company the right, but not the obligation to enter into an interest rate swap agreement.

Futures contracts

An *interest rate futures* contract has two parties, one who agrees to receive the interest on a set principal sum of money on a predefined date at an agreed rate and the other who agrees to pay the interest on the principal sum of money on the predefined date at the agreed rate. One of the counterparties will make a profit, the other an equal loss, depending on how market interest rates move. The futures contract is totally independent of the principal debt amount, indeed, the holders of futures contracts do not have to have any debt at all. They just have to agree to pay or receive interest on a notional amount of principal. When futures are used to hedge interest rate risk, the interest payments are set up in the opposite direction to the interest payments on the underlying principal amount. Therefore, when the company makes a loss on the actual interest being paid in the money markets (relative to the interest rate target), this will be offset by an equal profit being made on the futures contract. In general, when a company expects interest rates to rise, they will sell futures (short hedge), and when they expect interest rates to fall they will buy futures (long hedge). When interest rates rise, the value of futures contracts fall, when interest rates fall the value of futures contracts rise. This is best explained using an example:

Worked example 18.10 (Futures contract – hedging interest rate exposure)

Gato plc is planning to borrow €/£10 million in three months time for a three-month period. The finance manager in Gato plc reckons that interest rates are going to rise steadily over the next year. Therefore, it is decided to enter into futures contracts to minimise exposure to fluctuations in interest rates in this period. The current interest rate is 7% (day one, month one). The market is expecting interest rates to

Continued

increase to 8% in three months time and to 8.5% in six months time and so the futures market is currently quoting interest rate futures at 92.00 in three months time and 91.50 in six months time. The standard size of an interest rate futures contract is €/£500,000.

REQUIRED

(a) Explain how the finance manager of Gato plc can hedge the company's exposure to unexpected interest rate fluctuations.

(b) Assume that interest rates in two months time move to 10%. Show how a hedge works.

Solution

a) As interest rates are rising, the company will need to sell futures contracts (short hedge). With every increase in interest rates a corresponding decline in the value of the futures contracts will result. Then close to the maturity date the company will buy a futures contract in the futures market with the same maturity date for a cheaper price (the market value of all the futures will have fallen to reflect the change in interest rates). The company will make a profit on this deal as it will buy futures at cheaper rates to those it holds. The exchange agreed to give it the lower interest rate, because it can buy higher in the market place, and therefore will make a profit on the futures contract. The company will receive this from the futures exchange. This profit compensates for the increased payment required to service the underlying debt.

b) Step 1. (Day one in month one) – identify the requirement and the potential cash flows. The current interest rate is 7%. Ideally the company would like to obtain the debt at this cost i.e. interest of €/£175,000 (€/£10,000,000 x 7% x 3/12). However, the loan is required in three months time, so the company will only be able to lock into getting the loan at 8%. The

Continued

market expects rates to move to 8% so the bank will not agree to any rate below this. This means an interest payment for the succeeding three months of €/£200,000 (€/£10,000,000 × 8% × 3/12) is expected. The company wants to hedge against the possibility of the interest payment being more.

Step 2. On day one of month one, the company can enter into 20 €/£500,000 short futures contracts (i.e. agreeing to sell futures in six months time at 91.50). The date selected will be six months time, as the debt will not be started in three months time and the maturity of the futures contract should be beyond this initial date.

Step 3. In five months time the company should close out the futures agreement by entering into 20 €/£500,000 long futures contracts (i.e. agreeing to buy futures contracts for €/£90.00 per 100 ticks – the cost of these futures will reflect current expected rates) with a maturity in one months time (this date is aligned with the date of the original short future contracts). Therefore, both contracts will expire at the same time.

Step 4. In month six, both sets of contracts are closed, with the company making a profit of €/£1.50 (€/£91.50 – €/£90.00) per 100 ticks. Therefore, the total profit on the overall futures transaction is €/£37,500 (€/£1.50 × 20 × 100 × €/£12.50 (€/£500,000 × 0.01% × 3/12)). This profit helps to mitigate the loss incurred on the change in interest rate which now results in an actual interest payment of €/£250,000 (€/£10,000,000 × 10% × 3/12).

Therefore the overall cost of the debt to the firm is now €/£212,500, as opposed to €/£250,000, which would have resulted had the exposure not been hedged.

When the futures market predicts future interest rates accurately, a perfect hedge can be obtained which will eliminate the total difference between the market rates paid to the bank and those expected at the start of the agreement.

Forward rate agreements (FRAs)

Forward interest rate contracts are OTC future contracts that are bespoke. They are usually arranged between a company and its bank. In a forward rate agreement, the counterparties to a contract agree to pay, or receive interest on a specified nominal sum at a prearranged date. The actual loan/investment is a different contract. Payments made or received on the forward rate contract are due on the maturity of the contract and only the difference between the agreed interest rates and the market rates is either paid to, or received from the bank — depending on whether the forward contract made a profit, or not. This is shown in the next example:

Worked example 18.11   (Forward rate agreement – hedging interest rate exposure)

Gato plc is planning to borrow €/£10 million in three months time for a three-month period. The finance manager in Gato plc reckons that interest rates are going to rise steadily over the next year. Therefore, it decided to enter into forward rate agreement with Pajaro Bank plc to minimise the company's exposure to fluctuations in interest rates in this period. The current interest rate is 7% and the bank agrees to provide debt at this rate in three months time (the bank will charge a premium for this, particularly if they feel that interest rates are going to rise).

REQUIRED

a) Assume that interest rates in three months time move to 10% and Gato plc loans the €/£10 million from Pero Bank plc on this date for a period of three months. Show how this can be hedged, assuming Gato plc enters into the forward rate agreement with Pajaro Bank plc now.

b) Assume that interest rates fall to 6% and Gato plc loans the €/£10 million from Pero Bank plc on this date for a period of three months. Show the cash flows that will result

Continued

assuming Gato plc enters into the forward rate agreement with the Pajaro Bank plc now.

Solution

a)   Step 1. – to hedge the transaction Gato plc enters into a forward rate agreement with the Pajaro Bank plc to borrow €/£10 million in three months time at 7%.

Step 2. – in three months time Gato plc borrows €/£10 million at the spot rate of 10%. This loan is sourced from Pero bank plc.

Step 3. – at the end of the three months Gato plc will have to pay Pero Bank plc €/£250,000 (€/£10 million × 10% × 3/12).

Step 4. – at the end of three months Gato plc will receive €/£75,000 (€/£250,000 − €/£175,000 (€/£10 million × 7% × 3/12)) from Pajaro Bank plc*.

The agreement states that Gato plc should pay interest of €/£175,000 and Pajaro Bank plc are guaranteeing this. If Gato plc has to pay more, the Pajaro Bank plc will compensate them with the difference.

b)   Step 1. – to hedge the transaction Gato plc enters into a forward rate agreement with the Pajaro Bank plc to borrow €/£10 million in three months time at 7%.

Step 2. – in three months time Gato plc borrows €/£10 million at the spot rate of 6%. This loan is sourced from Pero bank plc.

Step 3. – at the end of the three months Gato plc will have to pay Pero Bank plc €/£150,000 (€/£10 million × 6% × 3/12).

Step 4. – at the end of three months Gato plc will have to pay €/£25,000 (€/£175,000 (€/£10 million × 7% × 3/12) − €/£150,000) to Pajaro Bank plc*.

The agreement states that Gato plc should pay interest of €/£175,000. If Gato plc has less interest to pay, then they have to pay Pajaro Bank plc the difference.

Conclusion

Advances in technology (the world wide web) and improvements in transport have resulted in an active world economy. Most companies that are beyond a certain size are likely to transact with third parties in various countries throughout the world. Some countries have comparative advantage over other countries because of their natural resources, tax status, etc. If a multinational company does not take advantage of country-specific efficiencies they will be left behind in the profit race game. Companies that wish to be competitive on a worldwide basis have to adopt global strategies.

Dealing globally increases the number and level of risks to which a company is exposed. Increased risk leads to increased uncertainty in planning and controlling an entity's cash flows and profits. In particular, shifts in inflation and its corresponding impact on the price of goods, shifts in interest rates and movements in foreign exchange rates can have catastrophic consequences on a company's performance and indeed on its survival. It is argued that prices, interest rates and exchange rates are intertwined and ultimately all goods end up with the same value. If this were the case, then changes in inflation, exchange rates and interest rates would not be a problem. However, it is considered that these theories only hold true in the long-term, not in the short-term and many companies transact in the short-term. In addition, external interference such as government intervention in the economic system may thwart the free market's natural progression towards equilibrium — hence global markets are not in equilibrium and speculative profits can be made from dealing across different countries. Therefore, most companies adopt a policy to manage risk. The starting point in this process is the identification of risks. A company can have risks that are hedged internally. The key is to highlight risks that put the company's cash flows and value at risk and to take steps to hedge these. A variety of methods can be utilised, including in-house steps, such as netting, matching, aligning supply purchases in countries where sales take place, etc. Alternatively, financial derivatives can be utilised to hedge risk exposure, or to make speculative gains.

Derivatives have over the past 20 years received bad press, due to speculative trading going wrong for dealers in a number of companies. In these instances, it would seem that procedural error (lack of control) and fraud were more to blame than the actual derivatives themselves. There is no doubt about it, derivatives which are used for speculative purposes are risky. Indeed, derivatives work because two parties take bets on what will happen in the market place. For example, they may bet on the direction of the movement in interest rates. One bets that they will rise, the other that they will fall. Both parties have to have opposite views, and one will always win, while one will always loose. For this reason, derivatives are regarded to be a *'zero sum'* game. Derivatives reduce risk if they are utilised correctly, however, they are costly and a company has to weigh up the costs and benefits of getting involved in these instruments.

Examination standard question

Worked example 18.12   (Hedging)

Background

On 31 December 2007, Octavo plc needs to borrow €6 million in three months time for a period of six months. For the type of loan finance that Octavo would use, the rate of interest is currently 13% per year and the Corporate Treasurer is unwilling to pay a higher rate.

The treasurer is concerned about possible future fluctuations in interest rates, and is considering the following possibilities:

(a)   forward rate agreements;
(b)   interest rate futures;
(c)   interest rate guarantees or short-term interest rate caps.

The treasurer of Octavo plc decides to hedge the interest rate risk by using interest rate futures. Her expectation is that interest rates will increase by 2% over the next three months.

The current price of March euro/sterling three months time deposit futures is 87.25. The standard contract size is €/£500,000, while the minimum price movement is one tick, the value of which is 0.01% per year of the contract size.

REQUIRED

(a)   Set out calculations of the effect of using the futures market to hedge against movements in the interest rate and estimate the hedge efficiency:

Continued

(1)   if interest rates increase by 2% and the futures market price moves by 2%;

5 Marks

(2)   if interest rates increase by 2% and the futures market price moves by 1.75%

4 Marks

(3)   if interest rates fall by 1.5% and the futures market price moves by 1.25%

4 Marks

The time value of money, taxation and margin requirements are to be ignored.

b)   Calculate, for situations (1) to (3) from a), whether the total cost of the loan after hedging would have been lower with the futures hedge chosen by the treasurer or with an interest rate guarantee which she could have purchased at 13% for a premium of 0.25% of the size of the loan to be guaranteed.

The time value of money, taxation and margin requirements are to be ignored.

12 Marks
Total 25 Marks
(ICAI, FAE, MABF, 2007 Manual, page 500)

Solution

(a)

(1)   If interest rates rise by 2%, the extra interest cost for the six months is €/£60,000 (€/£6,000,000 × 2% × 6/12)

Therefore, a €/£60,000 gain from the futures contracts is required.

A 2% rise is an increase of 200 ticks (2% = 200 ticks).

In this instance one tick has a value of €/£12.50 (0.0001 × €/£500,000 × 3/12)

Therefore, a 2% (200 ticks) movement on one contract would produce a gain of €/£2,500 (200 × €/£12.50)

Continued

Therefore, to hedge the €/£60,000 exposure, 24 futures contracts are required (€/£60,000/€/£2,500).

Before maturity
24 €/£500,000 March euro/sterling time deposit futures contracts are sold at 87.25 (effectively 12.75% interest) on 31 December.

24 futures contracts are bought in March or when interest rates change to 85.25 (effectively 14.75% interest). This will close out the position. The difference is 200 ticks cheaper (87.25 − 85.25). Where a tick is valued at €/£12.50.

The gain is therefore €/£60,000 (24 × 200 ticks at €/£12.50).

There is 100% hedge efficiency (€/£60,000/€/£60,000) – The perfect hedge.

(2)   In this case, the futures gain is €/£52,500 (24 × 175 ticks at €/£12.50)

The hedge efficiency is 87.5% (€/£52,500/€/£60,000).

(3)   In this case, there is a gain on the cash market arising from the fall in interest rates, and a loss on the futures market. Cash market gain is €/£45,000 (€/£6,000,000 × 1.5% × 6/12)

A futures market loss arises from selling 24 futures contracts at 87.25 and closing out the position by buying 24 futures contracts at 88.50.

The futures market loss is €/£37,500 (24 × 125 ticks at €/£12.50) or €/£6,000,000 × 1.25% × 6/12.

The hedge efficiency is 120% (€/£45,000/€/£37,500).

b)   ***Interest rate guarantee***
This will involve two costs. Interest — the loan rate will be 13% for the six months. This will cost €/£390,000 (€/£6,000,000 × 13% × 6/12) and the guarantee fee which

Continued

will cost €/£15,000 (€/£6,000,000 × 0.25%). Therefore, the total cost of the interest rate guarantee is €/£405,000.

(1) Under this scenario the interest on the loan will have risen to €/£450,000 (€/£6,000,000 × 15% × 6/12) less the gain on the futures contract of €/£60,000 gives a total cost of €/390,000. This is €/£15,000 cheaper than the interest rate guarantee.

Interest (calculated in b) (1) is €/450,000 less the futures contract gain of €/£52,500 gives a total cost of €/£397,500. This is €/£7,500 cheaper than the interest rate guarantee (€/£405,000 – €/£397,000).

(3) Interest is now €/£345,000 (€/£6,000,000 × 11.5% × 6/12) add the futures contract loss of €/£37,500 gives a total cost of €/£382,500. This is €/£22,500 cheaper than the interest rate guarantee.

WEBSITES THAT MAY BE OF USE

For information on worldwide trading in financial derivatives visit:
http://www.bus.org/

For explanatory articles on financial derivatives visit:
http://www.finpipe.com/derivatives.htm

For more detail on the Daiwa Banks $1.1 billion loss from derivative trading visit:
http://www.erisk.com/learning/casestudies/daiwa.asp

For information on risk management visit:
http://www.erisk.com/

For information on futures contracts and their markets visit:
http://www.liffe.com/liffeinvestor/introduction/how/futures/index.htm

For information on options and futures visit the Chicago Board of Trade website:
www.cbot.com

To read up on articles related to finance visit:
www.sternstewart.com/journal/overview.shtml. This site is the host site for the Journal of Applied Corporate Finance.

KEY TERMS

American option
Binomial model
Bid price
Black-Scholes model
Call option
Cap
Centralised treasury function
Closed position
Collar
Contractual risks
Convertible bond
Corporate finance
Covered call
Credit default swap
Currency risks
Currency swap
Custody account statements
Dealer options
Derivatives
Economic risk
Employee share options
Equity management
Equity swap
European options
Exchange traded options
Exchange rate
Exchange rate risk

Exercise date
Exercise price
Expectations theory
Exposure
Financial instruments
Fixed-to-floating rate swap
Floor
Forward contracts
Forward discount
Forward interest rate contracts
Forward premium
Forward rate
Fundamental analysis
Funding
Futures contract
Hedging
Interest rate futures
Interest rate parity
International Fisher Effect
Legs of the swap
Listed options
Long position
Long and short butterflies
Marked-to-market
Market risk
Multinationals
Non-contractual risks
Offer price
Open position

Open Fisher
Options
Over-the-counter options
Plain vanilla swap
Purchasing power parity
Put option
Short
Spread
Spot rate
Straddle
Strap
Strike price
Strip

Swap
Swaptions
Tax haven
Technical analysis
Tick
Translation risk
Transaction risk
Total return swap
Treasury
Treasury management
Warrant
Zero sum game

REVIEW QUESTIONS

1. Why do companies use derivative financial instruments?
2. The price of a pint of beer now in Dublin is €3.50. The price of beer now in Belfast is £2.50. The exchange rate for euro to sterling is €1.40:£1. UK inflation is 4% and inflation in the ROI is 6%.

REQUIRED

(a) Use the law of one price to predict the relative price of a pint of beer in one years time in both cities.
(b) Using the results from a) determine the future sterling/euro spot rate assuming PPP.

3. A company purchased call options for 10,000 equity shares in ABC plc at 25c/p per share one year ago when the share price was €/£1.50. The exercise price on the call option is €/£1.80. The current price is €/£2.10.

REQUIRED

(a) Should the company exercise the call options?
(b) What is the profit/(loss) on the transaction?
(c) What would the profit/(loss) on the transaction be if the current price was €/£1.60?
(d) What could the profit/(loss) be if the monies that were invested in options were utilised instead to purchase shares? *Note: assume the current price is €/£2.10, then rework assuming it is €/£1.60.*

4. Use the binomial model to determine the price of a call option that has one year to maturity, given that the market price of the underlying equity share at present is €/£4.00, the exercise price is €/£5.00, the expected value on the exercise date is either €/£2.00 or €/£7.00 and the rate of return on Government bonds is 8%.
5. What are the determinants of an option's value?

6. Determine the value of a call option on an equity share (that does not pay a dividend) using the Black-Scholes model, using the following information.

The current share price is €/£7.50, the exercise price is €/£8.00, the exercise date is six months time, the risk free-rate of interest (continuously compounded) is 7% and the standard deviation of returns on the share in the past has been 40%.

7. Stimpy plc a ROI company wants to borrow £10 million for seven years at a fixed rate to finance a capital investment in Manchester. The cheapest rate that Stimpy plc can obtain on the money markets is 10.25% per annum. This is cheaper than borrowing in the ROI. Stimpy plc can borrow euro at a floating rate of LIBOR + 0.5%.

Stimpy plc's bankers suggest that one of their UK customers (Wrent plc) would be interested in a swap agreement which would match the capital value in full. Wrent plc requires a floating rate euro loan. They have been pricing the market in the UK and the best deal they have been offered is LIBOR + 1.5%. It could borrow in sterling at the fixed rate of 11.5%. The bank charges a set arrangement fee of 0.15% each year, payable by both Stimpy plc and Wrent plc. The current exchange rate is €1.25 = £1.

REQUIRED

Create a swap agreement which would be agreeable to both Stimpy plc and Wrent plc.

CHALLENGING QUESTIONS

1. RECEIVING FOREIGN CURRENCY

Tartan plc (a UK company) has been invited to tender for a contract in the ROI with the bid priced in euros. Tartan plc thinks the contract will cost £1,850,000. Because of fierce competition for the bid, Tartan plc is willing to price the contract at £2,000,000. Since the exchange rate is currently €2.80:£1.00, it puts in a bid of €/£5,600,000.

The contract will not be awarded until after six months.

REQUIRED

Outline the cost/profit implications for Tartan plc assuming the following scenarios:

(a)   Tartan plc hedges the potential contract for currency risk using a forward rate contract, which is priced at the spot rate now and Tartan plc does not win the contract. The exchange rate in six months time has moved to €2.5:£1.

4 Marks

(b)   Tartan plc does not enter into a forward rate contract. Instead it waits to see what will happen. In six months time Tartan plc is awarded the contract. At this time the value of the euro has fallen to €3.20:£1.

4 Marks

(c)   Tartan plc takes out a put option costing £40,000 to sell €5,600,000 in six months time at €2.80:£1. Evaluate Tartan plc's position now assuming:

    (i)   Tartan plc fails to win the contract.

4 Marks

    (ii)   Tartan plc is awarded the contract. Exchange rates move to €3.20:£1

4 Marks

    (iii) Tartan plc is awarded the contract. Exchange rates move to €2.50:£1

4 Marks
Total 20 Marks
(ICAI, MABF, Adapted from FAE manual, 2007)

2. PAYING FOREIGN CURRENCY

Tartan plc (a UK company) is trying to purchase a plot of land in the ROI. The closing date for the auction is six months. Bids have to be by closed envelope, which will only be opened in six months time. Tartan plc thinks the land is worth €1,850,000. However, is willing to price the contract at £2,000,000 because of fierce competition. Since the exchange rate is currently €2.80:£1.00, it puts in a bid of €/£5,600,000.

REQUIRED

Outline the cost/profit implications for Tartan plc assuming the following scenarios:

(a)   Tartan plc obtains the sterling funds by way of a loan (at 7%) and converts the funds to euro now and invests the euro in a currency account through the local bank. The bank offers a return on 5% per annum on the euro deposit account. Evaluate Tartan plc's position assuming:

   (i) Tartan plc fails to win the contract and has to convert the euro back to Sterling to repay the six-month loan. The value of the euro has remained the same.

3 Marks

   (ii) Tartan plc is awarded the contract. The value of the euro has fallen to €3.20:£1 by this time.

3 Marks

   (iii) Tartan plc is awarded the contract. The value of the euro appreciates to €2.50:£1 by this time

3 Marks

(b)   Tartan plc hedges the potential contract for currency risk using a forward rate contract, which is priced at the spot rate now and Tartan plc does not win the contract. The exchange rate in six months time has moved to €2.5:£1.

3 Marks

(c)   Tartan plc does not enter into a forward rate contract. Instead it waits to see what will happen. In six months time Tartan plc wins the sale at the auction. At this time the value of the euro has fallen to €3.20:£1.

3 Marks

(d)   Tartan plc takes out a call option costing £40,000 to buy €5,600,000 in six months time at €2.80:£1. Evaluate Tartan plc's position now assuming:

   (i) Tartan plc fails to win the contract.

3 Marks

   (ii) Tartan plc is awarded the contract. Exchange rates move to €3.20:£1

3 Marks

(iii) Tartan plc is awarded the contract. Exchange rates move to
€2.50:£1

3 Marks
Total 24 Marks

3. COMPUDISK/LEEMAN

Background
It is 1 May 2008 and you have just been appointed Financial Accountant of a large family-owned group of companies established by a local entrepreneur, John Ferguson. The Group consists of two companies: COMPUDISK Ltd. ('COMPUDISK') and WOOLMILL Ltd. ('WOOLMILL'). The group is based in the UK.

Compudisk
The Group's main trading company, COMPUDISK, manufactures components used in the production of computers. The company currently has an annual turnover in excess of £30 million, due partly to a long association with its main customer INVER Ltd., a local subsidiary of one of the world's leading PC manufacturers COMPUDISK has also developed a close relationship with its two major materials suppliers based in Canada and Germany, each of which accounts for approximately 30% of cost of sales. This has resulted in a continuous supply of quality raw materials at the lowest possible price, which has enabled it (COMPUDISK) to maintain a constant gross margin over the last number of years. Supplies of raw materials are paid for in the currency of the country from which the materials are sourced.

Leeman - Supply contract
WOOLMILL has recently secured a lucrative three-year contract to supply high quality woollen fashion accessories to LEEMAN, an international fashion house with shops in Canada and the USA.

The contract will not require any additional capital expenditure. However, it will involve the use of a high-grade wool in the manufacturing process. This wool can be sourced directly from Italian suppliers or, depending on availability, from a local wholesaler (who also supplies other wools to WOOLMILL). This wool can only be purchased in May of each year.

The LEEMAN supply contract is divided equally into two separate sub-contracts priced in each of the respective currencies i.e. US dollars and Canadian dollars. Details of the US contract are shown in APPENDIX II along with information on current exchange and interest rates.

A specific clause in the contract requires delivery of the orders to Canada and the US at any time between 1 June and 31 July 2008 (at LEEMAN's option). In return for this flexibility regarding deliveries, LEEMAN has guaranteed to pay the amount due under the contract on 31 July 2008.

Foreign exchange exposures

The two companies in the group have no exposures to foreign exchange other than those indicated above.

John Ferguson has also read a recent newspaper article on 'The Euro, The Single European Currency'. This article suggests that the UK is about to join the EMU. John Ferguson is unsure of the possible foreign currency exposure implications for the Group arising from its introduction in the UK.

APPENDIX II

LEEMAN CONTRACT - US $ EXPOSURE

Contract price	US $ 750,000
Exchange rates:	
Spot (at 30 April 2008)	US $ 1.64 - US $1.66
Forecast spot at 31 July 2008	US $ 1.66 - US $1.68
Interest rates (£ rate 6% per annum)	US 10%

Note:

A US $ option could be purchased at a premium of £300 per $100,000, at a strike rate of $1.67 to £1, effective on 31 July 2008.

APPENDIX III

COMPUDISK LTD. - SALES INFORMATION - QUARTER ENDED 31 MARCH 2008

Product	Actual Sales	Actual Unit Contribution	Total Contribution	Actual Budgeted Sales	Budgeted Contribution	Budgeted Total Contribution
	Units 000	*£*	*£ 000*	*Units 000*	*£*	*£ 000*
A	2,200	0.15	330	2,200	0.15	330
B	1,700	0.18	306	1,500	0.19	285
C	4,000	0.14	560	3,900	0.13	507
Total	7,900		1,196	7,600		1,122

REQUIRED

Prepare an internal memorandum to the managing director (John Ferguson) setting out your response to the following matters:

c) (i) Calculate the outcome of two alternative hedging strategies available to WOOLMILL in respect of the US dollar exposure and compare with the out-turn if a no-hedging strategy was adopted, using the forecast spot rate at 31 July 2008. Based on your calculations, recommend the optimum method of hedging this currency receipt. Recommend the most appropriate strategy to protect against any other foreign currency exposures that might arise in relation to the LEEMAN contract.

18 Marks

(ii) Advise on the foreign exchange exposure implications of the introduction of Economic and Monetary Union (EMU) on the Group's activities, assuming that the UK joins the EMU.

6 Marks
Total 24 Marks
(ICAI, MABF, FAE, Extract from Autumn 1998)

4. INSTRUMEDIX Ltd.

NOTE: In this question reference is made to a fictitious overseas country and its related fictitious currency. Details of the names which you will encounter in the text are as follows:

Country	Currency
Rotina	*The rot*

Background

You are a recently qualified chartered accountant and have just commenced employment as a Finance Manager with INSTRUMEDIX Ltd. ('INSTRUMEDIX' / 'the company'). INSTRUMEDIX is a prosperous private company whose four directors each own 25% of the share capital. The company is engaged in the distribution of healthcare equipment and acquires and supplies all its products locally.

Future developments: FINNCARE

A former colleague of one of the directors has opened a clinic, FINNCARE, in Rotina. INSTRUMEDIX has been invited to tender for a contract to supply healthcare equipment to this clinic. All tenders must be quoted in Rotina rot. The equipment can currently be sourced directly from the United States for $500,000. INSTRUMEDIX will undertake to re-engineer the equipment in a form suitable for distribution to FINNCARE. It is estimated that additional engineering, administration and distribution costs associated with this contract will be €/£60,000, incurred and payable in euro/pounds (€/£'s).

The directors have agreed that the contract price should be quoted at an amount that will yield a profit of 20% of sales, in euro/pounds (€/£'s), based on current exchange rates.

It will take one month for FINNCARE to determine who should be awarded the contract. If it is successful with its tender, the company will order the equipment, re-engineer and distribute it to FINNCARE within a further two weeks. It is expected that payment will be made, and monies received, two months after the contract has been awarded.

The banks are quoting the following spot and forward rates:

	US dollar (US$)		Rotina rot (RR)	
	Offer	Bid	Offer	Bid
Spot rate	1.680	1.700	6.950	6.975
One-month forward rate	0.020	0.015 premium	0.400	0.450 discount
Three-month forward rate	0.030	0.025 premium	0.550	0.600 discount

The following estimates have been made as to what future spot rates and forward contracts will be at various intervals over the next three months:

	US dollar (US$)		Finnish markka (FM)	
Spot rates	Offer	Bid	Offer	Bid
One months time	1.620	1.630	7.000	7.150
Two months time	1.575	1.600	7.200	7.300
Three months time	1.540	1.560	7.600	7.750
Forward rates in one months time				
Two-month forward rate	1.600	1.625	7.700	7.875
Three-month forward rate	1.580	1.595	7.750	7.928

Three foreign exchange strategies are currently being considered by the directors:

(1) Enter into a forward exchange contract immediately.
(2) Wait until the contract has been awarded (i.e. one month), before entering into a forward exchange contract.
(3) Do nothing.

The directors have expressed concern about the consequences of future rate movements being contrary to predictions, when adopting a particular exchange policy and about the fact that they are not guaranteed the FINNCARE contract.

REQUIRED

Prepare a memorandum for the Board of Directors dealing with each of the following:

(d) In relation to the FINNCARE contract, consider the three foreign exchange strategies currently under review by the Board and outline the potential consequences of each strategy. Suggest and describe alternatives, if any, that may be more appropriate in the circumstances.

24 Marks

Total 24 Marks

(ICAI, MABF, FAE, Extract from Autumn 1996)

N.B. *Show clearly all assumptions and workings.*

5. INTERGLAZE

NOTE: In this question reference is made to four fictitious overseas countries and their related fictitious currencies. Details of the names which you will encounter in the text are as follows:

Country	*Currency*
Saxonia	*The sax*
Ruritania	*The rur*
Kostalonika	*The kosta*
Dalmatria	*The dal*

Background

INTERGLAZE Ltd. ('INTERGLAZE') is a large family-owned company that specialises in the design, manufacture, and fitting of glass windows. The company has expanded rapidly over the past five years, due to the unprecedented growth in the Irish construction sector. The company's main customers are Irish construction companies which sub-contract the glazing element of building contracts to INTERGLAZE.

Aware of the possibility of a downturn in the Irish construction market, the directors recently decided to undertake some contracts outside Ireland. Although smaller in size compared to many of its foreign competitors, INTERGLAZE quickly developed a reputation as a high quality operator. In particular, the company's ability to produce tailor-made glass capable of meeting the stringent design requirements of leading international architects led to the award of a number of high profile contracts, including the glazing of the Louvre museum in Paris.

Over the past number of years, INTERGLAZE has successfully developed long-term trading relationships with all the major Irish construction companies. However, because INTERGLAZE has only recently entered into foreign markets, it has not yet been able to develop similar relationships with key foreign target customers, most of whom are construction companies operating in their respective countries. Consequently, the directors do not have the same degree of knowledge about potential foreign customers compared to their Irish equivalents.

This lack of background knowledge on foreign customers was recently demonstrated when INTERGLAZE suffered a bad debt on a glazing contract completed in Saxonia. The Saxonian company had sent brochures detailing some of its previous contracts, and looked on paper to be a very strong company. On this basis no other research was undertaken. However, the Saxonian company was extremely slow in making payment, which was due on completion of the contract. It subsequently transpired that the Saxonian company had incurred a major loss on another building contract which ultimately caused it to go into liquidation. Eventually INTERGLAZE received approximately three million sax out of a total four million sax due from the Saxonian company.

Previously, the directors had considered the foreign markets as having good long-term growth prospects. However, in light of the bad debt experience in Saxonia, the directors are now extremely wary of undertaking any more contracts outside the Irish market, or with contractors with whom they do not have a previous trading/business relationship.

Ruritanian contract

Recently, INTERGLAZE has been offered the opportunity to tender for a large contract in Ruritania. Although the contract would be very lucrative, the directors are unsure as to whether to proceed with this tender, given the concerns regarding possible bad debts. In view of the continued growth in the Irish market, some of the directors are proposing to abandon the expansion into overseas markets and, instead, concentrate on the Irish market. The directors have now commissioned an external review of the company's operations to determine future strategy. You are a senior consultant in a local firm of management consultants that has been appointed to undertake this exercise.

A leading firm of worldwide building contractors, which has heard of INTERGLAZE's reputation for design and quality, has invited the company to tender for this prestigious contract in Ruritania. The tender must be priced in rurs. The contract will be awarded in three months time, with payment being received nine months after the date on which the contract is awarded.

The sales director has priced the contract at €/£1 million, and the directors have decided to quote a price in rurs based on the current spot rates. Besides their fears over the possibility of another bad debt, INTERGLAZE's directors are concerned about the degree to which the rur has weakened in recent months. In addition, the directors are keen to minimise foreign exchange risk associated with any further weakening in the rur, and are considering the following strategies:

   (i)   Enter into a forward exchange contract now; or

   (ii)   Enter into a currency option now; or

   (iii)   Wait until the contract has been awarded and then enter a forward exchange contract.

The Directors have asked for your recommendation as to the most appropriate strategy. Exchange rate details (€/£ vs. Rur) are shown in APPENDIX 1.

Kostalonikan (Kosta) loan

On 31 August 1999 INTERGLAZE took out a 200 million kosta loan to pay for a new glass-cutting machine that was purchased in Kostalonika. The loan was taken out in kostas in order to avail of low Kostalonikan interest rates that were available at that time. In addition, the directors negotiated a repayment structure whereby the loan was repayable in a single repayment of 200 million kostas on 31 August 2005, with interest costs being met on a normal quarterly basis.

However, in the last couple of years, Kostalonikan interest rates have increased sharply and the directors are concerned that INTERGLAZE's higher interest costs are now having a negative impact on profitability. In order to reduce interest costs, the directors are now considering repaying the kosta loan by taking out a new bank facility, possibly in €/£s or Dalmatrian dals. Both Irish/UK and Dalmatrian interest rates are now significantly below Kostalonikan rates (details shown in APPENDIX II),

If the loan was converted to €/£, the Directors would propose to increase the company's existing €/£1 million overdraft facility to accommodate the Kostalonikan loan. As a result of the failure to collect the remaining one million Sax (approximately €/£300,000) due from the Saxonian contract, and the continued growth of the business, the overdraft facility has been fully drawn down for the past six months. The company does not have any other bank facilities besides the overdraft and the Kostalonikan (kostas) loan. The directors have asked for your advice on their proposal to repay the Kostalonikan (kostas) facility. (Assume no penalties on early repayment.)

APPENDIX I

RURITANIAN CONTRACT

(€/£ vs. Rur)

	The Rur	
	Offer	Bid
Current Spot and Forward Rates		
Spot Rate	1.250	1.300
3 month forward rate	0.050	0.060 discount
9 month forward rate	0.150	0.180 discount
12 month forward rate	0.200	0.220 discount
Estimated Forward Rates in 3 Months Time		
9 month forward rate	1.500	1.535
12 month forward rate	1.515	1.550

Options

12 month options can currently be obtained at the following prices:
Rur Put option at €/£ 1 : *Rur* 1.51 - Premium €/£ 500 per 100,000 *Rur*
Rur Call option at €/£ 1 : *Rur* 1.51 - Premium €/£ 450 per 100,000 *Rur*

Interest Rates

It should be assumed that irish Interest rates are currently 6%

APPENDIX II

KOSTALONIKAN (*KOSTA*) LOAN

	Ireland	*Kostalonika*	*Dalmatria*
Date loan was drawn (31/Aug/99)			
Exchange rates	€/£1	*Kosta* 200	n/a
Interest rates	12%	5%	n/a
Current (31/Aug/02)			
Exchange rates	€/£1	*Kosta* 150	n/a
Interest rates	6%	10%	4%

REQUIRED

Draft a report to the managing director setting out your advice on the following matters:

a)

(i) Advise the directors on whether they should continue the expansion into foreign markets, outlining the reasons for your answer.

(Note: Ignore any capacity constraints.)

6 Marks

(ii) Assuming that INTERGLAZE decides to proceed with the expansion into foreign markets, suggest ways in which the company could minimise the possibility of incurring any further bad debts.

12 Marks

(iii) Assuming that INTERGLAZE proceeds with the Ruritanian tender, determine the price (in rurs) that the company should submit for this tender.

4 Marks

(iv) Calculate the outcome of each of the three proposed foreign exchange strategies, and recommend which strategy you consider most appropriate in the circumstances.

16 Marks

(v) Advise the directors on their proposal to convert the Kostalonikan (kostas) loan into €/£s by way of an increase to the company's existing overdraft facility, or into a Dalmatrian (dals) facility. Outline any other recommendations you would make as regards the structure of the company's existing bank facilities.

12 Marks
Total 60 Marks
(ICAI, MABF, FAE, Extract from Autumn 2002)

6. PROPERTY HOLDINGS

Interest rate protection
PROPERTY HOLDINGS has a significant level of long-term bank loans that were used to assist in funding the acquisition of the company's investment property portfolio. The directors are concerned about the possibility that long-term interest rates may increase, which would lead to a significant increase in the interest payable on the company's bank borrowings. You have been asked to outline to the Board some possible options for protecting the company from adverse interest rate movements.

REQUIRED

(a) (iv) Outline three alternative ways to protect the company against possible increases in interest rates on the company's long-term loans, indicating the merits and demerits of each alternative.

10 Marks
(ICAI, MABF, FAE, Extract from Autumn 2003)

7. DRAINCO Ltd.

Background
You are the Finance Director of DRAINCO Ltd. ('DRAINCO') a company that manufactures a range of drainage products which are used

mainly in the residential house building sector. From its base in Ireland, DRAINCO has been able to service its customers, which comprise a range of residential house builders in Ireland and the UK. DRAINCO is now considered the leading supplier of drainage products in this market.

The Board recently hired a firm of management consultants to advise on the strategic direction that DRAINCO should take over the next five years. As part of this exercise, the management consultants reviewed the opportunities available in a number of potential new geographical markets, including continental Europe, the US and the Far East. The firm concluded its report by recommending that DRAINCO should consider an overseas acquisition in either the Chinese or US markets, which are currently the two fastest growing international markets for drainage products in the world. Both markets are heavily fragmented, with low barriers of entry, potentially allowing a new entrant such as DRAINCO to establish a significant presence in these markets.

For the past six months you have been undertaking some research looking at potential acquisition targets in the Chinese and US markets. You have identified a preferred acquisition target in each of the markets, which is of a suitable size, and which might be available for purchase on 31 December 2006.

Shanghai Pipes Inc. ('SPI')

SPI is a large manufacturer of drainage products in the Chinese market, which is the fastest growing market in the world, due to the construction boom currently taking place in China's main cities.

The relatively cheap labour costs in the Chinese market mean that total operational costs are significantly below those incurred in the European or US markets. In addition, the low cost of production enjoyed by Chinese companies means that the Chinese market is protected from imports and, in effect, only Chinese-based companies can service this market.

SPI is currently a subsidiary of a large Chinese owned conglomerate. The senior management team in SPI currently do not have any shareholding in the company. There would be relatively little rationalisation cost associated with the acquisition of SPI.

The purchase of SPI can be structured on a deferred consideration basis, whereby a portion of the purchase price would only be paid at the end of three years, depending on the sales performance of the company over this time. The exact details surrounding the deferred consideration element (including the amount and sales targets that must be achieved) have yet to be agreed and are still subject to negotiation.

East Coast Drains Inc. ('ECD')

ECD is a long established company based in New Jersey. From its base, the company services the main cities along the east coast of the US.

ECD has a very successful track record. However, its manufacturing plant has not been updated in a long time, and is probably due for a major overhaul. The shareholders of ECD occupy the main senior management positions in the company and they have indicated that, should the company be acquired, they would wish to retire immediately. In addition, the purchase price of the company is payable up-front, with no element of deferred consideration.

It has been noted that there would need to be a rationalisation of some of ECD's product range. This would involve ceasing to produce some unprofitable product lines, with a resultant rationalisation cost of US $ 0.5 million.

Expected unit selling price, production costs (variable and fixed) and other costs are set out in APPENDIX I. Expected sales volumes are set out in APPENDIX II.

US Investments

Some years ago the directors of DRAINCO purchased some shares in major US-based blue chip companies. The Managing Director believes the US stock market has now peaked, and has requested that you dispose of the shares now, which would realise proceeds of US $1 million on 30 September 2006. The managing director has decided that the proceeds will be placed on deposit in US dollars until 31 December 2006 when they will likely be converted to €/£.

You have been asked to advise on a suitable hedging strategy for converting the US dollars back to €/£ at 31 December 2006.

Details of the forecast exchange rates are set out in APPENDIX III.

APPENDIX III

Hedging Strategy for US dollar Investments

Amount of US $ to be received on
30 September 2006   US $ 1 million

Exchange rates
Current €/£ spot at 30 September 2006   US $ 1.53 - US $ 1.55
Forecast €/£ spot at 31 December 2006   US $ 1.55 - US $ 1.56

Interest rates
US interest rates
- borrowings   7%
- savings   6%

Irish/UK interest rates
- borrowings   5%
- savings   4%

Note:
A US $ option could be purchased on 30 September 2006 at a premium
of €/£500 per US $100,000, at a strike rate of US $1.57 to €/£1.00,
effective on 31 December 2006.

REQUIRED

Prepare an Internal Memorandum to the board setting out the following:

b) (i) Calculate the proceeds of the US investments in €/£ at the appropriate spot rate at 31 December 2006. Suggest TWO alternative
hedging strategies for the US dollar proceeds, and calculate their
outcome. Based on the results of your calculations, recommend
which is the optimal strategy, assuming the acquisition of SPI or
ECD does not take place.

Note: For the purposes of this requirement, candidates should assume that today's date is 30 September 2006.

20 Marks

(ii) Assuming that the acquisition of either SPI or ECD takes place. advise on what the company should do with the US dollar proceeds, received on 31 December 2006, in relation to the funding of each of these acquisitions.

10 Marks
Total 30 Marks
(ICAI, MABF, FAE, Extract from Autumn 2006)

SECTION SIX

DIVIDEND DECISION AND SHAREHOLDER WEALTH MAXIMISATION

Chapter 19   Dividend Policy

DIVIDEND POLICY

19

Debt   10,000,000

Equity   15,000,000

Market Value   25,000,000

LEARNING OBJECTIVES

Upon completing this chapter, readers should be able to:

♣ Explain market protocol in respect of the pricing of shares before and after dividend distributions;

♣ Discuss the traditional, residual and irrelevancy dividend theories, highlighting the differences between the three;

♣ Calculate whether share price is in equilibrium, using the dividend valuation model;

♣ Calculate growth using either retentions or the past pattern of dividend distributions;

♣ Discuss the practical factors that influence dividend policy, highlighting influences on low and high dividend payouts;

♣ Explain scrip issues, stock splits and share repurchases and identify reasons for undertaking each and differences between them; and

♣ Comment on empirical research findings in respect of the relevancy of the dividend decision, with special reference to Lintner's model.

Introduction

In chapter 12, 'Cost of Capital', the dividend valuation model is explained. A key assumption to this model is that investors' value equity shares based on the future stream of dividends expected to be received. To this juncture in the text, this future stream of dividends is taken as given, however, in reality the situation is not so clear cut. This chapter discusses theories on the impact of dividend payout policy on equity holder wealth. There is debate as to whether there is an optimal dividend policy. What is evident from academic literature is that the majority of plcs choose a stable payout policy and equity holders consider deviations from a chosen policy as signals about a company's future. The chapter explains dividends, dividend policy, M&M's irrelevancy theory, traditional theory, residual theory practical issues surrounding the dividend payout decision and the use of share repurchase as an alternative to distributing dividends.

General information on dividends

Dividends are distributions out of earnings. The most common type is cash dividends, which are declared and paid on each issued share. Scrip dividends, scrip issues or share repurchases are also deemed to be forms of distributions (explained later in this chapter). Dividend distributions are either half yearly, or as is currently becoming vogue, quarter yearly. This practice is more common in the US. Indeed, some companies choose not to distribute any dividends at all. Distributions throughout a company's accounting year are referred to as *interim dividends*. The *final dividend* is agreed by equity holders at the Annual General Meeting (AGM), when the financial statements for the year are also presented. Though the final dividend is agreed at the AGM by the equity holders; they only have the power to reduce the distribution, not to increase it. Therefore, the board of directors is the dominant influence on the level of dividends a company distributes. When dividends are declared and agreed at an AGM, they become a liability of the company that has to be accrued immediately. Therefore, they impact on company liquidity.

It is not a simple world and dividends cannot be paid to equity holders at the exact time of being declared. The administrative process behind paying a dividend takes time. In this period the stock market continues to trade the company's shares. This causes confusion as to who gets the dividend, the seller of a share or the buyer and also causes problems for brokers. Therefore, to deal with this problem the stock market sets an ex-dividend date, or a cut-off date. This is usually two days before a company's declared date of record. On the *declared date of record* a company lists the equity holders that, according to their records, are entitled to dividends. The two days set by the stock exchanges, are to allow companies to update their records in light of the buying and selling transactions that have taken place to the ex-dividend date. The *payment date* is usually a couple of weeks after the declared record date. Around these dates, shares are advertised and traded as either ex-dividend or cum-dividend. *Ex-dividend* refers to purchases made after the ex-dividend date and highlights the fact that the share does not have a right to the impending dividend. When shares are traded as *cum-dividend* this means that they are being traded after the dividend has been declared, but before the ex-dividend date. Therefore, if purchased, the purchaser would have rights to the impending dividend. The distinction is important as it impacts on the value of a share. When a dividend is declared the share price will reflect the company's value, including the amount of the cash dividend that is about to be paid; therefore, it is expected that the value of the share will fall due after the dividend distribution.

Dividend policy

Dividend policy refers to the pattern of dividend payments made by a company over time. It encapsulates patterns in the *payout policy*, which is the *percentage of the current years earnings that are distributed* and consequently the *retentions policy* (*the percentage of the current year's earnings that are retained*) and the actual *dividend paid per share*. An underlying assumption in this text is that business finance decisions should be made which maximise equity holders' value (i.e. company value). Dividend policy is considered as one of the three main decisions to be taken by a business finance manager. It is argued by some that dividend policy is a key determinant of company value. M&M consider dividend policy to be irrelevant. Another school of thought suggests that dividends should only be paid when there are funds available that have no other productive use (residual theory). These three views are explained in turn.

Relevancy view

The dividend valuation model assumes that the value of a share (hence the value of equity) is related to the future stream of dividends that are receivable. It could be interpreted then, that a company with greater dividends would be higher valued. However, a component of the model is growth in dividends. An analysis of growth (under the traditional theory) shows that it is related to the level of retentions (see chapter 12, 'Cost of Capital'). When a larger proportion of profits are retained by a company for investment; the growth in earnings, hence dividends, is expected to be higher. In addition, the higher the return from new investments, the higher the growth in earnings. This is reflected in the following example.

Worked example 19.1   (Growth in dividends)

Vienta plc has a payout ratio of 40%, and retains the rest for investing in projects which yield 15%.

Trienta plc has a payout of 80%, and retains the rest for investment at 15%.

REQUIRED

a)   What is the estimated annual rate of growth in dividends, for both companies?
b)   What would the rate of growth change to if the yield increased to 20%?

Solution

a)   The formula for calculating growth in dividends is:

$$g=br$$

Where, g is growth, b is the proportion that is retained and r is the expected return on new investments.

Vienta plc
Growth is: $60\% \times 15\% = 9\%$

Trienta plc
Growth is: $20\% \times 15\% = 3\%$

Continued

b)   *The rate of growth increases in both instances.*

Vienta plc
Growth is: $60\% \times 20\% = 12\%$

Trienta plc
Growth is: $20\% \times 20\% = 4\%$.

Therefore, there are various factors that can impact on variables which are used in the dividend valuation model and consequently impact on company value. Under the relevancy theory (traditional theory), boards have to choose a policy which maximises equity holders' value and it is assumed that an optimum dividend policy exists. Porterfield (1965) uses a simple formula to apply when determining the level of dividend to distribute, or not. He claims that you should distribute when:

$$d_1 + P_1 > P_0$$

Where d_1 is the cash value to the equity holder of the dividend to be paid, P_1 is the expected equity share price value after the dividend has been paid (ex-dividend) and P_0 is the equity share price before the dividend was paid (cum-dividend). The value of d_1 to equity holders will be impacted on by their tax status, i.e. an equity holder with surplus personal allowance available will value a dividend higher, compared to an equity holder who pays income at the higher rate tax band. Therefore different equity holders will value a company differently. P_0 is the markets perception about the future profitability, growth and consequential dividend payments expected from the company, before the dividend is declared. P_1 will change due to the loss of resources associated with paying the dividend and may also change in light of the level of d_1, which may be different to market expectations, causing the market to revise their expectations of future dividend flows. P_1 and P_0 are derived using the dividend valuation model as discussed in chapter 12, 'Cost of Capital'. This model is rearranged to derive P_0.

$$P_0 = \frac{D_0(1+g)}{Ke - g} + D_0$$

Where D_0 is the dividend that is about to be paid, g is growth in dividends and Ke is the cost of equity (equity holders' required rate of return).

When calculating the value of equity ex-dividend (P_1) the formula changes to:

$$P_1 = \frac{D_0(1+g)}{Ke - g}$$

Worked example 19.2 (Relevancy theory)

Tantrum plc has achieved earnings of €/£800,000 this year. The company intends to pursue a policy of financing all its investment opportunities out of retained earnings. There are considerable investment opportunities, which are expected to be available indefinitely. However, if Tantrum plc does not exploit any of the available opportunities, its annual earnings will remain at €/£800,000, in perpetuity. The following figures are available:

Proportion of earnings retained %	Growth rate in earnings %	Required return on all investments by equity holders %
0	0	14
25	5	15
40	7	16

The rate of return required by equity holders would rise if earnings are retained, because of the risk associated with the new investments.

REQUIRED

What is the optimum retention's policy for Tantrum plc? The full dividend payment for this year will be paid in the near future in any case.

Solution

The question states that the dividend will be paid in the near future. Therefore, the value of equity at present is cum-dividend. The dividend

Continued

valuation model calculates the value of equity ex-dividend (P_1); therefore the dividend value (d_1) has to be included to find the current cum-dividend value (P_0).

$$d_1 + P_1 > P_0$$

Scenario 1 (Growth is zero, retentions are zero, and the cost of equity is 14%). In this scenario, equity holders' value will amount to:

$$P_0 = \frac{€/£800,000(1+0)}{0.14-0} + €/£800,000 = €/£6,514,286$$

Scenario 2 (Growth is estimated at 5% per year, retentions are usually 25% of net earnings, and the cost of equity is 15%). As 25% of earnings (which are €/£800,000) are retained, then 75% or (€/£800,000 × 75% = €/£600,000 are distributed).

In this scenario, equity holders' value will amount to:

$$P_0 = \frac{€/£600,000(1+0.05)}{0.15-0.05} + €/£600,000 = €/£6,900,000$$

Scenario 3 (Growth is estimated at 7% per year, retentions are usually 40% of net earnings, and the cost of equity is 16%). As 40% of earnings (which are €/£800,000) are retained, then 60% or (€/£800,000 × 60% = €/£480,000 are distributed).

In this scenario, equity holders' value will amount to:

$$P_0 = \frac{€/£480,000(1+0.07)}{0.16-0.07} + €/£480,000 = €/£6,186,667$$

The optimum policy is scenario two as this maximises equity holders' overall wealth.

Irrelevancy theory (Modigliani and Miller theory)

The link between retentions and growth is questioned under M&M's irrelevancy theory (1961). They consider that where investment opportunities are favourable to a company, the funds for this investment can be obtained from new long-term sources; hence, this should not impact on the dividend decision. They consider that company performance and growth is related to the availability and quality of projects undertaken (i.e. they should have positive NPVs). The financing of projects does not have to be sourced from retained earnings, indeed due to the benefit of the tax shield, they consider debt (to a point) to be the optimum source of funds to obtain, to maximise company value (see chapter 15, 'Capital Structure'). Therefore, the use to which surpluses from projects are utilised, is irrelevant, so long as the cost of capital is covered.

Worked example 19.3   (M&M irrelevancy theory)

Setenta plc is an ungeared company. The directors plan to dissolve the company in three years. The expected cash inflows over the next three years are €/£20,000 per year. Equity holders expect a return of 10% on their investment.

Applying M&M's theory, show that dividend policy, is irrelevant. Assume that the current policy is to distribute all available cash flows per year. Compare this to a scenario in which the company decides to distribute €/30,000 of the total available (€/£60,000) in year one (assume that this distribution does not breach any legal restrictions placed on dividend distributions), €20,000 in year two with the remainder in year three. In this situation M&M would suggest paying the dividend in year one and obtaining the €/£10,000 shortfall, by either issuing equity, or loan stock. Assume the extra €/£10,000 is raised by an equity distribution.

REQUIRED

a)   Calculate the market value of equity based on the current policy.

b)   Calculate the existing equity holders' worth, if the new dividend policy is pursued (applying M&M's irrelevancy theory).

Continued

Solution

a) The current policy is to distribute all net cash flows each year
    (i.e. €/£20,000 per year). Therefore, equity holders will value
    the company based on the future stream of cash flows, dis-
    counted to their present value at the equity holders' required
    rate of return (10%):

$$€/£20,000/(1.10)+€/£20,000/(1.10)^2$$
$$+€/£20,000/(1.10)^3 = €/£49,737$$

b) Under the revised policy, wherein €/£30,000 is distributed
    in year one to the current equity holders, a trade off is taking
    place. An additional €/£10,000 has to be raised. These new
    equity holders will require a 10% return also, therefore in
    future the return to current equity holders will fall by the new
    equity holders' requirements, which is $€/£10,000 \times 10\% =$
    €/£1,000 in year two and year three; leaving a future distri-
    bution of €/£19,000 to the current equity holders in year two
    and €9,000 in year three (being the €10,000 less the divi-
    dend to the new equity holders of (10% of €/£10,000)).

    The value of the company to the current equity holders
    based on this future stream of expected cash outflows, is as
    follows:

$$€/£30,000/(1.1)+€/£19,000/(1.1^2)$$
$$+€/£9,000/(1.1^3) = €/£49,737$$

Therefore, regardless of the pattern of payout, the value of
equity after taking account of the time value of money at the
equity holders' required rate of return, will remain the same.

The assumptions

M&M argue that dividend policy can be irrelevant in a world where there
are no taxes, no transaction costs, where equity holders have all the information about a company and do not misinterpret it, and where there is a
constant interest rate that is equal for companies and investors.

Residual theory

Residual dividend theory assumes that raising external finance is costly; therefore retentions are required to enable a company to invest in projects. The assumption is that before a dividend is considered all available projects with positive NPVs should be invested in. When these have been exhausted, the residual can be distributed. This allows equity holders the option of investing the funds that the company cannot provide the required return on, in other companies that can provide their required return. Therefore, this maximises equity holders' value. If the funds were retained and not invested in projects that provide a return over and above the equity holders' required rate of return, then equity holders' value would diminish over time.

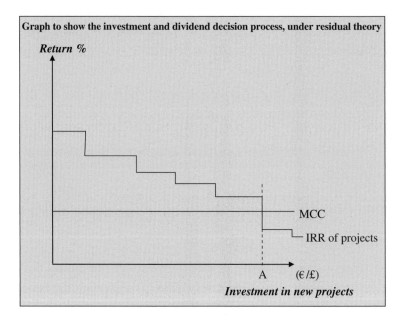

As depicted in the above graph, all available earnings should be invested in suitable projects, starting with those considered to have the highest IRR and ending at point A. At this point the IRR equals the equity holders' required return (Ke or their marginal cost of capital (MCC)). After this point the available projects' returns are less than the equity holders' current required rate of return. Any surplus funds should be distributed as a dividend. Under this theory, no dividend is an acceptable policy, when appropriate investment opportunities exist.

Issues affecting dividend policy

There are many factors that, depending on the company would suggest that either a low distribution or a high distribution is best for equity holder wealth. These are discussed later in this chapter under *'other practical issues'*. The two main factors that are argued to support paying either low or high levels of dividend, which are relevant for most companies, are *'taxation rates'* and *'transaction costs'*.

Factors supporting low distributions

Taxation levels

Dividends are subject to income tax, whereas returns on share sales are subject to capital gains tax. When a government's *capital gains tax* rates are lower than their *income tax* rates, low distributions are preferable as this will maximise an equity holder's financial position as low distributions result in higher capital gains (this argument is relevant where the majority of equity holders are individuals). Elton and Gruber (1970) report empirical evidence to support the argument that high income equity holders are attracted to companies with low pay-out policies.

Transaction costs (company)

When a company distributes funds to investors, this depletes the funds that are available for investment. In reality, raising new funds, for example issuing shares is costly and companies that distribute more will have to incur larger costs when they undertake new projects, relative to companies that retain more funds. There is been evidence to support a preference by companies to amass retained earnings and use these for investment purposes (pecking order theory is discussed in chapter 15, 'Capital Structure').

Factors supporting high distributions

Taxation

When a government's *income tax rates* are lower than their *capital gains tax* rates, high distributions are preferable as this will maximise equity holder value as high distributions result in lower capital gains (this argument is relevant where the majority of equity holders are individuals). However, this policy does reduce equity holders' ability to manage their tax affairs, as dividends are taxable when receivable, whereas equity holders can elect whether to sell shares, or not, in any particular tax year. Elton and Gruber (1970) report empirical evidence to support the argument that low income equity holders are attracted to companies with high payout policies.

Transaction costs (investors)
In some instances, equity holders will prefer high distributions, as distributions do not have transaction costs. When an equity holder is dependent on their shareholdings for yearly income they will incur high transaction costs if they have to sell shares to provide themselves with a steady income. In these circumstances, a high dividend payout policy is preferable.

Bird in the hand theory
Gordon (1959) argues that investors value dividends (near cash) at a higher premium than they value distant, more risky, capital gains. Gordon integrated this theory into the dividend valuation model (he added a growth variable), which values equity with higher growth in dividends, at a premium, to equity that has lower growth in dividends.

Taxation: clientele effects

In the latter sections it is argued that taxation is likely to impact on an equity holder's valuation of equity depending on government taxation policy. However, an individual's personal income position will also influence the value of a particular type of dividend policy to them. Each person is entitled to a tax-free allowance for taxable income and separately each person has a tax-free capital gains allowance. Therefore, the attractiveness of a company's dividend policy will depend on the other types of income that an individual receives. The consequence of this is that a company cannot predict a policy to maximise an individual equity holder's return.

It is argued by some (see for example, Elton and Gruber (1970) and Lewellen, Stanley, Lease and Schlarbaum (1978)) that management decide on a particular policy to attract a particular type of investor and that investors choose companies to invest in because their dividend policy matches their desired income type. This is known as the *clientele effect*. It might be thought that changes in dividend policy once established will be penalised by the market; however, M&M argue that theoretically this is not the case, suggesting that it is a matter of demand and supply. So long as the market has sufficient numbers of high payout and low payout policy companies to satisfy current demand, changing dividend policy will not impact on share price. The current equity holders will just sell their shares and purchase shares in a company that suits their preference. However, in the real world, a company that changes policy regularly will be penalised as equity holders will incur transaction costs when they sell shares. This means that most companies will try to keep a stable policy, even if their net earnings fluctuate.

The signalling power of dividends

Hakansson (1982) suggests that dividend payout is used as a means of conveying information to the market. A change in dividend policy is a *signal* to the market in respect of management's views on expected future cash flows. An increase in dividend payout may reflect managerial optimism about future net cash flows, or management's views that the market has not valued the company's investment portfolio correctly. A decline in the dividend payout might reflect pessimism about maintaining net cash flows in the future. However, in most countries, the market is usually well informed in respect of expected dividend distributions. Miller (1986) suggests that it is only variations from an expected dividend policy that can be regarded as signalling. In these circumstances much publicity usually surrounds the diverging dividend payout, making it difficult for management to use this as a means of manipulating company value. Therefore, when divergences from the expected occur, they can be assumed to be ethical signalling.

Other practical issues

Legislation
Section 263 in Part VIII of the Companies Order (Northern Ireland) 1986, which deals with the distribution of a company's profits and assets, restricts the maximum dividend that a limited company can distribute

to: its accumulated realised profits less its accumulated realised losses. A further restriction is placed on plcs in section 264 to ensure that sufficient funds are also retained to cover unrealised losses. Section 264 allows a plc to make a distribution up to the point at which the company's net assets are equal to the aggregate of its called-up equity share capital and undistributable reserves. A company's **undistributable reserves** include: the share premium account; the capital redemption reserve; the excess of a company's accumulated unrealised profits, over its accumulated unrealised losses; and any other reserve identified by legislation as not distributable. A distribution should not reduce the net asset total below the balance on the latter accounts. The reasoning for this restriction is to protect the creditors of a company, by ensuring that equity holders cannot get distributions, when creditors are owed more than the assets of the company are worth. The same restrictions are contained in Part IV, sections 45 and 46 of the Companies Act 1983 (ROI).

Liquidity
As mentioned earlier in this chapter, dividends are payable out of distributable earnings and are usually made in cash. Therefore liquidity is a key influence on dividend policy. Being profitable may not be synonymous with having cash. Indeed, many growing profitable companies have cash shortages and this will influence the directors' decision in respect of the dividend policy to adopt. As discussed earlier, theoretically, it can be argued that a profitable company, with profitable projects, can borrow in the capital markets and pay a dividend. However, in practice, directors prefer to service dividend payments from a company's current resources, as there are costs and control issues associated with raising capital in the markets that are not considered in the theory.

Inflation
Linked to the previous paragraph, inflation may influence dividend policy, because of its impact on the liquid resources of a company. Inflation usually increases the working capital requirements of a company and has a direct cash requirement. In a country where inflation rates are low, this issue is not as problematic as in countries where inflation rates are quite high. Therefore, it is likely that companies located in countries with high inflation rates will adopt a more conservative payout policy.

Covenants/debt capital/long-term finance

When a company issues debt capital, it is common practice to include legally binding restrictions, called *'restrictive covenants'*, into the debt capital agreements. These restrictions serve to protect the prospective purchasers of debt capital, from actions that may erode the potential for the debt to be redeemed in the future. Restrictive covenants may limit dividends that can be paid by a company, or may require that certain minimum liquidity ratios are maintained.

Aside from covenants, a company's directors need to ensure that sufficient liquid funds are available to redeem debt capital, or pay off other types of long-term finance. In some instances directors may elect to provide for the redemption of loan stock by setting aside a portion of each year's earnings into a sinking fund. This usually requires that a higher level of earnings are retained, impacting on the level of dividends that can be distributed. Where a company is financed by a long-term loan, it will have yearly non-negotiable cash outflows, which will impact on the ability to pay cash dividends.

Stability of profits

As discussed under clientele effects, equity holders are attracted to companies based on their dividend payout policy. Due to differing marginal rates of tax, some equity holders will be attracted to companies with low payout policies, whereas other equity holders will be attracted to companies with high payout policies. The market will penalise companies that vary their policy, as there will be less demand amongst equity holders for this type of share. In the 'real world' equity holders incur transaction costs, and changing holdings in response to changes in dividend payout policy is likely to be uneconomical. Therefore, equity holders like constant, stable dividend policies and directors try to set their policy so that a constant or increasing level of dividends can be paid (Lintner, 1956). Therefore, the stability of profits from year to year is likely to impact on the level of dividend that directors choose to set. The more volatile a company's profits, the more likely that a company's directors will select a low payout policy.

Investment potential

Different companies are faced with differing investment opportunities. In addition, depending on their standing, or age, companies may incur variant levels of capital rationing. For example, it is more difficult and costly, for a young emerging company to raise capital for small projects, than it is for a large established company to raise capital for a large project. There are economies of scale associated with capital market costs. Therefore, directors will be influenced by current and predicted cash requirements for investment opportunities when deciding on the dividend payout level. It is more likely and more acceptable by the market, for a young, growing company to have higher retention levels.

Ownership and control

Particularly in smaller companies, it is likely that control of the company is held by a small number of equity holders. They may not be happy if the company issues more share capital, as this may dilute their control. In these circumstances, equity holders would be supportive of a low payout policy, ensuring that investments and future growth are financed from retained earnings.

Other distributions

Scrip dividends/Bonus issues

A **scrip dividend** is a **scrip issue**, or **bonus issue** that pays a dividend in shares. A scrip dividend capitalises distributable profits i.e. transfers an amount equal to the scrip dividend from retained earnings to equity share capital. The equity holders are allocated additional shares and can choose either to add them to their portfolio, or to sell them and release cash. Some companies that wish to maintain their liquid resources can offer a choice of either a cash dividend or an enhanced scrip dividend. An **enhanced scrip dividend** is a scrip dividend that is issued at a premium to the cash dividend. An example of a very attractive scrip dividend, was that offered by British American Tobacco industries (BAT), in 1993. BAT industries offered either: a cash dividend, or shares to the value of 1.5 times the dividend amount. 92% of their equity holders elected to receive the scrip dividend. Most enhanced scrip dividends are not as attractive, for example in the year to December 2005, Guinness Peat Group plc offered a scrip dividend alternative of one new share for every 90 shares held instead of the interim cash dividend of one pence per equity share. The value of the scrip per share turned out to be 1.06p per share, only 6% higher than the cash dividend (http://www.gpgplc.com. au/stockevents/).

Worked example 19.4   *(Bonus issue)*

At the start of 2007 Cocina plc had one million issued ordinary shares. No new shares had been issued in the prior three years. The company paid a €/£200,000 dividend in 2005, €/£210,000 in 2006 and €/£230,000 in 2007. Assume that Cocina plc made a 'one-for-two' bonus issue in 2007. Ms. Marido owns 2% of the shares in Cocina plc.

REQUIRED

Determine the impact the bonus issue will have on Ms Marido's *number of shares*, *dividend per share* and *total dividend*, in 2007; by considering the dividend she would have received had the bonus issue not taken place, compared to the situation where it has taken place.

Solution

Marido's position prior to the bonus issue was that she owned 2% of the shares in Cocina plc (1,000,000 × 2% = 20,000 shares). Had the bonus issue not taken place Marido would have been entitled to 2% of the total dividend distribution (€/£230,000 × 2% = €/£4,600). This amounts to a dividend of 23.00c/p per share.

After the bonus issue Marido holds 30,000 shares (i.e. for every two shares held, Cocina plc issued another one). Her dividend will still be 2% of the distributable amount which has not changed (dividend entitlement is €/£4,600; the dividend per share is now 15.33c/p (€/£4,600/30,000).

Therefore, though Marido holds 50% more shares, the overall value of her total holding will not increase, nor will the value of her total dividend.

Theoretically, as highlighted in example 19.4, the overall value of a company, hence equity holders' holdings will not change, as the distribution is just a paper transaction that alters the number of shares in issue. However, in many instances equity holders assume that the company will maintain the dividend per share; therefore assume that the future stream of dividends due to them will increase. This may cause share price to rise.

Stock splits

A **stock split** is where the number of shares in a company is increased by a set proportion. For example, a 'two-for-one' split, wherein two new equity shares are issued for each old share held. It may seem that this paper transaction is like a bonus/scrip issue, however, unlike a bonus issue/scrip dividend which involves a transfer from retained earnings to equity share capital, a stock split leaves the balance sheet accounts unaffected, just changing the number of shares making up the equity share capital account. The value of a stock split can be questioned from a logic perspective; however, in practice it usually does increase equity holder wealth, particularly in companies that have very high individual share prices. A split in share value makes the shares more marketable and attractive to more investors. This increases demand for the shares, hence share price. There are costs associated with a stock split and management usually only employ this technique if they consider a positive outcome will result.

Share repurchases

Share repurchases have increasingly become part of the long-term strategies of some companies. Under legislation, a company can repurchase its own shares, either by buying them in the stock market, making an offer to all equity holders, or by approaching individual equity holders. Before a share repurchase can take place, a company's management needs to obtain permission from its equity holders and holders of any stock options or warrants and also from the *Take Over Panel (UK)*. In the ROI the repurchase has to conform to the *Market Abuse Regulations, 2005*. Companies either hold the shares they buy back (as treasury shares), or cancel them. In some instances, companies transfer the repurchased shares into a trust scheme for their employees.

The reasons for share repurchase are now considered. It is argued that a share repurchase is another form of distributing earnings to equity holders. As discussed earlier, equity holders are attracted to companies with stable dividend policies, even so, they will penalise companies that hold cash that is not earning a suitable return. From the company's perspective distributing this cash as a dividend, is not a suitable option, if the company is unable to maintain that dividend level in the future. The company has two options, to distribute a well publicised *special dividend* (one-off payment) or a share repurchase. A share repurchase, though more costly to a company, has benefits. It reduces the number of shares in issue; this will drive up the earnings per share for the remaining equity holders, a factor that may affect share price.

In other instances management may feel that the market is not valuing the company's cash flows correctly, resulting in the shares being undervalued. In these instances where the company has surplus cash it may be regarded as a good investment to buy back shares and cancel them. The company will no longer have to pay a dividend on these shares. The result of the additional share activity may be interpreted as a positive signal by the market, hence driving up share price.

Where a company has volatile profits and cash flows, it may use share repurchases in years where the company has excess cash, to reduce the risk of being unable to maintain a constant dividend policy in the long term. Share repurchase can also be used to manipulate the capital structure of a company, in instances where the goal is to increase the gearing levels of the company i.e. by obtaining debt to repurchase equity. It is argued though that this may increase the risks pertaining to those remaining equity holders and the existing debt holders. Finally, share repurchases can target individual equity holders; hence can be used to buy out unwelcome equity holders.

Worked example 19.5   *(Share repurchase versus dividend payment)*

Aseo plc is an ungeared company with 1,000,000 equity shares, that are worth €/£2,000,000 (market value). The company has surplus earnings of €/£100,000 in 2007 and currently has €/£500,000 in the bank. These funds were built up to purchase a competitor; however, this investment has fallen through. The funds are only earning 2% per annum and there are no immediate investment opportunities available to the company. The company has a track record of paying a set amount of dividend per share, which increases slightly, each year. Earnings fluctuate from year to year.

Continued

REQUIRED

a) Discuss the options available to the company.

b) Show using an example of an equity holder (Ms. Mujer) who owns 10% of the share capital of the company; that theoretically her wealth will not alter if the company were to distribute all the surplus cash, either as a dividend or as a capital repurchase (ignore taxation)?

c) Which option would the equity holder prefer if she were a higher rate tax payer?

Solution

a) As there are no immediate investment plans, the company would be best placed by returning the excess funds to equity holders, for them to invest, to earn a return that is equal to, or above, their cost of capital. The company is currently earning a return of 2%, which is low. In the long term retaining funds which earn such a low premium will damage equity holder wealth and the value of the company.

The surplus funds were accumulated for a major investment. This has fallen though. Therefore the excess cash position is a one-off scenario. The company should treat it as such and should either issue a one-off large special dividend payment, or should repurchase its shares. Both methods will return funds to the equity holders, but will not impact on the required payout ratio that is expected by equity holders. Given the volatile nature of the company's earnings it might be argued that, after paying the yearly dividend, a share repurchase is the best option, as this reduces pressure on the company to maintain its policy of distributing a growing dividend per share in the future.

b) *Scenario 1*
In the first scenario it is assumed that Aseo plc distributes the surplus €/£500,000 by way of a dividend.

Continued

Before the distribution, the value of Ms. Mujer's equity will be €/£200,000 (€/£2,000,000 × 10%). Ms. Mujer will receive a dividend of €/£50,000 (€/£500,000 × 10%). The effect of the distribution on company value will be to reduce it by the resource outflow i.e. the €/£500,000, to €/£1,500,000. Therefore, Ms. Mujer's equity will now be worth €/£150,000 (€/£1,500,000 × 10%), though she will also have the €/£50,000 dividend leaving her overall value unchanged. The difference is that she can take the €/£50,000 and invest it in other companies to earn a return in excess of the return the funds were earning in Aseo plc.

Scenario 2

In the second scenario it is assumed that Aseo plc buys back 25% of its own shares and cancels them. It is assumed that all equity holders are tendered for the buy back and all accept.

As in scenario one, before the share buyback, the value of Ms. Mujer's equity will be €/£200,000 (€/£2,000,000 × 10%). When the share buyback takes place, 25% of Ms. Mujer's shares will be repurchased by the company. This will equate to €/£200,000 X 25% = €/£50,000. The company will experience an outflow of its value equal to the total share repurchase amount i.e. the €/£500,000 leaving it worth €/£1,500,000. Ms. Mujer will be left with shares worth €/£150,000 and will also have the cash received from the sale of her shares (€/£50,000), which she can invest elsewhere.

The difference between the two options is that the number of shares in issue under scenario one will remain the same, and the future dividend payout will keep rising. Under scenario two the number of shares in issue will fall; therefore, there will be large reduction in the next cash outflow that Aseo plc has to distribute, without the payout policy changing and the *earnings per share* will increase.

Continued

c)   If Ms Mujer is a higher rate tax payer who is paying income tax at the high tax bracket, she may be more interested in the share buyback option. The sale of shares are treated as a capital gain by the tax authorities and the tax payable will be calculated on the difference between the cash received and the amount paid for the shares (indexed for any time allowances relating to the number of years the shares are held). In addition, each individual has a capital gains tax annual exemption allowance. If Ms. Mujer has not made any other capital sales in the year, then the whole allowance may be available for set-off against any net income made on the sale of these shares.

Research findings in relation to dividend policy

Prior to M&M's theoretical irrelevancy paradigm, the business world operated on the assumption that high dividend payout policies were optimal for equity holder wealth. Even though M&M's irrelevancy paradigm is set in an unreal world, where there are many assumptions, this theory and the residual theory ideals did impact on the attitudes of many in the business world. In particular, management started to question the logic of distributing a dividend, when the funds could be utilised by the company to earn high returns, which in turn would increase equity holder wealth. The result is that some companies adopt a policy of no distributions, claiming that they can invest the monies better than equity holders could (for example, Microsoft).

Theoretical models are usually given credence with empirical results. The impact and relevance of the dividend decision has stimulated many researchers to investigate empirically the relationship between earnings and dividends. A simple overview would suggest that earnings are a key determinant of dividend policy. However, due to the behaviour of management i.e. maintenance of a constant policy, this relationship is difficult to test appropriately. Risk is considered important, with in general, low-risk companies electing to payout higher dividends and high-risk companies electing to payout lower dividends.

In respect of setting dividend policy, an influential study is Lintner's research, published in (1956). He interviewed 28 companies and reported that management considered that the dividend decision was important.

Based on the information obtained from management interviews, he developed a simple model to capture the expected change in dividends from managements' perspective. He found that, last year's dividend provides the basis for the current year's dividend and that management believe that equity holders prefer a stable payout policy, which does not reduce the dividend level and indeed, increases it slightly. The dividend level is a set proportion of current earnings. He also found that management incorporated a safety factor into their calculations, to reduce the impact of fluctuations in yearly earnings. The model he suggested is as follows:

Dividend change in year = Annual upward drift + (safety factor
× (current earnings × target ratio))
− dividend of the previous year.

Later empirical studies reported findings that support Lintner's model (one example is, Farrelly Baker and Edelman, 1986).

Worked example 19.6   *(Target payout dividend)*

Despacho plc earned €2,000,000 in the year. Last year it paid a dividend of €/£600,000. The annual growth in Despacho plc's dividend is about 5%. The directors have indicated that they aim to pay out 40% of the company's earnings, though have a safety factor of 80%.

REQUIRED

Calculate the dividend to distribute in the current year using Lintner's model?

Solution

Lintner's model:

Dividend change in year = Annual upward drift + (safety factor
× (current earnings × target ratio))
− dividend of the previous year.

Continued

Where the annual upward drift is: €/£30,000 (€/£600,000 × 5%)
The safety factor is: 80%
Current earnings are: €/£2,000,000
The target ratio is: 40%
The prior year dividend is: €/£600,000

Therefore the
Dividend change in year = €/£30,000 + (80%
× (€/£2,000,000 × 40%))
− €/£600,000
= €/£70,000
The current year dividend = €/£600,000 + €/£70,000
= €/£670,000

Conclusion

Dividend policy is a complicated issue that is influenced by various factors, which taken together, result in differing policies being more appropriate for companies depending on their differing situations with, in some instances, a policy of zero payout being considered acceptable. There is support for the ideals of M&M; however, it is recognised that in the real world their assumptions undermine their theory. Residual theory also has informed the debate and may, in part, explain why younger companies with greater investment opportunities are expected to have lower payouts. Empirical research on dividend policy has reported that dividend policy does influence company value and earnings and risk are also considered major influences.

The practicalities of setting a dividend policy is that management have to predict their cash flow requirements for many years in advance. This process separately considers expected cash outflows to service current operations and planned investment (and its corresponding expected cash flows). Other repayments are also factored into the equation. The resultant pattern of cash flows will influence management as to the dividend policy that they can adopt. Underlying the whole process is the belief that a constant dividend policy is most appropriate. The risks associated with the projections, including the variability in net cash flows will influence management's decision as to the target percentage to set and the safety factor to build into their calculations.

In general, younger companies with many growth opportunities are more able to set a low payout policy; older more established companies that may have less growth opportunities are expected to distribute more each year. As discussed, tax is also important and changes in government policy in respect of the difference between income tax rates and capital gains tax rates may influence dividend policy. However, if a company were to change their policy it is considered more appropriate to do it gradually over time, or to use other means of manipulating their payout, such as share repurchases, bonus issues or special dividends. These actions are not usually read as signals by the market; hence share price should remain in equilibrium (assuming it was in the first place).

Examination standard question

Worked example 19.7

REX COVERINGS Ltd. is a family owned business engaged in the distribution of bedroom furnishings and accessories. The company was established 60 years ago and 34 descendants of the founder now own all the equity shares.

The company has recently appointed John Smith as Managing Director. He is not a member of the family which owns the business and does not have an equity holding in the company.

The family members do not wish to dispose of their equity holdings as they are content with the receipt of annual dividends. There is however an internal market for shares in REX COVERINGS Ltd. between family members. This allows any individual who requires liquidity to dispose of his/her equity holding.

Continued

The equity structure of REX COVERINGS Ltd. is as follows:

500,000 equity shares of €/£1	€/£500,000
450,000 preference shares of €/£1	€/£450,000

The equity shares, which are owned by family members, carry entitlement to vote, participate in a winding-up and control the appointment of Directors.

The preference shares are owned by a merchant bank, WESTBANK plc. Some years ago REX COVERINGS Ltd. experienced financial difficulties and WESTBANK plc provided a loan to the company. This loan was paid off. However, as part of the rescue package, the bank subscribed for preference shares. These shares have no rights, except that an annual dividend of €/£75,000 must be paid. If the dividend is not paid, the preference shares are convertible into 15% of the enlarged equity share capital of the company.

REX COVERINGS Ltd. has bank funding of €/£4.5 million (overdraft and term loan). The overdraft is used to fund short-term working capital requirements and to enable payment of annual dividends.

Up to now the company distributed its annual profits by way of dividend. In 20X7 the equity dividends totalled €/£2 per share.

John Smith is keen to expand the business and undertake new projects. He is concerned about a number of issues including the following:

(i) Whether he can invest in projects which require significant initial costs and which would, therefore, reduce profits for a period with consequent dividend implications?

(ii) What discount rates he might use to evaluate projects?

He has retained you to advise him on these matters.

REQUIRED

a) Explain why the views of equity holders and John Smith might differ on the growth strategy for REX COVERINGS Ltd.

5 Marks

Continued

b) Draft, for John Smith, the key points he should include in a document which he might send to equity holders suggesting a change in dividend policy and the reasons for such a change.

10 Marks

c) Calculate, assuming absence of any change in existing dividend policy, the discount rate which John Smith should use in evaluating new projects. Assume a required rate of return on equity of 20% and a Corporation Tax rate of 40%.

5 Marks

Total 20 Marks

(ICAI, MABF II, Questions and Solutions Manual, 2000/01)

Solution

a) In the absence of a remuneration package linked to the achievement of the equity holders' objectives, John Smith is likely to have views on the company's growth strategy which are quite different to those of equity holders.

Significant growth by re-investment of profits is likely to be favoured by John Smith. This would increase his profile as managing director. This desire is apparent from his desire to expand the business and undertake new projects.

The equity holders appear to be quite content with the sizeable dividend income, and they have no desire to realise capital by obtaining a stock exchange quotation. There is, in any case, an internal market to cater for such a need. The growth envisaged by John Smith; however, will require substantial financing. The company is already heavily borrowed and the equity holders are unlikely to inject capital into the company. A stock exchange quotation seems therefore to be a logical objective as far as John Smith is concerned. This is likely to direct his management decisions towards the expectations of potential institutional investors.

Continued

In an overall sense, John Smith will look to investment opportunities as providing the basis for long-term growth. This contrasts sharply with the attitude of the family equity holders, for whom dividends are of primary importance, with reinvestment being a mere residual.

b)   A document addressing possible change in dividend policy should address the following:

(i)   *Ability to pay dividends*
The policy of distributing annual profits by way of dividend may cause the company liquidity problems, as profit does not necessarily equate to a cash surplus.

(ii)   *Taxation*
A reduction in dividends might have the beneficial effect of reducing some equity holders' marginal income tax rate on distributions.

(iii)   *Historic pattern of dividends*
A policy of paying out all of the current year's earnings as dividends results in an erratic and unpredictable return for equity holders.
The policy has also resulted in increased borrowings and interest charges.

(iv)   *Impact of a more orthodox dividend policy*
A dividend of a fixed amount per share with an annual dividend growth rate would have the following advantages:
- Stability of income for equity holders.
- Ability of company to re-invest profits for future growth, thus securing future dividend payments.

(v)   *Raising finance*
- The cost of debt finance, used to pay dividends, is likely to be higher than borrowings for capital investment purposes.

Continued

- A policy of full dividend payout is unlikely to facilitate a flotation in the future. A flotation might allow family members easier access to a market for their shares and a better price per share.

(vi) Conversion of loan stock

A full payout policy restricts the ability of management to ensure profitability on an annual basis, thus increasing the risk of conversion of the loan stock.

The annual cost of conversion to the family equity holders could be estimated, based on the 20X7 dividend of €/£1m (500,000 × €/£2), plus the preference dividend saved of €/£75,000:

	€/£
Total dividend	1,075,000
Receivable by family (85%)	913,750
Received by family 20X7 (100%)	1,000,000
Reduction of annual family income on conversion	86,250

c)   Discount rate for new projects

One approach in deriving a discount rate is to calculate a company's WACC:

(i) Valuation

Ordinary shares

Dividend (D_1): €/£2 per share (assume zero growth)

Required return on equity (Ke): 20%

$$P_0 = \frac{D_1}{Ke}$$

$$\text{Equity value} = \frac{€/£2}{0.2} = €/£10$$

$$\text{Total value} = €/£10 \times 500,000$$
$$= €/£5,000,000$$

Continued

Preference shares

On the assumption that the dividend of €/£75,000 represents a reasonable market rate and that conversion is unlikely, then the nominal value of €/£450,000 can also be taken as the market value.

Term loan

It is assumed in this solution that long-term loans comprise €/£3m of total bank borrowings.

(ii) Cost

- Equity shares   20.00%
- Preference shares
  (€/£75,000/€/£450,000)   16.67%
- Loans
  (interest rate of 13% assumed)   7.80% $(13\% \times (1-0.4))$

(iii) WACC

	Market value €/£'000	Cost €/£'000
Equity capital	5,000	1,000
Preference shares	450	75
Loans	3,000	234
	8,450	1,309

$$\text{WACC} = \frac{€/£1,309,000}{€/£8,450,000} \times 100 = 15.49\%$$

This WACC is a valid discount rate, only for projects which have the same level of risk that is on average incurred on the company's existing projects.

KEY TERMS

Bird in the hand theory	Payment date
Bonus issue	Payout policy
Clientele effect	Relevancy theory
Cum-dividend	Residual dividend theory
Declared date of record	Retentions policy
Distribution	Scrip issue
Dividend	Share repurchase
Enhanced scrip dividend	Signal
Ex-dividend	Special dividend
Final dividend	Stock split
Interim dividend	Traditional theory
Irrelevancy theory	Undistributable reserves
Lintner's model	

REVIEW QUESTIONS

1. Describe the process, companies and markets adopt, to clarify who is entitled to a dividend, given that share trading does not cease.
2. According to the relevancy theory, should a dividend of 10c/p be distributed, if the value of the share cum-dividend is €/£1.80 and is predicted to move to €/£1.68 ex-dividend?
3. What are the assumptions underlying M&M's irrelevancy theorem?
4. Salon plc has earnings of €/£5,000,000 and a cost of capital amounting to 15%. In the past it has paid out 50% of its earnings as a dividend. In this current year, three investment projects are available as follows:

Project	Cost €/£'000	Expected return %
A	1,500	12%
B	2,000	18%
C	2,500	22%

REQUIRED

Assuming the company is going to apply residual dividend theory, indicate the dividend payout percentage that will result.

5.   Explain the clientele effect.

6.   Optimal Ltd. currently has a share price of €/£1.25 per share. The Board of Directors is currently considering the level of dividend that should be proposed in respect of the year ended 31 December 20X8. The board has researched the market's reaction to the dividend levels under consideration, and the resulting expected ex-dividend share prices are estimated as follows;

Dividend	Expected ex-dividend share price
Nil	100c/p
4.0c/p	117c/p
4.5c/p	120c/p
5.0c/p	134c/p
5.5c/p	136c/p
6.0c/p	128c/p

A dividend of 4.5c/p per share was paid in respect of the year ended 31 December 20X7. The average rate of income tax which Optimal Ltd.'s equity holders will pay on dividend income is estimated at 30%.

REQUIRED

Calculate the level of dividend which should be proposed by Optimal Ltd., for 20X8.

7.

a)   Discuss briefly the factors that might influence a private company's choice as to whether or not to pay a dividend and the amount of such dividend.

6 Marks

b)   The managing directors of three profitable listed public companies discussed their companies' dividend policies at a business lunch.

COMPANY A

Has deliberately paid no dividends for the last five years.

COMPANY B

Always pays a dividend of 50% of earnings after taxation.

COMPANY C

Maintains a low but constant dividend per share (after adjusting for the general price index) and offers regular scrip issues and shareholder concessions.

Each managing director is convinced that his company's policy is maximising shareholder wealth.

REQUIRED

What are the advantages and disadvantages of the alternative dividend policies of the three companies? Discuss the circumstances under which each managing director might be correct in his belief that his company's dividend policy is maximising shareholder wealth. State clearly any assumptions that you make.

<u>12</u> Marks
Total <u>18</u> Marks
(ICAI, MABF II, Summer 2006, Q7)

CHALLENGING QUESTIONS

1.   DEAKIN plc

a)   The M&M dividend irrelevance theorem is based upon a number of assumptions including the absence of taxation and transactions and flotation costs.

Critically discuss the assumptions upon which the irrelevance proposition is based.

6 Marks

b) DEAKIN plc, a quoted textile manufacturer, has followed a policy in recent years of paying out a steadily increasing dividend per share as shown below:

Year	Earnings per	Dividend (net)	Dividend
20X3	11.8c/p	5.0c/p	2.4
20X4	12.5c/p	5.5c/p	2.3
20X5	14.6c/p	6.0c/p	2.4
20X6	13.5c/p	6.5c/p	2.1
20X7	16.0c/p	7.3c/p	2.2

DEAKIN plc has recently made the 20X7 dividend payment and, therefore, the shares are currently quoted ex-dividend. The Board of Directors is considering a change in strategy whereby more of the company's financing will be generated from internal sources. This will involve reducing the dividend payout in 20X8 to 5c/p (net) per share.

The investment projects thus funded will increase the growth rate of the company's earnings and dividends to 14%, although some operating managers have suggested that the rate of growth is unlikely to exceed 12%. The overall return required by the company's equity holders, is 16%.

REQUIRED

(i) Estimate the market price per share for DEAKIN plc prior to the change in policy, using the dividend growth model.

4 Marks

(ii) Assess the likely impact of the proposed change on the company's share price.

4 Marks

(iii) Discuss the possible reaction of the equity holders and the market to the proposed change in the light of the previous dividend policy.

4 Marks
Total _18_ Marks
(ICAI, MABF II, Autumn 1998, Q6)

2.   BOTANIC plc

a)   M&M claim that a company cannot affect the market value of its equity by altering its dividend policy.

REQUIRED

Discuss the assumptions necessary to sustain this proposition.

8 Marks

b)   BOTANIC plc, a quoted engineering company, has just announced its final results for the year ended 31 December 20X7. Earnings Per Share (EPS) and Dividends Per Share (DPS) for the past five years are as follows:

	20X3	20X4	20X5	20X6	20X7
EPS (c/p)	61	64	71	73	76
DPS (c/p)	38	40	41	42	44

The board of directors believes that the future annual growth rate in dividends will be consistent with the average growth rate in dividends above.

BOTANIC plc's Beta factor has been calculated at 1.4.

The risk-free rate of interest is 7% and analysts are forecasting a 12% per annum return on the stock exchange index over the next few years.

REQUIRED

(i) Using the CAPM and Gordon's dividend growth model, calculate the share price that might be expected.

5 Marks

(ii) Give reasons why the share price might react differently to (i) above.

5 Marks
Total 18 Marks
(ICAI, MABF II, Autumn 1997, Q7)

3.   M&M

Most quoted companies attempt to maintain a relatively stable dividend payout policy, despite M&M's contention that dividend policy is irrelevant for company valuation purposes.

REQUIRED

a)   Critically appraise M&M's argument suggesting reasons why, in practice, corporate management appear to regard dividend policy as an important financial strategy decision.

10 Marks

b)   Suggest situations in which you would *not* recommend the pursuance of a stable dividend policy.

5 Marks

c)   Assume that a new system of taxation was introduced which favoured the distribution of profits and penalised retained earnings. Discuss how this development might influence:

(i) Corporate financial management.

(ii) Equity holders.

10 Marks
Total 25 Marks
(ICAI, MABF II, Autumn 1994, Q5)

4.   BEL plc

BEL plc was formed in 20X0 as a result of a management buyout by two employees of their former company. The buyout was funded with the assistance of venture capital institutions which were issued with 0% €/£100 convertible debentures while the founders were issued with equity shares.

It was agreed at the time of the buyout that the founders would seek a full stock exchange listing within a certain timeframe and the convertible debentures would be converted to fully paid equity shares just prior to the listing. The agreement also precluded BEL plc from issuing any long-term debt or paying any dividends while the convertible debentures were outstanding.

On 7 December 20X4 BEL plc obtained its stock exchange listing and on that date the company's issued share capital consisted of 10,000,000 ordinary shares of €/£1 each. The company's earnings and dividends since the listing have been as follows:

Year ended 31 May	Profits after tax €/£	Dividends per share
20X5	5,066,000	9.7c/p
20X6	6,133,000	12.0c/p
20X7	8,875,000	14.0c/p

The company's profits after tax are expected to be in the region of €/£10 million for 20X8 and are expected to grow by 13% per annum. The company's share price is currently 380c/p.

REQUIRED

a) Consider whether BEL plc's shares are under or overvalued at 380c/p, using the CAPM and the dividend valuation model.

8 Marks

b) Comment on BEL plc's dividend policy since the company went public and suggest factors, which should be taken into account by the board, in formulating a dividend policy for the future.

6 Marks
Total 14 Marks
(ICAI, MABF II, Questions and Solutions Manual, 2000/01)

5.   RACKETT plc

a) Recent empirical evidence suggests that dividend decisions in Irish companies are taken with reference to the factor of dividend stability, but some consideration is also given to other factors.

REQUIRED

Outline the main factors involved in the dividend decision and explain why the factor of dividend stability is seen to be most important.

10 Marks

b)   RACKETT plc distributes 20% of all available profits annually. The company is financed by 500,000 €/£1 ordinary shares and €/£150,000 10% fixed rate debentures. One of the conditions imposed by RACKETT plc is that the debentures are to be repaid by a series of equal annual payments (including interest and principal) over three years. Annual payments are to be made at the end of each year.

The profits before interest for the three year period, for which the debentures are being repaid, are as follows:

	Year 1	*Year 2*	*Year 3*
	€/£'000	*€/£'000*	*€/£'000*
Profit before interest	150	170	190

The rate of corporation tax is 18%.

REQUIRED

Calculate the annual average growth rate in dividends payable by RACKETT plc over the three-year period.

8 Marks
Total 18 Marks
(ICAI, MABF II, Autumn 2000, Q7)

6.   **WILLIAMS plc**

WILLIAMS plc is a company involved in the software industry. The company has been in existence for seven years and has been very successful to date specialising in the development of e-learning educational products. The company makes average annual operating profits of €/£450,000. Income from investments amounts to €/£20,000 per annum. Corporation tax is charged at a rate of 30% per annum. The company is financed by 400,000 €/£0.50 equity shares and €/£20,000 of 8% irredeemable debentures.

The directors are considering the company's dividend policy and the following views emerged from discussions at the recent Board meeting.

Director A is concerned that the company has not paid any dividend to the equity holders to date. He is concerned that, if the company does not distribute some profit soon, it will reflect poorly on the company's share price. Director A is proposing a dividend of €/£0.10 per share next year with a growth rate thereafter of 1% per annum.

Director B is of the view that the company should distribute 100% of its profits each year and that, if the company requires additional finance for future investments, such finance could be raised from external sources.

Director C is of the view that the company should eliminate the need to pay dividends by re-purchasing all of its equity and replacing it with debt. He has recently read in an academic journal that *'to maximise equity holder wealth in a world with tax, a company should gear itself as much as possible.'*

The company's required rate of return on an investment in the e-learning business is 18%.

REQUIRED

a) Discuss each of the proposals that the directors have made in relation to the future dividend policy of the company.

9 Marks

b) Calculate, using the dividend valuation model, the market price of the company's share under each of the following scenarios:

   (i) A dividend of 10c/p per share is paid out in the current year, with annual growth thereafter of 1%.

   (ii) A dividend of 100% of the annual profits is paid out annually.

5 Marks

c) Comment on the results to part b). Include in your comments an explanation as to why the actual market price of the company's shares may not be the same as the figures calculated above.

4 Marks
Total 18 Marks
(ICAI, MABF II, Summer 2002, Q6)

7.   DIVIDEND POLICY

'......dividends......cannot increase shareholder wealth; only good investment decisions increase shareholder wealth.'

Sharipo and Barbirer: Modern Corporate Finance 2000

a)   Discuss briefly the above quotation.

4 Marks

b)   Outline FOUR factors which a company is likely to take into account in deciding on its dividend policy.

4 Marks

c)   Describe whether each of the following is likely to increase, decrease or be irrelevant to the amount of dividends paid by companies. Give brief reasons for your answer in both cases.

(i) An increase in the rate of capital gains tax with no corresponding increase in the rate of income tax.

2 Marks

(ii) The sudden onset of a sharp economic downturn.

3 Marks

d)   Outline the reasons why three different external parties might wish to forecast an organisation's future financial performance.

5 Marks
Total 18 Marks
(ICAI, MABF II, Autumn 2004, Q7)

8.   SAYANG plc

b)   SAYANG plc ('SAYANG') has earnings available for equity shareholders of €/£ 2,000,000 and has 500,000 equity shares in issue. The current share price is €/£60 per share. The company is currently considering the payment of €/£2 per share in cash dividends.

REQUIRED

(i)   Calculate the company's current earnings per share (EPS) and price/earnings (P/E) ratio.

2 Marks

(ii) If the company can buy back its own shares at €/£62 per share, how many shares can be purchased in lieu of making the proposed cash dividend payment?

1 Mark

(iii) How much will the EPS be after the proposed buy-back? Explain your reasoning.

2 Marks

(iv) If the P/E ratio prior to the buyback continues to apply, what will the market price of the shares, be (after the buy back)?

1 Mark

(v)   Compare and contrast the EPS before and after the proposed buyback.

2 Marks

(vi) Compare and contrast the equity holders' position under the dividend payment and buyback alternatives.

_3 Marks
Total 11 Marks
(ICAI, MABF II, Autumn 2007, Q6(b))

APPENDICES

APPENDIX 1

FINANCIAL MATHEMATICS FOR ASSESSING THE TIME VALUE OF MONEY

An appreciation of the time value of money is crucial for business finance decision making. All business finance financial decisions involve determining the current value of future cash flows. There are several formulae and index tables which can assist in this evaluation. The formulae are used to calculate the Present Value (PV) of cash flows and the Terminal Value (TV) of cash flows (otherwise known as the Future Value (FV)). The tables are reproduced in appendices three to five.

Terminal value

The *TV* of a cash flow represents the future value of that cash flow. It is the actual amount of cash that a company expects to receive. The TV is calculated using the following formula:

$$TV = PV(1+r)^n$$

Where PV is the present value, r is the discount rate and n is the number of years the cash flows will be received in the future. For example:

Worked example 1   (TV)

Primavera Ltd. has just placed €/£500,000 in a four-year fixed interest deposit account earning 6% per annum.

REQUIRED

What is the TV of this investment on its maturity?

Solution

The TV will equal: €/£500,000 $(1.06)^4$ = €/£631,238.

Worked example 2   (TV)

In addition to the €/£500,000 deposited as in worked example 1, Primavera Ltd. plans to put a further €/£500,000 in the same account next year and to leave it deposit it for the remaining three years. The bank has guaranteed the fixed rate of interest of the second deposit.

REQUIRED

What is the TV of this investment on its maturity?

Solution

The TV will equal: €/£500,000 $(1.06)^4$ + €/£500,000 $(1.06)^3$ = €/£1,226,746.

Terminal value factors $((1+r)^n)$ are included in appendix five 'Terminal Value Factor Tables' for rates ranging from 1% to 20% for a 20 year period.

Present value: discount factors

Cash is worth more the sooner it is received, as cash can be invested to earn a return. Receiving cash in the future is the same as receiving the TV of a current cash flow. Indeed, there is a direct link between PV and TV which can be obtained by rearranging the previous formula:

$$PV = TV/(1+r)^n$$

Where PV is the present value, r is the discount rate, n is the number of years the cash flows will be received in the future and TV is the expected future cash flow. This formula is commonly split into two parts for ease of calculation with the TV being separated from the portion of the formula which makes the adjustment for the time value of money. This portion of the formula is commonly referred to as the discount factor and is expressed as follows:

$$\text{Discount factor} = 1/(1+r)^n$$

Where r is the discount rate and n is the number of years the cash flows will be received in the future. The discount factors for rates ranging from 1% to 20% for a 20 year period are provided in appendix three 'Present Value Discount Factor Table'. Each discount factor is calculated in the following manner:

Worked example 3   (PV discount factors)

Assume that the annual time value of money is 8%.

REQUIRED

a)   Calculate the PV discount factor that should be applied to a cash flow expected in one year's time.

b)   Calculate the PV discount factor that should be applied to a cash flow expected in five years time.

Solution

a)   The PV discount factor is $1/(1.08)^1 = 0.926$

b)   The PV discount factor is $1/(1.08)^5 = 0.681$

These PV discount factors can then be utilised to determine the PV of a future cash flow as depicted in the next example:

> **Worked example 4**   (PV)
>
> Assume that the annual time value of money is 8%.
>
> **REQUIRED**
>
> a)   Calculate the PV of €/£500,000 to be received in one year's time.
> b)   Calculate the PV of €/£500,000 to be received in five years time.
>
> **Solution**
>
> a)   The PV is €/£500,000 × 0.926 = €/£463,000
> b)   The PV is €/£500,000 × 0.681 = €/£340,500

This example shows the importance of taking into account the time value of money. If €/£340,500 were received by the company now, it could be invested at a discount rate of 8%, which will result in a TV of €/£500,000 in five years time.

Annuities

An *annuity* describes a certain pattern of cash flows, wherein a set amount of cash flow is received, or paid, over a set period of time. For example, receiving €/£10,000 every year for five years would be described as a five-year annuity of €/£10,000. In business finance, it is important to be able to work out the PV of an annuity. The principles outlined in the previous section can be applied to the cash flows and the PV of each individual receipt calculated and then totalled to give a single PV figure. Alternatively, an annuity factor can be applied to the annuity amount to determine the overall PV. These two approaches are now examined.

Worked example 5   (Annuities)

Primavera Ltd.'s insurance company has agreed to pay the company €/£320,000 each year for the next three years.

Assume that the annual time value of money is 8%.

REQUIRED

a)   Calculate the present value of the annuity assuming the first payment will be received on the last day of the year (Use two approaches – (i) calculate the present value of each individual cash flow then total these to find the overall PV of the annuity; (ii) calculate the PV using the annuity factor tables – showing how the annuity factor is determined).

b)   Calculate the PV of the annuity assuming the first payment will be received on the first day of the year (use the quickest approach).

Solution

a)   (i) The PV of the cash flow received at the end of the year is:
        €/£320,000 × 0.926 = €/£296,320.

     The PV of the cash flow received at the end of year two is:
        €£320,000 × 0.857 = €/£274,240.

     The PV of the cash flow received at the end of year three is:
        €/£320,000 × 0.794 = €/£254,080.

     The PV of the annuity is the sum of these outcomes:
        €/£296,320 + €/£274,240 + €/£254,080 = €/£824,640.

     (ii) The annuity factor provided by the annuity factor tables, for an annuity of three years at 8% is 2.577. This factor represents the sum of the discount factors for the years one to three (0.926 + 0.857 + 0.794). The annuity cash flow is multiplied by this factor to give a PV of €/£824,640 (€/£320,000 × 2.577).

Continued

> b)   In this scenario the first receipt does not need to be adjusted for the time value of money, as it is received immediately. Therefore, the cash flows will be €/£320,000 received immediately, followed by a two year annuity of €/£320,000. The PV will be €/£320,000+(€/£320,000×1.783)=€/890,560.

Annuity factor tables are provided in appendix four for rates ranging from 1% to 20% for annual periods up to 20 years.

Perpetuities

A *perpetuity* is a term to describe a pattern of cash flows, wherein a set amount of cash will be received, or paid, at regular even intervals (usually yearly) indefinitely. The PV of a perpetuity can be determined using the following formula:

$$\text{Perpetuity} = \text{Periodic cash flow}/r$$

Where r is the discount rate.

Worked example 6   (Perpetuity)

Primavera Ltd.'s insurance company has agreed to pay the company €/£320,000 each year in perpetuity. Assume that the annual time value of money is 8%.

REQUIRED

a)   Calculate the PV of the perpetuity assuming the first receipt will be received on the last day of the year.
b)   Calculate the PV of the perpetuity assuming the first receipt will be received immediately.

Solution

a)   The PV is: €/£320,000/0.08=€/£4,000,000.
b)   The PV is: €/£320,000+(€/£320,000/0.08)=€/£4,320,000.

Some of the models used to estimate a company's share price or bond price are adjustments to the perpetuity formula. They use expected future dividend receipts or interest receipts as proxies for the annual cash flow expected.

Integrated examples

Worked example 7

Primavera Ltd.'s insurance company has agreed to pay the company €/£320,000 each year for the next three years, commencing one year from now. Primavera Ltd. invests these sums immediately to a fund that earns at 6% and matures at the end of the three years. Assume that the annual time value of money is 8%.

REQUIRED

a)   Calculate the TV of this annuity.
b)   Calculate the PV of this annuity.

Solution

a)   The TV is $(€/£320,000 \times (1.06)^2) + (€/£320,000 \times 1.06) + €/£320,000) = €/£1,018,752$.

b)   The PV is $€/£1,018,752/(1.08)^3 = €/£808,718$.

Worked example 8

Primavera Ltd.'s insurance company has agreed to pay the company €/£320,000 each year for the next three years, the first receipt commences one year from now, followed by €/£500,000 in perpetuity, commencing at the start of year four (the first receipt being at the end of the year). Assume a discount rate of 8%.

Continued

REQUIRED

Calculate the PV of these cash flows.

Solution

The PV of the annuity is: €/£320,000 × 2.577 = €/£824,640

The PV of the perpetuity at the start of year four is: €/£500,000/0.08 = €/£6,250,000. This has to be discounted to the present time. The first day of year four equates to the last day of year three. Therefore, the PV of the perpetuity is: €/£6,250,000/$(1.08)^3$ = €/£4,961,452.

Therefore the PV of the total cash flows is: €/£824,640 + €/£4,961,452 = €/£5,786,092.

APPENDIX 2

USEFUL FORMULAE

Accounting rate of return (for company/share valuation)

$$\text{Company value} = \frac{\text{Estimated future profits}}{\text{Required return on capital employed}} \times 100$$

Accounting rate of return (for investment appraisal)

$$\text{ARR (total investment)} = \frac{\text{Average annual profit}}{\text{Initial capital invested}} \times 100$$

$$\text{ARR (average investment)} = \frac{\text{Average annual profit}}{\text{Average capital invested}} \times 100$$

Where the average annual profit is the total profit for the whole period (after depreciation) divided by the life of the investment in years and the average capital invested is the initial capital cost, plus the expected disposal value, divided by two.

Adjusted present value

$$\text{APV} = \text{Vu} + \text{Dt} - \text{PV of issue costs}$$

Where Vu is the present value of the cash flows from a project discounted using an ungeared cost of equity, Dt is the present value of the interest tax shield, for the debt being used to finance that particular project and PV is the present value of the issue costs.

Asset replacement

An asset should be replaced when:

$$(b) + (c) < (a)$$

Where (a) is the cost of owning the asset; (b) is the replacement cost of the asset; and (c) is the cost of owning the new asset.

Average inventory (manufacturing entity)

$$\text{Average inventory} = \frac{\text{Reorder level} + \text{Batch size} - \text{Demand during production period}}{2}$$

Average number of days' inventory

$$\text{Average number of days' inventory} = \frac{\text{Inventory value} \times 365}{\text{Cost of sales}} = \text{Days}$$

Average trade payables period

$$\text{Average trade payables period} = \frac{\text{Trade payables} \times 365}{\text{Credit purchases}} = \text{Days}$$

Average trade receivables period

$$\text{Average trade receivables period} = \frac{\text{Trade receivables} \times 365}{\text{Credit sales}} = \text{Days}$$

Baumol model

$$Q = \sqrt{\frac{2FS}{i}}$$

Where Q is the amount to be released from the deposit account or securities each time the cash balance reaches zero, i is the interest rate on the deposit account/securities that is being lost by not having the cash in the higher-rate option, S is the usage or demand level for the period being considered and F is the fixed cost per withdrawal or purchase/sale of security.

Baumol model (interest forgone)

$$\text{Interest forgone cost} = \text{Average cash balance} \times \text{Interest rate}$$

$$= \frac{Q}{2} \times i$$

Where Q is the amount to be released from a deposit account or from securities and i is the interest rate on the deposit account or return on the securities.

Baumol model (total cash holding costs)

$$\text{Total costs} = \text{Opportunity cost of interest forgone} + \text{Transaction costs}$$

Baumol model (total transaction costs)

$$\text{Total transaction costs} = \text{Number of withdrawals} \times \text{Fixed cost per transaction}$$

$$= \frac{S}{Q} \times F$$

Where S is the cash usage or cash demand level for the period, Q is the order amount of cash and F is the fixed cost per withdrawal/purchase/sale of securities.

Binomial model

$$C_0 = H(P - P_L/(1+r))$$

Where C_0 is the value of the call option with one period to the exercise date, P is the current share price, P_L is the lower value of the share expected at the end of the period, r is the risk-free rate of return and H is the hedging ratio.

Black-Scholes option valuation model

$$P_0 = PN(d_1) - \frac{E}{e^{rt}} N(d_2)$$

Where P_0 is the current value of the option, P is the current value of the asset, E is the exercise price, e is the exponential constant (2.7183), r is the risk-free rate of interest for the period and t is the time (in years) remaining in the option contract. $N(d_1)$ and $N(d_2)$ are values of the cumulative normal distribution, defined as:

$$d_1 = \frac{Ln(P/E) + (r + \sigma^2/2)t}{\sigma t^{1/2}}$$

and

$$d_2 = \frac{Ln(P/E) + (r - \sigma^2/2)t}{\sigma t^{1/2}}$$

Where Ln is the natural logarithm, σ^2 is the variance of the return on the share (i.e. the changes in market value and income) and σ is the standard deviation of the return on the share.

Capital asset pricing model

$$r_j = r_f + \beta(r_m - r_f)$$

Where r_j is the expected return on the equity share (it equates to Ke), r_f is the risk-free rate, r_m the average expected market return and beta (β) the estimated level of systematic risk for the equity share.

Cash conversion cycle (manufacturing firm)

$$\begin{array}{c} \text{Operating/cash} \\ \text{conversion cycle} \end{array} = \begin{array}{c} \text{Raw materials} \\ \text{conversion period} \end{array} + \begin{array}{c} \text{Work-in-progress} \\ \text{conversion period} \end{array} + \begin{array}{c} \text{Finished goods} \\ \text{conversion period} \end{array}$$

$$+ \begin{array}{c} \text{Trade receivables} \\ \text{conversion period} \end{array} - \begin{array}{c} \text{Trade payables} \\ \text{conversion period} \end{array}$$

Cash conversion cycle (retail firm)

$$\begin{array}{c} \text{Operating/cash} \\ \text{conversion cycle} \end{array} = \begin{array}{c} \text{Inventory conversion} \\ \text{period} \end{array} + \begin{array}{c} \text{Trade receivables} \\ \text{conversion period} \end{array} - \begin{array}{c} \text{Trade payables} \\ \text{conversion period} \end{array}$$

Company valuation (using the WACC)

$$\text{Market value of a company} = \frac{\text{Earnings}}{\text{WACC}}$$

Company value (when the market values of debt and equity are known)

$$MV = D + E$$

Where MV is the total value of a company, D is the market value of its debt and E the market value of its equity.

Dividend level (Porterfield)

$$d_1 + P_1 > P_0$$

Where d_1 is the cash value to the equity holder of a dividend to be paid, P_1 is the expected equity share price value after the dividend is paid (ex-dividend) and P_0 is the equity share price before the dividend is paid (cum-dividend).

Discount factor

$$\text{Discount factor} = 1/(1+r)^n$$

Where r is the discount rate and n is the number of years the cash flows will be received in the future.

Dividend valuation model (no growth – finding the value of equity)

$$P_0 = \frac{D_1}{Ke}$$

Where P_0 is the market value of equity, D_1 is the annual dividend and Ke is the equity holders required cost of equity.

Dividend valuation model (no growth – finding the cost of equity)

$$Ke = \frac{D_1}{P_0}$$

Where P_0 is the market value of equity, D_1 is the annual dividend and Ke is the equity holders required cost of equity.

Dividend valuation model (with growth – finding the cost of equity)

$$Ke = \frac{D_0(1+g)}{P_0} + g$$

Where D_0 is the last dividend paid, P_0 is the market value of equity on issue, g is the constant growth rate and Ke is the cost of equity capital.

Dividend valuation model (with growth – finding the value of equity)

$$P_0 = \frac{D_0(1+g)}{Ke - g}$$

Where D_0 is the last dividend paid, P_0 is the market value of equity on issue, g is the constant growth rate and Ke is the cost of equity capital.

Earnings yield

$$\text{Earnings yield} = \frac{\text{Earnings} \times 100}{\text{Share price}}$$

Economic batch quantity

$$\text{EBQ} = \sqrt{\frac{2FU}{CP\,(1 - d/r)}}$$

Where EBQ is the most economical batch size to produce every time the machines are set up, d is the demand rate per day, r is production per day, F is set-up costs, U is demand in the period and CP is the holding cost for one unit.

Economic order quantity model

$$\text{EOQ} = \sqrt{\frac{2FU}{CP}}$$

Where EOQ is the quantity that should be ordered, F is the fixed cost per order, U is the total usage (i.e. demand/sales) in units for the period and CP is the holding cost per unit.

Economic order quantity model: average inventory (zero lead time and no safety stock)

$$\text{Average inventory} = \frac{\text{EOQ}}{2}$$

Economic order quantity model: average inventory (zero lead time, safety stock)

$$\text{Average inventory} = \frac{\text{EOQ}}{2} + \text{safety stock}$$

Economic order quantity model: inventory reorder level (no safety stock)

$$\text{Reorder level} = \text{Lead time in days/weeks} \times \text{Usage in days/weeks}$$

Economic order quantity model: inventory reorder level (with safety stock)

$$\text{Reorder level} = (\text{Average usage} \times \text{Average lead time}) + \text{Safety stock}$$

Economic order quantity model: (total holding costs)

$$\text{Total holding costs} = \text{Average inventory} \times \text{Holding cost per unit}$$

$$= \frac{Q}{2} \times CP$$

Where Q is the quantity ordered and CP is the holding cost per unit.

Economic order quantity model (total inventory costs)

$$\text{Total costs} = \text{Holding costs} + \text{Ordering costs}$$

Economic order quantity model (total ordering costs)

$$\text{Total ordering costs} = \text{Number of orders} \times \text{Fixed cost per order (F)}$$

$$= \frac{U}{Q} \times F$$

Where U is the usage or demand for the period, Q is the reorder number of units and F is the fixed cost per order.

Equivalent annual annuity

$$\text{Annual annuity equivalent of the NPV} = NPV \times \frac{i}{1-(1+i)^{-n}}$$

Where i is the discount rate and n is the number of years that the investment lasts for.

Equivalent annual cost

$$\text{Equivalent annual cost} = \frac{NPV}{\text{Annuity factor}}$$

Expectations theory of exchange rates

$$\frac{\text{Forward}_{euro/stg}}{\text{Spot}_{euro/stg}} = \frac{\text{Expected spot}_{euro/stg}}{\text{Spot}_{euro/stg}}$$

Therfore the:

Forward $_{euro/stg}$ = Expected spot $_{euro/stg}$

Expected net present value (ENPV)

$$Y = \sum_{i=1}^{n} p_i X_i$$

Where Y is the expected value of Event X, X_i is the outcome i from event X and p_i is the probability (p) of outcome i occurring and n is the number of possible outcomes.

Gearing

$$\text{Gearing \%} = \frac{D}{D + E} \times 100$$

Where D is the market value of debt (including preference shares) and E is the market value of equity.

Growth in dividends (using historic actual dividend information)

$$g = \sqrt[y]{\frac{D_{t0}}{D_{t0-y}}} - 1$$

Where g it the growth rate, D_{t0} is the dividend that has just been paid and D_{t0-y} is dividend that was paid y years ago.

Growth (using retentions)

$$g = br$$

Where b is the percentage of earnings that are retained for investment and r is the return on the company's investments i.e. the return on capital employed.

Hedging ratio

$$H = \frac{(C_u - C_L)}{(P_u - P_L)}$$

Where H is the hedging ratio, C_u is the upper value on the option at the end of the period, C_L is the lower value on the option at the end of the period, P_L is the lower value of the share expected at the end of the period and P_u is the upper value of the share at the end of the period.

Interest rate parity

$$\frac{1 + r_{euro}}{1 + r_{stg}} = \frac{Forward_{euro/stg}}{Spot_{euro/stg}}$$

This equation can be rearranged to determine the expected forward rate, given the spot rate and the interest rates (r) in two different countries.

$$Forward_{euro/stg} = Spot_{euro/stg} \times \frac{1 + r_{euro}}{1 + r_{stg}}$$

International Fisher Effect

$$\frac{1 + r_{euro}}{1 + r_{stg}} = \frac{1 + i_{euro}}{1 + i_{stg}}$$

Where r is the interest rate and i is the inflation rate. When this is linked to the interest rate parity equation the follow relationship results:

$$\frac{1 + i_{euro}}{1 + i_{stg}} \times Spot_{euro/stg} = Forward_{euro/stg} = Spot_{euro/stg} \times \frac{1 + r_{euro}}{1 + r_{stg}}$$

Interpolation (IRR)

$$IRR\ rate = Rate\ 1 + \frac{NPV\ 1\ (Rate\ 2 - Rate\ 1)}{NPV\ 1 - NPV\ 2}$$

This is the correct formula to use where the first trial discount rate lies below the IRR (positive NPV) and the second lies above the IRR (negative NPV). In this instance Rate 1 will be the lower rate used and NPV 1 will be its associated positive NPV. Rate 2 is the second trial rate that is used (higher rate) and NPV 2 is its corresponding negative NPV.

Irredeemable debt (market value of debt)

$$D = \frac{i}{K_d}$$

Where D is the market value of the bond, i is the yearly coupon rate and K_d is the bond holders required return, or the cost of debt.

Irredeemable debt (cost of debt)

$$K_d = \frac{i(1-t)}{D}$$

Where D is the market value of the bond, i is the yearly coupon rate, t is the current tax rate and K_d is the bond holders required return, or the cost of debt.

Lintner's model

$$
\begin{aligned}
\text{Dividend change in year} \quad = \quad & \text{Annual upward drift} + (\text{safety factor} \\
& \times (\text{current earnings} \times \text{target ratio})) \\
& - \text{dividend of the previous year.}
\end{aligned}
$$

Where the annual upward drift is last year's dividend payment multiplied by growth in dividends.

Margin of safety (€/£)

$$\text{Margin of safety (€/£)} = \text{Worst value} - \text{Estimated value}$$

Margin of safety (%)

$$\text{Margin of safety \%} = \frac{\text{Worst value} - \text{Estimated value}}{\text{Estimated value}} \times 100$$

Miller Orr model target balance

$$\text{Target balance} = \text{Lower limit (L)} + (1/3 \times \text{spread (H}-\text{L)})$$

Or

$$Z = \sqrt[3]{\frac{3FV}{4i}} + L$$

Where Z is the target balance, F is the fixed transaction cost, V is the variability of cash flows as measured by the variance in cash flows, i is the daily interest rate and L is the lower limit (which is set by a company).

Miller Orr model spread

$$H - L = 3 \times \sqrt[3]{\frac{3FV}{4i}}$$

Where (H−L) is the spread, F is the fixed transaction cost, V is the variability of cash flows as measured by the variance in cash flows, and i is the daily interest rate.

Miller Orr model – upper limit

$$H = 3Z - 2L$$

Where H is the upper limit, Z is the target balance and L is the lower limit.

Modigliani and Miller: sources and uses of resources

$$P + F = D + I$$

Where P is profit, F is new sources of financing, D is dividends/distributions and I is investment.

Modigliani and Miller (proposition 1 – without tax)

$$Vg = Vu$$

Where Vg is the market value of a geared company and Vu is the market value of a similar ungeared company.

Modigliani and Miller (proposition II – without tax)

$$Keg = Keu + \frac{D}{E}(Keu - Kd)$$

Where Keg is the cost of equity in a geared company, Keu is the cost of equity in a similar ungeared company, Kd is the cost of debt, D is the market value of debt and E is the market value of equity in the geared company.

Modigliani and Miller (proposition III – without tax)

$$WACCg = WACCu$$

Where WACCg is the WACC of a geared company and WACCu is the WACC of a similar ungeared company.

Modigliani and Miller (proposition 1 – with tax)

$$Vg = Vu + Dt$$

Where Vg is the market value of a geared company and Vu is the market value of a similar ungeared company. Dt is known as the interest tax shield – D is the market value of debt and t is the tax rate.

Modigliani and Miller (proposition II – with tax)

$$Keg = Keu + \frac{D}{E}(Keu - Kd)(1 - t)$$

Where Keg is the cost of equity in a geared company, Keu is the cost of equity in a similar ungeared company, Kd is the cost of debt, D is the market value of debt, E is the market value of equity in the geared company and t is the tax rate.

Modigliani and Miller (proposition III – with tax)

$$WACCg = WACCu \times \frac{Vu}{Vg}$$

Where WACCg is the WACC of a geared company, WACCu is the WACC of a similar ungeared company, Vg is the market value of a geared company and Vu is the market value of a similar ungeared company.

Or

$$WACCg = Keu\left(1 - \frac{Dt}{E + D}\right)$$

Where WACCg is the WACC of a geared company, Keu is the WACC or cost of equity in a similar ungeared company, D is the market value of debt in the geared company, E is the market value of debt in the geared company and t is the tax rate.

Modigliani and Miller (proposition 1 – with tax and financial distress costs)

$$Vg = Vu + Dt - PV \text{ (financial distress costs)}$$

Nominal discount rate

$$\text{Nominal discount rate} = ((1 + \text{Real rate}) \times (1 + \text{Inflation rate})) - 1$$

Perpetuity

$$\text{Perpetuity} = \text{Periodic cash flow}/r$$

Where r is the discount rate.

Preference share (cost)

$$K_P = \frac{D_1}{P_p}$$

Where K_p is the cost of the preference shares, D_1 is the annual dividend and P_p is the market value of the shares.

Present value

$$PV = FV \times \frac{1}{(1+r)^n}$$

Where PV is the present value, r is the discount rate, n is the number of years the cash flows will be received in the future, and FV is the future value of the cash flow.

Or

Where the cash flow is the result of an investment that will have a terminal value (TV) the formula is (basically the same – just different notation):

$$PV = TV/(1+r)^n$$

Profitability index (NPV)

$$\text{PV per euro/pound of scarce resource} = \frac{\text{NPV of inflows}}{\text{Initial outlay}}$$

Purchasing power parity (PPP)

$$\frac{1+i_{euro}}{1+i_{stg}} = \frac{\text{Expected spot}_{euro/stg}}{\text{Spot}_{euro/stg}}$$

The expected difference in the inflation rate (i) between two countries equals the expected change in the spot rate between the two countries.

Redeemable bonds (market value)

$$P_0 = \frac{I_1}{(1+K_d)} + \frac{I_2}{(1+K_d)^2} + \cdots\cdots + \frac{R_n}{(1+K_d)^n}$$

Where P_0 is the market value of the bond in year 0, K_d is the discount rate or return on the bond, I is the annual interest paid by a company (coupon rate multiplied by the nominal value), R is the redemption value of the bond and n is the number of years to maturity.

Redeemable bonds (cost/return)

$$K_d = \frac{I_1}{P_0} + \frac{(R-P_0)/n}{P_0}$$

Where K_d is the discount rate or return on the bond, P_0 is the market value of the bond in year 0, I is the annual interest paid by a company (coupon rate multiplied by the nominal value), R is the redemption value of the bond and n is the number of years to maturity.

Standard deviation

The square root of the variance (σ^2), which is:

$$\sigma^2 = (X_1-Y)^2 p_1 + (X_2-Y)^2 p_2 \cdots\cdots (X_n-Y)^2 p_n$$

Where X_1-Y is the variation of outcome one (X_1) from the mean value (Y) and p_1 is the probability of observation X_1 occurring.

Terminal value/future value

$$TV = PV(1+r)^n$$

Where PV is the present value, r is the discount rate, n is the number of years the cash flows will be received in the future, and TV is the terminal value of the cash flow.

Untraded debt (cost)

$$K_{dt} = i(1-t)$$

Where K_{dt} is the net cost of debt after tax, i is the interest rate and t is the current tax rate.

Valuing equity (Free cash flow approach)

$$\text{Value of an equity share} = \frac{\text{NPV of the estimated free cash flows} - \text{debt}}{\text{Number of shares in issues}}$$

Valuing equity (NBV approach)

$$\text{Value of an equity share} = \frac{\text{Total assets} - \text{total liabilities}}{\text{Number of equity shares in issue}}$$

Valuing equity (NRV approach)

$$\text{Value of an equity share} = \frac{\text{Total assets at NRV} - \text{total liabilities at NRV}}{\text{Number of equity shares in issue}}$$

Valuing equity(Replacement cost approach)

$$\text{Value of an equity share} = \frac{\text{Total assets at replacement value} - \text{total liabilities}}{\text{Number of equity shares in issue}}$$

Weighted average cost of capital (WACC)

$$\text{WACC} = \frac{E(K_e)}{(D+E)} + \frac{D(K_d(1-t))}{(D+E)}$$

Where E is the market value of equity, D is the market value of debt, K_e is the cost of equity, K_d is the cost of debt and t is the current tax rate.

Working capital

$$\text{Working capital} = \text{Inventories} + \text{Trade receivables} + \text{Bank} + \text{Cash} - \text{Trade payables} - \text{Overdraft}$$

or

$$\text{Working capital} = \text{Current assets} - \text{Current liabilities}$$

Z score

$$Z = 1.2A + 1.4B + 3.3C + 0.6D + 1.0\ E$$

Where A is working capital/total assets, B is retained earnings/total assets, C is profit before interest and tax/total assets, D is market capitalisation/book value of debts before interest and tax/total assets, and E is sales/total assets.

Zero coupon bonds (annualised return)

$$K_d = \sqrt[n]{\frac{R}{IP}} - 1$$

Where K_d is the annualised return, R is the redemption value, IP is the issue price and n is the number of years to maturity.

APPENDIX 3

PRESENT VALUE DISCOUNT FACTOR TABLE

Present value of 1, i.e. $(1+r)^{-n}$

Where r is the discount rate and n is the number of periods until payment.

Periods	Discount rates (r)									
(n)	1%	2%	3%	4%	5%	6%	7%	8%	9%	10%
1	0.990	0.980	0.971	0.962	0.952	0.943	0.935	0.926	0.917	0.909
2	0.980	0.961	0.943	0.925	0.907	0.890	0.873	0.857	0.842	0.826
3	0.971	0.942	0.915	0.889	0.864	0.840	0.816	0.794	0.772	0.751
4	0.961	0.924	0.888	0.855	0.823	0.792	0.763	0.735	0.708	0.683
5	0.951	0.906	0.863	0.822	0.784	0.747	0.713	0.681	0.650	0.621
6	0.942	0.888	0.837	0.790	0.746	0.705	0.666	0.630	0.596	0.564
7	0.933	0.871	0.813	0.760	0.711	0.665	0.623	0.583	0.547	0.513
8	0.923	0.853	0.789	0.731	0.677	0.627	0.582	0.540	0.502	0.467
9	0.914	0.837	0.766	0.703	0.645	0.592	0.544	0.500	0.460	0.424
10	0.905	0.820	0.744	0.676	0.614	0.558	0.508	0.463	0.422	0.386
11	0.896	0.804	0.722	0.650	0.585	0.527	0.475	0.429	0.388	0.350
12	0.887	0.788	0.701	0.625	0.557	0.497	0.444	0.397	0.356	0.319
13	0.879	0.773	0.681	0.601	0.530	0.469	0.415	0.368	0.326	0.290
14	0.870	0.758	0.661	0.577	0.505	0.442	0.388	0.340	0.299	0.263
15	0.861	0.743	0.642	0.555	0.481	0.417	0.362	0.315	0.275	0.239

Periods	Discount rates (r)									
(n)	11%	12%	13%	14%	15%	16%	17%	18%	19%	20%
1	0.901	0.893	0.885	0.877	0.870	0.862	0.855	0.847	0.840	0.833
2	0.812	0.797	0.783	0.769	0.756	0.743	0.731	0.718	0.706	0.694
3	0.731	0.712	0.693	0.675	0.658	0.641	0.624	0.609	0.593	0.579
4	0.659	0.636	0.613	0.592	0.572	0.552	0.534	0.516	0.499	0.482
5	0.593	0.567	0.543	0.519	0.497	0.476	0.456	0.437	0.419	0.402
6	0.535	0.507	0.480	0.456	0.432	0.410	0.390	0.370	0.352	0.335
7	0.482	0.452	0.425	0.400	0.376	0.354	0.333	0.314	0.296	0.279
8	0.434	0.404	0.376	0.351	0.327	0.305	0.285	0.266	0.249	0.233
9	0.391	0.361	0.333	0.308	0.284	0.263	0.243	0.225	0.209	0.194
10	0.352	0.322	0.295	0.270	0.247	0.227	0.208	0.191	0.176	0.162
11	0.317	0.287	0.261	0.237	0.215	0.195	0.178	0.162	0.148	0.135
12	0.286	0.257	0.231	0.208	0.187	0.168	0.152	0.137	0.124	0.112
13	0.258	0.229	0.204	0.182	0.163	0.145	0.130	0.116	0.104	0.093
14	0.232	0.205	0.181	0.160	0.141	0.125	0.111	0.099	0.088	0.078
15	0.209	0.183	0.160	0.140	0.123	0.108	0.095	0.084	0.074	0.065

Periods	Discount rates (r)									
(n)	21%	22%	23%	24%	25%	26%	27%	28%	29%	30%
1	0.826	0.820	0.813	0.807	0.800	0.794	0.787	0.781	0.775	0.769
2	0.683	0.672	0.661	0.650	0.640	0.630	0.620	0.610	0.601	0.592
3	0.565	0.551	0.537	0.525	0.512	0.500	0.488	0.477	0.466	0.455
4	0.467	0.451	0.437	0.423	0.410	0.397	0.384	0.373	0.361	0.350
5	0.386	0.370	0.355	0.341	0.328	0.315	0.303	0.291	0.280	0.269
6	0.319	0.303	0.289	0.275	0.262	0.250	0.238	0.227	0.217	0.207
7	0.263	0.249	0.235	0.222	0.210	0.198	0.188	0.178	0.168	0.159
8	0.218	0.204	0.191	0.179	0.168	0.157	0.148	0.139	0.130	0.123
9	0.180	0.167	0.155	0.144	0.134	0.125	0.116	0.108	0.101	0.094
10	0.149	0.137	0.126	0.116	0.107	0.099	0.092	0.085	0.078	0.073
11	0.123	0.112	0.103	0.094	0.086	0.079	0.072	0.066	0.061	0.056
12	0.102	0.092	0.083	0.076	0.069	0.063	0.057	0.052	0.047	0.043
13	0.084	0.075	0.068	0.061	0.055	0.050	0.045	0.040	0.037	0.033
14	0.069	0.062	0.055	0.049	0.044	0.039	0.035	0.032	0.028	0.025
15	0.057	0.051	0.045	0.040	0.035	0.031	0.028	0.025	0.022	0.020

APPENDIX 4

ANNUITY FACTOR TABLE

Present value of an annuity of 1, i.e. $\dfrac{1-(1+r)^{-n}}{r}$

Where r is the discount rate and n is the number of periods.

Periods	Discount rates (r)									
(n)	1%	2%	3%	4%	5%	6%	7%	8%	9%	10%
1	0.990	0.980	0.971	0.962	0.952	0.943	0.935	0.926	0.917	0.909
2	1.970	1.942	1.913	1.886	1.859	1.833	1.808	1.783	1.759	1.736
3	2.941	2.884	2.829	2.775	2.723	2.673	2.624	2.577	2.531	2.487
4	3.902	3.808	3.717	3.630	3.546	3.465	3.387	3.312	3.240	3.170
5	4.853	4.713	4.580	4.452	4.329	4.212	4.100	3.993	3.890	3.791
6	5.795	5.601	5.417	5.242	5.076	4.917	4.767	4.623	4.486	4.355
7	6.728	6.472	6.230	6.002	5.786	5.582	5.389	5.206	5.033	4.868
8	7.652	7.325	7.020	6.733	6.463	6.210	5.971	5.747	5.535	5.335
9	8.566	8.162	7.786	7.435	7.108	6.802	6.515	6.247	5.995	5.759
10	9.471	8.983	8.530	8.111	7.722	7.360	7.024	6.710	6.418	6.145
11	10.368	9.787	9.253	8.760	8.306	7.887	7.499	7.139	6.805	6.495
12	11.255	10.575	9.954	9.385	8.863	8.384	7.943	7.536	7.161	6.814
13	12.134	11.348	10.635	9.986	9.394	8.853	8.358	7.904	7.487	7.103
14	13.004	12.106	11.296	10.563	9.899	9.295	8.745	8.244	7.786	7.367
15	13.865	12.849	11.938	11.118	10.380	9.712	9.108	8.559	8.061	7.606

Periods	Discount rates (r)									
(n)	11%	12%	13%	14%	15%	16%	17%	18%	19%	20%
1	0.901	0.893	0.885	0.877	0.870	0.862	0.855	0.847	0.840	0.833
2	1.713	1.690	1.668	1.647	1.626	1.605	1.585	1.566	1.547	1.528
3	2.444	2.402	2.361	2.322	2.283	2.246	2.210	2.174	2.140	2.106
4	3.102	3.037	2.974	2.914	2.855	2.798	2.743	2.690	2.639	2.589
5	3.696	3.605	3.517	3.433	3.352	3.274	3.199	3.127	3.058	2.991
6	4.231	4.111	3.998	3.889	3.784	3.685	3.589	3.498	3.410	3.326
7	4.712	4.564	4.423	4.288	4.160	4.039	3.922	3.812	3.706	3.605
8	5.146	4.968	4.799	4.639	4.487	4.344	4.207	4.078	3.954	3.837
9	5.537	5.328	5.132	4.946	4.772	4.607	4.451	4.303	4.163	4.031
10	5.889	5.650	5.426	5.216	5.019	4.833	4.659	4.494	4.339	4.192
11	6.207	5.938	5.687	5.453	5.234	5.029	4.836	4.656	4.486	4.327
12	6.492	6.194	5.918	5.660	5.421	5.197	4.988	4.793	4.611	4.439
13	6.750	6.424	6.122	5.842	5.583	5.342	5.118	4.910	4.715	4.533
14	6.982	6.628	6.302	6.002	5.724	5.468	5.229	5.008	4.802	4.611
15	7.191	6.811	6.462	6.142	5.847	5.575	5.324	5.092	4.876	4.675

Periods	Discount rates (r)									
(n)	21%	22%	23%	24%	25%	26%	27%	28%	29%	30%
1	0.826	0.820	0.813	0.806	0.800	0.794	0.787	0.781	0.775	0.769
2	1.509	1.492	1.474	1.457	1.440	1.424	1.407	1.392	1.376	1.361
3	2.074	2.042	2.011	1.981	1.952	1.923	1.896	1.868	1.842	1.816
4	2.540	2.494	2.448	2.404	2.362	2.320	2.280	2.241	2.203	2.166
5	2.926	2.864	2.803	2.745	2.689	2.635	2.583	2.532	2.483	2.436
6	3.245	3.167	3.092	3.020	2.951	2.885	2.821	2.759	2.700	2.643
7	3.508	3.416	3.327	3.242	3.161	3.083	3.009	2.937	2.868	2.802
8	3.726	3.619	3.518	3.421	3.329	3.241	3.156	3.076	2.999	2.925
9	3.905	3.786	3.673	3.566	3.463	3.366	3.273	3.184	3.100	3.019
10	4.054	3.923	3.799	3.682	3.571	3.465	3.364	3.269	3.178	3.092
11	4.177	4.035	3.902	3.776	3.656	3.543	3.437	3.335	3.239	3.147
12	5.278	4.127	3.985	3.851	3.725	3.606	3.493	3.387	3.286	3.190
13	4.362	4.203	4.053	3.912	3.780	3.656	3.538	3.427	3.322	3.223
14	4.432	4.265	4.108	3.962	3.824	3.695	3.573	3.459	3.351	3.249
15	4.489	4.315	4.153	4.001	3.859	3.726	3.601	3.483	3.373	3.268

APPENDIX 5

FUTURE VALUE FACTOR TABLE

Future value of 1, i.e. $(1+r)^n$

Where r is the discount rate and n is the number of periods.

Periods	Discount rates (r)									
(n)	1%	2%	3%	4%	5%	6%	7%	8%	9%	10%
1	1.010	1.020	1.030	1.040	1.050	1.060	1.070	1.080	1.090	1.100
2	1.020	1.040	1.061	1.082	1.103	1.124	1.145	1.166	1.188	1.210
3	1.030	1.061	1.093	1.125	1.158	1.191	1.225	1.260	1.295	1.331
4	1.041	1.082	1.126	1.170	1.216	1.263	1.311	1.361	1.412	1.464
5	1.051	1.104	1.159	1.218	1.276	1.338	1.403	1.469	1.539	1.611
6	1.062	1.126	1.194	1.265	1.340	1.419	1.501	1.587	1.677	1.772
7	1.072	1.149	1.230	1.316	1.407	1.504	1.606	1.714	1.828	1.949
8	1.083	1.172	1.267	1.369	1.478	1.594	1.718	1.851	1.993	2.144
9	1.094	1.195	1.305	1.423	1.551	1.690	1.839	1.999	2.172	2.358
10	1.105	1.219	1.344	1.480	1.629	1.791	1.967	2.159	2.367	2.594
11	1.116	1.243	1.384	1.540	1.710	1.898	2.104	2.332	2.580	2.853
12	1.127	1.268	1.426	1.601	1.796	2.012	2.252	2.518	2.813	3.138
13	1.138	1.294	1.469	1.666	1.886	2.133	2.410	2.720	3.066	3.452
14	1.150	1.320	1.513	1.732	1.980	2.261	2.579	2.937	3.342	3.798
15	1.161	1.346	1.558	1.801	2.079	2.397	2.759	3.172	3.643	4.177

Periods	Discount rates (r)									
(n)	**11%**	**12%**	**13%**	**14%**	**15%**	**16%**	**17%**	**18%**	**19%**	**20%**
1	1.110	1.120	1.130	1.140	1.150	1.160	1.170	1.180	1.190	1.200
2	1.232	1.254	1.277	1.300	1.323	1.346	1.369	1.392	1.416	1.440
3	1.368	1.405	1.443	1.482	1.521	1.561	1.602	1.643	1.685	1.728
4	1.518	1.574	1.631	1.689	1.749	1.811	1.874	1.939	2.005	2.074
5	1.685	1.762	1.842	1.925	2.011	2.100	2.192	2.288	2.386	2.488
6	1.870	1.974	2.082	2.195	2.313	2.436	2.565	2.700	2.840	2.986
7	2.076	2.211	3.353	2.502	2.660	2.826	3.001	3.186	3.379	3.583
8	2.304	2.476	2.658	2.853	3.059	3.278	3.512	3.759	4.021	4.300
9	2.558	2.773	3.004	3.252	3.518	3.803	4.108	4.436	4.785	5.160
10	2.839	3.106	3.395	3.707	4.046	4.411	4.807	5.234	5.695	6.192
11	3.152	3.479	3.836	4.226	4.652	5.117	5.624	6.176	6.777	7.430
12	3.499	3.896	4.335	4.818	5.350	5.936	6.580	7.288	8.064	8.916
13	3.883	4.364	4.898	5.492	6.153	6.886	7.699	8.600	9.596	10.699
14	4.310	4.887	5.535	6.261	7.076	7.988	9.008	10.147	11.420	12.839
15	4.785	5.474	6.254	7.138	8.137	9.266	10.539	11.974	13.590	15.407

Periods	Discount rates (r)									
(n)	**21%**	**22%**	**23%**	**24%**	**25%**	**26%**	**27%**	**28%**	**29%**	**30%**
1	1.210	1.220	1.230	1.240	1.250	1.260	1.270	1.280	1.290	1.300
2	1.464	1.488	1.513	1.538	1.563	1.588	1.613	1.638	1.664	1.690
3	1.772	1.816	1.861	1.907	1.953	2.000	2.048	2.097	2.147	2.197
4	2.144	2.215	2.289	2.364	2.441	2.521	2.601	2.684	2.769	2.856
5	2.594	2.703	2.815	2.932	3.052	3.176	3.304	3.436	3.572	3.713
6	3.138	3.297	3.463	3.635	3.815	4.002	4.196	4.398	4.608	4.827
7	3.798	4.023	4.259	4.508	4.768	5.042	5.329	5.630	5.945	6.275
8	4.595	4.908	5.239	5.590	5.961	6.353	6.768	7.206	7.669	8.157
9	5.560	5.987	6.444	6.931	7.451	8.005	8.595	9.223	9.893	10.605
10	6.728	7.305	7.926	8.594	9.313	10.086	10.915	11.806	12.761	13.786
11	8.140	8.912	7.749	10.657	11.642	12.708	13.863	15.112	16.462	17.922
12	9.850	10.872	11.991	13.215	14.552	16.012	17.605	19.343	21.236	23.298
13	11.918	13.264	14.749	16.386	18.190	20.175	22.359	24.759	27.395	30.288
14	14.421	16.182	18.141	20.319	22.737	25.421	28.396	31.691	35.339	39.374
15	17.449	19.742	22.314	25.196	28.422	32.030	36.063	40.565	45.588	51.186

APPENDIX 6

CUMULATIVE PROBABILITY [N(*d*)] THAT A NORMALLY DISTRIBUTED VARIABLE WILL BE LESS THAN *d* STANDARD DEVIATIONS FROM THE MEAN

(*d*)	0.00	0.01	0.02	0.03	0.04	0.05	0.06	0.07	0.08	0.09
0.0	0.5000	0.5040	0.5080	0.5120	0.5160	0.5199	0.5239	0.5279	0.5319	0.5359
0.1	0.5398	0.5438	0.5478	0.5517	0.5557	0.5596	0.5636	0.5675	0.5714	0.5723
0.2	0.5793	0.5832	0.5871	0.5910	0.5948	0.5987	0.6026	0.6064	0.6103	0.6141
0.3	0.6179	0.6217	0.6255	0.6293	0.6331	0.6368	0.6406	0.6443	0.6480	0.6517
0.4	0.6554	0.6591	0.6628	0.6664	0.6700	0.6736	0.6772	0.6808	0.6844	0.6879
0.5	0.6915	0.6950	0.6985	0.7019	0.7054	0.7088	0.7123	0.7157	0.7190	0.7224
0.6	0.7257	0.7291	0.7324	0.7357	0.7389	0.7422	0.7454	0.7486	0.7517	0.7549
0.7	0.7580	0.7611	0.7642	0.7673	0.7704	0.7734	0.7764	0.7794	0.7823	0.7852
0.8	0.7881	0.7910	0.7939	0.7967	0.7995	0.8023	0.8051	0.8079	0.8106	0.8133
0.9	0.8159	0.8186	0.8212	0.8238	0.8264	0.8289	0.8315	0.8340	0.8365	0.8389
1.0	0.8413	0.8438	0.8461	0.8485	0.8508	0.8531	0.8554	0.8577	0.8599	0.8621
1.1	0.8643	0.8665	0.8686	0.8708	0.8729	0.8749	0.8770	0.8790	0.8810	0.8830
1.2	0.8849	0.8869	0.8888	0.8907	0.8925	0.8944	0.8962	0.8980	0.8997	0.9015
1.3	0.9032	0.9049	0.9066	0.9082	0.9099	0.9115	0.9131	0.9147	0.9162	0.9177
1.4	0.9192	0.9207	0.9222	0.9236	0.9251	0.9265	0.9279	0.9292	0.9306	0.9319

Note: If d is 1.23, then [N(d)] is 0.8907. This means there is a 89.07% probability that a normally distributed variable will be less than 1.23 standard deviations above the mean.

(*d*)	0.00	0.01	0.02	0.03	0.04	0.05	0.06	0.07	0.08	0.09
1.5	0.9332	0.9345	0.9357	0.9370	0.9382	0.9394	0.9406	0.9418	0.9429	0.9441
1.6	0.9452	0.9463	0.9474	0.9484	0.9495	0.9505	0.9515	0.9525	0.9535	0.9545
1.7	0.9554	0.9564	0.9573	0.9582	0.9591	0.9599	0.9608	0.9616	0.9625	0.9633
1.8	0.9641	0.9649	0.9656	0.9664	0.9671	0.9678	0.9686	0.9693	0.9699	0.9706
1.9	0.9713	0.9719	0.9726	0.9732	0.9738	0.9744	0.9750	0.9756	0.9761	0.9767
2.0	0.9772	0.9778	0.9783	0.9788	0.9793	0.9798	0.9803	0.9808	0.9812	0.9817
2.1	0.9821	0.9826	0.9830	0.9834	0.9838	0.9842	0.9846	0.9850	0.9854	0.9857
2.2	0.9861	0.9864	0.9868	0.9871	0.9875	0.9878	0.9881	0.9884	0.9887	0.9890
2.3	0.9893	0.9896	0.9898	0.9901	0.9904	0.9906	0.9909	0.9911	0.9913	0.9916
2.4	0.9918	0.9920	0.9922	0.9924	0.9927	0.9929	0.9931	0.9932	0.9934	0.9936
2.5	0.9938	0.9940	0.9941	0.9943	0.9945	0.9946	0.9948	0.9949	0.9951	0.9952
2.6	0.9953	0.9955	0.9956	0.9957	0.9959	0.9960	0.9961	0.9962	0.9963	0.9964
2.7	0.9965	0.9966	0.9967	0.9968	0.9969	0.9970	0.9971	0.9972	0.9973	0.9974
2.8	0.9974	0.9975	0.9976	0.9977	0.9977	0.9978	0.9979	0.9979	0.9980	0.9981
2.9	0.9981	0.9982	0.9982	0.9983	0.9984	0.9984	0.9985	0.9985	0.9986	0.9986
3.0	0.9986	0.9987	0.9987	0.9988	0.9988	0.9989	0.9989	0.9989	0.9990	0.9990

APPENDIX 7

SOLUTIONS

CHAPTER 2

SOLUTIONS TO REVIEW QUESTIONS

1.   Strategic management is defined as:

> 'a systematic approach to positioning the business in relation to its environment to ensure continued success and offer security from surprises' (Pike and Neale, 2003).

2.   Typical non-financial objectives pursued by a company might include:

The provision of a service: Most utility companies will strive to achieve a particular standard of service to the public as a key objective. Companies such as Viridian Group plc, British Telecom plc, Eircom and the Electricity Supply Board (ESB) pursue minimum standards of service. These service standards are agreed with government regulators and are monitored by them.

The welfare of employees: Many companies pursue a policy of ensuring their employees are treated well. They do this by providing competitive wages, a strong pension policy, adequate training, a clear career development path, perks, a suitable induction programme, good redundancy and retraining initiatives when necessary, comfortable working facilities and pursuing a strong health and safety policy.

The welfare of society: Many companies, that have the potential to pollute the environment pursue policies to ensure that damage to the environment is minimised as far as possible. Manufacturing companies introduce processes to reduce air and waste pollution; car companies commit resources yearly for research into the creation of more economical vehicles that can run on environmentally friendly sources of energy, such as electricity and bio-fuel; and many retail outlets pursue a policy of recycling plastic bags or providing a 'bag for life'.

The welfare of directors: Otherwise known as 'agency theory'. Some companies may end up taking decisions that are primarily to benefit directors. This usually happens when decisions are made to maximise profits in the short term to the detriment of long-term profitability. Directors' salary bonuses may be pegged to profitability, resulting in this type of sub-optimal decision making.

The maintenance of strong supplier and customer relationships: Some companies will strive to maintain certain quality standards, to advance the products being produced, for the benefit of customers. Dealing ethically with both customers and suppliers may also be an aim. Establishing agreed terms of trade and sticking to them will benefit both customers and suppliers. The government has acted for the benefit of suppliers by allowing them to legally charge interest on overdue amounts that are not paid by an agreed payment date. Even so, withholding cash from a small supplier may cause them severe liquidity problems and many large companies pursue policies of being respectful to their suppliers by paying for supplies on time.

3.   Non-financial objectives do not replace financial objectives. They are usually secondary objectives, and in most instances place constraints on the extent of achievement of the financial objectives. In business finance, value creation/equity holder value maximisation is assumed to be the primary financial objective, yet all financial decisions have to be mindful of the rights and responsibilities of a company to act ethically towards other stakeholders. When a company is mindful of its responsibilities to the various stakeholders, this will usually restrict short-term profitability; however, in the long term, it is likely to be congruent with value creation. For example, not paying suppliers will leave cash in the company that can be used to earn a quick return; however, this will not do any favours for ensuring the future of that supply, is likely to result in the loss of discounts and may even push up the price of future supplies. Not providing good working conditions for employees, or awarding pay increases below the inflation rate, will increase company profitability in the short term, but is likely to lead to high staff turnover, sickness and lower productivity from the employees – hence lower long-term profitability.

4.   **Efficiency levels**
      In 1970 an economist called Fama suggested that market efficiency be analysed using three levels of efficiency. The ideal situation he termed 'strong-form efficiency'. When a market is operating with strong-form efficiency, all relevant current information, including information that is not available publicly, is reflected in current share price. As all internal information is reflected in share price, there is no scope for gains to be made from insider trading. The second level of efficiency is called 'semi-strong-form efficiency'. This level of efficiency suggests that all publicly available information is reflected in share price; however, insider information is not. This would suggest that insider trading can reap rewards, but market traders cannot make gains as all the gains are reflected in the share price immediately. The final level of efficiency Fama termed 'weak-form efficiency'. This suggests that share price fully reflects all the information contained in past share price movements. As this information is already reflected in share price, there are no gains to be made from charting the share price movements in the past, in an attempt at predicting future price movements.

5.   In Ireland and GB the governments use indirect means to influence company decision making, for example:

      Legislation: The governments put in safeguards to help promote ethical decision making within companies. Legislation places a duty of care on companies in respect of their actions with all stakeholders and potential stakeholders. For example, legislation promotes responsible, reliable company reporting; good governance and the ethical treatment of employees, creditors and customers. It also protects the general public by setting environmental requirements and ensuring that companies do not abuse their positions.

Taxation: The governments set several taxes, which influence company decision making. Examples include corporation tax (tax on company profits), capital gains tax (tax on share price increases when sold), income tax (tax on dividends received), value added tax (tax on supplies, collected by company on behalf of the government); capital allowances (tax-allowable deductions for capital expenditure), pay as you earn (tax on salary deducted by company on behalf of government); and national insurance (tax on salary deducted by company on behalf of government). Corporation tax and capital allowances affect the yearly costs and cash flows of a company; income tax and capital gains tax (and allowances) influence equity holder preferences in respect of dividend policy, and salary taxes influence direct company costs and, hence, profitability.

Economic policy: The governments and central bank try to control growth in the economy using micro-economics. For example: inflation influences cash flow requirements; interest rate changes influence company finance costs and options, and hence inflation; foreign exchange rate policy influences exporting and importing costs, and, again, inflation.

Grants: To encourage new investment in a particular industry, governments might provide grants for capital expenditure or staff training, or might grant accelerated capital allowances that allow a quicker tax deduction for capital expenditure. To encourage the private sector to invest in particular industries, the government might introduce tax incentives for investors (for example, the business expansion scheme: BES).

Encouraging share ownership: The governments in Ireland and Britain have actively encouraged private investment in equity markets by providing tax incentives for individuals who invest in certain types of companies; for example, start up companies (BES). In the 1980s and 1990s the governments privatised many public companies using methods that promoted private share ownership.

6. **Taxation**

Taxation is relevant to every decision taken under business finance. When deciding on dividend policy, the business finance manager has to be mindful of changes in the income tax and capital gains tax rates. A change in dividend policy, which does not take equity holders' tax position into account, is likely to result in a detrimental reaction by the markets.

When deciding on the type of finance to obtain, knowledge of tax is also required. Interest is tax deductible by companies, reducing the overall cost of debt, whereas as dividends are not tax deductible. Therefore, the level of corporation tax affects the cost of debt (so long as a company is profitable).

When considering a new investment, the profits to be made will be subject to tax, and expenditure on capital subject to capital allowances. Corporation tax is usually a cash outflow and a business finance manager needs to be able to determine the amount of the expected outflow to find the true net present value of a project. As tax is a real cost to companies, business finance managers need to be aware of any concessions or tax breaks that are available for companies so that the investment decision can be tailored to take advantage of these.

Finally, when a company has overseas branches, or subsidiaries, knowledge is required of any double taxation agreement in existence between the country of the parent company and the country where its branches/subsidiaries are located. Knowledge of taxation in these countries is also required.

Law

The business finance manager requires knowledge of several areas of law. These areas are now considered (this list is not exhaustive).

Contract law: The law of contract is relevant to all activities involving stakeholders. These include customers, suppliers, employees and financiers.

Civil law: Civil law will require that companies observe the terms of their contracts with the various stakeholders.

Company law: Company law constrains decisions that can be taken on behalf of a company so that stakeholders are not disadvantaged unfairly. Company law requires that a company's principal activities are consistent with those laid down in its Memorandum and Articles of Association. Company law ensures that: directors do not raise more capital than the limits laid down in these documents without equity holder agreement; distributions are not made out of non-distributable profits (to protect the loan creditors); and responsible reporting is followed by the company.

Environmental law: Environmental law places requirements on companies not to pollute or damage the environment beyond certain agreed levels.

Other legislation is also relevant and might be considered in a solution: health and safety law, employment law, law specific to an industry and equality laws. Mention might also be made of debenture trusts, deeds and covenants.

Mathematics

A business finance manager usually has to take account of economic events; quantitative techniques are best placed to analyse such information. For example, time-series analysis can be used for forecasting, correlation and regression analysis can be used to analyse the behaviour of costs, indices may be used to examine the impact of inflation and probability calculation can be used for the assessment of risk and return. In addition, specific mathematical formulae can be used to back up decision making, for example: the economic order quantity model can be used to determine the optimum inventory order quantity; the Baumol model can be used to determine the optimum amount of short-term investments to meet cash requirement demands; linear programming can be used in capital budgeting decisions when there are several constraints; and simulation models can be used to determine the outcome when there is variation in inputs.

Economics

Business finance decisions usually involve the allocation and use of scarce resources to achieve a desired outcome. Knowledge of economics would greatly assist in decision making as there are various models and theories on the behaviour of variables when changes are made (for example the price elasticity of demand) and models to determine the appropriate use of scarce resources. Areas where economics is particularly relevant include investment appraisal and the determination of an appropriate cost of capital.

Having knowledge of micro-economics improves the quality of forecasting, as the business finance manager is more likely to better predict cash flows based on expectations in respect of inflation rates, interest rates and foreign exchange rates.

7.   (a) *Inefficient market:* The market initially overreacts to the good news about the break-through, causing share price to increase to €/£6.50. After a period of time, the share price returns to its 'true value' of €/£5.75.

(b) *Efficient market:* This is evidence of a 'semi-strong-form efficient market', wherein the good news is reflected immediately with the share price rising to €/£5.75 when the information is made public. The share price before the announcement was €/£5.00, reflecting the situation before the announcement.

(c) *Inefficient market:* This is evidence of an inefficient market as the market is slow to react to the announcement.

8.   *Essay*

Introduction

The financial environment does impact on financial decision making. The financial environment encapsulates the economic environment within which a company operates and the financial markets in which a company's long-term funds are sourced and traded. As this company is Ltd. the focus of this essay will be to discuss the potential impact of economic influences on its finances. The first part of this essay considers this issue, the second part focuses on explaining how changes in economic factors might directly impact on financial decision making. It focuses on the impact of inflation, interest rate changes and foreign exchange rate changes. The latter part of the essay considers the proposal put forward by Ian Smart. In particular the focus is on the ethical issues that surround the proposal.

Economic influences

Inflation has been earmarked by governments as a major influence on a country's economic growth. Inflation results when demand for a good outstrips supply. In these circumstances a supplier can increase the price of the good, without loosing sales. The consequence is that the good becomes more expensive to purchasers who see the real value of their wages and capital fall. Purchasers will subsequently put pressure on their employers to increase their wages so that they can maintain their current spending power (capital maintenance). Due to the fall in the purchasing value of individuals' incomes, demand for products will fall. Individuals may become conservative and reduce overall spending – which will result in an economic downturn in the economy. When the purchaser is a company, pressure grows to increase the price of the end product, due to the increased production/supply costs. This may result in a loss of sales for the company and financial difficulties. When there are financial difficulties companies will try to cut costs, which can mean job losses.

Interest rate changes are used as a means of controlling demand for goods, hence inflation. The assumption is that interest rate increases will reduce the overall spending power of consumers (who usually have a reasonable amount of debt) bringing demand for goods down to a level which does not encourage companies with excess demand to increase prices. Therefore the price of goods does not increase, just the price of debt.

Foreign exchange rates are also of great influence to a company that imports supplies, exports goods, borrows, or invests in other countries. When the value of a currency in one country rises, the subsequent cost of goods exported from that country increases, resulting in a loss of demand for the country's goods (assuming that demand is related to price) and vice versa.

Economic influences and business finance decision making

Inflation and foreign exchange rate changes affect: asset values; costs; and revenues, making it difficult to accurately predict future cash flows, hence the outcomes from any financial decision making, with certainty. Where inflation causes the value of assets to rise an additional financing requirement will result, as replacement assets (such as inventories, trade receivables, or machinery) will be more expensive to purchase. Business finance managers should be aware of the financing implications of inflation and should ensure that sufficient financing is in place to meet future increased cash demands. Where inflation causes the costs of production to rise, an analysis of the impact on profitability should be undertaken. A strong knowledge of the competitive market for the good being sold by the company is vital, as the business finance manager would need to be able to estimate the reaction of customers and competitors to price changes. If this reaction is wrongly interpreted, the company could loose market share and profitability.

When interest rates increase the required return by company financiers will also increase. This is because the risk-free rate of interest (the guaranteed return on a risk-free investment such as a bank deposit account) has increased, therefore the premium required by financiers (equity holders and debt holders) will increase the overall return expected. When the expected return by a company's financiers increases; the number of potential investments that can be undertaken by a company falls, as only those investments that cover the new higher required return by the financiers will be accepted. All existing investment and assets will need to be reviewed and any that are not meeting the new higher required rate of return should be liquidated and utilised to reduce current debt levels. The cash outflow on debt finance cannot be waived; hence debt finance increases financial risk.

Finance managers would tend to place more importance on having hedging policies in place to reduce the exposure to loss in company value caused by changes in exchange rates. One simple, yet commonly used technique is to have a bank account located in the foreign country. Exchange rates can be fixed using derivative financial instruments such as forward rate contracts, futures contracts or swap contracts.

The ethical dilemma suggested by Ian Smart

The suggestion put forward by Ian Smart (assuming no country risk) will more than likely increase the profitability of the company in these hard times. However, the board of directors should consider the ethical consequences. Ethical practices can restrict the extent to which a company can achieve its primary objective. In the global economy in which we operate, there is much to be made by companies who have products that can be made in countries that have no employment laws. Profits and company value will theoretically increase if a company is able to access cheap labour, or even child labour, for next to nothing. In these circumstances, companies justify their actions by arguing that some income to a family is better than none; or by highlighting the fact that, though the salaries paid are low, they are higher than those paid by indigenous companies. Many companies also use some of the profits made for social purposes in the communities that they are located in by for example: building schools; building churches; building hospitals; or getting running water. These are all deemed to be signs of these companies acting ethically. However, this does not get away from the fact that the local population is being abused for financial gain. Whether the board feels that the financial gain is worth the drop in ethical standards, is a matter for discussion. Given that this company is an Irish/Northern Irish company, I would suggest that this action is not consistent with how we should be running a company. In addition, the consequences of this action becoming public might be great. There is likely to be an adverse reaction from the union, the public and from the government.

The use of bribery or corruption may be seen as part and parcel of normal trade within certain countries. In a global economy when there is much pressure to perform, unethical approaches (such as bribery) might be considered to be 'fair game' when attempting to achieve the company's primary objectives. However, unethical behaviour cannot be defended on the grounds of it being normal practice in a country, nor can it be defended by the argument 'if I did not do it, someone else would', or 'we would loose the business to a competitor, who does it'. Taking bribes is not considered to be appropriate in Ireland (all of it) and is not appropriate behaviour for Irish/Northern Irish companies. Evidence of the public interest and distaste with this sort of behaviour is clear from the current tribunals that are being theatrically played out on news programmes most nights. Were the use of bribery to become public, the company might be subject to the same attention and enquiry.

All in all these unethical actions may end up with the company in a worse financial state. However, on a positive note looking globally to obtain cheaper running costs and labour is an option that we should discuss, however, child labour and bribery should not form part of any investment package.

Conclusion

This essay has considered the impact of changes in economic influences on the potential demand and profitability of a company. It has also highlighted the increased uncertainty caused by changes in these variable factors on financial decision making. My role as financial manager will be more difficult with a greater focus going on hedging the company's exposure to inflation (by forward buying) to interest rate risk (by using swaps, options, future contracts, fixing interest rates) and foreign exchange exposure (by using swaps, options, futures contracts, etc). I hope you find the above discussion of benefit. If you have any other specific queries do not hesitate to contact me for clarification.

CHAPTER 3

· ·

SOLUTIONS TO REVIEW QUESTIONS

1. Inflation impacts on various parts of the financial statements in different ways. This can cause distortions when interpreting ratios. For example, inflation will increase the profitability of a company; however, changes to the value of historic assets are not updated. Therefore, the reported return on assets for two companies with identical assets and profits may be quite different, where the companies have purchased the assets years apart. A way round this might be to use the fair values of the assets; however, this information may not be readily available and can be costly to obtain.

2. Solvency deals with the ability of a company to meet their debts as they fall due for payment. It covers both the long and short-term ability of a company to settle its debt and creditor repayments. Information on solvency can be obtained from cash budgets, the cash flow statement, the gearing ratio and liquidity ratios.

    Liquidity deals with the ability of a company to meet its short-term liabilities from its short-term sources of funds. Information on the liquidity position of a company can be obtained from the current ratio and the acid test ratio. Causes of shifts in liquidity can be ascertained from an analysis of the trade receivables period, the trade payables period, the inventory holding period, and changes in cash levels.

3. **Alpha and Omega**

	ALPHA	OMEGA
ROCE	€/£340/€/£2,000=17%	€/£404/€/£2,160=18.7%
Gross profit margin	€/£1,440/€/£6,000=24%	€/£1,584/€/£7,200=22%
Net profit margin	€/£340/€/£6000=5.66%	€/£404/€/£7,200=5.61%
Total asset turnover	€/£6,000/€/£2,900=2.07	€/£7,200/€/£4,000=1.8
Inventory turnover	€/£4,560/€/£1,200=3.8	€/£5,616/€/£1,800=3.12
Trade receivables period	(€/£720/€/£6,000) × 365 =43.8 days	(€/£1,200/€/£7,200) × 365 =61 days
Trade payables period	(€/£900/€/£4,760) × 365 =69 days	(€/£1,040/€/£5,916) × 365 =64 days
Current ratio	€/£2,110/€/£900=2.34 : 1	€/£3,000/€/£1,840=1.63 : 1
Quick ratio	€/£910/€/£900=1.01 : 1	€/£1,200/€/£1,840=0.65 : 1
Gearing ratio	€/£500/€/£2,000=25%	N/A

*Note – figures are in millions

Profitability

Given the results of the analysis of the ratios it would seem that Alpha is more profitable than Omega, as it has a greater gross profit margin (24%) relative to Omega's gross profit percentage of 22%. The sales mix of Alpha may include more profitable lines relative to Omega, or Alpha may be availing of discounts, or may be able to charge a higher price due to better service. More information is required. Alpha also has a higher net profit margin (5.66%) relative to Omega's 5.61%, though the difference in the reported gross profit percentage has fallen. This may signify that Alpha has higher fixed administration and distribution costs relative to Omega.

In contrast, Omega has a greater ROCE than Alpha. This may be down to the accounting policies that are being adopted in respect of the depreciation of non-current assets, or may indicate a need for Alpha to invest in new more up-to-date efficient assets to achieve higher returns. Again more information is required about the assets before a final conclusion can be obtained. At this stage it can be said that Omega is generating more sales from each euro/pound invested in assets.

Efficiency

An analysis of the result of the working capital ratios would suggest that Alpha is more efficient in their management of working capital. Alpha gets paid from customers sooner (within 43.8 days compared to 61 days for Omega), pays its suppliers later (every 69 days compared to 64 days for Omega) and turns its inventories over faster (3.8 times per year, or every 96 days; compared to 3.12 times for Omega (every 117 days)). As Alpha reports a higher gross profit margin, it would seem that the efficiencies have not been at the expense of providing discounts to customers, or at receiving discounts from suppliers (the trade payables period is longer).

Liquidity

Alpha also has a stronger liquidity position. Its current ratio is 2.34 : 1, compared with 1.63 : 1 for Omega. If the industry average were known a better conclusion on the current ratio could be reached. If the industry averages were the benchmark for the current ratio, of 2 : 1, then it could be concluded that Alpha has too much invested in current assets, whereas Omega has too little. As Alpha only has a small balance in the bank, this would mean that its levels of trade receivables and inventory, though lower than the levels kept by Omega in relative terms, are still too high and need to be reduced. Alpha has a quick ratio of 1.01 : 1, which is close to the benchmark quick ratio of 1 : 1. Omega's reported quick ratio is much lower at 0.65 : 1. Omega has a large bank overdraft and no cash, whereas Alpha has €/£190 million in the bank. This lower ratio seems to be a result of Omega's financing policy, which is discussed next.

Gearing

Omega's long-term financing is equity. Omega has no long-term debt. However, Omega seems to be using its overdraft as a source of finance for the company. Working capital is a permanent requirement which should be financed by an equally permanent source of finance; however, Omega is financing it with an overdraft. Alpha seems to be financed in a less risky manner. It has €/£1,500 million in equity and a long-term loan of €/£500 million. Alpha has adopted a policy of financing part of its working capital requirement using long-term sources. This has resulted in Alpha having a more liquid position, with cash in the bank.

c)   Three possible limitations of ratio analysis might include any of the following:

- Ratios do not give the whole picture of a company's condition.
- Ratios cannot be used to interpret non-financial information such as employee morale or future developments.
- Companies with different accounting policies will end up with different ratios making comparison meaningless.
- The balance sheet is only a 'snapshot' of a company at a moment in time, the next day the balance sheet will be different. The problem is most accentuated when the company's trade is seasonal in nature, as the ratios will not be representative of the year being reported on.
- Ratios do not take into account the changing business environment. For example an increase in profitability may be below a country's inflation rate, hence, in real terms – profitability has fallen.
- Short-term fluctuations in the market may distort ratios, in particular, the investment ratio – the price-earnings ratio.
- The calculation of ratios does not take into account the change in the value of money (inflation).

CHAPTER 4

· ·

SOLUTIONS TO REVIEW QUESTIONS

1. In a balance sheet, assets are disclosed according to the length of time a company intends to keep them. Assets with an expected term (to the company) of less than one year are categorised as current assets, whereas assets the company intends to hold for more than one year are categorised as non-current assets. Current assets typically include inventories, trade receivables, short-dated securities, prepayments, bank deposit account balances, current account balances (if positive) and cash. Non-current assets are usually sorted into three categories: tangible (which typically includes land, buildings, plant and machinery, fixtures and fittings, motor vehicles and office equipment), investments (which typically includes shares in subsidiaries, joint ventures, associates, financial investments and derivatives) and intangible assets (which typically includes purchased goodwill, capitalised development expenditure, patents and purchased quota).

2. In most companies, current assets are a permanent feature of the balance sheet. Most companies have to carry inventories and have to sell goods on credit (trade receivables). This means that all year round the company has to invest in a minimum level of working capital to support its operating activities. This is a permanent requirement and is regarded as the permanent portion of current assets. In addition to the permanent requirement, most companies will have temporary increased demand for additional working capital, termed 'temporary current assets'. The best way to explain temporary current asset requirements is to consider a company that has seasonal sales, such as an umbrella company (though not one based in Fermanagh or Donegal, as demand would be constant all year round!). Production would be constant all year round, yet sales would take place mostly in the winter months. Therefore, there would be a large inventory build up during the year, needing short-term financing, and a surplus of cash in the winter when sales would outstrip production.

3. There are two types of costs: opportunity costs and shortage costs. An opportunity cost is revenue lost from not investing monies in non-current assets. This can be compared with shortage costs that would result when insufficient levels of current asset are held because a higher proportion of funds are invested in non-current assets. Shortage costs might include: lost sales from stock-outs, lost sales caused by disruptions in production, lost sales from having too aggressive a credit policy or default payments from having to cash in securities before their maturities.

4. If a company were to pursue a neutral policy in respect of their asset mix, they would hold sufficient levels of current assets to ensure that limited shortage costs occurred, yet not hold too much so as to be regarded as inefficient. A company pursuing a flexible approach would hold high levels of current assets. This would involve holding high levels of inventory, granting long credit periods and holding cash reserves in short-dated securities. A company pursuing a restrictive approach would hold low levels of current assets and high levels of non-current assets. The company would experience many shortage costs. This is a risky strategy as the liquidity of a company is related to the level of its current assets relative to its current liabilities.

5.   A company adopting a matching approach to the financing of its investments would match the term of the finance to the term of the investment. This adopts a 'self-liquidating loan' approach wherein the investment financed by the finance should be structured in such a manner as to repay the finance requirement, without having to rely on resources from other parts of the company. A company adopting a flexible approach would have sufficient long-term finance arranged to finance all its requirements (permanent and temporary). When temporary demand reduces, the excess finance funds would be invested in short-term securities. A company pursing a restrictive policy would finance its short-term requirements solely by short-term means, but would also use short-term sources to finance permanent current assets and possibly some non-current assets.

6.   Disintermediation refers to a move away from the use of intermediaries for bill finance. Intermediaries usually guarantee and sell finance bills in the markets, on behalf of a company. Disintermediation refers to a situation where a company arranges the finance bill and approaches the market itself. This reduces the cost of obtaining finance. Only large, listed, reputable companies can successfully cut out the financial intermediaries.

7.   Any two of the following will suffice: commercial banks will provide short-term finance as will factor companies, discount houses and acceptance houses. These are normally subsidiaries of commercial or merchant banks.

8.   Overdrafts, short-term loans, factoring, invoice discounting.

9.   *Factoring* is where an outside company, usually a financial institution, provides finance to a company on the strength of the trade receivables of the company. The factor also takes over the administration of trade credit, vets customers, issues invoices and statements and chases up late payers. Customers are normally fully aware of the factor's involvement with the company.

Under *a confidential factoring* agreement, the factor's involvement is not visible; the company remains responsible for the administration of the trade receivables ledger and issues invoices, statements and letters using its own stationery. The company still sells the invoices to the factor; however, it acts as an agent for the factor company in the collection of the debts.

10.   Two ways of externally financing trade debtors are:

- the assignment of debts (invoice discounting); or
- the selling of debts (factoring).

Invoice discounting is characterised by the fact that a lender not only has a lien on debts, but also has recourse to the borrower (seller), i.e. if the person or company who bought the goods does not pay, the selling company must take the loss. In other words, the risk of default on the trade balances pledged remains with the borrower. In addition, the buyer of the goods is not usually notified about the pledging of the debts.

Factoring, on the other hand is frequently undertaken 'without recourse', i.e. the factor must bear the loss in the event that the customer who bought the goods does not pay.

There are advantages and disadvantages to factoring and invoice discounting as a method of raising funds for an individual company.

- First of all, the flexibility of these sources of finance is an advantage – as the company's sales expand and more financing is needed, the amount of readily available financing increases. The client company of a bank can convert up to 80% of its book debts into cash immediately. The company can be in charge of its funding management, since funds can be drawn down only as required, and it can rely on the invoice discounter to fund quality debts, when the need arises. At the same time, this will enable companies to pay their suppliers sooner and to take advantage of bulk discounts.

- Secondly, trade receivables or invoices, provide security for a loan (provided by the discounting bank) that a company might otherwise be unable to obtain.
- Thirdly, factoring provides the services of a credit department that might otherwise only be available under much more expensive conditions. Invoice discounting is particularly beneficial to new companies, where significant equity holder investment is not evident, and young companies, where the balance sheet, or lack of track record, precludes or restricts traditional bank lending. Other potential users include expanding companies whose growth demands additional working capital, exporting companies where export sales can be funded and seasonal companies, which experience peaks and troughs in their cash flow requirements.
- Finally, any company which uses the facility prudently will be able to expand and increase profits, without having to increase the capital investment in the company.

Invoice discounting and factoring also have disadvantages.

- When invoices are numerous and relatively small in value, the administrative costs involved may render these methods of financing inconvenient and expensive.
- For a long time, factoring of trade receivables was frowned upon by suppliers and, indeed, was regarded as a confession of a company's unsound financial position, whereas invoice discounting is confidential.

Some companies such as small and medium-sized enterprises are unaware of the potential of these forms of finance. Some companies consider that having a good credit management system in place reduces the need to use invoice discounting. In fact, a prerequisite of invoice discounting is that good credit management systems must be in place. A traditional reliance by Irish companies on bank overdrafts and loans has meant that there is often a reluctance to accept other forms of finance.

Although both factoring and invoice discounting can be attractive to companies, particularly small companies, and can give flexibility in terms of the provision of finance and assistance in credit management and credit intelligence, these techniques may impede the overall ability of the company using them to raise overdraft finance, because the prospective lending bank is unable to take a floating charge on the accounts receivable of the company.

11.   The arrangement that affords the most protection to the exporter, whilst providing credit to the importer while the goods are in transit, is an *irrevocable documented letter of credit*, which has been confirmed. This is a legally binding arrangement that outlines the payment to be made, the documents to be delivered and the dates on which the documents should be delivered. The payment terms should be on a sight draft basis, meaning that the importer's bank has to pay the sum due when the letter is presented and the goods arrive. The contract cannot be altered or cancelled without the consent of all parties. When the arrangement is for payment on sight of the letter, the bill of lading is usually withheld and passed with the confirmed documented letter of credit to the importer's bank when payment is processed.

CHAPTER 5

∙∙

SOLUTIONS TO REVIEW QUESTIONS

1.   A *revolving credit facility* is a flexible term loan. Repayments made reduce the capital element of the debt; however, the funds are accessible again by a borrower. With notice, a borrower can draw down on the loan again, up to the original agreed level, within the timescale of the initial agreement. This flexibility means that this type of facility is more expensive relative to a straight term loan, as the bank has to keep additional reserves to be able to cater for the additional demand for cash.

2.   **Advantages to a hiree company of using hire purchase:**
     (see chapter for more detail)
     - *Easy to arrange*
     - *Quick source of finance*
     - *Availability*
     - *Cash flow certainty/easier budgeting*
     - *Not repayable on demand*
     - *Cash flow advantage*
     - *Tax relief*
     - *Ownership*

     Disadvantages to a hiree company of using hire purchase finance:
     (see chapter for more detail)
     - *Cost*
     - *Lack of flexibility*
     - *Cancellation is costly*
     - *Maintenance/insurance*
     - *Risks of ownership*
     - *Underutilisation*

3.   **Main motives for lease finance**
     (see chapter for more detail)
     - *It is an alternative source of funds that can be obtained when other sources are exhausted.*
     - *It is quick and easy to arrange and obtain.*
     - *The finance house does not require security.*
     - *It has cash flow advantages.*
     - *Where the lease is an operating lease, it is a form of off-balance-sheet finance.*
     - *It may be cheaper than other sources of finance and is tax deductible (the deduction differs depending on whether the lease is an operating or a finance lease).*

4.   As the interest rate is the flat rate, it will be applied to the €/£50,000 for three years. Therefore the total interest, which is calculated at the start of the agreement, will be €/£50,000 × 10% × 3 = €/£15,000. The total repayments per year will be €/£21,667 (€/£16,667 (€/£50,000/3) plus interest of €/£5,000 (€/£15,000/3).

5.   **Key differences**

- *Substance of the transaction/control:* Where control of an asset remains with the lessor, not the lessee, the transaction is more likely to be regarded as an operating lease.
- *Purpose of the asset:* If the asset is required for a one-off job, or requires specialist maintenance that can only be provided by the lessor, then it is more likely to be an operating lease.
- *Cost:* Operating leases are usually more expensive than finance leases.
- *Cancellation:* An operating lease can be cancelled easier and at less cost, when compared with a finance lease.
- *Obsolescence:* In a finance lease, the lessee takes over this risk, whereas it remains with the lessor when the lease is an operating lease.

6.   Report

To:	A Client
From:	A Student, Financial Consultant
Date:	30 May, 20X2
Re:	Short-term and medium-term sources of finance

As requested, I have prepared this report to offer advice on short-term and medium-term sources of finance. The report will first address factors that should be considered when selecting an appropriate source of finance and will then outline the main features of a number of sources of finance.

The factors that should be considered when selecting an appropriate source of finance may be summed up by a series of questions:
For how long is the finance required?
How much finance is required?
What will it cost?
For what purpose is it required?

For how long is the finance required?
Finance that is repayable within one year is regarded as short term, whereas finance repayable between one and seven years is considered to be medium-term financing.

The determination of the period over which finance is required facilitates the choice of short-term or medium-term sources: for example, €/£10,000 required for ten days until a customer settles an account suggests a short-term source, rather than a medium-term source.

How much finance is required?
A company must assess the amount of finance required to facilitate selection of the source of finance. For example, if an amount of €/£75,000 is needed, a medium-term loan for four years may be more appropriate than a bank overdraft for up to a year.

What will it cost?
It is important to establish the costs of similar sources of finance so that the most economical source may be selected for the particular circumstances.

For what purpose is it required?
This aspect deals with the matching principle, i.e. the purpose of the finance should be matched by the type of financing selected. For example, the purchase of a non-current asset

986 FINANCE: THEORY AND PRACTICE

expected to have a useful economic life of five years would be more appropriately matched with a medium-term source of finance, than with a short-term source of finance.

There are various sources of short-term and medium-term finance; however, this report will outline the main features of four of the main sources:

- Bank overdraft (short-term source)
- Medium-term bank loan (medium-term source)
- Hire purchase (medium-term source)
- Leasing (medium-term source)

(The solution should refer to the following key points.)

a) **Bank overdraft**
- Flexible – the lender may borrow as much, or as little, as is required.
- Relatively cheap – interest is charged only on the amount used.
- Overdraft interest is deductible for taxation purposes.
- Variable interest rate applies.
- Usually requires security or guarantee.
- In some instances, the bank account must be in credit for 30 days during the year.
- This financing is repayable on demand.
- Suitable and commonly used for financing short-term working capital requirements.

b) **Medium-term bank loan**
- Usually contract based.
- Requires security, which may be a fixed or floating charge on assets.
- May have to adhere to a financial covenant requiring a specific level of interest cover or a minimum current asset ratio.
- Repayable in a lump sum or by instalments.
- Loan may allow 'rest periods' when instalments may not be payable and no penalty applies.
- Interest rate attaching to the loan may be fixed or variable.
- Commonly used for purchase of non-current assets.

c) **Hire purchase**
- Commonly used for purchase of non-current assets such as plant and machinery.
- A hire purchase company purchases the asset and, in return for regular instalments, supplies the asset to a hiree.
- Hiree gains immediate use of asset, without high initial capital payment.
- Hire purchase payments include both capital and interest elements.
- Legal ownership remains with the hire purchase company until all instalments have been paid.
- Generally considered to be an expensive source of finance.

d) **Leasing**
- A lease conveys the legal right to use an asset in return for payment of a fee.
- Ownership of asset remains with the owner, the lessor.
- Lease agreements may be for less than a year or for the entire life of an asset.
- There are two types of lease: an operating lease and a finance lease.

- An operating lease is a type of rental – the lessee is not responsible for insurance or maintenance of the asset being leased.
- Operating leases are usually used for smaller assets; for example, office equipment, etc.
- Finance lease agreements require that the lessee is responsible for the insurance and maintenance of the asset being leased.
- Finance leases are typically used for larger non-current assets, such as vehicles, plant and machinery, etc.

When operating a company, it is very important to ensure that proper financing is in place. It is necessary to consider for how long the finance is required, how much is required, what the associated costs are and why the finance is required. Once these questions have been answered, it should be clear whether a short or medium-term source of finance is required and it will be possible to make a choice between the various sources available. This report has highlighted the features of the most commonly used sources of short-term and medium-term finance, each should be considered carefully before making a selection.

I hope that this report has provided all the information that you require. If you have any further questions about any aspect of the report, please do not hesitate to contact me.

A Student
Financial Consultant

CHAPTER 6

••

SOLUTIONS TO REVIEW QUESTIONS

1.   The purpose of a *restrictive covenant* is to restrict the extent to which management (who act on behalf of equity holders) can 'engage in opportunistic behaviour' to increase the value of equity at the expense of the other main collective investors in the company – for example, creditors and debt holders. The more restrictive the covenants, the less risky the debt, hence this debt will be valued higher by the market.

2.   A *trust deed* sets out the terms of the contract between a company and its bond holders and establishes the identity of a trustee and sets out his/her powers. It contains information such as the coupon rate, date interest should be paid, redemption date, right to receive financial statements and restrictive covenants.

3.   The company could set up a sinking fund. It could stagger the repayment by issuing a band of redemption dates (for example, redeemable 2015–2025). It could repurchase some of the bonds on the market, or make an offer to repurchase the bonds to the bond holders. It could issue the bonds as irredeemable and buy them back when it suits. It could issue equity capital and use the proceeds to redeem the bonds.

4.   Fallen angel.

5.   There will be fifteen payments into the sinking fund. The terminal value of the fund should be €/£2,500,000 × 1.05 = €/£2,625,000. The future value of an annuity factor for 15 payments that earn a fixed rate of 15% is 47.580. Therefore, the required yearly repayment (X) is:

$$X \times 47.580 = €/£2,625,000$$
$$X = €/£55,170$$

So long as the sinking fund earns the target return of 15%, then a transfer of €/£55,170 every year for 15 years will result in the sinking fund having a terminal value of €/£2,625,000.

6.   The current return on Jock plc's bonds is:

$$r = \frac{€/£9}{€/£90}$$

$$= 10\%$$

Therefore, this is a very good investment for the investor, as his expected return is 8%.

7.   The cash flows in relation to each bond are as follows:

Year	Cash flow
	€/£
0	(95)
0.5	5
1	5
1.5	5
2	5
2	100

This information can then be used to find the exact half-yearly discount rate, which can then be converted into an annual rate.

Year	Cash flow	Discount factor	Present value	Discount factor	Present value
	€/£	Try 5%	€/£	Try 8%	€/£
0	95	1.000	95	1.000	95
1–2 (4)*	(5)	3.546	(17.73)	3.312	(16.56)
2	(100)	0.823	(82.30)	0.735	(73.50)
			(5.03)		4.94

*Though the cash flows occur over a two-year period, it is a four-period annuity that needs to be used at half the rate.

Using interpolation, a more precise estimate of the half-yearly rate is:

$$5\% + \frac{-5.03(8-5)}{-5.03-4.94} = 6.51\%$$

This half-yearly rate is then converted to an annual rate:

$$(1+0.0651)^2 - 1 = 13.44\%$$

This rate is gross and can be reduced for the bond holder's tax rate to get the net return to the bond holder.

8.   The approach is to find the discount (compound interest rate) 'r' that would be achieved if €/£50 were to be invested now to achieve a terminal value payment of €/£100.

This is represented by the following:

$$€/£50(1+r)^{10} = £100$$

This can be rearranged to:

$$r = \sqrt[10]{100/50} - 1$$

$$r = 0.0718(7.18\%)$$

Therefore, an investor is receiving an annual gross return of 7.18% (before tax).

CHAPTER 7

....

SOLUTIONS TO REVIEW QUESTIONS

1.   *Book value of equity:* This represents a combination of the investment made by equity holders and undistributed gains made by the company. It includes the book value of the equity share capital, the share premium account, the capital redemption reserve, the revaluation reserve and revenue reserves. The total of these will equate to the book value of a company's total assets less its total liabilities. It bears little relationship to market value, which will factor in unrecorded items such as intellectual capital, the quality of the management team and expectations about future earnings.

   Nominal value: Each share a company issues has a nominal value (otherwise known as par value). The nominal value is established by the directors of a company when it is being incorporated, with the value and number of shares authorised for issue being stipulated in a company's articles of association. The nominal value can only be changed using a special resolution at an annual general meeting with the agreement of equity holders.

   Market value: The nominal value bears no relationship to market value which is the price that the market places on the equity of the company.

2.   In the UK the main exchange is the London Stock Exchange. It has two equity trading markets – the 'main market', which is used by very large companies and an over-the-counter market, the 'AIM', which is used mostly by small and medium-sized companies. It is mostly financial intermediaries that trade in these markets. In the UK an independent market, called the PLUS Market also operates as an over-the-counter exchange. It is tailored to suit small and medium-sized companies that wish to raise equity from financial institutions and is also used more by private individuals. In Ireland, the exchange is the 'Irish Stock Exchange'. It has two markets: the 'official list', which has mostly large companies and government bonds listed and the 'IEX', which caters for small to mid-medium-sized companies. All of these exchanges adopt the European guidance on exchanges and follow the recently enacted European Directive on prospectuses; therefore their conditions and rules are similar.

3.   **Advantages**
   (Expand on these points in your solution – see the chapter)
   - *Access to growth capital.*
   - *Access to an acquisitions platform.*
   - *An exit for equity holders.*
   - *Increased credibility.*
   - *Increased public profile.*
   - *Attract, reward and incentivise staff.*

   Disadvantages
   (Expand on these points in your solution – see the chapter)
   - *Market risk.*
   - *Costs.*

- *Agency theory.*
- *Loss of control.*
- *Regulatory burden.*
- *Managerial time tied up.*
- *Employee de-motivation.*

4. *Pre-emptive rights* refers to a stock exchange rule that became a legal requirement. It requires that companies that want to make a further issue of equity for cash, must offer the new shares to the existing equity holders in proportion to their current holding, in the first instance. This gives current equity holders the chance to maintain their percentage holding in a company.

5. The net earnings available for distribution to equity holders under both methods of financing is as follows:

	Preference shares €/£,000	Debentures €/£,000
Earnings before interest and tax	2,000	2,000
Interest: (€/£2,000,000 × 14%)	–	280
Earnings before tax	2,000	1,720
Taxation @ 40%	800	688
Earnings available for distribution	1,200	1,032

Therefore, equity holders are better off were the company to issue debentures.

6.

a) *Before:*

Each lot of two shares is currently worth: (2 × €/£5.00)	€/£10.00
The new issue will be priced at: (1 × €/£4.00)	€/£4.00
The total holding is worth:	€/£14.00

After:

Therefore, after the issue the theoretical ex-rights share price expected will be: (€/£14.00/3)	€/£4.67

b) The value of the right attached to each existing share will be:
    €/£5.00 – €/£4.67 = €/£0.33 per existing share.

c) The value of the right were it assumed to be attached to the new share is:
    (€/£4.67 – €/£4.00) €/£0.67 per new share. *(This can also be found by multiplying the existing shares required to qualify for a new share by the value of the rights per current share: €/£0.67 (€/£0.33 × 2) (rounded)).*

d)   *Before:*
The equity holder owned 2,000 shares valued at
€/£5.00 per share: (2,000×€/£5.00)   €/£10,000

To receive the 1,000 new shares the equity holder
will have to pay the company: (1,000×€/£4.00)   €/£4,000

After:
The equity holder will own (2,000+(2,000/2))
3,000 shares valued at €/£4.67. Total value:
(3,000×€/£4.67)   €/£14,000

Therefore the equity holders wealth has not increased, but the company will have
€/£4,000 additional cash to invest in projects.

e)   *Before:*
The equity holder owned 2,000 shares valued at
€/£5.00 per share: (2,000×€/£5.00)   €/£10,000

After:

The equity holder decides to sell his rights.
He is issued with 1,000 rights which he can sell for €/£0.67 each
so he gets cash worth: (1,000×€/£0.67)   €/£670

He still has his 2,000 shares though they are worth €/£4.67 each
after the issue: (2,000×€/£4.67)   €/£9,340

Total equity holder value: €/£10,010

(The difference is rounding.)

f)   The number of shares the equity holder can purchase is calculated using the following
formula:

$$\frac{\text{Rights price} \times \text{Number of shares allotted}}{\text{Theoretical ex-rights price}}$$

(€/£0.67 × 1,000)/€/£4.67 = 144 shares

Therefore the equity holder will have to sell (1,000−144) 856
rights providing him with cash of: (856×€/£0.67)   €/£574.00

Which he will use to purchase 144 shares at €/£4.00 each:
(144×€/£4.00)   €/£576.00

(The difference is rounding.)
After the sale the equity holder will have 2,144 shares valued at
€/£4.67: (2,144×€/£4.67)   €/£10,012

Equivalent to his original investment of €/£10,000.
(The difference is rounding)

g)   The company will sell the rights at an auction and reimburse the equity holder the proceeds, net of costs incurred selling the rights: €/£670 (€/£0.67 × 1,000). A cheque for €/£670, less any auction fees, will be issued to the equity holder, by the company.

7.   According to Simpson (2001), venture capitalists will base their decision on four fundamental areas of the proposed venture: the strengths of the management team; the entrepreneur leading the team; the product; and market opportunities. Simpson goes on to state that the integrity and quality of the management team is the most-significant influence.

Having a clear exit strategy is also very important. Venture capitalists will want a high return and will want to be able to liquidate it within about five to seven years. The most lucrative means is by flotation and venture capitalists are more open to investing in companies with this objective in mind.

CHAPTER 8

SOLUTIONS TO REVIEW QUESTIONS

1. *Working capital* is a company's investment in net current assets. It is the difference between a company's operating current assets and its operating current liabilities.

2. *Over trading* occurs when a company grows too quickly with insufficient long-term finance to support the increased level of assets that should be held, given the higher level of operational activity.

3. *Over capitalisation* is the over investment in current assets, whilst paying suppliers in a timely manner, i.e. an over investment in working capital. It describes a situation whereby too much inventory is held and credit periods allowed are too long, yet trade payable days are short.

4. The solution is split into three parts, the first considers the profitability assumed by the directors, the second identifies the change in overall working capital requirements and the third considers the changes in each of the components of working capital.

   i. *Profitability*

	Current year	Next year
	€/£'000	€/£'000
Sales	500,200	580,000
Cost of goods produced	420,050	500,000
Profits	80,150	80,000

   As is highlighted in the question, it would appear initially, that the absolute amount of profit made in the current year will be maintained in the coming year. However, this does not mean that the company is as profitable, as the profits are only possible if the increase in sales is achieved. The gross margin achieved from each pound/euro of sales has actually fallen from 16c/p in the euro/pound to 13.8c/p in the euro/pound.

   Gross profit percentage

	Gross profit	80,150	80,000
	Sales	500,200	580,000
		= 16%	= 13.8%

   ii. *Change in working capital.*
   The above analysis does not take into account the potential cost/savings from an increase/decrease in working capital requirements. The working capital requirements are as follows:

	Current year	Next year
	€/£'000	€/£'000
Finished goods inventory	60,000	70,000
Work-in-progress inventory	45,000	80,000
Raw material inventory	80,000	150,000
Trade receivables	62,500	65,000
Trade payables	(42,000)	(60,000)
Working capital requirement	205,500	305,000

An additional cash requirement of €/£99,500 (€/£305,000 – €/£205,500) is predicted based on the budgeted figures for the coming year. This will not be without cost. The question does not indicate whether the company has an overdraft. In addition, it does not mention the return that can be made by the company in other investments. However, it is assumed that a finance cost will be incurred due to the increase in working capital requirements. For example, if the company has an overdraft that charges 10%, then the increase in working capital requirements would lead to an additional interest charge of €/£9,950 per year. This reduces profitability by almost 12.5% (i.e. €/£9,950/€/£80,000). Based on this information it would seem that the company is not going to perform as well in the next period and equity holders should be made aware of the expected fall in profitability.

iii. *Assessment of working capital management*
The working capital policy pursued by the company can be evaluated for its efficiency using changes to the operating cycle of each of the components.

	Current year	Next year
	€/£'000	€/£'000
Finished goods inventory	60,000	70,000
Operating cycle		

$$\frac{\text{Finished goods}}{\text{Cost of goods sold}} \qquad \frac{60,000 \times 365}{420,050} \qquad \frac{70,000 \times 365}{500,000}$$

Finished goods conversion period	52.14 days	51.1 days

Finished goods are expected to be held for 51 days next year, relative to 52 days this year. This is a sign of efficiency and may lead to a reduction in storage costs that are normally associated with finished goods.

Work-in-progress inventory	45,000	80,000

Operating cycle

$$\frac{\text{Work-in-progress}}{\text{Cost of goods sold}} \qquad \frac{45,000 \times 365}{420,050} \qquad \frac{80,000 \times 365}{500,000}$$

Work-in-progress conversion period	39.1 days	58.4 days

The production period has increased by almost 19 days. This indicates a problem area. Production is expected to be less efficient in the coming year. This may account for the reduction in finished goods days. The company should investigate the production process to highlight reasons for the increase in work-in-progress period and take steps to reduce this.

Raw material inventory	80,000	150,000

Operating cycle

$\dfrac{\text{Raw materials}}{\text{Purchases of raw materials}}$	$\dfrac{80,000 \times 365}{280,000}$	$\dfrac{150,000 \times 365}{340,000}$
Raw material inventory conversion period	104.28 days	161.03 days

There has been an increase in the level of raw material held. Now 161 days worth of purchases are being held, compared to 104 days in the prior year. This is an indication of over-buying and tying up funds unnecessarily. It also suggests that the increase in the work-in-progress period is not attributed to delays/stock-outs of raw material and is more associated with the other costs of production such as staff costs and overheads. The purchasing manager may have availed of high discounts – however, this is not clear from the profitability analysis in part i. This area should also be investigated and the planned expenditure and inventory levels reduced.

Trade receivables	62,500	65,000

Operating cycle

$\dfrac{\text{Trade receivables}}{\text{Sales}}$	$\dfrac{62,500 \times 365}{500,020}$	$\dfrac{65,000 \times 365}{580,000}$
Trade receivables conversion period	45.61 days	40.9 days

The trade receivables conversion period has fallen by approximately four days. This means that the credit manager is receiving funds in quicker than in the prior year. So long as the manager is not giving discounts that adversely affect profitability, this is a sign of efficient credit management, which actually releases funds.

Trade payables	42,000	60,000

Operating cycle

$\dfrac{\text{Trade payables}}{\text{Purchases}}$	$\dfrac{42,000 \times 365}{280,000}$	$\dfrac{60,000 \times 365}{340,000}$
Period of credit granted by suppliers	54.75 days	64.42 days

The trade payables conversion period has increased by almost ten days. This is a source of funds to the company, as credit purchases do not have to be paid for as quickly. This increase in credit period allowed may be as a result of an agreement to purchase larger quantities, if so then it is a false saving, as the funds are just tied up in raw materials, which have to be stored at a cost. If the credit period taken is not agreed and is assumed; then the company runs the risk of annoying the supplier, possibly affecting the supply price, discounts and even supply in the long run.

Overall

The main area of concern is the level of raw materials being held and work-in-progress (production). These components need to be investigated to determine where the suspected inefficiencies are going to occur; corrective action should be taken.

CHAPTER 9

. . . .

SOLUTIONS TO REVIEW QUESTIONS

1. In a manufacturing company it is normal to find four types of inventory: finished goods; work-in-progress; raw materials; and consumables. In a retail company two types of inventory are typical: purchased finished goods and consumables.

2. The purpose of inventory management is to minimise the cost of holding inventory and ordering inventory, whilst ensuring there are no stock-out costs.

3. There are several negative consequences associated with not having an appropriate inventory management system. Some key consequences are outlined:

    The inventory costs and hence production costs may not be properly recorded and therefore the financial information on production and inventory will not be reliable. In addition, where there is no system to record inventory movement accurately, it is harder for managers to monitor and control costs.

    Where an appropriate monitoring system is not used, there may be excessive use of inventory in the production process, resulting in excessive waste.

    If inventories are stored without proper planning, then there may be:

    -   Stock-outs;
    -   Time costs associated with searching for inventory;
    -   Physical deterioration of inventory where there is no system to use older items first, etc;
    -   A higher risk of theft; or
    -   A higher risk of hazard where the inventory is of a hazardous nature, for example, the inventory may be flammable or poisonous.

4. A company uses the EOQ model to determine the optimum level of inventory to order to minimise the total inventory holding costs and ordering costs. It is used to determine optimum inventory levels.

5. JIT is an inventory management system that aims to minimise inventory holding costs. It requires strong quality procedures and is dependent on a company having good relationships with its suppliers and a sophisticated inventory management system to allow fast communication between all the parties involved with the inventories.

6. a) (i)   EOQ = square root of $((2 \times F \times U)/CP)$

        Where: U = Annual demand
                 F = The cost of placing an order
                 CP = The holding cost per annum

        The EOQ is the square root of $((2 \times 200{,}000 \times €/£32)/ (€/£8 \times 10\%) = 4{,}000$ units

The number of orders=200,000 units/4,000 units per order=50 orders

The annual ordering cost=number of orders×cost per order=50×€/£32=€/£1,600

Holding cost per annum=average inventory×holding cost per unit=4,000/2×(€/£8×10%)=€/£1,600

(ii)   To consider the impact of retaining the existing order quantity, we must compare the holding and ordering costs that would be incurred at the existing economic order quantity, to the costs that would be incurred if the order quantity was changed to the new EOQ.

Costs of ordering at the existing order quantity:

Order in batches of 4,000 units

		€/£
Order costs:	((242,000 units/4,000 units)×€/£32)	1,936
Holding costs:	((4,000 units/2)×€/£0.80)	1,600
Total costs:	(€/£1,936+€/£1,600)	3,536

Costs of ordering at the new EOQ:
The new EOQ is the square root of:
  ((2×242,000×€/£32)/(€/£8×10%))=4,400 units

Order in batches of 4,400 units

	€/£
Order costs:	
((242,000 units/4,400 units)×€/£32)	1,760
Holding costs:	
((4,400 units/2)×€/£0.80)	1,760
Total costs: (€/£1,760+€/£1,760)	3,520

The impact of retaining the order quantity of 4,000 units when annual demand increases to 242,000 units, is an excess of holding and ordering costs of €/£16. For a variation in the demand of 42,000 units from the estimated forecast of 200,000 units; an increase of €/£16 is immaterial. Although the EOQ is based on a precise number, it should be recognised that there is a range within which the total costs of inventory will not vary a great deal: this is known as the Economic Order Range (EOR). The implication of this is that the EOQ model can still be successfully used in situations where demand is not completely certain.

(iii)   The EOQ model is not appropriate in the following circumstances:

• When ordering costs are not known;
• When fixed inventory holding costs are not known;
• When demand cannot be reasonably forecast;

- Where there are discounts for bulk buying;
- Where other inventory systems are used such as JIT; and
- Where goods are manufactured internally (use EBQ).

(b) The ABC inventory classification system classifies inventories into three categories:

A - high-value inventory items;

B - medium-value inventory items; and

C - low-value inventory items.

It has been found that in many organisations, the profile of their inventory is such that a high percentage of the value of their inventory is represented by a small quantity of the inventory and conversely, a large quantity of inventory represents a small percentage of the total value of their inventories.

By analysing inventories into ABC categories, management can identify high-value items easily. They can then use the inventory classification to assist them in their inventory control. High-value items, which are often a small quantity of inventory, represent the greatest asset and hence risk to the organisation. Thus, in their inventory control they may decide to operate very strict control over their Category A inventories, compared to the controls in place for Category C inventories.

CHAPTER 10
••

SOLUTIONS TO REVIEW QUESTIONS

1. The 80/20 rule is a form of credit management wherein the small number of customers who account for the majority of sales from a company (80%) are identified and given priority attention in the credit-collection process. The aim is not to press them more than other customers for payment and to foster strong customer goodwill.

2. This can signal that a customer is starting to become higher risk, particularly if this is a new customer. They may have exceeded their credit periods with other companies that subsequently restrict supply, resulting in an increase in demand. Alternatively, it may signal that the credit limit for this customer is set at too low a level. If an appropriate level is not set, then this may cause a customer to seek their supplies elsewhere, resulting in lost contribution.

3. The *credit period* is the amount of time customers are allowed before they have to make payment.

4. *Credit quality* refers to the probability that customers will not pay their accounts on time and potentially become bad debts.

5. The cost of granting credit includes: the opportunity cost of finance tied up in trade receivables – these funds could be used to reduce an overdraft or be invested to earn a return; the risk of bad debts; the possibility of having to allow a discount; and the cost of administration time spent chasing up outstanding accounts. The benefit to be gained from granting credit is the contribution earned from the sale. If credit is not awarded, a customer may just take their custom elsewhere.

6. The average collection period is calculated as follows:

Collection period		Proportion of good debts	Expected days
36	×	10%/90%	4
45	×	60%/90%	30
72	×	20%/90%	16
			50

The investment in trade receivables that needs to be financed is therefore:

Credit sales (net of bad debts) × Trade receivables cash conversion ratio

$$(€/£5,000,000 - €/£500,000) \times 50/365 = €/£616,438.$$

7.   *Proposed expansion into new market*
      Insight Limited's proposed expansion into a new market can be evaluated as follows:

      (i)   *Calculate the direct effect on the income statement*

	€/£'000	€/£'000
Sales		10,000
Less:		
Variable costs	8,000	
Bad debts	500	
Collection costs	100	(8,600)
Net profit before deducting financing costs		1,400

      (ii)   *Financing costs*
      Increase in debtors: sales less bad debts × 60/365

= (€/£ 10m − €/£0.5m) × 60/365	1,561.6
Increase in inventory	1,000
Less increase in creditors:	
€/£10m × 80% × 30/365	(657.5)
Increase in working capital	1,907.1

      (iii) *Integration of income statement effect and financing costs*

Net profit before deducting financing costs	1,400
Less financing costs:	
Increase in working capital × 12%	
€/£1.907m × 12%	(229)
	1,171

      (iv)   *Conclusion*
      Expansion into the new market should increase annual net profit by approximately €/£1.2 million. Insight Limited should proceed with its expansion plans.

8.   a)   (i)   An aggressive working capital management policy involves financing part of the permanent portion of current assets using temporary short-term credit. In addition, a company pursuing such a policy will attempt to minimise its holdings of current assets, through maintaining the minimum level of safety stocks and trying to strictly control levels of trade receivables.

                  The net investment in working capital is minimised, but the return on the investment will be affected by the extent to which the restriction on current asset levels, particularly inventories, may have impacted on the sales levels achieved. The excessive reliance on short-term credit, and the matching of short-term finance with long-term uses, makes this a risky strategy.

            (ii)   A defensive working capital policy involves using long-term capital to finance the permanent portion of current assets and some part of the seasonal variations (that are temporary and could be financed by short-term self-liquidating loans). Relatively large balances of cash and marketable securities, such as government bonds, are maintained, large amounts of inventories are kept on hand and sales are stimulated by the use of a credit policy that provides liberal financing to customers, resulting in a high level of trade receivables.

This is an excessively conservative approach to working capital management, resulting in high levels of cash holdings. It will harm profits, because the opportunity to make a return on the assets tied up as cash will have been missed.

b)   (i)

	Jan–June 2006 (€/£'000s)	Jan–June 2008 (€/£'000s)
Interest costs:		
Trade receivables:		
(€/£700,000 × 8.5% × 0.5)	29.75	
Trade receivables:		
(€/£1,350,000 × 17% × 0.5)		114.75
Inventories: (€/£420,000 × 8.5% × 0.5)	17.85	
Inventories: (€/£420,000 × 17% × 0.5)		35.70
	47.60	150.45

Interest costs have increased by 3.16 times (€/£150,450/ €/£47,600). The directors' estimate is correct, with interest costs increasing for a number of reasons

- The annual costs of overdraft finance have doubled from 8.5% to 17%.
- The proportion of sales on credit terms has increased from 85% to 95%, requiring increased financing.
- Average trade receivables have increased by 93% ((€/£1,350,000/ €/£700,000) – 1).

(ii)

	Six-month period 2006	Six-month period 2008

Trade receivables conversion period:

$$\frac{\text{Average trade receivables}}{\text{Credit sales}} \times 365 \text{ days}$$

	Six-month period 2006	Six-month period 2008
$\dfrac{€/£700,000}{(€/£3,300,000 \times 0.85)} \times 365$	91 days	
$\dfrac{€/£1,350,000}{(€/£3,600,000 \times 0.95)} \times 365$		144 days

Inventory holding period:

$$\frac{\text{Average inventories}}{\text{Total sales (Note 1)}} \times 365 \text{ days}$$

$$\frac{€/£420,000}{€/£3,300,000} \times 365 \qquad\qquad 46 \text{ days}$$

$$\frac{€/£420,000}{€/£3,600,000} \times 365 \qquad\qquad 43 \text{ days}$$

The trade receivables cash-conversion period must be reduced: it has increased by over 50% ((144/91) − 1), from 91 days two years ago to 144 days now. This has fuelled an increase in average trade receivables, causing higher interest costs than when trade receivables were lower.

The inventory holding period has reduced somewhat over the past two years, due to a reduction in the inventory of finished goods. The company should investigate whether levels could be reduced further without significantly influencing customer service. The reasons for the increase in raw materials inventory by 26.3% ((120/95) − 1)) over the past two years should be investigated, given that sales levels have only increased by 9% ((€/£3,600,000/€/£3,300,000) − 1).

The company should look into the feasibility of operating Just-in-Time (JIT) purchasing for raw material supplies and JIT production in the manufacturing process. Work-in-progress levels are the most significant component of total inventories and are indicative of, perhaps, poor production control, allowing inventories to build up, or else a long manufacturing cycle time. Both of these factors need investigation by management and the true cause of high work-in-progress inventory levels should be discovered and addressed.

Note 1:

The cost of sales figure is unavailable for the work-in-progress and finished goods inventory turnover calculations. The purchases figure is unavailable for raw material inventory turnover calculations. Sales is used as a proxy for the unavailable information.

9.   The *risk assessment checklist* could include the following questions.

- Has the customer exceeded the agreed credit limit?
- Has the customer exceeded the agreed credit period?
- Have any of the cheques received from the customer bounced?
- Has the customer requested a longer credit period?
- Is the customer in the habit of disputing invoices (delay tactic)?
- Does the customer offer post-dated cheques?
- Has the customer's order quantities reduced with little explanation?

- Have there been any newspaper articles or web stories that would cause questions to be asked in respect of the financial position of a customer?
- Have there been negative rumours from other companies in respect of the customer's payment.
- Does the customer only pay for goods when the invoice for the next sales order is received?
- Is there an increase in the customer's staff turnover, particularly management?
- Does the customer state that the cheque is in the post, when experience dictates that it is not?
- Do the credit control staff have difficulties contacting the customer?

10.   The main aim of *creditor management* is to obtain good quality, keenly priced supplies using the longest credit period possible, whilst minimising the cost of administering and managing the supplies. These costs are interrelated and a balance has to be obtained that results in the maximisation of equity holder wealth. The following *key* points should help to ensure that the objective is achieved:

- Foster a strong credit reputation and ethical approach to creditor management.
- Ensure staff are appropriately trained.
- Put in place strong procedures and controls to ensure documentary and computer processes are efficient and effective.
- Ensure the credit period and limit received is formally documented in a credit agreement from each supplier.
- Review the policy and negotiate any changes with each supplier.

CHAPTER 11

$\cdots\cdots\cdots\cdots\cdots\cdots\cdots\cdots\cdots\cdots\cdots\cdots\cdots\cdots\cdots\cdots\cdots\cdots$

SOLUTIONS TO REVIEW QUESTIONS

1.   *Transaction motive:* Holding sufficient cash to cover the operational transaction costs of a company.

Precautionary motive: Holding a cash buffer to allow payment of unexpected one-off cash outflows.

Speculative motive: Holding an additional amount of cash to allow management to take advantage of profitable opportunities when they arise at short notice.

2.   *Transmission delay:* Delays in the time between a supplier writing a cheque and it getting to a company's premises.

Lodgement delay: Delays in the time between receiving a cheque and lodging the cheque to a bank.

Clearance delay: Delays in the time between a cheque being presented to a bank and the cash being available for use.

3.   There are many factors that can result in cash shortages. The answer might include:

- Inflation;
- Growth;
- Losses;
- Capital expenditure;
- Dividend payments;
- Seasonal fluctuations in operations;
- Taxation; or
- Debt repayments.

4.   The *Baumol cash management model* assumes there is certainty in the consumption of cash, that it is consumed by a company at a constant rate over time and when cash reaches the minimum level, it is replenished by an optimum amount. This model aims to ensure that a company always has cash for its predetermined requirements, and minimises the overall cost of keeping cash.

The *Miller Orr model* is a stochastic model that assumes cash usage is variable over time. It predicts this variability based on historic patterns and uses this to identify two action points, which automatically induce the purchase or sale of securities to meet a predetermined target balance. The minimum level of cash is predetermined by a company. The Miller Orr model calculates the spread, which allows the calculation of the target level and ceiling level of cash. Only when the cash balance reaches the ceiling or floor level will a purchase or sale of securities take place.

5.   *Current policy*

The cost of the current lodgement policy is the interest saving forgone for each day that takings are not lodged. It is assumed that the company's overdraft rate is higher than their cost of capital/investment return potential; hence this is the appropriate opportunity rate to use when quantifying the cost of not lodging.

Therefore, the cost of not lodging every day is the amount that could be lodged multiplied by the daily overdraft rate. The daily takings are the yearly sales divided by the number of days the shop earns income. It is open six days each week for every week in the year. Therefore, the total income is generated over 312 (6×52) days in each year and the daily takings are €/£12,500 (€/£3,900,000/312).

The daily overdraft rate is approximated from the yearly rate 0.0329% (12%/365).

Therefore, the daily interest forgone is €/£4.1125 (€/£12,500 × 0.0329%).

The number of days' interest lost is as follows:

Day sales arise	Days until banked*
Monday	6
Tuesday	5
Wednesday	4
Thursday	3
Friday	2
Saturday	1
Total	21

The monies are banked on Monday morning so will be eligible for deduction when that day's interest is calculated.

The total cost for the week is €/£86.3625 (€/£4.1125 × 21).

The total cost each year is therefore €/£4,490.85 (€/£86.3625 × 52).

Proposed policy
As the takings are lodged at the close of business every day, the only interest forgone is the Saturday takings, which are lodged with Monday's takings at the close of business on a Monday. Therefore, the cost will be: €/£427.70 (2 × €/£4.1125 × 52).

By implementing the accountant's suggested policy, Thomas stands to save €/£4,063.15 (€/£4,490.85 − €/£427.70).

6.   In this question the lower limit (L) is set by the company at €/£10,000. The variance in daily cash flows is €/£1,000,000; the fixed transaction cost (F) is €/£50; and the daily interest rate (i) is 0.025% (9.125%/365).

The spread is:

$$\text{Spread} = 3 \times \sqrt[3]{\frac{3FV}{4i}}$$

$$\text{Spread} = 3 \times \sqrt[3]{\frac{3 \times €/£50 \times €/£1,000,000}{4(0.025\%)}}$$

$$= €/£15,940$$

The ceiling level is therefore the minimum balance plus the spread.

$$\text{Ceiling level} = €/£10,000 + €/£15,940$$
$$= €/£25,940$$

$$\text{Target level} = €/£10,000 + (1/3 \times €/£15,940)$$
$$= €/£15,313$$

The company will purchase €/£10,627 (€/£25,940 − €/£15,313) of securities when the cash balance reaches €/£25,940, and sell €/£5,313 (€/£15,313 − €/£10,000) of securities when the balance reaches €/£10,000.

CHAPTER 12

•••

SOLUTIONS TO REVIEW QUESTIONS

1. The value of Enero plc's shares (P_0) to be used in the calculation of the WACC is €/£900,000 ((€/£2.05 − €/£0.15 − €/£0.10) × 500,000).

2. The expected net cash inflow from issuing one share will be €/£2.30 (€/£2.50 − €/£0.20).

    The company pays constant dividends of 46c/p per share. Therefore, the cost of equity is 20% (€/£0.46/€/£2.30).

3. Abril plc's cost of equity (Ke) is:

    $$\frac{8c/p(1+0.06)}{90c/p} + 0.06 = 0.1542(15.42\%)$$

4. Mayo plc's ROCE (r) is 20%. Its retentions (b) are 50%. Therefore, expected growth in dividends (g) is 10% (50% × 20%).

5. The market value (P_0) is the earnings per share multiplied by the price-earnings ratio of a similar quoted company: €/£900,000 (500,000 × (€/£0.20 × (10 × 90%))).

6. The current market value of the debentures is €/£112.00 for each €/£100.00 block. There is no mention of issue costs and the debentures are trading cum-interest. Therefore, the market value of a single debenture to be included in the WACC is €/£102 (€/£112 − (€/£100 × 10%)). The total market value of the debentures is: €/£10,200,000 ((€/£1,000,000/€/£100) × €/£102).

    The cost of the debentures is as follows:

Year	Cash flows	Discount Try 5%	NPV	Discount Try 10%	NPV
	€/£		€/£		€/£
0	102	1.000	102.00	1.000	102.00
1–8	(10(1–0.3))	6.463	(45.24)	5.335	(37.35)
8	(100)	0.677	(67.70)	0.467	(46.70)
			(10.94)		17.95

    $$Kd = 5\% + \frac{-€/£10.94(10\% - 5\%)}{-€/£10.94 - €/£17.95} = 6.89\%$$

7.   The WACC can be used as an appropriate discount rate for capital investment appraisal when the WACC reflects the company's long-term optimal capital structure, the investment being financed is of the same business risk to that of the company, the project is small, the finance being raised is in the same proportion to the current level of debt and equity in the company (this can be achieved over time – so short-term fluctuations are assumed to happen), and all the information is readily available (i.e. there is a market value for debt capital and the equity capital).

8.   Crystal plc

a)   The after-tax weighted average cost of capital should be calculated.

Calculation of the cost of equity:

(i)	Equity shares	€/£
	Market value of shares cum-dividend	3.27
	Less dividend per share: (€/£810,000/3,000,000)	0.27
	Market value of shares ex-dividend	3.00

The formula for calculating the cost of equity when there is dividend growth is:

$$Ke = \frac{Do(1+g)}{Po} + g$$

Where: Ke = cost of equity
   Do = current dividend
   g = rate of growth
   Po = current ex-dividend market value.

In this case, the future rate of growth (g) in dividends is estimated from the average growth in dividends over the past four years.

$$€/£810,000 = €/£620,000\,(1+g)^4$$

$$(1+g)^4 = \frac{€/£810,000}{€/£620,000}$$

$$(1+g)^4 = 1.3065$$
$$(1+g) = 1.069$$
$$g = 0.069\,(6.9\%)$$

The cost of equity is:

$$Ke = \frac{€/£0.27 \times 1.069}{(€/£3.27 - €/£0.27)} + 0.069 = 0.165(16.5\%)$$

(ii)   *7% debentures*
   In order to find the after-tax cost of the debentures, which are redeemable in ten years time, it is necessary to find the discount rate (IRR) that will give the future after-tax cash flows a present value of €/£77.10

The relevant cash flows are:

(1)   Annual interest payments, net of tax, which are €/£60,970 (€/£1,300,000×7 %×67%), for ten years; and

(2)   A capital repayment of €/£1,300,000 in ten years time.

It is assumed that tax relief on the debenture interest arises at the same time as the interest payment. In practice the cash flow effect is unlikely to be felt for about a year, but this will have no significant effect on the calculations.

IRR calculation

	€/£'000
Try 8%	
Current market value of debentures:	
(€/£1,300,000 at 77.1%)	(1,002.3)
Annual interest payments net of tax:	
(€/£60,970×6.710)	409.1
Capital repayment:	
(€/£1,300,000×0.463 (8% in ten years time))	601.9
NPV	8.7
Try 9%	€/£'000
Current market value of debentures:	
(€/£1,300,000 at 77.1%)	(1,002.3)
Annual interest payments net of tax:	
(€/£60,970×6.418)	391.3
Capital repayment: (€/£1,300,000×0.422)	548.6
NPV	(62.4)

$$\text{IRR} = 8\% + \frac{€/£8,700 \times (9\% - 8\%)}{€/£8,700 - (-€/£62,400)}$$

$$= 8.12\%$$

(iii)   *The weighted average cost of capital*

	Cost	%	€/£,000
Market value	€/£'000		
Equity	9,000	16.50	1,485
7% debentures	1,002	8.12	81
	10,002		1,566

$$\frac{€/£1,566,000}{€/£10,002,000} \times 100 = 15.7\%$$

The above calculations suggest that a discount rate in the region of 16% might be appropriate for the appraisal of new investment opportunities.

b) Difficulties and uncertainties in the above estimates arise in a number of areas.

The cost of equity: The above calculation assumes that all equity holders have the same marginal cost of capital and the same dividend expectations, which is unrealistic. In addition, it is assumed that dividend growth has been, and will be, at a constant rate of 6.9%. In fact, actual growth in the years 2005/6 and 2008/9 was in excess of 9%, while in the year 2007/8 there was no dividend growth. 6.9% is merely the average rate of growth for the past four years. The rate of future growth will depend more on the return from future projects undertaken than on the past dividend record.

The use of the weighted average cost of capital: Use of the weighted average cost of capital as a discount rate is only justified where the company in question has achieved what it believes to be the optimal capital structure (the mix of debt and equity) and where it intends to maintain this structure in the long term.

The projects themselves: The weighted average cost of capital makes no allowance for the business risk of individual projects. In practice some companies, having calculated the WACC, then add a premium for risk. In this case, for example, if one used a risk premium of 5%, the final discount rate would be 21%. Ideally, the risk premium should vary from project to project, since not all projects are equally risky. In general, the riskier the project the higher the discount rate, which should be used.

CHAPTER 13

··

SOLUTIONS TO REVIEW QUESTIONS

1. Investment appraisal involves making decisions now, on whether to invest in investments which will provide a stream of future cash flows/profits to a company. The fact that the analysis considers *expected* outcomes is an underlying limitation which exists with every appraisal technique.

    The reliability of the appraisal process is influenced by the reliability of the estimates made.

    Another steering influence in the decision making process is the strategic aim of a company. Only projects that have outcomes that are aligned with the strategic goals of a company should be undertaken.

    Only relevant cash flows should be considered when appraising a project. Therefore, sunk costs should be ignored; the focus being on analysing the incremental cash flows relative to the project. This is complicated slightly by the need to include opportunity costs (loss in cash flows elsewhere) due to an investment being implemented.

    As the appraisal process considers estimates made about the future, the process should take the time value of money into consideration. This is also problematic, as determining an accurate discount rate is not straight forward. The company's current cost of capital is subject to fluctuation due to the influence of the external economy/markets and the investment being analysed may not be of a similar type to the projects/business undertaken by a company. The new project might be riskier, or less risky and determining an appropriate rate is to some extent subjective.

2. *Advantages of using the ARR for investment appraisal*

    - The ARR is simple to calculate.
    - The ARR is readily understandable by management who are familiar with performance being assessed using ratios calculated from financial statements. These ratios are usually based on profits not cash flows, for example the ROCE.
    - An ARR can be set by management and used as a cut-off point when assessing a number of projects.

    Disadvantages of using the ARR for investment appraisal

    - This technique ignores the time value of money.
    - The ARR ignores the timing of cash flows.
    - The size of an investment is not reflected in the resulting rate.
    - The duration of the project is not reflected in the resulting rate.
    - The ARR is not influenced by the pattern of profits expected.

3. *Advantages of using the payback period method for investment appraisal*

    - The payback period method is quick and easy to calculate.
    - The method focuses on cash flows, not profit.
    - It provides useful information to help a manager decide between two projects, which have similar ARRs.

- It is a useful screening device for selecting projects for further analysis, particularly where a company has liquidity issues.
- It is regarded as a useful risk screening device. The risk associated with cash flow estimates is deemed to increase time, i.e. the further away an estimated cash flow, the greater the risk that the actual cash flow will be different.

Disadvantages of using the payback period method for investment appraisal

- This method focuses on cash flows and ignores profitability.
- The payback period method ignores cash flows expected after the payback period, which may be substantial.
- The time value of money is ignored.
- The size of the project does not influence the resultant ranking of the projects.

4. In this instance the discount rate should be the company's cost of capital – 18%. As there is no inflation the current value of the cash flows will equal their future value in money terms.

Year	Sales (€/£)	Costs (€/£)	Net cash flow (€/£)	Discount factor (12%)	NPV (€/£)
0	–	(200,000)	(200,000)	1.000	(200,000)
1	200,000	(120,000)	80,000	0.893	71,440
2	200,000	(132,000)	68,000	0.797	54,196
3	200,000	(145,200)	54,800	0.712	39,018
4	200,000	(159,720)	40,280	0.636	25,618
5	200,000	(175,692)	24,308	0.567	13,783
				NPV	4,055

As the project yields a positive NPV of €/£4,055, the investment should be undertaken.

5. There are two approaches to the appraisal of these cash flows. In the first approach, the cash inflows are deflated by the inflation rate (5%) to get the current value of the expected cash flows which are then discounted at the company's cost of capital – 12%. This cost of capital equates to the real rate required, as it does not take into account inflation.

Year	Net cash flow (€/£)	Deflation of cash flows (5%)	Deflated cash flows (€/£)	Discount factor (12%)	Inflation-adjusted present value (€/£)
0	(200,000)	1.000	(200,000)	1.000	(200,000)
1	80,000	0.952	76,160	0.893	68,011
2	68,000	0.907	61,676	0.797	49,156
3	54,800	0.864	47,347	0.712	33,711
4	40,280	0.823	33,150	0.636	21,083
5	24,308	0.784	19,057	0.567	10,805
				NPV	(17,234)

When inflation is taken into account, the project becomes unviable, as a negative NPV of €/£17,234 is now reported.

Alternatively, the real rate and the inflation rate can be combined using the formula provided in the chapter, to give a single nominal/money rate which can then be used to discount the cash flows.

Nominal rate = $((1 + \text{Real rate})(1 + \text{Inflation rate})) - 1$
Nominal rate = $((1.12)(1.05)) - 1$
Nominal rate = 17.6%

Year	Net cash flow (€/£)	Discount rate (17.6%)	Present value (€/£)
0	(200,000)	1.000	(200,000)
1	80,000	0.850	68,000
2	68,000	0.723	49,164
13	54,800	0.615	33,702
4	40,280	0.523	21,066
5	24,308	0.444	10,793
		NPV	(17,275)

Using the formula to calculate the nominal/money discount rate and applying this to the expected actual cash flows yields the same result as is obtained when the cash flows are deflated and then discounted at the real rate of return. The small difference between the two reported NPVs is as a result of rounding in the discount rates.

6. The *nominal/money discount rate* is the resultant rate, after adjustment for expected inflation. This rate will always be greater than the real rate, unless an economy suffers deflation, which is unlikely.

The *real discount rate* is the rate before being adjusted for expected inflation.

7. a) In selecting a discount rate for project appraisal: the rate chosen should reflect the risk of the investment being appraised and also the financial risk of the business as a whole. The risk of an individual project is a function of operating leverage and the cyclical nature of the cash flows, whereas the financial risk of a company as whole is a function of its capital structure.

   • Using a company's overall WACC as the discount rate for evaluating a new project, is only appropriate when the new project has the same business risk, as existing projects. Thus, if the risk of a new project is different to the risk on existing investments, then the risk of that project will not adequately be captured in the investment appraisal if the overall WACC is used as the discount rate. The advantage; however, to using the existing WACC as its discount rate, is that is easily calculated and there is no subjectivity regarding the calculation as it is based on market values and the costs of existing funds.

   • Using a system of multiple cut-off rates overcomes the major disadvantage associated with using the WACC. Using a specific rate appropriate to reflect individual project risk usually involves adjusting the WACC upwards or downwards. As the specific discount rate is based on the WACC, the financial risk of a company as a whole is captured in the analysis and additionally the risk of an individual project is captured by adjusting the WACC to reflect that risk. This approach is easy to understand, but the difficulty is assessing the risk of an individual project and adjusting the WACC appropriately. One way of calculating the adjustment required to the WACC to arrive at a specific discount rate, is to use the CAPM. However, there may be arbitrariness involved in calculating risk premiums and also beta factors are based on historic data and may not reflect future risks.

- Basing a discount rate for a project on the specific cost of funding that project is inappropriate. While the approach may capture the investment risk associated with the individual project it fails to capture the financial risk of a company. For example, if it was proposed that a new project would be fully financed by debt funding, the cost, and hence the risk to a company as a whole, is not simply the cost of debt finance. It also includes any increase in return required by equity holders who perceive an increase in financial risk due to increased leverage in the company.

For the reasons set out above (in option two) multiple cut-off rates that reflect the risk of each investment should be adopted for appraising new projects.

b)   *NPV calculations:*

	Year 0	Year 1	Year 2	Year 3	Year 4	Year 5
	€/£'000	€/£'000	€/£'000	€/£'000	€/£'000	€/£'000
Plant	(1,500)	–	–	–	–	40
Equipment	(500)	–	–	–	–	–
Working capital	(40)	–	–	–	–	40
Cash inflows *(W1)*	–	415	635	975	1,015	–
Tax payable *(W2)*	–	–	8.5	(13.5)	(47.5)	(55.5)
Net cash flow	(2,040)	415	643.5	961.5	967.5	24.5
Discount @ 18%	1.000	0.847	0.718	0.609	0.516	0.437
Present value	(2,040)	352	462	586	499	11

NPV   (€/£130,000)

As the NPV is negative the project should be rejected.

W1: Calculation of annual cash flows:

	Year 1	Year 2	Year 3	Year 4
	€/£'000	€/£'000	€/£'000	€/£'000
Operating cash flows	400	620	960	1,000
Loan interest	15	15	15	15
Relevant cash flows	415	635	975	1,015

W2: Calculation of tax:

	Year 1	Year 2	Year 3	Year 4
	€/£'000	€/£'000	€/£'000	€/£'000
Relevant cash flows	415	635	975	1,015
Capital allowances	(500)	(500)	(500)	(500)
Balancing charge				40
Taxable profits	(85)	135	475	555
Tax at 10%	(8.5)*	13.5	47.5	55.5
Tax payable (receivable) in	Year 2	Year 3	Year 4	Year 5

*NOTE: The approach taken in this suggested solution with regard to the tax loss is to obtain a refund of the amount. An alternative treatment of this loss would be to carry it forward to the following year to reduce the tax charge of that year.

IRR

To calculate the IRR we need to discount the net cash flows at two discount rates. Therefore, the cash flows are now discounted at 12%:

	Year 0	Year 1	Year 2	Year 3	Year 4	Year 5
	€/£'000	€/£'000	€/£'000	€/£'000	€/£'000	€/£'000
Net cash flow	(2,040)	415	643.5	961.5	967.5	24.5
Discount @ 12%	1.000	0.893	0.797	0.712	0.636	0.567
Present value	(2,040)	371	513	685	615	14

NPV   €/£158,000

$$IRR = 12\% + \frac{€/£158,000 \times (18\% - 12\%)}{(€/£158,000 - (-€/£130,000))} = 15.3\%$$

The IRR calculation confirms the decision that the project should be rejected as the IRR (15.3%) is below the cost of the project (18%).

CHAPTER 14

··

SOLUTIONS TO REVIEW QUESTIONS

1.   Both of the terms – *risk* and *uncertainty* – refer to the likelihood that actual cash flows and/or discount rates are different to the estimated cash flows or discount rates used in the initial project evaluation. *Risk* occurs when probabilities can be assigned to the various possible outcomes. When the outcomes are regarded as *totally uncertain*, no probabilities can be assigned to the outcomes.

       The two terms are sometimes used interchangeably as the probabilities assigned to possible outcomes are sometimes determined in a very subjective manner, making them quite uncertain. This usually occurs when a project is new to a company and no prior experience is available to allow an objective assessment of the probabilities of various outcomes.

2.   The *margin of safety* is a term used to signify the extent of change that can affect a variable, before the project starts to make a negative NPV. It is the point at which the project breaks even. It can be stated either in whole pounds or as a percentage change in the amount by which a variable's cost/price can change.

3.   *Simulation analysis* is being more widely used due to advances in computer technology regarding speed at which computer packages can perform calculations and provide a wide range of possible NPV outcomes for a project. Each project can be modelled (this includes pre-programming impacts of changes in, for example, the relationship between units and price and time – the various potential amounts and probabilities of occurrence are input) and then the computer performs hundreds of separate NPV calculations. The computer uses *Monte Carlo Simulation* techniques, wherein it randomly selects a variable to change, runs the calculation and plots the resultant NPV and its probability of occurring. At the end of the process, a probability distribution is plotted, which highlights the expected return from the project and its related risk.

4.   Two steps that might help to reduce country risk when investing in a capital project in a foreign country might include:

       •   Using a foreign manager, a foreign workforce and sourcing materials in the foreign country;
       •   Forging links with the government of the foreign country and involving them in the project; or
       •   Partnering with a local company in the foreign country.

5.   *Foreign exchange risk* is the risk that the actual exchange rate will be different to that estimated in the initial cash flow projections. A change in exchange rate will affect the cash flows of a project; a rise in the value of the foreign country's currency will have a beneficial effect (assuming a net cash inflow situation). For example, assume that €/£1 is worth $0.80. This means that a cash inflow of $1,000 received in the US is worth €/£1,250. You are told that the dollar has strengthened so now €/£1 is worth $0.70. In this instance, the $1,000 cash flow will

be worth €/£1,428. Similarly, a fall in the value of the foreign currency will have a negative impact on the cash flows. In this instance, one dollar buys less euros/pounds – for example, €/£1 is worth $0.90. In this instance, the $1,000 cash flow will be worth $1,111.

6.   a)   *The NPV of the 'most likely' outcome is as follows:*

Year	Cash flows €/£	Discount (10%)	Present value €/£
0	(200,000)	1.000	(200,000)
1	110,000	0.909	99,990
2	110,000	0.826	90,860
3	160,000	0.751	120,160
		NPV	111,010

b)   *Sensitivity analysis:* The first variable being analysed is sales price. There are two approaches – both are covered in this solution.

    (i)   *Break-even point (sales price):* The first approach uses the IRR to determine the sales price that will result in the investment breaking even. A lower sales price of €/£3.50 is used as the sales price of €/£4.20 gives a positive NPV.

The NPV when sales price is €/£3.50:

Year	Cash flows €/£	Discount (10%)	Present value €/£
0	(200,000)	1.000	(200,000)
1–3	40,000 (W1)	2.486	99,440
3	50,000	0.751	37,550
		NPV	(63,010)

W1: The yearly cash inflow is now:

	€/£	€/£
Sales: (100,000 × €/£3.50)		350,000
Labour	210,000	
Materials	80,000	
Other direct costs	20,000	310,000
Net cash flow		40,000

Using interpolation, the break-even sales price is:

$$€/£3.50 + \frac{-€/£63,010 \ (€/£4.20 - €/£3.50)}{-€/£63,010 - €/£111,010} = €/£3.75$$

Therefore, the margin of safety is €/£3.75 – €/£4.20 = (€/£0.45)

Sales price can fall by 45c/p before break-even point is reached.

Or can fall by 10.7% (45c/p/€/£4.20).

A second approach can also be adopted. The first step is to find the PV of the variable that is changing – in this case sales.

The PV is €/£1,044,120 (€/£420,000 × 2.486).

The NPV is 10.63% (€/£111,010/€/£1,044,120) of the PV of the variable; therefore, sales price can fall by 10.63% before the project reaches break-even point.

Sales price can fall by 44.6c/p (€/£4.20 × 10.63%) to €/£3.75 before the project starts to make a loss.

ii)   *Break-even analysis: labour*
      The IRR is again used.

A trial cash outflow of €/£270,000 is utilised, as follows:

Year	Cash flows	Discount factor	Present value
	€/£	(10%)	€/£
0	(200,000)	1.000	(200,000)
1–3	50,000 *(W2)*	2.486	124,300
3	50,000	0.751	37,550
		NPV	(38,150)

W2: Yearly cash inflow now:

	€/£	€/£
Sales: (100,000 × €/£4.20)		420,000
Labour	270,000	
Materials	80,000	
Other direct costs	20,000	370,000
Net cash flow		50,000

Using interpolation, the break-even labour cost is:

$$€/£270,000 + \frac{-€/£38,150 \ (€/£210,000 - €/£270,000)}{-€/£38,150 - €/£111,010}$$

$$= €/£254,654$$

Therefore, the margin of safety is €/£44,654 (€/£254,654 − €/£210,000).

Labour can increase by €/£44,654, before break-even point is reached.

Or can increase by 21.26% (€/£44,654/€/£210,000).

The second approach is also adopted. The first step is to find the PV of the variable that is changing – in this case, labour.

The PV is €/£522,060 (€/£210,000 × 2.486).

The NPV is 21.26% (€/£111,010/€/£522,060) of the PV of the variable. Therefore, labour costs can increase by 21.26% before break-even point is reached.

Labour costs can rise by €/£44,654 (€/£210,000 × 21.26%) to €/£254,646 before the project starts to make a loss.

iii) *Material costs*
      The second method is utilised for the next two variables as it is quicker to calculate:

The PV of the material costs is €/£198,880 (€/£80,000 × 2.486).

The NPV as a percentage of the PV of the material costs is 55.8% (€/£111,010/€/£198,880).

Therefore, material costs can increase by 55.8% before the project reaches break even.

Material costs can rise by €/£44,640 (€/£80,000 × 55.8%), to €/£124,640 (€/£80,000 + €/£44,640) before the project starts to make a loss.

iv)   *Other direct costs*

The PV of other direct costs is €/£49,720 (€/£20,000 × 2.486).

The NPV as a percentage of the PV of other direct costs is 223% (€/£111,010/€/£49,720).

Therefore, other costs can increase by 223% before the project break-even point is reached.

Other costs can rise by €/£44,600 (€/£20,000 × 223%) to €/£64,600 (€/£20,000 + €/£44,600) before the project starts to make a loss.

v)   *Discount rate*

The IRR is utilised to find the sensitivity in the discount rate. A rate of 43% is utilised as an alternative estimate.

Year	Cash flows	Discount factor	Present value
	€/£	(43%)	€/£
0	(200,000)	1.000	(200,000)
1–3	110,000	1.530	168,300
3	50,000	0.342	17,100
		NPV	(14,600)

$$10\% + \frac{€/£111,010 \ (43\% - 10\%)}{€/£111,010 - €/£14,600} = 39.16\%$$

The discount rate can increase from 10% to 39.16% before the project starts to make a loss.

The riskiest variable affecting this project is sales price, as a fall of above 10% in sales price will result in the project returning a negative NPV.

c)   *Scenario analysis*

	Best case scenario		Worst case scenario	
	€/£	€/£	€/£	€/£
Sales:				
(130,000 × €/£4.25)		552,500		
(80,000 × €/£3.80)				304,000
Labour	200,000		230,000	
Materials	76,000		50,000	
Other direct costs	18,000	294,000	22,000	302,000
Annual net cash flow		258,500		2,000

Year	*Best case scenario*			*Worst case scenario*		
	Cash flow	*Discount factor (10%)*	*Present value*	*Cash flow*	*Discount factor (13%)*	*Present value*
0	(200,000)	1.000	(200,000)	(200,000)	1.000	(200,000)
1–3	258,500	2.486	642,631	2,000	2.361	4,722
3	50,000	0.751	37,550	50,000	0.693	34,650
			480,181			(160,628)

The scenario analysis would therefore have the following results:

Outcomes	NPV
Best case	€/£480,181
Most likely	€/£111,010
Worst case	€/£(160,628)

CHAPTER 15

....

SOLUTIONS TO REVIEW QUESTIONS

1. The *capital structure* of a company is its mix of long-term debt and equity.

2. The *WACC* of a company is the return required by a company to cover the average return required by its investors. The investors are the holders of debt and equity capital in the company, i.e. their investment makes up a company's capital structure. In general, equity investors require a higher return relative to debt investors, as they face higher risks. Therefore, as the different sources of long-term finance in a company cost different amounts the level of each type held will impact on the overall WACC.

3. *Financial risk* captures the additional sensitivity in returns available to investors arising due to the level of debt in a company's financial structure.

4. a) The question provides the reader with information on equity share price and earnings for the two companies. This is sufficient to use the dividend-valuation model to calculate the cost of equity. The question states that all earnings after interest are distributed as dividends, hence there is no growth. As share price is given ex-dividend, the only workings required are to find dividends.

	Pero plc	*Gato plc*
	€/£'000	*€/£'000*
Earnings	300	300
Interest		
(€/£1.2m × 10%)	–	(120)
Dividend	300	180

	Pero plc	*Gato plc*
Cost of equity	$\dfrac{€/£300,000}{(€/£1.40 \times 1,600,000)}$	$\dfrac{€/£180,000}{(€/£1.60 \times 800,000)}$
Cost of equity	*13.39%*	*14.06%*

b) Pero plc is an all-equity-financed company. Its WACC is the same as its cost of equity (13.39%).

Market value of equity and debt:

	Pero plc	*Gato plc*
	€/£'000	*€/£'000*
Equity: 1,600,000 × €/£1.40	2,240	
800,000 × €/£1.60		1,280
Debt	–	1,200
Total company value (D+E)	2,240	2,480

Gato plc's WACC is as follows:

$$\frac{\text{€}/\text{£}1,280,000}{\text{€}/\text{£}2,480,000}(14.06\%) + \frac{\text{€}/\text{£}1,200,000}{\text{€}/\text{£}2,480,000}(10\%) = 12.10\%$$

c)   Gato plc has a higher cost of equity (14.06%) compared to Pero plc (13.39%) as its equity holders require a higher return to compensate them for the financial risk they bear due to gearing. However, Gato plc has an overall lower WACC because its capital structure includes debt, which is at a lower cost, and the additional premium commanded by its equity holders is more than compensated for by the cheaper debt.

d)   M&M (without taxes) would argue that the WACC in both companies should be the same, as a company's capital structure does not determine its value. The cost of equity in one of the companies is out of equilibrium. As the return/dividend is known, then the only explanation is that the equity is mispriced. It may be undervalued in Pero plc or overvalued in Gato plc, or a mixture of both.

5.   There are two views of the cost of capital. The *traditional view* states that the cost of capital is a function of a company's capital structure; therefore, a company's overall cost of funds can be reduced by a judicious use of debt finance. The *M&M view* states that in a world with no taxes, there is no gearing effect on market value, i.e. the cost of capital is independent of gearing because the advantages of using cheaper debt are exactly offset by the disadvantages (increased financial risk) of that increased debt.

Certain restrictive assumptions govern the M&M view:

- Perfect capital markets exist, where companies can borrow unlimited amounts at similar rates of interest.
- There are no taxes or transactions costs.
- Personal borrowing is a perfect substitute for corporate borrowing.
- Companies exist with the same level of business or systematic risk but different levels of gearing.

M&M put forward three propositions:

Proposition I
The cost of capital and market value of a company are independent of its gearing. This is because the market value of any company is given by capitalising its expected total earnings at the capitalisation rate appropriate to an all-equity company of that risk class. The income generated by a company from its business activities is that which determines value rather than the way in which it is split between the providers of capital.

$$K_o = \frac{\text{EBIT}}{\text{MV}}$$

K_o = Overall cost of capital
MV = Market value of the company in total
        (This should be independent of capital structure.)
EBIT = Earnings before interest and tax or net operating income.

Proposition II

The introduction of debt into the capital structure immediately increases the financial risk of the equity holders, who require a premium to compensate. This exactly offsets the apparently lower cost of debt and leaves Ko and the MV of the company constant.

This means that the expected return on the equity of an enterprise is equal to the expected return on a pure equity stream, plus a financial risk premium proportioned by the ratio of debt to equity. The effect on the cost of equity of introducing debt into the capital structure is that the cost of equity rises linearly to offset the lower cost debt directly, giving a constant overall cost of capital irrespective of the level of gearing.

Note: This is derived as follows.
As debt is introduced, the market value of equity in an ungeared company is given by:

$$E = \frac{EBIT - (K_d \times D)}{K_e}$$

> $E =$ Market value of equity
> $K_d =$ Cost of debt capital
> $D =$ Market value of debt
> $K_e =$ Cost of equity capital

Therefore, the equity cost of capital is given by:

$$K_e = \frac{EBIT - (K_d \times D)}{E} \ \textit{(through cross multiplication)}$$

From Proposition I, EBIT = Ko (E+D), so substituting into the above we obtain:

$$K_e = \frac{K_o(E + D) - (K_d \times D)}{E} = \frac{(K_o \times E) + (K_o \times D) - (K_d \times D)}{E}$$

$$K_e = \frac{(K_o \times E) + D(K_o - K_d)}{E}$$

Dividing by E, we get: $K_e = K_o + (K_o - K_d)\dfrac{D}{E}$

Note that Ko here is the overall cost of capital before debt introduction and is therefore the same as Keu used in the chapter.

Proposition III

To be accepted, projects will have to have a rate of return (k*) greater than or equal to the overall cost of capital Ko. To achieve this, M&M rests on the arbitrage assumption – if there are two enterprises, X and Y, each with the same EBIT, they must be valued equally, whether the payments are made to equity holders or debt holders. If they are not, then arbitrage profits can ensue.

6.   a)   Under M&M theory, capital structure will not impact on the WACC or the value of a company. Therefore WACCg = WACCu = Keu, which is 18%.

    b)   Using M&M proposition II the cost of equity in Marron Plc, the geared company, is:

$$= 18\% + \frac{20\%}{80\%}(18\% - 8\%)$$

$$= 20.5\%$$

7.   a)   The WACC is 12%.
    b)   The cost of equity in Rosa plc is:

$$= 12\% + \frac{40\%}{60\%}(12\% - 10\%)$$

$$= 13.33\%.$$

8.   Violeta plc has a WACC and Keu of 12%.

Under M&M proposition I (without taxes) the WACC of Amarillo plc is also 12%.

Amarillo plc has debt (D) with a market value of ($€/£2,000,000 \times 50\% = €/£1,000,000$) and equity (E) worth ($1,000,000 \times €/£3.00 = €/£3,000,000$). Its cost of debt is:

$$\frac{i}{P_d} \quad \frac{€/£4}{€/£50}$$

$$= 8\%$$

Using proposition II the cost of equity works out as:

$$= 12\% + \frac{1}{3}(12\% - 8\%)$$

$$= 13.33\%$$

9.   a)

$$WACCg = 18\%\left(1 - \frac{20\%(30\%)}{100\%}\right)$$

$$= 16.92\%$$

    b)   Using M&M proposition II the cost of equity in Marron plc, the geared company, is:

$$= 18\% + \frac{20\%}{80\%}(18\% - 8\%)(1 - 0.30)$$

$$= 19.75\%$$

10.   a)

$$WACCg = 12\%\left(1 - \frac{40\%(40\%)}{100\%}\right)$$

$$= 10.08\%$$

b)   The cost of equity in Rosa plc is:

$$= 12\% + \frac{40\%}{60\%}(12\% - 10\%)(1 - 0.40)$$

$$= 12.8\%.$$

11.   Violeta plc has a WACC and Keu of 12%.

Amarillo plc has debt D with a market value of (€/£2,000,000 × 50% = €/£1,000,000) and equity E worth (1,000,000 × €/£3.00 = €/£3,000,000). Its cost of debt is:

$$\frac{i}{Pd} \quad \frac{€/£4}{€/£50}$$

$$= 8\% \text{ (before tax)}$$

Using proposition II the cost of equity works out as:

$$= 12\% + \frac{1}{3}(12\% - 8\%)(1 - 0.3)$$

$$= 12.93\%$$

The WACC is:

$$\frac{€/£1,000}{€/£4,000}(8\%)(1 - 0.3) + \frac{€/£3,000}{€/£4,000}(12.93\%) = 11.10\%$$

Or:

$$WACCg = 12\%\left(1 - \frac{25\%(30\%)}{100\%}\right)$$

$$= 11.1\%$$

CHAPTER 16

1. The value of a company is the value of its total assets (non-current and current). The value of a company's equity is its total assets less all outstanding liabilities, such as current liabilities and long-term liabilities (including preference shares).

2. The expected free cash flow is as follows:

	€/£m
Net revenue	50
Depreciation	7
Interest[1]	–
Taxation[2]	(11.75)
Investment	(6.0)
Increase in working capital	(1)
Free cash flow	*38.25*

1. Interest is not deducted when calculating the free-cash flows.

2. Taxation = €/£50 − €/£3 = €/£47 × 25% = €/£11.75

3. a) The value of Greenan plc's equity can be calculated using the dividend valuation model.

   The dividend (Do) is 20% (1–80%) of the EPS, which is 5c/p (20% × 25c/p).

   Growth (g) is calculated using the formula g=br where b is the retentions percentage (80%) and r is the return earned by the investments (16%). Therefore, g=12.8% (80% × 16%).
   The cost of equity (ke) is 14%.

   $$P_0 = \frac{D_0(1+g)}{Ke-g}$$

   $$P_0 = \frac{5c/p(1+0.128)}{0.14-0.128}$$

   $$P_0 = €/£4.70$$

   b) Now Ke is 16%

   $$P_0 = \frac{5c/p(1+0.128)}{0.16-0.128}$$

   $$P_0 = €/£1.7625$$

4. The advantages of using the dividend yield ratio approach are now outlined.

   Straightforward to calculate: On the face of it this approach is simple to calculate.

   Constant dividend policy: This approach works best when companies pursue a constant dividend policy. This approach will value the company's shares according to the cash flow benefit expected to be received by shareholders, in the form of dividends. This is argued to be the most relevant value to minority shareholders

The disadvantages of using this approach are now outlined.

Sourcing a similar quoted company: In practice it is difficult to find a company to benchmark against as no two companies are ever the exact same.

Dividend policies: Different companies will have different dividend policies. Some companies do not pay a dividend at all and private companies typically have lower payout policies when compared to plcs.

Dividends: Dividends represent a portion of a company's earnings and a valuation based on dividends only may not represent the full value of the company, particularly if the company does not adopt a steady dividend payout policy.

5.   a)

Estimated data for year 1	€/£'000	Value drivers
Revenue	1,500	Sales growth
Operating costs	(1,000)	
Gross profit	500	Margin
Tax	(200)	Tax rate
Operating income after tax	300	
Depreciation	180	
Capital expenditure	(220)	Investment
Increase in working capital	(100)	Investment
Free cash flow	160	

b)

Year	Cash flows €/£'000	Discount rate 14%	PV €/£'000
1	160	0.877	140.3
2	200	0.769	153.8
3	220	0.675	148.5
4	250	0.592	148.0
5	280	0.519	145.3
5	3,000	0.519	1,557.0
		NPV	2,292.9

Using the shareholder valuation analysis approach, a company value of €/£2.2929 million results.

c)

Year	Cash flows €/£'000	Discount rate 14%	PV €/£'000
1	(120)*	0.877	(105.2)
2	200	0.769	153.8
3	220	0.675	148.5
4	250	0.592	148.0
5	280	0.519	145.3
6	290	0.456	132.2
7	290	0.400	116.0
8	290	0.351	101.8
9	290	0.308	89.3
9	5,000	0.308	1,540.0
		NPV	2,469.7

*€/£160,000 + €/£220,000 − €/£500,000

Under this scenario the company is valued at €/£2.4697 million, €/£0.1768 million more than under part b).

6.   An analyst usually takes seven to eight steps when valuing a company/share holding. These are listed and explained:

1.   Review the valuation methodologies and determine which of these is the most appropriate, given the purpose of the valuation (i.e. if the valuation is for a minority holding, then the dividend yield basis might be considered to be a starting point. If the valuation is for a controlling holding then an earnings or cash flow basis such as the P/E ratio basis might be first choice. When the purpose of the valuation is to purchase a company for break-up, then the assets basis might be the most appropriate approach).

2.   Review any prior IPOs, mergers, takeovers or company sales of similar type companies. This will give a strong guide as to the expected value to place on the entity.

3.   Find suitable benchmark companies. These companies should be in the same industry, in the same type of business within the industry and sensitive to the same economic influences to the entity being valued.

4.   Select a suitable multiple (influenced by the outcome of one above) and adjust it to take into account differences between the entity being valued and the benchmark entity. For example, there may be a size adjustment, or a marketability/liquidity adjustment.

5.   Where a factor of earnings is being used to value the entity, adjust these so that they reflect the expected equilibrium earnings from the entity in the future. Exceptional items should be removed, additional expected expenses included and economies of scale deducted.

6.   Determine the expected value using the chosen methodology using the adjusted figures from steps four and five. Identify a ceiling and floor value to offer and justify the value chosen.

7.   Consider market demand, market sentiment and the willingness of the company to enter into sale negotiations when deciding on the value to place on the company.

8.   Be prepared to negotiate. Valuations rarely are accepted first time around. Indeed this knowledge usually influences the first bid.

CHAPTER 17
• •

1.   The approach to be taken should include:

- Setting out and clarifying the company's strategic aim in respect of pursuing a takeover policy as a means of growing/investing.
- Detail how a takeover can achieve the strategic aims stipulated.
- Identify possible target companies and perform an analysis of each one to determine which would achieve the strategic aim of the takeover.
- Determine how the target company selected will fit within the group and plan for the future integration of the target company.
- Contact the directors of the target company to determine their views on a takeover. This meeting will include an offer for the company. It is not just a 'touchy feely' meeting.
- Perform a due diligence audit.
- If they are hostile to this, announce the takeover offer publicly.
- If the equity holders accept the offer, then complete the takeover.
- Set up an integration team and act quickly to integrate the new company into the group.
- Perform a post-audit of the whole takeover and integration process.

2.   a)   Market value of A plc is €/£20,000,000 (1,000,000 × €/£20)

Market value of B plc is €/£4,000,000 (400,000 × €/£10)

A plc offers €/£4,500,000 (400,000 × €/£11.25) for B plc, giving a premium of €/£500,000 (400,000 × (€/£11.25 − €/£10.00)).
NPV of the project expected (the present value of the synergies):

$$= \frac{\text{Net earnings from synergies per annum}}{\text{Cost of capital}}$$

$$= \frac{€/£140,000}{0.20}$$

$$= €/£700,000$$

b)   The proportion of the premium going to the equity holders in B plc is 71.42% (€/£500,000/€/£700,000), with the remainder 28.58% (€/£200,000/€/£700,000) going to the equity holders in A plc.

3.   A management buy-out (MBO) is where the current management team of a business purchase that business from the equity holders, usually for cash. The business is normally a subsidiary, branch or small business within a much larger company.

A management buy-in (MBI) is where the management team of a different company (usually in a similar line of business), purchase that part of the company from the equity holders, usually for cash. They normally consider that they can run the business more effectively than it is currently being run by the internal management team.

4. To acquire the equity shares of Target Company plc, Bidding Group plc will have to issue fewer shares. Bidding Group plc's shares have a market value of €/£30.00 per share and Target Company plc's shares now have a market value of €/£7.50, which means that only one share in Bidding Group plc has to be issued to acquire four shares in Target Company plc. So Bidding Company plc can purchase Target Company plc for 50,000 shares (200,000/4).

Summary of the impact of the changes to the value of Target Company plc on the acquisition and on the reported performance of the resultant amalgamated company.

	Bidding Group plc €/£'000	Target Company plc €/£'000	Bidding (post acquisition) €/£'000
Total net earnings	400	400	800
Total market value	6,000	1,500	7,500
Number of shares in issue	200	200	250
Market price per share	€/£30.00	€/£7.50	€/£30.00
Earnings per share	€/£2.00	€/£2.00	€/£3.20
Price-earnings ratio	15 times	3.75 times	9.375 times
Earnings per €/£ invested	6.67%	26.67%	10.67%

Workings	Target Company plc	Bidding Group plc (Post acquisition)
Market price per share	$\dfrac{€/£1,500,000}{200,000}$	$\dfrac{€/£7,500,000}{250,000}$
=	€/£7.50	€/£30.00
Earnings per share	$\dfrac{€/£400,000}{200,000}$	$\dfrac{€/£800,000}{250,000}$
=	€/£2.00	€/£3.20
Price-earnings ratio	$\dfrac{€/£7.50}{€/£2.00}$	$\dfrac{€/£30.00}{€/£3.20}$
=	3.75 times	9.375 times
Earnings per €/£ invested	$\dfrac{€/£2.00}{€/£7.50}$	$\dfrac{€/£3.20}{€/£30.00}$
=	26.67%	10.67%

The impact of a fall in the value of Target Company plc is to make this company cheaper to purchase by Bidder Group plc. As the earnings have not changed, this means that the earnings per share of Bidder Group plc after the acquisition will increase (the total number of shares in issue is now lower than before). This means that an uninformed investor may believe that Bidder Group plc's earnings per share increased by 60% in the period of the acquisition. The reduction in the price-earnings ratio should provide some hints as to the quality of this growth in earnings.

5.   a)   Fox plc is offering a premium of €/£5.00 per share for each share held by equity holders in Hen plc. This amounts to a total premium over market value of €/£2,500,000 (€/£5.00 × 500,000). Therefore, Fox plc expects that the synergies to be made have a minimum net present value of €/£2,500,000.

b)   Assuming that Fox plc's cost of capital is 20%, this means that Fox plc expects yearly net synergy gains (over and above the combined earnings of Fox plc and Hen plc's current earnings) to be a minimum of €/£500,000 per year, calculated as follows:

The present value of the future earnings must at least equal €/£2,500,000. This is equivalent to the synergy gains discounted at 20% into perpetuity. Assume the synergy gains (earnings) are X. They can be found by solving the following perpetuity:

$$\text{Present value} = \frac{\text{Earnings}}{\text{Cost of capital}}$$

$$\text{€/£2,500,000} = \frac{X}{0.20}$$

$$X = \text{€/£2,500,000} \times 0.20$$

$$X = \text{€/£500,000}$$

This represents the minimum expected synergy gains – as the equity holders of Fox plc will not agree to the acquisition unless they also stand to gain a portion of the synergy gains expected.

6.   When a company elects to purchase another entity using cash, the acquisition price is known with certainty and synergy gains do not impact on the cost – it remains static.

When a company purchases another entity using a share exchange deal, then the cost of the acquisition will be affected by the expected synergy gains to be made, as these will be reflected in the bidding company's share price, post-acquisition (assuming perfect capital markets). They increase the cost of the acquisition.

7.   A business that has been demerged and purchased by management (a MBO) might be more successful than it had been when it was part of the group, for the following reasons:

- The management team may be more motivated now that they are the owners (goal congruence).
- The management team have total control. They can make decisions quicker and have more flexibility in their decision making.
- The management team can undertake speculative investments (for example, purchasing supplies at a large discount from a company that is going out of business) and can pursue stricter debt collection policies, or can write off 'no-hope' debts, rather than chasing them up in the courts (it may have been the group's policy to pursue every debt through the courts regardless of size).
- The business will not have to contribute to central costs.
- If profitable, the business can retain profits for investment, rather than transferring it to the parent.

3.   A MBO might fail because:

- The price paid for the business was too high.
- The management team do not have the expertise or contacts to run an independent company.
- Key employees may leave the demerged company – this is likely to happen when employees are unsure about their future.
- Employee pension rights agreed in the original company may be crippling for the new company.
- The finance obtained to back the buyout may not have been sufficient. It may have covered the initial purchase price, but not the set-up costs, working capital, capital investment, etc.
- An economic downturn at this embryonic stage may adversely impact on the demerged entity.

4.   The questions an investor might ask about a buyout include:

- Does the management team have sufficient expertise to take the new company forward?
- Is the price being offered for the business good value, or is it too high?
- What exactly is being purchased – shares in a spin-off company, or assets?
- What contribution to the financing of this buy-out is coming from the management team?
- What is the expected performance of the demerged business?
- What are key assets in the demerged business?
- Why is the group selling this business?
- What has the performance of the business been like in the past?
- Have the management made sufficient provision for the finance of the new independent company (in terms of capital investment, working capital, etc)?
- Is the new business reliant on any key employees?

CHAPTER 18

....

1.   Many companies use derivative financial instruments to reduce risk. Most companies trade with a variety of different customers in a variety of different countries. In addition, most companies have debt. Having to deal with third parties, foreign countries and having debt opens a company up to various types of risk, including commodity risk, exchange rate risk, credit risk and interest rate risk. Risk is defined as the chance that actual outcomes will differ from expected outcomes. If there is too much risk in a company's cash flows, it is difficult for it to plan. Therefore, a company will take a variety of steps to reduce risk by hedging transactions using derivative financial instruments to make cash flows more certain.

2.

   a)   The expected price of a pint of beer in Dublin in one year's time is €3.71 (€3.50 × 1.06). The expected price of a pint of beer in Belfast in one year's time is £2.60 (£2.50 × 1.04).

   b)   The expected forward exchange rate assuming PPP holds will be €3.71/£2.60 = €1.43:£1.00.

3.

   •   The company should exercise the call option as the market value of the share on the exercise date is higher than the exercise price.

   •   ABC plc should buy 10,000 shares at €/£1.80 and then sell them immediately on the open market for €/£2.10 per share.

   Return on the purchase of the call option

Purchase 10,000 call options at 25c/p	(€/£2,500)
Purchase 10,000 shares at €/£1.80	(€/£18,000)
	(€/£20,500)
Sell 10,000 shares at €/£2.10	€/£21,000
Profit on sale	€/£500
Return on investment (€/£500/€/£2,500)	20%

   c)   In this instance ABC plc will not exercise the option, so the loss is the price paid for the option.

   Return on the purchase of the call option assuming the market price is €/£1.60

Purchase 10,000 call options at 25c/p	(€/£2,500)
Loss on investment	(€/£2,500)

   d)   *Assume the company purchases shares in ABC plc.*
        Assume current sale price is €/£2.10

Purchase 1,667 shares	
(€/£2,500/€/£1.50)	(€/£2,500)
Sale value on exercise date	
(1,667 × €/£2.10)	€/£3,500
Profit on investment	€/£1,000

Return on investment	
($€/£1,000/€/£2,500$)	40%

Assume current sale price is €/£1.60
Purchase 1,667 shares

($€/£2,500/€/£1.50$)	($€/£2,500$)
Sale value on exercise date	
($1,667 \times €/£1.60$)	$€/£2,667$
Profit on investment	$€/£167$
Return on investment (($€/£167/€/£2,500$)	6.7%

4.   a)

$$C_0 = \frac{H(P - P_L)}{(1+r)}$$

Where:

C_0 is the value of the call option with one period to the exercise date (?)
P is the current share price ($€/£4.00$)
P_L is the lower value of the share expected at the end of the period ($€/£2.00$)
r is the risk-free rate of return (8%) and
H is the hedging ratio:

$$H = \frac{(C_u - C_L)}{(P_u - P_L)}$$

P_u ($€/£7.00$) and P_L are given in the question. However, C_u and C_L need to be calculated. The maximum value of the option C_u will be the maximum market value less the exercise price, which in this case is $€/£2.00$ ($€/£7.00 - €/£5.00$), the lowest option value C_L will be zero as the option will not be exercised if the share price falls below $€/£5.00$. Therefore:

$$H = \frac{(€/£2.00 - €/£0)}{(€/£7.00 - €/£2.00)}$$

$$H = 0.4$$

And the value of the option is:

$$C_0 = \frac{0.4(€/£4.00 - €/£2.00)}{(1+0.08)}$$

$$C_0 = €/£0.86$$

5.   Option value is usually impacted on by three variables:

a.   *The exercise price listed on the option* – when the exercise price is low, relative to the market value of the asset, then the option will have a high value.

b.   *The length of time to the exercise date* – a call option is a cheap way of obtaining an asset now, but paying for it at some future stage. Therefore, it provides free-credit.

However, this is factored into the price of the option, the longer the period to exercise date, the more valuable the option.

c.   *The variability of returns on the underlying asset* – a call option will only be exercised if the share price rises above the exercise price. In these instances the holder of the option will not exercise the option and the holder will loose the monies paid out to obtain the option. However, if share prices rise above the exercise price, the holder of the option will exercise the option and can avail of unlimited profits. Therefore, an asset with volatile returns is likely to be attractive as the potential for greater profits is higher.

6.   The value of the option is calculated using the Black-Scholes model:

$$P_0 = PN(d_1) - \frac{E}{e^{rt}} N(d_2)$$

Where:

P_0 is the current value of the option (to find)
P is the current value of the asset (€/£7.50)
E is the exercise price (€/£8.00)
e is the exponential constant (2.7183)
r is the risk-free rate of interest for the period 7%
t is the (in years) remaining in the option contract (0.5 years)
σ is the standard deviation of returns expected (40%)

$$d_1 = \frac{Ln(P/E) + (r + \sigma^2/2)t}{\sigma t^{1/2}}$$

$$d_1 = \frac{Ln(750/800) + (0.07 + 0.4^2/2)0.5}{0.4 \times 0.5^{1/2}}$$

$$d_1 = 0.037$$
$$N(d_1) = 0.515*$$

This value is obtained from Appendix six 'Area under the normal curve up to t standard deviations above the mean.

$$d_2 = \frac{Ln(P/E) + (r - \sigma^2/2)t}{\sigma t^{1/2}}$$

$$d_2 = \frac{Ln(750/800) + (0.07 - 0.4^2/2)0.5}{0.4 \times 0.5^{1/2}}$$

$$d_2 = -0.246$$
$$N(d_2) = 1 - 0.5971* = 0.4029$$

This value lies between 0.24 and 0.25 in the tables – found using interpolation.
Therefore the value of the option is:

$$P_0 = 750(0.515) - \frac{800}{2.7183^{0.07 \times 0.5}} \times 0.4029$$

$$P_0 = 386 - 314$$
$$P_0 = €/£0.72$$

7. Stimpy plc wants £10 million. This is the equivalent of €12.5 million at the current exchange rate of £1:€1.25 (£10 million × 1.25).

The interest options open to both are highlighted in the following table.

Can borrow at a	Stimpy plc	Wrent plc
Fixed rate of :	10.25%	11.5%
Variable rate of:	LIBOR + 0.5%	LIBOR + 1.5%

Stimpy plc wants fixed-rate debt from the swap but knows that Wrent plc wants floating-rate debt. Stimpy plc could borrow in the domestic market at LIBOR + 0.5% for the purposes of swapping. Wrent plc's interest options are more expensive than Stimpy plc's options. Wrent plc could borrow in the UK at the fixed rate of 11.5%, however, Stimpy plc will not agree to pay more than 10.25% (the rate it can currently obtain in the home markets). Therefore, the 10.25% becomes the rate that forms part of the swap agreement. Wrent plc will have to make up the shortfall.

Therefore, Stimpy plc should borrow the €12.5 million euro at the variable rate of LIBOR + 0.5%. Wrent plc should borrow £10 million at the fixed rate of 11.5% and then both parties can swap the capital sums and pre-agreed interest payments.

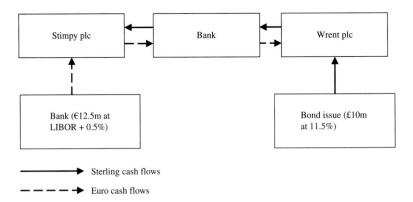

| ─────────▶ | Sterling cash flows |
| ─ ─ ─ ─ ▶ | Euro cash flows |

With the above arrangement the following interest payments will result:

Interest payments	Stimpy plc	Wrent plc
Interest on loan to bank	LIBOR + 0.5%	11.5%
Swap		
Agreed to pay	10.25%	LIBOR + 0.5%
Receives	LIBOR + 0.5%	10.25%
Net interest cost		
before commission	10.25%	LIBOR + 1.75%
Commission	0.15%	0.15%
Total interest to pay	10.4%	LIBOR + 1.9%

Finally, in seven years time Stimpy plc will refund the £10 million to Wrent plc who will use it to pay of the bank and Wrent plc will refund the €12.5 million to Stimpy plc who will also use it to repay the bank. The capital value of the loan has been hedged 100% in this instance against currency fluctuations.

CHAPTER 16

· ·

SOLUTIONS TO REVIEW QUESTIONS

1. It takes time for companies to update their records when share exchanges take place. It is considered that two days is ample time for this administrative process to be completed. Therefore, the market sets a cut-off date which is two days before the company's declared date of record. Buyers before this date are considered to purchase shares cum-dividend, hence are entitled to the distribution. Buyers after this date are trading in the shares ex-div (they have no right to the dividend). This process allows brokers to market the shares clearly as either cum-dividend or ex-dividend.

2. The dividend should not be distributed, as $d_1 + P_1$ is not greater than P_0. The equity holders will be worse off by 2c/p for every share that they own.

3. M&M argue that dividend policy can be irrelevant in a world where there are no taxes, no transaction costs, where equity holders have all company information (and do not misinterpret it), and where there is a constant interest rate (that is equal for companies and investors).

4. The company's cost of capital is 15% and projects B and C's expected returns exceed this target rate.

    Therefore, these projects should be invested in. This amounts to an investment of €/£4,500,000 in the year.

    The remainder of the years earnings: €/£500,000 (€/£5,000,000 − €/£4,500,000), should be distributed as a dividend, resulting in a payout ratio of 10% (€/£500,000/€/£5,000,000).

5. The *clientele effect* is where management decide on a particular policy to attract a particular type of investor, and investors choose companies to invest in because the company's dividend policy matches their desired income type. For example, high income tax payers would be more attracted to a company that pursues a low payout ratio, as increases in that equity holders' value will be reflected in increases in the company's share price. The higher-rate tax payer can then plan the sale of the shares over time taking into consideration other capital transactions, so as to maximise their net tax income position. Individuals have an annual capital gains tax exemption and high-income tax paying individuals will be keen to use this yearly exemption.

6. Optimal Ltd.

Dividend level	Estimated ex-dividend share price	Dividend (net of income tax)	Total value
Nil	100c/p	Nil	100.00c/p
4.0c/p	117c/p	2.80c/p	119.80c/p
4.5c/p	120c/p	3.15c/p	123.15c/p
5.0c/p	134c/p	3.50c/p	137.50c/p
5.5c/p	136c/p	3.85c/p	139.85c/p
6.0c/p	128c/p	4.20c/p	132.20c/p

The optimal dividend level is 5.5c/p. This probably reflects sentiment in the market that a rise in the dividend level will be required to justify an increase in share price. However, too high a dividend may cause the market to view the company as adopting an imprudent dividend strategy.

7. Because a private company does not need to concern itself with such things as the information content of dividends or the clientele effect, it is freer than public companies to decide whether and how much of a dividend to pay. However there are certain factors that will tend to influence those decisions

- *Tax differential* - shareholders may prefer capital gains to dividends due to the lower tax rate on capital gains. In this instance the company may decide to issue low dividends or no dividends at all.
- *Investment opportunities* – if a company has a project or projects that require investment but that will generate returns in excess of the company's cost of capital then it would make financial sense to use whatever cash is required to pursue these opportunities. This may in turn leave a smaller amount of cash for distribution as a dividend.
- *Available cash* – following from the previous point, if a company does not have surplus cash it will not be in a position to pay dividend, unless it seeks to borrow the money.
- *External factors* – there may be various other external factors which limit the amount of dividend that a company can pay. Examples of this would be loan terms & conditions, where a financial institutions specify limits on the level of dividends declared in order to protect their own interest.

b)

Company A

This company is espousing the Tax Differential policy. With this approach investors can expect to maximise the capital appreciation of their shareholding at the expense of dividend payouts. The advantage of this is that if they cash in their investment the gain will be taxed at a lower rate than the dividends would have been taxed at. The disadvantage is that individual investors have to wait to take all their gains at once. They don't get a regular income. Also if an investor pays income tax at the standard rate the tax differential is likely to be so small that, after broker's commission and other associated charges, the investor may actually be worse off.

Where a company has an investor base that doesn't rely on its investments for regular income and is pays income tax at the marginal rate this policy may be the most appropriate.

Company B

By having a fixed percentage payout policy this company is giving a very strong signal to investors. Investors can always be sure of where they stand with the company and what their entitlements are regarding dividend payment. The disadvantage is that the company is locked into this level of dividend payment. If an attractive investment opportunity arose which required an investment of more than 50% of retained earnings, the company may not be able to avail of the opportunity.

This policy would be most likely to maximise shareholder wealth where the company is in a stable environment, it knows the level of shareholders funds it needs to retain and it is not likely to suffer any opportunity losses.

APPENDIX 7. SOLUTIONS   1041

Company C

This company is making its main payouts in the form of scrip issues. The shareholders can, if they wish, sell the newly issued shares at market value. While they may not make a large capital profit on the sale they will also not have to pay much (or any) capital gains tax. The disadvantage is that if they do choose to generate income by selling their shares their overall percentage holding will decrease and their future entitlement to both dividends and scrip issues will reduce.

This policy is likely to maximise shareholder wealth where the shareholders want control over the timing of the revenue generation of their investment.

ABBREVIATIONS

ACCA	Association of Chartered Certified Accountants
AGM	Annual General Meeting
APR	Annual Percentage Rate
APV	Adjusted Present Value
ARR	Accounting Rate of Return
BACS	Bankers Automated Clearing Services Limited
BBA	British Bankers Association
BBAA	British Business Angels Association
BES	Business Expansion Scheme
BIMBO	Management Buy In and Buy Out
BOE	Bill of Exchange
BOGOF	Buy One Get One Free
BPPG	Better Payment Practice Group
BVCA	British Venture Capitalists Association
CBI	Confederation of British Industries
CHAPS	Clearing House Automated Payment System
CIMA	Chartered Institute of Management Accountants
CPA	Certified Public Accountants
DCF	Discounted Cash Flows
DETE	Department of Enterprise, Trade and Employment
DETI	Department of Enterprise, Trade and Industry
EBIT	Earnings before Interest and Taxation
EBQ	Economic Batch Quantity
ECF	Enterprise Capital Fund
EIS	Enterprise Investment Scheme
EMU	European Monetary Union
EOQ	Economic Order Quantity

EPS	Earnings Per Share
EU	European Union
EUA's	European Union Carbon Allowances
Euribor	Euro Inter-Bank Offered Rate
EVA	Economic Value Added
EVCA	European Private Equity and Venture Capital Association
FDI	Foreign Direct Investment
FLA	Finance and Leasing Association
FRA	Forward Rate Agreement
FRN	Floating Rate Notes
FTSE 100	The Financial Times Stock Exchange 100 Stock Index
FV	Future Value
FRC	Financial Reporting Council
GB	Great Britain
GDP	Gross Domestic Product
IAS	International Accounting Standard
IASB	International Accounting Standards Board
IBF	Irish Bankers Federation
ICAI	Institute of Chartered Accountants in Ireland
ICAEW	Institute of Chartered Accountants in England and Wales
ICAS	Institute of Chartered Accountants in Scotland
IFSRA	Irish Financial Services Regulatory Authority
IPO	Initial Public Offering
IRR	Internal Rate of Return
ISEQ	Irish Stock Exchange Quotation
ITP	Irish Takeover Panel
JIT	Just-In-Time Inventory Management
LBO	Leveraged Buy-Out
LIBOR	London Inter-Bank Offer Rate
LIFFE	London International Financial Futures and Options Exchange
LSE	London Stock Exchange
M&M	Modigliani and Miller
MBI	Management Buy In
MBO	Management Buy Out
MRP I	Materials Requirement Planning
MRP II	Manufacturing Resources Planning
NBV	Net Book Value

NI	Northern Ireland
NPV	Net Present Value
OFT	Office of Fair Trading
OTC	Over-The-Counter
PAYE	Pay As You Earn
PBIT	Profit before Interest and Taxation
PI	Profitability Index
PE ratio	Price Earnings Ratio
PLC	Public Limited Company
PPP	Purchasing Power Parity
PV	Present Value
ROCE	Return on Capital Employed
ROI	Republic of Ireland
RVCF	Regional Venture Capital Fund
TV	Terminal Value
SEC	Securities and Exchange Commission
UK	United Kingdom
US	United States
VAT	Value Added Tax
VC	Venture Capital
VCT	Venture Capital Trusts
WACC	Weighted Average Cost of Capital
WCC	Working Capital Cycle
WDA	Written Down Allowance

BIBLIOGRAPHY

Alkaraan, F. and Mitchell, F., (2006), 'Strategic Capital Investment Decision Making: A Role for Emergent Analysis Tools? A Study of Practice in Large UK Manufacturing Companies', *British Accounting Review*, 38, 2, June, 149–174.

Allen, K., (2007), 'Revamped Morrisons Increases its Supermarket Share', *Guardian*, Guardian.co.uk, December 2007 (accessed 21/05/08).

Altman, E. I., (1968), 'Financial Ratios, Discriminant Analysis and the Prediction of Corporate Bankruptcy', *Journal of Finance*, 7.

Altman, E. I., (1983), *'Corporate Financial Distress'*, Wiley.

Arnold, G., (1998), *'Corporate Financial Management'*, FT Prentice Hall.

Arnold, G. and Hatzopoulos, P., (2000), 'The Theory-Practice Gap in Capital Budgeting: Evidence from the United Kingdom', *Journal of Business, Finance and Accounting*, 27, 5&6, 603–626.

Ashton, D. and Acker, D., (2003), 'Establishing Bounds on the Tax Advantage to Debt', *British Accounting Review*, 35, 4, December, 385–400.

Asquith, P. and Mullins, D., (1983), 'The Impact of Initiating Dividend Payments on Shareholders' Wealth', *Journal of Business* (January), 76–96.

Atrill, P., (2000), *'Financial Management for Non Specialists'*, Second Edition, Essex: England, FT Prentice Hall – Financial Times.

Atrill, P., (2005), 'Valuing Company Shares', *Student Publications*, ACCA, 14/07/05, http://www.accaglobal.com/students/publications/finance_matters/

Balcaen, S. and Ooghe, H., (2006), '35 Years of Studies on Business Failure: an Overview of the Classic Statistical Methodologies and their Related Problems', *British Accounting Review*, 38, 1, March, 63–94.

Barnes, E. and Cahill, B., (2005), 'Private or Public Debt? Drivers of Debt Priority Structure for UK Firms', *The Irish Accounting Review*, 12, 1, Summer, 1–14.

Barnes, E. and Linehan, S., (2006), 'The Timing of Seasoned Equity Offerings: Evidence from UK Markets 1990–2002', *The Irish Accounting Review*, 13, 1, Summer, 1–22.

Barrett, T. and Cotter, D., (1990), 'The Dividend Strategy of Irish Manufacturing Companies', *Irish Business and Administrative Research*, 11, 77–90.

Baskin, J., (1989), 'An Empirical Investigation in the Pecking Order Hypothesis', *Financial Management*, 18, 26–35.

Baumol, W., (1952), 'The Transactions Demand for Cash: An Inventory Theoretic Approach', *Quarterly Journal of Economics*, November.

Beaver, W. H., (1966), 'Financial Ratios are Predictors of Failure', *Journal of Accounting Research*, 4.

Beaver, W. H., (1968), 'Alternative Accounting Measures as Predictors of Failure', *The Accounting Review*, January.

Beesley, A., (2006), 'Ambition Grows as Riverdeep Moves Forward', *The Irish Times*, 27 October 2006.

Berry, A. and Robertson, J., (2006), 'Overseas Bankers in the UK and their use of Information for Making Lending Decisions: Changes from 1985', *British Accounting Review*, 38, 2, June, 175–192.

Bills of Exchange Act, (1882), HMSO.

Bills of Exchange Act, (1882), Irish Statute Book, Office of the Attorney General.

BIS, (2008), *BIS Quarterly Review (June 2008); International Banking and Financial Market Developments*, Bank for International Settlements: Monetary and Economic Department, http://bis.org/

Bishopgate Corporate Finance, (2007), 'Valuing Private Companies', Viewpoint: The Newsletter of Bishopgate Corporate Finance Limited, Iss. 4, Spring 2007.

Black F, and Scholes, M., (1973), 'The Pricing of Options and Corporate Liabilities', *Journal of Political Economy*, May-June.

Booz, Allen and Hamilton, (2007), 'Seven Reasons Divestitures are Harder than you Think', *Chief Executive*, http://www.boozallen.com/media/file/seven_reasons_divestures.pdf.

Brealey, R. A., Myers, S.C. and Marcus, A. J., (2001), *Fundamentals of Corporate Finance*, Third Edition, Irwin/McGraw Hill,

Bream, R. and Firn, D., (2002), 'Elan Down to Junk Bond Status', *Financial Times* (London, England), 16 November 2002.

Bridle, A., (2005), 'Is Lords Insolvency Ruling a Threat to SME Funding?' *Irish News*, 20 September 2005.

Brown, P., Izan, H., and Loh, A., (1992), 'Fixed Asset Revaluations and Managerial Incentives', *Abacus*, 28, 1, 36–57.

DETE, Mergers and Takeovers (Control) Acts, 1978 to 1996: Twenty-Fourth Annual Report (Being the report for the year ended 2002), www.entemp.ie

DETI, (accessed 09/02/2007), *'Equity Finance'*, Business link http://www.businesslink.gov.uk/

DETI, (accessed 09/02/2007), *'Floating on a Stock Market: Your Options'*, Business link http://www.businesslink.gov.uk/

DETI, (2007), 'Implementation of the EU Directive on Takeover Bids: Guidance on Changes to the Rules on Company Takeovers', Department of Trade and Industry, Issued February 2007.

Dey, I., (2007), 'Shortlist May Make the Future Look Turquoise', *The Sunday Telegraph* (London), 4 February 2007.

Donaldson, G., (1961), *'Corporate Debt Capacity'*, Harvard University Press.

Done, K., (2006), 'High Hopes of no Big Problems for Aer Lingus IPO', *Financial Times* (London, England), 6 July 2006.

Drury, C., (1996), '*Management Accounting*', International Thompson Business Press, London.

Drury, C. and Braund, S., (1990), 'The Leasing Decision: A Comparison of Theory and Practice', *Accounting and Business Research*, Summer.

Drury, C., Braund, S., Osborne, P., and Tayes, M., (1993), 'A Survey of Management Accounting Practices in UK Manufacturing Companies', *Research Report No. 32*, ACCA.

Elton, E. and Gruber, M., (1970), 'Marginal Stockholder Tax Rates and the Clientele Effect', *Review of Economics and Statistics*, February.

Farrelly, G., Baker, H., and Edelman, R., (1985), 'A Survey of Management Views on Dividend Policy, *Financial Management,* Autumn, 78–84.

FRC, (2003), '*Combined Code on Corporate Governance*', July, Financial Reporting Council.

FRC, (1999), '*Internal Control: Guidance for Directors on the Combined Code (Turnbull Guidance)*', Financial Reporting Council.

FRC, (2005), '*Internal Control: Revised Guidance for Directors on the Combined Code*', October, Financial Reporting Council.

FRC, (2004), '*The Turnbull Guidance as an Evaluation Framework for the purposes of Section 404(a) of the Sarbanes-Oxley Act*', December, Financial Reporting Council.

Gordon, M., (1956), 'Dividends, Earnings and Stock Prices', *Review of Economics and Statistics*, May.

Green, I. and McIlkenny, P., (1991), 'Intertemporal Dividend Models: An Empirical Analysis using Irish Data', *Irish Business and Administrative Research*, 12, 124–135.

Green, P., Pogue, M., and Watson, I., (1993), 'Making the Dividend Decision', *Studies in Accounting and Finance*, 1, 1.

Guinness Peat Group PLC, (2006), '*Information in Respect of the Company's Stock Events in 2006*', http://www.gpgplc.com.au/stockevents/

Henderson, S. and Goodwin, J., (1992), 'The Case Against Asset Revaluations', *Abacus*, 28, 1, 75–86.

Horngren, C., Foster, G., and Datar, S., (2005), '*Cost Accounting: A Managerial Emphasis*', Prentice Hall.

Hotten, R., (2006), 'Review of 2006 From the Sale of YouTube to the Detention of Sportingbet's Chairman', *The Daily Telegraph*, 29 December 2006.

Howard, J. (Prime Minister of Australia), (2002), 'Howard's warning to business on corporate governance', *Australian Politics*, http://www.australianpolitics.com/news/2002/08/02-08-06.shtml

Howe, J. and She, Y., (1998), 'Information Associated with Dividend Initiations: Firm-Specific or Industry-Wide? Special Issue: Dividends', *Financial Management*, Financial Management Association, Autumn.

Hutson, A., (2008), 'Tata's Jaguar takeover hailed by workers', Coventry Telegraph, 27/05/2008, http:www.coventrytelegraph.net/news/

IASB, (1989), '*Framework for the Preparation and Presentation of Financial Statements*' IASCF.

IASB, (1997), *'International Accounting Standard 33: Earnings per share'*, IASCF.

Institute of Certified Public Accountants, (2007), 'Business Expansion Scheme Survey Results 2006', *CPA Bulletin*, 30 January 2007.

InterFinancial Limited, (2002), 'Valuing Private Companies', *Interfinancial Limited*, Vol.2, Iss. 3, pp. 1-4, July 2002.

ICAI, (2005), Anti-Money Laundering Guidance: Republic of Ireland, *Miscellaneous Technical Statement M42*, September 2005, ICAI, Dublin.

Irish Financial Services Regulatory Authority, (accessed 14/02/2007), *'Who We Are/ What We Do'*, http://financialregulator.ie/

Irish Stock Exchange, (2006), *'Annual Statistical Review'*, ISE, http://www.ise.ie/

Irish Takeover Panel, (2007), *'Irish Takeover Panel Act, 1997, Takeover Rules 2007'*, http://www.irishtakeoverpanel.ie/.

Jameson, R., (2008), 'Case Study: Daiwa', http://www.erisk.com/learning/casestudies/Daiwa.asp

Jensen, M. and Meckling, W., (1976), 'Theory of the Firm: Managerial Behaviour, Agency Costs and Ownership Structure', *Journal of Financial Economics*, October.

Jones, C.S., (1982), *Successful Management of Acquisitions* (Derek Beattie Publishing).

Jones, C.S., (1986), 'Integrating Acquired Companies', *Management Accounting*, April.

Jones, M. E. and Sutherland, G., (1999), *'Implementing Turnbull – A Board Room Briefing'*, The Centre for Business Performance, ICAEW, September 1999.

Kussan, M., (2007), *'Benefits to a Company of Flotation'*, London Stock Exchange, Xenos Technical Sheet.

Leeladhar, V., (2006), *'Corporate Governance in Banks'*, http://www.rbidocs.rbi.ord.in/rdocs/bulletin/DOCS/59405.doc

Lefley, F., (1994), 'Capital Investment Appraisal of Manufacturing Technology', *International Journal of Production Research*, 32, 12, 2751–2756.

Lewellen, W., Stanley, K., Lease, R., and Schlarbaum, G., (1978), 'Some Direct Evidence on the Dividend Clientele Phenomenon', *Journal of Finance*, December, 1385–1399.

Linfield, A., (2006), 'City Law in Practice: The Battle for BAA', *The Lawyer*, 08/11/2006. http://www.thelawyer.com/

Linsley, P. M. and Shrives, P. J., (2006), 'Risk Reporting: A Study of Risk Disclosures in the Annual Reports of UK Companies', *British Accounting Review*, 38, 4, December, 387–404.

Lintner, J., (1956), 'Distributions of Incomes of Corporations among Dividends, Retained Earnings and Taxes', *American Economic Review*, May, 97–113.

McCluskey, T., Burton, B., and Power, D., (2003), 'Evidence on Irish company Managers Views about Dividend Policy', *The Irish Accounting Review*, 10, 2, Winter, 29–52.

McKillop, D., Goth, P., and Hyndman, N., (2006), *'Credit Unions in Ireland: Structure Performance and Governance'*, Institute of Chartered Accountants in Ireland, Dublin.

Miller, M. and Modigliani, F., (1961), 'Dividend Policy, Growth and the Valuation of Shares', *Journal of Business*, 34, October, 411–433.

Miller, M. and Orr, D., (1966), 'A Model of the Demand for Money by Firms', *Quarterly Journal of Economics*, August, 413–435.

Miller, M., (1986), 'Behavioural Rationality in Finance: The Case of Dividends', *Journal of Business*, October.

Mills, R. W., (1988), 'Capital Budgeting Techniques Used in the UK and USA', *Management Accounting*, January.

Modigliani, F. and Miller, M., (1958), 'The Cost of Capital, Corporation Finance and the Theory of Investment', *American Economic Review*, 48, June, 261–297.

Modigliani, F. and Miller, M., (1963), 'Corporate Income Taxes and the Cost of Capital: A Correction', *American Economic Review*, 53, June, 433–443.

Modigliani, F. and Miller, M., (1969), 'Reply to Heins and Sprenkle', *American Economic Review*, 59, September, 592–595.

Murdoch, B., (2000), 'Stabilisation Sounds Alert for Investors', *The Irish Times*, 7 August 2000.

Morris, R., (1998), 'Forecasting Bankruptcy: How Useful are Failure Prediction Models?', *Management Accounting*, May.

Murray, L., (2001), 'Exchange Control Deregulation and Relationships Between UK and Irish Equity Markets', *The Irish Accounting Review*, 8, 1, Spring, 33–50.

Myers, S. and Majluf, N., (1984), 'Corporate Financing and Investment Decisions when Firms have Information that Investors do not have', *Journal of Financial Economics*, 13, 187–221.

Norris, G. and O'Dwyer, B., (2004), 'Motivating Socially Responsive Decision Making: the Operation of Management Controls in a Socially Responsive Organisation', *British Accounting Review*, 36, 2, June, 173–196.

O'Halloran, B., (2003), 'Greencore Borrows €259m in Private Placement', *The Irish Times*, Business and Finance (City Edition), pp 16, 29 October 2003.

O'Neill, L., (2008), 'FBD Shares Soar on Takeover News', *Farmers Journal*, 12/04/2008, http://www.farmersjournal.ie/2008/0412/agribusiness/company-coop/index.shtml.

Pike, R., (1988), 'An Empirical Study of the Adoption of Sophisticated Capital Budgeting Practices and Decision Making Effectiveness', *Accounting and Business Research*, Autumn.

Pike, R., (1996), 'A Longitudinal Survey of Capital Budgeting Practices', *Journal of Business, Finance and Accounting*, 23, 1, January.

Pike, R. and Neale, B., (2003), *'Corporate Finance and Investment: Decisions and Strategies'* (4th edition), FT Prentice Hall.

PLUSMarket Group PLC (accessed 30 June 2007), *'Rules for Issuers (No. 23)'*, http://www.plusmarketsgroup.com/

Porter, M. E., (1985), *'Competitive Advantage'*, New York, Free Press.

Porterfield, J.T., (1965), *'Investment Decisions and Capital Costs'*, Upper Saddle River, New Jersey, Prentice Hall.

Power, T., Walsh, S., and O'Meara, P., (2001), *'Financial Management: An Irish Text'*, Gill and Macmillan.

Puxty, A. and Dodds, J., (1991), *'Financial Management: Method and Meaning'*, Chapman and Hall, London.

Rappaport, A., (1986), *'Creating Shareholder Value: The New Standard for Business Performance'*, Macmillan.

Ross, S., (1977), 'The Arbitrage Theory of Capital Asset Pricing', *Journal of Economic Theory*, Vol. 13, No. 3.

Ross, S., Westerfield, R., and Jordan, B., (1999), *'Essentials of Corporate Finance: International Edition'*, Irwin McGraw-Hill.

Schuler, A. J., (2003), 'You Bought It, So Don't Break It: Five Best Practices in Post Acquisition Integration', http://www.schulersolutions.com/html/post_acquisition_integtration.html

Simpson, D., (2001), 'Mid-term Report: Why Northern Ireland needs to Raise the Stakes and Venture into a Competitive Marketplace', *Belfast News Letter* (Northern Ireland), 7 August 2001.

Smith, G., (2008), 'Health Concerns over Takeover Trend', *Independent,* 27/03/2008. http://www.independent.ie/ (accessed 21/05/08).

Smith, P., (2000), 'African Diamond Company Plans Listing on London Stock Exchange', *World Business Archive*, BBC Broadcast, 26 May 2000.

Solomons, D., (1965), *'Divisional Performance: Measurement and Control'*, Homewood, IL, Richard D. Irwin.

Sridhar, V., (2002), 'Power Games', *Frontline*, 19, 4, February 16–March 1.

Stark, A., (2004), 'Estimating Economic Performance from Accounting Data – a Review and Synthesis', *British Accounting Review*, 36, 4, December, 321–344.

Stern, J., Stewart, G., and Chew, C., (1995), 'The EVA Financial Management System', *Journal of Applied Corporate Finance*, 8, 2, Summer, 32–46.

Stevenson, S., (2000), 'The Efficiency of the ISEQ Index: Empirical Tests Using Daily Data', *The Irish Accounting Review*, 7, 1, Spring, 69–100.

Taffler, R. J., (1983), 'The Assessment of Company Solvency and Performance using a Statistical Model – a Comparative UK-Based Study', *Accounting and Business Research*, Autumn.

Taffler, R. J. and Tisshaw, H., (1977), 'Going, Going, Gone – Four Factors which Predict Failure', *Accountancy*, March.

The Associated Press, (2007), 'Bid for London Exchange Fails a 2nd Time', *The New York Times*, 11 February 2007.

The Irish Times, (2000), 'Boo.com Ireland wound up by Court', *The Irish Times*, 8 June 2000.

Timmons, H. and Anderson, J., (2006), 'Betting Big On a Buyout in London', *The New York Times*, 23 November 2006.

Timmons, H. and Kanter, J., (2006), 'British Shun A New Offer by Nasdaq', *The New York Times*, 21 November 2006.

Whittred, G. and Chan, Y., (1992), 'Asset Revaluations and the Mitigation of Underinvestment', *Abacus*, 28, 1, 58–74.

Whittred, G. and Zimmer, I., (1986), 'Accounting in the Market for Debt', *Accounting and Finance*, November, 1–12.

Yarr, J., (2008). 'Size Matters', *The Lawyer*, 05/02/08, http://www.thelawyer.com/ (accessed 21/05/08).

INDEX